Great Days Out

WHICH?
BOOKS

Acknowledgements

Consultant editor: Nick Trend
Other contributors: Rose Aston, Marian Broderick, Christopher Catling, David Hancock, Sasha Heseltine, Ralph Johnstone, Tim Locke, David Mabey, Laurence Main, Fred Mawer, Julie Meech, Judith Samson, Caroline Sanders, Gilbert Summers and Nia Williams

The publishers wish to thank the many tourist information offices and site curators who have helped to verify information in the Guide.

Which? Books are commissioned and researched by
Consumers' Association and published by
Which? Ltd, 2 Marylebone Road, London NW1 4DF

Distributed by The Penguin Group:
Penguin Books Ltd, 27 Wrights Lane, London W8 5TZ

First edition April 1996
Copyright © 1996 Which? Ltd

British Library Cataloguing in Publication Data
A catalogue record for this book is available from the British Library

ISBN 0 85202 599 8

Designed by Sarah Watson

Maps by David Perrott Cartographics

Printed and bound in Great Britain by Scotprint Ltd, Musselburgh, Lothian

For a full list of Which? books, please write to:
Which? Books, Castlemead, Gascoyne Way, Hertford X, SG14 1LH

Contents

Great days out

Photographs

With thanks to the following people and agencies for the use of their photographs. For each Great Day Out, the credits are generally given in the order that the photos appear.

Treat yourself to some Great Days Out

All aboard the Beamish tram (Great Day Out 125)

Britain is richly endowed with world-class attractions. Our countryside has been celebrated in art and literature for centuries, visitors flock to see everything and anything with royal associations, while places such as Stratford-upon-Avon, Oxford, Cambridge, York, Windsor, Edinburgh and Bath are on every tourist's itinerary.

But there is much more to Britain than these deservedly popular sights: no matter how well you know the country you are bound to alight, as you look through this book, upon fascinating facts and surprising revelations that will make you want to get out and about to see these places for yourself.

We have tried to cater for everyone: families, people travelling by car, bicycle or public transport, and those with mobility difficulties. Not everyone wants to restrict their excursions to the height of summer, so we have included plenty of recommendations for trips out of season, and also numerous suggestions taking into account that a planned day out may not be blessed with fine weather. In addition, we have attempted to give a good countrywide spread, so that wherever you are – at home, on holiday, visiting friends or relatives away from home – you should find something of interest within striking distance.

For details of how to use the book, see the inside covers, both front and back. In addition, the contents pages and especially the Index (on page xvi) will help you pinpoint a particular sight. And following this introduction we list nature reserves, zoos, astronomical sights, and military, naval and airforce museums and steam railways – not forgetting Great Days Out at theme parks and at the beach.

Most of the Great Days Out include more sights than you could or would even want to visit in the space of any single day, but this way you can tailor your own plans to the season and the inclinations of the members of your party.

TO WHET YOUR APPETITE

The era of musty museums with faded, illegible labels is gone. Britain is at the forefront of bringing museums and other sights into the technological age: throughout these pages you will come upon places that help you find out how things work or that give you a vivid idea of what it was like to live at a particular period, through sights, sounds, activities – even smells. Among many exciting examples are the Celtica Museum at Machynlleth (71), at the Museum of the Moving Image in London (43), and at Bradford's plethora of high-tech hands-on 'experiences' (110).

Here are some other ideas:

♦ Exploring the superb gardens in south Cornwall (3), rural Dorset (12) and Inverewe in north-west Scotland (150)

♦ Discovering our naval and seafaring heritage at Portsmouth (24), Chatham (39), Gloucester (59) and Humberside (108)

♦ Following in the footsteps of literary figures such as Thomas Hardy (17), the Brontë sisters (111), Dylan Thomas (67), Beatrix Potter and Arthur Ransome (122), Wordsworth (123), and the Bloomsbury Group (33)

♦ Revelling in some of our greatest art collections, including those at Glasgow (135), Manchester (106), London (45) and Birmingham (80)

♦ Marvelling at our industrial heritage at Ironbridge (79), the Potteries (77), Leeds (109) and the Rhondda Valley (65)

♦ Going underground at Wookey Hole (11), the Eurotunnel Exhibition (37) and the Dolaucothi Gold Mines (69)

♦ Wandering around some of the best of our country houses, such as the wonderful examples in Derbyshire (96, 98 and 100), Norfolk (93) and south-west London (48).

We also suggest ways to avoid the crowds at some of Britain's most popular attractions, for instance at Land's End (1), the Trossachs (140), the southern Cotswolds (58) and Stratford-upon-Avon (81).

Other Great Days Out that may inspire you to take a break are the theatre-lover's tour of London (43), beachcombing on the Gower Peninsula (66), ambling round pretty Norfolk fishing villages (92), wallowing in the nostalgia of the public transport vehicles of days gone by (97), going on a distillery crawl on Speyside (147), and of course getting better acquainted with our finest cities and towns, such as Durham (124), St Andrews (143), Chester (103), Wells (11), Canterbury (38) – and London (47). Whatever your interests, we are sure you will find something to please in *Great Days Out*.

Theme parks

If it's a day when nothing will please the family except hurtling down a roller-coaster, plummeting down a water shute or careering round a go-kart track, then you're in need of the nearest theme park. Inspired by the great Disneyland concepts, Britain now has several large-scale versions of its own – notably Thorpe Park, Alton Towers and Blackpool Pleasure Beach. But there are plenty of others, particularly in the fading seaside resorts, which will take the edge off a rainy day on the promenade. Here's our county-by-county round-up.

ENGLAND

CORNWALL
Flambards Village Theme Park, Culdrose Manor, Helston (01326) 574549 An award-winning park on the theme of a Victorian village, plus a Britain in the Blitz exhibition and Aero Park with helicopters, aeroplanes and an Exploratorium.
Holywell Bay Leisure Park, Trevornick, Holywell Bay (01637) 830095 Highlights include go-karts, skid pan, battle boats, crazy golf, scorpions, bumper boats and an indoor adventure play area.

DERBYSHIRE
American Adventure, Pit Lane, Ilkeston (01773) 531521 More than 100 rides such as the Great Niagara Rapids, Cherokee Falls Log Flume, the Missile and the Canyon Trip.
Gulliver's Kingdom, Temple Walk, Matlock Bath (01629) 580540 Among the highlights are the cable car ride, Royal Cave Tour, Wild West Street, Ghost Hotel, Alpine Log Flume and Double Decker Carousel.

DORSET
Tower Park, Poole (01202) 723671 This is a big leisure complex with a ten-screen cinema, water park, ice pad, 30-lane megabowl and nightclub.

EAST SUSSEX
Fort Fun, Royal Parade, Eastbourne (01323) 642833 A fun park with a runaway train, roller-coaster, grass sledges, bouncy castle, 'Concorde' jet ride, western railway and crazy golf.

HAMPSHIRE
Paultons Park, Ower, Romsey (01703) 814442 Attractions include bumper boats, pets' corner, go-kart track, Kiddies' Kingdom, Romany Museum, Land of the Dinosaurs, Astroglide and trampolines.

HUMBERSIDE
Pleasure Island Theme Park, Sea Front, Kings Road, Cleethorpes (01472) 211511 Attractions include the Tinkaboo Sweet Factory Water Ride, as well as pirate adventures.

KENT
Dreamland, Marine Terrace, Margate (01843) 227011 Take your pick from American-style adventure golf course, Bounty Ship, dodgems, log flume, big wheel, gallopers and waltzers. There is also an open-air market on Wednesdays and Saturdays.
Rotunda Amusement Park, The Seafront, Folkestone (01303) 245245 There's a good variety of family rides such as a roller-coaster, log flume, dodgems, mini-skooters, giant slide, toy rides, ghost train and two large amusement centres.

A GREAT DAY OUT AT THE BEACH

We list below those resort beaches that were given Seaside Awards by the Tidy Britain Group in 1995. The Group based its assessments on four main criteria: safety (including first aid facilities, safety equipment and so on); good management (e.g. availability of toilets, telephones, facilities for disabled people, good access and parking, and dog control); cleanliness (no litter, industrial waste, oil or rotting seaweed); and provision of up-to-date information. In all cases the beach area also had to comply with all appropriate legislation, including the Bathing Water Directive.

For further information and a list of an additional 100 or so rural beaches (which have to fulfil a limited number of similar criteria but which would not be expected to have the same level of supervision or facilities), send a stamped addressed envelope to the Seaside Award Office, Tidy Britain Group, Lion House, Muspole Street, Norwich NR3 1DJ.

South-West England
Bournemouth (Durley and Fisherman's Walk beaches); Burnham-on-Sea; Christchurch (Friar's Cliff); Corbyn Head, Torbay; Crinnis; Dawlish Warren; Goodrington South Sands; Meadfoot, Torbay; Oddicombe; Poole (Sandbanks); Porthmeor; Redgate, Torquay; Sennen Cove; Swanage; Teignmouth (main beach); Weston-super-Mare; Weymouth (Central); Woolacombe

South-East England Bexhill; Bognor Regis; Eastbourne; Hayling Island West; Leysdown (Grove Avenue); Littlehampton; Margate Bay; Minnis Bay, Birchington; Ryde (East); Sandown; Shanklin; Sheerness (Beach Street); Viking Bay, Broadstairs

East Anglia Hunstanton; Lowestoft South; Mundesley; Southend-on-Sea (Three Shells); Southwold; Wells-next-the-Sea

East Midlands Mablethorpe (Central); Skegness (Tower Esplanade); Sutton on Sea (Central)

Yorkshire and Humberside Bridlington (North and South beaches); Filey; Scarborough (North Bay); Whitby (West Cliff)

North-East England Sandhaven

North-West England Ainsdale

Wales Aberystwyth North (Traeth y Gogledd); Barmouth; Dinas Dinlle; Llandudno (North Shore); Pembrey (Cefn Sidan); Rhyl; St David's (Whitesands); Tenby (North); Treaddur Bay

Scotland Aberdour (Silver Sands); Elie; Fraserburgh; Nairn (Central); St Andrews (West Sands); Troon (South)

LANCASHIRE
Blackpool Pleasure Beach, 525 Promenade, Blackpool (01253) 341033 This is one of Europe's biggest theme parks, with over 150 rides from the terrifying Big One roller-coaster to Space Invader, Tokaydo Express, Avalanche, water chute, log flume, swamp buggies, Grand National and Beaver Creek water ride.

Camelot Theme Park, Charnock Richard, Chorley, Preston (01257) 453044 A log flume, Tower of Terror, Mad Monastery, Dragon Heights, Pirate Galleon, ball pool and serpent water slide are among the attractions.

Frontierland Western Theme Park, Marine Road, Morecambe (01524) 410024 The Percolator, Texas Tornado, Skyride, log flume, Wild Mouse Waltzer, Santa Fe train, Stampede roller-coaster, fun house and joy wheel.

LINCOLNSHIRE
Funcoast World, Roman Bank, Skegness (01754) 762311 There is a fun-splash sub-tropical waterworld with lagoons, rapids and flumes, a Prokon Super X simulator, funfair rides and a children's theatre.

MERSEYSIDE
New Palace Amusement Park, Marine Promenade, New Brighton 0151-639 6041 In this large, covered complex is a Space Mountain, Rolling Rocket, waltzers, dodgems, Astroglide and Dead Drop Slide.

Pleasureland Amusement Park, Marine Drive, The Fun Coast, Southport (01704) 532717 Look out for the large log flume and Rainbow ride, Cyclone, Himalaya, Wild Cat, river caves and fun house.

NORTH YORKSHIRE
Atlantis, North Bay, Scarborough (01723) 501560 The water theme park sited here boasts two of the world's largest water slides, plus river rapids ride, whirlpool bath and many other watery amusements.

Flamingo Land Family Theme Park, Zoo and Holiday Village, Kirby Misperton, Malton (01653) 668287 Skytrain, big top circus, Billy Bob Animated Show, the Corkscrew, roller-coaster, Crazy Water Creek top the bill of rides.

Lightwater Valley Theme Park, North Stainley, Ripon (01765) 635321 The Ultimate – a huge roller-coaster – is the chief attraction, plus Rat Ride, fun boats, chair-o-plane, Devils' Cascade and Quadracers.

SHROPSHIRE
Telford Wonderland, Telford Town Park, Telford (01952) 591633 This park is based on nursery rhymes and fairy stories including Snow White, Robin Hood, Humpty Dumpty, *The Wind in the Willows* and Little Red Riding Hood.

SOMERSET
Crinkley Bottom at Cricket St Thomas, Cricket St Thomas (01460) 30755 A wildlife park, heavy horse centre, playground, woodland railway, Crinkley Bottom, Blobbyland and Victorian shopping arcade can be explored here.

STAFFORDSHIRE
Alton Towers, Alton (01538) 702200 One of Britain's biggest theme parks with more than 125 rides and attractions including the Corkscrew, Black Hole, Nemeses, Grand Canyon rapids, Skyride and the Gloomy Wood.

SUFFOLK
Pleasurewood Hills Family Theme Park, Corton, Lowestoft (01502) 508200 This park has an American theme with a Pirate Ship, Close Encounters, miniature railway, Bouncing Bed and a Western train.

SURREY
Chessington World of Adventures, Leatherhead Road, Chessington (01372) 727227 Attractions at this theme park include Toytown Truckers, Runaway Mine Train, Mystic East, Dragon River, Circus World, 5th Dimension – and of course Chessington Zoo.

Thorpe Park, Staines Road, Chertsey (01932) 562633 Another front-ranking park featuring rides such as Depth Charge, the UK's first four-lane waterslide, Flying Fish roller-coaster, Carousel Kingdom, Thorpe Park Rangers show.

TYNE & WEAR
Metroland, MetroCentre, Gateshead 0191-493 2048 This massive indoor theme park features roller-coaster, dodgems, swinging chairs, waterfalls and a nine-hole golf course.

WEST SUSSEX
Harbour Park, Seafront, Littlehampton (01903) 721200 Among the many rides are Cyclone, dodgems, UK rockets, castle slide, waltzer, twister and Matterhorn.

Southcoast World, Bognor Regis (01243) 822445 Owned by Butlin's, this site includes an Aquasplash sub-tropical waterworld, Wizzy's World giant indoor adventure playland and funfair rides.

SCOTLAND

STRATHCLYDE
Wonderwest World, Dunure Road, Ayr (01292) 265141 This is a Butlin's-owned theme park featuring Wondersplash sub-tropical waterworld and over 25 funfair rides.

WALES

DYFED
Oakwood Adventure Park, Canaston Bridge, Narberth, Dyfed (01834) 891373 There are three areas: the Main Park with mini-golf, bobsleigh ride and much more; play area with bouncers, slides and a spider's web; and Jake's Town with goldmine, trading post and music hall.

GWYNEDD
Starcoast World, Pwllheli (01758) 701441 Among the amusements are a waterworld, funfair, Prokon Super X simulator, White Knuckle Boomerang and cable car rides.

Zoos and wildlife parks

A day out at the zoo is not what it used to be. Led by the advent of safari parks in the 1970s, and spurred by debate as to the merits of keeping wild animals in cages, most zoos have found ways to improve living conditions and introduce programmes for breeding rare and endangered species. There is also much more emphasis on making the animals more accessible to visitors — special enclosures where children can touch or get close to farm and domestic animals are becoming more common. Several zoos and parks have added alternative attractions in the shape of steam railways or funfair rides.

ENGLAND

AVON
Bristol Zoo Gardens Clifton, Bristol (0117) 973 8951 Tigers, lions, snakes, monkeys, polar bears, elephants, apes, plus a children's corner.

BEDFORDSHIRE
Whipsnade Wild Animal Park Dunstable (0990) 200123 A large open zoo with over 2,000 animals and a steam railway.
Woburn Wild Safari Park Woburn Park, Woburn (01525) 290407 A drive-through safari park with boating lake and pets' corner.

BUCKINGHAMSHIRE
Flamingo Gardens and Zoological Park Overbrook House, Weston Underwood, Olney (01234) 711451 Over 150 species of birds include flamingoes and vultures, as well as bison, wallabies and wild sheep.

CAMBRIDGESHIRE
Hamerton Wildlife Centre Hamerton, Huntingdon (01832) 293362 Animals include lemurs, marmosets, meerkats and wallabies.
Linton Zoo Hadstock Road, Linton (01223) 891308 This zoo is home to big cats, lynx, servals, llamas, toucans, tarantulas, binturong and giant tortoises.

CHESHIRE
Chester Zoo Chester (01244) 380280 Among the varied species of animals here is the largest group of chimpanzees in the UK, and a baby elephant. (GDO 103)

CORNWALL
Cornwall Animal World Trenance Park, Newquay (01637) 873342

Look out for capybara, lemurs, lynx, deer, pumas, bears, camels; there are also aviaries and a Tarzan trail.

DERBYSHIRE
Riber Castle Wildlife Park Matlock (01629) 582073
The animals at Riber Castle include rare and endangered species and a large lynx collection.

DEVON
Combe Martin Wildlife and Dinosaur Park Higher Leigh Manor, Combe Martin (01271) 882486 Snow leopards, parrots, monkeys, otters, seals, and the largest enclosure for meerkats in the world.
Dartmoor Wildlife Park Sparkwell, Plymouth (01752) 837343 Falconry displays, pony rides, an adventure playground and over 1,000 species of animals, reptiles and birds.
Paignton Zoological and Botanical Gardens Totnes Road, Paignton (01803) 557479
Many rare and endangered species are housed here. There is also a tropical house and miniature railway.
Shaldon Wildlife Trust Ness Drive, Shaldon, Teignmouth (01626) 872234 This zoo specialises in breeding rare and endangered species.

EAST SUSSEX
Drusillas Zoo Park Alfriston (01323) 870234 Over 400 animals and birds including otters, beavers, owls and penguins. (GDO 33)

ESSEX
Basildon Zoo London Road, Vange, Basildon (01268) 553985 The collection includes big cats, llamas, guanaco and rare poultry, plus aviaries and rare plants and trees.
Colchester Zoo Stanway Hall, Maldon Road, Stanway, Colchester (01206) 330253 A large zoo featuring leopards, lions, chimpanzees, rhinoceros, zebras and elephants.
Mole Hall Wildlife Park Widdington, Saffron Walden (01799) 540400 This park has a varied collection of mammals, birds, wildfowl and butterflies.

HAMPSHIRE
Isle of Wight Zoo Granite Fort, Yaverland Seafront, Sandown, Isle of Wight (01983) 403883 This zoo houses big cats, snakes, parrots, monkeys and aviaries.
Marwell Zoological Park Colden Common, Winchester (01962) 777406 This zoo specialises in breeding rare animals and organises special events throughout the year.

HEREFORD & WORCESTER
West Midland Safari and Leisure Park Spring Grove, Bewdley (01299) 402114 Exhibits include a reptile house, sea lion show, Cine 180 show, pets' corner, miniature railway and garden centre.

HERTFORDSHIRE
Paradise Wildlife Park White Stubbs Lane, Broxbourne (01992) 468001 Among 16 acres of woodland are lions, llamas, wallabies, Shetland ponies, goats, donkeys and pumas.

HUMBERSIDE
Sewerby Hall and Gardens Sewerby, Bridlington (01262) 673769
Watch out for llamas, penguins, macaws, coatimundi, wallabies, pheasants, deer and flamingoes at the children's zoo.

KENT
Blean Bird Park and Children's Zoo Honey Hill, Blean, Canterbury (01227) 471666 The birds on display include cockatoos, macaws, pheasants and owls.

Brambles Wildlife Park Wealdon Forest Park, Herne (01227) 712379 A 26-acre woodland park with rare English farm animals, rabbits, wallabies, owls, foxes, deer and Scottish wildcats.

Howletts Wild Animal Park Bekesbourne, Canterbury (01227) 721286 The wild animals include big cats, Indian deer and antelope, gorillas, pongos and lemurs.

Port Lympne Wild Animal Park, Mansion and Gardens Lympne, Hythe (01303) 264647 Many animals, especially rare breeds, plus a mansion housing an art gallery, and a safari trailer journey.

LANCASHIRE

Blackpool Zoo Park East Park Drive, Blackpool (01253) 765027 The animal kitchen is open to the public and the park also has a miniature railway.

LINCOLNSHIRE

Mablethorpe's Animal Gardens and Seal Trust North End, Mablethorpe (01507) 473346 Genets, raccoons, monkeys, parrots, seals and owls are among the mammals and birds bred here – there's also a wildlife hospital.

LONDON

London Zoo Regents Park 0171-722 3333 Despite doubts over its financial future, London Zoo still has over 8,000 animals and a daily programme of events.

MERSEYSIDE

Knowsley Safari Park Prescot 0151-430 9009 This offers five miles of game reserve to drive through with lions, tigers, zebras, monkeys, bison and white rhino roaming in 400 acres of parkland.

NORFOLK

Banham Zoo and Monkey Sanctuary The Grove, Banham, Norwich (0891) 321297 (premium rate service) An international collection of animals and birds, with many rare and endangered species.

Norfolk Wildlife Centre and Country Park Great Witchingham (01603) 872274 There is a range of European animals, a pets' corner, steam railway and electric theme hall.

Thrigby Hall Wildlife Gardens Thrigby Hall, Filby, Great Yarmouth (01493) 369477 A swamp house contains a large collection of crocodiles, and there are plenty of mammals, birds and reptiles – mainly from Asia.

NORTH YORKSHIRE

Flamingo Land Theme Park and Zoo Kirby Misperton, Malton (01653) 668287 This is Europe's largest privately owned zoo, housing sea lions, parrots, bears, flamingoes and zebras.

OXFORDSHIRE

Cotswold Wildlife Park Bradwell Grove, Burford (01993) 823006 There is a tropical house, reptile house, tigers, rhinos, leopards, monkey and a children's farmyard.

SOMERSET

Crinkley Bottom at Cricket St Thomas Cricket St Thomas (01460) 30755 *To the Manor Born* was filmed at this site, home to heavy horses, a country life museum, wildlife valley and tropical aviary.

SUFFOLK

Suffolk Wildlife Park Kessingland, Lowestoft (0891) 321298 (premium rate service) This park contains lions, cheetahs, monkeys, chimpanzees, oryx, otters and Poitou donkeys.

SURREY

Birdworld and Underwaterworld Holt Pound, Farnham (01420) 22140 Underwaterworld is a large aquarium of tropical fish, and birds on show range from penguins to ostriches.

Chessington World of Adventures Leatherhead Road, Chessington (01372) 727227 About 480 animals are housed at this famous wildlife park including wallabies, monkeys, polar bears, big cats and sea lions.

Gatwick Zoo Russ Hill, Charlwood (01293) 862312 There are birds, wallabies, monkeys, penguins, flamingoes and butterflies, as well as tropical gardens.

WARWICKSHIRE

Twycross Zoo Twycross, Atherstone (01827) 880250 The first ever Bonobo chimps to reside in Britain are on display here, as well as gorillas, orang-outangs, elephants, giraffes, sea lions and reptiles.

WEST MIDLANDS

Dudley Zoo and Castle 2 The Broadway, Dudley (01384) 215300 Near medieval castle ruins over 1,000 animals are on display, including many rare species.

WILTSHIRE

Longleat, Warminster (01985) 844400 The only white tigers in Britain are here, as well as lions, rhinos, hippos, elephants, gorillas, zebras and monkeys.

SCOTLAND

CENTRAL

Blair Drummond Safari and Leisure Park Blair Drummond, Stirling (01786) 841456 As well as large game reserves, there is a sea lion show, pet farm, chimpanzee island cruise and natural wildfowl sanctuary.

DUMFRIES AND GALLOWAY

Wildlife Park Kirkcudbright Lochfergus Plantation, Kirkcudbright (01557) 331645 Zoological park and nature reserve with over 100 animals in a hillside forest parkland.

HIGHLAND

Black Isle Wildlife and Country Park The Croft, Drumsmittal, North Kessock (01463) 731656 In spring and summer months, chicks develop in the egg and hatch incubators and there are goats, sheep, cattle, llamas, pigs, deer and wallabies at this park.

Cluanie Park By Beauly (01463) 782415 Birds of prey include an American bald eagle. Rare breeds of cows, sheep and deer are also kept.
Highland Wildlife Park Kincraig (01540) 651270 This drive-through park is set in 260 acres of beautiful countryside containing bison, red deer and wild horses.

LOTHIAN
Edinburgh Zoo Corstorphine Road, Edinburgh (0131) 334 9171 This is home to Europe's largest penguin pool and over 1,000 different species of animals. (*GDO 134*)

STRATHCLYDE
Argyll Wildlife Park Inveraray, Argyll (01499) 302264 A large collection of wildfowl, plus a variety of owls and an emphasis on Scottish wildlife. (*GDO 139*)
Glasgow Zoo Glasgow 0141-771 1185 The large collection at this city zoo includes reptiles, birds, mammals, fish and insects.

TAYSIDE
Camperdown Wildlife Centre Camperdown County Park, Dundee (01382) 432689 The indigenous wildlife collection includes deer, wildcats, pine martens, European brown bear and lynx.
The Scottish Deer Centre By Cupar, Fife (01337) 810391 Rangers take guided tours to see the stags; also a tree-top walkway, information on red deer and falconry displays.

WALES

CLWYD
Welsh Mountain Zoo and Flagstaff Gardens Colwyn Bay (01492) 532938 Tropical houses and a Jungle Adventure Land are surrounded by gardens and woodland.

GWYNEDD
Anglesey Sea Zoo Brynsiencyn, Anglesey (01248) 430411 Fish and sea animals are on display in large walk-through tanks.

WEST GLAMORGAN
Penscynor Wildlife Park Cilfrew, Neath (01639) 642189 Mammals, a tropical house, pets' corner and aviaries.

Nature reserves

Whether you want to take the children to watch tadpoles hatching, or clamber up a mountainside in search of rare wild flowers, Britain's hundreds of nature reserves are an ideal environment in which to enjoy and learn about flora and fauna. Many reserves offer free admission (although there may be a charge at the car park or visitor centre), and most will offer some sort of marked nature trail and information boards (but check details with the owner or manager before visiting).

It is worth being a little wary of what you are visiting since there is no official definition of what constitutes a 'nature reserve'. The sites of major national importance are designated as National Nature Reserves (NNR) by English Nature (01733 340345), the Countryside Council for Wales (01248 370444) and Scottish Natural Heritage (0131-447 4784) – contact them direct for more detailed information.

The other 'official' category is that of Local Nature Reserves. These are designated and often managed by local authorities or local Wildlife Trusts. The Royal Society for Nature Conservation (01522 544400) oversees local Wildlife Trusts, which are organised on a county-by-county basis and which administer, own or manage some 2,000 nature reserves nationwide, from small urban sites to more extensive rural conservation projects. For details of local Wildlife Trusts, contact the RSNC.

The Forestry Commission (0131-334 0303) is another useful source of information; it manages 14 Forest Parks, from Argyll to the New Forest, as well as dozens of woodland nature reserves in England, Scotland and Wales.

We list here a selection of some of the most interesting nature reserves owned or managed by the other national bodies. Use the contact numbers given for information on membership, or details of more local numbers.

NATIONAL TRUST
The National Trust (0171-222 9251; public affairs department) owns 26 National Nature Reserves (although some are managed by other bodies), many smaller reserves, and 28 per cent of its land is of special scientific interest. The following is a selection of what the Trust has to offer:
Formby, Merseyside. The dunes and pine woods are one of the last refuges of the red squirrel in England.
Hatfield Forest, near Bishop's Stortford, Hertfordshire/Essex border. This remnant of the ancient broadleaf woodland which once formed part of the royal Essex forest has an observation hide and a nature walk.
Malham Tarn Estate, near Ribblesdale, North Yorkshire. Breeding birds such as wheatear, curlew and grebe stalk the wetland, and the estate is also rich in wild flowers.

Sandscale Haws, near Barrow-in Furness, Cumbria. The beach, sand dunes and marshes are home to rare natterjack toads and the equally scarce coral root orchid.
Sharpenhoe Clappers, near Barton-le-Clay, Bedfordshire. This stretch of Chiltern scarp, including an Iron Age hill fort, is noted for its wild flowers on the grassy hillside, and beech and ash woodland.
Studland Beach and Nature Reserve, Dorset. The beach is one of Britain's best, while the heath, dunes and chalk cliffs provide a varied habitat for seaside flora and fauna.
Wicken Fen, near Ely, Cambridgeshire. The nation's oldest nature reserve, one of the last stretches of undrained East Anglian fenland, is rich in plant, insect and bird life.

Witley Common, near Godalming, Surrey. A full-scale Nature Information Centre stands in the pine woods on the edge of the common, while the marked nature walks explore and explain the wild flowers and wildlife.

NATIONAL TRUST FOR SCOTLAND

The National Trust for Scotland (0131-226 5922) owns and manages two mainland National Nature Reserves. In addition, like the National Trust, much of its land forms important habitats for plants and wildlife. For full details see its *Guide to Properties*.

Ben Lawyers National Nature Reserve, Perth and Kinross, Tayside. Forms part of Perthshire's highest mountain (3,984 feet), home to a rich variety of mountain plants and birdlife including ring-ouzel, ptarmigan and curlew.

St Abb's Head National Nature Reserve, Berwickshire, Borders. Forms a spectacular headland of 300-foot cliffs – nesting sites for shags, puffins and razorbills among many others.

THE ROYAL SOCIETY FOR THE PROTECTION OF BIRDS

(01767) 680551 Has over 130 bird reserves throughout the UK. Some of the more important ones include:

Abernethy Forest, near Aviemore, Highland. This is a famous osprey nesting site, as well as home to breeding pairs of crossbills and capercaillies.

Arne, Poole Harbour, Dorset. One of the last remaining areas of Dorset heathland, home to the nightjar, stonechat and Dartford warbler, as well as all six species of British reptiles.

Bempton Cliffs, near Bridlington, Humberside. Two miles of chalk cliffs attract razorbills, puffins, shags and many other sea birds.

Elmley Marshes, near Sheerness, Kent. Freshwater fleets and saltmarshes with many waders including curlew and dunlin and winter visitors such as the hen harrier, merlin and short-eared owl.

Leighton Moss, near Morecambe Bay, Lancashire. Reedswamp and wooded limestone slopes are the habitat of rare bitterns, osprey and marsh harriers. Otters are also seen regularly.

Nagshead, Forest of Dean, Gloucestershire. The oak-dominant mixed woodland is an ideal habitat for many smaller birds, including tits, blackcap, garden warblers and treecreepers.

Vane Farm, near Kinross, Tayside. Loch Leven is a top spot for migrating waders, geese and ducks, while woodpeckers, owls and tree pipits nest in the woodland.

Ynys-Hir, head of the Dyfi estuary, Dyfed. Saltmarsh, peat bog and woodlands are home to a wide variety of birds of prey – peregrines, merlins, buzzards, kestrels and sparrowhawks – as well as badgers and polecats.

WILDFOWL AND WETLANDS TRUST

(01453) 890333

Arundel, West Sussex. More than a thousand ducks, geese and swans from all over the world can be found on and around the River Arun.

Caerlaverock, Dumfriesshire. Barnacle geese spend the winter on the Solway Firth around Caerlaverock, making this site one of the most important for wintering wildfowl in the UK.

Llanelli, Dyfed. Home to a wide variety of wild birds, including the oystercatcher, redshank, curlew, little egret and sometimes osprey.

Martin Mere, Lancashire. This is one of Britain's most important wetland sites: visitors can see a variety of ducks, geese and swans from all over the world as well as two flocks of flamingoes.

Slimbridge, Gloucestershire. Founded in 1946 by the late Sir Peter Scott, Slimbridge is home to a large collection of exotic wildfowl and the only place in the UK where visitors can see all six types of flamingo.

Washington, Tyne & Wear. A rare haven for birds in a busy industrial area on the north bank of the River Wear.

Welney, Cambridgeshire. This internationally important wetland site on the beautiful Ouse Washes is a winter ground for a wide variety of wild ducks, geese and swans.

ASTRONOMICAL SIGHTS

As well as our list of top attractions for star-gazers and space fans, we have listed museums and other institutions which have planetaria (and sometimes observatories) which are open to the public. Planetarium shows begin at fixed times, and there may be only a very limited number during the day, so it is vital to phone ahead and book, or at least check the timings. If you want to do some star-gazing, most observatories are open on one or two evenings each week in the winter.

CHESHIRE

Jodrell Bank Science Centre and Arboretum (01477) 571339 Home to the world's second-biggest fully steerable radio telescope, Jodrell Bank also has a lively visitor centre with space and astronomy exhibitions, interactive videos and a Planetarium. Outside is a 35-acre arboretum.

LONDON

Old Royal Observatory, Greenwich, London SE10 (0181-858 4422) Charles II's observatory, designed to help perfect navigation and astronomy, stands on the Greenwich Meridian. The building houses a historic collection of astronomical instruments.

LOTHIAN

Royal Observatory Visitor Centre, Edinburgh (0131-668 8405) From the present-day solar system back to the beginning of space and time, the visitor centre explains the intricacies of modern astronomy.

STRATHCLYDE

Coats Observatory, Paisley (0141-889 2013) The observatory was built in 1882, but thanks to a major technological update it has resumed its role as one of Britain's key centres for astronomical, meteorological and seismic monitoring.

Other planetaria and observatories

- Central Museum and Planetarium, Southend-on-Sea, Essex (01702) 215640
- Goonhilly Satellite Earth Station (01326) 221333 (see *Great Day Out 1*)
- Liverpool Planetarium, Liverpool Museum, Liverpool (0151-207 0001)
- London Planetarium, Marylebone Road, London NW1 (0171-935 6861)
- Natural Sciences Centre, Newchapel Observatory, Stoke-on-Trent, Staffordshire (01782) 785205
- York Observatory, Museum Gardens, York (01904) 629745

Steam railways

Many of these railways have special events aimed at children – Thomas the Tank Engine weekends in summer for instance, and Santa Specials in December (although they may otherwise be closed during the winter). Attractions for adults sometimes include evening dinner trips in restored dining cars. Many also have visiting locomotives, as well as their own engines and rolling stock, and diesel galas using preserved mainline engines are becoming more and more common. For a full list of Britain's steam railways see *Railways Restored* published by Ian Allen.

Other steam railways that form part of the *Great Days Out* themselves include the Bluebell Line in Sussex (*31*), the North York Moors line (*117*) and the Settle to Carlisle Railway(*121*).

50 different engines, wagons and carriages but there is also a mile of steam-driven line.

ENGLAND

BEDFORDSHIRE
Leighton Buzzard Railway, Leighton Buzzard (01525) 373888 This former sand-carrying line now operates a variety of narrow-gauge locomotives from around the world.

BUCKINGHAMSHIRE
Buckinghamshire Railway Centre, Quainton (01296) 655720 Principally a museum with rolling stock and engines from around the world.

CAMBRIDGESHIRE
Nene Valley Railway, near Peterborough (01780) 782854 The 7½ miles of riverside railway is operated by both British and European engines.

CORNWALL
Launceston Steam Railway, Launceston (01566) 775665 The old mainline to Padstow has been relaid with narrow-gauge track, and trains on the 5-mile round trip are now pulled by locos from the Welsh slate mines – all around 100 years old.

CUMBRIA
Ravenglass and Eskdale Railway, Ravenglass (01229) 717171 This narrow-gauge track was laid to carry iron ore over a hundred years ago. Now it offers a stunning 7-mile ride through the Lake District.
South Tynedale Railway, Alston (01434) 381696 There are hopes to extend the track on this short, narrow-gauge line along the South Tyne Valley.

DERBYSHIRE
Midland Railway Centre, Ripley (01773) 747674 This combined museum and 3½-mile working steam line celebrates the Midland Railway from the nineteenth century to the days of diesels and electrification.

DEVON
Paignton and Dartmouth Steam Railway, Paignton (01803) 555872 The 7-mile run along the former GWR line between Paignton and Kingswear includes stops at the beach at Goodrington Sands and at Churston, where you can take the short ferry ride to Dartmouth.
South Devon Railway, Buckfastleigh (01364) 642338 The railway has former GWR rolling stock and engines which operate the 7 miles of track along the Dart Valley to Totnes.

DORSET
Swanage Railway, Swanage (01929) 425800 Six miles of the former Wareham branch line between Swanage and Norden have been preserved for steam trains.

CO DURHAM
Tanfield Railway, Tanfield (0191-274 2002) Reputedly the oldest existing line in the world, Tanfield dates from 1725. Three miles of track remain and the oldest locomotive still working dates from the 1870s.

ESSEX
Colne Valley Railway, Castle Hedingham (01787) 461174 The main attraction is the museum, with about

GREATER MANCHESTER
East Lancashire Light Railway, Bolton Street Station (0161-764 7790) The 1¾ hour journey along the Irwell Valley from Bury to the moors takes in some wonderful scenery; the track engineering (viaducts and tunnels) is impressive too. Trains are hauled by either steam or diesel locomotives.

HAMPSHIRE
Isle of Wight Steam Railway, Havenstreet (01983) 882204 A high spot for tank engine fans – several versions run on the 5-mile line.
Mid-Hants Railway, Alresford (Watercress Line) (01962) 733810 There are period-style stations and ten miles of track through the rolling Hampshire countryside between Alton and Alresford. The oldest engines date from the early 1920s and there are a few Southern Railway coaches in working order.

LEICESTERSHIRE
Battlefield Line Railway Market Bosworth (01827) 880754 Visit the field of the Battle of Bosworth by steam train from Shackerstone Station. There is also a railway museum and Victorian tea room.
Great Central Railway, Loughborough (01509) 230726 The eight miles of track between Loughborough and Leicester are operated by diesels and main-line steam engines.

MERSEYSIDE
Southport Railway Centre, Southport (01704) 530693 The Lancashire and Yorkshire engine shed is home to a variety of railway and other commercial engines, and there is a short stretch of track.

NORFOLK
North Norfolk Railway, Sheringham (01263) 822045 Originally dubbed the 'Poppy Line' to rival Sussex's Bluebell Line; trains

still run between the seaside resort of Sheringham and the Georgian town of Holt through the rolling, wooded countryside of north Norfolk. A wide range of locomotives operate – from tank engines to mainline locos.

OXFORDSHIRE
Didcot Railway Centre, Didcot (01235) 817200 A haven for GWR enthusiasts with an extensive museum of locos and rolling stock, but there are also two short lengths of track for steam rides.

SHROPSHIRE
Severn Valley Railway, Bridgnorth (01299) 403816 One of the most important preservation railways in Britain, the track runs for a full 16½ miles; there are 28 engines (mainly ex-GWR and LMS mainline locomotives) in the collection, of which 14 are still in operation.

SOMERSET
East Somerset Railway, Cranmore (01749) 880417 There are only three miles of track, but five different working steam locomotives at this small railway near Shepton Mallet.
West Somerset Railway (Bishop's Lydeard to Minehead). (01643 704996) The 20-mile track runs vintage steam and diesel locomotives.

WEST YORKSHIRE
Keighley and Worth Valley Railway, Haworth (01535) 645214 This is certainly the most romantic way to reach Brontë country. From Keighley BR station you can ride to Haworth – or continue for five miles to Oxenhope – by steam train pulled by one of half a dozen working locomotives. Used as the setting for the film of *The Railway Children*.
Middleton Railway, Leeds (0113) 271 0320 This line was the first rail road to be authorised by Parliament in the mid-eighteenth century.

CENTRAL
Bo'ness and Kinneil Railway, Bo'ness (01506) 822298 A 7-mile ride through woodlands combines a tour of Birkhill Fireclay Mine and a visit to the impressive collection of locos and historic railway buildings.

HIGHLAND
Mull and West Highland Narrow Gauge Railway, Craignure, Mull (01680) 812494 The tiny 10¼-inch gauge line which runs the 1½ miles to Torosay Castle has dramatic views of the island.
Strathspey Steam Railway, Aviemore (01479) 810725 Take a trip on an 1899 Caledonian Railway Engine for the 5-mile ride between Boat of Garten and Aviemore.

CLWYD
Llangollen Station, Llangollen (01978) 860979 Both steam and diesel trains run from this former GWR station on the 5-mile track to Glyndyfrdwy.

GWYNEDD
Bala Lake Railway, Llanuwchllyn (01678) 540666 The former slate-quarry locos now haul passenger coaches for four miles along the lake.
Fairbourne Railway, Fairbourne (01341) 250362 This narrow-gauge railway was built for horse-drawn wagons. Now four different steam locomotives haul carriages the mile and a half along the coast to the Barmouth ferry.
Ffestiniog Railway, Porthmadog (01766) 512340 The narrow-gauge

steam railway that used to serve the slate mines – there is an original locomotive dating from the 1860s in the museum – is now perhaps the most scenic of the North Wales lines.
Llanberis Lake Railway, Llanberis (01286) 870549 Another narrow-gauge Welsh slate line with two miles of track along Padarn Lake.
Snowdon Mountain Railway, Llanberis (01286) 870223 This 100-year-old rack and pinion railway has wonderful views and is the lazy man's route to the top of Snowdon.
Talyllyn Railway, Tywyn (01654) 710472 This steep narrow-gauge line includes stops at the Dolgoch Falls and the Nant Gwernol forest.

MID GLAMORGAN
Brecon Mountain Railway, Merthyr Tydfil (01685) 722988 A revived stretch of former British Rail track runs through the National Park to Taf Fechan reservoir – the train is pulled by a 1908 East German locomotive.

POWYS
Welshpool and Llanfair Railway, Llanfair Caereinion (01938) 810441 The 16-mile steam-hauled round trip through wonderful mid-Wales scenery runs on narrow-gauge tracks. There are stations along the A458 Shrewsbury–Dolgellau road.

Military, naval and airforce museums

It would be hard to beat military museums for the sheer size and scale of the exhibits, so whether you are interested in seeing round a battleship, sitting in a fighter's cockpit or examining a tank at close quarters, you will find here some of the most important armed forces museums around Britain. However, many of the more specialist regimental museums have not been included – for details contact the local tourist board – and don't forget that others such as the historic dockyards at Chatham (39) and Portsmouth (24) and the Bovington Tank Museum (19) feature in the Great Days Out themselves.

AVON
International Helicopter Museum, Weston-super-Mare (01934) 635227 More than 50 helicopters and autogyros form the heart of the collection; also a roller-coaster ride simulator.

CAMBRIDGESHIRE
Duxford Airfield, Duxford (01223) 835000 Once a Battle of Britain fighter station, now a branch of the Imperial War Museum; the hangars are home to a vast collection of military aircraft and to the first prototype *Concorde*. Regular flying displays take place.

CLEVELAND
HMS Trincomalee, Hartlepool (01429) 223193 One of the oldest British warships still afloat, *Trincomalee* was launched in 1817. (Next door are PSS *Wingfield Castle* and the historic quay.)

DORSET
Royal Signals Museum, Blandford Forum (01258) 482248 Learn about the history of army communications.

HAMPSHIRE
Aldershot Military Museum, Aldershot (01252) 314598 Museum devoted to the town's extensive connections with the army.
Museum of Army Flying, Middle Wallop (01980) 674421 Museum aircraft often fly at weekends; otherwise, the range of extensive exhibits covers the history of military aircraft since before the First World War.

HERTFORDSHIRE
Mosquito Aircraft Museum, London Colney (01727) 822051 Museum of the De Havilland heritage including *Mosquitos*, a *Tiger Moth* and a *Venom*.

HUMBERSIDE
Museum of Army Transport, Beverley (01482) 860445 From horse-drawn supply wagons, to Field Marshal Montgomery's Rolls-Royce.

KENT
Kent Battle of Britain Museum Trust, Hawkinge (01303) 893140 This shrine to the 'Few' has full-sized replicas of the fighters.

LINCOLNSHIRE
Battle of Britain Memorial Flight Visitor Centre, Coningsby, (01526) 344041 Here you can see *Lancaster*, *Spitfires* and a *Hurricane* – all in working order. Check before going that they are not on operational duties.

LONDON
Cabinet War Rooms, King Charles Street, London SW1 (0171-930 6961) Churchill's bomb-proof operations rooms are preserved much as they were at the end of the Second World War.

HMS Belfast, near Tooley Street, London SE1 (0171-407 6434) Launched in 1938, *Belfast* took a leading role in naval engagements during the Second World War. Ring for details of special events for children.
Imperial War Museum, Lambeth Road, London SE1 (0171-416 5000) The Museum houses a national record of wars fought by British forces since 1914. Its previously rather stuffy, staid atmosphere has been improved by restoration and the introduction of more high-tech displays.
National Army Museum, Royal Hospital Road, London SW3 (0171-730 0717) Battle scenes, models, the skeleton of Napoleon's horse, medals, photographs and uniforms – everything you could possibly want to know about soldiery over the last 500 years.
Royal Airforce Museum, Colindale, London NW9 (0181-205 2266) The heart of the museum is the collection of over 75 military aircraft dating back to the early days of flight. Among the sideshows is a *Tornado* flight simulator.
Museum of Artillery, Woolwich, London SE18 (0181-316 5402) The rotunda (designed by John Nash) houses a superb display of guns and ammunition over a period of 700 years.

NORTH YORKSHIRE
Yorkshire Air Museum & Allied Air Forces Memorial, Elvington (01904) 608595 Aircraft on display include the last *Lightning*, and visitors can enter the original flying control tower which served the allied airforce during the Second World War.

NOTTINGHAMSHIRE
Newark Air Museum, Newark-on-Trent (01636) 707170 More than 40 training and reconnaissance aircraft, jet fighters, bombers and helicopters are on show; also an undercover aircraft display hall.

SHROPSHIRE
Aerospace Museum, Cosford (01902) 374872/374112 This large aviation collection includes *Victor* and *Vulcan* bombers.

SOMERSET
RNAS Yeovilton, near Ilchester (01935) 840565 This Fleet Air Arm museum has displays of aeroplanes which range from Sopwith *Camels* to a *Concorde* prototype.

SUFFOLK
Norfolk and Suffolk Aviation Museum, Flixton (01508) 480778 A *Spitfire* replica, used in the film *The Battle of Britain*, *Sea Vixen* and a USAF *Super Sabre* are housed in this East Anglian museum.

WEST SUSSEX
Tangmere Military Aviation Museum Trust, Tangmere (01243) 775223 Seventy years of military aviation are recorded in photographs, documents, models, uniforms and other relics.

SCOTLAND

HIGHLAND
Museum of Flight, East Fortune (01620) 880308 A Supermarine *Spitfire* MK16, De Havilland *Sea Venom*, Hawker *Sea Hawk* and *Comet* are arranged in a former airship base.

TAYSIDE
HM Frigate Unicorn, Dundee (01382) 200900 Aboard one of Britain's oldest floating warships – a 24-gun frigate launched in 1824 – is a museum of life in the Royal Navy.

WALES

POWYS
South Wales Borderers and Monmouthshire Museum, Brecon (01874) 613310 Among the collections is a Zulu War room devoted particularly to the battle at Rorke's Drift in 1879.

INDEX AND PHONE DIRECTORY

In this index you will find the phone numbers of all places in *Great Days Out* with an asterisk by their names. Some of these phone numbers are seasonal so you will need to contact the tourist information office mentioned in the relevant day out where applicable. (Note that 0891 numbers are charged at premium rates.) The index also includes other main sights which you cannot telephone, as well as certain towns and villages, which of course have no phone numbers. The **bold numbers** in the middle column refer to the number of the Great Day Out.

From Land's End to Lizard Point

St Michael's Mount and Mont St Michel were chosen as monastery sites by the same Benedictine order

Bracing cliff walks, hidden coves and golden sandy beaches, plus a dramatic cliff-top open-air theatre, a sub-tropical garden and a magical island surmounted by a fourteenth-century castle, are among the ideas for a great day out away from the crowds in the far west.

The drive described here, plus some fine walking, starts amid the spectacular scenery of Land's End, takes in Penzance and the majestic St Michael's Mount, gloriously set in Mount's Bay, and ends with the delights of the windswept west coast of the unspoilt Lizard peninsula, with its towering cliffs, sandy coves and traditional fishing villages.

Land's End, the westernmost point on mainland England, lures countless visitors to its dramatic cliff scenery and rather exploited headland complex of hotels, exhibitions and family attractions. You could escape the crowds by strolling on the cliff path to appreciate this magnificent stretch of coastline in relative solitude.

Head east from Land's End to the unique **Minack Open Air**

♦ **GOOD FOR** Those who appreciate dramatic coastal scenery; the beaches will appeal to youngsters
♦ **TRANSPORT** Car essential: this is a one-way trip of around 45 miles
♦ **ACCESS FOR DISABLED PEOPLE** Suitable only at Trengwainton Gardens
♦ **BEST TIME TO VISIT** Spring, summer and autumn for NT properties and most museums, and to see gardens at their best; all year for invigorating cliff walks

Theatre* at Porthcurno. Hewn out of the cliff-face in classical Greek style by Miss Rowena Cade in 1931, the 750-seat auditorium enjoys a breathtaking backdrop of sea, sand and cliff scenery. The story of its creation is told in the Exhibition Centre, using photographs, models and audio-visual techniques. Performances are put on in summer;

either attend a matinée or watch a play by moonlight.

Below the theatre and reached by a steep coastal path (road access for the faint-hearted) is a sheltered beach of white sand – ideal for a summer swim – and the village of **Porthcurno**. It was here that the first transatlantic cable was brought ashore, and an interesting **Telegraph Museum*** is housed in the once-secret Second World War underground telegraph station behind the car park.

Those so inclined can extend their cliff-path walk for a further mile to incorporate the headland of Treryn Dinas, with its fine example of an Iron Age cliff castle and the **Logan Rock**, a 65-ton boulder that teeters on the cliff edge. In 1824, one Lieutenant Goldsmith and a group of sailors pushed it off its perch, but after a local outcry the Admiralty ordered him to replace it. A footpath leads inland across fields to the attractive hamlet of **Treen** and the friendly Logan Rock Inn.

In direct contrast to the harsh granite landscape that predominates on the peninsula, the peaceful **Trengwainton Gardens*** (NT), to the north-west of Penzance, are a gardener's delight, notable for their magnolias and rhododendrons. Owing to the mild maritime climate, this unique complex of five walled gardens, with views across Mount's Bay, also contains rare exotic shrubs and trees that are not cultivated outdoors anywhere else in Britain. Light refreshments are available in the farmhouse garden.

Penzance, the westernmost town in England, overlooks Mount's Bay and has an interesting maritime museum and a helpful **tourist information office***. It is the departure point for day trips to the Isles of Scilly aboard the Scillonian ferry*, or by helicopter*.

Dominating Mount's Bay east of Penzance is one of Britain's most treasured landmarks, **St Michael's Mount***, a little granite island rising 250 feet above the bay and crowned by a fairy-tale fourteenth-century castle. Originally the site of a Benedictine priory founded by Edward the Confessor in the twelfth century, it became a fortress at the time of the Dissolution of the Monasteries in 1535 and later was a Royalist stronghold during the seventeenth century. Since 1660 it has been home to the St Aubyn family and was bequeathed to the NT in 1954.

St Michael's Mount is approached on foot by a splendid granite causeway at low tide, so time it right to avoid getting your feet wet, or at high tide use the small ferry* (which operates only in favourable weather conditions). Beyond the tiny harbour and hamlet, a steep climb leads you to the priory church and castle which affords superb views towards Land's End and the Lizard. Friezes, paintings and portraits by famous artists decorate the various rooms of the castle, with the eighteenth-century Blue Drawing Rooms featuring elegant Chippendale furniture.

To avoid the crowds in the height of the season, arrive early. Make time for refreshments in the excellent Sail Loft Restaurant, or the Island Café,

The Minack Theatre puts on everything from Shakespeare to opera

and to view the audio-visual presentation explaining the history of the castle.

Before the masses descend on the Mount, escape further south-east, beyond Helston to the isolated and beautiful Lizard peninsula, to experience some of the grandest coastal scenery in Britain. If time allows, your first stop could be the Halzephron Inn at **Gunwalloe** (signed off the A3083 south of Helston), for its imaginative food and far-reaching views across Mount's Bay. A mile beyond the inn lies the sheltered **Gunwalloe Church Cove** (NT), with good parking and a safe sandy beach. Standing alone amongst the sand dunes is the charming fifteenth-century Church of St Winwaloe, with its unusual detached bell tower.

Further south, there are soaring cliffs and pinnacles of Serpentine rock interspersed with delightful little coves. The solid granite piers of the tiny harbour in **Mullion Cove** or Porth Mellin (NT) were built in the 1890s and jut out from beneath steep, cave-pocked cliffs. The NT maintains the charming old net store, the winch house and the wooden fish cellar in this picturesque, traditional fishing hamlet, and owns most of the coastline. You can bathe near the cove, but Mullion is the ideal location from which to undertake a wonderful cliff walk southwards over **Predannack Head**, which is covered in scented thyme and sea thrift. The NT leaflet 13 (available locally) gives details of the area and the 1½-mile circular walk from Mullion Cove.

An interesting indoor venue not far away is the **Goonhilly Satellite Earth Station***. Guided tours of the station and its massive satellite dishes, as well as an impressive visitors' centre and audio-visual show, give a good insight into how the global communications network functions. There is a licensed café here.

Walking enthusiasts may prefer a ramble along the breathtaking cliff path from Mullion. Head south for four exhilarating miles to view the wonderful seascape at **Kynance Cove** (NT), a popular yet beautiful place, especially out of season. For the less adventurous, there is a spacious clifftop car park reached by a toll road across the Lizard Downs. A beach café operates here in the summer to quench thirsts.

Our route culminates at the wild landscape around **Lizard Point**, the southernmost tip of Britain. Famous for its prized Serpentine rock, the area is worth exploring for the many rare plants which thrive here, the clifftop walks and the far-reaching views along the Cornish coast which extend on clear days right over to Bolt Head in Devon.

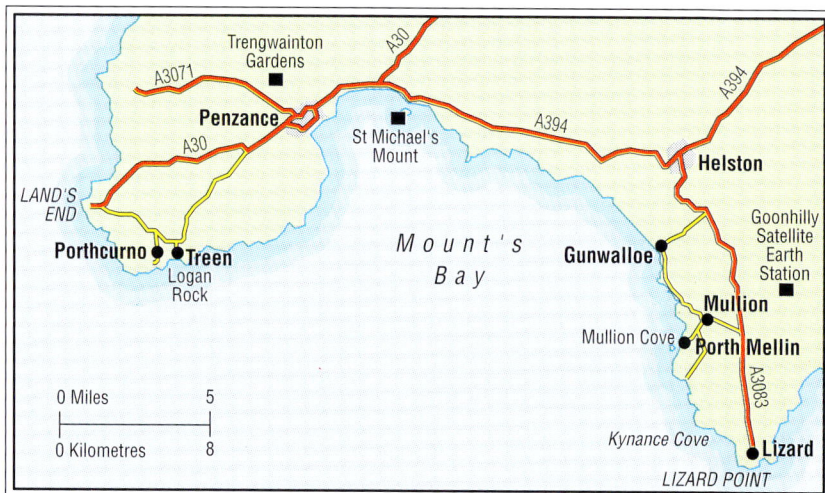

St Ives: sun lovers' and art lovers' mecca

Sophisticated art and mass tourism make an unlikely combination in this historic fishing port, with its winding cobbled lanes. Visitors are lured by the splendid beaches and the new Tate Gallery St Ives.

On a summer bank holiday the narrow lanes are overwhelmed by the sheer volume of people

♦ **GOOD FOR** Families with young children who like beaches, and those who like modern art

♦ **TRANSPORT** A car is not necessary: the railway station is near the town centre. If you're in a car, park it and walk

♦ **ACCESS FOR DISABLED PEOPLE** Access is good for the Tate, limited for the Barbara Hepworth Museum

♦ **BEST TIME TO VISIT** St Ives can be unpleasantly crowded in the height of summer. The Tate and the Barbara Hepworth Museum are open all year (except during re-hanging; ring the Tate for dates), closing on Mondays from October to March

Since its heyday in the middle of the nineteenth century, when some 400 boats fished for pilchards from its harbour, St Ives' fishing fleet has become virtually extinct. Artistic pretensions have lasted better. Turner, Whistler and Sickert came here to paint in the nineteenth century, but it was from the 1920s to the 1950s that St Ives' art really blossomed, with figures such as potter Bernard Leach, husband and wife Ben Nicholson and Barbara Hepworth, and later Terry Frost, Patrick Heron and Peter Lanyon to the fore. The Tate Gallery St Ives, opened in 1993, is devoted primarily to exhibiting works from the St Ives school. These can be found, too, in some of the numerous high-quality commercial galleries, which also bear witness to the thriving contemporary arts scene.

BEARINGS AND BEACHES

At the southern end is **Porthminster Beach**, the best in St Ives for families, with a protected big crescent of sand and everything from beach huts to watersports. Between it and the harbour lie characterful backstreets like The Warren and St Andrew's Street, the latter with a number of little galleries. The **tourist information office*** is on Street-an-Pol, just south of the harbour.

Westcott's Quay has a magnificent view over the arc-shaped **harbour**, which is St Ives at its most touristy, with amusement arcades, surf shops and downmarket cafés jostling for space. There are plenty of fishing trips and cruises, and self-drive motor boats for hire.

Running parallel with the harbour's western side is **Fore Street**, St Ives' often incredibly busy main thoroughfare. Here the aroma of baking pasties wafts from every other window, and shell and fudge shops sit cheek-by-jowl with art galleries of mostly dubious taste. If you are interested in shopping, head out to the St Ives Pottery on Lower Fish Street, where you will find ceramics, jewellery and mirrors.

North of the harbour lies **Downalong**, a maze of tiny streets and alleys, where the fishing community used to live. Many of the town's best galleries are here. Teetotal Street recalls the importance

The façade of the Tate Gallery was designed to echo the form of the old gasometer that used to stand on this site

of the Methodist movement, which took root here in the eighteenth century, while The Digey leads to **Porthmeor Beach**. This dazzling giant expanse of sand is flecked in fine weather with holidaymakers as far as the eye can see, like a seaside version of a Lowry painting. It is famous for its surf: surfing equipment can be hired, and TJ's School of Surfing* provides instruction. Directly behind is the Tate Gallery St Ives (see below).

The northern end of the beach abuts **The Island**, a misnamed grassy promontory with a diminutive sailors' chapel and the best views of Porthmeor Beach. On its other side nestles **Porthgwidden Beach**, a pretty, sheltered sandy cove, which can be very crowded.

MAJOR ART GALLERIES
The **Tate Gallery St Ives*** provokes strong reactions from almost all who visit. There are few who do not appreciate the aesthetics of the building, whose vast glass frontage makes the most of its position over Porthmeor

Beach. But their appreciation of the exhibits – mainly from the London Tate's permanent collections, changing repeatedly and focusing primarily on the best of St Ives' modern art – is more debatable. The editor of the local paper has described the gallery as 'an alien spacecraft landing from planet London', and you will have to make up your own mind as to whether you find the abstract canvases which dominate wonderful, inexplicable or simply not your cup of tea.

The **Barbara Hepworth Museum*** (joint admission with the Tate) is more accessible. The sculptress lived, worked and died (in 1975) here. Many of her abstract pieces in bronze, marble and wood are incredibly tactile and earthy, and they are enhanced by their location, ranged around her lovely airy house and bosky, palmy garden, just where she wished them to be. In her workshop, piles of half-chiselled

Barbara Hepworth designed many of her works to be displayed in her garden

marble lie around, and her overalls hang on the wall, as if she's just popped out.

HISTORICAL ST IVES
The **parish church of St Ia** is well worth seeing for its splendid wagon roof with coloured bosses and gold paintwork, its fifteenth-century carved bench ends and a Hepworth *Madonna and Child*.

St Ives Museum*, in a building between the harbour and Porthgwidden Beach which has served as a pilchard factory, laundry, cinema and sailors' mission house, has a marvellous assortment of local memorabilia. You'll find everything from old bathing costumes and fishing nets to typewriters and miniature home-made anchors, as well as lots of evocative old photographs of ships, shipwrecks, fishermen, miners and artists.

Botanical treasures of southern Cornwall

Trelissick Garden has an extensive park, woodland walks and rare plants

The secluded valleys of southern Cornwall boast several eighteenth- and nineteenth-century horticultural treats. In the five gardens described here are many plants more usually found in the tropics, so you can feast your senses on magnolias, bamboos and palms.

I n contrast to Cornwall's windswept, rocky north coast and its harsh granite interior the less rugged landscape of the southern coastline features gently rolling farmland and deep-water estuaries hiding an intricate network of wonderful wooded creeks. Here, protected from the worst of the westerly gales, and benefiting from a mild, generally frost-free climate and a strongly acidic soil, the land has been ideal for the cultivation of many exotic plants and the development of some of Britain's finest gardens.

This day out highlights five gems, including the award-winning Lost Gardens of Heligan, which are being painstakingly restored to their nineteenth-century glory after seventy years of neglect; the National Trust parkland and garden of Trelissick overlooking the Fal

♦ **GOOD FOR** Gardeners and garden-lovers seeking inspiration and relaxation
♦ **TRANSPORT** Car essential
♦ **ACCESS FOR DISABLED PEOPLE** Trelissick has good access; two wheelchairs and a self-drive buggy are available. Access may be difficult in the other gardens
♦ **BEST TIME TO VISIT** Spring and early summer for the vibrant colours and heady perfumes. Heligan and Trebah can be visited throughout the year

estuary; and the three gardens – Penjerrick, Glendurgan and Trebah – created by Alfred Fox close to the peaceful, wood-fringed Helford River. Most of these fine gardens were established by prominent Cornish families at a time when botanists were exploring the globe and collecting new exotic plants, many of which were acquired by the influential estate-owners of the day.

THE LOST GARDENS OF HELIGAN*

These gardens, splendidly situated at the head of a picturesque valley with views across the historic fishing harbour of Mevagissey, were created by the Tremayne family. Originally part of a grand self-contained estate, the 57 acres of pleasure grounds were once considered the finest Victorian gardens in Cornwall, if not in the whole of England. However, after the First World War, the estate was tenanted. From then on the larger part of the great garden gradually fell asleep under a thick blanket of bramble, ivy and rampant laurel, and the house was sold in 1970 as flats. In 1990, the gardens were rediscovered and their value as a unique time capsule realised. Thus began the largest and most important garden reclamation project in Britain, to restore a museum of nineteenth-century horticulture.

You can make your own fascinating discoveries by wandering along the Ride, where 18 inches of loam and ivy were peeled back to reveal the original paths and drains in perfect condition; exploring the Ravine, a hundred-yard man-made rockery complete with Victorian water system; or strolling across Flora's Green, a grassy sward flanked by a fine collection of rhododendrons, many of which were grown from seeds gathered by the explorer Sir Joseph Hooker between 1847 and 1851. Make sure you see the set of bee boles, precursors of bee hives, dating from 1830, and the only surviving pineapple pit in Britain, now fully restored and growing pineapples again after a gap of 100 years.

Another highlight of your visit is likely to be the magical sub-tropical valley garden known as the Jungle. A boardwalk winds around lakes and across swampland vegetation, revealing the largest collection of tree

The Lost Gardens of Heligan - a sleeping beauty awakened after 70 years

palms, about 60 varieties of bamboo and exotic trees and shrubs. Up the trunk of one of the largest trees here (the *Podocarpus totara*), you will see one of the many bat boxes in the gardens – part of an attempt to preserve native bats. Stout footwear is essential in wet weather. Take care on the uneven and sometimes overgrown paths.

TRELISSICK GARDEN*

Occupying 390 acres of parkland and woodland, with magnificent views across the beautiful Fal estuary, Trelissick Garden is one of the National Trust's most popular botanical attractions in Cornwall. The extensive park was landscaped in the eighteenth and early nineteenth centuries, and the 25 acres of tranquil garden were developed between 1937 and 1955 by the Copeland family, who inherited the elegant nineteenth-century house (not open) with its Grecian façade. In spring and early summer over 100 kinds of camellias, magnolias, rhododendrons and hydrangeas can be seen in the course of a gentle stroll around the garden. Also easy on the eye are many unusual and exotic plants and shrubs, a dell full of giant cedar and cypress trees and a large walled garden with fig trees. Fine oak and beech woodland lapped by the deep waters of the Fal estuary make this splendid walking country and the 4½-mile perimeter walk can be enjoyed all year round.

THE THREE FOX GARDENS

The wood-fringed charm of the serene Helford River, with its deep, sheltered creeks and winding inlets, is the setting for three of Cornwall's most remarkable gardens. Penjerrick, Glendurgan and Trebah were just some of eight estates within five miles of each other that were owned by the Fox family during the late eighteenth and nineteenth centuries.

Penjerrick* is a luxuriant 15-acre valley-garden with glorious sea views featuring ponds in a wild woodland setting. It is home to the glorious Penjerrick rhododendron hybrids that can be found in hundreds of gardens across the country. You will also find magnificent camellias,

bamboos, tree ferns and lawns flanked by purple beeches and conifers in this delightful garden.

The garden at **Glendurgan*** (NT) is another botanical wonder. You can walk through the stunning valley, rich in fine trees and rare and exotic shrubs – notably camellias, magnolias and enormous tulip trees – to reach the tiny waterside hamlet of Durgan. Children will enjoy the Giant's Stride (a pole with ropes to swing from) and the laurel maze.

Only a few hundred yards from Glendurgan lies the dramatic **Trebah Garden***. Its 26 sub-tropical acres occupy a deep ravine that drops over 200 feet to a private beach – which visitors to the garden may use – on the Helford River. Ambling through the dense network of paths, you come upon ponds full of giant Koi carp, waterfalls and unusual water plants; many species of rhododendron; and a range of tender trees and shrubs, such as the Chilean laurel, varieties of eucalyptus, tree ferns, Chusan palm trees and a Chinese fir. Children will have fun in the play area enclosed within a tree canopy and the 'Trebah Trail' and the 'Time Trail'.

> **LUNCHBOX**
>
> In Trelissick, the Garden Arts and Crafts Gallery and the excellent Barn Restaurant offer light lunches and afternoon teas. There are also cafés at Heligan, Glendurgan and Trebah, and plenty of suitable picnic places at all the gardens.

The restored cherry laurel maze of 1833 at Glendurgan

Picturesque Padstow and the North Cornish Coast

The working fishing port and civilised little resort of Padstow, a couple of grand country houses, heady coastal scenery and fine beaches present a varied day out on Cornwall's north coast.

We suggest spending the morning wandering around Padstow's port, and certainly having lunch here (see Lunchbox). If the weather is poor or you fancy a bit of culture head off to the local country houses in the afternoon. If the weather's fine, you could walk along the coast from Padstow, or take the car to better beaches nearby and to grandiose Carnewas.

PADSTOW

John Betjeman rightly describes Padstow as being 'less touristy than other [Cornish] fishing towns like Polperro and St Ives' and, lying snugly within the sandy Camel Estuary, 'less dramatic than Boscastle and Tintagel'. Though tourism has certainly made its impact on the

- ♦ **GOOD FOR** Pottering around a picturesque fishing town – with excellent restaurants – and taking in country houses and beaches
- ♦ **TRANSPORT** Car essential to get to Carnewas and Pencarrow House
- ♦ **ACCESS FOR DISABLED PEOPLE** Only limited access to Prideaux Place and Pencarrow House
- ♦ **BEST TIME TO VISIT** Padstow doesn't become as crowded as some other Cornish ports in high season. Prideaux Place and Pencarrow House are open only certain hours Sunday to Thursday between Easter and September/October. Padstow's May Day celebrations are special (see overleaf)

semi-circle of slate-hung houses round the harbour, the fudge, shell and gift shops and the cafés here are

not a gaudy bunch. The names of quayside enterprises, such as the Old Custom House Hotel and the Shipwright's Inn, recall Padstow's heyday as a port, before ships became too large to navigate the estuary's sands and the railway arrived.

If the weather is suitable, you can take a pleasure cruise or fishing trip. Otherwise, browse around the narrow backstreets and alleyways behind the harbour and in the art galleries and antique shops. The little **Padstow Museum** above the library on the Market Place will tell you more about the port's history and the 'Obby 'Oss, a pantomime-like horse, led through the streets during May Day celebrations, all the while hassled by a 'teazer' with a club. This ancient musical festival is said to originate from ancient pagan fertility rites.

Directly south of the harbour, ocean-going netters and trawlers may be moored at the docks (or even unloading their catch if you're lucky). You can look at tanks of conger eels, lobsters and crabs in one quayside warehouse. Another has been converted into the **Padstow Shipwreck Museum***, which is full of photos of old wrecks and artefacts salvaged from the *Lusitania* and the *Medina*, liners sunk in the First World War.

BEACHES AND DRAMATIC COASTAL SCENERY

Padstow doesn't have a beach it can call its own – the nearest good sandy strip is a pleasant 20-minute walk north along the estuary. It's a gentle further half-hour stroll from the beach on to **Stepper Point**, whose double aspect takes in a gaunt, cliffy coastline and the yellow, estuarine shoreline. You can drive to a car park (closed out of season) between the beach and the point to cut down on the walking.

▲ *The Bedruthan Steps have been renamed Carnewas after the family that owns them*

Further west are much more impressive beaches. Take your pick from the vast sands at **Harlyn Bay**, the even bigger, dune-backed **Constantine Bay** (with dangerous currents in places), and a deep sandy cove, **Porthcothan Bay**.

If you're not interested in swimming, head for **Carnewas**, a beach famous for the giant rocks spattered across it. The geological explanation is that these granite stacks have withstood the erosion by the sea while the softer surrounding rock has disappeared, but according to legend put about for nineteenth-century tourists the rocks were stepping stones for the giant Bedruthan. It's a five-minute walk from the National Trust's tea rooms and **tourist information office*** to the top of the steep flight of steps (which has recently been reopened) down to the beach. Bathing is not advised because of the strong currents, and the beach is completely covered at high tide. However, even then the trip is worth it for the walks along the spectacular clifftops.

TWO COUNTRY HOUSES

Amid a deer park on the hill above Padstow stands Elizabethan **Prideaux Place***, still very much the home of the Prideaux-Brune family who have been in residence (originally as Prideaux) since it was built in 1592. The hour-long tour of a small selection of the house's many rooms (80 in total, including broom cupboards) introduces over-the-top Strawberry Hill Gothic and Georgian alterations, a panoply of family portraits, works by the distinguished Cornish portrait painter John Opie, and the Great Chamber, with its incredible plaster ceiling painted with biblical images.

An hour-long spin around **Pencarrow House and Gardens*** also offers a behind-the-scenes look at the lives of Cornish gentry. The head of the resident Molesworth-St Aubyn family is the fifteenth baronet; the fourth baronet began

'Obby 'Oss dancing takes place on May Morning, and the crowd joins in the chorus and last line of each verse of the Morning Song

the house in the mid-eighteenth century. The house is littered with portraits, including what is claimed to be the most important family set by Joshua Reynolds, and fine furnishings, many with interesting histories, such as curtains acquired by the sixth baronet after a sea battle with a Spanish ship off the Philippines. The 50 acres of formal and woodland gardens, with trails through the woods to a lily-covered lake, boast some 570 types of rhododendron, as well as camellias and azaleas.

Boscastle, Tintagel and Arthurian legend

One of Cornwall's prettiest harbours, Boscastle lies close to a touristy but dramatic spot — Tintagel, with its ruined headland castle.

This stretch of the north Cornish seaboard holds some of Britain's most inspirational coastal scenery. Sheer cliffs, pummelled into shape by the Atlantic, contrast sharply with the pint-sized port of Boscastle, secret in its deep ravine. While Boscastle is prim and neat in typical National Trust tradition (the NT owns most of the harbour), Tintagel is over-commercialised. But at both places the primary attraction is the exhilarating coastal scenery, which you can appreciate only if you are willing to walk a little.

BOSCASTLE

Boscastle is now a serene and picturesque place, but before the railway reached nearby Camelford in 1893 it was a bustling port, with hundreds of schooners and ketches laden with limestone, slate and china clay negotiating its sinuous inlet.

Park behind the harbour and before setting off consider popping

♦ **GOOD FOR** Combining an interest in the Arthurian legend with cliff-top walks; children will enjoy Tintagel
♦ **TRANSPORT** A car is essential: Boscastle is 4 miles from Tintagel
♦ **ACCESS FOR DISABLED** Access is good at the Heritage Coast Visitor Centre and King Arthur's Great Halls
♦ **BEST TIME TO VISIT** Out of season; Tintagel and Boscastle get very crowded in the summer, but even then you can leave the crowds behind if you go on to the cliffs. Tintagel Castle and King Arthur's Great Halls stay open all year; others shut from November to Easter

into the **Heritage Coast Visitor Centre*** for an introduction to local history, geology and wildlife. The rear of the harbour is indubitably quaint, with an old mill converted into a crafts centre and the likes of the Pixie Cottage selling lucky charms and unicorn heads. Follow the frothing stream past more sagging, slate-roofed cottages converted into gift

shops and tea rooms to the curved arm of the **harbour** proper, where the tweeness soon dissolves. Steep, brackeny sides hem in the harbour and a pair of ancient walls defend it from the sea.

The path on the northern side provides the best harbour view if you are willing to scramble on to the slate fist of **Penally Point**. If you take the southern path, you can continue on a pleasant half-hour circular walk. Climb up to the white, defunct lookout on Willapark, from which there are unbeatable views along the coast. Then cut inland to Forrabury Church with its piscine weathervane, and follow the road from the less touristy upper village back down to lower Boscastle.

A three-mile drive north-east of Boscastle brings you to **St Juliot Church**, a medieval building neatly restored by Thomas Hardy in 1872. His architectural drawings are on show, as is a memorial to the novelist and his wife Emma, the rector's sister-in-law.

TINTAGEL

According to legend, the site of the ruins of **Tintagel Castle*** was King Arthur's birthplace and his Camelot; Merlin is supposed to have lived in a cave underneath. Yet even English Heritage, which manages the site, admits 'the bald facts provide no basis for Arthurian romance', and the National Trust asserts that there is not a shred of evidence that Arthur ever came here. The association was fabricated in writing first by Geoffrey of Monmouth in the twelfth century, perpetuated by Sir Thomas Mallory 300 years later, and re-endorsed by Tennyson in Victorian times.

Experts agree that the visible remains come from the thirteenth century, but the site's pre-medieval

▲ *Tintagel Castle is best seen from the opposite cliff for an overall view*

history is still uncertain, despite the ongoing archaeological work. What is known is that there has been a settlement here since Roman times, and that in the Dark Ages there may have been a Cornish king's castle or a Celtic monastery on the site.

Actually, the Arthurian cult is superfluous to the castle's allure. While the medieval remains are scanty, just enough still stand to give you a flavour of the fortress. But more remarkable is their position, above colossal cliffs, accessed by steep staircases and spread across a miniature isthmus, half on a virtual island, half on the mainland. To reach the castle, it is a steep ten-minute walk down from the village, or you can take a ride in a Land Rover.

Walk south along the cliffs for half a mile to the isolated **Tintagel Church**, where little stone walls prop up the wind-battered gravestones. The early Norman building has interesting features, such as a Saxon doorway, miniature windows and a carved Norman font.

A half-mile stroll inland from the church along a lane takes you back to Tintagel village, where Arthurian links are milked for all they're worth. Among the rather touristy shops try the King Arthur Book Shop for its enormous selection of books on British legends and mysticism. Otherwise, scurry into the sanctuary of the National Trust's **Old Post Office***, a tiny fourteenth-century manor house with an improbably sloping roof. Its dolls'-house-sized rooms, one of which reconstructs the post office that was here in the nineteenth century, are best visited early or late in the day, when the place is relatively peaceful.

Lastly, Tintagel's most bizarre expression of the Arthurian legend is **King Arthur's Great Halls***, built by a millionaire custard manufacturer in 1933. In the first hall, dated special effects and pre-Raphaelite-style paintings relate the Arthurian story, and in the second, 73 stained-glass windows show the knights' heraldic devices and their deeds.

If you want to spend time on the beach, head for **Trebarwith**, just south of Tintagel, which is big and sandy except at high tide.

LUNCHBOX

Boscastle has tea shops round the back of the harbour; its most appealing pub is the Napoleon Inn at the top of the village. Rather than try to find a good place in Tintagel, you would do better seeking out the good fishy menus of the Port William pub at Trebarwith.

▲ *One room in this manor house was established as a post office as early as 1844*

Exploring the verdant Dart estuary

The Dart estuary ferry traces a route through the most distinctive scenery in south Devon

The sinewy, multi-tentacled Dart estuary is best seen from the water, whether you are on a yacht or an organised cruise boat. The river connects the genteel, historic ports of Dartmouth and Totnes, both of which deserve some hours of exploration.

The view of Dartmouth from across the estuary is one of colourful houses rising in rows up the hillsides. The wide waterway between it and Kingswear could hardly be busier, being packed with boats, car ferries plying between the two sides, hundreds of sleek yachts, fishing boats loaded with lobster pots and buoys, and the training vessels of the landmark Britannia Royal Naval College. Downstream you pass Bayard's Cove on the way to Dartmouth Castle (both of which you can visit – see overleaf). Upstream you see ship-repair yards before coming to the Dart's peaceful reaches, where banks, intersected by finger-thin creeks, are covered by thick woodland. In the TV series *The*

♦ **GOOD FOR** Wandering through two old towns on foot and viewing them from the river; Totnes is good for browsing, especially for those interested in New Age issues

♦ **TRANSPORT** Ferry services connect Totnes to Dartmouth (see below). The towns are 13 miles apart by road, and are best explored on foot

♦ **ACCESS FOR DISABLED PEOPLE** Access is good for River Link and Red Cruisers' boats Driving Ferry services

♦ **BEST TIME TO VISIT** Ferry services between Totnes and Dartmouth operate from April to the end of October. From November to March circular cruises from Dartmouth are infrequent, and the castles and small museums are closed or have limited hours. The three-day Dartmouth Royal Regatta is at the end of August

Onedin Line this scenery masqueraded as Amazonian rainforest. The area is rich in birdlife (bring binoculars); you can see herons, cormorants, shags, oystercatchers and curlews, especially in the mudflats. Watch carefully to see a seal's head poking out of the water like a periscope. The commentary on board the boat points out various grand houses half-visible behind the screen of trees, one of which is Greenway, the former home of Agatha Christie, and provides anecdotes relating to picturesque villages such as Dittisham, with its thatched waterside cottages.

DARTMOUTH

The second and third Crusades sailed from here in the twelfth century, as did ships that were to fight the Spanish Armada and a large proportion of the D-Day fleet. Nowadays, it is a well-to-do holiday town, with art galleries, craft shops, yacht chandlers and some classy restaurants.

Over the centuries it has grown on reclaimed land (basically the flat part of the town). Visitors naturally gravitate first towards the **Boat Float**, a pretty little inner harbour surrounded by tall, colourfully plastered Victorian houses. Just north on Duke Street is the timbered, richly carved, slate-hung Tudor **butterwalk**, so called because the projected first floor created a shaded arcade which stopped traders' butter below from melting. One of its houses contains the small **Dartmouth Museum***, covering much maritime history and with model ships on display in beautiful panelled rooms. Further north lie lanes bursting with flower displays, such as pedestrianised Foss Street, and stepped **Brown's Hill**, once a packhorse route.

South of the Boat Float lie Dartmouth's most notable medieval houses, particularly on Higher Street,

The Cherub Inn, in Higher Street, is Dartmouth's oldest remaining building

the old centre of the town. Some of the tottering, timbered buildings here were originally the shambles, or butchers' shops. The beamy **Cherub Inn**, dating from 1380, was originally a merchant's house. Further south on Lower Street stands **Agincourt House**, an antiques and coffee shop dating from the same period. But the favourite corner of Dartmouth for most visitors is the stone and cobbled jetty of **Bayard's Cove** just beyond; superficially, it seems to have changed little since the *Mayflower* moored here in 1620 on its way to America.

About a mile south (also reachable by ferry from the main quay), **Dartmouth Castle***, the first castle to be designed for artillery, rises out of the rocks near the estuary mouth. You can clamber around the considerable building work, which dates from medieval times, but the views are the main attraction.

TOTNES

In Tudor times Totnes was one of the country's richest towns, thanks to a profitable export trade in wool-cloth and tin. As a result, the main streets of this hilly town are rich in slate-hung and gabled merchants' houses, the best now housing the **Elizabethan Museum***, which is local, extensive and varied. Other sights include another **butterwalk** further up, and, just off the High Street, the interesting **guildhall**, with a fine courtroom and council chamber to view. The Norman motte and bailey **castle*** above the town has a complete circular keep, as it never saw battle, from which there are extensive views over the town's roofs and the Dart beyond. Totnes' riverside aspect is less

The heron is just one of the many breeds of bird seen from the ferries that cruise up and down the River Dart

appealing, but on Steamer Quay you might nose around the **Totnes Motor Museum***, a good collection of vintage children's and racing cars, bicycles and motorbikes.

Totnes is also a paradise for browsers. Amid elegant clothes shops and traditional gift shops, other stores either sell books or the latest health foods, and many tout New Age therapies. In addition, advertisements offer palm-reading, Chinese medicine and astrology courses. On Tuesday mornings in summer traders don Elizabethan costume. For more information, visit the Totnes **tourist information office***, situated on The Plaines, near the river.

Dartmoor: isolation and idyllic hamlets

Dartmoor is the largest uninhabited region in the south of England

From the desolate beauty of Dartmoor to the picture-postcard villages that nestle in its wooded valley fringes, this scenic drive explores the landscape of southern England's wildest tract of open country.

The best way to appreciate Dartmoor is to combine a drive with a series of easy strolls. This tour crosses the high moorland with its ancient stone clapper bridges (made with raised stones), lofty granite tors, prehistoric settlements and panoramic views, then meanders through river valleys on the eastern flanks, via high-hedged lanes strung with villages of thatch and stone. Here we describe the places of interest along the way, and worthwhile diversions and the principal spots for short rambles.

The drive starts from the fine cathedral city of **Exeter**. You could easily spend much of the day wandering around its cobbled streets, admiring the Elizabethan buildings and enjoying the excellent shops. Focal points include the Norman

- ♦ **GOOD FOR** Those who are keen walkers and lovers of olde worlde villages
- ♦ **TRANSPORT** Car essential: approximately 70-mile round trip
- ♦ **ACCESS FOR DISABLED PEOPLE** Possible at some sights – phone to check
- ♦ **BEST TIME TO VISIT** All year, although Dartmoor can be an inhospitable place to drive across in winter, as weather conditions can change rapidly

cathedral*, the fourteenth-century guildhall* and the **Maritime Museum*** in the lively quay area. Free guided tours of the city begin from the Cathedral Close throughout the year and the Quay House Interpretation Centre in the summer.

Within minutes of leaving the city confines you begin the gradual ascent towards Dartmoor, first crossing the edge of the wooded Haldon Hills to reach the village of **Dunsford** in the Teign Valley. Nearby Steps Bridge, where the River Teign emerges from its steep and wooded gorge, is a good place for a short woodland or riverside stroll – particularly reputed in spring when the wild daffodils, ransoms (wild garlic) and bluebells are out. Superb views unfold across the valleys as you approach the small market town of **Moretonhampstead**, one of the 'Gateways to Dartmoor'.

Four miles north-west of the town, near **Drewsteignton**, stands the granite **Castle Drogo*** (NT) on a crag 900 feet above the valley, commanding wonderful views of Dartmoor from its gardens. Designed by Sir Edwin Lutyens and built between 1910 and 1930, it is a bizarre combination of medieval might and twentieth-century luxury. Starting from the Angler's Rest pub, which is situated by the sixteenth-century **Fingle Bridge** over the Teign, you can enjoy a superb riverside ramble.

North Bovey, a mile south of Moretonhampstead, is a typical Dartmoor village, with beautifully preserved cob and thatch cottages flanking a green, complete with an ancient cross, pump and commemorative oaks.

The **Miniature Pony Centre*** (near North Bovey), where children can mingle with an assortment of animals from Shetland ponies and pygmy goats to dwarf rabbits, is worth a visit. It has an indoor play area, lakeside restaurant and local craft shop. High up on the moor is impressive **Grimspound**, a fine example of a Bronze Age shepherd settlement with well-preserved remains of 24 huts. The tiny hamlet of **Postbridge**, renowned for its fourteenth-century clapper bridge, is a good place for a walk and a

Haytor is the most visited tor in Dartmoor

picnic alongside the East Dart River, as is nearby **Bellever**, which has forest trails and a riverside picnic area. Climb Bellever Tor for far-reaching views over the emptiest parts of the moor.

If you wish to find out more about Dartmoor's landscape, wildlife and development from prehistoric times, visit **Princetown** and the fascinating **High Moorland Visitor Centre***. From **Two Bridges**, just to the east, an easy one-and-a-half mile walk along the West Dart River leads to Wistman's Wood, where 500-year-old mis-shapen and stunted oak trees form the last remains of the primeval forest that once covered Dartmoor. Beyond **Dartmeet**, a famous beauty spot with a clapper bridge, café and footpaths, you soon descend from the bleakness of the moor into the softer and more sheltered landscape of Dartmoor's eastern fringe, where small rivers tumble through deep wooded valleys, and tiny country

lanes link some of the moor's prettiest villages. (Many of the lanes are narrow and steep with high hedges, so take great care as you drive along them.)

Unspoilt **Buckland in the Moor** lies enveloped in woodland, a cluster of granite and thatch cottages beside a rocky stream. Surrounded by high ridges and tors, **Widecombe in the Moor** is probably the best-known and most visited of the Dartmoor villages. Immortalised by the song 'Widecombe Fair', it is dominated by the 120-foot tower of its fourteenth-century church, the Cathedral of the Moor; the next-door **Church House*** (NT), originally a brewhouse dating from 1537, is occasionally open to the public.

Haytor is the most accessible and most loved of the moor's jagged tors. Your reward for making the short climb from the car park is the views across the lowlands of Devon to the

coast and into the tor-strewn heart of Dartmoor. Further exploration will lead you to a number of interesting relics of Dartmoor's industrial past, such as the route of an old granite tramway which transported stone from nearby quarries.

Tucked away in the Bovey Valley on the fringes of the moor the small town of **Bovey Tracey** is a useful stopping place, not only for refreshment but for the excellent craft centre (**Devon Guild of Craftsmen***) housed in a former watermill. Parke Estate (NT) on the edge of the town is home to the headquarters of the Dartmoor National Park Authority (**Information Centre***). For more information phone the Exeter **tourist information office***.

OTHER PLACES WORTH SEEING
Investigate the lovely Bovey Valley, especially the village of **Manaton**, once the home of novelist John Galsworthy, and idyllic **Lustleigh** where old cottages, a thatched inn and a tea room cluster around the historic church and village green. Nearby are the **Becka Falls***, where the Becka Brook plunges 70 feet down a boulder-strewn wooded valley; it is best seen after heavy rain.

Another good place for a family excursion would be **Canonteign Falls and Country Park***, set in 100 acres of ancient woodland. It boasts the highest waterfall in England, nature trails, lakes, licensed restaurant and excellent children's play facilities.

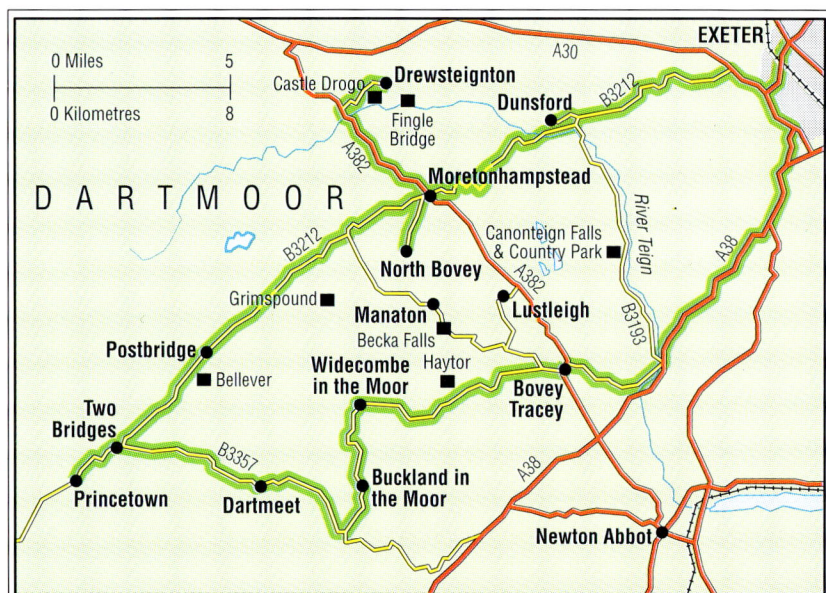

LUNCHBOX
The isolated Warren House Inn (on the road between Moretonhampstead and Postbridge), England's third-highest inn, is good for snacks. The peat fire there is said to have been burning continuously for over 100 years. Otherwise, seek out the Rock Inn at Haytor Vale, Cridford Inn at Trusham, Manor Inn at Lower Ashton and the Nobody Inn at Doddiscombsleigh, the timeless Drewe Arms in Drewsteignton and the Rugglestone Inn at Widecombe in the Moor.

Tea rooms abound, including the one at Castle Drogo, the elegant lounge or terrace at the splendid Gidleigh Park Hotel near Chagford, Primrose Cottage in Lustleigh and the Granary Café in the Riverside Mill at Bovey Tracey.

On the Tarka Trail 'twixt the Taw and the Torridge

Broughams and other carriages in the Loft at Arlington Court

The Tarka Trail meanders along tranquil estuaries, peaceful river valleys, fields and hedges that hide hamlets and forgotten lanes – the landscape that inspired Henry Williamson to write Tarka the Otter.

Henry Williamson (1895–1977) came to north Devon on a motorcycle to escape from the drudgery of suburbia. While living in a rented cottage he encountered an orphaned otter cub, and it is his experiences nurturing the cub that form the heart of his novel, *Tarka the Otter*, published in 1927. In 1978 this minutely observed and moving tale was made into a film.

Although you will see much mention of Tarka hereabouts, you are unlikely to see any real otters. (Far more common is the imported mink, similar but smaller.) Those intent on seeing an otter should head over to the **Otter Trust Sanctuary*** at North Petherwin, three miles north-west of Launceston (about 25 miles from Barnstaple).

The long-distance **Tarka Trail** (180 miles in all) forms a large figure-of-eight centred on the historic town of **Barnstaple**, the perfect base from which to begin your day. Spend part of the morning

♦ **GOOD FOR** Walkers and cyclists. Gentle inclines and a good surface, especially between Barnstaple and Great Torrington, make the Trail particularly suitable for wheelchair-users and families with young children on bicycles. A series of leaflets, 'Mid Devon Country Walks and Villages', is ideal for those exploring this rural backwater by car

♦ **TRANSPORT** BR station at Barnstaple, connected to the main Exeter line

♦ **ACCESS FOR DISABLED PEOPLE** Good access for most sights; adapted cycles can be hired for use on the Tarka Trail

♦ **BEST TIME TO VISIT** Excellent walking and cycling all year. Most sights are open from Easter to November

strolling round Barnstaple's narrow streets, enjoying the variety of small specialist shops and the bustling, lofty Victorian Pannier Market, or visit the **Museum of North Devon***, with its Tarka Gallery.

Then make your way to the railway station and the start of the

This day out concentrates on the southern part of the Tarka Trail but information about the area, including details of the myriad of walks, as well as the Tarka Line, can be obtained from the **Tarka Country Tourism Association*** or the **tourist information office*** at Barnstaple.

trail's southern loop. Take the Tarka Line railway which runs south from here (see box), or walk or cycle (bikes can be hired from **Tarka Trail Cycle Hire***) along the westward part of the loop which follows the disused line towards Petrockstowe.

SOUTH-WEST OF BARNSTAPLE

The 23 traffic-free miles pass through a rich variety of countryside, from the open saltmarsh of the Taw/Torridge estuary to the rolling farmland and ancient woodland of the inland valleys.

Rewarding diversions along the way include the pretty estuary village of **Instow**, where you can visit the Italianate garden at **Tapeley Park*** or take the summer ferry across the estuary to **Appledore**, a small boat-building village with narrow cobbled streets, pastel-coloured Georgian cottages, lovely harbour and the **North Devon Maritime Museum***, comprising several rooms, each displaying different aspects of Devon's maritime history, with steam and motor coasters.

The quiet hillside town of **Bideford** was Britain's third-largest port in the sixteenth century and, like Barnstaple, it comes complete with medieval bridge, historic covered market and antique shops. Beyond Bideford the trail explores the deeply wooded **Torridge Valley**; diversions can be made to the attractive villages of Monkleigh (pottery), Frithelstock (site of ancient priory) and Weare Giffard.

Shy, nocturnal creatures, otters are hard to find

Beyond Canal Bridge, the fictitious birthplace of Tarka, is the ancient market town of **Great Torrington**, set high above the river and affording magnificent views from its well-tended commons. In the town, you can join a guided tour at the

Dartington Crystal* factory to see glass-blowers at work as well as an exhibition tracing the history of glass over the past 300 years. Garden enthusiasts should not miss the **RHS Rosemoor Garden*** (1 mile south-east), which nestles in a sheltered wooded valley and contains fine collections of rare shrubs and trees and 2,000 varieties of rose.

Beyond Petrockstowe the trail takes to footpaths, eventually reaching Okehampton and the wild fringes of Dartmoor. The villages of Hatherleigh (pottery and crafts), Sheepwash, Black Torrington, Iddesleigh and Winkleigh are particularly charming and worth a browse.

Keen cyclists can follow peaceful country lanes from Petrockstowe, possibly linking up with the Sticklepath Cycle Route before making good use of the innovative **Bike Bus***, a summer-only service (No. 361), which stops at Okehampton, Hatherleigh and Meeth on its way back to Barnstaple.

NORTH-WEST OF BARNSTAPLE

An easy excursion north-west of Barnstaple is to follow the trail along the Taw/Torridge estuary to Braunton and **Braunton Burrows National Nature Reserve***, an area of sand dunes, saltmarsh and pasture that provides an important habitat for many species of birds and wild flowers. Other notable places to visit within easy reach of Barnstaple include **Arlington Court and Park*** (NT; 7 miles north-east of Barnstaple on the A39), a magnificent early nineteenth-century house set in 30 acres of landscaped gardens and parkland. There are splendid collections of models, costumes, shells and early horse-drawn carriages, as well as woodland and lakeside walks.

THE TARKA LINE

The **Tarka Line*** is one of the prettiest branch lines in Britain; it follows the gentle river valleys of the Taw and Yeo between Barnstaple and Exeter. Those seeking the peace and tranquillity of the Taw Valley should alight at **Eggesford Bridge** for the Tarka Trail, easy waymarked forest walks and cycle trails; bikes can be hired from **Eggesford Country Centre***.

LUNCHBOX

Excellent lunches are served at the Lynwood House restaurant in Barnstaple. Along or just off the trail try the Quay at Instow, the Clinton Arms in Frithelstock, the Cyder Press in Weare Giffard and the Black Horse in Great Torrington for reliable bar lunches, or, further afield, the Half Moon in Sheepwash, the Tally Ho! in Hatherleigh and the thatched Duke of York at Iddesleigh. Good teas are available at Tapeley Park at Instow, Honey Beam Cottage Tea Room in Weare Giffard, Acorn Tea Rooms in Hatherleigh, Eggesford Country Centre, and at the NT restaurant at Arlington Court.

From moorland to sea on the Somerset coast

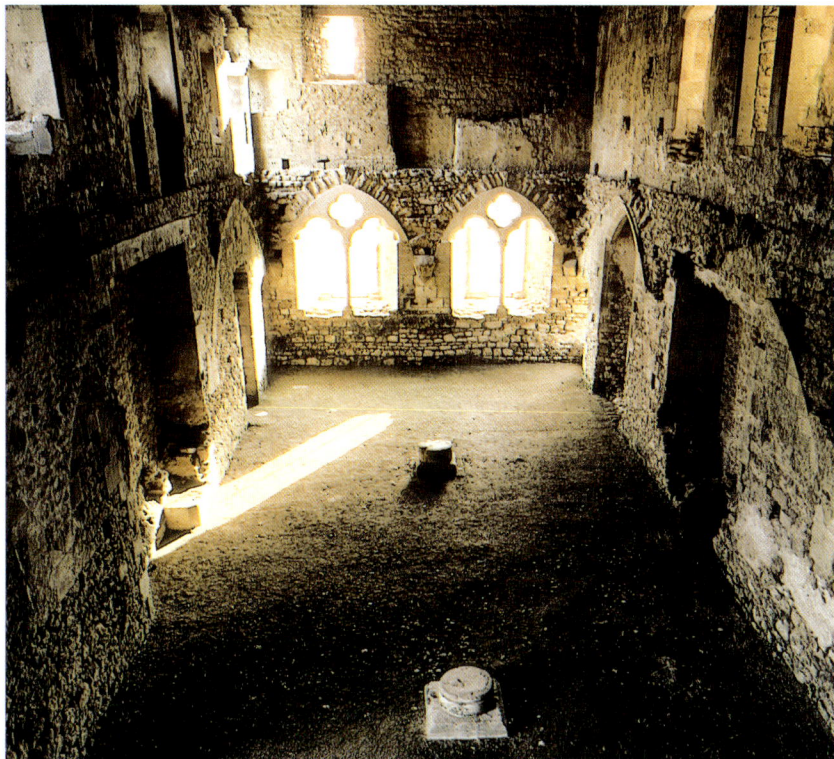

Some 700 years on, Cleeve Abbey still boasts a complete set of cloisters

Magnificent walks, stunning views, picture-book villages, a bustling seaside resort and a clutch of literary associations — Exmoor and the Quantocks are blessed with all these, making for a varied day out.

A leisurely drive along the scenic A39 between Lynton in Devon and Bridgwater in Somerset must be one of the most rewarding car journeys in the West Country. After crossing the rolling heather-covered uplands of Exmoor with its spectacular views of rugged hogback cliffs and the deep inland combes of Doone country, it plunges into the Vale of Porlock, surrounded by wooded hillsides. Further east, beyond Minehead, it skirts the undulating fields and forests of the Brendon Hills to reach the unspoilt Quantock Hills, familiar to Coleridge and Wordsworth.

Having ascended Countisbury Hill just east of Lynton to be greeted by breathtaking views over the Bristol Channel to the Welsh coast, *Lorna Doone* fans can make a short detour to explore the valleys, villages and landmarks immortalised by R.D. Blackmore. Fact and fantasy merge as

♦ **GOOD FOR** An ideal family motoring tour which will appeal to walkers too
♦ **TRANSPORT** Car necessary – one-way trip about 30 miles
♦ **ACCESS FOR DISABLED PEOPLE** Dunster watermill: access to lower floor only, steps with handrails to upper levels; Cleeve Abbey: ground floor only; Combe Sydenham: ground floor only; Coleridge Cottage: steps up to building
♦ **BEST TIME TO VISIT** All year for walking, particularly in autumn; most sights are open between Easter and October

you follow the tortuous narrow lane beside the East Lyn River, linking Oare Church (scene of Lorna's tragic wedding), Malmsmead and its footpath access deep into Doone country, and Robbers' Bridge, before rejoining the A39 near the top of the notorious Porlock Hill. To appreciate the outstanding coastal views and abundant wildlife of this area,

descend into Porlock via the winding wooded toll road, well worth the small fee.

Enclosed on three sides by hills, **Porlock**, with its narrow streets, is a good place to pause for refreshment. There is an exhilarating 1½-mile walk from the harbour village of **Porlock Weir** along the wooded cliff path to tiny **Culbone Church**, England's smallest complete parish church at 35 x 12 feet. It lies hidden in a wooded combe and boasts a pre-Norman leaded window and a fourteenth-century bell.

The Vale of Porlock is an area of chocolate-box cottages of thatch and cob. The 12,400-acre Holnicote Estate (NT) takes in some 4½ miles of coastline between Porlock and Minehead. **Allerford** is famous for its double-arched packhorse bridge and the **West Somerset Rural Life Museum*,** housed in the old thatched school, which gives a fascinating insight into Victorian village school life and displays domestic and farming tools of the period. Even more attractive is **Selworthy**, a charming collection of thatched white cottages around a walnut-shaped green. Sheltering beneath majestic Selworthy Beacon – ideal walking country – the village looks out across the lush valley to Dunkery and the Exmoor Hills. Buildings of note are the old tithe barn, fifteenth-century almshouses and the fourteenth-century church topped by a magnificent wagon roof.

Those who like walking can leave their cars at Horner or Webber's Post car parks and explore the many waymarked paths, notably the Cloutsham Woodland Trail, that exist in these ancient wooded valleys. If you have the energy, climb to the top of **Dunkery Beacon**, the highest point on Exmoor, for some awe-inspiring views extending to the Brecon Beacons and Bodmin Moor.

The picturesque packhorse bridge in Allerford is built of rough stones

Minehead's sandy beach and promenade make it a popular holiday resort, and it is also one of the termini of the **West Somerset Railway***, Britain's longest private line: diesel and steam trains run for 20 miles along the coast to Watchet, then inland through glorious countryside – a good way to admire the Brendon and Quantock Hills.

Nestling between two hills on the eastern boundary of Exmoor is **Dunster**. Dominated by the battlements of its ancient **castle*** (NT), this fine medieval village is ideal to walk around in and for lunch or tea. Its treasures include an eight-sided Yarn Market, erected in 1609 when Dunster was an important cloth centre; the Old Nunnery, a fourteenth-century jettied and tile-hung building; a seventeenth-century **watermill***; and a thirteenth-century circular dovecote. The **National Park Visitor Centre*** next to the main car park can provide

you with more information on the history of Dunster and what to see.

At **Washford** you will find the ruins of **Cleeve Abbey*** (EH), a late twelfth-century Cistercian abbey with a well-preserved gatehouse, dormitory and refectory, plus medieval wall paintings and a fine timbered roof. An old BBC transmitting station near Washford has been transformed into an indoor jungle, complete with 15-foot waterfall and tropical plants – at **Tropiquaria*** you can see snakes and spiders, lizards and free-flying birds. An outdoor playground and the Shadowstring Puppet Theatre make it an ideal destination for families.

Combe Sydenham Country Park* lies on the edge of the Brendon Hills and is well worth the short detour off the A39, along the B3188 between Watchet and Wiveliscombe. You can visit the splendid sixteenth-century house, once the home of Sir Francis Drake's

second wife, Lady Sydenham, watch corn being ground into flour in the restored medieval corn mill and explore 500 acres of unspoilt woodland, via a network of well-signposted trails.

Beyond Williton, home to the fascinating **Orchard Mill Museum***, which displays rural and domestic bygones in a seventeenth-century watermill setting, the A39 rounds the striking ridge of rolling moor and woodland of the Quantock Hills. Fringed by villages, notably **East Quantoxhead**, with its cluster of cottages by a duck pond and Court House, once the seat of the Luttrell family, and **Holford**, where William Wordsworth rented Alfoxton House (now a hotel) in 1797, it is a peaceful and unspoilt area to explore on foot. Samuel Taylor Coleridge lived in neighbouring Nether Stowey and, like his friend and walking companion Wordsworth, he found the landscape inspirational: it was in his small **cottage*** (NT) in 1797–1800 that he wrote 'The Rime of the Ancient Mariner' and 'Kubla Khan'. There are good walks from Holford and from the tiny road that crosses the moor between Nether Stowey and Crowcombe.

LUNCHBOX

For reliable bar food try the Ship in Porlock or the historic Luttrell Arms in Dunster. Good places for tea (and lunch) include Periwinkle Cottage Tea Rooms in Selworthy; Horner Tea Rooms, the Old Tea Shoppe and the Watermill Tea Room, all in Dunster; and the Orchard Mill Museum restaurant at Williton. The Combe Sydenham Country Park also offers refreshments.

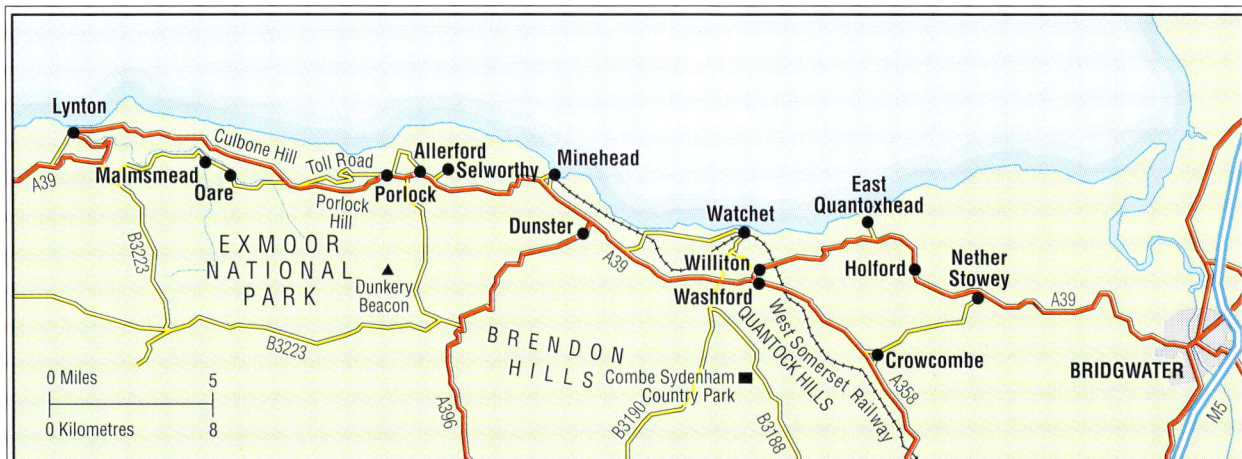

Myth, legend – and a shopping bonanza

A Benedictine monastery for part of its life, the abbey was destroyed in the Reformation

♦ **GOOD FOR** A varied day out, including walking, a tour round the abbey and shopping for unusual purchases
♦ **TRANSPORT** The nearest railway station to Glastonbury is Castle Cary (8 miles away), then there are taxis and a limited bus service. In Glastonbury a bus service runs from the Market Place to the Tor (half a mile away) from the beginning of July to the end of August. There is also a bus service from Glastonbury to Street
♦ **ACCESS FOR DISABLED PEOPLE** There is access to the abbey
♦ **BEST TIME TO VISIT** One weekend at the end of June Church of England and Roman Catholic pilgrimages proceed to the abbey. The abbey also hosts mystery plays in July. The abbey is open daily all year, as is Clarks Village. Most of the smaller sights have limited winter opening hours. There is a large influx of people into the town in the last week of June for the Glastonbury Festival of Performing Arts, a musical and counter-culture extravaganza

Glastonbury, once an island within a sea that covered the surrounding area, is an extraordinarily spiritual place, infused with a concoction of myth, legend and history. There is plenty here for visitors who wish to immerse themselves in this atmosphere.

Some people say that Glastonbury is the Celtic Avalon, the meeting-place of the dead, others that Joseph of Arimathea arrived here on a Christmas Day some years after Christ's crucifixion (some stories even suggest that he was Christ's uncle and visited Somerset with his nephew). When he planted his staff in nearby Wearyall Hill, the Glastonbury Thorn miraculously sprang up. Joseph also brought with him the chalice from the Last Supper and this became the Holy Grail of Arthurian legend. Furthermore, some say that

Arthur and Guinevere could have been buried here. Added to all this is much talk of ley-lines and the Glastonbury Zodiac (in which the local geography marks out the signs of the zodiac), as well as centuries of reliable ecclesiastical history, during which time Glastonbury Abbey became the richest in the land. Literature in the town's New Age shops will familiarise you with the basic tenets of all the history and legends.

Joseph of Arimathea is alleged to have built the first Christian church

on the site of the **abbey**, although its accountable history dates from AD688, when the Saxon King Ine founded the first monastery. In 1191, seven years after a fire had destroyed the abbey completely, monks 'found' the tomb of Arthur and Guinevere (the site is marked), quite possibly as a publicity ruse to attract pilgrims and their money. The abbey was dissolved in 1539, and the head of its abbot was, rather gruesomely, mounted on the gate.

The superb visitor centre* at the abbey tells you much more, and its information is complemented by archaeological finds such as possible souvenirs from visiting pilgrims and monks' paint palettes made from oyster shells. The majestic grounds are vast. Just enough of the abbey church and adjoining Lady Chapel still stand to convey the scale of what was once England's longest monastic church. Remains of the domestic buildings are very scanty, except for the wonderfully complete fourteenth-century Abbot's Kitchen. The thorn tree in the grounds is said to be a descendant of the original Glastonbury Thorn.

There is something mystical about the very shape of the **Tor**. It is no surprise, therefore, that this landmark hill has been associated with the Cosmic Mother, a fairies' glass mountain, the entrance to the underworld, and a hill-fort presided over by the King of the Summer People in Arthurian times. Alternatively, some claim that it is covered with an ancient maze and others that it is hollow and contains a druid temple. Whatever the case, the bracing climb (either from Wellhouse Lane or a steeper, shorter ascent from Stone Down Lane) is rewarded by expansive views from the top. The tower is all that remains of a fourteenth-century church.

Close to the western base of the Tor, the **Chalice Well*** lies at the top of a pretty garden. As spring water flows from the well through the garden, both above and below ground, iron deposits turn the rocks red – hence the legend that Joseph hid the chalice containing the blood of Christ here after the Last Supper. For centuries now the water has been believed to have healing powers, and

New Ageists hang out in the garden meditating. Just outside the garden on Wellhouse Lane a makeshift shrine of lockets of hair, feathers and a joker playing cards has been erected where the spring tumbles over a rock.

The **Somerset Rural Life Museum***, housed in the fine fourteenth-century abbey barn, has tableaux of local agricultural scenes – of peat-digging, cider-making and basket-weaving – along with old agricultural implements. The **Glastonbury Lake Village Museum***, above the **tourist information office*** in a fifteenth-century town house, has a fine exhibition on the discovery in 1892 of an Iron Age settlement just outside Glastonbury. The fascinating finds include ladles, wheel spokes and bracelets.

SHOPPING

Many a shop window in Glastonbury advertises crop circle symposiums, Tarot study groups and healing

Conjectures about what the Tor was used as add to its allure

workshops. Inside, you'll find buddhas, joss-sticks, New Age music and plenty of esoteric paraphernalia. Gothic Image, next to the tourist information office, has the best collection of literature on Glastonbury. The greatest concentration of way-out shops (and people), including a healing centre and **Avalon Information***, which offers guided tours round Glastonbury, can be found at **The Glastonbury Experience** in a pretty courtyard off the bottom of the High Street. At Star Child, one of the shops here, the incense is so thick you can hardly breathe.

AN EXCURSION TO STREET

To bring you down to earth, head the two miles over to **Street**, an unlovely town placed on the map by the Clark family, who founded Clarks shoe factory here in the nineteenth century. The big attraction, luring over two and a half million people annually, is the dazzlingly smart **Clarks Village***. The UK's first purpose-built factory shopping complex, it has some three dozen outlets, from Black & Decker to Benetton and Laura Ashley. All sell seconds and end-of-line stock at knock-down prices. The adjacent **Shoe Museum*** is a vast and thoroughly absorbing collection of footwear from Roman to contemporary times.

LUNCHBOX

Glastonbury has a surfeit of interesting cafés, the most stylish being the Blue Note Café (modernist in style, jazz posters on the wall) at the bottom of the High Street. Across the way is the George & Pilgrims, a fifteenth-century inn which began life as a guest house for abbey visitors; it serves teas and has an inexpensive brasserie.

Did the Chalice well-head cover hide the Holy Grail?

Exploring medieval Wells and ancient caves

The west front of Wells Cathedral dominates the little city

- ◆ **GOOD FOR** Families with older children
- ◆ **TRANSPORT** The nearest railway stations are Bristol and Bath. There is a very good bus service from both stations to Wells. Buses also run from Wells to Cheddar Gorge (9 miles away) and Wookey Hole (2 miles away)
- ◆ **ACCESS FOR DISABLED PEOPLE** Access is good for most of Wells Cathedral; at Wookey Hole there is access to the fascinating mill and at Cheddar there is very limited access to the caves
- ◆ **BEST TIME TO VISIT** Wookey Hole and Cheddar Gorge become very crowded in the school summer holidays, though the attractions cope well with large numbers. Throughout the year, the cathedral hosts many evening concerts and lays on daytime tours (except Sundays). Bishop's Palace has very limited opening hours

The tightly knit cluster of outstanding medieval buildings in Wells, England's smallest city, includes one of the country's most gorgeous cathedrals. A morning spent wandering around Wells is followed by a trip underground, at Wookey Hole or Cheddar Gorge, for this day out.

'A peaceful village, little more,' a commentator said about Wells in 1894. A century later, this tiny city feels no more important than a modest market town. Its sights are few in number but high in quality; allow little more than half a day to make a thorough exploration. Devote most of your time to the Gothic cathedral, which has a number of sublime features; ideally, take a cathedral tour. You need a couple of hours to see the caves and associated attractions at Wookey Hole or Cheddar Gorge so it is best to visit one or the other, not both.

CITY WALK

Start in the handsome **Market Place** (market days Wednesday, Thursday and Saturday). Its few antique shops include Bernard G. House's Scientific Instruments, which has a wonderful collection of old telescopes and barometers. The **tourist information office*** is also in Market Place. Dominating the square are two medieval arches; pass through the one called the **Penniless Porch** (where beggars used to – and still do – congregate) to the **Cathedral Green**, a great swathe of grass with seventeenth- and eighteenth-century buildings on three sides.

On the fourth side stands the **west front** of the **cathedral***, the most memorable of the building's five outstanding features. This vast monument still has on display three-quarters of its 400 thirteenth-century statues, the finest collection of medieval statuary in Britain. The front would have been even more stunning in its original colours of gold, crimson and white (visit the museum to see an exhibition of this). Biblical scenes, and knights, bishops and popes, rise in tiers to a modern replacement of *The Risen Christ* at the top.

Inside, the eye is immediately drawn down the nave to the second highlight, the **scissor arches**, appearing like a kestrel's face. Added in the fourteenth century to prevent the tower from collapsing, they still look brand new owing to the cleanliness of the stone.

The **carving** on the cathedral's capitals – the third highlight – is as fine as anywhere in Britain, mingling fantasy with scenes of everyday life, including two sufferers from toothache. In the south transept you can follow a cartoon-book sequence showing a couple of thieves stealing fruit and getting their come-uppance. In the north transept, the famous **medieval clock**, the fourth item to look out for, dates from 1390 (though its mechanism is late Victorian). Every quarter Jack Blandiver kicks a pair of bells with his heels, and the knights above perform a jousting tournament while the pair outside (c.1475) strike their bells with their halberds.

Finally, follow the flight of worn steps up to the **Chapter House**. This ethereal space has a spider's web of vaulting and intricate carving round the stone stalls which line the sides of the octagonal room.

Return to the Cathedral Green and enter the **Wells Museum***. Its most enjoyable displays are those of the cathedral's west front – you can study the statues at close quarters and get an impression of how it might have looked when painted – and of Wookey Hole (see below), with the so-called Witch of Wookey's bones among the archaeological finds.

Directly north of the cathedral lies the city's loveliest street, a cobbled cul-de-sac called **Vicar's Close**. Its cottages were built in the fourteenth century to house the Vicar's Choral, the men of the choir. Although the cottages (except for no. 22) been considerably altered over the centuries, together with the street they make a remarkable medieval ensemble.

Pass back through the cathedral and its cloisters to **Bishop's Green**. Ahead of you is the moated and walled **Bishop's Palace***, which is

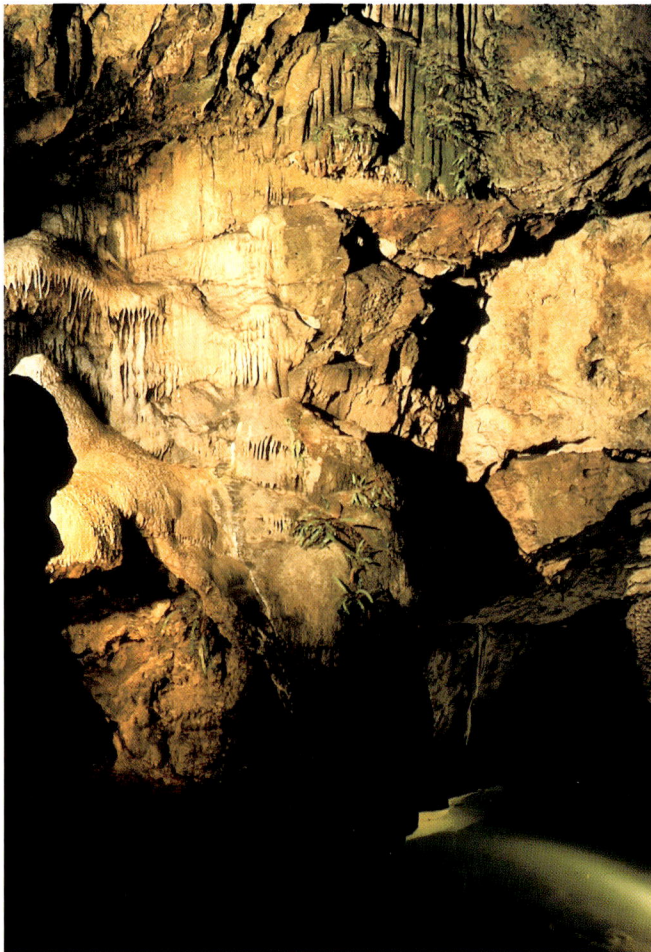

The witch of Wookey petrified in the caves – allegedly by a monk from Glastonbury

the residence of the Bishop of Bath and Wells. As you enter, look for the little bell with a dangling rope on the left-hand side of the gatehouse; before they became too well-fed by tourists, the resident swans used to ring this when they were hungry. The palace grounds comprise vast gardens with a croquet lawn, magnificent trees, picturesque ruins and the Wells, where a large pool of spring water reflects the cathedral. The rooms that are open to the public in the thirteenth-century palace itself are grand affairs, full of portraits of bishops and Victorian Gothic décor.

You return to your starting point, the Market Place, through the medieval gate of the Bishop's Eye.

WOOKEY HOLE AND CHEDDAR GORGE

A fun 40-minute guided tour takes you through **Wookey Hole**'s* sequence of caverns. The guide milks the centuries-old legend of the Witch of Wookey, inspired by the sinister shape of a stalagmite and lent

credence by the discovery in 1912 of the medieval remains of a woman, the skeletons of a goat and a dog, a dagger and an alabaster ball. However, the tour's highpoint is seeing the crystalline blue underground river, the Axe. The entrance fee includes admission to a Victorian papermill, which still makes rag paper, and to an olde-worlde fairground, with garish carousels, a maze of mirrors, and Edwardian penny slot machines. Much of **Cheddar Gorge**, a 1¼-mile-long cleft between high limestone cliffs, is saturated with gift shops and tea rooms. The most popular purchase is, of course, Cheddar cheese. At the Cheddar Gorge Cheese Co. (open Easter to end of October) there's cheese-making to watch and cheeses to taste and buy. However, as at Wookey, the main attraction is underground.

A single ticket gives access to **two cave systems*** with pretty pools, stunning stalagmites and stalactites. Gough's Cave is the larger; Cox's Cave ends with goblins and snorting dragons in the Crystal Quest. You can wander around both the caves unaccompanied. The ticket also allows access to a modest museum which focuses on early man's habitation of the caves, and to Jacob's Ladder, whose 274 steps climb to a tower on the clifftop – you may not think the view was quite worth the effort.

LUNCHBOX

Wells' High Street, Sadler Street and Market Place have a large number of old coaching inns. The Fountain Inn, east of the cathedral, on St Thomas Street, serves quality food including a dozen versions of ploughman's with speciality cheeses. Richter's, the city's best restaurant, does remarkably good-value lunches. The cathedral's self-service Cloisters Restaurant is in a stunning location along one side of the cloisters.

The contrasting gardens of rural Wessex

Areas of tranquil beauty abound in Stourhead despite the crowds

The temple-dotted landscape at Stourhead, the more intimate scale of Tintinhull, Montacute's formality, the cottage-garden fecundity of East Lambrook Manor and Barrington Court's classic style — the variety of this day out will delight any garden enthusiast.

The skill of the English as garden-makers is clearly demonstrated by this cluster of gardens on the Somerset/Wiltshire border. The gardens span several eras and styles, and all five could be seen in one day if you set off early, following the suggested route in order to make the most of the different opening times. Stourhead is open all year, but the other gardens are open only from Easter to October, and each is closed for one or two days during the week (Barrington Court Friday, East Lambrook Sunday, Montacute Tuesday, and Tintinhull Monday and

♦ **GOOD FOR** Families with young children will enjoy the treasures that are to be found in the gardens of these historic houses
♦ **TRANSPORT** A car is needed if you plan to visit more than one of the gardens (a one-way trip of about 45 miles)
♦ **ACCESS FOR DISABLED PEOPLE** Excellent at all the sites except East Lambrook Manor. At Stourhead, wheelchair routes have been mapped out and an electric vehicle is available to take visitors from the car park to the house, restaurant and garden entrances
♦ **BEST TIME TO VISIT** Spring and autumn for Stourhead's trees and May to early July for the azaleas and rhododendrons

Tuesday); Wednesday, Thursday and Saturday are the only days when all five can be visited.

STOURHEAD

Hidden in a secret valley in the depths of the Wiltshire countryside, Stourhead* (NT) is England's finest example of the eighteenth-century landscape style, even more romantic than its near contemporary, the Stowe Landscape Gardens (see *Great Day Out 53*). The gardens were created by the immensely rich Henry Hoare (1705–85), who inherited the village and house at Stourhead, along with the family banking business, at the age of 19. On return from a grand tour of Italy, he set about transforming the medieval fishponds on his land into today's lake, planting rare and beautiful trees on the perimeter and building a series of temples, grottoes and bridges modelled on those he had seen during his travels. The result is a magnificent landscape of 100 acres that is magical at all times, whether wreathed in autumnal mists or blazing with colour in May–early July, when the massed azaleas and rhododendrons are in flower.

It is best to arrive at Stourhead as soon as it opens so as to have the place to yourself. The story of Henry Hoare and the making of the gardens is told through exhibits in the new visitor centre by the car park. Here, you will be given a map with a recommended route that begins at the house (very much of secondary interest to the gardens). It takes you anti-clockwise round the lake to the various follies and temples, all deliberately sited to make the most of the views. In the boggy margins of the lake look out for moisture-loving plants, such as ragged robin, orchids and asphodels. Children will love the Temple of the Nymph, the artificial cave in which the clear spring waters of the River Stour gush from

Barrington Court boasts many delightful gardens

the hillside into a pool by which lies the statue of a sleeping water nymph. Swans and ducks demand to be fed along the route, as do fish, such as carp and rudd, at the Iron Bridge. The tour ends in Stourhead village, where the parish church contains monuments to members of the Hoare family.

BARRINGTON COURT

A drive 34 miles along the A303 will take you to Barrington Court* (NT), an Elizabethan estate beautifully restored in the 1920s when Gertrude Jekyll (1843–1932) designed the gardens. Again, the E-shaped house, built in golden Ham stone, is of less interest, except that it forms a fine backdrop to the marvellous gardens. These were designed as contrasting 'rooms' with separate colour schemes: the famous White Garden that inspired Vita Sackville-West's Sissinghurst garden (see Great Day Out 36) is a dazzling

display of cream, white and silver. In the Buss garden, the planting achieves a glorious but subtle patchwork effect, and in the kitchen gardens there are many unusual plants for sale.

EAST LAMBROOK MANOR

A 4-mile drive through shady lanes brings you to the garden at East Lambrook Manor* created by Margery Fish and her husband in the years 1937–69, and made famous in a series of well-regarded books, such as *Carefree Gardening*, *Gardening in the Shade* and *Cottage Garden Flowers*. Informality is the keynote here, since plants are allowed to self-seed and create new and ever-changing combinations. Although not large, the garden is crammed with plants and riddled with footpaths, which

An ornamental astrolabe in the garden at Tintinhull

children will explore with delight. The nursery alongside specialises in hardy geraniums.

MONTACUTE

Seven miles on (via South Petherton) is Montacute* (NT), an Elizabethan H-plan house built, like the village outside its gates (and Barrington Court), from the golden-yellow Ham stone that is still quarried from the hills that overlook the house. Such a strongly coloured stone needs bold and colourful planting to complement it, and the gardens, replanted in the 1950s, are full of bright roses and clematis, partnered by hot-coloured achilleas, montbretias and lilies. Colour reigns in the house as well, in the form of Elizabethan and Jacobean portraits on loan from the National Portrait Gallery, in which the artists often lavished more attention on the gorgeous clothing of the sitters than on their physical features. The house also contains elegant furniture from the seventeenth and eighteenth centuries and samplers from the seventeenth century.

TINTINHULL

This last garden, less than 2 miles from Montacute, is the creation of several hands, notably Phyllis Reiss, who lived here from 1933–62, followed by Penelope Hobhouse, the well-known gardening writer. The garden at Tintinhull* (NT), which surrounds a seventeenth-century house, is small but full of ideas that can be copied or adapted for your own garden, especially the container planting. Well-placed seats invite you to linger and take in the subtle plant combinations, enjoying the fragrance and the sound of bees.

LUNCHBOX

Bring a picnic or eat at Barrington Court, which has an informal café and a very good restaurant using produce grown in the Walled Garden. At Stourhead snacks and lunches are available at the Spread Eagle Inn or at the National Trust café in the stable block alongside. Montacute has a restaurant in the grounds, and two good pubs in the village itself, the Phelips Arms in the main square and the King's Arms by the church.

Brunel's Bristol and urban culture

The Clifton Suspension Bridge was designed by Brunel but completed in 1864, after his death

BRUNEL: ENGINEER PAR EXCELLENCE
Bridges, tunnels, ships, railways...Isambard Kingdom Brunel (1806–59) designed and built them all. Famously innovative, he was involved in the building of the Thames tunnel, the first line of the Great Western Railway (to Bristol) with all the bridges and tunnels, and the first steamships for regular transatlantic travel.

Bristol boasts a unique maritime and architectural heritage and excellent modern facilities, as well as exciting nightlife, shopping and entertainment. Our suggested tour explores the rejuvenated harbour and a varied selection of the city's sights.

The best way to discover Bristol, and in particular Brunel's most famous landmarks within the harbour area, is to follow the Maritime Trail, or use one of the traditional wooden ferry boats* plying the harbour waters to visit specific attractions. Alternatively, view the city and sights from on board one of the waterbus round-trips, then concentrate on just a few sights.

Bristol developed around its harbour on the River Avon, and as a port has influenced world exploration and trade since the Middle Ages. John Cabot set sail for the New World from its quay in 1497 and later the port flourished, trading in wool, tobacco, sugar and, from the

♦ **GOOD FOR** Maritime history, art, architecture, shopping, entertainment – Bristol has something to appeal to everyone
♦ **TRANSPORT** By rail to Bristol Temple Meads; walk or use public transport once in the city
♦ **ACCESS FOR DISABLED PEOPLE** Most sights (except ferry)
♦ **BEST TIME TO VISIT** All year

seventeenth century, slaves. The port suffered when the slave trade was abolished in the nineteenth century. However, under the influence of the great designer and civil engineer Isambard Kingdom Brunel, the city prospered as a transatlantic port, famed for its construction of

passenger ships and as the terminus of the Great Western Railway.

Though most of Brunel's great achievements in Bristol can be viewed in the dockland area, one of his major contributions to the city landscape, the spectacular **Clifton Suspension Bridge**, lies further west. Spanning the Avon Gorge, 245 feet above the water, it is best reached by bus or car.

A suitable starting point for a day's exploration of the revitalised dockland is at the **SS Great Britain***, Brunel's magnificent vessel, built and launched in Bristol in 1843 and the world's first propeller-driven ocean-going iron ship. Here there is a large car park and a convenient ferry-landing stage. Those arriving by train at Temple Meads Station can board a ferry at the adjacent landing stage. The ship first carried passengers to New York, then to Australia, and ferried troops to the Crimea, before being abandoned in the Falklands in 1886. In 1970 her rusting carcass was towed back to Bristol and is currently being restored to its former condition in her original dry dock.

You can use the same admission ticket next door, where you will find the **Maritime Heritage Centre***, which explores 200 years of Bristol shipbuilding, from the days of wood and sail to modern steel and plastics.

For the main sights in the docklands, follow the Trail eastwards along the quayside, parallel to the tracks of the Bristol Harbour Railway; trains run on alternate summer weekends. Watch out for mooring ropes and other dockside obstacles as you make your way past Brunel's Buttery, a cafeteria with views across the harbour to the Amphitheatre, where huge tobacco bonds once stood, and the starkly contrasting modern building housing the headquarters of Lloyds Bank, to reach the **Industrial Museum***. Occupying a converted dockside transit shed, it displays various horse-drawn and motor vehicles from the area, locally constructed aircraft and numerous steam exhibits, such as the Fairbairn Steam Crane and the 'Mayflower' Steam Tug.

Cross Princestreet Bridge, keeping to the Trail as it proceeds alongside St Augustine's Reach, and past the **Arnolfini Arts Complex***, a thriving cultural site, including a contemporary art gallery, created out of old tea warehouses. Further artistic diversions, such as photographic exhibitions, galleries, cinemas and a café/bar, can be enjoyed at the **Watershed Media Centre*** at the head of the old dock basin. At this point (Neptune's Statue) you are a stone's throw from the bustling city

The docks in Bristol, crucial to the development of the city's fortunes

centre, and options abound for additional exploration of this cosmopolitan city. Elegant Park Street has the best shops, restaurants and wine bars, and is near the **City Museum and Art Gallery***, **Georgian House*** (a museum of eighteenth-century life) and **Harveys Wine Museum***.

From Neptune's Statue it is also a short stroll to the historic heart of the city, St Nicholas Quarter, with its narrow streets, fascinating markets crammed with stalls selling flowers, antiques and second-hand curios, and the eighteenth-century Church of St Nicholas, which now houses the **tourist information office***.

Alternatively, hop aboard one of the historic ferry boats that tour the waterway through the centre of the city. Savour the view of the graceful St Mary Redcliffe Church with its 285-foot spire, pass Redcliffe Quay and the site

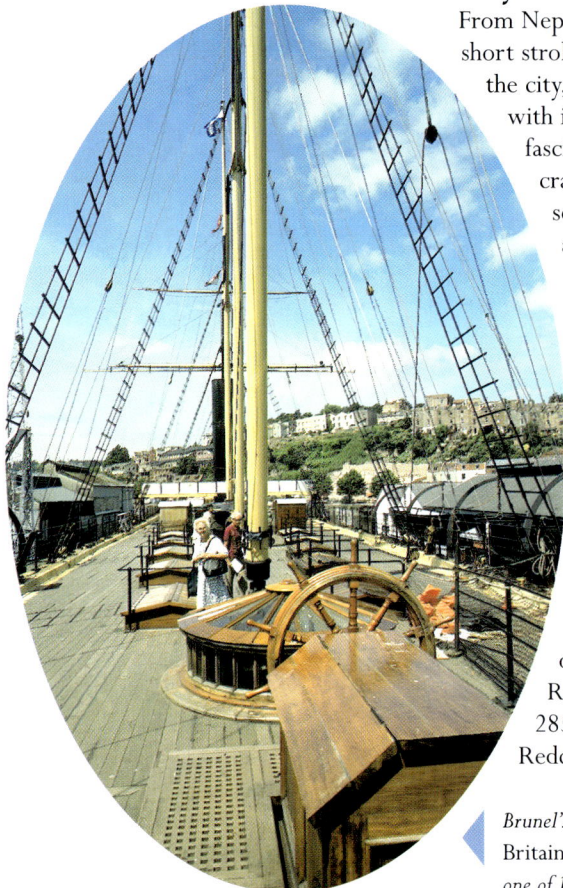

Brunel's masterpiece, the SS Great Britain, an innovation in its day, is one of Bristol's foremost attractions

where Cabot's ship, **The Matthew***, is being rebuilt, and alight at Welsh Back to wander along King Street, Bristol's oldest thoroughfare and home of the Old Vic Theatre. Continue walking to Bristol Bridge landing-stage for the St Nicholas Quarter and easy access to Broadmead, the city's principal shopping centre.

You could remain on the ferry to Temple Meads Station to take in **Bristol Old Station**, the original terminus of the Great Western Railway, built in 1839–40 to the designs of Brunel and now the oldest surviving railway terminus in the world. Housed on two floors of the building is the captivating **Exploratory Hands-on-Science Centre***, which invites visitors to try out over 150 experiments, involving phenomena associated with devices as diverse as lasers and lenses, bridges and bubbles and machines and mirrors. It's a venue for all the family to enjoy.

LUNCHBOX

The dockland area boasts some well-sited historic pubs and a few floating restaurants. The Maritime Heritage Museum's café provides welcome refreshment, while the excellent and airy café/bar with its al fresco harbourside benches makes the Arnolfini an ideal stop-off point for a light lunch or afternoon tea.

Georgian Bath and Jane Austen

☂ ❄ 🚐 ♿

The wonderful, sweeping Royal Crescent, a legacy of John Wood the Younger

JANE AUSTEN'S BATH

Apart from Beau Nash (see below), Bath's most famous resident was probably the novelist Jane Austen, who lived here between 1801 and 1805. Bath and its social life formed a backdrop to parts of *Persuasion* and *Northanger Abbey*, both published in 1818. Following in the footsteps of Austen's characters is still perfectly possible: the Pump Room, the Assembly Rooms (known to her as the Upper Rooms), the shops of Milsom Street, and the grand houses of Great Pulteney Street, Laura Place and Camden Crescent have changed relatively little since Austen's days – at least from the outside.

The house where Jane Austen lodged at No. 4 Sydney Place is marked by a plaque, but is not open to the public.

The Celts discovered the three hot springs and the Romans developed them, but it was the Georgian architects and socialites who embellished Bath with the wonderful sandstone terraces and Palladian façades which grace the city today.

Given Bath's terrible parking problems and traffic congestion, arriving by rail is probably the best way of getting your day off to a good start. To take account of this, our walk starts at the station. Exit via Dorchester Street and follow the road west and northwards round the corner into Southgate and Stall Street – the beginnings of the pedestrianised centre of the city.

If you take the second right, towards Abbey Green and the Abbey Church Yard, you will be approaching the heart of historic Bath. The great west front of the much-restored fifteenth-century **abbey**, embellished with reliefs of ascending and descending angels, is directly on your right. Although the abbey may not be quite as impressive as its sister cathedral at Wells (see *Great Day Out*

♦ **GOOD FOR** Families with children over 10 or so, and those who appreciate elegant architecture
♦ **TRANSPORT** Bath has excellent rail services. Getting around the city is easier without a car; if you do have one, use one of the park-and-ride sites on the outskirts and take the frequent shuttle bus into the city centre
♦ **ACCESS FOR DISABLED PEOPLE** Most of the sights – except the Roman Baths – are accessible. Some of the streets in the city are very steep
♦ **BEST TIME TO VISIT** All year

11), it is still worth taking a few minutes to explore the interior – look out for the fine renaissance fan-vaulting of the choir.

Tours of the **Roman Baths*** begin from just across the Abbey Church Yard. The first part of the

visit takes you through the museum, which displays some of the most important finds (mosaics, coins, and fragments of stone and bronze sculpture), as well as parts of the original Roman building and its foundations, including some of the Temple steps. But the highlight is the Great Bath, the original showpiece of the Roman Temple. About 250,000 gallons of warm water per day (at a constant 46.5°C) still pour into the main pool. Astonishingly, this massive complex, surrounded by the foundations and hypocausts which served the saunas, cooling and curative rooms, lay lost and forgotten until it was rediscovered in 1880.

You can exit through the **Pump Room***, with its imposing Corinthian columns and a statue commemorating Beau Nash, the English dandy who in 1704 was made master of ceremonies here. Now an excellent tea room and restaurant, the Pump Room dates from 1795, when Georgian Bath was at its very peak. The windows overlook the King's Bath, used by the Georgians at a time before the Great Bath was re-discovered, and you can buy glasses of the pungent spring water piped directly from the source.

Heading back through Abbey Church Yard, you come out into York Street just opposite **Sally Lunn's House***. Reputedly the oldest house in Bath (*c*.1482), it is now run as a kitchen museum (the first Bath buns were baked here in the seventeenth century), teashop and restaurant. Cutting through from Sally Lunn's to Orange Grove, you reach Grand Parade and a pleasant walk north along the gardens lining the River Avon. From here you have an excellent view of **Pulteney Bridge**, Robert Adam's fanciful design which echoes the Ponte Vecchio in Florence. It is worth taking at least a short detour across the bridge to see the grand, wide terraces of Laura Place and Great Pulteney Street. (If you are prepared for a longer diversion continue to Sydney Place – where you can visit the **Holburne Museum and Crafts Study Centre*** in an imposing building – and into the eighteenth-century Sydney Gardens before returning to the main route.)

After re-crossing the bridge, continue along Bridge Street, then turn left into High Street (note the restored façade of the 1778

Guildhall) and cut through the Corridor – narrow alleys lined with small shops and stalls. On reaching Union Street continue northwards, taking in the shops of Old Bond Street, Upper Borough Walls and the surrounding streets before moving on to **Milsom Street**. This was (and still is) one of Bath's most fashionable shopping parades.

Following Bartlett Street at the top of Milsom, you can cut through to the Assembly Rooms and the Museum of Costume. (However, those interested in the history of Bath's architecture could make a detour up the steep pavements of the Paragon to the **Building of Bath Museum***. Continue to the Assembly Rooms via Hay Hill.) The **Assembly Rooms*** rivalled the Pump Room as a meeting place and entertainment centre for Georgian socialites. The grand Ball Room with its five chandeliers is usually open to the public and still serves as an occasional concert venue, while the yellow and white Octagon Room was where smaller gatherings and card games were held (it features in Jane Austen's *Persuasion*). In the basement, the **Museum of Costume*** has an extensive collection of garments and accessories reflecting the 'progress' of fashion from sixteenth-century ruffs to mini-skirts and flared trousers.

The next stretch of the walk takes in some of the finest buildings in Bath. Take time to admire the **Circus**, a superb circular terrace beautifully embellished with contrasting pillars and roundels. This was perhaps the greatest achievement of architect John Wood the Elder. Famous former residents include Dr Livingstone, Clive of India and Gainsborough. Next head along Brock Street and into the **Royal Crescent**, more restrained but more imposing than the Circus, and still the best address in Bath. The interior of **No. 1 Royal Crescent*** has been brilliantly restored as a Georgian townhouse with basement kitchen and first-floor drawing-room.

Huguenot refugee Sally Lunn made brioches in the basement kitchen here

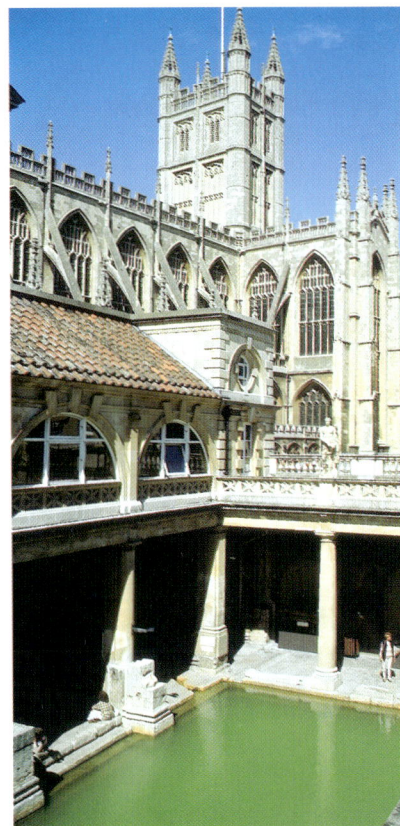

The therapeutic Roman Baths, built nearly 2,000 years ago

The route continues south along the Gravel Walk which lines the Royal Victoria Park. You pass the **Georgian Garden** – restored to its 1770 appearance by the replacement of grass with the gravel that was used to protect the hems of long skirts – and head down towards Westgate Street, via Queen Square (note the imposing pedimented design of the north side in particular) and Barton Street. From Westgate take the alley down towards the Cross Bath, where Mary of Modena, wife of James II, erected a cross in thanksgiving for her pregnancy, and the Hot Bath, the third of the city's hot springs. Follow the Colonnades of Bath Street and you will come out opposite the Pump Room. From here you can return directly to the station or take time to enjoy the shops around Stall Street.

LUNCHBOX

Bath has several good teashops such as Sally Lunn's. For a more substantial lunch at a reasonable price try Beaujolais on Chapel Row, off Queen Square, or Woods on Alfred Street. For more ideas try the **tourist information office*** in Abbey Church Yard.

Fossils and famous works of fiction, in Lyme Regis

The Cobb, built for fishermen in about 1300, and harbour at Lyme Regis

To appreciate Lyme Regis properly, a little preparation is in order. Read *The French Lieutenant's Woman* (or watch the video), a romantic story set in 1867 largely in the town and filmed here in 1980. And read Austen's last novel, *Persuasion*, part of which is set here; when it was written in 1815, Lyme was a fashionable resort for visitors from Bath. In 1994 *Persuasion* was made into a BBC drama involving more local filming in this pleasant seaside town.

Fossils, John Fowles' The French Lieutenant's Woman *and Jane Austen's* Persuasion *have made this picturesque resort on Lyme Bay, west Dorset, well-known the world over.*

With its snaking breakwater, the Cobb, Regency houses and snug position between the wooded Undercliff to the west and great folds of cliffs like frozen waves to the east, Lyme is seductively pretty. The beaches around Lyme are not the best for relaxing, but the coastline is the country's premier fossil-hunting region. Booklets in the **tourist information office*** (in Church Street, near the guildhall) advise on what to look for and where to look.

LYME REGIS
Park in the car park next to the **Cobb**. Lyme's most famous landmark, a presence in various forms on the coastline since at least the fourteenth century, curves mysteriously into the sea to protect a little harbour. At its end a caped

♦ **GOOD FOR** Fans of the sea, dense woods and fossils
♦ **TRANSPORT** Nearest railway station is at Axminster, 5 miles away
♦ **ACCESS FOR DISABLED PEOPLE** Most of Lyme's attractions are not easily accessible for disabled visitors
♦ **BEST TIME TO VISIT** Spring and late summer are best: the resort can be very congested in the height of summer; museums are closed or have limited opening hours between November and March; Lyme's big events are the Lifeboat Week (first week of school holidays), the regatta and carnival (second week in August) and the Jazz Festival (early July)

Meryl Streep stood precariously in the most memorable image from *The French Lieutenant's Woman* (in fact the film's art director stood in for her as

the weather was so rough). On the inside of the Cobb wall look for the uneven steps called Granny's Teeth, where the fictional Louisa Musgrove in *Persuasion* is reckoned to have fallen. Having taken in the superb coastal views from the Cobb, you could allow yourself to be persuaded to take a fishing trip or coastal cruise, or you might pop into the **Marine Aquarium***. It stands behind a little fishing fleet moored to the quay by bollards made from up-ended and buried cannon. You may find the fish tanks inside far less interesting than the photo displays and the long-time owner's chat on the filming of the town's literary claims to fame.

The Cobb is connected to the town by **Marine Parade**, above the sand and shingle beach (which disappears at high tide). Towards the parade's eastern end look out for a gigantic ammonite fossil set into the front wall of Sundial House. The pink, thatched cottages just further on featured in *Persuasion*; two are named after characters in the novel.

First port of call in Lyme's centre should be the little town museum on Bridge Street, called the **Philpot Museum***. It was built on the site of the house of Mary Anning, the town's celebrated Victorian fossil-finder. Alongside models of the Cobb and old prints and photos of local scenes, there is a fine collection of fossils, notably ammonites, brittle stars and belemnites.

Just as enjoyable is the **Fossil Shop** opposite, the best of the town's clutch of commercial fossil collections. You might fall in love with dinosaur-dung book-ends, dinosaur eggs, a brontosaurus femur or perhaps a megalosaurus footprint.

Head up Coombe Street to visit **Dinosaurland***. This is an excellent place to learn about the surrounding coast's evolution, why it is such a treasure trove for fossils, and how fossils are formed. A plethora of fossils is displayed in various states of restoration, next to models of the creatures they represent. Ask here about guided fossil walks.

Head back down Coombe Street and turn right into **Riverside Walk** for a brief, scenic stroll alongside the River Lym up to **Sherborne Lane**. This pedestrianised back street, the oldest part of the town, leads to **Broad Street**, the largely late-Georgian high street. Near the bottom on the right is another good fossil store, the Old Forge Fossil Shop, and Serendip Bookshop, still with the Victorian frontage it acquired for the filming of *The French Lieutenant's Woman*.

TWO COASTAL WALKS

Lyme itself is unlikely to detain you for a full day, so here are a couple of coastal walks from which to choose. From behind the bowling green by the Cobb's car park, a steep flight of

Lynsey Baxter and Jeremy Irons in the 1981 film of The French Lieutenant's Woman, *directed by Karel Reisz*

steps leads up through the woods and over meadowland to the **Undercliff** (20 minutes away), a wild and densely wooded tract of coast known for remarkable landslips. One of these, in 1839, caused 40 acres to disappear into a mile-long chasm. It was to the Undercliff that Charles Smithson (played by Jeremy Irons in the film) in *The French Lieutenant's Woman* came, first to hunt for fossils, then to meet Sarah Woodruff. A coastal path continues along the cliffs westwards for five miles. Keep well clear of the flaking cliff edges.

Two hours either side of high tide you can walk along the boulder-strewn beach (stout shoes essential) between Lyme and Charmouth below charcoal-black **Black Ven** cliff. It was here that in 1811 Mary Anning (see above), at the age of 12, found a fossilised ichthyosaurus. Check the tides before you set off, because it is easy to be cut off. The journey takes about 45 minutes one way without stopping; an uninteresting inland route partly following roads round the back of the cliff takes about 1½ hours. The cliff has suffered from landslips and mudflows, so searching for fossils in it or on it is very dangerous. But the movement of the cliff means a fossil-rich beach below, where you will find lots of people literally bent on bagging a prize discovery.

At **Charmouth**, a former coach-stop, the beach is quite sandy and the **Heritage Coast Centre*** provides further informative introductions to local geology and fossil finds.

LUNCHBOX

There are plenty of adequate cafés, pubs and restaurants. Fish dishes at probably the best-known pub, the Pilot Boat Inn on Bridge Street, have a good reputation. Buddles is an interesting delicatessen nearby on Coombe Street, while there are a couple of pleasant tea rooms at the bottom of Broad Street.

Typical ammonite fossils (Oistoceras wrighti, Asteroceras obtusum and Tragophylloceras loscombi) from Jurassic rocks near Lyme Regis

Around Dorchester: glorious gardens and a giant

Although designed in the 1880s, the gardens at Athelhampton blend with the Tudor house

Chocolate-box villages and beautiful landscaped gardens nestle amid the unspoilt rolling countryside around Dorchester. Our suggested itinerary for garden-lovers takes in three splendid gardens, a downland stroll and a celebrated Dorset village.

Like that of *Great Day Out 17*, the recommended route starts at Dorchester. Choose one sight, or combine a few, whether the gardens and grounds surrounding grand Athelhampton House; the Farm Park, nature trail and classical gardens at Kingston Maurward; the ancient Giant cut into the chalk down, high above Cerne Abbas; or the eighteenth-century landscaped gardens at Minterne Magna.

A mile east of Dorchester, signposted off the A35, is **Kingston Maurward House***, a fine Georgian mansion set in 35 acres of gardens and lawns and housing the

♦ **GOOD FOR** Garden enthusiasts
♦ **TRANSPORT** Public transport limited: there is a railway station in Dorchester, and buses run to Puddletown, after which there is a mile-long walk along a main road to Athelhampton House. A bus service runs between Dorchester and Minterne Magna
♦ **ACCESS FOR DISABLED PEOPLE** Parts of Kingston Maurward grounds are not accessible; at Athelhampton the ground floor only is accessible and there are steps in the garden; the gardens at Minterne Magna are not suitable for wheelchairs
♦ **BEST TIME TO VISIT** All the gardens are open between April and October. Cerne Abbas is a good place to visit all year

Dorset College of Agriculture. The gardens are designed in the *jardin anglais* style, with separate, intimate gardens divided by yew hedges and balustrades. Rolling parkland sweeps down to a five-acre lake with the River Frome and its watermeadows beyond. You can wander round the grounds and follow the mile-long nature trail by the lake and river, a perfect habitat for abundant wildlife and a rich variety of plants. The beautiful Edwardian gardens contain a huge selection of tender and hardy perennials. Children will enjoy helping to feed the animals in the Farm Animal Park, where some unusual breeds are kept.

Venture a short distance further north-east along the A35, via Puddletown and the church with its wonderfully intact seventeenth-century interior (see *Great Day Out 17*), to spend a memorable afternoon exploring **Athelhampton House*** and its 20 acres of imaginative formal gardens. The gargoyled and turreted manor, built on the legendary site of King Athelstan's palace, is regarded as one of the finest examples of fifteenth-century domestic architecture in the country. Ham Hill stone, creamy Portesham ashlar and local stone slates were used in its construction. Meandering passages and numerous staircases link sumptuously furnished, linenfold-panelled rooms – in particular the King's Room, the Great Chamber and the Green Parlour – all with a distinctly lived-in feel. The glory of the manor is its baronial Great Hall with a magnificent timbered roof, tapestries, minstrels' gallery and fine heraldic glass. The house was used as the setting for two of Thomas Hardy's poems and his macabre short story, 'The Waiting Supper'.

The grounds of Athelhampton House are just as intriguing, with eight walled gardens, as well as

▲ *A balustraded bridge at Minterne Magna, where water has been used to stunning effect*

fountains, pavilions, a fifteenth-century dovecote (the roof of which is inscribed with Thomas Hardy's signature) and topiary pyramids in the Great Court, all encircled by the River Piddle.

Directly north of Dorchester, attractive rolling chalk downland and hidden valleys dotted with idyllic villages beckon visitors. A drive or cycle ride through the picturesque Cerne Valley will help to capture the essence of this area, and just north of the village of Cerne Abbas on the A352 you will get a particularly good view of the 180-foot outline of the naked **Cerne Giant**, etched into the chalk turf of Giant's Hill and overlooking Cerne Abbas, one of Dorset's showpiece villages. Grasping a club, the figure is believed to be 1,500 years old and is associated with ancient fertility rites.

Cerne Abbas derives its name from a Benedictine abbey founded here in AD987, the remains of which – a fifteenth-century mullioned guesthouse and part of a fourteenth-century tithe barn – form the nucleus of this settlement. Pretty flint, brick and colour-washed cottages fringe the main street, with an impressive terrace of unusual sixteenth-century timber-framed houses gracing historic Abbey Street. The stone-roofed Pitchmarket is well preserved, as is St Mary's Church, which has a fifteenth-century tower and a splendid heraldic east window, probably originating from the abbey.

Visitors not content with a leisurely amble around the village can seek out the waymarked footpath beside Cerne Abbey House and the graveyard. This traverses sheep-grazed pastures before ascending steeply, passing the Giant, to the top of Giant's Hill. Effort will be rewarded by characteristic downland views and the opportunity to investigate the ancient rectangular earthwork known as the Trendle. The steep, grassy path may be very slippery in winter.

The last destination on the journey are the landscaped gardens that surround the fine Edwardian Hamstone manor house at **Minterne Magna***, two miles north of Cerne Abbas. The original house was formerly the home of the Churchill family, but since 1768 the Digby family have landscaped 29 acres of glorious valley gardens. Maximum use has been made of the tumbling river, with various small lakes, a series of cascades, dams and bridges on different levels, creating a peaceful and lush environment for many rare plants and shrubs. Scent and the soothing sounds of water are held by the valley. Over one and a half miles of woodland paths weave through outstanding collections of Himalayan rhododendrons, bamboos, azaleas, maples and magnolias, superb in both spring and autumn.

▲ *Thomas Hardy used Minterne Magna as a model for Hinstock House in* The Woodlanders

LUNCHBOX

Refreshments are served at Kingston Maurward House and at Athelhampton House. Alternatively, try one of three good pubs or the tea room at Cerne Abbas. In the Cerne valley, the diminutive fifteenth-century thatched Smiths Arms at Godmanstone, reached via the A352 Sherborne road, is reputedly England's smallest inn. Legend has it that Charles II stopped to have his horse shod at this one-time smithy, and having been refused a drink granted the blacksmith a licence on the spot. Set beside the River Cerne, it makes a good refreshment stop.

A walk and a drive through Thomas Hardy's Wessex

> Thomas Hardy's great-grandfather built the cottage at Higher Bockhampton in 1801. Here the novelist was born 39 years later

Thomas Hardy's Wessex was modelled so closely on towns and villages in his native Dorset that exploring the sights from his novels can feel more like a historical tour than a visit to scenes from fiction.

Our walk around Dorchester and short tour of the countryside nearby take in some of the locations and buildings most evocative of three of Hardy's greatest novels, *Far from the Madding Crowd*, *The Mayor of Casterbridge* and *Tess of the d'Urbervilles*. Details of places in Hardy's other novels can be gleaned from the **tourist information office***.

DORCHESTER

Dorchester, which Hardy called Casterbridge, plays a key role in many of his novels. This was where he went to school and served his apprenticeship as an architect. It is a good place in which to spend an hour or two at the start of your day exploring some of the scenes and sights he used as a backdrop in much of his work.

♦ **GOOD FOR** Steeping yourself in the towns, villages and countryside that Thomas Hardy took for the setting of his novels
♦ **TRANSPORT** Car or bicycle
♦ **ACCESS FOR DISABLED PEOPLE** No
♦ **BEST TIME TO VISIT** Summer, when National Trust properties are open to the public and the surrounding countryside is at its most beautiful

Although much has changed since Hardy knew it, a good deal – especially the High Street with its stone and brick façades, boxy shop fronts, hanging signs and bow windows – retains much of the atmosphere of a nineteenth-century market town. Hardy himself is commemorated by a statue at the west end of the High Street, and there is a re-creation of his study,

removed from his house at **Max Gate*** (National Trust), along with pictures, furniture, photographs and other memorabilia, in the **Dorset County Museum*** a little further down the street.

Just to the east, where Corn Hill meets the High Street, is where much of the crucial action of *The Mayor of Casterbridge* was set. The corn exchange and town hall, with its distinctive steeple-like clock tower and barrel-vaulted roof, was where Henchard (who had secretly sold his wife at a fair many years before becoming Mayor) was exposed in public by the old furmity dealer. Henchard's grand house, now a branch of Barclays Bank, is just down the road in South Street. On the High Street, the exterior of the King's Arms with its 'spacious bow window' remains unchanged. Here Henchard's wife stays when she returns to Casterbridge and learns of his lofty social status. Henchard's bankruptcy proceedings were also heard here.

TOUR OF INNER WESSEX

Our tour of inner Wessex includes sights from Hardy's life and from both *Tess of the d'Urbervilles* and *Far from the Madding Crowd*. Just off the ring road, a couple of miles to the east of Dorchester at **Stinsford** (called Mellstock in the novels), is the little church where Hardy was baptised. Although he wanted to be buried here, only his heart is interred in the graveyard: his body is in Westminster Abbey. His birthplace – everybody's idea of the perfect thatched cottage – is just down the road at **Higher Bockhampton** (Upper Mellstock). You can reach it by a ten-minute walk along a rough track, or, much more scenically, take a woodland path from the car park. It is owned by the National Trust: part of the garden is open to the public in

Farmer Gabriel Oak (Alan Bates), red Gladstone bag in hand, strides with his dog across Casterbridge (Dorchester) market in the 1967 film of Far from the Madding Crowd

summer and the interior can be visited by appointment*.

Heading back south through **Lower Bockhampton** (Lower Mellstock) and over the River Frome, you reach the heart of Valley of the Great Dairies from *Tess of the d'Urbervilles*. Here Hardy cast an idyllic interlude in the tragic life of Tess, when she finds work as a milkmaid and meets Angel Clare. Although Hardy doesn't name it specifically, the little stone-roofed, vaulted church in the middle of West Stafford seems to be the church where she and Angel were married. He took the name of Talbothays, where Tess worked, from his father's farm, but the imaginary farmhouse was more likely to have been based on a building at Lower Lewell, a few miles further on, where you can still see a magnificent thatched barn from the road.

From Lower Lewell continue northwards along narrow, winding back roads to **Puddletown** (Weatherbury). The centre of the village is rather marred by the busy A35, but away from the main street it is much quieter and prettier. Hardy used the village church as the setting for a pathetic scene from *Far from the Madding Crowd*. Sergeant Troy – lover of both Fanny Robin and Bathsheba – sleeps in the porch to escape the rain after planting snowdrops and crocuses on Fanny's grave. But, with classic Hardy irony, the water that streams overnight from the gargoyles at the corners of the tower washes them away. The gargoyles are still there, although they do not seem as fearsome as in Hardy's description.

At this point you can make a seven-mile detour to **Bere Regis (Kingsbere) church** to see the tombs of the Turberville family (Hardy called them d'Urberville) – one of the most evocative sights in Hardy's Wessex. His description of the tombs is still accurate: 'canopied, altar-shaped and plain; their carvings being defaced and broken; their brasses torn from the matrices.' The stone where Tess reads the inscription about her ancestors is so worn that it is now virtually illegible, but a brass plaque to Robert Turberville, who died in 1559, and the Turberville stained-glass window with the coats of arms of twenty of the family, are still here. The homeless and destitute Tess and her family unload their furniture and camp beneath this window, only to be disturbed by Alec d'Urberville – heralding the beginning of the end for Tess.

On the way back to Puddletown along the Piddle Valley (B3142) you pass the stunning Jacobean mansion **Waterston Manor** (not open to the public), which Hardy used as a model for Bathsheba's farmhouse in *Far from the Madding Crowd*. Glimpsing it through the trees, you can make out the massive stone frontage: 'fluted pilasters, worked from solid stone, decorated its front, and above the roof the chimneys were panelled or columnar, some coped gables with finials and like features still retaining traces of their Gothic extraction.' From here return to Dorchester along the B3143.

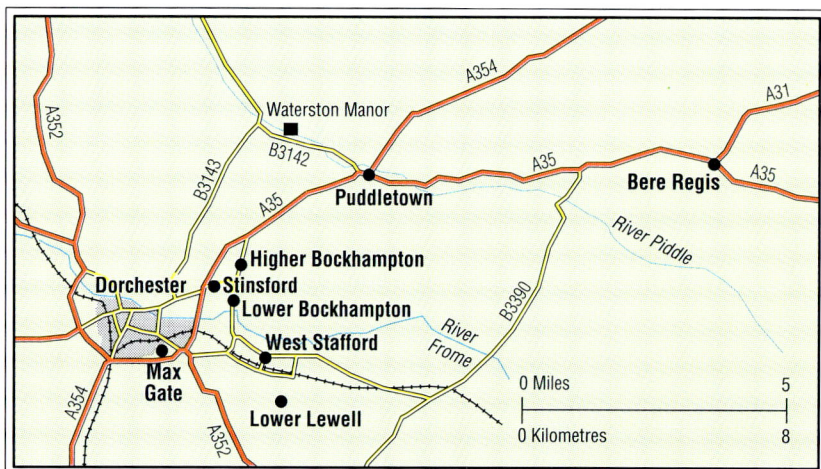

LUNCHBOX

Dorchester itself has various places for lunch, and the nearby villages have country pubs, most of which serve food.

Weymouth, Abbotsbury and Chesil Bank

A snowy sliver of Chesil Bank seen from Portland, just south of Weymouth

- ◆ **GOOD FOR** All-year activities and interest, inside and out
- ◆ **TRANSPORT** A car is necessary if you are going beyond Weymouth
- ◆ **ACCESS FOR DISABLED PEOPLE** Ring attractions to check access
- ◆ **BEST TIME TO VISIT** Summer, but some sights (such as the Timewalk and Sea Life) are open all year. Major annual events in Weymouth include the International Beach Kite Festival (end April), the Trawler Race and Water Carnival (first May bank holiday) and the Weymouth Carnival (mid-August). In Abbotsbury, the gardens are open all year but the Swannery is open only March to October; June is the cygnet month

Devote half a day to Weymouth, whether idling on the beach, pottering round its pleasing harbour, or visiting the first-rate Timewalk attraction, and half a day to Abbotsbury's sub-tropical gardens and 600-year-old Swannery.

Weymouth's appeal comes in various guises. If the weather is fine, you may make it no further than the 'peach of a beach', as the tourist board puts it. But the town is worth visiting at any time, both for its busy, historic harbour and for its Georgian flourishes. George III favoured the resort and in 1789 was the first monarch to plunge into the sea in a bathing machine here.

In high summer, the **beach**'s arc of sand provides a classic slice of the British seaside, with donkey rides, Punch and Judy shows, and hot dogs and candyfloss sold from brightly striped stalls. A sweep of Georgian buildings runs along the esplanade behind, but your eye is drawn to the town's two most famous and colourful landmarks: a statue of George III in all his regalia, and Queen Victoria's Jubilee Clock.

Immediately south of the beach, the long channel of the **harbour** shelters ferries bound for the Channel Islands, sleek yachts and a sizeable fishing fleet. Along Custom House Quay on its northern flank you will find the active Victorian fishmarket, and **Deep Sea Adventure***, an exhibition of diving through the ages, from a replica of a seventeenth-century diving bell to a modern one-man submarine. The southern side of the harbour (walk round or take the tiny ferry across the harbour mouth) is the more appealing, lined with Georgian cottages and pleasingly workaday with its little wharves and smart lifeboat. Wander along to **Nothe Fort***, built in 1860. Its guns, panoramic views, warren of tunnels and underground chambers filled with reconstructions of soldiers' lives in Victorian times and Second World War days are likely to be of interest to all.

Just south of the harbour, **Brewers Quay*** is a Victorian brewery stylishly converted into a mini-mall of quality craft shops and eateries. Here also is the **Timewalk***: if you visit just one attraction, make it this, an excellent multi-sensory experience which brings to life Weymouth's rich history. For 50 minutes you are coaxed past superbly detailed tableaux which recreate scenes from Weymouth's past, from medieval days when the plague and smuggling were rife to Georgian times when the king went

Georgian waterfront buildings by Weymouth's busy harbour

LUNCHBOX

Weymouth has a wide choice of pubs and inexpensive seafood restaurants round the harbour. There is *al fresco* eating and drinking round the square outside Brewers Quay, and a good delicatessen inside. In **Abbotsbury**, the Swannery and Sub-Tropical Gardens have tea rooms. The comfortable old Ilchester Arms serves a wide range of upmarket pub grub.

For more suggestions ask at the **tourist information office***.

bathing and high society went to the ball. All the while, ropes creak, the wind whistles, seagulls screech.

Another place that is particularly geared to families is **Sea Life***, an adventure park east of the town centre where you can see (and touch) all sorts of marine creatures at close quarters.

ABBOTSBURY

The yellow-stone and much-thatched village of Abbotsbury to the west of Weymouth takes its name from the Benedictine abbey founded here in the eleventh century. Heavy traffic can be a blight, and virtually nothing remains of the abbey itself, dissolved in 1541. But the abbey has bequeathed a number of absorbing attractions (see below), and the surrounding scenery is memorable.

For an overview of Abbotsbury and around, make the 15-minute climb from a lane just west of the Ilchester Arms up to the bare, once-monastic fourteenth-century **St Catherine's Chapel**. Perched high on downland, it commands wide views that take in **Chesil Bank**, a remarkable 18-mile-long pebble mound of a beach which separates the Fleet, a long saline lagoon, from the sea. From the chapel you can take a path down to the **Swannery*** at the western end of the Fleet; otherwise, return to the village and drive down. Begun by the monks at least 600 years ago, this is the world's only managed colony of mute swans.

Paths take you via thick woodland, carefully preserved wild flowers and rustling reedbeds (the harvested reed is still used for thatch in the village) to a bird-watching hide and ancient duck-decoy pipes. Birds are lured into these peculiar frames, which cover water outlets like the shell of a great animal, in order to be

Swans in the Fleet, a lagoon that runs parallel with the sea for seven miles

ringed. But the highlight of course is the swans themselves. They are at their most impressive at feeding time (noon and 4pm), when hundreds make straight for the Fleet and form a dense white mass over the water.

Returning to the village, you come to the abbey's magnificent fifteenth-century **Tithe Barn***. Of almost cathedral-like proportions at 272 feet long, it claims to be the largest thatched barn in Britain. More amazing still is the fact that in its prime it was twice as long – half now stands in ruins. The intact half contains a lovingly displayed collection of agricultural and domestic bygones.

Just west of the village lie the glorious eighteenth-century **Sub-Tropical Gardens***. A network of paths meanders round 20 acres of magically tranquil woodlands and formal gardens, via gunnera-fringed lily ponds, along azalea and hydrangea walks, and areas such as the Sino-Himalayan Glade. A lane continues past the gardens to Chesil Bank, where you can clamber to the crest of the shingle up a boardwalk.

EAST FLEET

Little remains of this village, just west of Weymouth, which suffered in a great storm in 1824 known as 'the Outrage'. A 30-foot tidal wave breached Chesil Bank and virtually destroyed the church, the chancel of which now survives as a tiny chapel; however, the seventeenth-century Mohun family brasses are still there. The village has had real and fictitious connections with smuggling: the Mohun vault in the old church has a secret passage used by smugglers, and John Meade Falkner's smuggling novel *Moonfleet*, published 1898, is set here.

Scenery and militaria on the Isle of Purbeck

The geology of the area is spectacular, with chalk cliffs, contrasting rock layers and fossils

An island only by name, this largely unspoilt corner of Dorset has much to offer visitors no matter what their interests are, including a couple of good historical and cultural attractions.

The Isle of Purbeck's scenery is at its most rewarding along the coast. Inland, its mix of low-key downland and heathland does not make for particularly interesting driving, apart from the back lanes between Corfe Castle and East Lulworth (sometimes closed), which run through army ranges. The hillsides here are crossed by sand-covered tank-lanes made by the army and marked by giant numbers. Distances between the focal points are fairly short, so if you choose between

- ♦ **GOOD FOR** Walkers, explorers, history enthusiasts and tank fans
- ♦ **TRANSPORT** A car is necessary: a tour via the Tank Museum, Corfe Castle and Lulworth Cove is about 24 miles
- ♦ **ACCESS FOR DISABLED PEOPLE** To the Tank Museum and Knoll Beach
- ♦ **BEST TIME TO VISIT** The Tank Museum and Corfe Castle are open throughout the year. The Tank Museum holds its Battle Day on the last Sunday in July. Clouds Hill is open afternoons Sunday and Wednesday to Friday between April and October

Studland Bay and Lulworth Cove you could do everything described here in one busy day. Further information and details of walks are available from the **tourist information office*** at Lulworth Cove.

LULWORTH COVE

This is an overvisited tourist honeypot in high summer. Then, as many as 1,300 vehicles descend on its car park (which levies an exorbitant charge), while the tiny village loses its charm under a welter of beach shops and ice-cream stalls. However, the big cove itself – a remarkably neat horseshoe with chalk, sandstone and limestone cliffs above a shingle beach – is so spectacular that it justifies the visit. Keats was inspired to write what turned out to be his last sonnet after a visit here in 1820.

Boat trips start every half-hour from the cove along the coast to **Durdle Door**; most people choose the strenuous walk (25 minutes one way) instead. Return to the back of the car park, then make a steep ascent and descent over the clifftop. The views all the way to Portland Bill are breathtaking. The giant natural limestone arch of Durdle Door is almost dwarfed by the surrounding cliffs, and either side of the arch are expansive, picturesque shingle beaches, reached by long flights of steps. The arch was created by the action of the waves which will one day cause its destruction.

CORFE CASTLE*

The same name belongs to both the dramatic ruined stronghold standing on a hillock in a gap in the Purbeck Hills, and the village that surrounds it. Much of the sturdy masonry used to build the village's houses was taken from the castle after Parliamentarians demolished it in 1646 following a heroic six-week siege against the Royalist owner, Lady Bankes.

The castle has Saxon origins (King Edward the Martyr was murdered here in AD979), but the ruins date mainly from the Norman era. A tapestry at the entrance outlines its history well. Enough of the bailey walls, gatehouses and towering keep survive to make an hour-long wander very rewarding, and the 360-degree view from the keep over the Isle of Purbeck's chequered fields and Corfe village is lovely.

BOVINGTON TANK MUSEUM*

The museum is situated at Bovington Camp, the army's tank training centre. A chronological layout takes you from a mock-up of Leonardo da Vinci's prototype tank to the only surviving example of the first type of tank used in the First World War, to Sherman, Panzer and Tiger tanks from the Second World War, and then to terrifyingly large present-day tanks and guided-missile vehicles. Unusual specimens include experimental tanks, amphibious tanks and a mini 'airportable' tank, as well as cutaways to allow you to inspect engines, vehicles to climb into and simulated rides. Don't miss the video explaining the amazing technology

Bovington Tank Museum holds what is claimed to be the largest collection of armoured fighting vehicles in Britain

used in contemporary tanks and showing comical blunders through the decades.

All that said, many visitors might find the museum a chilling, soulless place: little attention is given to the men who fight cooped up inside these machines. The human-interest angle is better dealt with at the Tank Museum by a text-heavy exhibition on the soldier and writer T.E. Lawrence (Lawrence of Arabia), who was a member of the Tank Corps here from 1923 to 1925.

The exhibition works well in conjunction with a visit to **Clouds Hill***, just north of Bovington Camp, where Lawrence lived periodically until his death in a motorbike accident in 1935. The very modest, even ascetic, cottage is a wonderfully evocative place. It is furnished much as it was when Lawrence had it, with additional photos and curios such as an Arab robe (donated by Sir Alec Guinness) which Lawrence wore as a dressing-gown, and a plethora of books matching those he would

Corfe Castle is now a museum: exhibits include a model of the village and castle prior to its annihilation

have had on his shelves. The knowledgeable caretaker trades in books by and about Lawrence and relates fascinating stories about the cottage's ghost and MI5 plots associated with Lawrence's death. If you have caught the Lawrence bug, ask for the Lawrence of Arabia Trail leaflet, which leads you to churches associated with him at nearby Moreton and Wareham.

BEACH WALKS AND WATERSPORTS

The National Trust owns three miles of superb sandy beaches along Studland Bay. They are backed by a protected heathland (beware of adders) and woodland, and enjoy panoramic views across Poole Bay. The main strand is Knoll Beach, with direct access from the car park, a visitor centre, where there are hands-on displays, and watersports facilities. Middle Beach and South Beach are smaller and more charming, and also have simple sports facilities.

LUNCHBOX

The Castle at West Lulworth is a lovely thatched pub with a pretty garden, serving good food. The Fox Inn at Corfe Castle also has a pleasant garden, along with features originating from the castle itself. Bovington Tank Museum and Studland's beaches have cafés. The best café at Lulworth Cove is the Old Boat House directly over the beach, while there are virtually no facilities at Durdle Door except in the caravan park up on the hillside.

Salisbury: medieval town planning at its best

The grace, delicacy and height of this famous landmark owe much to an unknown master mason

England's tallest cathedral spire and largest close are Salisbury's proud boasts, together with fine eighteenth-century houses, a first-rate museum and a medieval grid of shopping streets.

The 404-foot spire simply soars above the Close, the vast swards of which are of field-like dimensions. The explanation for the Close's spaciousness is that Salisbury was a planned city. First called New Sarum, it was founded in 1220 with the beginning of the cathedral's construction. Nearby Old Sarum was abandoned because its hilltop site was exposed and short of water.

The **Cathedral*** is remarkable due to the fact that it is virtually in one style (Early English), built between 1220 and 1258. Only the tower, spire, cloisters and Chapter House were added later, in the subsequent hundred years.

Inside, the absence of a choir screen allows for an unbroken view the length of the whole building, the

♦ **GOOD FOR** Mixing sightseeing with enjoyable shopping
♦ **TRANSPORT** The railway station is about a mile from the city centre. All the sights are within walking distance
♦ **ACCESS FOR DISABLED PEOPLE** There is access to the cathedral but to only some of the Close's museums and open houses
♦ **BEST TIME TO VISIT** May for the arts festival, April to October for Mompesson and Malmesbury houses. The Chapter House is shut for the first three weeks in December and there are no tours of the cathedral. Services restrict cathedral sightseeing on Sundays and Malmesbury House, Salisbury and South Wiltshire Museum are also closed on Sundays (except July and August)

nave lined with austere pillars of Purbeck marble. Individual works of art or monuments are few, primarily

due to the architect James Wyatt's massive restoration programme, carried out during 1789–92. He removed chantries, medieval stained-glass and the choir screen, hid medieval painting under whitewash and shifted tombs of armoured knights and bishops. However, remnants of the choir screen can be seen in the Morning Chapel, most tombs now lie neatly along the nave, and nineteenth-century roof paintings over the choir partially convey how tremendously colourful the church might have been. Look, too, for possibly the oldest working clock in the world (dated 1386). Consider a general guided tour and also a roof tour, up to the base of the spire.

The stunning **Chapter House**, off the largest cloisters in Britain, threatens to steal the show. You can peruse one of the four remaining copies of the Magna Carta or admire the fan vaulting, but much more entertaining is the frieze of 60 thirteenth-century stone bas-reliefs running round the octagonal room, vividly depicting Old Testament stories.

The River Avon and a wall, erected in the fourteenth century to keep the masses at bay, bound the **Close**. Many of its flint and red-brick houses are as old as the cathedral, but the finest were revamped in the late seventeenth and early eighteenth centuries.

On the west side of the Close the King's House, so named because James I visited it twice, holds the excellent **Salisbury and South Wiltshire Museum***. If you have limited time, focus on the exhibitions devoted to Stonehenge (including irreverent cartoons and interesting early photos of the site), to Early Man, with well-displayed Stone and Bronze age, Roman and Saxon finds, and to Salisbury's history. This last has watercolours of the cathedral by

Turner, a fascinating collection of medieval objects found in the city's old drainage channels, and the 12-foot-high Giant and the Hob-Nob hobby horse, both used in the medieval tailors' pageant. **The Wardrobe***, once used by the bishop to store documents and clothes, is now a regimental museum with medals and silverware.

On the north side of the Close **Mompesson House*** (NT) is a tasteful Queen Anne residence redecorated with much baroque plasterwork in 1740, and complemented by period furnishings. Just south of the medieval North Gate, glance at **Matrons College**; possibly designed by Sir Christopher Wren, it is still used to house clergy widows as it was originally intended. In the north-east corner by St Ann's Gate stands **Malmesbury House***, half medieval, half added to between 1698 and 1702 according to a Wren design. You can take a half-hour tour to inspect much rococo plasterwork and a Strawberry Hill gothic library.

High Street Gate leads from the cathedral to the town

BEYOND THE CLOSE: COMMERCIAL SALISBURY

Most old English towns have evolved in a higgledy-piggledy fashion, but as Salisbury was a planned 'New Town' its commercial centre is laid out on a neat grid.

From St Ann's Gate walk about 300 yards along St Ann's Street to Jacobean **Joiners' Hall** to see the strange bearded and big-breasted men carved below its windows. One block north on Trinity Street hides tiny Trinity Hospital, almshouses founded in 1379 and restored in

Queen Anne style (you can enter its chapel). North-west on New Canal stands Salisbury's strangest edifice – **John Halle's Hall**, a fifteenth-century banqueting hall that serves as the foyer for a cinema. Walk down Fish Row to **John a' Port's House**, built in 1425 for a rich wool merchant; as it is a shop you can inspect its interior timbers. Since 1361 the handsomely large **Market Square** has been occupied by market traders, who now sell every Tuesday and Saturday everything from pork pies to fresh flowers and fish to curtains. Walk south to the crown-shaped **Poultry Cross** at Butcher Row and Minster Street, where poultry was once sold.

Salisbury's top sight outside the Close is **St Thomas' Church**. Its 'doom painting', dated 1475, covers the whole wall of the chancel arch. It shows Christ passing judgement over mortals either ascending to heaven with angels or descending to hell into the jaws of dreadful beasts. The church also has lovely roofwork to admire.

The **High Street** leads you back to the Close, past a clutch of gift shops; fourteenth-century D.M. Beach at No. 54 is a fine second-hand bookshop, which also sells prints of the city. Alternatively, for majestic cathedral views, walk west over Crane Bridge to the Town Path across the watermeadows. The **tourist information office*** is situated behind Guildhall, which is on Market Square.

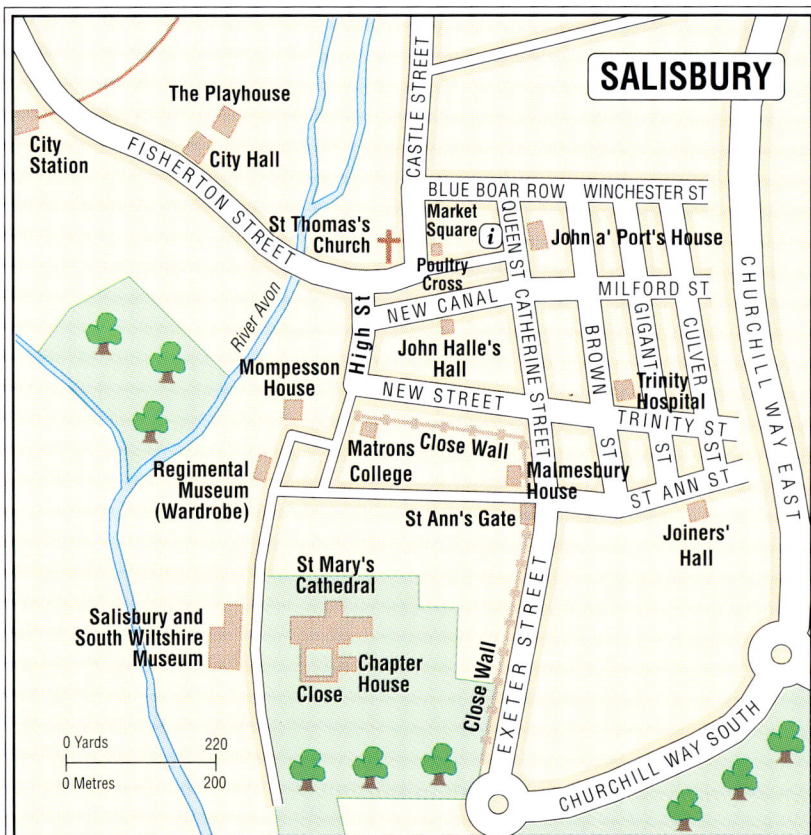

LUNCHBOX

The cathedral and the Close's four museums/open houses all have cafés. The most appealing is that of the National Trust, in Mompesson House's pretty garden. In town, Michael Snell Tea Rooms sell hand-made chocolates, amazing cake selections and have good lunch menus. The Haunch of Venison is a snug beamed pub with interesting bar and restaurant menus; a severed eighteenth-century hand and photos of the playing cards it clasped were discovered in 1903 during renovations

Prehistoric mysteries in rural Wiltshire

Where sheep may safely graze … amongst the standing stones of Avebury

Stone Age shrines or solar computers? Individual temples or points in a giant grid fusing the energies of heaven and earth? The standing stones and stone circles at this ancient site still grip the human imagination some 5,000 years after their construction.

STONEHENGE

Although the present standing stones are roughly 3,500 years old, excavations at Stonehenge suggest that a circular monument was built here as long ago as 2600BC. This consisted of the outer ditch and bank as well as the 56 'Aubrey holes', the ring of inexplicable holes named after the seventeenth-century antiquary who first discovered them.

About 2000BC, an avenue of earth banks was built from the circle to the River Avon, and 60 holy 'bluestones' brought from the Prescelly Mountains in South Wales were erected in a double circle. Two hundred years later they were joined by the great 'sarsen' (sandstone) blocks and 'hanging stones' that later gave Stonehenge its name. Although the sarsen blocks came only 20 miles from the Marlborough Downs, their sheer size throws up hurdles in the challenge to explain Stonehenge.

Since 1000BC, Stonehenge has been slowly disintegrating, but in 1918 it was given to the nation and its future safeguarded; now, together with the other monuments on Salisbury Plain, it is designated a World Heritage Site by UNESCO.

(The **Salisbury and South Wiltshire Museum*** contains galleries dedicated to Stonehenge and early man: see *Great Day Out 20*.)

AROUND STONEHENGE

Fifteen **long barrows** lie within three miles of Stonehenge; one of the best, at Winterbourne Stoke, can be reached along a footpath beside the A303. Another footpath from Stonehenge car park leads to the **Cursus**, two parallel banks marking an enclosure that may have been used for processions or ritual races. The Stonehenge gift shop sells a leaflet which details the routes to surrounding monuments.

Drive up the A345 to **Old Sarum**, one of the busiest settlements in medieval England, where the vast earthworks of an Iron Age hill fort and the abandoned remains of a Norman castle and cathedral — forerunner to the 'new' cathedral in Salisbury — are spread over 56 acres of green countryside.

AVEBURY

It is best to visit Avebury first thing in the morning, when the still light and early mists add extra magic to the place. As at Stonehenge, many of the original stones were lost in the seventeenth and eighteenth centuries, smashed up to build the village of Avebury and neighbouring farms. Most of the village is within the circle of standing stones that forms what has been described as a

- ♦ **GOOD FOR** Being out of doors, trying to fathom early man's preoccupations
- ♦ **TRANSPORT** A car is essential
- ♦ **ACCESS FOR DISABLED PEOPLE** You need to walk short distances to see most of these sites close up
- ♦ **BEST TIME TO VISIT** The monuments are impressive in all seasons, although poor weather may spoil visibility and comfort

ceremonial enclosure, and enough remains of the original construction for it to have been identified as the largest stone circle in Europe. As John Aubrey told Charles II in 1663, 'Avebury doth as much exceed Stonehenge in grandeur as a cathedral doth an ordinary parish church.'

Covering over 28 acres, the site consists of a huge earth bank and ditch 1,300 feet in diameter, between them 50 feet tall, with entrances at the four compass points to a Great Circle of sarsen stones and two inner circles. Originally, the outer circle contained about 100 stones and the inner circles about 30 each; today there are 27 stones in the outer circle and a few stray monoliths scattered in the gardens of Avebury village.

Associated with the earlier stones on the site is an avenue of standing stones alongside the B4003.

The preservation of Avebury is faithfully recorded at the **Alexander Keiller Museum** (EH), named after the archaeologist who bought the site and re-erected the surviving stones in the 1930s. The museum (in an outhouse of Avebury Manor) illustrates Keiller's momentous excavations in the 1920s and 1930s.

The foundations of the cathedral at Old Sarum

SILBURY HILL

The most mysterious site in the region is this symmetrical, flat-topped mound less than a mile to the south of the Avebury circle alongside the Bath road (A4). At 130 feet high and covering over five acres, the uncanny hillock (once described as 'a great, green plum-pudding') is the largest prehistoric artificial mound in Europe. It is thought to have been a burial mound, although numerous excavations have failed to uncover any trace of a burial, except for a comparatively recent one near the summit. Other possible reasons for its existence are that it served some astronomical or religious purpose.

Another important site is **West Kennet Long Barrow**, one of Britain's largest neolithic tombs, situated south of Avebury on the south side of the A4. This 350-foot

A winter view of the unmistakable sandstone constructions that have made Stonehenge world-famous

burial site, 8 feet in height, dates from 3700BC and has five internal chambers, in which excavations suggest that about 45 people, possibly all from one family, were buried here over a 1,000-year period. Entry to the barrow is possible at its eastern end. Inside, glass covers have been let into the 'roof' to allow natural light to penetrate, and you can go deep into the interior. The enormous stone at the entrance formerly sealed the barrow, which was excavated over a whole century, from 1859 to 1956. Finds from this and other barrows in the area are on show at the **Archaeological and Natural History Museum in Devizes***, just down the A361.

LUNCHBOX

Salisbury has a number of fine old pubs serving decent meals, or for more upmarket fare try the White Hart in St John Street, which claims to have been serving food for over four hundred years. In Marlborough, light meals are available from the Polly or Tudor Tea Rooms in the High Street, and more extensive meals from Morans Restaurant in London Road and Bentleys in Kingsbury Street. Avebury has its own eatery, Stone's Restaurant, next to the stone circle, and a seventeenth-century pub.

The legacy of medieval and Georgian Winchester

Cheyney Court, a fifteenth-century house, seen from Priory Gate

Georgian red-brick streets and old flint walls characterise this serene city. Its top sights — a superb cathedral, famous public school and the remains of great castles — are testament to Winchester's importance in medieval times.

By the reign of Alfred the Great, Winchester was the capital of Wessex and thereafter, for about 200 years before the Conquest, of England. In early Norman times kings were crowned both here and in London. Yet nowadays this compact little city's streets soon give way to watermeadows, and tweedy schoolmasters and cloaked choristers lend the place an old-fashioned air.

Winchester is best appreciated on foot. The **tourist information office***, at the Guildhall in Broadway, offers various services including guided tours (daily in summer) and self-guided walks. Otherwise, start at the **cathedral***.

♦ **GOOD FOR** Those interested in fine architecture and medieval history
♦ **TRANSPORT** Winchester station is about a ten-minute walk from the cathedral
♦ **ACCESS FOR DISABLED PEOPLE** To the cathedral and some other sites
♦ **BEST TIME TO VISIT** Some small museums close in winter, and Winchester College tours take place only in summer. On Sundays there are no cathedral tours, the Hospital of St Cross is closed all day and Winchester College is closed in the morning

The present building was started in 1079, though the cathedral predates the Conquest, and work appears to have continued ever since. From its bulk and its disproportionately squat tower, you would find it hard to guess what lies within: the **nave**, in soaring, slender Perpendicular style, takes up much of the longest Gothic church in Europe (575 feet). Note the elegant ribs and bosses of the ceiling. The cathedral's other pleasures come in smaller-scale artistic and historic detail, best discovered on one of the free, hourly guided tours (not Sunday; specialised roof and tower tours are also offered).

If you want to explore on your own, in the nave aisles search out **Jane Austen's grave** and two of the cathedral's six superb **chantry chapels**. One commemorates Bishop Wykeham, who was largely responsible for the creation of the inspirational nave. The transepts are the only complete parts of the original Norman church. In the north transept is the entrance to the crypt, which you can tour when it is not flooded. The choir boasts the oldest medieval stalls in Britain. Behind it, the **Great Screen** drips with tracery (its statuary is Victorian), while the **mortuary chests** contain relics of pre-Conquest monarchs such as Canute.

The retrochoir housed the shrine of **St Swithun** until the Reformation (a modern canopy covers the site). This ninth-century bishop wished to be buried humbly outside his cathedral. When his body was moved inside, a great storm erupted; by tradition, it will rain for the next 40 days if it rains on St Swithun's Day (15 July). Of the retrochoir's four splendid chantries, the most interesting is that of Bishop Fox, whose bony representation was intended to reflect his frail mortality. In front of Bishop Langton's Chapel

'King Arthur's Round Table', in Winchester's medieval Great Hall

stands a statue of William Walker, who in 1906–11 dived into the muddy waters under the cathedral to replace rotten timbers with cement to save the building from collapse.

Don't miss the **Jacobean library**, in the south transept. Its chief treasure is the twelfth-century **Winchester Bible**; you can pore over its pages of handwritten Latin script and sublime illustrated initial letters. The **Triforium Gallery** above exhibits restored original statues from the Great Screen and fragments from St Swithun's shrine.

The cathedral close was described by Keats as 'two college-like squares, garnished with grass and shaded with trees'. In the outer close alongside the cathedral the Anglo-Saxon Old Minster has been outlined. Cross to the Square, a happy jumble of pubs, cafés and shops, and walk through to the pedestrianised High Street. Turn left up to the **Westgate Museum*** in one of the city's two surviving medieval gateways. Seventeenth-century graffiti are etched into the walls of this former debtors' prison. The vast **Great Hall*** nearby was built in 1222, the only surviving part of a medieval castle begun by William the Conqueror and demolished in the Civil War. Hanging on one wall like a giant dartboard is the so-called **Round Table of King Arthur**. Dating from 1522, it depicts a Tudor King Arthur and the names of his knights in Gothic script.

Return to the cathedral and make your way round to the **inner close**. This peaceful sanctuary has handsome buildings of pre-Reformation monastic origin (generally viewable only from the outside). The most picturesque of them is the fifteenth-century gabled and half-timbered **Cheyney Court**.

Pass through the close's gate and turn left through **Kingsgate**, the other medieval city gate. The shop under its arches sells appealing prints of the city. Just yards away, **College Street** is one of Winchester's loveliest, lined with colourful Georgian buildings; Jane Austen died in No. 8 in 1817.

Just beyond, **Winchester College*** is England's oldest school – and looks it. Founded in 1382 by Bishop Wykeham as a place to train clergy, it became the model for the English public school system. Its pupils are called Wykehamists and its motto is 'Manners makyth man'. Seventy scholars have traditionally lived round the beautiful yet austere Chamber Court, while full fee-paying 'commoners' reside elsewhere. Visitors can inspect the court and the fan-vaulted chapel independently, but need to take a guided tour of the cloisters, uniquely surrounding a chantry, and to School, a vast classroom possibly designed by Christopher Wren.

East on College Street a sign suggests a scenic diversion across the watermeadows to the serene **Hospital of St Cross*** – a two-mile round trip. This walk inspired Keats' 'Ode to Autumn'. The hospital is the country's oldest charitable institution, founded in the 1130s. Brothers in black gowns (or red if they are members of the later Noble Order of Poverty) live in its flint cottages. Their only obligation is to attend chapel daily – no hardship as it is a fine, simple Norman building. Also visit the old hall, kitchens and manicured walled garden. Wayfarer's Dole of bread and ale is still served at the main gate on request, but in small, symbolic quantities.

Return to College Street. **Wolvesey Castle***, the bishop's palace in the Middle Ages, still has just enough masonry to convey the scale of the residence. Follow the River Itchen and the city wall to the National Trust's **City Mill***, Winchester's last working waterwheel, and its pretty island garden. Just to the west stands a splendid **statue of King Alfred**, who was buried at Winchester in 901. Turn left opposite it into Abbey Gardens and thence to the cathedral, where you might end the day at **Evensong** (5.30; 3.30 on Sunday), sung (except Wednesday) to flickering candlelight in the choir.

LUNCHBOX

The Cathedral Refectory is a stylish, modern cafeteria with an outdoor terrace alongside a medieval wall. The Wykeham Arms is the city's ultra-civilised pub, with no-smoking rooms and sophisticated fare.

Museums and walks in the New Forest

The lawns in front of the houses at Buckler's Hard were used to stack ships' timbers

WALKING IN THE NEW FOREST

The area is a walkers' paradise as the unique laws here allow access to any trail or track on the open forest (unless you are advised otherwise). You do not have to venture far from any of the 150 Forestry Commission car parks to feel the peaceful seclusion of the forest and open heathland. Waymarked walks with accompanying information leaflets are available from Rhinefield, Bolderwood and Ober car parks near Brockenhurst. Varied walks, often incorporating a visit to a country pub, can be enjoyed from Fritham, Linwood, Burley, Beaulieu Road Station, Brockenhurst and Minstead. Make sure that you acquire a large-scale map of the forest as there are few landmarks and you may find the area very disorientating.

Where the ancient heath and forest meet the peaceful waters of the Solent, a wealth of attractions waits to be discovered. The family day out on the New Forest fringe described here takes in the best of them.

You may wish to wander around the bustling cobbled streets, quaint shops and yacht-lined waterfront of Lymington; or stroll through the landscaped woodland gardens at Exbury; or explore the idyllic riverside section of the Solent Way, which links the historic ship-building hamlet of Buckler's Hard to Beaulieu, famous for its abbey and motor museum. This collection of ideas will help you plan your day out. All the sights are within easy reach of each other, but note that a visit to Beaulieu could well fill a whole day.

If you are interested in boats or browsing round a few specialist shops, the ancient town of **Lymington** would be the ideal place to begin your day. Take a gentle morning stroll up the wide High Street, lined with eighteenth- and nineteenth-century houses, to the

♦ **GOOD FOR** Combining a forest walk with visits to gardens and picturesque villages; the museums will appeal to children over 10

♦ **TRANSPORT** This is a 20-mile round trip so a car (or cycle) would be a great advantage. The nearest railway station is Brockenhurst. Alternatively, take a bus from Southampton to Lymington, and from Lymington to Beaulieu

♦ **ACCESS FOR DISABLED PEOPLE** Good access at most sites

♦ **BEST TIME TO VISIT** All year; Exbury Gardens are at their best during spring, early summer and autumn

imposing parish church. Wend your way via the **tourist information office*** and the **St Barbe Museum*** (local history) in New Street to the cobbled streets leading to the lively quay and marina, haven to hundreds of yachts.

Away from the hustle and bustle, signposted off the A337 north of Lymington, is the peaceful forest village of **Boldre**. Of particular interest is **St John's Church**, standing in woodland isolation a mile from the village. Inside, you will find memorials to HMS *Hood*, the warship that sank in 1941 with only three survivors, including a painting of the ship, a few lanterns and two carved benches. Garden enthusiasts may like to make a small detour to visit the nearby **Spinners Garden***, which was created in 1960 and contains many woodland and ground-cover plants, as well as a nursery known for its rare trees, shrubs and plants.

Further north, some seven miles north-east of Lymington, in the New Forest is **Beaulieu** with its picturesque position at the head of Beaulieu River. Enhancing the tranquil riverside setting are the ruins of the thirteenth-century **abbey** and its adjoining great gatehouse, now **Palace House** and the home of the Montagu family since 1538.

Beyond, beautiful gardens connect the National Motor Museum and other attractions, making this a good family destination. If you purchase an all-inclusive ticket, you can visit the abbey cloisters and ruins, and find out about the daily life of Cistercian monks through the Exhibition of Monastic Life. Next, take time to view the interior of Lord Montagu's splendid home and its family treasures, especially the fine paintings and furnishings.

With the same ticket you can trace the history of 100 years of motoring through state-of-the-art technology on an automated ride-through display called 'Wheels', as well as explore the heart of the **National Motor Museum***and its priceless collection of 250 classic, vintage and veteran motor cars and motor cycles. Among the exhibits you will find a petrol-driven car from 1892 and Sir Donald Campbell's *Bluebird*. Other attractions include a ride on the high-level monorail that transports you around the grounds, giving you a rooftop view of the museum, and taking a trip on a Veteran Bus.

If you would prefer a country ramble (see box), you could join the well-waymarked Solent Way, conveniently signposted beside the

▲ *Exbury Gardens benefit from their setting by river and forest*

Montagu Arms in Beaulieu, for a 2½-mile woodland and riverside walk to the charming eighteenth-century village of **Buckler's Hard**. Twin terraces of dwellings flank the descent to the river and look today much as they did when the village thrived as a ship-building yard. Buckler's Hard was the creation of the second Duke of Montagu, who originally planned a town and docks here to receive produce from his own extensive foreign estates. Some 60 wooden vessels, made of New Forest oak, were constructed and launched here between 1698 and 1818,

including some of Nelson's fleet that defeated the Franco-Spanish ships at Trafalgar.

To appreciate the history of the village, visit the **Maritime Museum***. On show are guns and other items of ships' equipment, prints and plans, and models of ships built here, such as Nelson's *Agamemnon*. You can re-live eighteenth-century life by setting foot in some of the cottages – stroll through the New Inn of 1793, complete with costumed figures, smells and conversation; look in on the family of a poor labourer at home, or Henry Adams, the Master Builder, at work. In the summer you can cruise the wood-bordered Beaulieu River, observing the wildlife, on board the *Swiftsure*.

Throughout the spring and early summer **Exbury Gardens***, on the east bank of the Beaulieu River, are a botanical treat. Unsurpassed displays of the famous Rothschild rhododendron, azalea, camellia and magnolia collection can be enjoyed in this 200-acre riverside woodland setting. A labyrinth of tracks and paths through a rock garden, rose garden and daffodil meadow and past ponds and cascades are there for the exploring. Jubilee Pond provides a good setting for a picnic.

▲ *The National Motor Museum will fascinate car enthusiasts of all ages*

LUNCHBOX

Bluebird at Lentune on Quay Street in Lymington offers decent snacks and teas. For a welcoming atmosphere and reliable bar snacks go to the Red Lion in Boldre, the Fleur de Lys (the oldest pub in the New Forest) at Pilley near Boldre, the Chequers at Pennington, just west of Lymington, and the Montagu Arms in Beaulieu, also noted for good afternoon teas in the conservatory or the pretty garden. Refreshments are also available in the Brabazon Food Court at Beaulieu and in the Yachtsman's Bar (open all day) of the Master Builder's House Hotel, or in the Mainsail Café at the Buckler's Hard Maritime Museum.

Salt and naval might at Portsmouth

Portsmouth Historic Dockyard's famous old ships and extensive exhibitions make it one of the best places to learn about Britain's naval heritage. A boat tour of the Royal Navy's fleet is also an absolute must on this maritime day out.

Ever since Henry VII constructed the world's first dry dock here in 1495, the kingdom's premier naval base has been sited at Portsmouth. Now past and present meet with historic ships such as the *Mary Rose* and HMS *Victory* within spitting distance of sleek frigates and colossal aircraft carriers. The city of Portsmouth has a small old quarter, and also encompasses Port Solent, the bulbous Portsea Island and the jaunty resort of Southsea, whose breezy promenade and pebble beach oversee the busy sea lanes into Portsmouth Harbour. Piers, a funfair

- ♦ **GOOD FOR** Naval history aficionados, of course, but most people will find plenty to interest them
- ♦ **TRANSPORT** Portsmouth Harbour BR station is only yards from the dockyard; boat and bus services go to other attractions (more details from the tourist information office*)
- ♦ **ACCESS FOR DISABLED PEOPLE** To all parts of the dockyard, including ships. Limited access to Submarine World
- ♦ **BEST TIME TO VISIT** Very busy in summer, especially at weekends. Boat tours take place between Easter and end October

HMS Warrior (1860) was the first warship to be iron-clad

and high-tech aquarium compete for custom with the more serious naval attractions.

We suggest you spend the morning and lunchtime at the Historic Dockyard, and take in a boat trip and one of the additional sights in the afternoon. Irritatingly, limited opening times won't enable you to do any more, and with adult admission fees of nearly £20 for the attractions featured here, you may not wish to. There is probably enough at the Historic Dockyard alone to fill a cheaper and more leisurely day.

PORTSMOUTH HISTORIC DOCKYARD*

This is the part of the 300-acre Royal Navy base open to the public, and comprises museums and exhibitions in handsome Georgian red-brick storehouses and boathouses, and three historic ships. You can visit everything on a single admission ticket. The ticket states a time to tour **HMS Victory**, which will be as soon after you enter the complex as possible, unless you ask otherwise. Gradually being restored to appear as it did in 1805, HMS *Victory* (whose photograph graces the front cover of this book) is the world's oldest commissioned warship. It is even more famous for being Nelson's flagship at the Battle of Trafalgar: the spot where the admiral fell and the place where he died are honoured. You can view the ship's gun decks (some cannon are fake), the hardy living areas for the ratings and the palatial suite of cabins for the admiral. Retired naval servicemen conduct the engaging 40-minute tours; they give you a good feel for the hardships of life at sea two centuries ago, showing off a cat-o'-nine-tails and telling tales of maggot-infested biscuits.

Next, visit the **Royal Naval Museum**. It contains an absorbing exhibition on the Battle of Trafalgar and a vast store of memorabilia relating to Admiral Lord Nelson. With limited time (and certainly with restless children in tow), you may choose to skip the rest of the museum's exhaustive trawl through the navy's history.

Head back past HMS *Victory* to the **Mary Rose Ship Hall**. The warship *Mary Rose*, built in 1509, sank just outside Portsmouth Harbour in 1545 while preparing to engage the French fleet. The extensive remains of her hull were delicately raised and brought ashore in 1982 and can now be seen in a covered dry dock. For at least the next fifteen years water and a mixture like antifreeze will be constantly sprayed from a vast sprinkler system to preserve and seal the timbers; eventually, the hull will be displayed dry.

HMS Ark Royal *has seen action in many theatres of war, including the Bosnian conflict*

The Solent silt preserved the artefacts on board the ship remarkably well. Many are displayed in the **Mary Rose Exhibition** (inconveniently located at the opposite end of the dockyard from the hull). First, watch the excellent accompanying film on the recovery of the ship and its objects, then allow a good hour to study the superb finds, which range from a backgammon board and a single domino to bronze guns emblazoned with the Tudor rose, and arrows and longbows.

The dazzlingly restored **HMS Warrior** (1860) was the world's most impressive warship when she was built. You can explore all the decks and the engine room on your own. This ship is built on a far grander scale than HMS *Victory*, but otherwise is strikingly similar in many respects, not least its posh cabins for officers and its messes squeezed in between the guns for the 655 ratings.

The centrepiece of **Submarine World*** is the surprisingly large submarine *HMS Alliance*, which was in service between 1947 and 1973. The forty-minute guided tour inspects the claustrophobic living quarters, the control and engine rooms and the

In memory of ADMIRAL SIR BERTRAM RAMSAY killed in action 1945 who commanded the seaborne forces at Dunkirk 1940

The Cathedral reflects Portsmouth's naval history, including this window and the grave of an unknown sailor whose body was lifted with the Mary Rose

BOAT TRIPS

A boat trip round Portsmouth Harbour may well be the highlight of your day. The most interesting trips sail within yards of such ships as the Royal Yacht *Britannia*, the aircraft carrier HMS *Ark Royal*, frigates, destroyers and an arctic patrol vessel. Bring binoculars with you. Fifty-minute **Waterbus*** tours are the most useful, allowing you to disembark at Submarine World and Old Portsmouth (a pleasant mile-long walk along the promenade to the D-Day Museum) and pick up a later ferry. They leave from alongside Portsmouth Harbour station every half-hour.

torpedo tubes. Alongside stand human torpedoes (two men seated on top of the torpedo would be carried to the target, attach the torpedo and swim off quickly), a gallery of models of prototype submarines through the ages and an exhibition on nuclear submarines. (The Waterbus – see box above – stops off at the jetty. It's a ten-minute walk from the Gosport terminal of the free passenger ferry connecting Portsmouth Harbour BR station with Gosport.)

The 272-foot Overlord Embroidery receives top billing at the **D-Day Museum***. Conceptually plagiarised from the Bayeux Tapestry, it tells the D-Day story in colourful set scenes. But this imaginative museum offers much else besides, including a good archive-footage film show and a 'Duck' amphibious landing craft to clamber over. Most memorable are the reconstructions of a living-room in a blackout, an Anderson shelter, and the map room near Portsmouth where the D-Day invasion's progress was charted.

Isle of Wight: a day out from Yarmouth

Away from the hustle and bustle of the traditional resort towns, the more rural and unspoilt area of West Wight offers a host of walking opportunities and numerous family attractions.

Enjoy peaceful country walks or cycle rides beside the Yar Estuary; tramp across magnificent chalk headland and hills with spellbinding coastal views; explore a castle and a cliff-top fort; visit a country park complete with aquarium and planetarium; and have fun in an exciting Pleasure Park. And if this is not enough, you can also swim and sunbathe, or take a boat trip around the Needles.

If you are beginning your day out from the mainland, leave your car at the Lymington Ferry Terminal and board the regular **Wightlink*** ferry for the 30-minute crossing of the Solent to the picturesque little town of Yarmouth. (For those who are on the island with a car, Yarmouth's main

- ♦ **GOOD FOR** Families, walkers, cyclists
- ♦ **TRANSPORT** On foot or Southern Vectis* bus service that runs from Yarmouth
- ♦ **ACCESS FOR DISABLED PEOPLE** Some sights difficult with wheelchair. Fort Victoria and Needles Pleasure Park accessible
- ♦ **BEST TIME TO VISIT** Excellent walking all year. Sights open Easter to October

car park is situated off River Road.) With its stone quays and charming old houses, **Yarmouth** is the perfect place to disembark, as the town square, complete with pier entrance, tea rooms and pubs, is only a short distance from the harbour, which in the summer months is a popular mooring for yachts. It was the main port on the Isle of Wight in the

twelfth century when it received a royal charter. It boasts a well-preserved **castle***, built during the reign of Henry VIII as a coastal defence against the ransacking French; it houses the Master Gunner's parlour and kitchen, and a small Great Hall. From the open gun platform you can savour the view of the harbour and the Solent.

This corner of West Wight is ideal for walking, with its wealth of estuary, coast and downland paths. Head for the **tourist information office*** by the harbour to buy one of the leaflets giving details of the various trails in the area, many of which can be linked for a full day's walking. However, if you would rather pedal round this part of the island, you can hire mountain bikes from **Wavells Delicatessen*** in the main square.

Not to be missed is the memorable **Yar Estuary** circular walk. This four-mile, level ramble explores both sides of the peaceful estuary, whose mudflats, saltmarsh and inlets support a diverse wildlife, notably wintering birds, and reed and marsh plants. Highlights en route include a three-storey eighteenth-century tide mill following the course of the now disused Newport–Freshwater railway, which closed in 1953; and the enchanting **All Saints' Church** in Freshwater, set on a hillock enjoying serene river views. The churchyard contains the grave of Emily Tennyson, wife of the poet laureate Alfred, Lord Tennyson, who lived at nearby Farringford House (now a hotel) between 1853 and his death in 1892. He composed 'Idylls of the King' and 'The Charge of the Light Brigade' on the island. Several eminent Victorians were regular guests at Farringford, including Lewis Carroll, Henry Longfellow, Edward Lear and even Garibaldi.

Enthusiastic walkers can link with the Freshwater Way at the causeway

The Needles: five chalk pinnacles gradually being eroded by the sea

by the River Yar and continue to **Freshwater Bay** on the island's south coast. Sheltered between dramatic white cliffs, the bay offers safe bathing and has several hotels and cafés.

If time and energy levels allow, follow the signposts for the **Tennyson Trail** at the western end of the bay to begin the most spectacular and exhilarating cliff walk on the island. Ascend past **Fort Redoubt***, now a superbly sited tea room, and climb the chalk downland to Tennyson's Monument, erected in memory of the poet at the highest point of **Tennyson Down**. Taking in unrivalled views of the Channel and the Solent, and along the Dorset coast, keep on the well-defined coast path, eventually reaching the **Needles Old Battery***. This Victorian fort was built in the early 1860s, 250 feet above the sea, and houses an exhibition of the history of the Needles headland in the old powder house. It is now owned by the National Trust. A 200-foot tunnel leads to a viewing platform and magnificent views of the Needles and

the lighthouse. If your enthusiasm waned at Freshwater Bay, or the beach beckoned, you can return to Yarmouth by open-top bus via the sights at Alum Bay and/or the Needles (summer only).

Alum Bay is a great family destination popular for its exciting chairlift ride down to the beach. The amazing sand cliffs are coloured white by quartz, red by iron oxide,

grey by carbonaceous remains and yellow by limonite. You can also take a summer boat trip to see the Needles and its lighthouse at close quarters. The bay is home to **Needles Pleasure Park***, where the attractions range from crafts like pottery and glass-blowing to the twenty-first-century world of simulator rides.

Just west of Yarmouth and easily reached on foot is the **Fort Victoria Country Park***. Here a waymarked circular walk, perfect for a family ramble, combines a nature trail and the wooded coastal path. Other attractions include a picnic site and stirring views over the water. During the summer you can join one of the guided wildlife tours of the park. The old fort itself, built around 1840 as part of the defences of the Solent, is home to a marine aquarium, displaying fish from around the island's shores, tropical fish and conger eels, the Isle of Wight Maritime Heritage Exhibition and a fascinating planetarium, where you can learn about space exploration and scientific adventure.

Yarmouth has plenty to offer the visitor and makes a good base for a tour

The watery splendour of Chichester harbour

Chichester harbour — once a busy port, now a yachtsman's paradise

This unspoilt and beautiful harbour with its many inlets forms a natural habitat for a wide variety of wildlife. The surprising mixture of Roman remains, historic villages and riverscape makes this one of the South Coast's finest recreational areas.

Quaint waterside villages, a shoreline that is home to an abundance of wildlife, and a magnificent Roman palace — Chichester harbour is a promising venue for a day in the open air.

The harbour has had a rich history as a commercial port since the Roman invasion of Britain in AD43. The Romans established a harbour at Fishbourne and by the Middle Ages goods such as wool and later cloth were being exported from the various quays around the adjacent 50 miles of shoreline. During the eighteenth and nineteenth centuries the area was noted for both its shipbuilding and its oyster industries.

Today, apart from a small fleet of professional fishermen, the main

- ♦ **GOOD FOR** Wildlife, picturesque villages, sailing, waterside rambles
- ♦ **TRANSPORT** Car, cycle or boat
- ♦ **ACCESS FOR DISABLED PEOPLE** Some sights; phone to check
- ♦ **BEST TIME TO VISIT** Summer for harbour water tours, winter for the best birdwatching; all year for walking, village exploration and most sights

users of the 17 miles of navigable channels and creeks are the people aboard the thousands of yachts and dinghies, out to enjoy themselves. Visitors wishing to sail in the harbour waters in their own vessels will find launching facilities at most of the quayside villages. Fees are payable, so contact the **Chichester Harbour**

LUNCHBOX

For the best views try the Royal Oak at Langstone, the Anchor Bleu in Bosham, the Crown and Anchor at Dell Quay and the Old House at Home in Chidham. Restaurant choices include Spencers and 36 On the Quay (harbour views) in Emsworth and the Millstream Hotel in Bosham, which is also a pleasant spot for a summer afternoon tea in the garden beside the millstream.

Conservancy* office for more information. If you do not have your own boat you can still appreciate the birdlife at close quarters by taking a peaceful 1½-hour cruise round the area by courtesy of the water tour company based at West Itchenor.

Landlubbers will also find much to see and do, as the harbour is virtually surrounded by scenic footpaths, linking the shoreline villages and offering a variety of circular walks of various lengths. Parking areas at the water's edge help visitors make the most of the watery landscape.

Good walks range from a short stroll around East Head near West Wittering (1¼ miles) and the lovely stretch of coastal path between West Wittering and Itchenor (2½ miles), to a lengthy ramble around Thorney Island (7½ miles), and between Itchenor and Chichester, incorporating the scenic Chichester canal towpath (5½ miles). Take care, for some paths become impassable at high tide. Information on historical guided walking tours and self-guided walks is available from **Havant** and **Chichester tourist information offices*** and also from the Harbour Conservancy.

You could combine a harbourside stroll with a visit to one of the historic villages dotted around the harbour. One of the oldest and most photogenic is **Bosham** (pronounced Bozzum), a flourishing yachting centre built on a piece of land jutting

The beaches and sand dunes of West Wittering are constantly under threat of erosion

out into an inlet, complete with village green, a splendid Saxon church (where King Canute's daughter is buried) and brick and tile-hung cottages. Browse round Bosham Walk Craft Centre with its collection of little shops and tea rooms, or picnic on the lovely **Quay Meadow** (NT). King Harold set sail for Normandy in 1064 from Bosham, an event recorded on the Bayeux Tapestry, and it was at Quay Meadow that King Canute unsuccessfully challenged the waves to withdraw. With this in mind, make sure you remove your vehicle from the harbourside car park before the tide turns.

For a stroll, you could head south alongside Bosham Channel to Smugglers Hard, then catch the summer ferry to Itchenor.

The ancient little port of **Emsworth**, tucked away between two of the many small creeks around the harbour, is a pleasant village of narrow streets lined with cottages, a busy harbourside and two old tide mills. Once a thriving boat-building and oyster-fishing centre, it is now a popular sailing destination which also attracts naturalists and walkers.

Visit **Emsworth Museum***, which details the maritime connections and history of the village, or look round the specialist shops in the village before setting out on the 2¼-mile coastal Wayfarers Walk to Langstone, via Warblington

and its Saxon church, for refreshment at the Royal Oak (open all day), a 500-year-old inn perfectly sited on the harbour edge.

On wet and windy days, forgo the harbour stroll and head for one of the indoor attractions in the area. Top of the list should be the magnificent **Roman Palace*** at Fishbourne, the largest known Roman residence in Britain (see *Great Day Out 29*).

Butterfly enthusiasts should include **Earnley Butterflies and Gardens*** on their itinerary. There, you can walk amongst free-flying tropical butterflies and birds and through 17 themed gardens, all under cover. This is an ideal family venue with farmyard animals, picnic and play areas and refreshments. At the **Sussex Falconry Centre*** at Birdham you can watch falcons fly, touch and handle owls and enjoy flying a hawk. Admirers of roses, both old-fashioned and modern, should ensure they have time to wander around **Apuldram Roses*** at Dell Quay, a specialist rose garden that is a riot of colour during the summer.

Sea- and sun-worshippers looking for a beach will find the best bathing beaches at West Wittering and on Hayling Island, located on either side of the harbour entrance. Hayling Island also boasts excellent windsurfing facilities.

A Georgian house and Norman church in Bosham

A tour of Chichester's Georgian centre

The south side of Chichester Cathedral from St Richard's Walk

◆ **GOOD FOR** Roman and Georgian architecture, elegant shops
◆ **TRANSPORT** The bus and railway stations are both by Southgate
◆ **ACCESS FOR DISABLED PEOPLE** Possible at all the sights apart from the walls; wheelchair users should encounter few problems
◆ **BEST TIME TO VISIT** All year

Encircled by defensive walls dating back to the Roman occupation, Chichester's compact centre contains many impressive medieval landmarks, a Norman/Gothic cathedral and some of the finest examples of Georgian town planning and architecture in England.

The best way to see West Sussex's county town is on foot. Though small, the elegant Georgian heart of the city, with its splendid spired cathedral, fascinating local museum, interesting art gallery and many specialist shops, has much to offer.

Our suggested walk begins at the long-stay Northgate car park next to the internationally acclaimed **Festival Theatre*** (opened in 1962 and ideal for anyone planning to round off their day by seeing a play). Pass beneath the subway into North Street and immediately turn right into North Walls, signposted Walls Walk (see box), to follow the well-surfaced promenade along part of the town walls that the Romans constructed in the second century AD; the surviving sections run for 1½ miles, enclosing the city's heart.

Pass the neo-classical (1936) County Council building and soon cross West Street, once the site of the ancient West Gate. A short distance along West Street on your left is **Ede's House** (1696), one of the city's most architecturally outstanding buildings. Endure a short section along the Ring Road, but soon after veer off to the left through the colourful **Bishop's Palace Gardens**, a tranquil place affording memorable views of the Tudor palace and cathedral. Instead of going up on to the walls, pass through the fine fourteenth-century gateway into Canon Lane, where ecclesiastical Chichester proper begins.

You can enter the **cathedral*** and cloisters by turning left along Vicars' Close, a narrow pathway lined with a row of fifteenth-century houses, built as homes for the vicars choral (the men who sang in the choir). The barrel-vaulted ceilinged cloisters now house a Visitors' Centre and Refectory, a useful refreshment stop with a sheltered walled garden. Then you reach the main entrance to the cathedral. This magnificent mainly Norman building has traces of a more modern Gothic style, particularly in its upper storey, which was repaired after two severe fires in 1114 and 1187. Do not miss the two superb Romanesque carvings on the south wall of the south choir aisle, depicting the raising of Lazarus and Christ arriving at Bethany. Twentieth-century treasures include a huge Aubusson tapestry, hanging behind the high altar, designed by John Piper

Georgian houses in Lion Street

in 1966, and a glowing stained-glass window by Marc Chagall which was installed in 1978.

From the unique detached fifteenth-century **Bell Tower**, home to a peal of eight bells and the cathedral shop, turn right along West Street to reach the **Market Cross**, an octagon surmounted by a crown of stone pinnacles, which marks the centre of the city. It was given by Bishop Story in about 1500 so that the town's market folk and their goods would have shelter. Here you turn right along South Street, passing the timber-framed White Horse Inn, which dates from 1416, before bearing left into Theatre Lane to reach the Pallants.

(At this point, for a longer walk, you could leave the city confines for a stroll along the **Chichester canal**: continue along South Street, turning left into Market Avenue to reach Basin Road on your right, which leads to the Canal Basin. Here you can hire a rowing boat or take a canal boat trip, or walk along the towpath.)

The smart area known as the **Pallants** consists of four narrow streets all lined with fine Georgian buildings, whether modest

cottages or elegant merchants' houses. The grandest, with its red-brick pillars and black iron railings, is **Pallant House***, which was built in 1712 by Henry Peckham, a prosperous wine merchant; it is a combination of historic house and art gallery, containing fine furnishings, an Edwardian kitchen, an important collection of Bow porcelain and works by Picasso, Gainsborough and Henry Moore.

North Pallant leads to East Street, one of the main pedestrianised shopping streets. Return to the Market Cross and walk along North Street where you can see the **Buttermarket**, built in 1807 to a design by John Nash, and **St Olave's**, the oldest of Chichester's medieval churches (now a bookshop). Built in about 1050, and restored in 1850, it still retains some Saxon work. The centrepiece of North Street is the **Council House**, an imposing red-brick building, built in 1731 and arcaded at street level. The Neptune and Minerva stone, which once adorned a small classical temple, is set in the walls outside.

Turn right along Lion Street beside the Council House to enter St Martin's

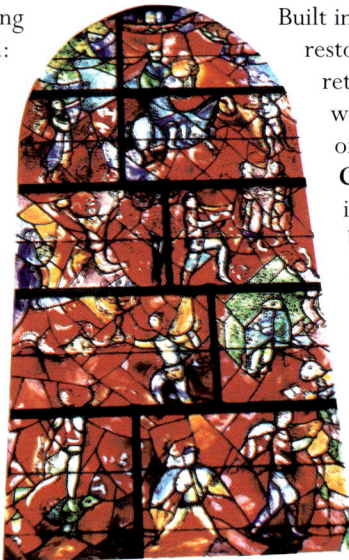

The action-packed Chagall window in Chichester cathedral

Square, with the almshouses to thirteenth-century **St Mary's Hospital*** opposite. The chapel and parts of this early hospital are open by appointment only. Proceed down St Martin's Street back to East Street, turning left, then left again into **Little London**, a name reputedly bestowed by Queen Elizabeth I because its hurly-burly reminded her of London. The street, lined with attractive cottages, brings you to the **Chichester District Museum***, which traces the city's history from prehistoric times to the present day; exhibits include a Roman lead coffin in which you can see the impressions left by its occupant's leg bones and pelvis.

At the end of East Row, either climb the steps back on to the city walls, or follow East Walls left, soon to cross Priory Road into Priory Park. Nestling against the city walls is the grassy mound which marks the site of the Norman motte and bailey castle. This was probably little more than a timber stockade that was captured by the French in 1216 and destroyed by the English the following year. In the centre of the park is the medieval **Guildhall***, originally the chancel of a thirteenth-century Franciscan friary and later the court where William Blake was tried for sedition. Benches on the castle mound and on the city wall promenade are perfect spots from which to savour the view across the city and cathedral. Stroll along the walls, shortly leaving the park to return to your starting point.

Goodwood, gardens and an open-air museum

Be prepared for a good deal of walking in the open-air museum

Compare rural domestic life in medieval, Tudor and Victorian times by visiting the fascinating Weald and Downland Open Air Museum and grand Goodwood House, or stroll around tranquil gardens for a delightful day out in beautiful Sussex.

You don't have to travel the length and breadth of the Weald and Downland between Kent and Hampshire to appreciate the rich architecture in the region. Over three dozen buildings have been rescued and re-erected on a glorious 40-acre downland site, along with a medieval farmstead. Rural collections and crafts can also be seen here.

In completed contrast, two miles across the downs is the lavishly furnished Goodwood House, the home of the Dukes of Richmond. A short distance from the open-air museum and Goodwood lies West Dean College with 35 acres of informal lawns and gardens. The proximity of the three attractions should allow you to combine two for a full day; but the museum could easily take up most of a day itself.

- ♦ **GOOD FOR** Families
- ♦ **TRANSPORT** Car necessary
- ♦ **ACCESS FOR DISABLED PEOPLE** Parts of the Weald museum may prove difficult for wheelchairs
- ♦ **BEST TIME TO VISIT** Museum open all year; special events take place between April and October. Limited summer opening at Goodwood House. (Avoid the five main race days at the end of July.) West Dean Gardens open April to October

WEALD AND DOWNLAND OPEN AIR MUSEUM*

This museum, in Singleton, five miles north of Chichester, was opened in 1971 with the principal aim of establishing a centre for rescuing neglected and endangered historic buildings, which would have otherwise been lost or destroyed.

Each dwelling has been carefully dismantled and painstakingly re-erected, and the museum illustrates the history of original building styles and types from medieval times to the nineteenth century. The main exhibits include a fine fifteenth-century timber-framed Wealden farmhouse, with a central hearth and replica domestic furniture showing how it might have looked in about 1540, a medieval shop and an exceptional seventeenth-century brick dwelling housing the museum's own shop. Add to this a Tudor market hall, a blacksmith's forge and a working watermill, and you get a museum which has the appearance of an idyllic, authentic village. There are also a seventeenth-century man-driven treadwheel for raising water; a school and a timber-framed weather-boarded stable, both from the eighteenth century; and a nineteenth-century plumber's workshop. The reconstruction of a flint cottage, based on archaeological evidence obtained from excavations of a deserted medieval village, is impressive. The collection is enhanced by displays of traditional rural crafts and skills.

Children will be enthralled with the museum's introductory exhibition, housed in the Hambrook Barn. A 'hands-on' gallery helps them explore building materials and techniques through activities such as weighing, sieving and joining. They will also enjoy the medieval farmstead with its livestock and traditional farm machinery. They can see flour being ground inside the seventeenth-century watermill and watch rural crafts like spinning demonstrated in some of the buildings, as well as thatching, flint-walling, sheep-shearing and ploughing on certain days during the summer. Wandering freely around so many remarkable buildings is a real treat.

The charming sunken garden at West Dean lies at one end of the pergola

GOODWOOD HOUSE*

Set in a magnificent estate of 12,000 acres at the foot of the South Downs, this imposing magnolia-covered flint-and-mortar house reflects a lifestyle worlds apart from the rustic one portrayed at the Weald and Downland Open Air Museum. Goodwood is famous for its associated downland racecourse, motor circuit, golf course and hotel. A visit here gives you a glimpse of the affluent lifestyle of a noble family from the eighteenth century to the present.

You can view the spacious and sumptuously furnished state rooms, which contain many fine paintings and mementoes of the family. There are remarkable works of art by Canaletto, Stubbs, Van Dyck and Reynolds, rare French furniture, rich tapestries, and a priceless collection of Sèvres porcelain. The ballroom is stunning with its gilded ostentation. Also of note are the fine eighteenth-century stables by the house.

The Shell House in the grounds is a small pavilion built in 1739 for Sarah, Duchess of Richmond. It is so called because it is covered with an amazing pattern of shells.

Make the most of Goodwood's unrivalled position on the South Downs by working off any excesses at lunch or tea with a parkland stroll. The 60-acre Country Park near the racecourse incorporates picnic areas, a children's play area and an information point.

WEST DEAN GARDENS*

Nestling in a tranquil setting within the attractive brick-and-flint village of West Dean, no more than a stone's throw from the Weald and Downland Open Air Museum, are 35 acres of top-notch lawns and gardens surrounding West Dean House, now a flourishing arts and crafts college. You could spend a peaceful couple of hours here enjoying the mixed and herbaceous borders, the many unusual trees – among them three cedars of Lebanon planted in 1748, more than half a century before the house was built – and the newly restored walled garden with its original glasshouses dating from the 1890s. Also worth seeking out are the 300-foot Harold Peto pergola and the unique collection of nineteenth-century tools and lawnmowers.

The 'wild garden', on which Gertrude Jekyll advised, lies beyond the pergola. It is, as its name suggests, natural in character, and harbours many streams which eventually join up with a fast-flowing river.

If you still have time and energy, follow the 2¼-mile Circuit Walk which ascends through the parkland to St Roche's Arboretum (which has many rare trees and shrubs), with splendid views across the Lavant Valley and unspoilt downland landscape.

Goodwood Racecourse has been in use for nearly 200 years

Roman lifestyle in deepest Sussex

Cupid riding a dolphin: an almost intact mosaic floor at Fishbourne Palace

Piece together your own picture of Roman life in Britain from the stunning mosaics discovered in a villa and a palace in West Sussex, then take a stroll along Stane Street, an old Roman road that crosses the Sussex Downs.

West Sussex was a favourite location for the rich and powerful among the Roman invaders. Traces of several villas have been found in the area, and the sites which have been most extensively excavated – at Fishbourne, a couple of miles west of Chichester, and Bignor, high in the Downs to the north-east – contain some of the most complete and important Roman mosaics in Britain. They reveal fascinating evidence of the lives of the wealthy landowners who occupied these islands nearly 2,000 years ago. Far from being only of interest to specialists, the sites have plenty to appeal to adults, and to entertain children from about the age of eight upwards, especially at Fishbourne.

FISHBOURNE ROMAN PALACE*

The remains at Fishbourne date from the beginning of the Roman

♦ **GOOD FOR** Anyone interested in the ancient past, and families with older children
♦ **TRANSPORT** Public transport is available to Fishbourne only (bus or train)
♦ **ACCESS FOR DISABLED PEOPLE** Yes
♦ **BEST TIME TO VISIT** Fishbourne open all year except one month over Christmas/ New Year period; Bignor closed end October to March

occupation of Britain, perhaps as early as AD43. What was initially little more than a harbour depot soon developed into what is now generally assumed to have been a palace – many believe it was used by King Tiberius Claudius Cogidubnus, a Briton with Roman citizenship who had considerable power in the area in the first century AD. With its four wings, colonnades, porticoes and about 100 rooms, most of which had mosaic floors, it was certainly grand enough to have been a royal palace. Since it

was rediscovered in 1960 in a field surrounded by housing estates, about 25 mosaics have been unearthed, representing the largest collection of Roman mosaics *in situ* in Britain.

Visits begin with some well presented display cases documenting the major finds, the progress of the excavations, and the history of the palace. The short introductory video (particularly good for children) helps to get you oriented, and explains the sheer size of the palace and its grounds; to date, only a small proportion of it has been permanently uncovered.

Once you have a grip on the history and the layout, go on to view the main excavations. Raised walkways have been built above the remains of the walls and the mosaic floors both to protect them and give visitors a good view. Take the central walkway and look to both left and right as you walk through.

The excellent guidebook identifies the key points of the palace with letters that correspond to those marked on the guard rails. Those

▲ *Winged cupids posing as duelling gladiators in a mosaic at Bignor Villa*

interested in how the Romans coped with the English weather shouldn't miss point B (near the entrance), which shows a fine excavated cross-section of the under-floor heating system (hypocaust). Among the mosaic highlights is point F with its virtually complete floor depicting at its centre Cupid riding a dolphin, surrounded by four elaborate sea-horses and four intricate vases. Evidence of the huge fire which finally destroyed the palace in the late third century can be seen in the scorched mosaics at point H, complicated designs which are among the earliest in this form on the site.

Relatively little of the palace walls remains, but those few patches of plasterwork which have survived show that the interior decorations were extremely elaborate. Rooms were painted to imitate inlaid marble and seem to have had a mock dado rail and painted cornices. In the far corner of the excavations a small dining-room has been recreated to give an impression of the decoration, and also the surprisingly modern-looking furniture. Near here children can exercise their creative skills by making their own mosaics.

The palace was originally built around a courtyard with formal gardens at its centre, in a design favoured by patrician Romans since the first century BC. The Roman bedding trenches marking the complicated patterns of low hedges which lined the paths have been unearthed. Some of these beds have been replanted, together with a cypress, roses, flowering trees, rosemary, lily and acanthus – just some of the Roman favourites likely to have been grown here.

BIGNOR ROMAN VILLA*

Bignor may not be quite as important as Fishbourne, but it has some impressive mosaics, and a stunningly beautiful location high up in the Sussex Downs, near Petworth and Pulborough. Thatched huts protect the mosaics, and convey a clearer idea of the individual rooms than the all-embracing cover at Fishbourne Palace.

The earliest remains date from about AD190, and it seems that for the next 200 years or so the farmers who owned the villa prospered from the rich soil and their location just off Stane Street, the Roman road which linked Chichester with London. In the fourth century AD, in particular, they used their wealth to extend the villa into one of the largest in Britain, and embellished it with some of the most wonderful mosaics.

The first stage of the tour is the small exhibition room which contains reconstructions of the villa and a scattering of finds from the various archaeological digs since its rediscovery in 1811. Next you will see the Ganymede mosaic, which formed part of the decorations around a central fountain and ornamental pool in the villa's summer dining-room.

A startling pair of geometric mosaics then leads to the most celebrated room of all, with its extraordinary mosaic of a melancholy Venus presiding over four scenes of duelling gladiators. Where the floor has collapsed with age you can clearly see the hypocaust heating system which indicates that this was probably the winter dining-room.

Among other mosaics at the site are the head of a man representing Winter – the only surviving panel from a depiction of the four seasons – and a small mosaic of a dolphin with the initials TR, which probably stood for Terentius, the name of the designer. Outside the main cluster of buildings are the remains of the baths, and a superb mosaic of Medusa, one of the three Gorgons, which used to decorate the heated changing-room for the baths.

▲ *Central heating Roman-style: the foundation of the hypocaust at Fishbourne*

LUNCHBOX
Refreshments are available at both sites.

The great country houses of the South Downs

The Great Parlour at Parham House, near Pulborough

Three glorious options for days out in and around the South Downs, incorporating a pretty village, a charming small town, scenic walks and, the highlight of each outing, a magnificent stately home — each of them filled with fine paintings and furniture.

The area north of Chichester, graced by the meandering Rivers Arun and Rother and the beautiful rolling hills of the South Downs, boasts three fine stately homes: Parham House, Petworth House and Uppark. Although they are within easy reach of each other on a relaxed car journey, it would be wise to focus your day out on a single house, as opening times are limited to the afternoons, and exploring the house and its gardens or parkland, plus taking tea, will more than fill the time available. With this in mind, ideas for a morning's activity and lunch-stop options before your arrival at these majestic houses are suggested below.

PARHAM HOUSE*

A morning spent in the ancient settlement of **Amberley** (two miles

♦ **GOOD FOR** Spending a day (or more) enjoying beautiful houses and parkland
♦ **TRANSPORT** You will need a car if you want to see more than one house in a day
♦ **ACCESS FOR DISABLED PEOPLE** Wheelchair hire is available at all the houses
♦ **BEST TIME TO VISIT** The houses are closed in winter, although the park at Petworth is accessible all year

to the west), lying on a low ridge above the watermeadows of the River Arun, will prove rewarding. The main village street, lined with pretty brick, stone and timber cottages — many of them thatched — leads to the Norman church of **St Michael** with its red-ochre, twelfth-century wall paintings and memorials to Edward Stott and Arthur Rackham, who lived nearby. Beyond the village stands **Amberley**

Castle, a fortified residence built in 1380 for the Bishops of Chichester. It is now a hotel.

Parham House, dating from 1577, is reached by a mile-long drive off the A283 Pulborough–Storrington road. This peaceful Elizabethan family home, built of stone and with walled gardens and eighteenth-century Pleasure Grounds, stands in a beautiful setting on a plateau beneath the South Downs. The house contains an important collection of paintings, furniture, oriental carpets and rare needlework within its principal rooms, which include the panelled Great Hall, Great Parlour and the 160-foot Long Gallery. Fine-weather visits warrant a stroll round the 11-acre grounds, complete with a large walled garden with herbaceous borders, a herb garden, orchard, mature trees, a lake and a brick and turf maze. Special events are held here during the year: ring for details.

PETWORTH HOUSE*

The 13-mile perimeter wall surrounding the 700 acres of Petworth Park encroaches right into the centre of Petworth, making this small town the ideal place to while away a few hours before you visit the splendid seventeenth-century mansion that dominates it.

Either browse around the many antique and bric-a-brac shops that line the attractive, if not traffic-free, streets, or pick up an informative (free) leaflet from the **tourist information office*** in the Market Square, and follow the historical walk around the town. Most of Petworth's old, timber-framed houses are in the narrow streets adjacent to the square, which itself dates from Tudor to Georgian times. Alternatively, go for open space and stunning views as you walk in Petworth Park (open from 8am). Anything from a gentle stroll to a five-mile hike can be enjoyed around the deer park, landscaped by Capability Brown in 1752–63.

The imposing 320-foot west front of Petworth House (NT) faces the lake and great park and is renowned for its collection of paintings and sculpture, assembled by the Percy family (the Earls of Northumberland) over 350 years and rivalling that of many London galleries. The impressive state rooms and galleries contain works by Gainsborough, Van Dyck, Holbein, Rembrandt, Reynolds and, in particular, Turner, who was a regular visitor here. Not to be missed are the rich carvings by Grinling Gibbons, said to be his finest, in the Carved Room.

UPPARK*

Although not dramatic, the landscape of the South Downs is certainly beautiful, alternating between undulating hills and lush woodland, with the extensive rounded escarpment affording unrivalled views across the Sussex Weald. There is probably no better place to experience the unspoilt charm of the Downs than the delightful area around **South Harting**, north of Chichester.

Begin your day with a saunter along a section of the **South Downs Way**, a 100-mile trail that links

Petworth House, a treasury of works of art, seen from its park

Eastbourne and Winchester. Park in the car park on top of Harting Down (NT) and explore the 520-acre stretch of chalk downland and woodland, which is rich in flora and fauna and commands magnificent views across the Rother Valley towards Midhurst.

Take a picnic or descend into the sleepy village of South Harting for lunch. A short drive back up the scarp brings you to Uppark, a seventeenth-century house with views south towards the Solent. Recently restored following a major fire in 1989, it houses an impressive collection of paintings and decorative art formed by members of the Fetherstonhaugh family, who bought the estate in 1747 and bequeathed it to the National Trust in 1954. The fine Georgian furniture and decoration, including some original wallpaper and fabrics, make Uppark a rare example of the period. One ante-room contains a remarkable classical dolls' house. Also on view are the servants'

Uppark, near Petersfield, where the novelist H.G. Wells lived as a boy

rooms, where H.G. Wells spent his early years while his mother was housekeeper to the former dairymaid who married Sir Henry Fetherstonhaugh.

Unfortunately, because of conservation requirements and the limited capacity of the property, entry is by timed ticket only, so expect to wait at busy times. If capacity is reached early in the day, the whole property, including the car park, will be closed, so it is best to book ahead.

The **Exhibition and Visitor Centre** tells the story of the six years of repair and restoration, including hands-on exhibits to aid children's appreciation of the work. Otherwise, take a walk round the woods or the landscaped gardens.

LUNCHBOX

Refreshments are available in the Big Kitchen at Parham House and there is also a picnic area; set lunches can be had at Amberley Castle. At Petworth House, light lunches and teas are served in what was once a sculpture gallery, built in 1837. If a pub lunch is more your style, the sixteenth-century White Hart at South Harting serves good food. You can get light lunches and cream teas at Uppark.

The Bluebell Line and Sheffield Park Garden

One of the Bluebell Line's beautifully restored locomotives leaves Horsted Keynes station

- ♦ **GOOD FOR** Families, steam nostalgics and tree lovers
- ♦ **TRANSPORT** If arriving by car, park at Sheffield Park station, the main headquarters of the Bluebell Line. There are no parking facilities at the end of the line (Kingscote). It is also possible to come by train from Victoria BR station in London and start the journey at the other end (East Grinstead; bus transfer to Kingscote)
- ♦ **ACCESS FOR DISABLED PEOPLE** Good access to station but limited on trains
- ♦ **BEST TIME TO VISIT** Trains run all year (but see Tickets and timetables box). The Sussex countryside is in its prime in spring when the bluebells are in flower. Santa specials run during December, and there are various steam days throughout the year. Sheffield Park Garden is particularly beautiful in autumn

Re-live the great age of steam on one of Britain's most scenic vintage railways, as it meanders for ten miles through the unspoilt Sussex Weald. Spend the afternoon revelling in one of Britain's most superb collection of trees, especially fine in autumn.

Travelling on board a slow-moving steam train must be about the best way to appreciate the delights of the wooded Sussex countryside; it is especially pleasurable in springtime because, as its name suggests, this picturesque valley route is carpeted with a mass of bluebells. Beginning at Sheffield Park station, where there is a fascinating locomotive museum, the steam trains wind their way north for ten head-turning miles, affording the opportunity to alight at two beautifully restored stations, Horsted Keynes and Kingscote, along the way. Here, we briefly trace the history of the preservation this charming country railway and outline how to make the best of a day on the Bluebell Line. An added attraction is the magnificent 100-acre landscaped garden at Sheffield Park (National Trust), only three-quarters of a mile from the main station.

The **Bluebell Line*** is part of the abandoned East Grinstead–Lewes line, one of the rural railways that were closed during the 1950s and 1960s. (For others that are once more up and running see the section devoted to steam railways at the front of the book.) Immediately after the closure in 1958, the Bluebell Railway Preservation Society bought the track and rolling stock and began the painstaking task of restoring it to its former Victorian glory, reopening the line in 1960 with the help of many volunteers. In the intervening years every minute detail has been considered in preserving the railway as it was in the age of steam, as well as developing the excellent locomotive museum and doubling the length of the track towards East Grinstead, the ultimate goal.

TICKETS AND TIMETABLES

Inclusive tickets can be bought from any Network Central station as well as from Bluebell Line stations themselves. It is worth noting that a full-line ticket gives you an unlimited number of journeys on the train – a great incentive for parents with enthusiastic train-loving youngsters who are keen to spend the whole day aboard. As one would expect, there are more trains running at summer weekends and during school holidays, with only a limited weekend service operating in the winter months – phone the special timetable information* number for more details.

Starting at **Sheffield Park station**, a marvellous example of Victorian railway architecture with cast-iron columns and a vast assortment of advertising signs from a bygone age, you can see the largest collection of locomotives and carriages away from the National Railway Museum in York (see *Great Day Out 120*). A walk around the engine shed will bring you into close quarters with gleaming locomotives as well as others awaiting restoration. Also on show are masses of artefacts and memorabilia relating to the steam age.

If you are arriving from London you will start your trip at the other end with a splendid fifteen-minute journey on board a 1950s bus from East Grinstead station to Kingscote.

Horsted Keynes is a perfect spot for children to let off some steam themselves. The station is worth close inspection as it is thought to be the best-preserved station in Britain, oozing with nostalgic charm. Also present here is the railway's award-winning carriage and wagon department, where carriages are renovated and safety standards checked. Beyond Horsted Keynes, peaceful country scenes are

The superb colours of autumn leaves reflected in one of Sheffield Park's lakes

interrupted as the train enters the dramatic half-mile long **West Hoathly tunnel**; it emerges beside Gravetye Woods, *en route* to the elegantly restored **Kingscote station** and the end of the line.

A stylish way to experience the Bluebell Line is to reserve a table on the **Golden Arrow Pullman*** and wine and dine in superbly refurbished 1924 Pullman cars. It operates on Saturday evenings and Sunday lunchtimes throughout the summer and is acknowledged to be one of best dining trains in Britain. Further special events and steam days often feature visiting locomotives and are well worth attending.

Although a visit to the Bluebell Line is likely to absorb the whole day, non-train buffs may be content with a half-day journey along the line to savour the views. After lunch you could stroll through the landscaped park at **Sheffield Park Garden*** (NT). The garden was originally

Some of the old fixtures and fittings at Sheffield Park Station

designed by Capability Brown for the first Earl of Sheffield in about 1775 and added to by the third earl, but a later owner, Arthur Gilstrap Soames, set about introducing numerous exotic trees and shrubs to add to the native species so that the park should be as fine an autumnal feast of foliage as you could imagine. Here, in a lakeland setting typical of an English landscape garden of the period, you can see fine specimens of sweet chestnut, tupelo, Scots pine, rowan, weeping birch, Japanese maple, redwood, swamp cypress – and many more. In spring rhododendrons, camellias – and bluebells, of course – are the lure.

LUNCHBOX

·The station complex at Kingscote offers the only refreshment facilities along the line. You have the choice of the Bessemer Arms for real ale and home-made pub lunches, or Puffers Restaurant, for self-service hot and cold fare. Visitors intent on having a picnic can spread their rugs in the extensive riverside picnic area here or in the ten-acre field near Horsted Keynes station at the other end of the line. Alternatively, after a morning's train ride, you may like to head for the attractive village of Fletching (three miles east) for a reliable pub meal at the Griffin Inn, reputedly the oldest licensed premises in Sussex.

Brighton: Regency buildings by the sea

The calm before sun-worshippers and pleasure-seekers take over the sea-front

Brighton has been called a city of candyfloss and culture. It is a seaside town of piers and slot machines and of elegant Regency squares built round the flamboyant Royal Pavilion.

In 1783 the tiny fishing village of Brighthelmstone received a royal visitor in the person of the Prince of Wales, the future King George IV. High society flocked there in his wake, and so began the transformation of this south-coast village into today's bustling city. The coming of the railway made Brighton less exclusive, and put it within easy reach of London; arriving by train is still the best option if you want to avoid the city's traffic-choked roads and expensive parking. Park-and-ride schemes are signposted from all the approach roads.

THE ESPLANADE

The sea-front is bracing, with strong breezes, even at the height of summer, stirring up the surface of the Channel. You can watch the waves break on the shingle beach from the main sea-front road, with a view of **West Pier** to the right. Built in 1866, this set a new standard in

♦ **GOOD FOR** Brighton is a popular destination with teenagers and those who enjoy lively, crowded places. Few people are unimpressed by the Royal Pavilion
♦ **TRANSPORT** Brighton is very well connected by train. The city itself is best explored on foot
♦ **ACCESS FOR DISABLED PEOPLE** Wheelchair access to most main sites; the Lanes are pedestrianised and can be negotiated with help
♦ **BEST TIME TO VISIT** Weekdays and out of season, to avoid the worst crowds. Preston Manor closed on Monday, Brighton Museum on Wednesday and Booth Museum on Thursday

seaside architecture but was damaged in the Second World War and never repaired. The West Pier Trust hopes to restore it by the millennium.

Palace Pier, to the left, built in 1891, is still a fully functioning pier, with karaoke bars, a fairground, fish and chip bars and amusement

arcades. Opposite the pier entrance, the old Brighton Aquarium, dating back to Regency times, has been transformed into the new **Sealife Centre***, where sharks and other creatures of the deep can be viewed from an underwater tunnel.

ROYAL PAVILION

From Palace Pier, negotiate the busy roads inland to Old Steine, with its public gardens and Victorian bronze fountain, and to the **Royal Pavilion***. This evolved from a simple seaside villa built for the Prince of Wales in 1787 into an exotic pleasure palace, designed by John Nash in 1815-22. The Pavilion, with its onion domes, minarets and Mogul-style windows, is all Indian on the outside but totally Chinese within, splendidly decorated with scarlet dragons and imitation bamboo furniture.

BRIGHTON MUSEUM AND ART GALLERY

The architectural theme of the Pavilion continues opposite in the Dome Theatre, with its peacock-tail windows. Behind the theatre, in Church Street, is the **Brighton Museum and Art Gallery***. Both are housed in the former Royal Stables built in 1803-8. The museum interior is a *tour de force* of ceramic work, again on an Indian theme, and the collections range from Burmese textiles, Mexican masks and Japanese teapots, to fashions in dress (from the Brighton Belles of 1804 to 1970s punk), Victorian slot machines and furniture by Salvador Dali (a 1936 sofa modelled on Mae West's lips). The museum has an especially good collection of art nouveau and art deco furnishings, plus paintings by such leading British twentieth-century artists as Duncan Grant, Vanessa Bell, Mark Gertler and Walter Sickert.

Indian soldiers injured in Europe in the First World War were housed in the Pavilion because it would 'remind them of home'

LANES AND LAINES

Confusingly, Brighton has both Lanes and laines. **The Lanes** are a maze of medieval streets, reached from the museum through the Pavilion Gardens, lined with chic shops and bistro-style restaurants. Part of the fun is in getting lost, but maps are available from the **tourist information office*** opposite the Town Hall.

A **laine**, by contrast, is the local word for the fields that once surrounded Brighton. If you follow signposts to North Laine you will pass down Bond Street, Gardner Street, Kensington Gardens and Sydney Street, all lined with shops selling antiques, crafts and designer clothes with all the bustle and atmosphere of an outdoor market (there is a real bric-à-brac market here on Saturday mornings). Dip into the streets on either side (especially Trafalgar Terrace or Frederick Gardens), and you will pass down narrow alleys (known locally as 'twittens') lined by Regency bow-fronted cottages which have very neat, minuscule gardens.

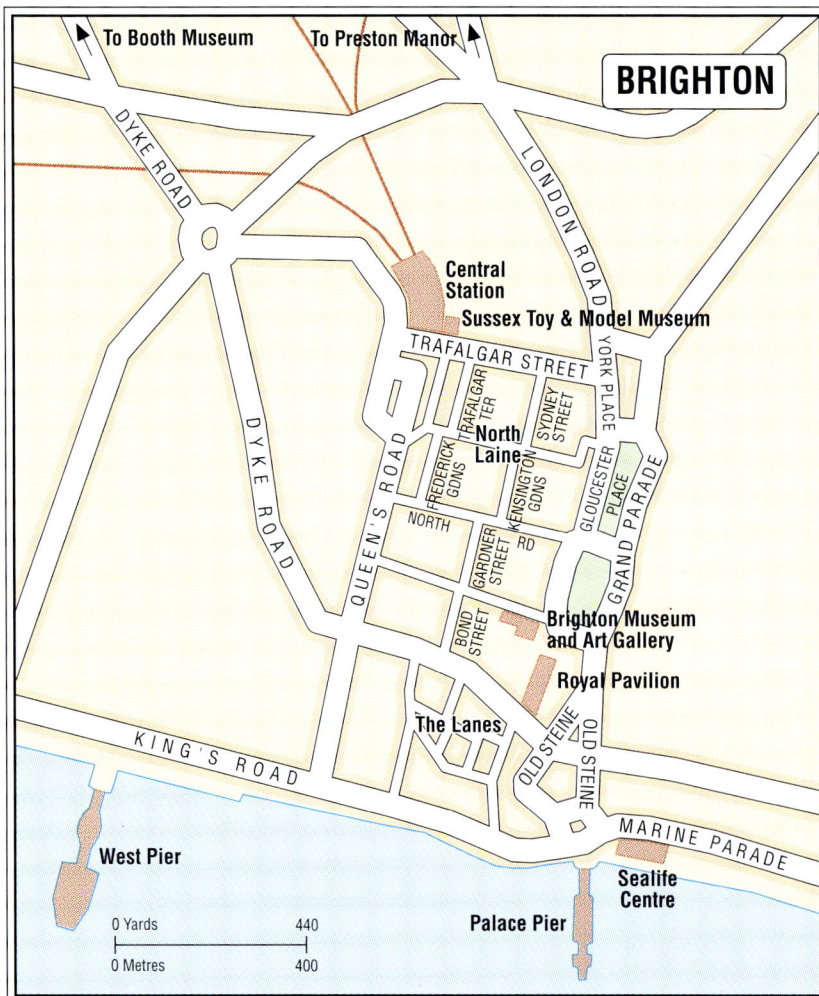

OTHER MUSEUMS

Immediately next to North Laine is Brighton station, where the **Sussex Toy and Model Museum***, housed beneath the railway arches, displays classic toys, from 1930s electric railways to bears and dolls.

At the **Booth Museum of Natural History***, less than a mile to the north-west, a huge collection of Victorian stuffed birds, in recreated natural settings, forms the core of a museum that also features butterflies, fossils, dinosaur skeletons and displays on ecology.

A short walk away is **Preston Manor***, which presents a vivid picture of Edwardian life, both in the stately rooms of the wealthy owners and in the servants' quarters 'below the stairs'.

LUNCHBOX

For lunch in the Lanes, Darcy's Fish and Seafood, Wheeler's and the Pump House pub in Market Street all offer tempting menus. The Queen Adelaide Tearooms do lunches and blow-out Regency teas with views across the Pavilion Gardens.

BRIGHTON map: To Booth Museum, To Preston Manor, Central Station, Sussex Toy & Model Museum, Dyke Road, London Road, Trafalgar Street, North Laine, Queen's Road, Brighton Museum and Art Gallery, Royal Pavilion, The Lanes, King's Road, West Pier, Palace Pier, Sealife Centre, Marine Parade, Old Steine.

Lewes and the green vistas of the South Downs

The Annunciation *by Vanessa Bell in St Michael and All Angels Church, Berwick*

Lewes is a good base for exploring the Sussex Downs. Choose between a grown-ups' day out, taking in the homes of Virginia Woolf and Vanessa Bell, or family treats, such as Drusillas Zoo Park and an exhibition on insects, followed by a walk to Cuckmere Haven.

M any people have appreciated the pleasures of the Sussex Downs, not least William Blake, who penned the words to 'Jerusalem', England's unofficial national anthem, while gazing up at the sheep-grazed pastures from his cottage window at Felpham. Roads and suburban sprawl have since scarred the coastline, but the area around Lewes still fits Blake's description of pleasant pastures and mountains green.

LEWES

From the walls of the **castle*** at the heart of Lewes there are commanding views down the River Ouse to the sea and to the steep escarpments of the South Downs, which seem to surround the town. The history of the town and castle are brought to life in the 'Lewes Living History' display in the castle gatehouse, a 20-minute

♦ **GOOD FOR** Art-lovers and nature-lovers alike are well catered for
♦ **TRANSPORT** Lewes, Glynde and Berwick have good rail links. You will need a car to visit all the sights
♦ **ACCESS FOR DISABLED PEOPLE** No access in Lewes; but Charleston Farmhouse will help if contacted in advance; Drusillas has full facilities; and adapted bikes can be hired* for exploring Cuckmere Haven
♦ **BEST TIME TO VISIT** Most of the country houses have limited opening times; phone to check. Bonfire night in Lewes is quite a spectacle, but is not for the faint-hearted: torch-lit processions through the town include burning crosses and are an expression of strong anti-Catholic sentiment, in memory of the town's Protestant martyrs

audio-visual show based on a wonderfully detailed Victorian scale model of the town. Archaeological

DRUSILLAS ZOO PARK
Immediately east of Berwick, Drusillas Zoo Park*, beside the A27, marks the start of the Cuckmere Valley. Children will love this award-winning park, where you can try milking a cow, learn about the rainforest or make animal masks in the craft workshops, as well as watch penguins, monkeys, otters and porcupines in naturalistic enclosures.

finds from all over Sussex are displayed in the Barbican House museum at the castle.

The High Street is a living textbook of Sussex architectural styles, with lots of good shops and places to eat at (see box). Leading off the High Street, numerous narrow lanes, known locally as 'twittens', give the town its unusual plan. Cobbled Keere Street, a picturesque, steep twitten, will take you to Southover High Street, where the timber-framed **Anne of Cleves House*** has been turned into a museum dealing with Sussex life and the local woodturning, charcoal and iron industries.

THE BLOOMSBURY GROUP IN SUSSEX

Though we tend to think of the Bloomsbury Group as a London phenomenon, some members of this élite circle of writers, intellectuals and artists spent the latter part of their lives living and working around Lewes. Southover High Street leads south for 4 miles to the pretty village of Rodmell. Here, at **Monk's House***, Virginia Woolf wrote many of her novels and letters, clutching her pen between freezing fingers, unable to afford adequate heating. The house is furnished with pieces made by her sister, Vanessa Bell, a leading light of the Omega Workshops, and there is a lovely garden that Virginia created with Leonard, her husband.

▲ *The 226-foot-high Long Man of Wilmington on the north side of Windover Hill*

More work by Vanessa Bell and her artistic circle of friends can be seen at **Charleston Farmhouse***, 5 miles east of Lewes, south of the A27. Allow plenty of time to enjoy the guided tour of this marvellous and inspiring house, every surface of which is decorated with paintings by Bell and Duncan Grant. There is also an excellent film, shown every 15 minutes, on life at Charleston, and a shop selling crafts in the Omega Workshops style.

The last Bloomsbury shrine is the little church at **Berwick**, 2 miles further east, an idyllic spot in the downs where Vanessa Bell is buried. The walls of the church and the pulpit are covered in murals painted by the members of her circle.

VILLAGES ON THE DOWNS
Further south, **Alfriston** is a picture-postcard village of thatched and timbered houses, now in danger of being overwhelmed by tourist shops, but there are plenty of places to eat at (see box). St Andrew's church is known as the Cathedral of the South Downs because of its size and magnificence. Alongside is the fourteenth-century **Clergy House***, a pretty Wealden house with cottage garden, the first property to be acquired by the National Trust after its foundation in 1895.

Litlington, to the south-east, has a Norman church that stands at the foot of the Lullington Heath Nature Reserve, a steep hill renowned for its chalkland flowers and dotted with prehistoric burial mounds.

Two fine country houses are tucked into the folds of the South Downs between Charleston and Lewes. **Glynde Place***, to the north of the A27, is a richly furnished Elizabethan manor, extensively altered in the eighteenth century (Glyndebourne, the famous opera house, lies just to the north, but is open only to opera-goers). **Firle Place***, south of the A27, is full of portraits, furniture and porcelain collected by the Gage family, which has owned it for the last 500 years.

Lullington church, just to the north, has a seating capacity of just 20, and is claimed to be England's smallest church. Just beyond is the downland village of Wilmington, where an enigmatic chalk-cut figure, the **Long Man of Wilmington**, strides across the hillside. Some say that he is a prehistoric fertility figure, others that he is possibly of eighteenth-century origin.

SEVEN SISTERS COUNTRY PARK
South of Litlington is Exceat, where you can visit the **Living World Exhibition*** on insects and marine life, ideal for children who like spiders and other creepy-crawlies. At the nearby visitor centre you can pick up trail leaflets and look at displays of the fascinating flora and fauna of the **Seven Sisters Country Park***, 690 acres of unspoilt downland and salt marsh. A path leads for 2 miles from the visitor centre along the banks of the meandering River Cuckmere to the shingle beach at Cuckmere Haven. From here there is a wonderful view of the Seven Sisters, a series of sheer chalk cliffs rivalling the more famous ones at Dover.

LUNCHBOX
In Lewes, try the Pelham Arms for home-made pub food, or Seasons for vegetarian dishes. More shops and cafés are to be found in the lower town, around the banks of the Ouse. At Alfriston, the Olde Smugglers Inne, the George and the Sussex Ox all serve bar meals, and Ashley's Village Store sells fresh-baked bread and picnic ingredients. Having climbed the hill at Litlington, you may want to recover over tea in the Victorian Pleasure Gardens in the grounds of the Litlington Tea House.

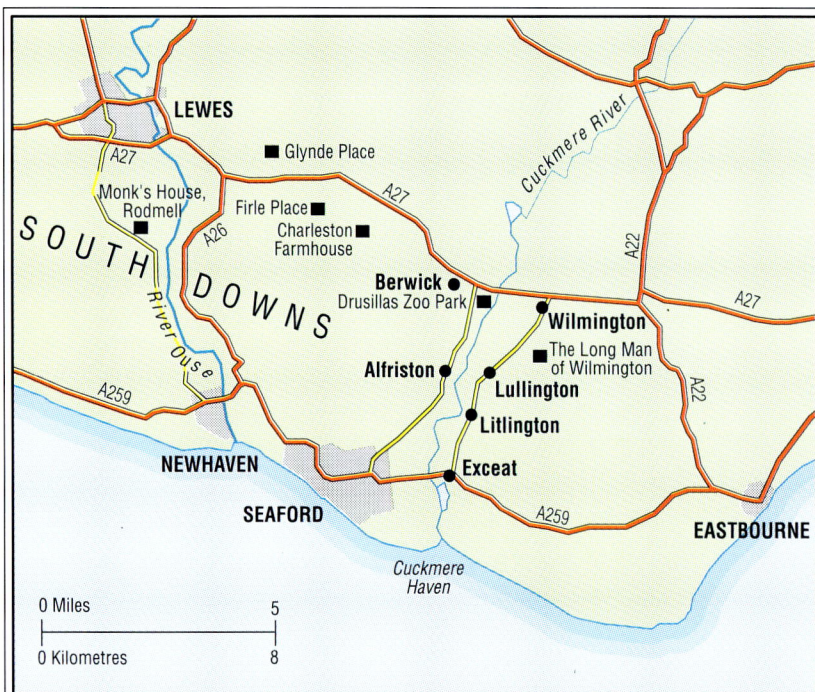

The Cinque Ports: sand, smuggling and 1066

Fairfield, in the wild, open space of Romney Marsh

Explore the steep cobbled streets of hilltop Rye and Winchelsea, take a dip in the sea — weather permitting — from the safe sandy beach at Camber Sands, then shop for fresh fish in Hastings and visit the site of the famous battle of 1066.

The Cinque Ports were established in the eleventh century to defend the narrowest part of the English Channel. In return for maintaining a fleet of warships, the ports were freed from paying certain types of tax, although they were not exempted from paying excise duties, and smuggling was rife along this coast in the eighteenth century, playing an important part in the local economy. Of the original Cinque Ports (the first five – Dover, Sandwich, Hastings, Romney and Hythe – were later joined by Rye and Winchelsea), only Dover (see *Great Day Out 37*) remains a major port today. Silt deposits have left Rye and Winchelsea high and dry, separated from the sea by the vast, flat expanse of Romney Marsh, renowned for its birdlife, giant frogs and Romney Marsh sheep, which are prized for their wool and for the salty (pré-salé) flavour of their meat.

♦ **GOOD FOR** A quiet, pottering sort of a day out
♦ **TRANSPORT** BR station at Hastings; otherwise a car is necessary
♦ **ACCESS FOR DISABLED PEOPLE** Difficult
♦ **BEST TIME TO VISIT** Summer weekdays to enjoy uncrowded streets and beaches; a Wednesday or Saturday from Easter to the end of October if you want to visit Lamb House in Rye

RYE

Amidst the untidy suburban sprawl that characterises the Kent and Sussex coast today, the ancient hill town of Rye is a gem. Its maze of cobbled streets is lined with medieval and Georgian houses. Once protected by a wall on one side and cliffs on the other, Rye has been left behind by the receding sea. The tidal rivers which almost encircle the town are busy at high tide, with yachts and fishing boats which still chug up the River Rother from the sea to unload their catch. The timber warehouses on the Strand Quay now house shops selling antiques and craftwork, including locally made pottery. Another has been converted into a heritage centre and **tourist information office***, where a scale model of the town serves as the centrepiece for an audio-visual introduction to Rye.

Cobbled **Mermaid Street** leads steeply up from the quay, past the Mermaid Inn, once the haunt of a notoriously bloodthirsty gang of smugglers, or 'owlers' as they were known (they used owl calls to signal to each other). Their story is told on information boards which you can read if you stop for coffee or lunch and find a seat beside the massive Tudor fireplace.

Mermaid Street leads to West Street where, on the right, you will find **Lamb House*** (NT), the home of Henry James from 1897 until his death in 1916. James wrote many of his best-known novels in the Garden Room, which also features in the entertaining Mapp and Lucia novels of E.F. Benson, who lived in the house after James; Benson used Rye (which he called Tillingham) as the setting for his books, and was mayor here three times.

It is a short step from Lamb House to the atmospheric **church of St Mary**, with its Burne-Jones stained-glass windows and splendid clock tower (the clock face dates from 1761, but the mechanism is the oldest turret clock still working in England). You can climb the tower to see for miles around, but excellent views are also to be had with less effort from the **Ypres Tower*** (built in 1250), located to the east of Church Square and now a rather good local history museum.

Rye's best-known thoroughfare, Mermaid Street, lined with old houses

From the tower you can look down southwards on to **Camber Castle*** (EH), distinguished by its unusual four-leaved clover shape, built by Henry VIII at a time when Counter-Reformationary Catholic monarchs in Europe were threatening to invade England. You may also be able to see **Camber Sands**, to the east. The gently shelving sandy beach is packed on summer weekends, but is often deserted during the week.

WINCHELSEA

Also visible from the Ypres Tower is Rye's hilltop neighbour, Winchelsea. Old Winchelsea lay on the coastal plain but was battered to destruction in the great storm of 1287. New Winchelsea was laid out as a planned town in 1292 on the adjacent hilltop, in 39 rectangular blocks. Merchants built fine houses with capacious cellars, for Winchelsea became the centre for wines and spirits in the Middle Ages, declining into genteel decay as the sea receded and the port gradually silted up.

Today, a 20-minute stroll will take you round the town's quiet lanes, lined with rose and wistaria-clad Regency houses, many with medieval wine vaults just visible through pavement grilles. The huge, but never-completed, **church of St Thomas** contains remarkably well preserved tomb effigies of fourteenth-century admirals who served with the Cinque Ports fleet. The town's history is told in the **Court Hall Museum*** in the High Street, just north of the church.

HASTINGS

If you continue down the same road you will reach the car park that serves **Hastings Country Park**, an unspoilt stretch of Sussex coastline that offers bracing clifftop walks, picnic spots and several sheltered coves, accessible only on foot, where you can have a swim from the shingle beaches.

If it is too cold for bathing, head for the **Cliff Railway**, which takes you up to the ruins of **Hastings Castle***. An audio-visual presentation on the Battle of Hastings is shown in the castle dungeons. The town's smuggling history is the subject of another atmospheric museum: the **Smugglers Adventure***, set in a series of chalk-cut caves on West Hill, on the opposite side of town, uses push-button models and waxworks to bring its subject-matter to life.

BATTLE

For the actual site of the most famous battle in English history, you must leave Hastings and drive north for 7 miles to Battle, a fine Sussex town of tile-hung houses, now serving as antique shops, art galleries and tea rooms. William the Conqueror founded **Battle Abbey*** on the site of his great victory in 1066, and although a school occupies the abbot's dwellings, the ruins of the Norman abbey, and the battle site itself, are now managed by English Heritage. Having watched the introductory audio-visual, you can tour the battle site, following the events of that fateful day in October by means of a series of informative signboards, ending up at the spot where King Harold lost his life, now the site of Battle Abbey's high altar.

The East Cliff lift at Rock-a-Nore, Hastings

LUNCHBOX

Fresh locally caught fish is a speciality of the Cinque Ports area. At Hastings you can eat fish and chips at numerous seafront cafés, or try the shellfish from the beachside stalls lining Rock-a-Nore Road. In Winchelsea, fish and seafood form the basis of bar snacks and full meals at the New Inn.

The castles and manors of west Kent

Knole House was built in the fifteenth century for Thomas Bouchier, Archbishop of Canterbury

Discover peaceful unspoilt villages and a hoard of stately homes, formal gardens and castles in this corner of the Weald of Kent, with its wooded hillsides, orchards, hops farms and occasional vineyards.

This tour includes the magnificent properties of Knole, Chartwell, Hever Castle and Chiddingstone Castle, plus the delightful Emmetts Garden. It would be impossible to visit them all in one day, so you are advised to focus on one, or combine a couple, and either pack a picnic lunch, enjoy a pub meal or make use of the excellent catering facilities to be found at all the sights.

The old Saxon market town of **Sevenoaks** is the perfect starting point for this tour. Cyclists can hire bicycles from **Bikes, Bikes, Bikes*** on the High Street. The great house of Knole dominates the town, but you might like to spend some time beforehand wandering around the old streets spotting notable historic buildings with the help of a *Town Trail* leaflet from the **tourist information office***.

♦ **GOOD FOR** This is a very good day out for cyclists; if you are in a car, consider mixing and matching places in this and *Great Day Out 36*, particularly Penshurst Place, just south-east of Chiddingstone

♦ **TRANSPORT** The route covers approximately 29 miles – cycle or drive

♦ **ACCESS FOR DISABLED PEOPLE** Facilities at all sights, although limited at Knole

♦ **BEST TIME TO VISIT** All properties are open between March/April and October. The gardens are at their best in spring and early summer. Knole Park is open daily all year

KNOLE HOUSE*

Opening out behind the High Street is the extensive 1,000-acre deer park that surrounds reputedly the largest private house in England (NT). It was acquired by Henry VIII and subsequently given to the Sackville

Diversions along the way for those who have had a surfeit of heritage for one day might include a visit to **Penshurst Vineyard***, one of the most modern vineyards in England, offering tours and free wine-tasting. West of Sevenoaks along the beautifully wooded Greensand ridge is **Emmetts Garden*** (NT), a charming hillside shrub garden noted for its rare trees and shrubs, its bluebells and rose and rock gardens. It is well worth visiting for the wonderful views across **Bough Beech Reservoir** and the Weald. Wildlife enthusiasts can explore the environs of the reservoir and visit the Nature Centre.

family by Elizabeth I in 1603. They transformed the original house into this mansion, a spectacular example of late medieval architecture overlaid with Renaissance embellishments. With 365 rooms, there is one for every day of the year, as well as 52 staircases (one for every week) and 7 courtyards (one for every weekday). The Sackville family still lives in one section of the house, while thirteen magnificent state rooms are open to the public, all rich in architectural detail from the seventeenth and eighteenth centuries, with the finest collection of Stuart furnishings in the world, and outstanding tapestries and works of art by Van Dyck, Reynolds and Gainsborough. Knole was the birthplace of the writer and gardener Vita Sackville-West and the setting for Virginia Woolf's novel *Orlando*. It has 26 acres of gardens to stroll through and footpaths that criss-cross the undulating pasture and parkland.

CHARTWELL*

Occupying a splendid position along the Greensand Ridge is the much-loved home of Sir Winston Churchill and his family for over 40 years. The house is comfortable and has the air of a still lived-in family home, with fresh flowers from the garden and log fires. The National Trust has turned two rooms into museums displaying gifts to Churchill from heads of state around the world, including Adenauer and Stalin, and the dress uniforms and medals of the statesman. Churchill's paintings can be seen throughout the house and in the garden studio. Entry to the house is by timed ticket only, so expect delays at weekends and in high summer. If you have to wait, make the most of the terraced gardens and the idyllic views over Kent and West Sussex (Churchill always maintained he bought the house, in 1922, for the views). Black swans swim on the lakes and golden orfe in the fishpools.

HEVER CASTLE*
Perhaps the most celebrated of the grand properties gracing the Kentish

Sculptures in Hever Castle's Italian garden, collected by Waldorf Astor

Weald is the enchanting thirteenth-century Hever Castle, which lies four or five miles south of Chartwell. Once the childhood home of Anne Boleyn (Henry VIII came here to court her), the moated castle acquired its present stately appearance through the investment and imagination of William Waldorf Astor, who bought the estate in 1903. You can explore the glorious interior, complete with superb collections of furniture and paintings, rich Edwardian wood-carving and plasterwork, various *objets d'art* and an exhibition on scenes from the life and times of Anne Boleyn. Attractions outside the house are plentiful: splendid Italian gardens filled with antique sculptures and fountains, a large lake and formal gardens with plenty of topiary as well as a walled rose garden. The yew tree maze and an adventure playground will keep children amused, and the unique model-house exhibition depicting life in English country houses from medieval to Victorian times will fascinate everyone.

CHIDDINGSTONE CASTLE*
The attractive and unspoilt National Trust village of Chiddingstone has a beautifully preserved row of half-timbered sixteenth- and seventeenth-century houses, including the post office and the tile-hung Castle Inn. At the top of the street is the castle. Originally a seventeenth-century house, it was added to in the early nineteenth century and heavily restored in the mid-twentieth century; it is now a romantic, neo-Gothic castle, with turrets and arrow slits. Inside, there are some fine Stuart and Jacobite portraits, intriguing Egyptian antiquities and a significant collection of Japanese armour and swords.

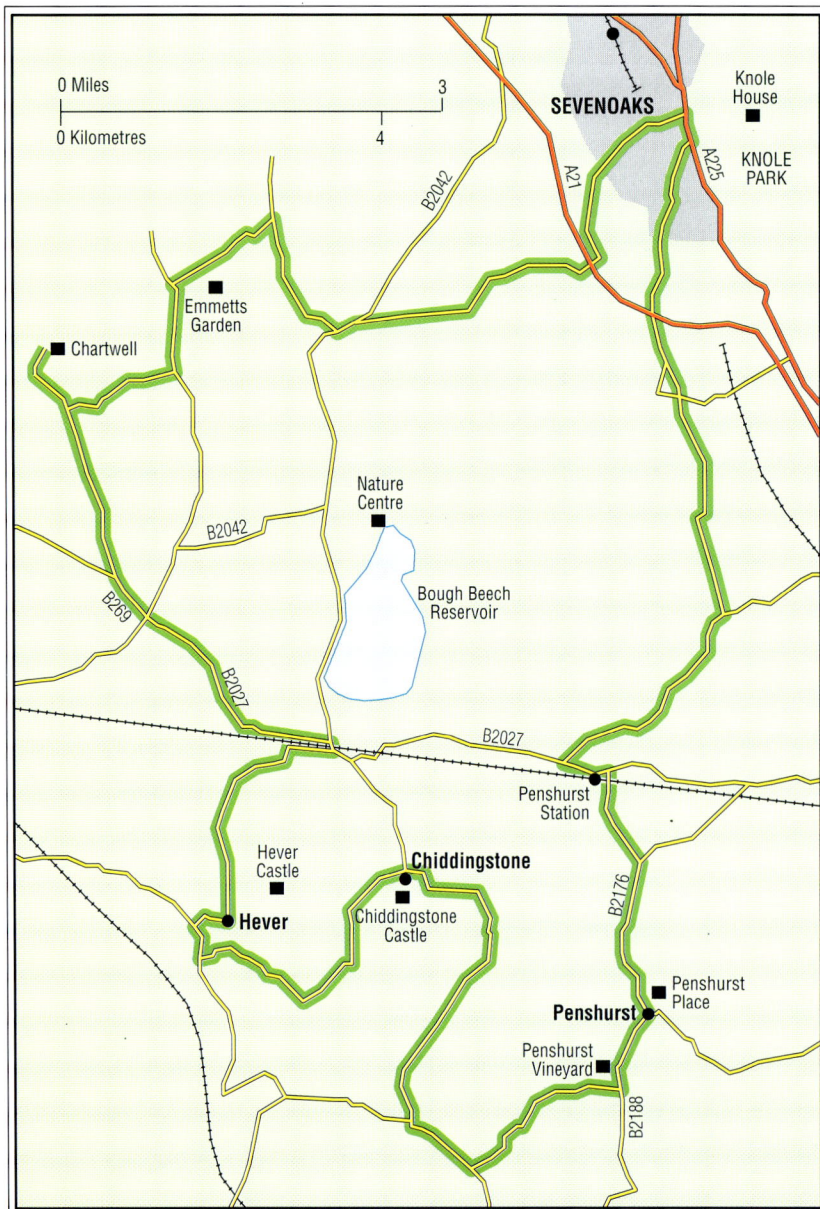

LUNCHBOX
For a reliable bar meal try the Royal Oak in Sevenoaks, the Henry VII at Hever, the Castle Inn at Chiddingstone, the Bottle House Inn at Smart's Hill, or the Little Brown Jug at Chiddingstone Causeway. Head for Coffee Call along Dorset Street in Sevenoaks for a good snack and Fir Tree House Tea Rooms in Penshurst for a traditional tea, and bike hire.

Mid-Kent's fabulous castles and gardens

Leeds Castle's setting is particularly spectacular seen from above

Kent is awash with intriguing castles and houses set in wonderful gardens; Leeds Castle is a must, while Sissinghurst, Scotney, Bodiam and Penshurst also offer many enticements.

The castles in this tour are best visited from east to west, starting with Leeds Castle to take advantage of its earlier opening times. Do not try to rush round all five in a day. Instead, we recommend that you visit Leeds Castle, which alone can take up the best part of a day, then choose one from among the others, allowing at least two hours to do it justice. Weekends are very busy, especially at Sissinghurst, where entry is by timed ticket, so you may have to wait, though once in the garden you can stay as long as you wish.

LEEDS CASTLE*

Apparently straight out of a fairytale, Leeds Castle (well signposted from the A20 and from junction 8 of the M20) rises from two linked islands in the midst of a placid lake. To reach the castle from the car park there is a walk of nearly a mile, partly through woodland dotted with garden statuary and partly beside a stream.

♦ **GOOD FOR** Active families and all those who love English castles and gardens; see also *Great Day Out 35*
♦ **TRANSPORT** Car essential
♦ **ACCESS FOR DISABLED PEOPLE** Steep and narrow paths at several sites, but there are recommended wheelchair routes, and special parking and set-down arrangements
♦ **BEST TIME TO VISIT** Weekdays in spring and summer are pleasant, but Sissinghurst closed Monday; Scotney Castle closed Monday (exc bank hols) and Tuesday

When the castle comes into view it fully lives up to its sobriquet of the 'Lady's Castle' – it once formed part of the dowry given by each English monarch to his queen upon their marriage. The castle's graceful aspects owe much to a nineteenth-century owner, Fiennes Wykeham-Martin, who added many of the medieval-style turrets.

Another owner, Lady Baillie, undertook a major restoration programme from 1925 and started the large collection of wildlife, including the elegant black swans that wander round the grounds and moat. Highlights include the Culpeper Garden (designed in 1980 by the renowned gardener Russell Page), which brims with herbs and cottage-garden plants; the castle itself, with its fine furnishings and portraits; the maze; grottoes; greenhouses; and the huge landscaped park, from which there are captivating views back to the castle. Eating in the self-service Fairfax Hall restaurant can involve queuing for a long time, but at least you can try wines produced on the Leeds Castle estate once you are there.

SISSINGHURST CASTLE*

Sissinghurst (almost 13 miles south of Leeds Castle by country lanes) is more than just a plant-lover's paradise, it is a place of pilgrimage. One of the most exciting of all gardens, it offers a chance to commune with the spirits of its eccentric creators, Harold Nicolson and Vita Sackville-West. Their story has been told in numerous biographies, but in case you need a beginner's or refresher course, there is an excellent exhibition in the barn next to the mellow red-brick castle where you can brush up on the less-sensational aspects of their history, as well as that of the castle, while waiting to visit the garden itself.

Different parts of the garden will catch your attention, depending on the season: in spring, the Bulb Garden is outstanding, and includes delightful species of tulips collected by Vita when she rode, on horseback, across Turkey and Iran to visit Harold while he was working in the British Embassy in Tehran. In summer the fiery scarlets of the Hot Garden contrast with the cool tones of the White Garden and the many velvety shades of purple from the clematis

The stocky ruins of Scotney Castle, lapped by its moat

which covers every wall. In autumn, the many different asters in the courtyard garden come into their own. For a different perspective on the garden, climb the tower for an aerial view, passing the study (with its framed photograph of Virginia Woolf) in which Vita Sackville-West wrote her many poems, stories and gardening articles. If you want to linger, the National Trust has mapped out a series of well-signposted walks round the Sissinghurst estate. The **Granary Restaurant*** has gained such a reputation that it is advisable to book if you want lunch.

SCOTNEY CASTLE*

Two castles were built at Scotney (9 miles west of Sissinghurst on the A262, then the A21): the upper one (closed to the public) was built in 1843 in Elizabethan style to take advantage of the extensive Bewl Valley views; the lower one, built in the fourteenth century, is now a creeper-clad ruin reflected in the still waters of its moat. Between the two is a series of garden terraces, cascading down the hillside, and a quarry from which the stone for the upper castle was extracted, where rock plants cling to the exposed stone. All around is a profusion of azaleas and rhododendrons, making a marvellous sight when they all flower together during May and June. For meals, try the excellent Brown Trout pub in nearby Lamberhurst, which specialises in seafood.

BODIAM CASTLE*

In 1385 Bodiam Castle (10 miles south-east of Scotney Castle) was built on the banks of the River Rother as a defence against an expected French invasion that never came. The roofless ruin now sits on an island, encircled by a wide moat filled with huge carp, and surrounded by the banks and hollows of a late-medieval water garden. An audio-visual presentation explains the history of the castle and the development of medieval armour. Refreshments are available in the castle tea rooms or in the Castle pub opposite (with a children's garden).

PENSHURST PLACE*

Penshurst Place (13 miles north-west of Scotney, via Tunbridge Wells) has changed little since the early seventeenth century when Ben Jonson wrote his poem 'To Penshurst', in praise of the hospitality of the owners, the Sidneys. Today there is an adventure playground and a toy museum, but the Mount is still there (resort of the dryads in Jonson's verse), and the Nut Garden, full of Kentish cobs (hazels) as well as the medieval Great Hall, with its open fireplace and impressive roof timbers. Other rooms are gorgeously furnished with heirlooms and family portraits, including one of Sir Philip Sidney, the author of the poem 'Arcadia', who was born at Penshurst in 1554.

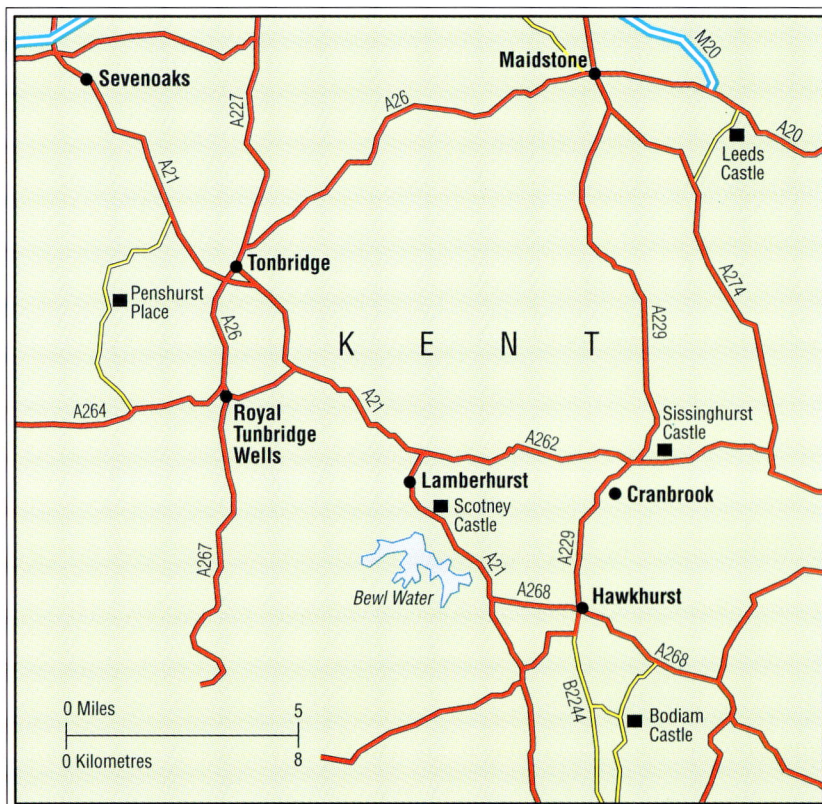

Entrée to Europe: Dover Castle and Eurotunnel

Dover Castle is one of the most important historical and architectural sights in Britain, to which the two modern attractions chosen for this day out make an excellent contrast.

It is perfectly possible to see the castle, the 'White Cliffs Experience' and the Eurotunnel Exhibition in a day, but if you are worried about children with short attention spans, it is probably best to start with the castle, or limit the day to just two sights.

DOVER CASTLE*

Dover's history as the gateway to Europe and stronghold against invasion from the Continent has been a turbulent one. Dominating the hill above the harbour, with clear views of the French coast, Dover Castle has been a fortress since the Iron Age, and besieged, battered and re-

♦ **GOOD FOR** Three contrasting sights form a fascinating picture of the history of British links with continental Europe
♦ **TRANSPORT** Railway stations at both Dover and Folkestone
♦ **ACCESS FOR DISABLED PEOPLE** Good at White Cliffs and Eurotunnel Exhibitions
♦ **BEST TIME TO VISIT** All year round

fortified many times in the following centuries. The sheer size of its ramparts make it seem daunting, so get your bearings by heading for the inner courtyard to watch the introductory video. This explains how the castle developed from a Roman fort to become perhaps the best defended stronghold in medieval England, before being adapted for defence against both Napoleon and Hitler.

The square-towered keep, built for Henry II in the 1180s as both fortress and sumptuous palace, is the historical showpiece. The architecture, although adapted in later years, is a fascinating mixture of late Norman (rounded arches) and Early English Gothic – note the decorated capitals of the pillars in the tiny chapel – and traces of a lead plumbing system show that Henry even enjoyed the luxury of running water. The main rooms are the Great State Chamber with the king's adjoining bedchamber, complete with private lavatory, and great Armour Hall, which was Henry's main public apartment.

After visiting the keep, follow your own route and explore the rest of the castle. Part of the Roman lighthouse, Pharos, still stands at the highest point of the castle grounds, and next to it is a Saxon church of about AD1000. Examine the eighteenth-century gun-emplacements and the original Avranches Traverse tower built to house defensive archers. Perhaps the most fascinating exhibit is Hellfire Corner with its underground vaults and tunnels, built deep into the chalk cliffs to house the operations rooms that were used as a command centre during the Second World War. The evacuation of Dunkirk was planned here, and Churchill visited to study the progress of the war. The visit to Hellfire Corner is by guided tour

▲ Dover Castle, described as 'the key to the kingdom', was first built in 1066

only. Also on show is the World War II Underground Hospital, constructed in 1941, which was used as a casualty dressing station. Finally, you may like to spend some time wandering around the grounds, enjoying the views over the Channel and the Kent hills

THE WHITE CLIFFS EXPERIENCE*

Although it traces the same historical span as that of Dover Castle, the Experience could hardly be more different. It is purpose-built around some minor Roman and Saxon ruins in the centre of Dover. Mini dramas, interspersed with written accounts and illustrations, are produced through the use of videos and life-size tableaux to bring crucial events in Dover's history alive. From the opening sequence – the narrative of

Julius Caesar's largely abortive invasions of Britain in 55 and 54BC which took place just along the coast at Walmer Beach – you are quickly drawn into the story. The conquest by Emperor Claudius, invasions by Saxons and Vikings, smuggling, Channel ferries and Dover at war are all covered. Among other diversions to keep children amused are a chance to make mosaics, and 'Gromet's Challenge', essentially an adventure playroom on the theme of an old square-rigged sailing ship. Perhaps the most entertaining section is a video of some of the most distinctive attempts to cross the Channel, from Blériot's first flight (customs recorded his arrival 'by yacht' since there was no heading on the form for 'aeroplane') to more bizarre efforts in amphibious cars, motorbikes and inflatable sail-powered wetsuits.

EUROTUNNEL EXHIBITION CENTRE*

Just off the M20 opposite the Channel Tunnel Terminal at Folkestone, five miles west along the coast, the exhibition charts the history and building of Britain's first permanent physical link with France and the longest undersea tunnel in the world. There to promote Le Shuttle and Eurostar trains, it has been put together in a way that will appeal to both adults and children, with interactive displays and games as well as guided tours and workshops. The entrance is surrounded by the slowly rusting machinery used to build the 84 kilometres of tunnels. All items are up for sale, but it is hard to imagine who would want to buy them. The centrepiece is the great cylinder of the tunnel-boring machine, headed with a revolving disc which cut through the chalk. As it bored, the machine installed the concrete rings which line the tunnel.

You can read a short account of previous failed attempts to bridge the channel, including the extraordinary exploits of the French engineer Thome de Gamond, who spent forty years during the nineteenth century attempting to devise a tunnel and charted the seabed by jumping out of a rowing boat with weights on his feet, olive oil in his mouth, and fat in his ears to protect himself against the water pressure.

Inside the Exhibition Centre you can sit at the controls of Le Shuttle or a construction train, play tunnel video games or walk on board a scale model of a shuttle peopled by talking dummies who describe their journey to France. The final exhibit is a wonderful model railway, showing both the Folkestone and Calais terminals, and a cross-section of tunnel, complete with fishtank representing the Channel above.

LUNCHBOX
Dover Castle and the 'White Cliffs Experience' both have sizeable cafés which serve decent hot meals. At the Eurotunnel Exhibition Centre you can buy light snacks or sandwiches or take a picnic and eat it in two specially preserved 1960s InterCity railway carriages which have been installed at the edge of the car park.

▲ The Roman invasion of Britain is vividly re-created at the 'White Cliffs Experience'

The religious and literary riches of Canterbury

Christ Church Gate, the vast, ornate entrance to Canterbury Cathedral

Here you can walk through nearly 2,000 years of history, discovering the birthplace of English Christianity and one of Europe's most celebrated places of pilgrimage for over 800 years.

Canterbury's compact and mostly pedestrianised city centre, with its plethora of fine buildings, shops and fascinating museums, is best explored on foot. You can walk beside the massive Norman walls that encircle the city, amble along narrow, winding streets lined with medieval houses, climb a fortified gatehouse, go underground to view the Roman foundations, step inside the majestic cathedral, or even glide lazily down the River Stour in a **boat*** to appreciate the history and charm of this magnificent city.

If you are arriving by car, park in one of the long-stay car parks just outside the city walls and make your way to the **visitor information centre*** on St Margaret's Street, which is perfectly positioned for the start of this walk. You can also join a

♦ **GOOD FOR** Tracing the history of the city on foot; children and adults alike will appreciate the museums

♦ **TRANSPORT** Bus or train to Canterbury

♦ **ACCESS FOR DISABLED PEOPLE** Canterbury Tales Visitor Attraction, Roman Museum, the cathedral and Canterbury Centre are accessible for wheelchairs; Canterbury Heritage Museum is accessible only at ground-floor level

♦ **BEST TIME TO VISIT** The attractions are open all year; during the summer the city gets very crowded

'Canterbury Walk' or other tour with an official **guide***.

One of Canterbury's greatest 'promoters' was Geoffrey Chaucer (1340–1400), author of the *Canterbury Tales*, the story of a group of pilgrims (including a Pardoner, a

Knight, a Clerk, a Reeve, a Miller and a Wife of Bath), travelling from London to Becket's shrine. They pass their time by recounting various tales, some heroic, some bawdy, some moral. At the **Canterbury Tales Visitor Attraction*** you can step back to the fourteenth century to join these pilgrims on their journey. Hire an audio-cassette and listen to the tales, read in modern English, while you watch entertaining tableaux, surrounded by the sounds and smells of the time.

One of the most memorable views in Canterbury is that from the High Street along Mercery Lane, with its fine, overhanging buildings, to the medieval splendour of Christ Church Gate, the main entrance to the cathedral. Equally arresting is the view along neighbouring Butchery Lane which frames the majestic **Bell Harry Tower**, dominating the city landscape. It is here that you will find the entrance to the **Roman Museum***. At the level of the Roman town, called Durovernum Cantiacorum, you can follow the discoveries of archaeologists, and walk through reconstructions of Roman buildings, including a market-place with stallholders' wares set out in authentic detail.

Queningate, or Queen's Gate, is the most impressive way to approach the city's crowning glory – the **cathedral***. Rebuilt around 1070 (it

The Weavers, which once housed refugees from religious persecution

was founded in 507), this spectacular building has been the destination of countless pilgrims since Becket's murder in 1170. Its unique features include an impressive high and narrow nave, fine medieval stained-glass, intricate carvings, the tombs of the Black Prince and Henry IV, a Norman crypt and the soaring splendour of the great fifteenth-century Bell Harry Tower. Near the cathedral are the ruins of the former Benedictine priory and the medieval **King's School**. Not to be missed in the environs of the school are the **Norman Staircase** and, opposite Mint Yard Gateway, **Sir John Boy's House** with its bizarrely warped doorway.

Some fine buildings line **Palace Street**, in particular the timber-framed **Conquest House**. Like many along the street it houses an antique shop in its beautifully restored interior. In St Alphege Lane you will find the **Canterbury Centre***, a converted church with exhibitions, slide shows and videos describing the city's past, present and visions of the future.

Many of the façades and shop fronts in **St Peter's Street** hide medieval origins, but the projecting upper floors, jettied timber-frames and tile-hung gables give the game away. The Saturday antique and collectors' market in the **Sidney Cooper Centre** may appeal; also, many of the narrow side-streets boast an array of galleries, gift and bric-à-brac shops. At the end of the street are the fourteenth-century **West Gate***, the city's only remaining fortified gatehouse, and the Guildhall. The Guard Chamber features displays of arms and armour from the Civil War to the Second World War, and from the battlements you can savour the views of the city and cathedral, including the River Stour running through **Westgate Gardens** – a peaceful place to picnic.

As you head back into the heart of the city, take time to admire the gabled Tudor cottages, known as **The Weavers**, which overhang the Stour at King's Bridge. These were built in the sixteenth century to house Flemish and Huguenot refugees, who settled in Canterbury to practise their weaving and dyeing skills. Standing opposite is the **Eastbridge Hospital of St Thomas**, one of the oldest buildings in the city, dating from 1180 and once used to accommodate poor pilgrims after their long journey.

Reached from Stour Street, via a beautifully tended kitchen garden, is the oldest Franciscan building in Britain. The **Greyfriars** was built in 1267 over a fork in the Stour and is all that remains of the Greyfriars Friary. The monks used to fish through a trapdoor in one of the ground-floor rooms, and on the first floor there is a quiet chapel. Before the monks moved into their island house they lived in the magnificent medieval **Poor Priests' Hospital**, now beautifully restored and home to the captivating **Canterbury Heritage Museum***. Excellent modern displays and vivid explanations guide you through Canterbury's history, from the building of the Roman town to the present day.

The Normans surrounded the city with a tower-studded wall and built a **castle** in about 1100. All that remains of the latter are the ruins of an impressive keep which guarded the ancient Wincheap Gate, but much of the encircling wall has survived. From here, you can follow a high-level footpath along the top of the wall, which overlooks public gardens, passes **Dane John Mound**, a pre-Roman burial ground, and affords splendid views across the city.

LUNCHBOX

Palace Street has a continental feel to it, with cafés and a first-class French pâtisserie. Elsewhere, among the best are: Il Vaticano on St Margaret's Street for fresh pasta dishes; Pierre Victoire in Best Lane for excellent-value set lunches; in Castle Street Flap Jacques for hearty snacks and the lively George's Brasserie; Morelli's Ice Cream Parlour on Sun Street for ice-cream, pastries and cappuccino. Liberty's store on Burgate offers reliable light lunches and decent afternoon teas.

The great historic dockyard at Chatham

◄ *The caulking of the warship* Valiant, *in the Wooden Walls Gallery*

Step back in time to enjoy a full day out exploring the world's most complete Georgian dockyard, now an award-winning living museum, tracing 400 years of illustrious Royal Navy shipbuilding history.

This fascinating 80-acre site at Chatham comprises the greatest concentration of historic buildings in Britain, all of which are beautifully restored, with the impressive main buildings housing various museums, galleries and working areas.

The **Historic Dockyard*** served the Royal Navy for over 400 years, from 1547 when storehouses were rented to Henry VIII for servicing the fleet at anchor on the River Medway, to its gradual demise and closure in 1984. Over the centuries it has played a vital role in supporting the Royal Navy – over 400 ships, ranging from sail-powered warships to steam-driven iron-clad battleships and twentieth-century submarines, were designed, built, refitted and repaired in the docks.

♦ **GOOD FOR** An intriguing overview of Britain's naval heritage
♦ **TRANSPORT** By train to Chatham BR station, then bus or taxi. Free car parking; the Dockyard is signposted from the M2, junction 3
♦ **ACCESS FOR DISABLED PEOPLE** Excellent facilities
♦ **BEST TIME TO VISIT** Open April to end October, some days in November, February and March; closed December and January

The most famous of all the ships constructed here was Lord Nelson's flagship, HMS *Victory*, launched in 1765. Other wooden warships that took part in the Battle of Trafalgar in 1805, HMS *Revenge*, *Temeraire* and *Leviathan* – the 'Wooden Walls of England' – were also built here.

When the docks finally closed, the Chatham Historic Dockyard Trust was formed to preserve the oldest part of the complex as a living museum. The remaining 300 acres were developed for commercial and residential use, with the outer reaches being operated as a commercial port. The Trust's phenomenal task was to conserve and restore more than 100 buildings and other structures of architectural, historical and archaeological importance, 47 of which are Scheduled Ancient Monuments.

The first port of call is the **Visitor Centre**, housed in the old Galvanising Workshop. Here the four centuries of dockyard history are recalled in the form of an audio-visual show, alongside models, maps and photographs. It is advisable at this juncture to assess how much time you wish to spend on your visit. The main galleries and buildings, the 'highlights' route, will absorb two hours, whereas a full tour will require at least four hours, plus refreshment stops along the way. Also, you may wish to allow time for particular demonstrations, listed on the blackboard.

The first of the principal displays and exhibitions on the main tour is the excellent **Wooden Walls Gallery** in the restored Mast Houses and Mould Loft. The sights, sounds and smells of the dockyard in 1758 are recreated as you follow William Crockwell, a young apprentice, on his first day at work. The story of the *Valiant*, a timber-hulled warship, is recounted as you are taken through

The former HMS Gannet, *now under restoration at Chatham*

LUNCHBOX
Excellent catering facilities on-site include the licensed Wheelwrights' restaurant, and in summer the Ropery Snack Bar and the Ordnance Mews Coffee Shop. Those who have brought a picnic have the choice of a spot overlooking the River Medway or an undercover eating area.

the stages of its construction, learn how many trees were needed for it and encounter some of the characters of the docks, including the Ratcatcher. The focal point of the display is the collection of artefacts recovered from the wreck of the *Invincible*, which sank in 1758.

Adjacent are the impressive Victorian covered slips in which many of the ships were built. **Slip No. 6** is home to the historic boat collection and steam centre, featuring, among others, a First World War coastal motor boat, a midget submarine and several steam traction engines, all of them being restored. Centre-stage in Chatham's dry docks is the former Royal Navy sloop HMS *Gannet*, the only Victorian sloop to survive. Constructed on the River Medway at Sheerness in 1878 and powered by both sail and steam, she is gradually being brought back to her former glory. Visitors are welcome on board to watch the painstaking work in progress, and a nearby gallery reveals the story of this unique vessel.

Beyond the Conservation Unit, where exhibits like figureheads are restored, are the beautifully renovated Clocktower Building, Admiral's Offices (not open) and the **Commissioner's House**, the oldest naval building to survive intact in Britain. This, surprisingly, has a peaceful walled garden, complete with an Italianate water garden and a 400-year-old mulberry tree. From

this vantage point Cromwell is reputed to have watched the Roundheads take the city of Rochester from the Royalists during the Civil War.

Behind the Anchor Wharf storehouses is the **Ropery**, one of the dockyard's most memorable attractions. Rope has been made on this site since 1618, although the present vast buildings were built in the eighteenth century. Here, on the quarter-mile rope walk, you can see rope being made using traditional methods and machines by the dockyard's own rope-making company, Master Ropemakers. In the nearby exhibition areas curious displays show how raw materials were combed, spun and twisted together to make rope.

The furthest point of the tour is the Lead and Paint Mill, now the

Historical Society Museum, a rich assembly of dock workers' memorabilia. Heading back to the visitor centre you will pass the Royal Dockyard Church, built in 1804, and the stables where the heavy horses are kept and from where horse-drawn wagon rides around the complex can be taken during the summer months. Next door is the **Sail and Colour Loft**, a museum gallery where you can watch flags being made, observe the techniques of sail-making and tie some knots.

Continue past splendid dockyard houses to reach the **Ordnance Gallery**, well worth a visit for its fine collection of naval muzzle-loading guns dating from the seventeenth century. If time allows, take a trip on board the paddle steamer *Kingswear Castle* from Thunderbolt Pier and cruise along the River Medway in style.

A few minutes' drive (or short walk) away from the Dockyard, at Chatham Maritime, is submarine *Ocelot*, the last 'O'-class (O for Oberon) submarine built at Chatham for the Royal Navy. Brought here in 1992 and fully restored, she is now presented jointly with English Partnerships, developers of Chatham Maritime.

Master Ropemakers forming 'strands' on the rope walk of the Ropery

Hampton Court, Henry VIII's palatial home

🚶 ☂ ❄ 🚐 ♿

The William and Mary additions to Wolsey's original palace seen from the formal gardens

The most varied and extensive of the Royal Palaces with easily enough activities – indoor and out – to fill an entire day

PRACTICALITIES

Hampton Court is so big that seeing the whole palace, including a break for lunch, exploring the gardens, strolling by the River Thames and getting lost in that most famous of mazes, could easily take up a whole day. So it pays to think ahead about how to pace your visit, making the most of the different touring 'routes', the extensive gardens and the facilities for children.

The first thing to realise is that although most famous as Henry VIII's extravagant Tudor palace, there is an astonishing architectural variety among the buildings which survive today. While the origins are essentially Tudor – Henry VIII's chief minister Cardinal Wolsey built most of the original structure in the 1520s – much of the rest of the palace dates from 1689.

Further major alterations for royal residents were made during the eighteenth and nineteenth centuries, and as a result Hampton Court provides a series of historical snapshots of some of the most stylish of the Royal Courts.

♦ **GOOD FOR** Bad weather as there is much to amuse inside. Children will enjoy the maze and trails
♦ **TRANSPORT** The palace is 1 mile south of Kingston-upon-Thames; parking is possible within the grounds or in Bushy Park. Hampton Court is the nearest British Rail station (5-minute walk)
♦ **ACCESS FOR DISABLED PEOPLE** There are ramps into the ground floor and lifts up to the other floors. There are also ramps into the cafés and wheelchair-accessible WCs both outside and inside
♦ **BEST TIME TO VISIT** All year round, as there is plenty to see both inside the palace and outside in the gardens

GUIDED TOURS

To reflect these historical contrasts, Hampton Court has been divided into six different sightseeing routes – plus the gardens. (Each route has a number from one to six, but if you feel like exploring them chronologically the order is: five, one, six, four, two, three!)

All the routes can be followed without a guide, but if you prefer guided tours some can be followed

accompanied by excellent 30-40 minute 'sound tours' on headphones (they are available from the information office in Clock Court; the cost is included in the admission price). Group tours are also available for Henry VIII's State Apartments and around the King's Apartments. Both last about 45 minutes, are free, of a high standard and led by guides in contemporary costume, but they have to be pre-booked by calling at the information office. Each tour leaves roughly once an hour but they are often full, so you may have to wait an hour or more to catch the next. Tours of the gardens, lasting about an hour, can be booked through the East Front shop (free to palace ticket holders). Call **Hampton Court Palace*** for the latest details.

SEEING ROUND THE PALACE – ROUTE BY ROUTE

Each route is clearly signed and starts from a different point around the central courtyard, Clock Court. If you don't take a tour, it's worth investing in a 'souvenir guide book' which explains the historical and architectural background to what you are seeing – relatively little information is given in the rooms themselves.

1. Henry VIII's State Apartments

(Sound and guided tour)
Sadly, little is left of Henry VIII's Hampton Court – and much of what does remain has been altered by successive kings. However, the Great Hall, which begins this tour, has changed little and is still hung with tapestries (of the story of Abraham), commissioned by the Tudor king. On the way to the Chapel, with its sumptuous vaulted ceiling, you pass two of the most important paintings in Henry's collection – a royal family group with Jane Seymour (his third

wife) and Edward VI, and **The Field of the Cloth of Gold**, which depicts Henry meeting the great French king François I.

2. The Queen's State Apartments

These rooms were intended for Queen Mary, wife of William III, but she died before they were finished. The result is a mixture of styles and décor as the rooms were fashioned and adapted by later monarchs. The room that remains closest to the original intentions is the Audience Chamber, which retains the crimson baroque throne canopy. Be sure not to miss the excellent views of the East Front Gardens from the Queen's Drawing Room.

3. The Georgian Rooms
(Sound tour)
These rooms, adorned and decorated by George II, are dominated by the enormous cartoon gallery, originally home to the great Raphael cartoons now housed in the V&A Museum (see *Great Day Out 44*), but now hung with seventeenth-century copies. Further on, the private rooms of Queen Caroline give perhaps the most intimate insight into royal domestic life. Her bedchamber (equipped with extraordinary locks on both doors which could be operated by levers from the bed) and bathroom, with its marble cistern, are preserved in their original state.

4. The King's Apartments
(Sound and guided tour)
The king in question is William III, who commissioned Sir Christopher Wren to knock down Henry VIII's original Privy Chambers and rebuild them between 1689 and 1700. This series of lavish rooms was badly damaged by the 1986 fire, but it

The King's Beasts line the way over the moat to the main entrance

would take an expert eye to spot the restorations. Among the highlights are the Presence Chamber, with William's original throne, and sixteenth-century tapestries from Henry VIII's Whitehall Palace; and the private dining-room hung with the 'Hampton Court Beauties', paintings of the most attractive of Queen Mary's courtiers. The apartments also have wonderful views over the recently re-planted Privy Garden, now restored to its original 1702 layout, down to the Tijou wrought-iron screen and the river beyond.

5. The Wolsey Rooms and Renaissance Picture Gallery

Two tiny wood-panelled rooms which Wolsey built for his own (short-lived) private use begin the tour, but the rest of the rooms are lined with renaissance paintings from the current Royal Collection. Highlights include a rather gawky Raphael self-portrait, Titian's *Boy with a Pipe*, Bellini's *Portrait of a Young Man*, *The Massacre of the Innocents* by Breugel and the only painting which historians are sure was hung by Henry VIII at the palace, *The Four Evangelists Stoning the Pope*, commissioned from Girolamo da Treviso after his acrimonious break with Rome.

6. The Tudor Kitchens
(Sound tour)
Arguably this is the most interesting route of all, and it certainly gives the best impression of everyday life in the palace. A staff of 200 once worked in 50 or more rooms (including 15 subsidiary kitchens), catering for up to 800 courtiers a day. Nowadays you can see only nine, but these include the magnificent Great Kitchens, extremely realistically laid out as if the staff were preparing a feast in 1542, with stuffed animals, original utensils and cooking pots. Real fires blaze in the hearths, and the 'dishes' being prepared includes roast boar and stuffed carp. Among the side rooms are the old boiling house butchery, the enormous cellar (three hundred barrels of wine were drunk each year), and the dressing and garnishing rooms complete with stuffed peacocks.

The Palace Gardens
(Guided tour)
The gardens of Hampton Court are almost a day out in themselves, especially if you include an exploration of Bushy Park and the formal gardens along the Great Canal, dug by Charles II, which leads up to the East Front. In practice, however, most visitors restrict themselves to the collection of gardens to the south of the main buildings. The neatly clipped rows of hollies and yews in William III's Privy Garden are the obvious attraction, but don't miss the Pond Garden, laid out by Henry VIII and perhaps the most tranquil of all. Nearby are William's Banqueting House overlooking the river and the Mantegna Gallery, home to the renaissance master's series of paintings *The Triumphs of Caesar*. The maze is on the north side of the palace, in an area known as the Wilderness, renowned for its dazzling display of spring bulbs.

Pomp and ceremony in royal London

Horse Guards Parade was built for the royal cavalry in 1750–8

Palaces, priceless jewels and pageantry – this day out is steeped in the sumptuous heritage of Britain's monarchy.

If the Royal Standard is flying above **Buckingham Palace***, you know that the Queen is in residence. The palace has been the main home of the royal family since Victoria moved in after succeeding to the throne in 1837, and it makes a good starting point for exploring royal London. When George III bought the building for the Crown in 1761, it was a country house on the edge of London; George IV commissioned the architect John Nash to turn it into a home fit for a monarch.

Since 1993, the public has been allowed in for two months each summer (August and September) to gaze at a dozen or so lavish state rooms where the Queen does much of her official entertaining. These include the Throne Room, the Picture Gallery, hung with priceless works by Rubens, Rembrandt and van Dyck among others, and the Music Room, where

♦ **GOOD FOR** Lovers of art, architecture, the monarchy
♦ **TRANSPORT** All sights are within central London; public transport is easier than driving and parking
♦ **ACCESS FOR DISABLED PEOPLE** Either none or limited, except Crown Jewels. For Buckingham Palace write to Visitor Office, Buckingham Palace, London SW1
♦ **BEST TIME TO VISIT** Some sights open only in summer months; the Changing of the Guard takes place daily from April to August, alternate days rest of year; Kensington Palace is open daily from May to September

guests are presented before banquets. The queues to get in are formidable, and the entry charge is steep, but some will take comfort from the knowledge that the money raised is helping to restore Windsor Castle, which suffered a serious fire in 1992.

Crowds gather all year round outside to watch the **Changing of the Guard***. At 11.30am the foot soldiers of the New Guard, kitted out in scarlet jackets and bearskins and accompanied by a regimental band and drummers, march through the palace gates and into the forecourt to take over from the previous day's guard. The ceremony lasts about 40 minutes, after which the Old Guard marches out of the forecourt and back to barracks. (A shorter guard-changing ceremony takes place every morning at **Horse Guards Parade*** on Whitehall.)

Her Majesty owns one of the most valuable art collections in the world, thanks in part to Anthony Blunt, who was her art adviser for 30 years. You can see more of this collection a few yards along Buckingham Palace Road in the **Queen's Gallery***, which has changing exhibitions based on a different theme each year. Unlike at Buckingham Palace, at the Gallery you can bypass the ticket office and visit the gift shop for free. If you hanker after souvenirs such as Buckingham Palace biscuits and jams, royal videos or crown-motif cufflinks, this is the place to come.

You can get a sense of the pomp of great royal occasions at the **Royal Mews*** (very restricted opening times, phone in advance to check), where a glittering line-up of royal coaches is displayed. The star attraction is the Gold State Coach, built in 1761 for George III and used for the coronation of every British monarch since. This vast, magnificent contraption is decorated with painted panels, weighs four tons and needs eight horses to pull it. Other splendid vehicles on show include the Glass Coach, in which Princess Elizabeth and Lady Diana Spencer travelled to their weddings. The royal horses are housed in John Nash's elegant stables.

▲ *Buckingham Palace was called the Queen's House during George III's reign*

Within walking distance are the remains of three other royal palaces; like Windsor Castle after them, all suffered disastrous fires which destroyed most of the original buildings. The Houses of Parliament stand on the site of Edward the Confessor's **Palace of Westminster**, by which name the complex is still known. You need to arrange a tour through your MP (see *Great Day Out 46*) if you want to look inside Westminster Hall, a vast room with a magnificent hammer-beam roof – virtually all that remains from medieval times. Sir Thomas More and Anne Boleyn were sentenced to death, and Charles I was tried here.

In the 1530s Henry VIII moved his court to Whitehall Palace, which he seized from the disgraced Cardinal Wolsey. This building was destroyed in 1698 when clothes left to dry in front of a fire caught alight. All that survived was Inigo Jones' **Banqueting House*** (see *Great Day Out 49*), with ceilings painted by Rubens for Charles I (who later walked from this room to his execution on a scaffold erected outside the palace).

St James's Palace on the Mall was built in 1532 as a hunting lodge for Henry VIII, who at the same time appropriated a huge swathe of land on which to indulge his favourite sport (these Tudor hunting grounds have since become the London royal parks – St James's, Green Park, Hyde Park, Kensington Gardens and Regent's Park). St James's Palace is still the official court, and you can still see Henry's turreted gatehouse in Cleveland Row. Next door is Clarence House, where the Queen Mother lives.

Kensington Palace* in Kensington Gardens is well worth a visit. William III and Mary moved here in 1689 after the damp river air at Whitehall Palace proved too much for William's asthma, and commissioned Sir Christopher Wren to enlarge the building. Guided tours are available through the state apartments to see such highlights as William Kent's painted ceilings and the wonderful King's Staircase, whose walls are decorated with paintings of the court personalities of the day. Princess Victoria was born and brought up in Kensington Palace, and

Princesses Diana and Margaret have private apartments here. The palace also houses a superb collection of coronation robes and court dress.

Every coronation since 1066 has been held in **Westminster Abbey***, and many kings and queens have been married and buried here. Don't miss Henry VII's beautiful fan-vaulted chapel, containing his tomb and that of Elizabeth I and her arch rival Mary, Queen of Scots; Edward the Confessor's shrine, where many medieval monarchs are buried; and of course, the Coronation Chair, last used in 1953.

No exploration of royal London would be complete without a visit to the **Tower of London*** (see *Great Day Out 42*) to see the Crown Jewels. After Charles I was beheaded in 1649, Cromwell ordered that the royal regalia be moved to the Tower and melted down, so most of the crowns, orbs and sceptres date from the restoration of the monarchy in 1660 and after.

To get to the jewels, you pass through an imposing pair of steel doors; visitors waiting in queues are entertained with a film of the Queen's coronation. Among the priceless items on show are the Imperial State Crown, worn by the monarch at major state occasions and encrusted with more than 2,800 diamonds, including the second largest diamond in the world (the largest, the First Star of Africa, is set in the Sceptre of the Cross, also on display). St Edward's Crown is used only at coronations, fortunately for the monarch as it weighs four-and-a-half pounds. The Queen Mother's Crown, the only one made of platinum, is set with the famous Koh-i-Noor diamond. To keep the queues moving, travelators glide visitors past glass cases containing the jewels.

LUNCHBOX

Only two of the sights mentioned here offer refreshments: at Kensington Palace the elegant Orangery, added by Queen Anne, is now a café; the wharf at the Tower of London also has a café. You will find cafés and sandwich bars in the streets near all the sights. Prêt à Manger in Kingsgate Road near Buckingham Palace sells delicious sandwiches for a quick lunch.

The Queen's Walk, Tower Bridge and Docklands

The Royal Naval College is a Baroque masterpiece, designed by Christopher Wren

A tour on foot along one of London's most dramatic stretches of riverside, a train ride through the transformed Docklands and a walk under the Thames to Greenwich.

Start from London Bridge (rail and tube at London Bridge stations nearby). The unremarkable **London Bridge** of 1968–72 spans what was for centuries the only crossing point of the Thames in London. In medieval times the bridge was covered by a slummy warren of houses. In 1971 a later version of 1823–31 was shipped to Arizona where it now spans Lake Havasu (one story, no doubt an urban myth, is that the purchaser thought he was buying Tower Bridge).

Take the steps down from the bridge by the large office block, built of salmon-pink polished granite and called No. 1 London Bridge, and follow the **Queen's Walk** along the riverside. Here are some of the best views of the City over the Thames, including the **Monument**, a slender classical column designed by Christopher Wren to commemorate the Great Fire of London of 1666. For centuries this structure was a soaring pinnacle that dominated the

- ♦ **GOOD FOR** River views, old and modern industrial architecture, and museums
- ♦ **TRANSPORT** All sights are near public transport
- ♦ **ACCESS FOR DISABLED PEOPLE** Steps at the start of the route, but the section as far as the Tower of London is otherwise feasible
- ♦ **BEST TIME TO VISIT** All year; Tower of London is best out of season

panorama; now it is apologetically squeezed between high-rise office blocks and backed by the NatWest Tower. Further to the east is the controversial **Lloyd's Building** (1978–86), designed by Richard Rogers, architect of the Pompidou Centre in Paris. Like its French cousin it displays its conduits on the outside. The route then passes **Hay's Galleria**, a splendid 1987 revival of Victorian warehouses built originally by Thomas Cubitt in 1857, with an arched roof. Inside are shops, craft stalls and David Kemp's sculpture *The*

Navigators, a very surprising ship-cum-fountain.

HMS Belfast*, the last big gunship of the Royal Navy, saw much action in the Second World War. Visitors can walk round its seven decks and see the punishment cells and the dental surgery.

Before crossing Tower Bridge it is worth walking a few yards further. The route momentarily loses sight of the waterfront as it enters **Shad Thames**, the street parallel to the river, which is criss-crossed by high catwalks leading from one warehouse to another; this atmospheric location has been used for many films and TV dramas. The street ends near the **Design Museum*** (1989), with its minimalist-style café and small but idiosyncratic shop selling designer gifts and design-related books. From here the view changes remarkably: the tower at Canary Wharf is visible ahead, and the City has vanished from sight. **New Concordia Wharf** has more warehouses, handsomely restored as flats but still Dickensian in appearance.

Tower Bridge*, opened in 1894 and perhaps the most famous of all city gateways, houses a small museum (the entrance fee is high, but you get the chance to follow the high-level walkway above the road section). Displays explain the swing mechanism, which raises the bridge to allow big ships through. One celebrated anecdote concerns a double-decker bus which drove on to the bridge just as it was being raised; it was too late either to reverse the bridge mechanism or for the bus to U-turn. With great presence of mind the driver accelerated, and the bus safely negotiated the gap of a couple of feet; a short delay would have been fatal.

Cross the bridge and take the steps down on the left at the last of the bridge's arches (leading past the museum entrance). Turn left at the bottom to join the riverside in front of the **Tower of London***. The best way of hearing the grisly history of the raven-inhabited Tower is to take a tour led by one of the distinctively attired Beefeaters. Tales of murdered princes and executions are told as you view the weapons, instruments of torture and Crown Jewels. Though parts of the structure date only from the nineteenth century, the centrepiece is one of Britain's finest Norman castles.

The route continues around the dry moat (you don't need to pay the entrance fee for this part) alongside the railings, round the north side of the Tower, passing the entrance to Tower Hill tube, where there is a chunk of medieval postern gate. Carry on under the pedestrian subway, following signs for the World Trade Centre, fork right on the other side and then turn left into **St Katharine's Dock**. First opened in 1828, it was restored in the late 1970s and is now well endowed with waterfront restaurants; historic ships, including Thames barges, are often moored here.

Return to Tower Hill tube and go across to Tower Hill Gateway to catch the **Docklands Light Railway** (DLR) to Island Gardens. On these toy-like trains you will cross the Isle

Gothic Tower Bridge provides extensive views of London from its covered walkway

of Dogs at high level. Beyond West India Quay the panoramas open out spectacularly over gleaming new office blocks, water and the former docks. Towering over all of them is **Canary Wharf** (1991), at 800 feet Britain's tallest building. In the 1960s London's docks slid into decline as a result of changes in cargo handling and trade. Only a few years after Sir Winston Churchill's funeral (1965) when the dock cranes were bowed in respect, the great docks were empty and the port effectively redundant; the last dock closed in 1982. You can get off at Mudchute station to visit **Mudchute City Farm***, where farm animals go about their business in a very incongruous setting.

At Island Gardens station, before taking the foot tunnel under the Thames, stop to admire the view of Greenwich from the gardens by the tunnel entrance. The journey through the tunnel itself is surreal, with every footstep echoing off the white lavatory tiles. A restored antique lift whisks you up into the very different atmosphere of **Greenwich**. There is enough here

Canary Wharf, after its problems in the early 1990s, now has a popular shopping centre

to occupy a full day. At weekends the lively market (crafts in one area, antiques, books and junk in another) promises many hours of browsing. The **Cutty Sark** is the last surviving tea clipper and makes an appealing contrast to the HMS *Belfast*. To the right of the *Cutty Sark*, on the riverside, is **Gipsy Moth IV**, the ketch on which Sir Francis Chichester sailed single-handedly round the world in 1966–7. For a magnificent view of the serpentine Thames, walk into Greenwich Park to look down from near the **Old Royal Observatory*** of 1675 to the **National Maritime Museum*** and **Queen's House***. The latter is the earliest truly classically proportioned building in Britain, designed by Inigo Jones. For more information, visit Greenwich **tourist information office***, situated in Greenwich Church Street.

The best, though not the cheapest, method of return is by river boat to central London. Trains run back from Greenwich to London Bridge, Waterloo East and Charing Cross.

LUNCHBOX
A wide range of food and drink, from a takeaway sandwich at the Tower to a gourmet meal on the river, is available at many of these attractions.

A theatre lover's tour of London

The National Theatre moved to its present location at the South Bank Centre in 1976

For a dramatic day in London visit Covent Garden's Theatre Museum and the Museum of the Moving Image, take advantage of the Royal Festival Hall's free events or take a backstage tour at the National Theatre. Finish by looking back in time at Shakespeare's Globe.

COVENT GARDEN

Covent Garden's long association with the theatre can be savoured by wandering the streets around the Theatre Museum. To the north is the **Royal Opera House**, while the **Piazza**, to the west, is the stage for street performers of all kinds, from clowns and jugglers to Chinese acrobats and musicians. **St Paul's Church** (designed in Tuscan style by Inigo Jones in the 1630s) stands on the west side of the Piazza and is known as the Actors' Church. It contains memorials to Charlie Chaplin and Noel Coward among others. The church faces the Punch and Judy pub, which stands close to

♦ **GOOD FOR** Fascinating contrasts and tours for theatre lovers
♦ **TRANSPORT** All the sights are close to underground stations, bus routes and Waterloo and Charing Cross railway stations
♦ **ACCESS FOR DISABLED PEOPLE** Indoor attractions all accessible, but help will be needed to get from Covent Garden to the South Bank
♦ **BEST TIME TO VISIT** All year round

where the first-ever Punch and Judy show was performed in London by Pietro Gimonde's marionettes on 9 May 1662 (Pepys was there, as he records in his diary). Mr Punch's 'birthday' is still celebrated on the same spot by performances every second Sunday in May.

THE THEATRE MUSEUM*, RUSSELL STREET WC2

(Covent Garden Underground)
The museum offers a range of daily events, such as guided tours, costume workshops and make-up demonstrations, and these help to bring the otherwise rather static displays to life, involving visitors (especially stage-struck children) in the magic of the theatre. These events are free, but it is advisable to book in advance since places are limited. The permanent collections require a lot of reading, but if you are interested in the history of the theatre from Shakespearean times to the present day, the detail is fascinating. Much of the material consists of contemporary engravings (including some humorous and very unflattering cartoons of audiences), but there are some impressive costumes as well, ranging from sequined outfits worn by eighteenth-century dancers to the hippyish tie-dye smocks of the dancers of Diaghilev's Ballets Russes at the première of *The Rite of Spring* in 1913.

THE SOUTH BANK

(Waterloo Underground)
From Covent Garden it is only a short stroll to the Strand and to **Waterloo Bridge**, with its excellent views. Because it straddles a bend in the river, there are fine vistas both to the east and west: to the City and the new skyscrapers of Canary Wharf on the one hand, and to the Houses of Parliament facing County Hall on the other.

By contrast with these stirring riverside panoramas, the **South Bank complex** looks as dreary as you might expect from an architectural style that some have called Brutalist. The traffic-free spaces around the stained, windowless concrete have been colonised by local communities, and skateboarding youths use the brick inclines to practise their manoeuvres, while markets, specialising in second-hand books and third-world arts and crafts, have sprung up along the riverbank. To the right, the **Royal Festival Hall*** offers further free entertainment in the form of foyer concerts and exhibitions of art, sculpture and photography. Something is always happening here, from 10am to10.30pm, while good shops selling books and music CDs, and coffee bars abound.

MUSEUM OF THE MOVING IMAGE (MOMI)*

(Waterloo Underground)
Like the Theatre Museum, it is the special events that make MOMI the fun place it is. You do not need to book ahead. Costumed actors appear out of nowhere, like the travelling players and mountebanks of old, and drum up an audience for their particular part of the museum by shouting, for example, 'Roll up for the magic lantern show…come and see my stupendous Phenakistoscope.' In the first part of the museum, devoted to the earliest forms of moving image, the hands-on working

Shakespeare's work can be experienced in its original setting at the Globe Theatre

models have impressive names such as Praxinoscope, Zoetrope and Fantasmagorie. Horror has been a consistent theme in film from the early days, and the museum has its fair share of monsters, from Frankenstein to the Daleks.

Adults can wallow in televisual nostalgia by watching old episodes of *Juke Box Jury* or *Z Cars* at the many monitors dotted around the museum. The most popular section by far is that devoted to television in the computer age, where you can try reading the news from an autocue, or star as the interviewee on a chat show. The rest of the museum deals in depth with a whole range of cinematic subjects, many of them quite sobering, such as the Correspondent at War, the Documentary, Soviet Realism, and German Expressionism.

THE NATIONAL THEATRE*

(Waterloo Underground)
Alongside MOMI is the National Theatre, which, like the Royal Festival Hall, has foyer concerts and numerous exhibitions. It also offers backstage tours, which are justly popular and must be booked in advance. Three to five tours take place on most days, lasting an hour and led by well-informed and enthusiastic guides who help you

All performances at the Royal Opera House Covent Garden are in their original language

appreciate the sheer scale of the task involved in mounting a National Theatre production.

THE GLOBE THEATRE*

(Mansion House Underground)
An amble along the Riverside Walk, under Blackfriars Bridge, will bring you to a circular timber-framed building, roofed in thatch and dwarfed by such towering neighbours as the Bankside power station and the Oxo tower. The Globe Theatre, brainchild of the late Sam Wanamaker, is an authentic reconstruction of Shakespeare's famous Globe, built in 1599 and burned down in 1613 after two cannon, fired during a performance of *Henry VIII*, set the thatch alight. Visitors can tour the theatre and learn about the raucous nature of playgoing in Shakespeare's day, when audiences barracked actors, who in turn departed from the script to tell jokes, juggle or generally court popularity with the audience, while unpopular actors were driven from the stage in a hail of rotten fruit and nuts. To consolidate your Shakespearean experience, you can attend a performance (the theatre is due to open September 1996). There is no artificial lighting so the productions take place only in summer, twice daily, in the afternoon and early evening.

LUNCHBOX
The National Theatre, MOMI, the Royal Festival Hall all have cafés and restaurants.

Four of the world's greatest museums

Tippoo's Tiger at the V & A: a small organ inside (unfortunately, not audible) imitates the victim's dying groans

Applied arts, the natural world, science and archaeology — take your pick from four world-class museums, which all present their subjects in exhilarating and imaginative ways.

The three South Kensington museums – the Natural History and Science Museums, and the V&A – owe their origins to the funds generated by the Great Exhibition of 1851 and to Queen Victoria's desire to commemorate her husband, Prince Albert, the driving force behind the Exhibition, who died of typhoid in 1861. The fourth attraction, the venerable British Museum, was founded nearly a century earlier in 1753 from the bequest of Sir Hans Sloane. Each of the four museums merits a whole day's exploration, though you could easily combine the Natural History and Science Museums in one visit.

VICTORIA & ALBERT MUSEUM

(South Kensington Underground)
Before he died, Prince Albert founded the **Victoria & Albert Museum*** (V&A) as an object lesson

- ♦ **GOOD FOR** Adults will enjoy all the museums; children are more likely to prefer the Natural History and Science museums
- ♦ **TRANSPORT** Use buses or London Underground
- ♦ **ACCESS FOR DISABLED PEOPLE** No problem
- ♦ **BEST TIME TO VISIT** Year-round attractions. In general, weekday mornings are the quietest

for commercial designers, bringing together outstanding examples of applied design to inspire future generations. The result is a wonderful bazaar of diverse treasures, from the ornately carved Great Bed of Ware, made in 1590, to Tippoo's Tiger in the Nehru Gallery, an animated model of a tiger shown devouring his luckless victim, an East India Company army officer.

The V&A is the kind of museum where it is best to wander and be

taken by surprise, but exhibits not to be missed are the Raphael Cartoons (due to re-open in 1996), the Dress Collection (fashions from 1540 right up to the present day), the Frank Lloyd Wright Gallery, with furniture, metalwork, ceramics and stained glass representative of his work, and the Turner paintings (including Salisbury Cathedral and Dedham Mill). The 20th Century Gallery features design classics of our age, and the shop sells crafts and jewellery made by contemporary young artisans. The V&A also runs an exciting programme of temporary exhibitions.

NATURAL HISTORY MUSEUM

(South Kensington Underground)
Since its inspired decision to create a section entirely devoted to dinosaurs, including a highly realistic animated tableau, the **Natural History Museum*** has become a firm family favourite. It is also a good place to teach your children the facts of life, with imaginative displays on human biology. The Creepy Crawlies section has a scorpion enlarged to nightmarish proportions, and an itch-inducing display of the insects you might find in a none-too-clean kitchen.

If that is not really your idea of beauty you might head instead for the Mineral Gallery for exquisite examples of fine crystals and gemstones. At the far end, spectacular specimens, some older than the Earth itself, invite close inspection in the Meteorite Pavilion. The first phase of the new Earth Sciences complex, with the promise of three state-of-the-art exhibitions, is due to open in 1996.

Diplodocus and Triceratops skeletons in the cathedral-like setting of the Natural History Museum's Central Hall

SCIENCE MUSEUM

(*South Kensington Underground*)
The little chunk of moon rock in the Natural History Museum may look insignificant, but the Exploration of Space display in the next-door **Science Museum*** drives home the immense achievement involved in bringing that little lump of rock down to Earth. The displays include the tiny and flimsy-looking *Apollo 10* space capsule and replica of the *Apollo 11* moon-landing craft. The theme of flight is continued in the huge aeronautics gallery, with its historic aircraft and executive jet. The Launch Pad, by contrast, is less about flight and more an opportunity for children to carry out their own experiments and let off steam. Many of the older parts of the museum contain quiet corners where you can quietly ponder everything from the oldest working clock in the world (from Wells Cathedral – see *Great Day Out 11*) to the artistry of nature, as manifest in the molecular structure of human DNA.

BRITISH MUSEUM

(*Russell Square or Tottenham Court Road Underground*)
Containing works plundered from every ancient culture in the world (including the Elgin Marbles, which Greece has demanded back), the **British Museum*** is unique by virtue of its sheer size and the diversity of its collections. A comprehensive tour in one visit is impossible, so pick up a free map at the entrance and select a few highlights.

The Elgin Marbles, for all their notoriety, may turn out to be disappointing, unless you are soaked in Classical history. For something truly awesome, head for the marvellous seventh-century BC Assyrian reliefs of winged bulls and lion hunts. On a different scale altogether are the intricately decorated helmets, bowls and crowns of the seventh-century AD Sutton Hoo treasure, or the

Court dress from the 1740s and 1750s: part of the extensive Dress Collection at the V & A

twelfth-century Lewis chessmen carved from walrus ivory. Another popular exhibit is the leathery corpse of Lindow Man (affectionately known as Pete Marsh), the body found preserved in a Cheshire bog where he had been thrown as a sacrificial victim by Celtic priests over 2,000 years ago.

Also save some time for browsing among the display cases of the British Library (due to move to new premises in St Pancras): the Lindisfarne Gospels of AD698 (see *Great Day Out 128*), letters from Jane Austen and Shakespeare's autograph are among the many precious items on show.

LUNCHBOX

Both Natural History and Science Museums have cafés catering for children. The V&A also has excellent catering facilities (though many thought that the advertising slogan 'A great café with a museum attached' was demeaning to the scholarly reputation of the museum).

The British Museum is a short stroll from numerous good pubs and restaurants: try the Museum Tavern, 49 Great Russell Street, where Karl Marx used to slip in for a pint while writing *Das Kapital*, or Wagamama, 4 Streatham Street (off Coptic Street), serving inexpensive Japanese food (including vegetarian).

Three of the world's greatest art galleries

During the Second World War the National Gallery's paintings were moved to a Welsh slate-quarry cave

Between them, London's National Gallery, National Portrait Gallery and Tate Gallery span the history of western European art from the Middle Ages to modern times. New technology has revolutionised the way in which art is presented, affording a more interactive, rewarding visit.

The experience of visiting London's great national art collections has been transformed by the advent of electronic audio guides. The National Gallery's CD-ROM *Gallery Guide Sound Track*, for example, provides a commentary on each of the thousand or so pictures on permanent display, adding up to over 40 hours' worth of listening. Visitors do not have to follow a pre-set route – if you see a picture that interests you, just key in the reference number and listen to the art experts' interpretation of the work. At the Tate Gallery, where many of the works are by contemporary artists, you can hear the likes of David

Hockney or Bridget Riley explaining the thought-processes that lie behind their paintings.

It is possible to spend a whole day at either the Tate or the National Gallery, browsing alone or following one of the many guided tours. The Tate offers ones on specific subjects at different times throughout the day, and the National Gallery has a twice-daily general tour of its collection. Lunchtime lectures are available at both galleries.

NATIONAL GALLERY
(*Charing Cross Underground*)
Founded in 1824, the **National Gallery*** houses Britain's national art collection covering most European schools and periods of painting (though British and twentieth-century art are largely the domain of the Tate Gallery). Shrewd purchases were made in the nineteenth century when medieval and Renaissance art were out of fashion, with the result that the National Gallery has an astonishingly rich collection from these periods, most of which is housed in the new Sainsbury Wing annexe. This wing also contains facilities such as cloakrooms, the Brasserie restaurant, the main shop, lecture theatre, information desk and the Micro Gallery, where computer terminals allow you to plan your own route through the gallery, taking in many well-known paintings.

Chronologically, it makes sense to start in the Sainsbury Wing, with its modern interpretation of Florentine Renaissance architecture; here the jewel-like colours of works by Botticelli, Uccello and Piero della

◆ **GOOD FOR** Art lovers and a rainy day in London
◆ **TRANSPORT** Use buses or London Underground
◆ **ACCESS FOR DISABLED PEOPLE** Access is good at all 3 galleries
◆ **BEST TIME TO VISIT** In general, weekday mornings are the quietest. All three galleries are closed on Sunday morning

Francesca are framed by arches of dove-grey stone imported from Tuscany. Leonardo da Vinci's entrancing cartoon *The Virgin and Child with St Anne and St John the Baptist* is now housed in its own darkened room behind bullet-proof glass, following damage caused by a shotgun-wielding malcontent in 1987. Don't miss the Wilton Diptych in Room 53, a richly symbolic portrait of the boy-king Richard II painted by an unknown artist in the fourteenth century, or Jan van Eyck's *Giovanni Arnolfini and his Wife* in Room 56.

In the main building, works familiar through countless reproductions abound. Among the most popular are Rembrandt's two self-portraits, which were painted at the ages of 34 and 63 (Room 27), Constable's *The Hay Wain*, a painting of his father's mill in Suffolk, and two of Turner's late masterpieces, *Rain, Steam and Speed* and *The Fighting Temeraire*. Often overlooked (literally, because they are on the floor) are Boris Anrep's mosaics on the staircases and landings, executed between 1928 and 1952. The one entitled *Awakening of the Muses* depicts

The Merry-Go-Round, *by Mark Gertler, is housed at the Tate Gallery, which is the nations's gallery of British art and museum of modern art*

Virginia Woolf as Clio (Muse of History) and Greta Garbo as Melpomene (Muse of Tragedy).

NATIONAL PORTRAIT GALLERY

(*Charing Cross Underground*)
Just around the corner from the National Gallery, the **National Portrait Gallery*** is a 'Who's Who' of famous British faces through the ages, including monarchs (splendid pictures of Henry VIII and Elizabeth I) and their lovers (Nell Gwynne and the Earls of Leicester and Essex), writers (Shakespeare, Byron and the Brontë sisters), artists (Holbein, Hogarth and Hockney) and scientists (Newton and Brunel). Much fun is to be had from comparing your mental images of these well-known names with their actual appearances.

Elizabeth I, artist unknown, is one of 9,000 portraits in the National Portrait Gallery, dating from Tudor times to the present day

TATE GALLERY

(*Pimlico Underground*)
An element of serendipity is involved in a visit to the **Tate Gallery***, because sections are rehung at regular intervals with a view to showing as much as possible of the huge twentieth-century art collection (by the year 2000 the Bankside Power Station will have been converted into a new branch of the Tate, and the collection will be split into British Art and Modern Art sections). Free plans are available at the entrance.

The British Art collection is represented by Constable, Stubbs, Blake and the Pre-Raphaelite artists Rossetti, Millais and Burne-Jones. The Modern Art exhibition ranges from seminal pieces by Matisse to highly controversial works, such as Carl André's infamous pile of bricks. The meeting point of representational and abstract is found in the Clore Gallery, designed by post-modern architect James Stirling to display works from the Turner Bequest. Traditionalists will have no quarrel with early Turner seascapes and views of the Thames, while followers of the avant-garde may be struck by abstract later works such as *Snow Storm*, which Turner painted after being lashed to a mast of a ship and exposed to the elements for four hours.

London for free (or very little)

A miniature bazaar stall and doll (c.1840) at the Bethnal Green Museum of Childhood

Among the many things you can see in London for next to nothing are puppets, plants, politicians and programmes being made.

MUSEUMS
Museum of Garden History*
(St Mary-at-Lambeth, Lambeth Palace Road, SE1; Waterloo, Lambeth North or Westminster Underground)
Housed in a church next to Lambeth Palace (London home of the Archbishop of Canterbury), this small museum was set up by a group of horticulturally minded volunteers in memory of John Tradescant father (1570–1638) and son (1608–62), renowned plant collectors and gardeners to Charles I. The family is buried beneath an elaborate tomb in the churchyard, where a small knot garden has been created using only plants known in the early seventeenth century. Inside the church, displays chart the changing tastes in garden design and tell the story of other famous gardeners. Ancient gardening implements continue the theme.

♦ **GOOD FOR** Your pocket and the range of things to do
♦ **TRANSPORT** All sights are on bus or Underground routes
♦ **ACCESS FOR DISABLED PEOPLE** Telephone in advance for Museum of Childhood and Bonhams; other locations are accessible to wheelchair users
♦ **BEST TIME TO VISIT** Any time of year, but London is quieter out of season

Bethnal Green Museum of Childhood*
(Cambridge Heath Road, E2; Bethnal Green Underground)
This offshoot of the V&A (see *Great Day Out 44*) contains a huge assortment of toys and games: teddy bears, intricate dolls' houses, trains, toy soldiers, and puppets and dolls from the seventeenth century to the present-day Action Man and Barbie.

The result is a collection that will delight youngsters and induce waves of nostalgia in their parents. A highlight is the section on board games and family entertainments from the pre-television era. The top-floor gallery is devoted to the history of childhood – clothes, nursery furniture and everyday objects, including an eighteenth-century baby walker and a tiny corset made for a Victorian girl, give an insight into child-rearing and care through the ages. The free children's art workshops on Saturdays are popular.

Geffrye Museum*
(Kingsland Road, E2; 15-minute walk from Old Street Underground)
The changing tastes in British interior design are the theme of the delightful Geffrye Museum, housed in an attractive set of almshouses built in 1715 for the Ironmongers Company. A series of living-room settings from different periods starts in the seventeenth century with oak furniture and magnificent panelling, and moves through the refined elegance of Georgian times and an ornate Victorian parlour to twentieth-century art deco and the 1950s. Outside, the grounds include a walled herb garden and a knot garden, the design of which is based on a motif taken from an oak cupboard in the Elizabethan and Jacobean room.

RADIO AND TELEVISION STUDIOS
Being part of an audience for a recording of a radio or television programme is an amusing way of spending an evening. Recordings of light entertainment shows for BBC Radios 2 and 4 – anything from *Just a Minute* to new, alternative comedy – take place most evenings at the Radio Theatre at **Broadcasting House*** in central London *(Oxford Street Underground)*. It is wise to reserve

The Victorian Room at the Geffrye Museum is filled with artefacts from that era

seats; write to BBC Radio Ticket Unit, London W1A 4WW for details of future shows. Sitcoms, quiz shows and other light entertainment TV programmes are recorded at **Television Centre** (*opposite White City Underground*). Write for details well in advance with an s.a.e. to Audience Services, Room 301, Design Building, BBC Television Centre, Wood Lane, London W12 7RJ, or chance your luck for returns at short notice.

To be part of the audience of London Weekend Television (LWT) programmes, send an s.a.e. to Audience Department, LWT, London Television Centre, Upper Ground, London SE1 9LT. For the most popular programmes, such as *Blind Date*, there is a waiting list.

HOUSES OF PARLIAMENT*
(*Westminster, SW1; Westminster Underground*)
Take a seat in the Strangers' Gallery at the House of Commons and watch Members of Parliament debate the issues of the day. Members of the public are allowed into the gallery while the House sits – usually 2.30–10pm or later on Mondays to Thursdays, 9.30am–3pm on Fridays, and on Wednesday mornings. Afternoons are busiest, particularly during Prime Minister's Question Time on Tuesdays and Thursdays, when you may have to queue for an hour or two for a seat. It is advisable

to write to your MP for tickets as far in advance as possible. Given enough warning, MPs can usually also arrange tours of the Palace of Westminster for their constituents. The address at which to contact MPs is House of Commons, Westminster, London SW1A 0AA.

AUCTION ROOMS
Bonhams* (*Montpelier Street, SW7*); **Christie's*** (*King Street, SW1*); **Phillips*** (*New Bond Street, W1*); **Sotheby's*** (*New Bond Street, W1*). Sales of everything from fine art and antiques to pop memorabilia, model cars and other collectables take place most weekdays at the four large London auction houses. Items are on view for three or four days before each sale. Anyone is welcome to visit the viewing and valuation halls of these auction houses, or watch the drama as the bids rise. There is no dress code – jeans are as acceptable as suits – and the bidding system is such that you do not have to worry about scratching your nose at the wrong moment. To find out about forthcoming auctions, phone the individual auction houses. Some newspapers also carry details.

CONCERT VENUES
Royal Festival Hall*
(*South Bank Centre, SE1; Waterloo Underground*)
Every lunchtime the main foyer of

the Royal Festival Hall is the venue for informal music performances by both up-and-coming and established artists. All musical styles are covered: a typical week's programme might include Latin jazz, American dance music and Renaissance choral works. An added bonus are the art exhibitions dotted around the foyer area. Details of free concerts are listed in the Festival Hall's monthly diary of events; alternatively you could phone the box office.

Other London venues with free concerts include the **Barbican** (its Sunday lunchtime jazz sessions are popular) and the **National Theatre**, where theatre-goers are entertained with live music before each performance. (For more about the South Bank, see *Great Day Out 43*.)

NO. 11 BUS
Not strictly free, but a bargain if you have a travel pass for the Underground and buses, is the No. 11 bus, which travels between Liverpool Street station and Fulham, passing or stopping off at many of London's top sights along the way. These include St Paul's Cathedral, the National Gallery and National Portrait Gallery (alight at Trafalgar Square), Downing Street and Horse Guards on Whitehall, the Houses of Parliament and Westminster Abbey, and the trendy clothes shops along the Kings Road. You can hop on and off all day, devising your own tailor-made tour of the capital.

A walk through the City of London

An autumnal glimpse into the collegiate setting of Lincoln's Inn

Founded by the Romans as Londinium, the area of London now known as the City is a patchwork of medieval churches and markets, Dickensian alleyways and high-tech financial institutions.

On weekdays the City bustles with workers, whether brokers employed in the financial markets, barristers hurrying between the law courts and their chambers, or porters in blood-stained aprons drinking in the pubs after a night's work in Smithfield meat market. All this activity adds to the appeal of an area that is full of fascinating buildings and places of historical interest. But with the exception of St Paul's Cathedral the City can be as quiet as a ghost town at weekends.

First make your way by tube to Holborn, and turn right out of the station into High Holborn. Take the second alley right, Little Turnstile, into Lincoln's Inn Fields. At Nos. 12 and 13 is **Sir John Soane's Museum*** (see *Great Day Out 49*). Look for the entrance to Lincoln's Inn at the bottom of the square on the left (if the gate is closed, go straight on and turn left in Carey Street, past the Seven Stars pub, haunt of lawyers).

- ♦ **GOOD FOR** Anyone interested in London's diverse history will enjoy the walk
- ♦ **TRANSPORT** Tube stations and bus connections at start and finish of walk
- ♦ **ACCESS FOR DISABLED PEOPLE** Wheelchair users will need help
- ♦ **BEST TIME TO VISIT** Weekdays for both the business bustle of the City and opening times of sights; the **tourist information office*** can supply more details

Walk through the gate into New Square, shaded by huge plane trees and lined with Georgian brick buildings. Just beyond the war memorial, head slightly left to visit the fine chapel, built in 1623. Back in New Square, turn left (south) to leave via the archway where the windows of Wildy & Sons, the legal booksellers, are enlivened by cartoons. The arch brings you out to Carey Street, once site of the bankruptcy courts (Carey was corrupted to Queer – hence 'to be in Queer Street', meaning to be in debt).

Turn left, admiring the view ahead of the **Public Record Office***, a fine Victorian building in the ornate Perpendicular Gothic style. A small museum inside exhibits the Domesday Book and Shakespeare's will, among other choice items. The second left, Chancery Lane, leads past the fifteenth-century Old Gatehouse to Lincoln's Inn. Just beyond this, turn right at Southampton Buildings, past the London Silver Vaults (base of antique dealers specialising in silver, plate and jewellery). At the end of the short street, go through gates into a rose garden, where a path bends to the left into Staple Inn. Pass through the courtyard and out through the gatehouse (a notice forbids entry to 'Old Clothes Men' and 'Rude Children') and look back. Built in 1545 as a hostel for wool merchants, this imposing timber-framed building is one of the few to have survived the Great Fire of 1666.

Bear right and cross High Holborn to the vast Prudential building. The next left will take you to Leather Lane, with its weekday street market. Hatton Garden, the next street left, leads to an area noted for its many jewellers and diamond merchants. Cross this street and bear left down Charterhouse Street. Walk all the way along (crossing Farringdon Road), past Smithfield meat market, a splendid Italianate building of 1857. Heading into Charterhouse Square, you will pass the Fox and Anchor pub, known for its hearty breakfasts and art nouveau tilework. The square is named after the medieval Charterhouse on the left, founded in 1084 and converted to Charterhouse School after the Reformation.

Go right in the square, down narrow Hayne Street, through the alley by the Olde Red Cow pub into Cloth Fair (excellent beer and pub food at the Hand and Shears on the left). Turn right in this characterful street, where John Betjeman once lived. Opposite is the Romanesque church of St Bartholomew the Great, burial place of Rahere, Henry I's court jester, who founded St Bartholomew's hospital in 1123. Walk through the churchyard and turn right, beneath a half-timbered pre-Great Fire gatehouse, to see the buildings of this famous hospital.

At the gatehouse turn left into Little Britain, walking down to the imposing General Post Office (GPO) headquarters on the right, home to the **National Postal Museum***. This is a good point at which to divert if you want to visit Wren's magnificent **St Paul's Cathedral***. Opposite the GPO is the charming Postman's Park. Walk through, noting the art nouveau tile memorials to ordinary people who have committed heroic deeds. Now turn left to visit the outstanding **Museum of London***, devoted to the City and its long history. Alternatively, turn right, then first left into Gresham Street and walk all the way up to the **Guildhall***, built in 1411 as the headquarters of the trade guilds which once controlled all the City's business. The main hall (open to the public) is where Lord Mayors are installed. Continue up Gresham Street to the fortress-like bulk of the Bank of England, designed by Sir John Soane to symbolise rock-solid dependability.

Smithfield meat market operates at night; most activity is over by 8am

Keep the Bank building on your right as you walk up Lothbury, with a view ahead of the Stock Exchange building and the NatWest Tower. Take Barth Lane right to find the **Bank of England Museum***, then continue into Threadneedle Street and right to Bank. On the left, the Royal Exchange (1843) is a temple to commerce, and the similar building on the southern side of the square is the Mansion House, the official residence of the Lord Mayor of London.

From the front of the Royal Exchange, walk left all the way down Cornhill. Cross Gracechurch Street into Leadenhall Street, and take the first right into Leadenhall Market, a graceful Victorian shopping arcade full of impressive food stalls. In the middle of the market, turn left to see the Lloyd's building (1986), a daring construction of glass and steel.

Turn right in Lime Street, out and across busy Fenchurch Street, across Eastcheap, right then first left. This takes you to the **Monument***, completed in 1677 as a memorial to the Great Fire. Climb to the top for views towards St Paul's in the west and the Tower of London in the east.

LUNCHBOX
Numerous pubs and sandwich bars on weekdays; few places open at weekends.

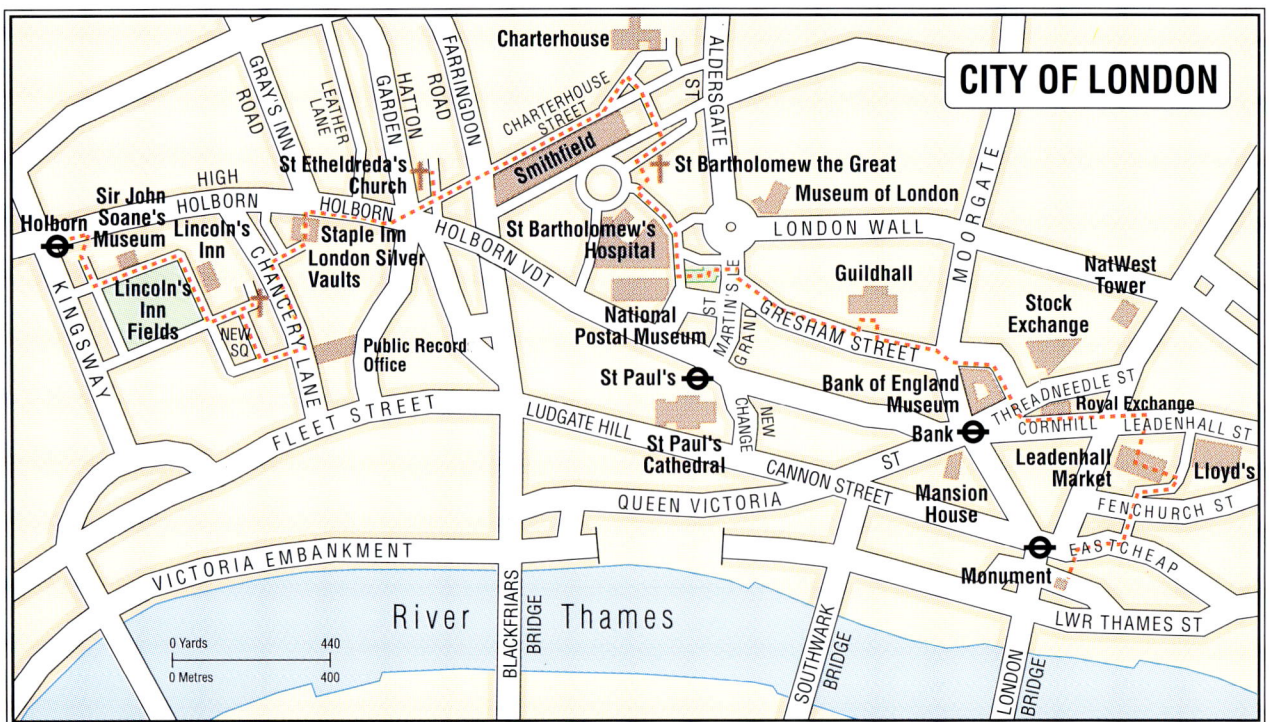

CITY OF LONDON

Charterhouse
GRAY'S INN ROAD
LEATHER LANE
HATTON GARDEN
FARRINGDON ROAD
CHARTERHOUSE STREET
Smithfield
ALDERSGATE ST
St Bartholomew the Great
Museum of London
MOORGATE
St Etheldreda's Church
HIGH HOLBORN
HOLBORN
Sir John Soane's Museum
Lincoln's Inn
Staple Inn
London Silver Vaults
HOLBORN
HOLBORN VDT
St Bartholomew's Hospital
LONDON WALL
Guildhall
NatWest Tower
Holborn
KINGSWAY
Lincoln's Inn Fields
CHANCERY LANE
NEW SQ
Public Record Office
National Postal Museum
GRESHAM STREET
Stock Exchange
ST MARTIN'S LE GRAND
St Paul's
CHANGE
NEW ST
Bank of England Museum
THREADNEEDLE ST
Royal Exchange
CORNHILL
LEADENHALL ST
FLEET STREET
LUDGATE HILL
St Paul's Cathedral
CANNON STREET
Bank
Leadenhall Market
Lloyd's
FENCHURCH ST
QUEEN VICTORIA
Mansion House
EASTCHEAP
VICTORIA EMBANKMENT
Monument
BLACKFRIARS BRIDGE
River Thames
SOUTHWARK BRIDGE
LONDON BRIDGE
LWR THAMES ST

0 Yards 440
0 Metres 400

South-west London's great houses

The Central Dome and West Wing of the Great Conservatory at Syon Park

Visiting the stately homes and gardens on the south-western fringe of London is an ideal way of escaping the metropolis for a breath of country air without having to travel very far.

Syon Park, with its house, gardens, steam railway and butterfly house, is a day out in itself (open daily year round). Alternatively, you could combine the Palladian splendours of Chiswick House (but see box for opening times) with the Adam interiors at Osterley. Jacobean Ham House (see box) could be taken in as part of a stroll along the Thames footpath from the 'villages' of Richmond or Twickenham.

SYON PARK*

(Gunnersbury Underground and bus 237 or 267; entry by car from Park Road)
Syon started life as a monastery, which Henry VIII seized at the Dissolution; he gave it to the Duke of Somerset, who ended up on the scaffold, as did several other people associated with the house, such as Catherine Howard, the king's fifth wife, and Lady Jane Grey. The estate passed to the Dukes (later Earls) of

♦ **GOOD FOR** Easy access from London means any one of these houses provides a welcome break from the bustle of the city
♦ **TRANSPORT** All the houses are easily reached by public transport
♦ **ACCESS FOR DISABLED PEOPLE** Access is good at Syon Park
♦ **BEST TIME TO VISIT** Syon House, Osterley Park and Chiswick House are closed Monday, Tuesday and in winter, and Ham House is closed Thursday, Friday and in winter. The summer months attract crowds to all sites.

Northumberland, who were very proud of their ancient lineage; thus, when Robert Adam came to remodel the house for them he was asked to include portrait medallions in the superb Long Gallery, illustrating their lineage back to Charlemagne, from whom they claimed descent. Adam's splendid interiors lend lightness to

the inside of a house that was rather unfortunately refaced in the late-nineteenth century, which left it with a dour exterior.

Capability Brown was hired to landscape the extensive grounds in 1767–73, and garden-lovers will be drawn to the magnificent rose beds, as well as the drifts of spring bulbs in and around the stately oaks and cedars planted by Brown. Banks of colourful rhododendrons flower in June, followed by massed hydrangeas, and the margins of the lake are planted with gigantic gunneras and other moisture-loving plants. A focal point of the garden is the Great Conservatory, designed during the years 1820–7 by Charles Fowler (the architect of Covent Garden market) and a major influence on Joseph Paxton's design for the famous Crystal Palace that housed the Great Exhibition of 1851. The domed Conservatory, with its two side wings, houses rare and exotic plants, and the raised demonstration beds outside are designed for wheelchair users to enjoy.

Nearby is a big, well-stocked garden centre and the restaurant. Children will enjoy the butterfly house, full of colourful tropical species, with an annexe full of insects and reptiles, including cockroaches, tarantulas and iguanas. There is also a miniature steam railway, but this runs only at weekends.

OSTERLEY PARK*

(Osterley Underground)
Though Osterley Park (NT) is open all year round, the house opening times are restricted. The exterior, with its Tudor brick turrets, looks as it did when the house was first built for Sir Thomas Gresham (1519–79), the fabulously wealthy merchant and founder of London's Royal Exchange. A later owner, Sir Francis Child, founder of Child's Bank, lived

elsewhere and used the house, with its capacious vaults, for storing large quantities of money. His grandsons, Francis and Robert Child, decided to take the house in hand in 1761 and employed Robert Adam to rework the interiors. The result is a perfectly preserved exemplar of the neo-classical style then in vogue, with tapestries, chairs and wallpapers influenced by Chinese, Egyptian, Grecian and Etruscan art. The result is not to everyone's taste (Horace Walpole thought it 'too theatric' and compared the style unfavourably to a Wedgwood vase). The grounds, landscaped at the same time, are full of stately trees and paths that meander round the heron-dotted shores of the lakes.

HAM HOUSE*

(*Underground or train to Richmond station, then walk 1½ miles along a well-signposted path that follows the Thames upstream, or train to Twickenham station and walk via Church Street and Riverside to the foot ferry that crosses to Ham House close to Eel Pie Island*)
Ham House was built in 1610 by the first Earl of Dysart, who was given the estate as his reward for being Charles I's childhood companion and whipping boy, taking the punishments meted out to the king when he misbehaved. The Earl escaped

The sweeping staircase leading to the entrance of Osterley Park, built by Sir Thomas Gresham

following the king to the scaffold, perhaps because his daughter, Elizabeth, was Oliver Cromwell's mistress. Elizabeth later married the Duke of Lauderdale and it was she who enlarged and refurnished Ham House in the 1670s.

In contrast to the cool elegance of Robert Adam's Osterley and Syon, this house is wonderfully ostentatious, full of ornate wood carvings and plasterwork and hung with costly tapestries. Such extravagance left subsequent generations almost penniless, so the house remained untouched – like Sleeping Beauty's castle, according to Horace Walpole – as a rare example

of Restoration taste, beautifully restored by the National Trust. The gardens are also being returned to their original splendour. The Orangery restaurant is open, and picnics are allowed in the Rose Garden.

CHISWICK HOUSE*

(*Chiswick Park or Turnham Green Underground, then walk for ½ mile, or take bus 190 and 290 or train to Chiswick station, then a five-minute walk*).
Though the Great West Road thunders not far away, Chiswick House, set in its fine Italianate gardens, is in another world. Lord Burlington, patron of the arts and an accomplished architect in his own right, built the house as a rural retreat in 1725–9. Inspired by Palladio's Villa Capra, near Vicenza in northern Italy, the house was a fitting showcase for Burlington's fine library and art collection.

As you approach the impressive pillared entrance, note the carvings; they, like the stone from which the villa is built, are enhanced by bright sunlight, which also reveals the gardens at their classical best.

More of the history of the building is coming to light as a result of comprehensive restoration, and the ground-floor rooms contain an exhibition, with video, on the life and times of Lord Burlington. The principal rooms are on the upper floor, which is richly decorated with ceiling paintings of scantily clad cherubs and classical deities by William Kent.

Kent also remodelled the gardens, creating the small lake (the prototype of the Serpentine, in Hyde Park), which is crossed by James Wyatt's elegant stone bridge.

In Chiswick itself, there is a delightful riverside stroll along Chiswick Mall, lined with fine eighteenth-century houses and several notable pubs, such as the Dove Inn (where Charles II and Nell Gwynn used to meet for secret rendezvous), the Old Ship, the Blue Anchor and the Black Lion.

Ham House, an important seventeenth-century house in beautiful grounds

London's hidden art treasures

A Bar at the Folies-Bergère *1881–2, by Edouard Manet (1832–83)*

You don't have to fight your way through the crowds at the National Gallery or the Tate to see great art in London. Some of the greatest works of art in London are in less famous museums and galleries.

Highlighted here are some outstanding collections in nine museums and galleries well off the tourist track. Whether you prefer Impressionists to Old Masters, or Pre-Raphaelites to seascapes, you can combine those that most appeal to you to make an uplifting day out.

♦ **GOOD FOR** Rainy and out-of-season visits – but phone individual galleries for opening times
♦ **TRANSPORT** The furthest sight is about 8 miles from central London; public transport is easier than driving and parking
♦ **ACCESS FOR DISABLED PEOPLE** Phone individual galleries for access details
♦ **BEST TIME TO VISIT** Year round

COURTAULD INSTITUTE GALLERIES*

(The Strand, London WC2; Temple / Covent Garden Underground)
Since its move from the old, cramped exhibition rooms in Bloomsbury to the impressive halls of Somerset House on the Strand, the Courtauld Collection has taken on a new lease of life. The new galleries are dominated by a remarkable collection of Impressionist and Post-Impressionist works. Among these are seminal works by Degas (*Woman Drying Herself*); Renoir (*La Loge*); Manet (*A Bar at the Folies-Bergère*); Pissarro (*Penge Station*); Van Gogh (*Self-portrait with Bandaged Ear* and *Peach Trees in Blossom*); Gauguin (*Nevermore*); Cézanne (*Route Tournante*); and Monet (*Autumn at Argenteuil*). Some Old Masters are also represented, including Botticelli, Bellini, Rubens, Tiepolo and Veronese.
♦ Refreshments in the basement cafeteria

SIR JOHN SOANE'S MUSEUM*

(13 Lincoln's Inn Fields, WC2; Holborn Underground)
Soane (1753–1837) – one-time architect to the Bank of England, and designer of Dulwich College Picture Gallery (see below) – was something of an eccentric; his house in Lincoln's Inn Fields has been preserved virtually as he left it, and it reflects his eclectic and highly individual taste. Among the huge collection of architects' drawings, books and antiquities are some excellent paintings. Most important are two series by Hogarth: *The Rake's Progress*, charting the downfall of a gentleman, and *The Election*, a satire on political corruption. Three views by Canaletto have recently been restored, and among numerous other works there are paintings by Watteau (*Les Noces*), Turner (*Refectory of Kirkstall Abbey*) and Reynolds (*Love and Beauty*).
♦ No refreshments

THE WALLACE COLLECTION*

(Hertford House, Manchester Square, W1; Bond Street Underground)
A few examples from just one room underline the extraordinary quality of the paintings in the Wallace Collection, which was largely compiled by Lord Hertford during the nineteenth century. Room 22 houses Frans Hals' best-known work, *The Laughing Cavalier*; the Velasquez masterpiece *A Lady with a Fan*, three Rembrandt portraits, and four by Van Dyck; *Rainbow Landscape*, a rare painting by Rubens of the countryside around his home and perhaps his greatest landscape; an unusual and striking mythological scene by Titian, *Perseus and Andromeda*; and several other important paintings by Poussin, Andrea del Sarto and Murillo. Throughout the other 24 galleries and rooms are some of Boucher's finest works, paintings by Canaletto, Guardi and Bronzino, and a strong collection of seventeenth-century Dutch paintings.
♦ No refreshments

WELLINGTON MUSEUM*

(Apsley House, Hyde Park Corner, W1; Hyde Park Corner Underground)
The Duke of Wellington's former home houses paintings from two sources – his own gifts and

purchases, and those captured from Napoleon's brother Joseph on the battlefield and later presented to Wellington by the Spanish king. The result is a fine collection, strong in Spanish and Flemish paintings. Highlights to look out for include the huge marble statue of a nude Napoleon by Canova (Napoleon didn't like it); Correggio's *Agony in the Garden*, one of the Duke's favourite paintings; some lively canvases by Jan Steen including *A Wedding Party* and *The Dissolute Household*; and Velasquez's *Waterseller of Seville* and *A Spanish Gentleman*.
♦ No refreshments

Sir John Soane Museum, London / Bridgeman Art Library, London

The Election III The Polling, *1754–5, by William Hogarth (1697–1764)*

THE BANQUETING HOUSE*
(*Whitehall, SW1; Embankment / Westminster Undergrounds*)
Inigo Jones was commissioned by Charles I to rebuild the Whitehall Banqueting House after it burnt down in 1619. Architecturally, it was of great importance, but it is the superb painted ceiling undertaken by Rubens which makes it an unmissable part of London's artistic heritage. Charles paid Rubens £3,000 for the works which celebrate the reign of his father James I, and they are generally recognised as the finest ceiling paintings in Britain. A video presentation in the undercroft and an audio tour are included in the admission price.
♦ No refreshments

WILLIAM MORRIS GALLERY*
(*Lloyd Park, Forest Road, E17; Walthamstow Underground*)
Most of this collection, housed in Morris's childhood home in Walthamstow, comprises examples of his craft work and designs – including tapestries, stained glass, wallpapers and textiles. But there are also several fine paintings and sketches by some of the leading Pre-Raphaelites. Choice examples are Rossetti's cartoons for the stained-glass at St

Martin's Church in Scarborough, *The Parable of the Vineyard*; and several watercolours by Burne-Jones. Look out also for the sketch of Rouen Cathedral by John Ruskin.
♦ No refreshments

DULWICH PICTURE GALLERY* (*College Road, SE21; West Dulwich BR station*)
The Dulwich collection rivals the Courtauld and Wallace galleries for the quality of its paintings. Founded in 1811 and designed by Sir John Soane, it is Britain's oldest purpose-built gallery. The collection contains some remarkable works, among them Rembrandt's *Girl at a Window*; important works by Poussin and Claude, Rubens, Van Dyke and Murillo; Watteau's dreamy *Le Bal Champêtre*; and works by Hogarth, Gainsborough and Reynolds are among the eighteenth-century paintings. The earliest painting is *Portrait of a Young Man* by Piero di Cosimo.
♦ Refreshments from cafés and restaurants in nearby Dulwich Village

THE IVEAGH BEQUEST*
(*Kenwood, Hampstead, NW3; 210 bus from Golders Green or Archway Underground*)
As with the National Maritime Museum at Greenwich (see below), a trip to Kenwood could be a day out in itself. The Earl of Iveagh's collection is housed in his elegant eighteenth-century house (partly designed by Adam), set in rolling

parkland on the edge of Hampstead Heath – a great place for a picnic or an afternoon's walk, and with open-air concerts on many summer evenings. The bulk of the collection is of the English school, including important works by Van Dyck, Gainsborough, Reynolds and Turner. The two great masterpieces are Rembrandt's self-portrait of 1663 and *The Guitar Player* by Vermeer, painted in about 1672. An interesting view of seventeenth-century London is provided in Claude de Jongh's *Old London Bridge* of 1630.
♦ Refreshments at the Kenwood cafeteria

NATIONAL MARITIME MUSEUM*
(*Romney Road, Greenwich, SE10; Greenwich / Maze Hill BR stations*)
The art collection of the National Maritime Museum is one of its great strengths – and it doesn't just consist of massive canvases of great sea battles, although the paintings depicting the Spanish Armada, and Turner's great account of Trafalgar, are not to be missed. There are some superb portraits, of Henry VIII, Elizabeth I and Drake, as well as works by Hogarth and Reynolds, and the famous view of Greenwich by Canaletto. The museum is also strong on works from the voyages of Captain Cook. Zoffany's *Death of Cook* is the best-known, but the paintings of William Hodges depicting Tahiti, New Zealand and Easter Island are fascinating visual documents of the eighteenth-century discoveries.
♦ Refreshments at the Bosun's Whistle Restaurant

Note that most collections rotate the paintings on display, or send them on temporary loan to other galleries, so it is best to phone beforehand if you want to see a particular work.

The essence of royal and aristocratic Englishness

English monarchs have lived and been buried at Windsor Castle for 900 years

♦ **GOOD FOR** Those with an interest in heritage and history
♦ **TRANSPORT** The nearest BR stations to Windsor Castle are Windsor and Eton Riverside, and Windsor Central; the nearest one to Dorney Court and Cliveden is Taplow
♦ **ACCESS FOR DISABLED PEOPLE** Access is good at Windsor Castle
♦ **BEST TIME TO VISIT** All year round, but ring ahead if you are visiting Windsor Castle as parts may well close at short notice if the Queen is in residence

The influence of Britain's monarchs may have diminished through time but the history and heritage associated with them still provide some of the most fascinating sights and stories in the land.

From the grandiose apartments of Windsor Castle to the stately gardens of Cliveden and Dorney Court, royal and aristocratic associations abound in this wealthy part of England. Here we describe some of the foremost attractions; see also *Great Day Out 51*.

WINDSOR CASTLE*

Any tour of this region – some say of the whole United Kingdom – would be incomplete without a visit to the magnificent precincts of Windsor Castle. Planned by William the Conqueror as the first of several fortresses that would form a defensive ring around London, the castle has been home to many kings and queens,

each of whom has left an idiosyncratic architectural mark. The best place to start is in the State Apartments, the opulently furnished rooms in which royalty has feasted for nine centuries. Since the fire of 1992, however, two of the rooms have been closed for restoration until 1998 or so.

The lavish furnishing of royal residences is neatly illustrated at the entrance to the State Apartments, where the exquisite **Queen Mary's Dolls' House** provides a tour-in-miniature of an eighteenth-century country house. From the dolls' house the visitor enters the castle proper up a sweeping Gothic staircase to the apartments – a series of huge reception and dining rooms hung

with magnificent paintings; the suggested route continues to Charles II's bedroom and private chambers, through to the baroque King's Dining Room.

From the state apartments the recommended route passes back to the castle's Lower Ward, where at 11am (not every day; ring the **tourist information office*** to check) visitors can watch the Changing of the Guard, which is accompanied by a cacophony of clashing cymbals, bawled orders and perfectly synchronised bootsteps.

On the northern side of Lower Ward is the entrance to **St George's Chapel**. In June, the chapel is the setting for one of the most spectacular of the nation's state ceremonies, when the Queen invests new Knights of the Garter to the ancient order.

Throughout the summer there is a host of colourful events at Windsor: marching bands, Sunday concerts and exhibitions from the immense Royal Collection. However, opening arrangements are subject to change at short notice. St George's is closed for Sunday services until 2pm. For up-to-date opening times, there is a **24-hour information line***.

WINDSOR

Elsewhere in the town there are some charming fifteenth-century buildings, although most have now become twee tea rooms and souvenir shops. Two buildings worth a visit are the St Albans Street **home of Nell Gwynn**, one of Charles II's mistresses, which is reputedly connected to the castle by tunnel, and the **Guild Hall** built by Sir Christopher Wren. At the **Crown Jewels Museum*** on Peascod Street is Windsor's latest attraction – a permanent exhibition of replica royal regalia from 15 different countries, worth £4 million.

ETON AND ETON COLLEGE*

For a different type of encounter with aristocratic England cross over the Thames to Eton, where the souvenir shops are replaced by art galleries and antique shops. The stretch of river dividing Windsor and Eton is an ideal place to rest on fine days, with a series of riverside restaurants and willow-lined walks, cruise boats plying the river, and **rowing boats for hire***.

Eton's main attraction, however, is the fifteenth-century college that has produced no fewer than 20 Prime Ministers, and now numbers a future king among its students.

The college offers interesting tours out of term-time, usually given by a member of staff, but if you do not have much time it is still worth visiting the famous chapel. From there, it is a short walk across the quadrangle – where the famous 'quad race' in *Chariots of Fire* was filmed – to the ancient courtyards and cloisters of inner Eton. Off one corner of the quadrangle is the **Museum of Eton Life**, which offers a foray into the college's illustrious history, from Wall Games and Eton Fives to the more dubious subjects of fags and flogging blocks.

DORNEY COURT*

From Eton, it is a three-mile drive west to Dorney Court, a red-brick Tudor house regarded by many as England's finest medieval manor. Built in 1440, Dorney

One of many grand views of Sir Charles Barry's gracious house, Cliveden

Court has been passed down through 13 generations of the Palmer family, who count among their blue-blooded ancestors Barbara Palmer, who was the Countess of Castlemaine and another of Charles II's mistresses.

The interior of the house is as distinguished as its own history. In musty, wood-panelled rooms with bowing ceilings old family portraits hang above handsome fifteenth-century oak furniture. The present generation is continuing to renovate the house, and today charges an admission fee to aid the cause. There is also a charming tea room behind the house, and from early June to late August you can pick a wide variety of fruit and vegetables from the gardens, with 10 per cent discounts for visitors to the house.

CLIVEDEN*

A short drive up the A4, three miles north of Maidenhead, brings you to another bastion of the English aristocracy. Set on wooded cliffs 200 feet above the Thames, this beautiful Italianate villa was home in the nineteenth century to

Lupton's Tower (1520) in School Yard, Eton College's main quadrangle

Frederick, Prince of Wales; it achieved notoriety in the 1960s as the setting for the indiscretions that led to the government-rocking Profumo Affair. The villa is now a luxury hotel but, thanks to the National Trust, the 375 acres of pristine gardens and ancient woodland remain open to non-residents. About half the park is formal garden, and all sections are within a half-hour stroll of the main car park north of the house.

Just east of the car park is the Water Garden, where Chinese carp cruise around a lakeside pagoda. North of the house, beside the opulent marble statue 'The Fountain of Love', designed for the first Lord Astor, is the Long Garden with elegantly sculpted hedgerows flanked by Italian statues. Nearer the house, the Rose Garden blends blossom and stone in equally classical surroundings.

The house itself is fronted by eight marble sarcophagi, some of which date from AD230. From here the non-resident must follow the path to the left of the house into the Duke's Garden, where the giant numbers '1668' commemorate a duel between the Duke of Buckingham and the Earl of Shrewsbury, whose wife had become the duke's mistress. From the terrace above are sweeping views over the magnificent parterre, the woodland and the river beyond.

If you have more time, the thick woodland provides a variety of inspiring walks. Sights of natural interest include the country's largest tree section, including a Californian redwood brought to Cliveden by the first Lord Astor, and a wide range of wildlife, including deer, badgers and Chinese ducks, the only species of duck that nests in trees.

LUNCHBOX

Windsor and Eton are full of pleasant pubs, cafés and picnic spots, especially along the riverbank. Monty's and the Sir Christopher Wren's House Hotel serve good lunches and traditional teas overlooking the main bridge between the two towns. Dorney Court has its own tea room while at Cliveden there is a 50-table restaurant beside the main house, which caters for non-residents from April to October, Wednesdays to Sundays, 11am to 5pm.

Three famous towns on the upper Thames

Emulate Jerome K. Jerome's Three Men in a Boat *by enjoying a lazy day out on the Thames; you can hire boats at Cookham, Marlow or Henley, take a river cruise or just stroll along the willow-fringed towpaths, with views of fine waterside buildings.*

> Henley, on a long straight stretch of the Thames, was the scene of the first university boat race in 1829

COOKHAM

Cookham is strongly associated with Stanley Spencer, the eccentric artist who spent much of his time here wheeling his canvases, easels and paints around in a battered perambulator. The pram is now on show in the tiny **Stanley Spencer Gallery*** housed in the former Wesleyan chapel at the eastern end of the high street. The displays in the gallery change regularly, although there are one or two permanent exhibits; all exemplify Spencer's predilection for depicting biblical events in a modern setting, as often as not in Cookham or one of the nearby villages.

From the gallery it is a short stroll to the parish **church** where Spencer has a memorial. At the church gate, the life-size stone angel on top of George Pendall's grave is familiar to lovers of Spencer's work as the subject of one of his best-known paintings. The church contains one or two fine memorials, including the brass to Robert Peche, who enjoyed the splendid title of Master Clerk of the Spicery to Henry VI.

From the church head for the river by turning left (along a very narrow path), then down some steps signposted as a public footpath on the left just before the bridge. This leads to the riverbank, where a ferry service operates on weekday

♦ **GOOD FOR** Walking and boat trips
♦ **TRANSPORT** A car is necessary to get from town to town
♦ **ACCESS FOR DISABLED PEOPLE** Access is possible at the Stanley Spencer Gallery
♦ **BEST TIME TO VISIT** All year; spring and autumn are delightful because of the colours of the Chiltern beechwoods. Stanley Spencer Gallery is open all year, but weekends only end Oct to Easter

afternoons linking Cookham with Marlow and Medmenham (leaves Cookham 3pm and returns at 6.30pm). The path continues through a park, where numerous leisure boats are moored; turn right at the end of the park to walk along a surfaced road leading to **Cookham Moor** and the western end of Cookham High Street. Pubs and restaurants abound, and several shops sell fashions, antiques and crafts.

From Cookham, the road due east passes through Cookham Dean to a wooded escarpment with extensive views over the Thames to Marlow. However, the A404 dual carriageway intrudes on the view. The road then drops quickly to the valley and leads across Marlow's fine bridge. To park, turn left at the first roundabout and follow signs for the Pound Lane car park.

MARLOW

Alongside the car park is the **tourist information office***, where you can pick up walk leaflets and town guides. To reach the river turn left, skirting the cricket pitch. At the towpath, turn left and walk for a mile or so through open countryside to take a look at the splendid riverside houses on the opposite bank. The white tower of Bisham church is the landmark to aim for. Just beyond the church is **Bisham Abbey**, a Tudor house built round the remains of the twelfth-century monastery.

Retracing your steps, you will find a fine view of Marlow's stately **bridge**, built in 1832 to the designs of Tierney Clarke, who built a similar bridge linking Buda and Pest in the Hungarian capital. Just before the bridge is the fine Georgian house, now the leisure centre, built in 1760 by the distinguished Dr Battie, who specialised in treating lunatics, hence the adjective 'batty'.

On the opposite side of the river is a luxury hotel, the **Compleat Angler**; one section is the original inn, founded in the sixteenth century. Rowing boats can be hired from this spot, and it is the embarkation point for 40-minute river trips that depart on the hour throughout the day (spring and summer only).

Head up the steps by the bridge and cross to look at the yellow brick church of **All Saints**, rebuilt in the nineteenth century because the river had undermined the foundations of the old church. Inside are several memorials of interest, including one high on the wall in the porch commemorating Sir Miles Hobart, the local MP who died in an accident in 1632 when his coach crashed on Ludgate Hill in the City of London.

Follow the churchyard path to the right to the Two Brewers pub, then take the path between high brick walls to the right of the pub. When you emerge in a lane turn right to return to the riverside at **Marlow Lock**, an attractive spot busy with boats of all kinds and offering fine views of Marlow Bridge. Retrace your steps to the Two Brewers and walk up St Peter Street for some of Marlow's finest medieval and Georgian houses, then turn left into Station Road to return to the high

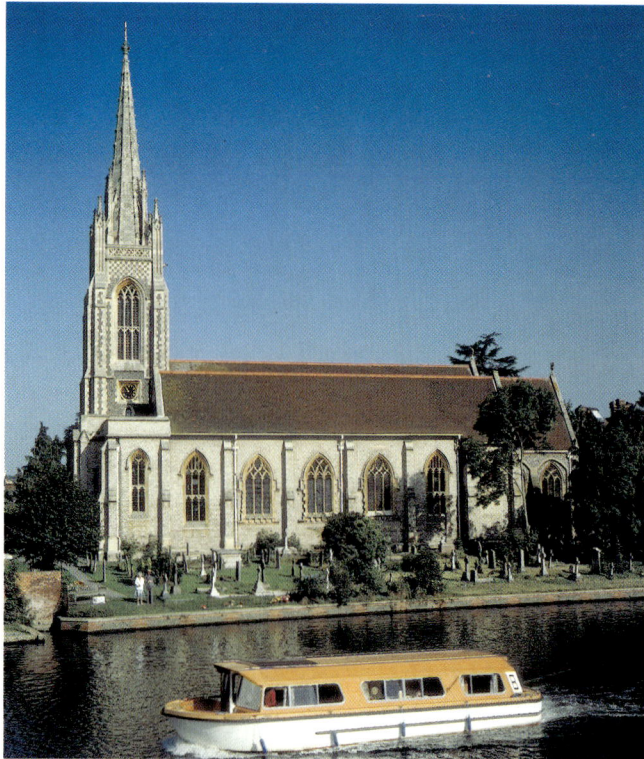

Marlow, Henley's more sedate neighbour, was once home to Shelley, T.S. Eliot and George II prior to his coronation

street and the car park. Marlow high street offers several up-market restaurants, or you can sample locally brewed Brakspear's beer over bar snacks at the Chequers.

The road to Henley passes through woodland to **Medmenham**, where the notorious Hellfire Club used to hold orgies in the mid-eighteenth century, now the site of a research centre. In Henley, try to park in the large car park behind Waitrose, off the Market Place.

HENLEY-ON-THAMES

The most prominent building in the market place is the **Town Hall**, a graceful neo-classical building (housing the **tourist information office***, closed during the winter) that faces downhill to a prosperous-looking group of eighteenth-century town houses. Many of them now serve as shops selling *haute couture* clothes and delicatessen provisions to those who flock for the summer regatta (held since 1839 in the first week in July).

The river lies at the opposite end from the market place, past the parish church at the end of Hart Street. Henley's **bridge** is an elegant stone structure with classical masks depicting the rivers Thames and Isis over the central arches. To the right, over the bridge, is the post-modernist boathouse that serves as the regatta headquarters, while the regatta course itself is the broad, straight sweep of river to the left of the bridge. Head right, before the bridge, if you want to hire rowing boats or perhaps take a stroll along the riverside out to Mill Meadows, the town gardens and on to wilder Marsh Meadows beyond.

Greys Court*, two and a half miles north-west of Marlow and three miles west of Henley, is owned by the National Trust and well worth a visit. A romantic garden has been created around the ruins of the Tudor tithe barn and other farm buildings, with an extensive walled garden full of fruit espaliers and vegetable gardens. A surprising survival is the massive donkey-wheel, a sixteenth-century 19-foot timber treadmill that was used to draw water up from a 200-foot well, supplying water to the house right up until 1914.

LUNCHBOX
Each village has a range of pubs and tea rooms to choose from. The tea room at Greys Court serves home-made cakes and is well up to the usual National Trust standard.

Henley Regatta plays host to serious sportsmen and revellers alike

Romans, roses, royalty – and a fine abbey

The ceiling of the Great Crossing Tower in the Cathedral and Abbey Church of St Alban

With a rich legacy from its Roman past and its vast medieval abbey, St Albans has a compelling charm. Visits just outside the city to a formal rose garden, a children's farm and one of Britain's most stately homes make for a varied day out.

One way of organising your day to see all that St Albans and its environs have to offer is to visit the abbey and the museum in the morning, and Hatfield House, the farm and the garden in the afternoon. Start your day at the site of former Roman excavations, which have been transformed into **Verulamium Park**, a lovely open space with trees, lake and waterbirds, and traversed by the pretty River Ver. The only extant relics of the Roman city of Verulamium are here — fragments of wall and a hypocaust (heating system) of a Roman house. The **Roman Theatre***, set among ploughed fields, is the only one in Britain. From the back of the grassy amphitheatre, visitors can look down on the stage, dressing room and arena.

♦ **GOOD FOR** Visiting attractions from different periods of history; children will enjoy the realism of the Verulamium Museum and the informality of Bowman's Open Farm

♦ **TRANSPORT** St Albans is very well connected by road (just off the M1, around 20 miles north of London) and rail (there are good connections to St Albans and Abbey stations). An all-day ticket for the St Albans Trail Bus (S1) from either St Albans or Abbey stations will enable you to visit all the sights within the city itself. Parking may be difficult on Wednesdays and Saturdays (market days)

♦ **ACCESS FOR DISABLED PEOPLE** Good to most sights, including Hatfield House (small wheelchairs only) and abbey

♦ **BEST TIME TO VISIT** Summer for Hatfield and the Rose Gardens, all year for other places

The **Verulamium Museum*** concentrates on the 400-year period of Roman occupation and ingeniously exhibits its outstanding archaeological finds (from leather vests and cooking pots to jewellery and coins) by relating them to such day-to-day activities as playing games, taking baths and doing business. An excellent series of tableaux shows people cooking, writing in wax or painting, surrounded by the excavated objects. Pride of place goes to the lovely mosaics, seemingly as fresh and bright as when they were made. The Romans' view of death is graphically illustrated by open coffins, skeletons and an audio-visual display. Avoid visiting this museum between 10am and 2.30pm in term-time as you may be swamped by schoolchildren.

To reach the **Cathedral and Abbey Church of St Alban***, about a mile away, walk either through the park or along St Michael's Street, perhaps visiting the restored sixteenth-century **Kingsbury Watermill** still pumping away water from the River Ver. Agricultural tools and a milling machine are displayed here. Continuing up Fishpool Street, note the variety of houses — pretty sixteenth-century cottages with tiny windows, grand Georgian mansions and ostentatious Victorian villas.

In AD209 St Alban became Britain's first martyr after being executed for sheltering a Christian priest. A Benedictine abbey was founded in AD793 on the site of the martyrdom by Offa, King of Mercia. In 1077 building began on a more substantial Norman church, using bricks from nearby Verulamium, and continued for about 300 years. The abbey prospered until 1539 when the monastic buildings were destroyed. However, the abbey was sold to the parishioners and much restoration work was carried out in the Victorian period. In 1877 the abbey was renamed a cathedral.

The impressive interior reveals Britain's longest medieval nave, lined by lofty columns. The variety of arch shapes – rounded Norman (some with zigzag patterns), pointed Early English and carved Decorated styles – clearly shows the different architectural periods. Note the paintings in the nave, on some columns and on the panelled ceiling of the Great Crossing Tower. The transepts are the best-preserved parts of the Norman church, and some pillars from Offa's early church are to be found high in the south transept. Behind the altar is an ornate stone screen protecting the tomb of St Alban, set on a carved marble base and covered by a red awning.

Energetic visitors can climb the 90 or so steps of the **Clock Tower***, built in 1410 and one of only two surviving curfew towers in Britain today, for a good view of the abbey and the town. Just opposite is French Row, a group of small timber-framed houses where, reputedly, French prisoners were kept during King John's War with France. Continue into Market Place, where the Georgian Town Hall, facing up St Peter's Street, now houses the **tourist information office***.

The **Museum of St Albans*** in the town centre is devoted to St Albans' post-Roman history. Most of the motley exhibits are of local origin, such as patterned water closet pans, straw trimmings and a £5 note issued by the Bank of St Albans, which functioned between 1830 and 1841. One section displays artefacts illustrating everyday Victorian activities; there is also a comprehensive collection of tools used by blacksmiths, wheelwrights and coopers.

The 1,100-acre **Bowmans Open Farm*** (at London Colney, south-east of St Albans on the A6) grows crops, rears livestock – cows, pigs and sheep – and

There are over 1,700 varieties of roses in the 12-acre Gardens of the Rose

has genuine rural smells. Children can touch and observe at close quarters piglets, chickens and rabbits, and they can follow a short trail to the milking parlour, calf house and grain store.

The **Gardens of the Rose***, the headquarters of the Royal National Rose Society, are a visual and fragrant delight with displays of ancient and modern varieties of roses set in beds amongst well-tended lawns (at Chiswell Green, 3 miles south-west of the city).

Hatfield House*, four miles to the east of St Albans, is a fine Jacobean pile built by Robert Cecil, whose father, William Cecil, was appointed Chief Minister by Elizabeth I. She had spent her childhood in the Old Palace, now in the gardens around the house and of which only the Tudor Banqueting Hall survives.

The huge Marble Hall, two floors high, is the grandest room,

The elaborately painted wooden ceiling of the presbytery at the abbey

with much carved wood and a minstrels' gallery, two famous portraits of Elizabeth I, and fine Brussels tapestries. Throughout the house, one richly furnished room follows another, with decorative plasterwork ceilings, chandeliers, and portraits by Europe's most renowned artists. Despite this, the house has a surprisingly friendly feel, perhaps because so many of the Cecil family's personal belongings are on display – footstools, lockets and fans. Don't miss Elizabeth I's gloves, hat and yellow stockings in crocheted silk or the illuminated parchment family tree tracing her line back to Adam. In the high-ceilinged kitchen are gleaming copper pans as well as lengthy menus and shopping lists from 200 years ago. At the side of the house are ornamental, sunken and herbaceous gardens. The knot garden is a recent addition.

LUNCHBOX

Food is available at several old pubs in town, particularly in Fishpool Street, in the Refectory in the Abbey's Chapter House, at Kingsbury Watermill (waffles are a speciality) and at Hatfield House. Alternatively, you could have a picnic at Hatfield, Bowman's Open Farm or in Verulamium Park. There is also a café at the Gardens of the Rose.

Temples of delight and canal curiosities

Spend the morning exploring England's largest work of art – the 750-acre landscape gardens at Stowe – then enjoy a canal-side lunch at Stoke Bruerne, followed by a walk or a narrowboat trip to the Blisworth canal tunnel, and end the day with visits to two manor houses.

Gardening is an art in which the English have excelled down the ages, and anyone interested in the evolution of English garden styles will find Stowe irresistible. The huge **gardens*** – or perhaps park would be a better term – were laid out at the beginning of the eighteenth century under the direction of Lancelot Brown, better known as 'Capability' (owing to his enthusiasm for the excellent 'capabilities' of his clients' gardens). The client in this case was Richard Temple, who, true to his name, poured his wealth into building numerous temples, grottoes and follies all over the gardens, employing such leading architects as Vanbrugh, Kent and Gibbs to design them.

♦ **GOOD FOR** Lots of walking outdoors at Stowe, so take the family on a fine day
♦ **TRANSPORT** 14-mile drive from Stowe to Stoke Bruerne; add 25 for Sulgrave Manor or Canons Ashby House
♦ **ACCESS FOR DISABLED PEOPLE** Stowe Landscape Gardens are unsuitable for manual wheelchairs, but electric self-drive cars are available free; there is access to the gardens at Sulgrave Manor and Canons Ashby House
BEST TIME TO VISIT Spring and autumn

Temple's magnificent house became **Stowe School*** in 1923 (the eighteenth-century state rooms are open to the public during the Easter and summer holidays). The school handed the gardens over to the National Trust in 1989, and an extensive programme of restoration work has been under way ever since. This does not detract at all from the pleasures of a visit. (The gardens are closed from the end of October until late March, apart from a ten-day period over the New Year.)

PATHWAYS THROUGH ARCADIA

On arrival visitors are given a map of the gardens showing three different routes (1, 2 and 3 miles long), all well signposted. The areas nearest the house contain a golf course. To get away from it and to more peaceful areas, do the medium walk. This walk takes about two hours, allowing time to sit and admire the harmonious views – for this is very much a place for reflection, where philosophers and poets might pass their hours contemplating eternal truths.

In fact, to understand the gardens fully, it helps if you have a classical education (failing that, buy the detailed National Trust guide), for every feature of Stowe is intended to evoke the world of ancient Greece and Rome. All three walks start at the Temple of Concord and Victory, which overlooks the man-made Grecian Valley. An eighteenth-century poet, Thomas Wateley, waxed lyrical about the shadows lengthening across this vale and the sun setting on the columns of the temple. A path leads down from here to the Temple of Ancient Virtue with its views over the River Styx (in reality the Alder) to a landscape dotted with bridges and grottoes, trees and grazing cattle, all strongly reminiscent of the heroic landscapes popularised by the French artist Claude (1600–82). The sense of pastoral serenity is completed by watery reflections and the sound of wind gently rustling the trees.

The museum at Stoke Bruerne offers a fascinating insight into canal history

LOCKS AND TOWPATHS

After visiting the gardens, head for Stoke Bruerne, a pretty village of thatched cottages 14 miles north-east of Stowe. The lock basin at Stoke Bruerne sits on the Grand Union Canal, between a flight of seven locks to the south and the 1¾-mile-long Blisworth Tunnel to the north. This is where thirsty boat people stopped

LUNCHBOX

There is a coffee shop serving light lunches at Stowe, but Stoke Bruerne has greater choice. The Boat Inn, alongside the lock basin, serves generous portions of food and traditional beers (children welcome). Other options include the Old Chapel Tearoom (serving salads, sandwiches and full meals) or the more formal Bruerne's Lock restaurant, both on the opposite side of the lock.

for refreshment in the canal's heyday, after 'legging it' through the tunnel (lying flat on their backs and pushing the boat by 'walking' along the tunnel walls). Over lunch you can decide whether to explore the canal towpaths on foot or by boat. Two **boat companies*** offer leisurely narrowboat trips to the entrance of the Blisworth Tunnel, lasting half an hour. Alternatively, you can walk there in just over ten minutes along a hard-surfaced towpath. If waterside flowers and wildlife interest you, consider taking the quieter southern towpath to watch pleasure boats passing through the flight of locks.

In a converted cornmill beside the lock basin, the **British Waterways Canal Museum*** covers the history of the canal system. Some of the displays on canalboat engines and boat lifts are quite technical but are brought to life by working models (for which 20-pence coins are needed). The most striking exhibits relate to the arts and crafts of the canal people, including the elaborate bonnets worn by women and girls to protect themselves from the sun and rain (horses had their own crocheted caps to keep the flies off their faces in summer). There are many examples of the distinctive style of painting, known as 'roses and castles', with which canal people covered everything, from the woodwork of their boats to milk jugs and water cans. You can usually watch people producing modern versions of this art in the canal basin outside, and the museum shop is stocked with just about everything ever written or produced featuring canals or narrowboats.

SULGRAVE MANOR AND CANONS ASHBY HOUSE

To extend the day, consider including a visit to **Sulgrave Manor*** (a 30-minute drive south-west of Stoke Bruerne, via Towcester and Helmdon). The house was home to the ancestors of George Washington, first US President, and is furnished in Tudor and Queen Anne style. It has a remarkable eighteenth-century kitchen, with an open hearth, cooking equipment and wooden furniture. Other rooms to visit include the Great Hall, the Tudor Great Chamber (a rather spartan bedroom) and two elegant bedrooms. The fine gardens are full of topiary, lavender, roses and herbaceous plants; there is also a kitchen garden. Living history recreations are a speciality of the Manor, so ring and check in advance if you want to take part in an American Indian rendezvous, a recreation of life in Tudor England or an American Civil War battle. Just 3 miles north is **Canons Ashby House***, owned by the National Trust. The house was built around 1550, and has rare and interesting Elizabethan wall paintings and Jacobean plasterwork. The eighteenth-century formal gardens are a vivid contrast to the more naturalistic style of Stowe.

Oxford: a walk round the hallowed lanes

The Bridge of Sighs, an elegant Edwardian bridge inspired by its Venetian namesake

Oxford is the city of dreaming spires and golden domes, a place full of wonderful architecture, entertaining museums, good shops and restaurants, plus quiet college cloisters, green meadows and two rivers.

As well as being a university town, Oxford is a bustling and prosperous city with a large population – many of whom come out to shop on Saturday, filling all the available car parks. Visiting on a Saturday can be a frustrating experience unless you use the park-and-ride schemes signposted at all entries to the city. Parking in the centre may be easier (though expensive) on other days.

Head straight for the **Ashmolean***, one of the best museums in Britain, with a huge collection ranging from the exquisite ninth-century enamelled jewel of King Alfred to paintings by Van Gogh and Picasso. Across from this classical temple to the arts is the Gothic Martyrs' Memorial, commemorating Archbishop Thomas Cranmer and Bishops Latimer and Ridley: during the reign of the Catholic Queen Mary they chose to be burned at the stake rather than renounce their Protestant beliefs. **Balliol College**, alongside the Memorial, is renowned for the great number of statesmen and high-ranking politicians it has produced.

♦ **GOOD FOR** Walking around the city is a pleasure in itself, so count good weather as a plus. The **tourist information office*** on Gloucester Green by the bus station can supply further ideas
♦ **TRANSPORT** Take the train to Oxford station, then catch the 52 bus (or walk) into the city centre. If you are driving, leave your car and make use of the park-and-ride system. Buses are good
♦ **ACCESS FOR DISABLED PEOPLE** Help essential
♦ **BEST TIME TO VISIT** Oxford is a good place to visit at any time of year, but it is also home to many students as well as local residents and there is a constant stream of tourists, making Oxford very busy even out of term-time (particularly on Saturdays)

After passing the church of St Mary Magdalen, turn left into **Broad Street**. On the right at No. 6 is the **Oxford Story***, where you ride in a car through tableaux illustrating 800 years of Oxford's history – an excellent guide to the city's key people and events. Broad Street is famous for its bookshops, notably the labyrinthine Blackwell's.

THE COLLEGES AND THEIR GARDENS
Oxford has dozens of cloistered college quadrangles and fine gardens but many are now closed to the public because they were being swamped by noisy tour groups. Some colleges open their gates in the afternoons, nearly all of them charging an entrance fee. Among the most rewarding to visit are Christ Church (described in the walk), Trinity (alongside Blackwells), New College, with its fine gardens, Magdalen, with its gardens and deer park, and Merton, for its thirteenth-century chapel.

Opposite is the marvellously eccentric **Sheldonian Theatre** (1662), an early design by Christopher Wren, used for university ceremonial events as well as concerts. It is fronted by 13 outsize heads, popularly said to be of Roman emperors, though nobody really knows whom they represent. To the right of it is the **Museum of the History of Science***, with exhibits on Alexander Fleming and the discovery of penicillin.

Go through the gate to the left of the Sheldonian into the beautiful Jacobean courtyards of the **Bodleian Library** (on Sunday the gates are closed, so take the next right, Catte Street, to reach the Radcliffe Camera). The entrance to the library is guarded by a seventeenth-century statue of a former Chancellor, the Earl of Pembroke. Go inside to see the magnificent fan-vaulted vestibule, look at displays of rare manuscripts and perhaps sign up for a guided tour of the library later in the day. As you head on through the courtyards you will emerge into Radcliffe Square with the exquisite baroque **Radcliffe Camera** straight ahead, designed by Hawksmoor and Gibbs in 1714–48 to house a science library. Beyond is the church of **St Mary the Virgin** (the tower can be climbed for fine views); to the right is Brasenose College, with All Souls opposite, notable for the fact that membership is restricted to distinguished graduate scholars.

Turn left and return up Catte Street, then right beneath the Bridge of Sighs, built in 1913 to link the two halves of Hertford College. A tiny alleyway on the left will take you to a favourite haunt of undergraduates and of the TV detective Inspector Morse, the excellent **Turf Tavern**, which has been serving food and beer since the thirteenth century. Back on New College Lane, just follow your nose down a twisting lane that retains all the atmosphere of the medieval city, with its high walls and views of **New College** gatehouse, plus an entertaining series of modern gargoyles high up along the flank of the college round the next bend.

Having emerged on the High Street (known universally as 'The High'), turn left and walk down to **Magdalen Bridge**, past Magdalen College with its high tower from which singers welcome the spring on May Day morning. Punts can be hired at the bridge.

Cross the road to the **Botanic Garden*** and explore this delightful

Two of Oxford's 'dreaming spires': the Radcliffe Camera and St Mary's

riverside site, with its glasshouses and varied planting. As you leave the Garden, turn left and left again, down Rose Lane, to enter **Christ Church Meadow**, a fine expanse of natural water meadow, grazed by longhorn cattle and threaded by the meandering courses of the River Cherwell. Ignore the first right but take the second, a broad avenue that

leads up to **Christ Church***. Here, it is well worth paying the admission fee to visit the college chapel, which is also Oxford's cathedral, a fine Norman building with outstanding stained glass by Morris and Burne-Jones telling the story of Oxford's patron, St Frideswide. You can also visit the wonderful medieval kitchens and hall, the Picture Gallery, with its outstanding collection of Italian Renaissance works, and the Great Quad, dominated by Christopher Wren's pepper-pot entrance tower.

Leave by the same entrance, turning right on St Aldates. The **Museum of Oxford*** on the right is devoted to the story of the town as opposed to the gown. Highlights include reconstructed rooms contrasting middle-class Oxford, all William Morris furnishings, with the homes of car workers in the suburb of Cowley, location of the famous Morris motor works.

Continue up St Aldates to Carfax, named from the Latin *quadrifurcus*, the meeting of four ways. Ahead and to the left lie Oxford's main shopping streets. Turn right down the High Street to find the entrance to Oxford's **covered market** on the left, a place for dedicated gourmets, with its stalls selling fish, fruit and vegetables, cooked meats, breads, cheeses and pastries. Then head back to the Ashmolean (see the map).

Map

OXFORD

- Pitt Rivers Museum
- University Museum
- MUSEUM ROAD
- ST GILES
- PARKS ROAD
- Lamb and Flag
- Ashmolean Museum
- Balliol College
- Martyr's Memorial
- Sheldonian Theatre
- Museum of the History of Science
- St Mary Magdalen
- Broad
- Oxford Story
- Bodleian Library
- MARKET ST
- CORNMARKET ST
- Brasenose College
- Covered Market
- Bus and railway stations and (i)
- Carfax
- QUEEN ST
- ST ALDATES
- BLUE BOAR ST
- Museum of Oxford
- Christ Church
- Cathedral
- Turf Tavern
- New College
- CATTE ST
- Hertford College
- All Souls College
- Radcliffe Camera
- St Mary the Virgin
- HIGH STREET
- River Cherwell
- Magdalen College
- ROSE LANE
- Magdalen Bridge
- Botanic Garden
- CHRIST CHURCH MEADOW

0 Yards 220
0 Metres 200

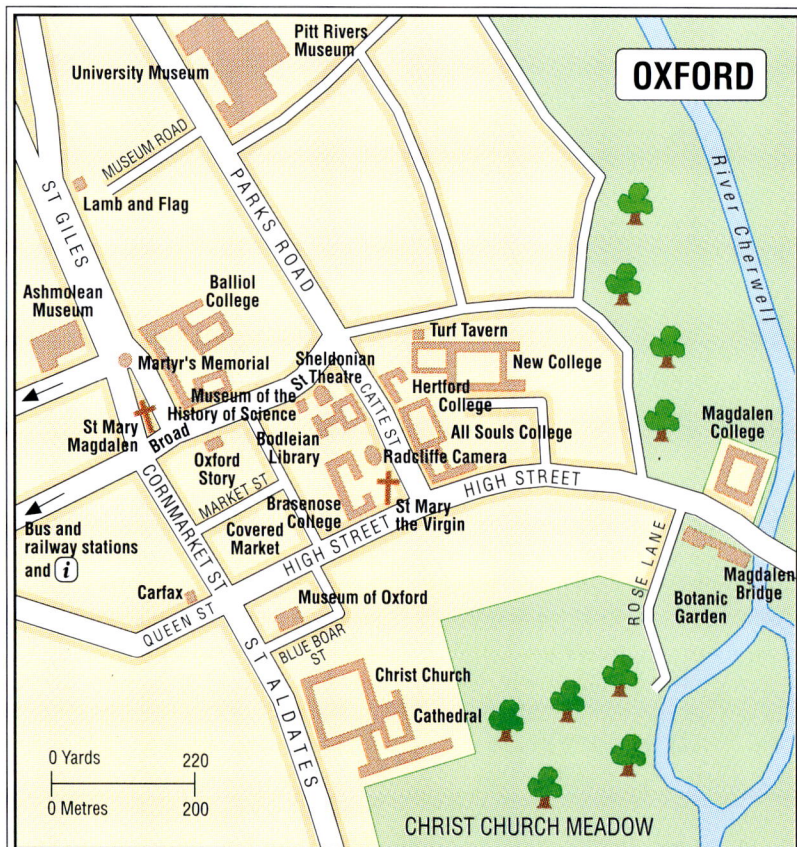

Woodstock and England's answer to Versailles

Blenheim Palace, a Vanbrugh masterpiece and birthplace of Sir Winston Churchill

Spend an hour or two exploring this historic small town just north of Oxford and finding out about the people and buildings of Oxfordshire, then tour magnificent Blenheim Palace, with its 2,000 acres of landscaped parkland and numerous attractions.

WOODSTOCK

On the A44 eight miles north of Oxford, Woodstock tends to be thronged with visitors leaving behind that 'city of dreaming spires' for the open expanse of parkland at Blenheim. An amble around the town, with its attractive stone-fronted Georgian houses and shops, charming tea rooms and historic inns, is a good way to while away an hour or so before visiting the palace, which opens at 10.30.

♦ **GOOD FOR** A truly grand day out
♦ **TRANSPORT** Bus from Oxford
♦ **ACCESS FOR DISABLED PEOPLE** The ground floor only of Blenheim Palace
♦ **BEST TIME TO VISIT** The Palace and Pleasure Gardens are open mid-March to end October, the park all year

From Saxon to Tudor times, the town was the site of a great medieval manor, the birthplace in 1330 of Edward, the Black Prince, and the site of Elizabeth I's imprisonment during the reign of Queen Mary. The manor fell into decay during the Civil War and was finally dismantled by the first Duchess of Marlborough after Blenheim Palace was built on a different site.`

Before setting out, pick up the informative free guide from the **tourist information office***. Notable buildings to look out for are the grand Town Hall, built in 1766 by Sir William Chambers; Chaucer's House (where Geoffrey, the poet, was a regular visitor, and his son Thomas lived) along Park Street; and the famous 750-year-old Bear Inn. In the **Oxfordshire County Museum*** at Fletcher's House, an elegant town house with tranquil walled gardens, you can trace the history of Oxfordshire and its people, and find out about the local industries of steel and glove-making. The museum has a bookshop and a coffee bar.

BLENHEIM PALACE*

Cross the quadrangle at the end of Park Street and pass beneath the triumphal arch to enter the landscaped parkland. Even though you know you are about to see one of England's most majestic buildings, nothing can prepare you for the first view of this staggeringly impressive mansion. Having been given the Royal Manor of Woodstock by Queen Anne in 1704, in recognition of his great victory over the Sun King, Louis XIV, and the French, at the Battle of Blenheim in that year, John Churchill, First Duke of Marlborough, set about building England's answer to Versailles.

Designed by Vanbrugh, with some participation by Hawksmoor, the house alone covers seven acres and is regarded as one of the finest examples of Baroque architecture in England. The opulent interior is rich

The Long Library, with its books, organ and statue of Queen Anne, at Blenheim Palace

in furnishings and art treasures, with gilded state rooms housing collections of fine tapestries, sculptures, European and Chinese porcelain, paintings by Reynolds, Van Dyck, Romney and Kneller, and numerous wood carvings by Grinling Gibbons.

Among the rooms you troop through are the Great Hall, its painted ceiling depicting the victorious Marlborough, the Saloon, renowned for its *trompe l'oeil* murals, and three state apartments. On the west side of the palace is the outstanding Long Library, which lives up to its name at 183 feet – one of the longest rooms in an English private house. Filling all that space are 10,000 volumes and an exceptional four-manual Willis organ.

Towards the end, the route takes you to the surprisingly plain bedroom where, in 1874, Winston Churchill was born. Various personal belongings, manuscripts, photographs and letters to his father are on display; Churchill himself is buried in nearby **Bladon churchyard**. If you visit his grave, use the official village car park and make the short climb to the church on foot.

You can choose to investigate the impressive interior of the house independently or join one of the frequent hour-long guided tours. But allow plenty of time to explore the remaining attractions, especially the formal Italian gardens.

With a family in tow you could hop on board the narrow-gauge railway that links the car park with the **Pleasure Gardens**, a complex of family-orientated activities based around the original Palace's walled kitchen garden. Children will inevitably gravitate towards the **Butterfly House**, where tropical butterflies and moths, as well as over twenty indigenous species, fly freely, and to the maze area. The **Marlborough Maze**, the world's largest symbolic hedge maze, was designed to reflect the history and architectural magnificence of the palace. Young visitors can also play a game of giant chess or draughts, look round a model of a Woodstock street, and use up any surplus energy at the adventure play area. (The maze and chess and draughts attract an extra charge.)

If the Pleasure Gardens do not appeal, escape for a long walk across the two thousand acres of **parkland**, complete with a large artificial lake spanned by Vanbrugh's 390-foot bridge, a Grand Cascade, hanging beech woods, a fine arboretum containing rare trees and shrubs, and a superb rose garden. Landscaped by Capability Brown, who is said to have based the tree planting scheme on a plan of campaign for the Battle of Blenheim, the park is a peaceful place in which to roam after a hectic day, especially in summer.

Otherwise, you might choose to take a trip around the lake on the motor launch, or hire a rowing boat on Queen Pool (again, there is an extra charge).

A converted drinking trough in Woodstock

Cotswold charm in and around Chipping Campden

Hidcote Manor Garden: a twentieth-century delight in the north Cotswolds

Warm golden-stone villages, a fine Jacobean manor house, a ruined abbey and a choice of two of England's most beautiful gardens make this a varied and rewarding day out in the northern Cotswolds, famed for the gently rolling nature of its serene limestone landscape.

Chipping Campden, tucked amid folds of rich farmland, is often regarded as the most beautiful of all the market towns in England. Its wide main street, the ancient Market Hall and the impressive gabled stone houses are the only indications today that the settlement was one of the great Cotswold wool towns during the Middle Ages.

A leisurely morning stroll along the High Street to the magnificent Church of St James will reveal the historic charm and former importance of this substantial village. Cotswold-stone dwellings dating from the fourteenth century line both sides, many featuring steeply

♦ **GOOD FOR** Walking and pottering around a beautiful village and gardens in local country houses
♦ **TRANSPORT** A car is a must unless you are planning to visit only one sight
♦ **ACCESS FOR DISABLED PEOPLE** Access at some sights
♦ **BEST TIME TO VISIT** Spring and summer are best to enable you to appreciate the full beauty of Hidcote Manor and Kiftsgate Court Gardens, and Stanway House is open only in the summer

pitched roofs, mullioned windows, gable-ends and other splendid examples of domestic architecture of bygone centuries. The grandest, built by the wealthy wool merchants, include the gargoyle-adorned Grevel's House and **Woolstaplers Hall***, the latter now home to an interesting museum displaying varied collections from years gone by. Pride of place in the centre of the street is the seventeenth-century gabled Market Hall, erected to provide shelter for stalls selling local produce.

Dominating the northern end of the High Street is the fifteenth-century perpendicular parish church with its lofty 120-ft pinnacled tower and large memorials to the noble wool merchants, who helped the village to prosper. Look out for the Jacobean lodges and gateway near the church: these and the banqueting rooms are the sole remains of Campden House, a sumptuous mansion that was occupied by Royalist troops during the Civil War and subsequently burnt down in 1645 to prevent it from falling into Parliamentarian hands.

Anyone who enjoys walking should seek out Hoo Lane (at the southern end of the High Street) to join the start of the well-waymarked Cotswold Way, a 100-mile trail that links Chipping Campden to Bath. Climb gradually out of the village for approximately 1 mile to reach the top of Dover's Hill (NT), which forms a natural amphitheatre on the spur of the Cotswolds. Your reward will be a panoramic view across the Vale of Evesham towards the Malvern Hills.

If you choose to walk up here on the first Friday after Whitsun Bank Holiday you will witness one of the oldest traditions in the Cotswolds, the Robert Dover's Games, or Cotswold Olympics. Held here since 1612, the event features rural games such as tug-of-war, shin kicking, greasy pole and pikes and cudgels, followed by a torchlight procession.

There is a colourful carnival the next day, called the Skuttlebrook Wake. The picturesque location and the charm of Chipping Campden are best appreciated on your walk downhill back to the village.

Among the many choices in this scenic pocket of the Cotswolds for an afternoon excursion are the delightful gardens of Hidcote Manor and Kiftsgate Court, which are situated four miles north-east of the village, off the B4632 (well signposted).

Hidcote Manor Garden* (NT), created by the great American horticulturist Major Lawrence Johnston, comprises a honeycomb of small gardens within its ten acres, all separated by walls and hedges of different species and each with a particular feature, whether avenues, long walks, terraces or rockeries. Hidcote is renowned for its rare shrubs, trees and herbaceous borders. Note that the garden can be unbearably crowded on Sundays and bank holidays.

Hidcote's neighbour **Kiftsgate Court Garden*** is spectacularly set on the edge of the Cotswold escarpment, affording far-reaching views over the Vale of Evesham from

A detail from the seventeenth-century Market Hall, which was an important venue in the wool trade

its terrace. Here, a series of interconnecting gardens has been developed over three generations, beginning in 1920, when a Heather Muir started collecting rare and exotic plants from around the world. Like Hidcote, each of the (six) gardens has a distinct character, notably the banks and Lower Garden with its Mediterranean feel; for many the chief attraction is the collection of old-fashioned roses, including the largest rose in England, the Rosa Filipes Kiftsgate.

If gardens, however beautiful, are not your interest, an alternative

outing involves driving south-west of Chipping Campden via the equally pretty villages of **Broadway** and **Buckland** to reach the unspoilt settlement of Stanway, lying beneath the western escarpment of the Cotswolds, signposted off the B4632 Broadway-to-Winchcombe road. **Stanway** is an enchanting collection of predominantly thatched golden-stone houses clustering close to its fine Jacobean manor, **Stanway House***, a jewel of a Cotswold mansion. Reached via an exquisite gabled and carved gatehouse built in 1630, the manor is a typical squire's residence, full of family portraits and unusual furniture. The Great Hall, with its vast window and minstrels' gallery, and the Great Parlour, are particularly impressive.

A walk through the formal landscaped parkland is to be recommended: behind the church is a splendid medieval Tithe Barn, built in 1370 to store tithes for the Abbots of Tewkesbury, who owned the manor at the time. Recent uses include music and arts festivals and the local flower show. Further investigation will reveal a thatched wooden cricket pavilion set on staddle stones.

Just south of Stanway are the beautiful ruins of **Hailes Abbey*** (NT, EH), a Cistercian monastery founded in 1246. It was a leading medieval pilgrimage destination because of its phial of blood, said to be Christ's own. You can do a 'sound tour', in which a friendly monk talks you through the history of the abbey.

Built of golden ashlar, Chipping Campden almost glows

LUNCHBOX

In Chipping Campden, try Forbes in the Cotswold House Hotel, or the Eight Bells along Church Street. For tea, two civilised places are the Lygon Arms Hotel in Broadway and the Buckland Manor Hotel at Buckland; booking is advisable. Teas are also available at Hidcote.

Cirencester and the glorious Cotswolds

The weavers' cottages in Arlington Row are now owned by the National Trust

The market town of Cirencester, with its majestic church and lively museum, makes an excellent starting point for a tour of the southern Cotswolds, a region of honey-coloured limestone villages, ancient churches and sheep-pasture bounded by drystone walls.

Cirencester was founded by the Romans and, indeed, retains its regular grid of streets, which are interrupted in places by the winding lanes of the medieval town. These are lined by characterful stone houses, which were built by wealthy wool merchants during the fifteenth, sixteenth and seventeenth centuries, when buyers came from as far away as the Netherlands and Tuscany in search of fine fleeces from the special Cotswold breed of sheep, the Cotswold Lion. The story of the town and its surrounding countryside can be explored at the Corinium Museum, at Chedworth Roman Villa and at the Cotswold Countryside Collection in nearby Northleach, after which there is a pleasant drive back to Cirencester via Bibury, dubbed by William Morris as England's prettiest village.

♦ **GOOD FOR** There is much for families to see, and the tour is particularly suitable when the weather is not so good
♦ **TRANSPORT** A car is necessary to do the whole tour; parking is possible in Cirencester. The nearest railway station to Cirencester is Kemble
♦ **ACCESS FOR DISABLED PEOPLE** Access to the museums
♦ **BEST TIME TO VISIT** Spring for the daffodils, summer, and autumn for the changing colours of the countryside, but this itinerary is very suitable in all weathers as there are many recommended museums

CIRENCESTER

Archaeologists have reaped a rich harvest of mosaic work, statuary and pottery from sites excavated in the town over the past 200 years, and their finds now fill the **Corinium**

LUNCHBOX
Cirencester has plenty of good shops. Most are found on either side of the Market Place, but do not miss the Brewery Yard, with its craft workshops, exhibition galleries and excellent coffee shop, serving home-made cakes and buffet lunches (including vegetarian). Other eating options include Harry Hare's, a bistro-style restaurant at 3 Gosditch Street at the back of the church, and Tatyans, an authentic Chinese restaurant at 27 Castle Street.
　Wonderful bread, Italian-style salads, salami and many other unusual picnic ingredients can be had from Gastromania, at 3 The Market Place next to the church.

Museum* in Park Street. Here, Roman life is vividly portrayed through reconstructions of Roman rooms, waxwork models of Roman soldiers and huge mosaics mounted on the walls. Cirencester was a major centre for mosaic production, and accomplished local artists turned their hands to the exotic in the form of tigers and lions depicted in the Orpheus mosaic, as well as to local wildlife, such as the hare in the charming Hare Mosaic.

Black Jack Street, left from the museum, leads to the parish **church of St John Baptist***, with its fan-vaulted porch and magnificent tower. This can be climbed, with prior permission, for views of the bustling Market Place (market days are Monday and Friday and the **tourist information office*** is here). Also visible are the Abbey Grounds, north of the church (the abbey was demolished at the Dissolution) and Cirencester Mansion, sheltered by what is claimed as the world's tallest yew hedge. Cirencester Park lies beyond: it was laid out in the early eighteenth century by the first Earl Bathurst, with the help of his friend, the poet Alexander Pope, and is open to the public every day.

Water for the villa came from a natural spring, where the Romans erected a shrine, the Nymphaeum

Chedworth Roman Villa*

In pursuit of further fine examples of Roman mosaic work, it is worth visiting Chedworth Roman villa (signposted off the A429 Stow road), which is owned by the National Trust and open most of the year. A short introductory film explains villa life, and the mosaic floors of the bath-house block include humorous depictions of the Four Seasons. The villa is set in an idyllic spot, backed by woodland; to the rear is a well-marked path leading up to an abandoned railway line where you can walk and study local wildlife.

The Cotswold Countryside Collection*

Farming methods changed very little from Roman times until the onset of mechanisation in the twentieth century, as can be seen from the rural life displays at the Cotswold Countryside Collection, housed in an eighteenth century 'House of Correction' on the A429 at Northleach. Excellent displays cover everything from farmhouse kitchens to the life of the shepherd, complete with tape recordings of farm labourers talking about their work in rich Cotswold accents.

In **Northleach** itself the main attraction is the fine church, with its outstanding series of memorial brasses commemorating the rich wool merchants whose money paid for the rebuilding of the church in the fifteenth century. Look out especially for the brass of Thomas Fortey and his wives, with its charming border depicting snails, pigs and hedgehogs and its unusual date (MCCCC47), combining Roman numerals with one of the earliest known uses of Arabic numerals in England. Nearby, at **Keith**

Harding's World of Mechanical Music* on the High Street, museum guides will demonstrate working pianolas and musical boxes from the era before radio was invented.

THE COLN VALLEY, BIBURY AND BARNSLEY

Returning along the A429 to Cirencester, turn left about 3 miles south of Northleach to follow signs to Coln St Dennis, Coln Rogers and Ablington, passing through the rural lanes and villages of the idyllic **Coln Valley**. **Bibury** can be crowded, especially around the Trout Farm and the Arlington Mill end of the village. Escape the crowds by visiting the fine church, which has numerous good examples of Saxon carving embedded in its walls, and then take a walk around the village to see the fourteenth-century weavers' cottages of Arlington Row. If you follow the Row uphill you can pick up a public footpath that turns left, skirting the village cricket pitch, with fine views down over Bibury Court Hotel, an ornate Jacobean building. The path continues down to the banks of the Coln, where it passes through the hotel grounds before returning to the village.

Garden lovers should stop at **Barnsley House***, in Barnsley, on the return to Cirencester; Rosemary Verey's garden here is known to many through her books and is a delight at all times of the year.

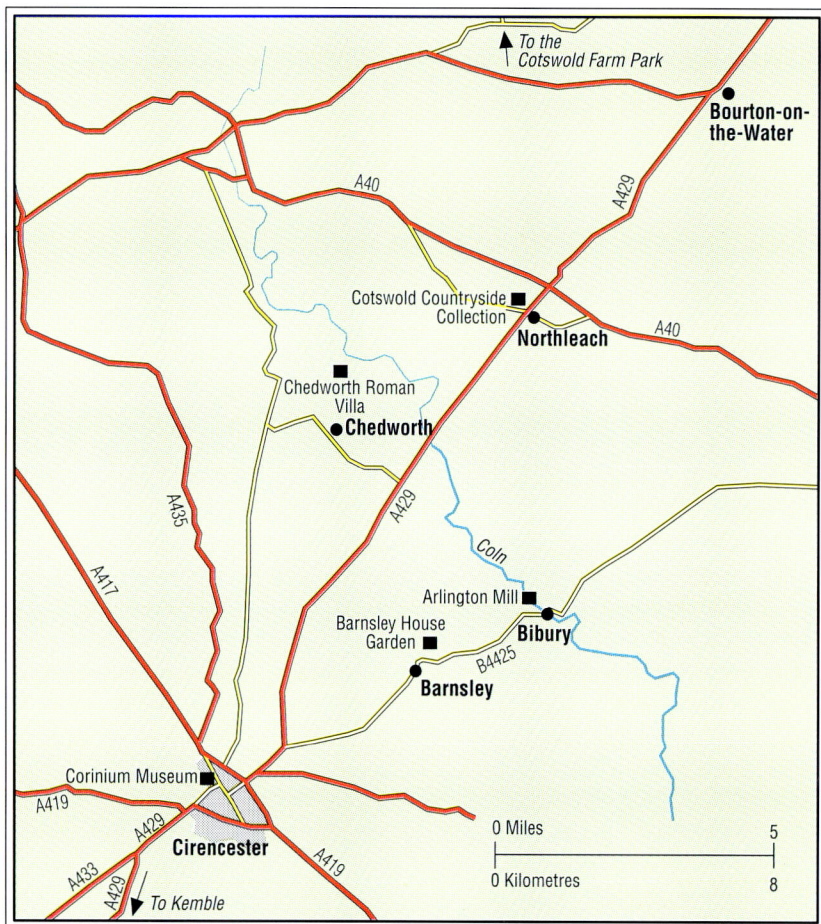

BOURTON-ON-THE-WATER

Touristy it may be but Bourton-on-the-Water (the next town north on the A429 after Northleach) has much to offer, especially for children, and nobody can deny the picturesque elegance of the numerous low bridges that cross the River Windrush as it flows through the village. Attractions include the **Model Village*** (a one-ninth scale replica of Bourton itself), the **Cotswold Motor Museum*** (home of the children's television character, Brum) and **Birdland***, with its macaws, parrots and flamingos. If you simply cannot bear crowds, then head for the **Cotswold Farm Park***, near Temple Guiting on the opposite side of the A429, where Cotswold Lions, the sheep on which the medieval wealth of the region was based, are among the rare breeds on display.

Off the beaten track in the southern Cotswolds

Legend has it that the Devil will kill the 100th yew tree in St Mary's churchyard

This lesser-known south-west corner of the Cotswolds is an ideal destination for admiring the scenery or simply pottering. Villages nestle in folds of wooded hills, sheep graze in meadows and fine churches bear witness to the profitable wool trade of the past.

Using Stroud as a base, this day out offers a choice of villages and viewpoints, two old, but not stately, houses (one remains eternally unfinished), an unusual garden and two commons. Motorists should drive with care on side roads, many of which are single track. Potential walkers should bring OS maps, Landranger series 162 and 163: in spite of many footpath signs, paths may be overgrown or peter out.

Painswick is a small town clustering round a hilltop, the perfect English period film backdrop, with sloping streets and dramatic views to the steep hills beyond. The substantial grey-stone houses with fine doorways, some of them shops now, and more simple terraced cottages span four centuries of English architecture. The fifteenth-century timber-framed Post Office occupies

♦ **GOOD FOR** Rural views, churches, gardens and manor houses
♦ **TRANSPORT** A car is necessary
♦ **ACCESS FOR DISABLED PEOPLE** No
♦ **BEST TIME TO VISIT** Easter to October for the houses; all year for the drive

the oldest building, and the **tourist information office*** is in the library, which was once a school.

In the centre of the town stands **St Mary's Church** surrounded by its famous churchyard, with many carved table tombs and impressive rows of 99 yew trees. An annual clipping ceremony takes place each September. St Mary's can trace its history back to Norman times, and the oldest surviving parts are the English perpendicular north aisle and the tower dating from 1480 (with a later steeple). Civil War damage can

still be seen on the tower. Behind the churchyard on the wall is a pair of iron 'spectacle' stocks.

North of Painswick are two short and worthwhile detours. The six-acre **Painswick Rococo Garden***, set in a hollow, claims to be the sole survivor of this brief period of garden design in Britain. It is being restored to its 1740 state, and is dotted with Gothic arches, pools and orchards. There are winding woodland walks, avenues of yew and beech and a splendid central formal vista. Climbing the spiral staircase of the two-storey octagonal pigeon house is a good way to enjoy the rural views. Some of the walking is quite steep. In late February and early March the woods and banks of the stream are carpeted with snowdrops.

One mile further north is **Painswick Beacon**, 250 acres of common land: a short climb up from the car park over sandy ground and a golf course will give fine views over the Severn Vale.

One route from Painswick to Bisley passes Slad, made famous by Laurie Lee in his autobiographical novel *Cider with Rosie*. **Bisley** itself is a large and prosperous-looking village, set in a south-facing bowl near the head of the Toadsmoor Valley. It has many handsome stone houses and an unusual Victorian twin-celled lock-up. **All Saints' Church** has a medieval chancel and tower, but was heavily restored in 1862. Outside stands a pointed stone structure, 'the Bonehouse', a twelfth-century wellhead, where alms were left for the poor, and where, on Ascension Day, garlands of flowers are arranged around the old well in a ceremony known as 'well-dressing'.

Sapperton, further south-east on minor roads, is a tiny village on the Bathurst estate. From a terrace above the church, views extend across the thickly wooded Frome Valley towards

Formal terraced gardens and magnificent yews complement the restored Owlpen Manor

Stroud. Had the Thames and Severn Canal survived, Sapperton might have developed, but its two-mile tunnel caused problems and the canal was abandoned. On its completion in 1789 the tunnel was the longest in Europe. You can walk to the entrance from nearby **Daneway** where, at the turn of the century, the arts and crafts movement leaders, the Barnsley brothers, Ernest and Sidney, and Ernest Gimson, set up their furniture workshops. All three are buried in the churchyard of St Kenelm's, restored in the early part of the eighteenth century and embellished with effigies of local worthies and much Jacobean woodwork.

An easier route south from Painswick is via **Stroud**, sited at the head of five valleys. At the upper end of the pedestrianised High Street is the Shambles, with the oldest stone market hall (Old Town Hall) in the Cotswolds, built in 1594. The **tourist information office*** is housed in the imposing Subscription Rooms, which are used for concerts and exhibitions and the annual October Arts Festival.

Further to the south-west is the Elizabethan **Owlpen Manor*** at Uley, set in a wooded valley and very much a family home. Restoration was started in the 1920s by Norman Jewson, a later exponent of the arts and crafts movement. His changes included remodelling the plasterwork ceilings and altering floor levels. The house is full of personal items, solid furniture from several periods and a lovely Tudor canvas painted with everyday scenes. **Uley Church** has lustrous mosaics and a gold-starred ceiling. Nearby **Woodchester Mansion***, often dubbed 'the forgotten masterpiece', stands in

The exedra is one of the decorative architectural features in the Painswick Rococo Garden

its own ancient and enclosed wooded valley. The exterior of this large stone house belies its history: one day in 1868 its workforce simply downed tools when the owner's money ran out. It now offers visitors the opportunity to see the construction methods of a grand building, from cellars to roof, and to marvel at the stone-cutting skills of the time. Everything is in stone – arches, bosses, window frames, even a bath.

Turning east brings you to **Minchinhampton Common**, nearly 600 acres of grassy plateau, fringed by trees and dotted with bushes and Iron Age remains. Locally owned cattle and ponies still enjoy their ancient right to graze in summer; they share the space with golfers, horse-riders and kite-fliers. You can walk anywhere, admiring the profusion of wild flowers and the surrounding views. Take note – the common can be windy.

The small market town of **Minchinhampton**, on the eastern side of the common, owes its prosperity to the wool industry and the first floor of Old Market House, where wool used to be sold, stands on stone columns. The old streets, some narrow and twisting, are lined with harmonious stone houses from the sixteenth to the eighteenth centuries – even the Post Office is a Queen Anne building. A short distance from the Market Square is **Holy Trinity Church**, the oldest sections of which – the tower, transepts and heavy stone tiled roof – date from the fourteenth century. The unusual truncated spire replaced the original one, which was too heavy for the supporting arches. The Victorians in their usual manner 'restored' the church by demolishing the nave, with its Norman arches and chancel, but luckily they spared the monumental brasses.

LUNCHBOX

There's a choice of pubs with gardens (two in Bisley, one in Sapperton, one in Daneway). Owlpen Manor has a fifteenth-century, elegantly converted Cyder House Restaurant (with garden), and lunch is also served in Painswick Rococo Garden. For a picnic on a windless day, Minchinhampton Common would be ideal.

Gloucester and its lively dock complex

A narrowboat moored in Barge Basin in colourful, revitalised Gloucester Docks

Explore the most complete Victorian docks in Britain, enjoy a canal cruise, learn to steer a narrowboat, walk through a wartime trench — all at Gloucester Docks. The city itself is steeped in history and the two sites are well endowed with unusual museums.

Running like a silver thread through Gloucester's history is the River Severn, the reason for the city's existence. Gloucester was, until recently, the lowest bridging-point on the river, a location of great strategic and commercial importance. It is fitting, therefore, that Gloucester's rejuvenation as a popular tourist centre in the last few years should be based on the refurbishment of the magnificent Victorian docks.

The day out described below starts at the docks, but does not end there: set aside time to visit some of Gloucester's other sights.

Finding your way around is easy. The city's four main streets — Northgate, Eastgate, Southgate and Westgate — meet at the Cross, where the medieval St Michael's Tower houses the **tourist information office*** (call in for free leaflets).

- ♦ **GOOD FOR** Excellent choice of things to do and see within the dock area and elsewhere in the city
- ♦ **TRANSPORT** Gloucester is well connected by train and has a good bus service
- ♦ **ACCESS FOR DISABLED PEOPLE** Good at most attractions; limited at the Antiques Centre and Folk Museum
- ♦ **BEST TIME TO VISIT** Boat trips run from Easter to October; the sights are open all year (some close on Mondays in winter)

GLOUCESTER DOCKS

The docks, now combining port and marina, may be approached from Westgate or Southgate Streets. The site is a large one, with three basins, two dry docks, several quays, 15 warehouses, the terminus of the Gloucester and Sharpness Ship Canal and a lock giving access to the Severn.

The dock complex is not merely a tourist attraction but a real, working landscape. Four of the warehouses are now council offices, and the dry docks are still in use for ship repairs. Commercial vessels continue to ply the canal, but leisure craft are far more abundant. Children especially enjoy watching **Llanthony Bridge** lift the road into the air to allow the passage of boats between the canal and Main Basin, while motorists wait with varying degrees of impatience. At the other side of the basin a lock performs a similar function, connecting the docks to the Severn.

Next to Llanthony Bridge, the **National Waterways Museum*** is housed in Llanthony Warehouse. Through an impressive mix of traditional memorabilia and interactive displays the museum vividly recreates 200 years of canal history. You can learn to steer a narrowboat here, using a genuine rudder in conjunction with a simulator. The indoor displays are superb. Outside, you can wander round workshops, a forge and an engine house; inspect old railway carriages and board the boats moored at the quayside; or visit Peter the shire horse, who occupies a stable in Llanthony Yard when not giving cart rides. You will also find a well-stocked shop, a café and an activity room for young children.

The museum is also the place to book a cruise on **Queen Boadicea II**, a Dunkirk veteran. Short trips on the canal last about 40 minutes, but longer ones are available too, on both the canal and the river. The longest cruise lasts six hours, so you would need to allow a whole day for this.

A few yards away, beyond the **Mariners' Church**, is Reynolds Warehouse, where you can visit **Glass Heritage*** to watch craftsmen making stained-glass windows in the traditional way.

Step back in time at the Robert Opie Collection of packaging paraphernalia

A short walk from here, overlooking Victoria Basin, stands Albert Warehouse, home to the **Robert Opie Collection** at the **Museum of Advertising & Packaging***. No one viewing the exhibits can fail to feel nostalgic: here are the packets and tins which filled our parents' and grandparents' larders, the enamel signs which once adorned shops and stations, and the TV commercials of the 1950s and '60s. This most colourful and fascinating of museums also incorporates a café and gift shop.

Not far from the docks is the former Custom House, now home to the **Soldiers of Gloucestershire Museum***. Military museums can be dull, but this one is not. In addition to the medals and uniforms you would expect, it houses a range of lively modern displays that enable you to join a tank crew in the North African desert, explore a First World War trench or lead a patrol through no-man's-land.

The **Antiques Centre*** in Lock Warehouse, close to the River Severn, resembles a museum in its scale and scope. With 47 display cases on the ground floor and 68 shops on four upper floors, this is a paradise for collectors and browsers alike – with a café attached. To shop for more modern items, head for the **Merchants Quay Shopping Centre** by Main Basin, which offers a range of small speciality shops. Just across the bridge near the

Antiques Centre you will find **Alney Island Nature Reserve**, between the twin channels of the Severn. Despite its urban location, it is an important wetland habitat, thanks largely to annual winter flooding. For more information about this and other green spaces in Gloucester ring the Environmental Services Department* of the city council.

CITY SIGHTS

The **Folk Museum*** in Westgate Street has an informal, child-friendly atmosphere and occupies a range of superb timber-framed buildings. The top floor of the museum was once a workshop for making brass pins by

hand. Its absorbing displays illustrate social history, folklore, agriculture, industry and crafts in Gloucestershire over the last 500 years. Reconstructions include a Victorian schoolroom, a dairy (producing the local cheeses), an ironmonger's shop and the workshops of a wheelwright and a carpenter.

Do not miss the **cathedral***, a sublimely beautiful building and the birthplace of English Perpendicular architecture. It started off as St Peter's Abbey under the Normans, but was upgraded to a cathedral by, ironically, Henry VIII after his visit to Gloucester in 1535.

Children may enjoy a short trip to the **House of the Tailor of Gloucester and Beatrix Potter Shop***, which has a display on the eponymous book and sells souvenirs based on various Potter characters.

The **City Museum and Art Gallery*** is also worth a visit. It contains, among other treasures, the famous Birdlip Mirror, an exquisite, engraved bronze mirror found in the grave of an Iron Age princess excavated near the city in 1879.

A tug with the innovative National Waterways Museum in the background

A tour of the magical Forest of Dean

Looking north across Herefordshire from Symond's Yat rock

There is a magic to the woodland and dappled sunlight of the Forest of Dean that captivates children and grown-ups alike, and this tour, taking in the industrial heritage and natural wonders of the region, makes for a full and satisfying day out.

This circular tour can be joined at any point along the route, but to make the most of opening times, it is best to start at the Dean Heritage Centre, midway between Lower and Upper Soudley, just north of the A48 Chepstow to Gloucester road. The route then goes west to the ancient iron mines at Clearwell Caves, with a short stop along the way to climb New Fancy View and look over the forest canopy. After Clearwell, you can visit the charming village of Newland, then head north to Symonds Yat for even more spectacular views before returning south to Speech House to follow the woodland sculpture trail. Maps of the trail, and of the whole Forest of Dean, are available at Coleford's **tourist information office*** and at all the attractions along the route, and the attractions themselves are very well signposted.

♦ **GOOD FOR** Choose a fine day in spring, summer or autumn to enjoy the Forest at its most enchanting
♦ **TRANSPORT** A car is essential for the 45-mile circuit
♦ **ACCESS FOR DISABLED PEOPLE** Special wheelchair routes at Symonds Yat rock and the Dean Forest sculpture trail, but Clearwell Caves are not accessible
♦ **BEST TIME TO VISIT** Spring and autumn for woodland colour; some sites are closed November to Easter

Gloriously located in the middle of mixed woodland and ancient iron workings, **Dean Heritage Centre*** occupies a converted mill of 1827. The exhibits deal with the history of the forest and its people in a very accessible way, with audio-visuals as well as reconstructions of the forest and its wildlife before man arrived on the scene; minerals, such as coal and

iron ore that you can handle; a suitably claustrophobic mock-up of a coal mine; and many other displays. Children will enjoy exploring the forester's cottage in the museum grounds, furnished with only the barest of necessities, and the pigsty in the backyard complete with Gloucester Old Spot occupant (and sometimes a litter of piglets).

Footpaths meander through the 'scowles' that surround the museum – great scoops in the ground created by centuries of digging for iron ore; some of these have been turned into an excellent adventure playground, others contain sculptures inspired by the woods, and one shows a charcoal burner's encampment. Nearby is a Natural History Cabin with beehives and a wood-ant's nest behind glass so that you can watch the busy insects at work.

From Upper Soudley, a minor road heads south through the forest to Blackpool Bridge. In May these woods are full of bluebells; foxgloves take over in June. Blackpool Bridge carries a disused tramline, one of several in the forest built in the nineteenth century to transport coal and iron ore down to the River Severn for further distribution. Two miles west you can divert right to visit the landscaped remains of the defunct **New Fancy open-cast coal mine**. The vast spoil tip has been turfed over to create an artificial hill from whose summit are extensive views over the top of the forest. Continuing west, the road passes through Parkend, where railway buffs will find it difficult to resist the signposts to the **Dean Forest Railway***, which has a museum at Norchard, and steam services to Lydney most weekends in the year.

As a detour off the route, about a quarter of a mile north of Clearwell, **Puzzle Wood*** is the site of unique pre-Roman iron workings. The area was landscaped in the 1800s to turn its network of paths into a natural maze, so you wander past rocks, through ferny glades and across little bridges over chasms.

Back on the route, **Clearwell Caves*** are a fascinating combination of natural caverns and man-made tunnels, created to exploit the rich mineral deposits that lie beneath the forest. The detritus of past mining activities lies all around, and the various mining practices are explained as you follow the waymarked route, including the underground life of the young children who had to haul the coal and ore trucks until this was made illegal in 1842. The temperature in the caves is a constant 10° Celsius, which feels decidedly cold in summer, so wear a sweater and sensible shoes.

The **Miner's Brass**, an image depicting a fourteenth-century miner, hod and pick-axe in hand and candle in mouth, has become the symbol of the Forest of Dean. You can see the original in the church at **Newland**, three miles north-west of Clearwell Caves. The vast church, known as the 'Cathedral of the Forest', is full of fine memorials, as is the surrounding churchyard.

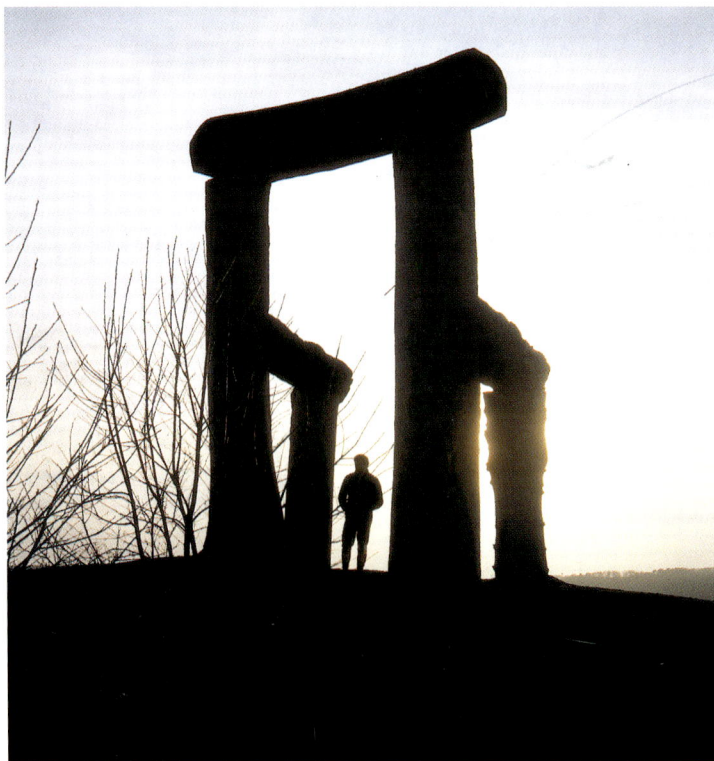

The Giant's Chair, one of several surprises on the Sculpture Trail

Symonds Yat rock lies some five miles north of Newland and is very popular – you are unlikely to enjoy the panoramic views in solitude. High above the River Wye, the rock overlooks a great oxbow bend in the river. Peregrine falcons nest on nearby cliffs, and the RSPB sets up telescopes in season so that, for a small donation, you can watch the birds nesting and feeding. A path is under construction from the rock down to the Wye, and from there a foot ferry will take you to the Jubilee Park, with its maze, museum of mazes, craft centre and butterfly farm (see *Great Day Out 61*).

Head back south from Symonds Yat to Coleford and follow signs to

Speech House. Once a court where miners and foresters could resolve disputes about land ownership, tree-felling and mineral extraction rights, Speech House is now a hotel. Just beyond, on the B4226, is the well-signposted car park at Beechenhurst Lodge, whose adventure playground and picnic facilities can become crowded at weekends. Now follow the intriguing **sculpture trail** through the woodland, coming upon monolithic sculptures made from natural forest materials, such as the magnificent oak Giant's Chair, like something out of a fairy story, the simple metal Melissa's Swing, and the huge hanging stained-glass window that depicts a forest scene. (The walk is four miles long but you could opt for a shortcut.)

If you are heading back in the direction of Gloucester, there are two further sights worth considering. Just east of Cinderford, the rather sparsely furnished but historically fascinating **Littledean Hall*** has some interesting displays on the history of the English manor house. Three miles further east, on the A48, is the beautifully restored water garden, built in the Dutch style in the late seventeenth century, at **Westbury Court Garden***, now maintained by the National Trust. It is planted with varieties of fruit tree that existed before 1700, including pear, plum and apple.

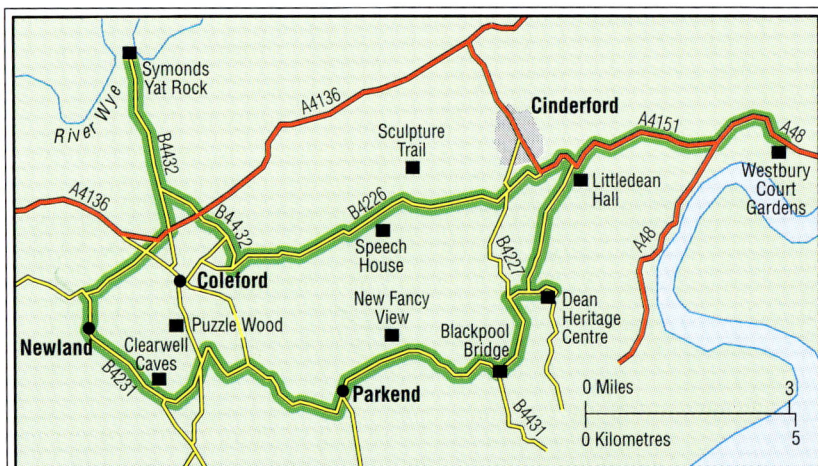

LUNCHBOX

There is a small restaurant at the entrance to Clearwell Caves that serves children's food. Alternatively, there are good places to eat at in Clearwell itself: the rather formal Tudor Farmhouse has an imaginative menu with good vegetarian choices, while the Wyndham Arms serves pub food and welcomes children. Puzzle Wood also offers refreshments. There is a picnic area at Westbury Court Garden.

The lower reaches of the Wye Valley

The magnificent red sandstone ruins of Goodrich Castle dominate the landscape

The River Wye straddles the borders of England and Wales. With beautiful countryside to explore and a choice of activities ranging from shopping and visiting museums to canoeing and ballooning, there is something for everyone in the Wye Valley.

This part of the Wye Valley has been popular with visitors since the eighteenth century, when the 'Wye Tour' was almost essential for poets, painters and the leisured gentry. The area is still lovely, with plenty of things to see and do. We outline the main attractions in the short stretch of the valley between Ross-on-Wye and Monmouth.

Ross is a friendly, lively little market town built on a sandstone hill above the River Wye. The mock-Gothic town walls and the Prospect Gardens provide good views of the valley, while the riverside meadows and parks offer opportunities for walks and picnics. The town centre is a cheerful jumble of brick, stone and timber-framed buildings crowding around the seventeenth-century double-gabled market hall (market

♦ **GOOD FOR** Shops, museums, castles, walks, cycling, canoeing
♦ **TRANSPORT** About 12 miles from Ross to Monmouth, and only short diversions are necessary to visit all the other sights; telephone Hereford and Worcester County Bus Line* for further details of buses on the route
♦ **ACCESS FOR DISABLED PEOPLE** Very good, but phone individual venues to check
♦ **BEST TIME TO VISIT** If your main interest is the countryside go between April and June, or September and November; otherwise, visit between Easter and the end of October, as some venues are closed outside this period

days are Thursday and Saturday). There are antique shops, and a candle workshop which is open to the public.

Palma Court contains several interesting shops, too, and also houses the **Lost Street Museum***, an atmospheric reconstruction of an Edwardian street. Shop frontages, fittings and goods are genuine, and there is also a pub, the Lillie Langtry, all etched glass, brass and mahogany. On Kyrle Street (named after John Kyrle, the seventeenth-century benefactor of the town) you will find the curious **Button Museum***, with around 10,000 buttons on display. Some are made from teeth or bone; others, notably the hand-painted enamel and porcelain ones, are miniature works of art.

Ross is a good centre for walking and cycling expeditions. Bike hire is available from **Little & Hall*** on Broad Street. If you prefer to see the countryside from the air, however, balloon trips over the area are available. The **tourist information office*** on Edde Cross Street can give you details.

Heading south from Ross you soon arrive at **Goodrich Castle*** (EH), perched high above the Wye on a rocky bluff. An abundance of rooms, passages and towers, together with a refreshing absence of 'keep off' notices, makes it a real hit with children. Most exciting is the climb up a steep spiral staircase to the top of the twelfth-century keep.

From Goodrich it is just two miles to the **Wye Valley Farm Park*** at Huntsham. Rare breeds of farm animals and poultry thrive in a traditional setting, and children are encouraged to get close and touch the animals.

A mile further south is **Symonds Yat** (see *Great Day Out 60*). If you want to enjoy the spectacular view from **Yat Rock** without the crowds go midweek or out of season.

Yat Rock is a good starting-point for walks, and some routes are outlined on leaflets available from the

The Market Hall, Ross-on-Wye is built of sandstone and boasts fourteen arches. The carved medallion represents Charles II

refreshments kiosk. Cross the river to the **Doward** to find even more walking opportunities. The crossing may be made by Biblins suspension bridge, or by hand-powered cable ferry – ask at the Saracen's Head or Ye Olde Ferrie Inne. **The Wye Valley Rural Heritage Centre*** is also on the Doward, and displays an impressive collection of vintage farm machinery, including gypsy caravans, vintage tractors, hand tools and horse-drawn farm implements.

Less than a mile north of the Doward, at Whitchurch, is the **Jubilee Park***, which includes a maze, a museum of mazes, a tropical butterfly house and a garden centre. If you are offended by commercialisation in such a setting, this attraction is not for you. If, on the other hand, you are looking for somewhere to spend a wet day, you may well find it ideal.

For those who do not mind getting wet, canoeing is an adventurous option, especially on the rapids below Yat Rock. If you prefer

something more sedate, boat trips are available. Contact one of the tourist information offices for details of various activity and hire centres.

And so to **Monmouth**. Built at the confluence of the Rivers Wye and Monnow, this border town has a long history, as you will appreciate if you visit the fascinating archaeological dig on Monnow Street. There are plenty of fine buildings to admire, notably the unusual thirteenth-century gatehouse on Monnow Bridge. Very little remains of the castle where Henry V was born in 1387, but the king's statue gazes out over Agincourt Square from the Shire Hall, where the **tourist information office*** is located.

Agincourt Square is the hub of the town, especially on market days (Friday and Saturday). Most of the main streets radiate from it, including Priory Street, where the **Nelson Museum and Local History**

Admiral Nelson on the quarterdeck of HMS Victory

Centre* has a unique collection of the admiral's memorabilia on view, including his fighting sword, battle plans, personal effects and letters.

Like the rest of this area, Monmouth is ideal for walkers, and even if you can manage only a short (if steep) walk, you should climb to the top of the wooded hill called **The Kymin** (800 feet) to enjoy a view which Lord Nelson himself declared to be one of the finest he had ever seen. Two follies stand on top, the Round House and the bizarre Naval Temple.

Charles Stuart Rolls, co-founder of Rolls-Royce, grew up on the Hendre estate near Monmouth. A pioneer aviator, balloonist and motor enthusiast, he has the dubious reputation of being the first Briton to die in an air-crash (Bournemouth, 1910). His aerial exploits are celebrated in the Local History Centre and a dashing statue of him was erected in the main square in 1911.

LUNCHBOX

In Ross you will find a wide range of possibilities including Oat Cuisine, a wholefood café, and Meader's, which is unusual in offering a Hungarian menu. In Monmouth, many of the most appealing choices are in Church Street.

Romantic ruins in the Severn Valley

Tintern Abbey, which for over 400 years was a grand and powerful monastery

Three of the best ruins on the Welsh side of the Severn Valley region are featured in this day out, namely Chepstow Castle, Tintern Abbey and Raglan Castle. Children will enjoy the freedom to explore and adults will appreciate the romantic settings.

Chepstow, Tintern and Raglan are all easily reached from the M4, but once you are off the motorway it is best to stick to the delightfully rural roads that thread through a landscape of gently rolling hills, interspersed with ancient woodland.

All three of the sites on this tour are managed by **Cadw***, which also produces a highly commendable series of guidebooks, one for each of the ruins, containing a full and detailed history, with recommended tour route, top-quality reconstruction drawings and numerous photographs. Excellent information boards are also dotted around the sites at strategic points, along with displays in the visitor centres, so those unfamiliar with the history of the area will not be at a loss.

♦ **GOOD FOR** People who enjoy visiting ruins set in beautiful scenery
♦ **TRANSPORT** A car is necessary if you plan to do all three sites in one day
♦ **ACCESS FOR DISABLED PEOPLE** Good at Raglan Castle and Tintern Abbey, but help will be needed to negotiate the steep paths at Chepstow
♦ **BEST TIME TO VISIT** All year (though the woodland around Tintern looks spectacular in autumn)

CHEPSTOW CASTLE

Chepstow Castle* is dramatically located on a clifftop above the winding River Wye, although you may not fully appreciate this fact until you enter the castle and look at the sheer drops that plunge to the river from its walls. The castle was built here not to defend the town, but to guard the river crossing. From here up to Monmouth, 16 miles away, there is no other point where the river can easily be crossed because steep cliffs rise from one or both sides of the river – in fact, the crossing used by the Romans was only ½ mile upstream of the current one. Chepstow was therefore the main crossing point from southern England into Wales, just as it is today – the Severn Bridge is only a mile away.

It was the Normans who built the first castle here: William the Conqueror gave Chepstow to William Fitz Osbern, his trusted friend from the Norman town of Breteuil, who used the town as his base for the conquest of the Welsh kingdom of Gwent. The first castle built by Fitz Osbern in 1067 has survived, making it something of a rarity, since many other early Norman castles were later demolished and rebuilt on a grander scale. Moreover, Chepstow Castle is unusual in that it is built of stone, rather than of timber and wood, the more common post-Conquest building materials. At Chepstow the original keep was simply absorbed into the expanding castle as it spread along the clifftop to reach the immense proportions you see represented by today's ruins. Models help to reconstruct castle life; for instance, maids chat as they prepare a banquet, unaware that a rat is nibbling on crumbs under the table. An exhibition of the history of the castle has a section where you can try on a pikeman's helmet, or handle a cross-bow.

Having explored the castle, you may like to visit the **tourist information office*** alongside the castle car park, which has displays on the Wye Valley Long Distance Footpath, or call in at the **Chepstow Museum*** on the opposite side of the road, full of material on the

Chepstow Castle exhibits a clear progression of styles spanning half a millennium

town's ancient and more recent history. Two displays are particularly worth seeking: one covers the local salmon fishing industry, and the other shows the contents of a now-defunct hairdressing salon in the town, complete with fearsome contraptions from the 1930s for creating perms and waves that look like instruments for experimentation devised by a crazed scientist. The town itself is a pretty place of Georgian buildings encircled by its medieval walls.

TINTERN ABBEY

At **Tintern Abbey*** (five miles north of Chepstow on the A466) the great game for children is to explore the monastic drains (bring a torch if you have one, though this is not essential), which form a series of tunnels below the medieval latrines and monks' dormitories. While the children disappear and re-emerge at unexpected points around the site, adults can enjoy the romantic wooded setting of this very well-preserved Cistercian abbey, a setting that inspired Wordsworth to one of his characteristically introspective poems, and Turner to a series of fine watercolours.

One of the views that Turner painted was of the west façade of the abbey church, a masterpiece of Gothic tracery and elaborate moulding. Built between 1296 and 1301, this church was far more decorative than its predecessor on the site, and is indicative of the decadence that would eventually lead to the order's demise: when it was founded in 1098, the Cistercian order eschewed all forms of luxury and sought to return to the austerity and simplicity of the monastic life defined by St Benedict in AD540.

The Cistercians sought out wild and uninhabited places, as the Wye Valley was in 1131 when they first settled here, but by their industry the monks became, ironically, a very wealthy and powerful order. Tintern Abbey was therefore a monastery of considerable grandeur and comfort.

Raglan Castle, combining elegance and functionality

LUNCHBOX
There are plenty of opportunities for picnics. Otherwise, several pubs serving bar snacks and full meals compete in all three centres.

RAGLAN CASTLE

Raglan is about nine miles north-west of Tintern, reached by any one of several rural roads. The **castle*** is not in the town, but on a hill high above the busy A40 to the north. The thrilling feature of this fifteenth-century castle is its completeness: there are scores of staircases and rooms to explore, as well as bridges spanning the lily-filled moat, and paths on different levels. Much of this results from aesthetic considerations, rather than the strict demands of warfare: Raglan is a very elegant, frenchified castle built at a time when the needs of defence were giving way to the desire for a show of prestige, hence the frilly machicolations (a series of arched openings at battlement level), fancy fireplaces, huge bay windows and fan-vaulted ceilings. The Elizabethan owners, the Herberts, used the castle for lavish entertainments on a scale that can be judged from the size of the kitchens and pantry. After the Civil War, however, when part of the castle was destroyed, they moved on to build a splendid new home at Badminton, and Raglan was simply left to moulder in genteel decay.

Circling the great peaks of the Brecon Beacons

Corn-Du is typical of the Beacons — smooth, grassy flanks rising to razor-sharp ridges

A DROP OF THE HARD STUFF
Did you know that Jack Daniels was a Welshman, and that he took his distilling skills to Tennessee to found the American bourbon industry? The long history of Welsh whisky-making from the sixth-century monastic distillery of Bardsey onwards is vividly displayed at the Welsh Whisky Visitor Centre*, just outside Brecon by the A40/A470 roundabout. Visitors are accompanied on their journey through alcoholic time by a high-tech robotic monk.

To explore the high peaks, forests, valleys and waterfalls in this, one of Britain's most dramatic National Parks, you will need a car that can cope with all the uneven surfaces, twists and turns.

The Brecon Beacons National Park is 520 square miles of barely tamed natural beauty between the Black Mountains to the east and Fforest Fawr to the west. The Beacons were originally used as sites for signal fires and they have lost none of their spectacular appeal. The sheer diversity of this landscape is what makes it so exciting: look around and you will see barren contoured hills, breathtaking escarpments in tiered ranks, high moorland and rocky gorges. Here, too, are billowing waterfalls, lakes and reservoirs, upland slopes pocked with balding patches of heather, immense swirling valleys and wildlife in abundance.

BRECON
Brecon is the perfect base for a day out. It is a thriving market town with a maze of narrow streets full of attractions. The **tourist information**

♦ **GOOD FOR** Enjoying great scenery and putting your car through its paces
♦ **TRANSPORT** About a 40-mile round trip from Brecon
♦ **ACCESS FOR DISABLED PEOPLE** Some museums; the views can be appreciated from the car
♦ **BEST TIME TO VISIT** April to October; the Brecon Jazz Festival is in early August

office* and the **National Parks Centre***, just behind the old cattle market, are worth a visit.

The town stands at the confluence of the Rivers Honddu and Usk and from the bridge you can see the ruins of the medieval castle. Displays of Brecon's past and present are on view in the **Brecknock Museum***: carved love spoons and Celtic crosses share the stage with landscape photographs and drawings of the renowned Brecon Jazz Festival. A short walk away is the **South Wales**

and Monmouthshire Regimental Museum*. You could stroll down to the wharf of the Monmouthshire & Brecon Canal, where **Dragonfly Cruises*** offer regular trips down to Brynich Aqueduct and back.

OUR SUGGESTED DRIVE
Set off on the A470 signposted to Merthyr Tydfil: this southward part of the journey, about 18 miles, is downhill most of the way. Leaving Brecon, you get your first panoramic glimpse of the Beacon peaks straight ahead of you. Pen-y-Fan — its highest point — looms majestically. From its summit, 2,907 feet above sea level, climbers can survey 14 counties, taking in the Malvern Hills, the Bristol Channel and the industrial valleys of south Wales.

First stop, some five miles out of Brecon, is the **National Park Mountain Centre*** at Libanus. On a moorland ridge some 1,100 feet above sea level, it is the perfect vantage point for a real look at Pen-y-Fan and its neighbour, Corn-Du.

A few miles on is **Storey Arms**, site of a youth hostel and one of the most popular base camps for those who plan to scale Pen-y-Fan on foot. From here the landscape begins to change as you pass the Beacons and Cantreff reservoirs. Great swathes of coniferous forest and mixed woodland begin to appear, getting denser as you approach the Taff Fawr Valley: the clearly signposted **Garwnant Forest Visitor Centre*** is a good place for a break. After Llwyn-on Reservoir, the industrial valleys begin to open up as you approach Merthyr Tydfil.

When you reach Cefn-coed, just before the main junction with the A465, turn sharp left towards Vaynor, Pont-sticill and Talybont. This is the

A view of Talybont Reservoir, one of the many bodies of water in this area

beginning of the tortuous route northwards through the heart of the Beacons. As the road climbs, it follows the western fringes of Pont-sticill Reservoir, then on past Pen-twyn Reservoir. Take the right fork and drive into Taf Fechan Forest. This is the trickiest drive of all – the road

is little more than a rough, rugged track, and it reaches its highest point at a perilous dog-leg just before Blaen-y-glyn. Here are some magnificent **waterfalls**. The forest road follows the river until it reaches **Talybont Reservoir**: built in the 1930s to supply Newport with water, this is now famous as a haven for wildlife, attracting hordes of wintering birds.

Make a detour into **Talybont-on-Usk**, where you can park the car and have a walk along the towpath of the **Monmouthshire & Brecon Canal**. From Talybont, pick up the B4558 and head for Pencelli (where stand the long-abandoned ruins of a medieval castle). Stay on the B road out of Pencelli and aim for Brynich. As the road crosses the canal, look for an eighteenth-century storehouse, now housing the **Waterfolk Canal Museum***, which has the largest collection of canal memorabilia in Wales, and where you can enjoy horse-drawn canal trips. Further north, don't miss Brynich Lock or the handsome stone aqueduct nearby. You are now Brecon bound: simply follow the signs into the town.

Re-creating Roman and medieval life

The name Caerleon is derived from castra legionis, meaning camp of the legion

Spend the day discovering what life was like after the Roman invasion of Wales in AD75 by looking round two settlements, and visit a Norman Welsh village of the fourteenth century brought back to life in authentic detail.

Caerwent and Caerleon, some eight miles apart, are among the most fascinating and complete Roman sites in Britain. Both are easily accessed from the M4 and are managed by Cadw, the government organisation that looks after public monuments in Wales (EH members are entitled to reduced admission rates in their first year of membership, and free entrance thereafter). As for all Cadw monuments, there are excellent guidebooks to both places, and informative boards at the sites themselves.

Cosmeston medieval village lies some 22 miles to the south-west of Caerleon, between Barry and Penarth. The village is at its best

◆ **GOOD FOR** History enthusiasts
◆ **TRANSPORT** Car necessary; no public transport
◆ **ACCESS FOR DISABLED PEOPLE** Access is good at the Museum of Welsh life, National Museum and Art Gallery, Cosmeston medieval village and the Roman Legionary Museum
◆ **BEST TIME TO VISIT** All year round

when hosting special events, featuring costumed 'villagers' who demonstrate medieval crafts and the skills of swordplay or archery.

CAERWENT

If you travel from east to west, Caerwent is the first of the three sites

that you will come to. The largest civilian settlement in Wales, it was established after a long and bitter war against the tribe known as the Silures, whom the historian Tacitus described as warlike, valiant and stubborn. Despite their superior armour and organisation, the Romans suffered heavy defeats before they finally quelled the Silures, establishing this town, known as Venta Silurum (the market of the Silures), to introduce the wild Welsh to the benefits of Roman civilisation.

Today, Venta Silurum, a town of 3,000 inhabitants, is little more than a one-street village, but its decline has meant that large areas of the Roman city have survived in the fields and back gardens (the sites are all in the open air, and access is unlimited). Park by the church, which has a small museum in its porch, and walk through the churchyard, keeping to the left, then cross over a stile into a farmyard and over another stile to the right and walk down the wide track straight ahead. This will take you to the best-preserved stretch of the Roman wall that encircles the town.

Turn left and climb the steps on to the wall, following the footpath until you reach the Norman castle mound. From here there are views to the east over to the huge twin towers of the new Severn Bridge, and to the west over a large area of the ancient Roman city. Follow the walls round to the east gate, then turn left up the village street until you reach the Roman temple site on the right. It is not known which god was worshipped here, but the temple of AD330 is an impressive sight; it stands beside the even more grandiose basilica and forum at the heart of the town. Continue on, past the church and village war memorial, and turn right into Pound Lane to see the remains of blacksmiths' shops and houses.

The Roman wall at Caerwent is still standing to a height of 17 feet or more

CAERLEON

Caerleon is the base from which the Romans finally succeeded in quelling the Silures after a thirty-year war in the latter half of the first century AD. Such a protracted war called for the establishment of a Roman legionary fortress and all the necessary support services, so Caerleon was founded as a garrison for some 5,500 men, women and children, and the Romans called it 'Isca' after the River Usk (then called the River Isca). The huge **baths complex*** has been discovered through a good deal of excavation; it functioned much as today's municipal leisure complexes do, with outdoor and indoor pools and exercise areas. Visitors view the remains from above, inside a covered building; Cadw has done a splendid job on the display, using taped commentaries, audio-visuals and lighting effects.

Equally imaginative is the **Roman Legionary Museum***, a short walk away (turn right from the baths' car park), run as part of the National Museum of Wales. This is full of

objects excavated from the fortress, and they provide an insight into Roman army life, from their armour and food to their tombstones and religious beliefs. The road directly opposite the museum leads to the amphitheatre on the left, and a Roman barracks block on the right, complete with cookhouse and latrines. In between is the town's rugby pitch, which occupies precisely the same site that the Romans used as their exercise and parade ground.

The amphitheatre, capable of holding every person in the garrison, is one of Britain's most impressive Roman remains, and visitors can imagine the brutal spectacles involving wild beasts and prisoners that once took place here. It is now used for various theatre productions and festivals.

COSMESTON MEDIEVAL VILLAGE*

Cosmeston was carefully reconstructed on the footings of a genuine medieval village, excavated in the 1980s. Restoration involved

building stone walls using traditional clay, straw and dung mortar, with cruck-built timber frames and thatched roofs, and reconstructing field boundaries, gardens, ovens and pig sties. Rare Dexter cattle, Ryeland sheep and wild-boar-cross pigs roam the village, and, on special occasions, villagers in period dress re-enact daily chores using only the utensils available in the fourteenth century (phone in advance to find out when these will be happening). The village stands next to the Cosmeston Lakes Country Park, which has a visitor centre displaying information on local wildlife, an adventure playground, and leaflets detailing various wildlife walks around the lakes.

'Land of My Fathers' from Caerphilly to Treorchy

The biggest castle in Wales, Caerphilly has a double concentric circuit of walls

South Wales is the land of choirs, cheese, castles and coalmines. Our day out in this fiercely Welsh area takes in the best of these.

To get the real flavour of Welshness, you could not have a better destination than the industrial valleys in the south of the country. This was once the stronghold of the coalmining industry, a tough region etched with pride, hardship and despair. You can still find echoes of this culture in almost every town and village in Mid Glamorgan, but there is also an unmistakable note of confidence and renewal. The mines and collieries may have gone, but the castles remain unmoved, the choirs sing as sweetly as ever and rugby still rules. This day out takes you through this rich landscape to discover some of its most enduring features.

CAERPHILLY CASTLE*

Wales is famed for its fortresses, but none is more majestic than Caerphilly Castle – a vast medieval monolith straddling 30 acres and set

♦ **GOOD FOR** Immersing yourself in Welsh Wales
♦ **TRANSPORT** Car necessary: about 15–20 miles from Caerphilly to Treorchy
♦ **ACCESS FOR DISABLED PEOPLE** The Rhondda Heritage Park and the Pontypridd Historical and Cultural Centre are fully accessible; access to Caerphilly Castle is limited
♦ **BEST TIME TO VISIT** Parks and castles in summer; Pontypridd during the Rugby season (September to Easter)

on three artificial islands. Built by 'Red Gilbert' de Clare, the Anglo-Norman Lord of Glamorgan, and his cohorts over two decades during the thirteenth century, it is an amazing feat of engineering and has proved impregnable throughout its history. Its four great gatehouses, ingenious fortifications and water defences are a wonder to behold. The famous

'leaning tower' (which manages to 'outlean' even Pisa's) is probably the result of subsidence, although some claim it is like that because Cromwell tried to blow it up during the Civil War. For more details on the castle and other sights contact the **tourist information office*** in Caerphilly.

After falling into decline, Caerphilly cheese is once again being produced in these parts. To taste some of the real stuff, walk from the castle to **Court House**, on Cardiff Road. This converted fourteenth-century longhouse is now a bar/restaurant serving real ales and genuine Caerphilly, which is made on the premises once a week by a local farmer's wife.

LIVELY PONTYPRIDD

From Caerphilly, head towards **Pontypridd**, 'The Gateway to the Valleys': take the B4600 or the A468 out of the town, then pick up the main A470 heading north. If there is time, visit **Nantgarw China Works*** (leave the A470 at Treforest Industrial Estate/Caerphilly exit and follow the signs). Set up by William Billingsley in 1813, the factory was for a while renowned for its high-quality porcelain. Today, you can see the restored works site, admire the archaeological finds and watch the resident potter at work.

Even if rugby is not your bag, to be in 'Ponty' on a Saturday during the rugby season (especially if Pontypridd is playing on its home ground, Sardis Road) is quite an experience. The sprawling town market – held on Wednesdays and Saturdays – has been dubbed 'the Petticoat Lane of Wales'.

In the nearby Market Tavern, advertisements celebrate the heyday of entertainment in the local Town Hall Theatre. In the 1950s, audiences were wowed by such acts as Yeaman's Famous Footballing Dogs, Arthur Pond ('the long ripple') and other

Experience the sights, sounds and smells of a colliery at the Rhondda Heritage Park

FEATS OF CLAY
A visit to John Hughes's **Grogg Shop*** is a must when you are in Pontypridd. His distinctive red and green building just out of town on the Broadway is filled with pottery effigies of legendary rugby players. Welsh heroes and villains jostle for position with big names from the international arena. John Hughes has also applied his talents to other famous faces: John Wayne swaggers past Winston Churchill, while Bob Dylan strums his guitar in a corner.

'scintillating stars of the future'. A star of today, the singer Tom Jones, was born in Pontypridd.

If you want to learn about Pontypridd and its people, visit the **Pontypridd Historical and Cultural Centre*** in a converted chapel by the town's Old Bridge. Working models, archive films and sound recordings are used to good effect here. One attraction is a life-size figure of the opera singer Sir Geraint Evans (born in this area), donning his 'Falstaff' costume.

Alternatively, if you fancy fresh air and outdoor pursuits, cross the Old Bridge and head for **Ynysangharad War Memorial Park***, which boasts glorious gardens set alongside a sweeping bend of the River Taff, not to mention a children's play area and the largest outdoor swimming-pool in Wales. Close to the bandstand is a memorial to Evan and James James, the father and son who wrote the words and music for 'Land of My Fathers', a song later adopted as the Welsh national anthem.

THE RHONDDA HERITAGE TRAIL

After lunch, head for the Rhondda Valley. The **Rhondda Heritage Park***, based at Lewis Merthyr Colliery, Trehafod, signposted between Pontypridd and Porth, will give you a very realistic insight into the life of a coalminer.

For years, Rhondda and coal were synonymous; the seams were first worked on this site during the 1850s. The colliery closed in 1983, but the Heritage Park has breathed new life into what had become a derelict industrial wasteland. 'The Black Gold Experience', a multi-media exhibition, recreates the local culture of the Rhondda as seen through the eyes of three generations of one mining family. If you really want to know what it was like underground, go for 'A Shift in Time' – a hair-raising subterranean trip that ends with an unforgettable ride as you hurtle through the maze of dark and twisting tunnels back to the surface (wear sturdy shoes and clothing). If the kids want to have fun of a different kind, they can play in the Energy Zone with its amazing adventure games.

A couple of miles further on is Porth, home of the **Welsh Hill Works**. To provide an alternative to the strong alcoholic brews sold to miners in the local pubs, William Evans (an ardent Chapel man) set up a factory producing non-alcoholic alternatives, including ginger beer and football stout – an initiative that eventually grew into a major soft drinks company, Corona Pop.

Regeneration has changed the face of the Rhondda landscape since many of the collieries closed. In their place you will find numerous country parks and picnic areas. Beyond Porth is **Clydach Vale Country Park**: laid out around the remains of the old Cambrian Colliery, it is a pleasant expanse of lakes, streams, native trees and copses. Further north, amid the rising mountain slopes near Glycornel is **Nantgwyddon Picnic Park**. Stroll through the oak woods, sit by the lake or make the strenuous two-mile trek to the site of a prehistoric settlement high on Mynydd y Gelli.

Further on, close to Treorchy, is **Bwlch Clawdd Picnic Park** and adventure playground tucked away in a pine forest (barbecue facilities are available here). It is also worth taking a walk to see the **Gorsedd Circle** that marks the site of the National Eisteddfod held here in 1928.

Treorchy itself is best known for its world-famous choir, whose home venue is the **Park and Dare Theatre***. Built between 1903 and 1913 using subscriptions from miners' wages, it now ranks as a first-rate centre for the performing arts. It also houses a curiously fascinating exhibition devoted to that 'adopted Welshman', the bass singer Paul Robeson. Don't miss the chance to hear the choir if it is performing.

LUNCHBOX
Have lunch in John & Maria's, a lively old-style Anglo-Italian restaurant directly opposite Pontypridd Railway Station. Alternatively, enjoy a picnic in Ynysangharad War Memorial Park.

Animal, vegetable and mineral on the Gower

Local delicacies proudly displayed at Swansea's indoor market

A day out on the Gower Peninsula is a chance to explore some of South Wales' finest scenery, encompassing beaches, coves, woodland, great reaches of sand and astonishing outcrops of rock.

The Gower Peninsula, a rugged rectangle of land stretching from Swansea and Mumbles westward to Rhossili and Worms Head, was earmarked as Britain's first Area of Outstanding Natural Beauty in 1956 and it is easy to see why. Our suggested day takes in some of the highspots, where you can indulge in almost any activity that takes your fancy – from poking around for shells to riding the waves on a surfboard. And if your beachcombing endeavours are to no avail, you can always cheat and buy something from Swansea's historic indoor market.

SWANSEA

Whatever else you decide to do, set aside time for Swansea, particularly if the weather is less than kind. The **tourist information office*** in Singleton Street should be able to provide you with details of events and sights worth seeing.

♦ **GOOD FOR** Beachcombing, treasure trove and wild food
♦ **TRANSPORT** Car desirable, or cycle: about 15 miles from Swansea to Rhossili
♦ **ACCESS FOR DISABLED PEOPLE** Some sights
♦ **BEST TIME TO VISIT** April to October; Swansea Market Cockle Festival early September

The great **indoor market**, between the two main shopping centres, is unmissable, especially if you are keen on local produce. Here you will find all kinds of seafood – cockles from Penclawydd, the seaweed called laver, and fish of every description. You will also find bakers selling Welsh cakes and bara brith, plus any number of crafts, curios, and knick-knacks with local connections.

Swansea also has its share of museums and other public attractions: **Swansea Museum***

SPOONFULS OF LOVE
Lovespoons – symbolic tokens of affection and loyalty carved out of wood – are one of Wales' most enduring craft traditions. You can feast your eyes on the finest display in the UK at the **Lovespoon Gallery***, 492 Mumbles Road, Mumbles.

itself, in Victoria Road, is the oldest in Wales and has some extraordinary prehistoric finds from the caves on the Gower Peninsula, as well as displays of local wildlife and a reconstructed traditional Welsh kitchen. In the revitalised Maritime Quarter, the **Maritime and Industrial Museum*** charts the city's nautical past, and various floating exhibits include the old Mumbles lifeboat as well as a steam tug and a lightship.

If flora and fauna are your passion, don't miss **Plantasia*** at Parc Tawe. This futuristic botanical extravaganza is housed in a spectacular glass pyramid that contains three climatic zones from tropical rainforests and deserts to humid areas full of rare orchids and carnivorous plants. Pineapples, bananas, coffee and ginger are quite at home in this city jungle; so too are snakes, lizards, tree frogs, stick insects and spiders.

THE GOWER PENINSULA
Head out of the city, following the coast road that leads towards **Mumbles**. This jovial playground of a village is famous for its lighthouse and also its 900-foot Victorian pier,

LUNCHBOX
Load your picnic hamper with produce from Swansea market if you are planning to spend most of the day on the Gower Peninsula. Otherwise, Swansea and Mumbles have numerous affordable eating places. There is also a tea room and picnic area at the Gower Heritage Centre.

The broad sweep of Rhossili Bay at the Gower's western tip

which has glorious views across the bay. Looming above it all, on a hill above the village, is **Oystermouth Castle***, the last seat of the Lords of Gower and still an impressive sight. There is an invigorating cliff walk nearby to Langland Bay and on to Caswell Bay.

From Mumbles, cut through Newton and Bishopston until you reach the B4436. Turn left and pick up the main A4118 towards Parkmill, which is now the focus of the **Gower Heritage Centre***. This is a rare example of a fully functioning complex of rural trades and crafts, centring on a historic water mill and corn-grinding machinery, and with blacksmiths, wheelwrights, masons and carpenters all in occupation.

Now head for the sand and seascapes of Oxwich Bay, first making a detour to **Oxwich Castle**, which is actually the remains of a courtyard house built during the sixteenth century. From here you can gaze across **Oxwich Bay** with its three miles of glorious sands and dunes.

The bay itself is tailor-made for all types of watersports and activities, especially canoeing and sailing; otherwise, you could hire a boat from one of the local skippers for a sea-fishing trip. You can also get absorbed in some fruitful beachcombing for shells, pebbles and anything else that the sea might wash up; foraging for laver (see the Seaside harvest box) is another favourite summer pastime. Oxwich also has a good nature trail, with walks across the dunes and woodland that skirt the bay.

At the end of the A4118 itself lies **Port Eynon**, a compact village of slate-roofed white cottages, with its recently excavated **Salt House***, where salt was reclaimed from the sea in Tudor times. But for the most spectacular sights and scenery of all, you need to drive further west along the B4247 towards **Rhossili**, Gower's dramatic 'Land's End'. The **National Trust Visitor Centre and Shop***, housed in the

A cockle-picker rakes through the mudflats on one of the Gower's northern beaches

Coastguard Cottage, is the ideal point from which to start.

Views from the village itself, which stands on a headland above three miles of superb sandy beach, are spectacular. Great Atlantic rollers crash in when the westerly winds are blowing, making the whole area a magnet for surfers and watersport fanatics. For something less strenuous, there is more excellent beachcombing to be had: several wrecks are buried in the sands, yielding up the occasional silver dollar.

For those who fancy walking, there are several good hikes from the main village car park (expect crowds in the height of summer) over the cliffs. To the north is the expansive curve of Rhos Bay, its smooth sands backed by a three-mile coastal hill walk to the hermit's cell of Burry Holms. Alternatively, head south along the high cliffs, past secluded Mewslade Bay and Paviland Cave, which may well have been dwelling places for our prehistoric ancestors. Some of these caves can be entered at low tide and are said to contain the roosts of rare bats, as well as remains of extinct animals such as the Irish elk, mammoth and woolly rhino.

And if you stand at Rhossili and look westward, you cannot fail to miss the curiously named islet of **Worms Head**, which can also be reached via a causeway when the tide is out.

Carmarthen and Dylan Thomas country

The wooden cliff-hanging shed above the Boat House at Laugharne where Dylan Thomas wrote

---

LUNCHBOX

Waverley Vegetarian Restaurant in Lammas Street, and the Old Curiosity restaurant at King Street, both in Carmarthen, welcome children.

Romance, legend, history and fiction are intertwined in this 'mussel pooled and heron priested shore', as the poet Dylan Thomas described the Taf Estuary below Laugharne (pronounced Larn) where he lived for four years until his death in 1953.

'**B**rown as owls', as in Dylan Thomas's 'Poem in October', the sandstone **Laugharne Castle*** (recently restored by Cadw) was erected on a site occupied by the great Rhys ap Gruffydd, the last Prince of South Wales. Its formidable outline was created by its Norman lords, the de Brians. The castle was later turned into a fine Tudor mansion by the Elizabethan courtier Sir John Perrot, but having been besieged by Roundheads in 1644, it was partly dismantled and never lived in again. A garden was established in the eighteenth and nineteenth centuries and one of its broad paths was covered with locally abundant cockleshells.

Richard Hughes, author of *A High Wind in Jamaica*, lived in **Castle House** in the grounds of the castle. The novelist invited the newly-weds Dylan and Caitlin Thomas to stay in

♦ **GOOD FOR** Fans of the life and works of Dylan Thomas; castles, markets
♦ **TRANSPORT** 25 miles one way from Laugharne to Kidwelly, plus 16 miles round-trip between Carmarthen and Llansteffan. Kidwelly and Llansteffan castles are served by buses from Carmarthen
♦ **ACCESS FOR DISABLED PEOPLE** Difficult steps to Boat House; tourist information office has free disabled access guides
♦ **BEST TIME TO VISIT** The Dylan Thomas Boat House Museum and Laugharne Castle are open all year, with reduced opening hours in winter. Kidwelly Castle closed Christmas and on New Year's Day

1938, but he was not generous with his wine. The Thomases soon discovered Hughes' wine cellar and proceeded to raid it after dark. One day Thomas was sipping some stolen

wine in the summerhouse when Hughes dropped by. The poet sat on the bottle and the wine slowly leaked out between his legs.

Dylan Thomas's short stories in *Portrait of the Artist as a Young Dog* were written here, while Hughes used the setting for his novel *In Hazard*.

Dylan and Caitlin and their two children Llewellyn and Aeronwy finally moved to Laugharne in 1949, where Dylan wrote his most famous work, *Under Milk Wood*, between cliff-top trips for a drink at Brown's Hotel. Although this radio play was probably based partly on New Quay in Cardigan Bay, the white clock-tower of Laugharne must have been where Myfanwy Price dreamt of 'her lover, tall as the town clock-tower'. Dylan turned a wooden shed, which was built on stilts over the cliff-edge and was once the garage for Laugharne's first motor car, into his 'workshack' after his patroness (Margaret Taylor, wife of the historian A.J.P. Taylor) bought it for him in 1949, along with the three-storey Boat House. This 'sea-shaken house on a breakneck of rocks', as he called it, would be worth a visit even if Thomas had not just come, 'one day, for the day, and never left; got off the bus, and forgot to get on again'. It is now open to visitors as a **heritage centre*** dedicated to the poet's life and work.

If you are at all keen on castles, a diversion to the one at **Llansteffan** will be a cherished bonus. It perches on a high ridge above the Tywi Estuary, and is open at any reasonable time with no admission charge. The twin-towered gatehouse is the most impressive remaining feature. Dylan

Laugharne Castle and the Taf Estuary: inspiration for both Thomas and Hughes

A delightful walk of about three-and-a-half miles can be taken from Kidwelly Castle. The Ordnance Survey Pathfinder map No. 1106 would be useful (Kidwelly Castle is at grid reference SN 409071).

Facing the entrance to the castle, go left to pass the old Moat House on your left and reach a crossroads. Go right along Water Street and take the second signposted path on your left, marked 'Ffordd yr Haf/Summer Way'. Follow this old green lane, turning right when signposted. Go ahead through a kissing-gate and bear left to the top right-hand corner of a field. Turn right beside a hedgerow on your right, cross over a stile and bear right, as signposted. Continue through a gap in a hedge and pass springs in an uncultivated area. Cross another stile to the right of a gate. Turn left and then right at a junction with a lane.

Descend to a road, with a view across the river to the battlefield of Maes-Gwenllian ahead. (Gwenllian was the wife of Gruffudd ap Rhys, Lord of Dyfed. When her husband was away in Gwynedd, in 1136, she led local Welsh resistance to a Norman advance. The heroine met her death at Maes-Gwenllian, where her headless ghost was observed walking the battlefield. One night somebody reunited her body with its head and her spirit was, at last, at peace.)

Turn right along the wide verge and take a lane on your left, following it around a sharp right-hand bend. As you approach Broadford Farm, on your right, turn right along an old green lane. Continue across a new road and through a gate. At the metalled lane turn right to climb to a road. Turn left to return to Kidwelly Castle.

Thomas was a regular visitor to Llansteffan as his mother came from nearby Llangain, and his short story 'A Visit to Grandpa's' immortalised one visit he made as a child.

Nestling on the banks of the River Tywi in lush countryside, **Carmarthen** is the ancient county town of the region. The Romans made it their administrative capital Moridunum. Market days are Wednesday and Saturday and the craft shops and specialist food shops are worth a browse. The **tourist information office*** can provide you with details of exhibitions and trips. Some say that Merlin (Myrddin) came from Carmarthen. He prophesied the drowning of the town 'when Myrddin's tree shall tumble down'. A few years ago the local authority removed the tree, by then reinforced with concrete and iron bars, as it was a traffic hazard …

Wales is rich in castles, so one more might go unnoticed, but **Kidwelly Castle*** (Cadw) is a real beauty. Its medieval masonry (four towers and a gatehouse) overlooking the River Gwendraeth provides a textbook illustration of castle development, with its walls-within-walls defensive system.

Not all of Kidwelly's history belongs to the Middle Ages. Gain an insight into the life of a handmill tinplate worker at the **Kidwelly Industrial Museum***, occupying the site of the tinplate works which functioned between 1737 and 1941. The riverside picnic site and playground are just the place for children to let off steam.

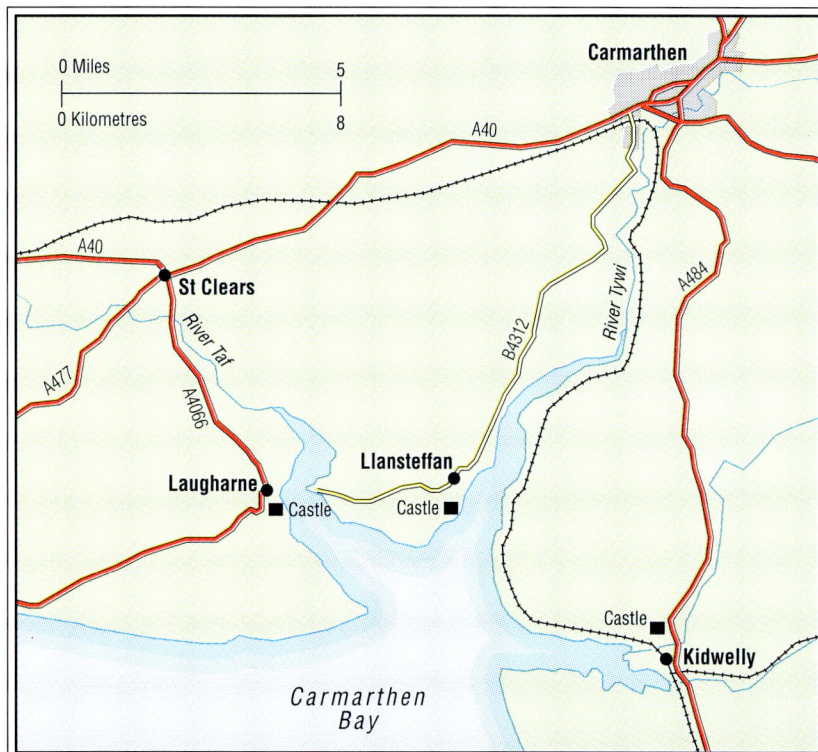

0 Miles	5
0 Kilometres	8

Carmarthen

A40

A40

St Clears

River Taf

A477

A4066

River Tywi

B4312

A484

Laugharne
■ Castle

Llansteffan
Castle ■

Castle ■
● Kidwelly

Carmarthen Bay

The Pembrokeshire Coast National Park

Dinbych-y-pysgod, the Welsh name for Tenby, means 'little fort of the fishes'

The 180-mile National Park in Pembrokeshire is the only coastal national park in Britain. This section of it covers some of the loveliest and least spoilt coastal scenery in Great Britain, a handful of medieval Welsh towns and includes an extraordinary centre of pilgrimage.

The old county of Pembrokeshire is one of cliffs and beaches, working harbours and ancient settlements, hills and woods. Inland are the Preseli Hills, high moorlands where the stones were quarried for Stonehenge in Wiltshire, but our route follows the coast itself and the long-distance Pembrokeshire Coast Path, taking in Britain's smallest city and a massive medieval castle, before finishing at the pretty beach of Tenby.

Begin at **Fishguard**, an attractive town built round the old fishing village known in Welsh as Abergwaun. From here it is a 16-mile drive along the A487, following the spectacular coast, with its rocky headlands, quiet inlets and small towns, to the cathedral city of St David's. This tiny city is almost always crowded with sightseers and hikers; parking can be a big problem. Many

- ♦ **GOOD FOR** Plenty of driving and walking, but select appropriate stretches of the coastal footpath and keep children under careful supervision
- ♦ **TRANSPORT** By car is best – 53 miles from Fishguard to Tenby; no railway at St David's
- ♦ **ACCESS FOR DISABLED PEOPLE** Access to a few sights
- ♦ **BEST TIME TO VISIT** Spring, summer, autumn; St David's all year

come to see the **cathedral***, built to honour the patron saint of Wales and all but hidden in a deep hollow. David is believed to have founded a monastery on this spot in the sixth century but this and later buildings had been destroyed by the time his shrine was found in the undergrowth in the eleventh century; the present cathedral was begun in 1181. One of

the most striking features of the interior is the early sixteenth-century Irish oak roof; look out, too, for the Abraham stone, carved with Celtic motifs, which marked the grave of Hedd and Isaacs, Bishop Abraham's sons who were killed by Vikings. This is kept in the south transept, along with a fine seventeenth-century Eastern Orthodox icon from Crete, showing Elijah being fed by ravens.

Next to the cathedral are the splendid ruins of the fourteenth-century **Bishop's Palace***. The arched, Decorated-style parapet, which Bishop Henry Gower had constructed to give the building unity, is still impressive, and in its heyday the palace's great hall was said to be big enough for all the bishops of Europe to dine in together.

About half a mile from St David's itself, which is crammed with gift shops and cafés, signs direct you to **St Non's Chapel and Well**, a peaceful spot overlooking the sea near a Catholic retreat. St Non, David's mother, and was said to have given birth to him here on the cliffs during a thunderstorm. The legend goes that a well sprung up as David was born. Its healing waters are now covered with a stone arch and guarded by a simple shrine.

WALKING

The **National Park Information Centre*** (open April to October) in St David's city hall is a good place to pick up maps and directions for walks along the coastal path. Out of season, visit the **tourist information office*** at Fishguard. You can start virtually anywhere along the coast and choose from gentle, relatively level stretches or more challenging routes that involve stiff climbing and run close to sheer drops. Having found the most appropriate section, take sensible precautions: wear sturdy shoes or boots and be prepared for sudden weather changes (the mists can roll in from the sea at an alarming rate).

One popular walk runs from **Whitesand Bay to St David's Head**. The starting point is just a couple of miles from St David's along the B4583; park at the car park behind the beach and climb the steps leading to the path on the right. This takes you along the cliff edge, with tremendous views of the reefs and islets around the bay, known as the Bishops and Clerks, to the promontory of **St David's Head**. Traces of an Iron Age fortress can be seen here, as well as the massive stones of the **Warriors' Dyke**.

You can extend the walk further along the coast (where the path is less defined and requires caution) to see **Arthur's Quoit**, a Stone Age burial chamber standing alone among the gorse and heather. For a more taxing extension, turn inland towards the rocky 595-foot peak of **Carn Llidi**. From here the track brings you back to the road leading to Whitesand Bay.

From St David's the A487 takes you to **Haverfordwest** (Hwlffordd), a useful stopping point for lunch. You then join the A4076, which passes the sinister-looking power station and oil refineries

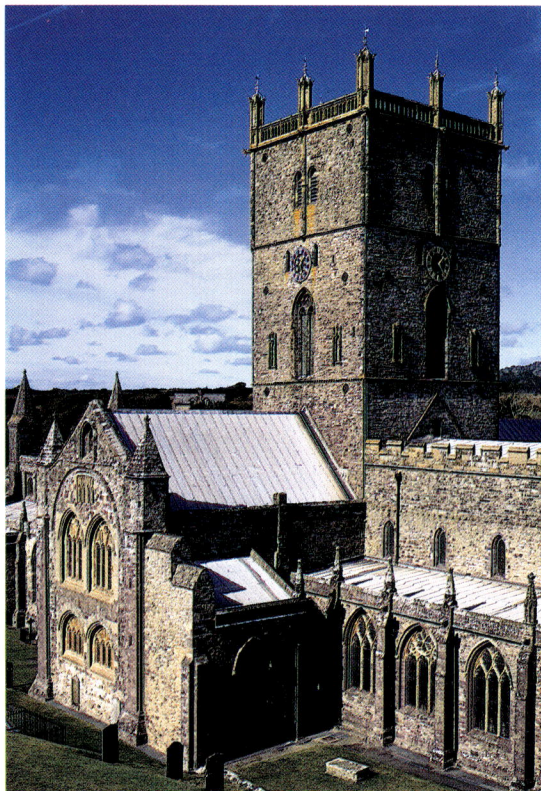

offshore at Milford Haven. Cross the Cleddau toll bridge and continue to the little market town of Pembroke. **Pembroke Castle***, the oldest fortress in West Wales, looms over the town and river, and can be reached from the main street or by climbing Westgate Hill from the car

The purple-coloured stone, used to build St David's Cathedral, was quarried from nearby Caerbwdi

park. Its earliest part, the round keep, built in about 1200, stands 75 feet high, with walls 19 feet thick. Harri Tudur (Henry Tudor), who was to take the throne in 1485 as Henry VII, was born here.

The final run of this journey is along the A4139 to the lovely seaside resort of Tenby (Dinbych-y-pysgod), where pastel-coloured houses crowd round the harbour, separating two wide swathes of sandy beach; one is the Blue Flag-flying North Beach, the other is the dune-backed South Beach, which is busy with windsurfers, kite-flyers and anglers. Tenby has immense appeal other than sand and sea. On the headland above the harbour (Castle Hill) are the ruins of a medieval castle and the small **Tenby Museum and Picture Gallery***, which houses a collection of paintings by Augustus and Gwen John. The town itself has a higgledy-piggledy medieval layout and parts of its defensive walls survive: on South Parade the Five Arches (six, in fact) straddle the pavement, and shops and houses have been built into the walls' recesses. On Quay Hill the National Trust runs the three-storey **Tudor Merchant's House***, one of Tenby's many interesting old houses. Remains of its original frescoes can still be seen inside.

Caldy Island, just a mile and half long, lies offshore to the south of Tenby and has been a religious centre for over 1,500 years. The Cistercian monks who now live here make a range of goods to earn their crust, including perfume, shortbread, yoghurt and chocolate, and visitors can take the short boat trip from Tenby Harbour to sample them. Only men are allowed to tour the monastery, but everyone can enjoy the island's wildlife, particularly the seals, and the cormorant colony nesting on nearby St Margaret's Island.

Poetry and mining in 'Wild Wales'

Strata Florida Abbey: the Latin name means 'carpet of flowers'

LUNCHBOX

If you prefer not to picnic at Strata Florida, aim to arrive in Tregaron in time for lunch. The **Talbot Hotel** is where George Borrow 'experienced very good entertainment, had an excellent supper and a very comfortable bed'. Bar meals are served, and there is also a restaurant. Children are welcome and can find swings in the beer garden. If you do not want to order Tregaron's famous ham, vegetarian dishes are always on the menu. Both mines also have refreshments.

On this day out you can visit a silver-lead and a gold mine, contemplate the history and poetry of past centuries in an abbey and two churches, and witness the raw beauty of two natural sights in the remote countryside of Cardiganshire.

This tour takes you into a remote part of Wales, mostly along solitary B roads, and gives you a vivid sense of an ancient land of Celtic mists and legends. The route hugs the western edge of the Cambrian mountains a dozen miles inland from Cardigan Bay, and starts east of Aberystwyth at Ponterwyd. It follows part of the tour that the East Anglian writer and traveller George Borrow made in the mid-nineteenth century and later recounted in his book *Wild Wales*, which was published in 1862.

When Borrow was making his way to Ponterwyd he sought the assistance of a local guide. He recorded the comment: 'We must find him one. It will never do to let him go by himself.' Nowadays, the

♦ **GOOD FOR** Literary associations and unusual mining history in some of Wales' least-known countryside; no under-5s in the mines
♦ **TRANSPORT** 54-mile one-way trip: car essential
♦ **ACCESS FOR DISABLED PEOPLE** No
♦ **BEST TIME TO VISIT** Both mines open Easter to October

Llywernog Silver-Lead Mine*, the first port of call for the visitor, is easy enough to find, just one mile west of Ponterwyd. This award-winning open-air museum has been restored to look as it if were still in its Victorian heyday. Allow two hours to follow the **Miners' Trail**: aim to be there when it opens at 10am. You can see, for instance,

what was involved in panning for the silver or lead. The play area will keep children amused.

Next head south along the A4120. Very soon you will come upon **Ysbyty Cynfyn** church. Set above the wooded gorge of the River Rheidol, the churchyard boasts five large standing stones, suggesting that the church was built within an ancient stone circle. Under a tree next to the railings on the left of the church porch is the last resting place not only of one Isaac Hughes, who died on 6 March 1856, aged 32 (he is thought to have been a miner at Llywernog), and of his young son and daughter, Hugh and Hannah, who died a few days either side of their father, but also of the first recorded quadruplets, Margaret, Elizabeth, Catherine and Isaac, who all died within six days of their birth on 17 February 1856. Only their mother, Margaret, survived that year's outbreak of typhoid.

A few minutes further south you will arrive at **Devil's Bridge*** (see *Great Day Out 70*), its bridges, waterfalls and punchbowls scoured by the water in the rocks. Coin-operated turnstiles allow daily admission to the gorge, where George Borrow noted: 'If pleasant recollections do not haunt you through life of the noble falls and the beautiful wooded dingles to the west

Miners' helmets and lamps are provided for your tour of the Dolaucothi Roman Gold Mines

of the bridge of the Evil One, and awful and mysterious ones of the monks' boiling cauldron, the long, savage, shadowy cleft, and the grey, crumbling, spectral bridge, I say boldly that you must be a very unpoetical person indeed.' Be warned – there are a great many steps.

Take the B4343 south to Pontrhydfendigaid, where you turn east along a lane to **Strata Florida Abbey***, an ideal place for a picnic on a sunny day. This ruined Cistercian abbey (in the care of Cadw*) still has some marvellously intact mosaic floors and a beautifully carved stone archway. Here Llywelyn the Great assembled all the Welsh lords to swear allegiance to his son Dafydd as Prince of Wales in 1238. Alongside the graves of some of the princes and princesses of the old kingdom of Ceredigion reposes a tramp who was found dead in the snow on the road to Rhayader in 1929.

He is in notorious company, if it is true that the fourteenth-century poet Dafydd ap Gwilym is also buried in the graveyard, under an ancient yew tree. He was a great womaniser, although you wouldn't think so from this verse: 'I am one of passion's asses, Plague on all these parish lasses! Though I long for them like

mad, Not one female have I had, Not a one in all my life, Virgin, damsel, hag or wife.'

Carry on down the B4343 for a late lunch in Tregaron. As Borrow approached the town, a local told him it was 'famed for very good ham; best ham at Tregaron in all Shire Cardigan'. The sleepy little town has a **tourist information office*** in the square.

Continue south along the B4343 to one of the most sacred spots in Wales. **Llanddewi Brefi's church** is built on the spot where St Dewi (St David) preached against the word of the monk Pelagius, who had promoted salvation by deeds rather than by divine grace. Some 4,000 years beforehand, Huw Gadarn, 'Huw the Mighty', had come here; the bellowing of his ox split open the Foelallt Rock to the east of the church.

Head now for **Pumsaint**, on the A482 between Lampeter and Llanwrda. The place name refers to five saints who set up a hermitage here shortly after the Roman occupation of Britain came to an end. The Romans were attracted here by gold, and you can see what brilliant engineers they were if you follow the Roman tour at **Dolaucothi Gold**

Mines*, the only known Roman gold mine in Britain. Now in the care of the National Trust, the mines prospered again in the nineteenth century and the beginning of the twentieth after years of neglect, which helped to preserve the Romans' work. Adits (horizontal shafts) were dug into the hillsides and a complex aqueduct system devised consisting of channels cut in the hillsides for carrying the water that washed the ore after crushing. The miners are thought to have been slaves, forced to live as well as work underground. A visitor centre explains the history of the mines and a trail leaflet gives details of a self-guided tour and walks round the Dolaucothi estate. Tours of the 1930s Mitchell Mine and the Roman tour (overground and underground in the Roman adit) are extra to the admission charge. The visitor can also see old machinery and try gold-panning: tiny pieces of real gold are hidden amongst the fools' gold – this is particularly popular with children. Be sure to arrive before 4.30pm to book a place on an underground tour, and wear stout footwear.

If you still have time and energy, finish off your day by driving up the valley of the River Cothi to reach the RSPB's Dinas Nature Reserve, just south of Llyn Brianne. Enjoy an easy ramble of two miles from the car park (leaflets are obtainable at the site); the route is waymarked and includes an exciting quarter-mile boardwalk over a marshy area. Halfway round the walk admire the 'white water' of the dramatic cataracts in the River Towy.

TWM SIÔN CATTI

Twm Siôn Catti used to live in a cave near the top of a cliff above the woodland in the Dinas Nature Reserve. Born in about 1530, the illegitimate son of Catti Jones of Tregaron, he is as legendary a figure in Wales as Robin Hood is in England, with the difference that we know Twm Siôn Catti really did exist. George Borrow said he was 'very different from other thieves; a funny fellow, and so good-natured that everybody loved him – so they made him magistrate, not, however, before he had become a very rich man by marrying a great lady who fell in love with him.'

Ceredigion: the ancient coast of Cardiganshire

Constitution Hill looks down on the seafront in Aberystwyth

The ancient princedom of Ceredigion was bounded by the Pumlumon mountains to the east and by the sea to the west, and its name is still applied to this predominantly Welsh-speaking area. This day out explores the coast from Aberystwyth to Cardigan.

From the cheerful attractions of an old-fashioned seaside resort to the unspoilt beauty of Cardigan Island, this is a section of the west Wales coastline that will appeal to everyone. A journey from Aberystwyth to Cardigan reveals the magnificent, sweeping Cambrian highlands, the quiet serenity of Ceredigion's bays and islets and the strong Welsh character of its towns and villages.

Sitting on the shore of Cardigan Bay, **Aberystwyth** is a useful base for exploring the coast and has plenty to occupy visitors for considerably more than a day. At heart this is still a Victorian seaside town: its curving seafront terrace of elegant three-storey houses has barely changed in a

♦ **GOOD FOR** Families who want a varied day, mostly outdoors
♦ **TRANSPORT** Railway station at Aberystwyth; a regular bus service runs from Aberystwyth to Cardigan via Aberaeron and New Quay
♦ **ACCESS FOR DISABLED PEOPLE** Limited at most attractions
♦ **BEST TIME TO VISIT** Spring, summer

hundred years. In the holiday season the promenade offers such traditional attractions as donkey rides, shows and concerts in the bandstand pavilion, a paddling pool, and fish and chips. The stub-end of the pier, most of which was washed away in a storm in the 1930s, has the usual games and

amusements arcades, but just across the road is a feature unique to Aberystwyth, the **Old College**, an incongruous mock-Gothic creation with turret and mosaic murals, originally built as a hotel but bought for the new University College in 1874 when its owner went bankrupt. It is still used by the university. At the same end of the promenade are the few ruins of thirteenth-century **Aberystwyth Castle**; opposite are the steep slopes of Constitution Hill, whose summit is accessible by foot or by the rumbling old electric **Cliff Railway***, which carried its first passengers in 1902 and is the longest-running railway of its kind in Britain. Your reward is a sweeping view of the bay and town and an even better panorama at the **Camera Obscura**, a restored Victorian curiosity, where an image of the outside world is reflected on to a round 'table' in a darkened room.

Aber, as it is known in Wales, is more than just a resort: this is a university town with a bustling life of its own and a large community of Welsh-speaking residents and students. The university's modern campus overlooks the sea from Penglais Hill and includes a well-run **Arts Centre***. Between campus and sea is a network of streets crowded with shops, B&Bs, hotels and chapels. In Terrace Road, a refurbished Edwardian music hall houses the **Ceredigion Museum***, which concentrates on local history. The museum is also accessible via the **tourist information office***.

For an excursion from Aberystwyth, make the 12-mile drive to **Devil's Bridge*** (see also *Great Day Out 69*), a lush gorge where three bridges have been built one over the other. The curious stack crosses four waterfalls that plunge 326 feet into the River Mynach. The first bridge, set up in the twelfth

One of the first planned towns in Wales, Aberaeron has a stone-walled harbour

century, was said to be the work of the devil; the second was built above it in 1753, when the original became unsafe, and in 1901 another version was constructed over the earlier two. Steps lead down beside the falls to a waterside walk, but take care – this can be a tricky, slippery descent, even in the best of weather..

You can also travel to Devil's Bridge by the **Vale of Rheidol Railway***, originally built to carry lead and timber. The steam train climbs over 600 feet on the hour-long journey, on an exceptionally narrow track, and passes through lovely mountain country.

Alternatively, after a morning in Aber you could take the coast road (the A487) south to **Aberaeron**, about 16 miles away. This smart little Georgian harbour town was built virtually from scratch in the early nineteenth century by the Reverend Alban Thomas Jones-Gwynne and his wife, Susan, who spent every last penny on their pet project. Brightly painted houses sit round a small quayside, where the **Hive on the Quay*** has an unusual exhibition of bees at work (honey ice-cream is on sale all over town). A pleasant riverside walk is signposted from town, along Heol y Dwr (Water Street). If it rains and you decide to go no further on this itinerary, other diversions in Aberaeron include the **Sea Aquarium*** and the **Clos Pengarreg Courtyard*** craft complex.

A short detour from the A487 will take you to **New Quay**, a picturesque resort village and erstwhile shipbuilding and fishing port. It boasts a crescent-shaped beach of golden sand and a sheltered harbour, from where, if you are lucky, you could spot a dolphin in the bay. The **New Quay Bird Hospital***, which treats wild birds and animals, especially seals and oiled seabirds, is open to the public.

Head south towards Cardigan, and follow the B4548, signed to Gwbert-on-Sea. A track leads from this tiny village to the **Cardigan Island Coastal Farm Park***, where pastureland and hayfields roll down to the rocky sea cliffs. Pay at the farmhouse or at a coin-in-the-slot turnstile and you can wander past goats, ponies, pigs, waterfowl and wallabies (strange but true), and even feed them titbits bought at the house. Follow the track down to the shore edge, divided by a narrow channel from Cardigan Island. Here you can watch the redshanks, guillemots, cormorants and other seabirds – you may even spot a sea-lion or two basking in the water.

Machynlleth and its Celtic history

The Celtica Museum of myths and legends is fully interactive without a written word in sight

From the 3,000-year-old history of the Celts in Machynlleth, once the capital of Wales, to back-to-the-future exhibits at the Centre for Alternative Technology, this is a day for finding out about Welsh culture, past and present.

Begin with the story of the Celts in the Celtica Museum at Machynlleth, then spend some time exploring the town, including the ancient Parliament House of Wales. Continue down the road to see some of the very latest energy-saving ideas at the open-air Centre for Alternative Technology and finish off the day with an 11-mile drive along the estuary to Aberdovey, a family resort with a beach that stretches for four miles and a picturesque harbour.

MACHYNLLETH

Should you need a good distraction for pestiferous children you couldn't do much better than the **Celtica Museum***. Opened in 1995, it was designed by the creator of the Jorvik

♦ **GOOD FOR** A day out for history lovers of all ages
♦ **TRANSPORT** This is a 30-mile round-trip from Machynlleth so a car is a must
♦ **ACCESS FOR DISABLED PEOPLE** Access is good at the Celtica Museum, Centre for Alternative Technology and the Corris Craft Centre
♦ **BEST TIME TO VISIT** Spring, summer, autumn; Wednesday is market day in Machynlleth

Viking Centre in York. The museum traces the history of the Celts through 3D film, theatre and interactive audio-visual equipment. The guiding voices are of Celtic youngsters, who appear at one stage as holograms, and computers are

available to pose and answer questions. The museum shows how the Celts lived 3,000 years ago and also suggests what their life-styles might be like in the future. You are led through various rooms, complete with their own sounds and smells: the Foundry, Origins Gallery, Corridor of Time, Village Settlement, and finishing in the *Yma o Hyd* Corridor (meaning 'we're still here'), with a choral sequence involving local characters. Parkland surrounds the museum and a tea room provides refreshment. For younger children, a playground and crèche are available.

It is best to leave your car at the museum and walk the few hundred yards into the centre of the market town of **Machynlleth**, where you will arrive at the nineteenth-century clock tower. Standing in its shadow you can see nearly the whole town; it is smaller than you might expect for a place of such significance to Wales. You could carry straight on to browse in the book and antiques shops, or, alternatively, head down the wide main street to the **Parliament House** on the left, one of three medieval houses in the town. It is usually open daily from 10am to 5pm but if you find it closed the **tourist information office*** next door will tell you when it is next open.

The small exhibition demands a lot of concentration as it tells in detail the story of Owain Glyndwr (Owen Glendower), a Welsh nationalist of the turbulent fifteenth century. Glyndwr is referred to by Shakespeare as being 'not in the roll of common men'; above all others he managed to crown himself Prince of Wales and set up a parliament in this building; he then proceeded to wage war on the English. Here, too, you can make a brass rubbing to take home, spending just a few pence for one of the Virgin Mary or a few pounds for Mary Queen of Scots.

Afterwards, there are numerous short walks to choose from; the tourist information office has details of many starting in the town, including one which takes you up the Roman steps for a panoramic view over the town and beyond to the coast. There is also an inexpensive historical guide if you prefer to follow a detailed town trail.

Visit the **Centre for Alternative Technology***, three miles north of the town, at lunchtime to see the animals being fed and other attractions that happen only once a day. The entrance is via a water-balanced cliff railway, which runs on water power. You then follow markers around the exhibits, which include wind generators, organic gardens and wave machines, which have all been designed to be environmentally friendly.

Hands-on activities, such as making a pump slow down by covering a solar panel with a huge cardboard cloud, keep children entertained. A trip down the mole hole, with its oversized worms and grubs and eerie subterranean noises, is very popular. There isn't much information at each station: for this you need to go to the shop or the information centre, open daily for a few hours in the early afternoon.

Aberdovey, a dinghy sailors' paradise, is renowned for its watersports and outdoor activities

ABERDOVEY AND BEYOND

A terrace of houses painted pale blue, nursery pink and yellow is crammed up against the cliff at Aberdovey, which is free of neon signs and amusement arcades. It is an old-fashioned resort: children make pebble fortresses on the sandy beach, regular visitors pass the time in their boats, and day-trippers wander about with ice-creams while small boys fish from the jetty.

On arrival, drive past the **tourist information office*** to the sea front, where you can park. Here you can hire canoes if you feel adventurous, or set off back up the estuary for a couple of miles along the shoreline until you reach picnic island, a small grassy area where it is sometimes possible to find yourselves alone.

You could, instead, follow the A487 northwards as it winds its way up through pine, beech and oak forest and visit **Corris Craft Centre*** about eight miles north of Machynlleth. The craft centre is a large site where you can eat and drink and watch craftspeople working with wood, clay and leather – abundant

materials in this area – and then buy some of the wooden toys, candles and calligraphy, or visit the caverns of King Arthur's Labyrinth, with an underground boat ride.

For a more energetic detour you could head for the famous mountain **Cader Idris**. The easiest route, though it still takes several hours, is the Tal-y-lyn path: take the A487 north, turn left on to the B4405 to Tal-y-lyn lake and park immediately on the right in the new landscaped car park; from here it is a steep but straightforward walk to the 2,927-foot summit of Cader Idris. The other well-trodden routes are the Fox's track, which starts at the Gwernan Lake Hotel, and the Pony track, which starts near the NCP car park further up the road. The best map is OS 1:25,000 Cader Idris/Dovey Forest. Walks range from waymarked family routes to tougher ascents.

LUNCHBOX

Machynlleth offers a good choice of cafés and pubs in the town, including a wholefood café on the main street. The Centre for Alternative Technology has a restaurant with seating both indoors and out, and serves good, cheap food between 12.30 and 2.30. Disappointingly, there are no fish and chip shops at Aberdovey, although you can take your pick from a number of inexpensive restaurants.

Cader Idris towers above the many lakes in the area, some of which are said to be bottomless

A sketch of Welsh history around Tremadog Bay

Portmeirion stands on a site that in 1925 was a rocky wilderness accessible only from the sea

A journey along the Cambrian coast, in the crook of the Llyn Peninsula, takes in medieval castles, wide beaches and stunning views over Tremadog Bay.

This coastal day out provides a brief outline of Welsh history, from Harlech, with its turbulent past of conquest and rebellion, through the purpose-built port of Porthmadog, where slate was carried for shipment abroad, to the eccentric village of Portmeirion, an exotic Italianate mini theme park. If you have the time, it would be well worth making the trip as far as Pwllheli, with its spacious beach and good fishing, on the Cambrian Coast Railway, which follows a dramatic route between the mountains and the sea. Otherwise, choose the well-signposted coastal drive, which can be extended to take in the whole of the magnificent Llyn Peninsula.

By starting at **Harlech** you can discover how this shoreline has

- ♦ **GOOD FOR** A day outdoors, with several indoor attractions if it rains
- ♦ **TRANSPORT** 9 miles from Harlech to Porthmadog, both have railway stations, and a further 25 miles to Plas yn Rhiw
- ♦ **ACCESS FOR DISABLED PEOPLE** Access is good at Portmadog Maritime Museum and Snowdon Mill
- ♦ **BEST TIME TO VISIT** Late spring, summer, early autumn, as many sites close in winter

changed over the centuries and the important role it played in the long conflict between Wales and England. **Harlech Castle*** is the place to begin; dominating the little grey-stone town and its bay, this impressive fortress was one of the chain of defences built by Edward I during his thirteenth-century

campaign of conquest in Wales. At one stage nearly a thousand men were working on the castle. Today, its views of the sea and Snowdonian mountains make it a delight for painters and visitors alike.

Accessed via a wooden walkway from the town, its remains are remarkably intact and still reveal the distinctive touches of its Savoyard architect, Master James of St George. In 1404 the Welsh rebel leader Owain Glyndwr (Owen Glendower) seized the castle and moved his court there until its recapture by the English in 1409. Sixty years later, its resistance under siege in the Wars of the Roses inspired the song 'Men of Harlech'. Climb the walls to appreciate its strategic site: on the western side, looking out over Tremadog Bay, the castle is balanced on a sheer cliff; this once dropped down to a channel where ships could deliver supplies at the Water Gate. The water has since receded, and the gate leads to the Harlech railway station and, beyond that, a wide golf course. A footpath crosses the golf links and dunes (an alternative, easier route is by road) to the long, sandy beach and safe bathing waters.

Several craft shops are packed into the few streets of Harlech, and the **tourist information office*** (closed in winter) has details of walks and inland sights and towns.

A 10-minute train journey or a short drive along the A496 brings you to **Porthmadog**, a busy, cheerful and thoroughly Welsh harbour town. (Turn on to the A487 at the Penrhyndeudraeth toll bridge for a faster approach which avoids Maentwrog.) Porthmadog was developed by nineteenth-century entrepreneur William Madocks, who reclaimed 7,000 acres of land across the Glaslyn estuary and built a causeway known as the Cob, now crossed by a road and the Ffestiniog

The railway that once carried slate from the quarries now ferries tourists between Portmadog (this is the harbour) and Blaenau Ffestiniog

Railway line (each car must pay a small toll for a day ticket to cross the Cob). His plan was to profit from tourists travelling to the Ireland ferries but it failed when Holyhead on Anglesey became the main ferry port, bypassing the Llyn.

In the event, the town flourished not because of tourists but as a result of the booming slate industry at the end of the nineteenth century. Ships left Porthmadog to carry cargoes all over the world, loading slate from the Blaenau Ffestiniog quarries, brought here by narrow-gauge train.

Another of the 'Great Little Trains of Wales' sets off from Porthmadog for a short trip to Pen-y-Mount. Once the longest narrow-gauge line in Wales, the **Welsh Highland Railway*** ran through Snowdonia to Dinas Junction, near Caernarfon, but was closed to traffic in 1937. Porthmadog volunteers have restored this section of the line and the old locomotive Russell, and guided tours are given round the Gelert Farm Works, showing the history of the railway and the restoration process.

Good on a rainy day, the **Porthmadog Maritime Museum***, on one of the harbour's old wharves, traces the history of the fine three-masted schooners once put together here; and the **Snowdon Mill***, on the edge of town, has a pottery and craft centre where you can throw your own pot, make candles or jewellery or print T-shirts. In the **Madog Motor Museum***, next door, is a collection of 70 vintage vehicles.

A few minutes' drive south of Porthmadog or a walk from

Minffordd railway station (ask at the **tourist information office*** for full public transport details) brings you to one of the oddities of Wales. **Portmeirion*** is a fantasy brought to life by architect Sir Clough Williams-Ellis, who created this Mediterranean-style village between 1925 and 1975. Its domes, statues and colonnades occupy a wooded peninsula overlooking the Dwyryd estuary, and the light-opera approach, as Williams-Ellis called it, extends to the terraced restaurant and quayside hotel. Among several gift and book shops are some selling the distinctive Portmeirion pottery. Wild gardens surround the village and include rare Himalayan flowering trees. The cult 1960s TV series *The Prisoner* was filmed at Portmeirion.

If you have more than a day to explore the Llyn you could make Porthmadog your base for a drive or train journey further along the peninsula, visiting **Criccieth Castle***, sacked in 1404 and never re-occupied, and the beach and continuing to Pwllheli, which gives access to the tip of the Llyn. Beyond Pwllheli (on the A497, then on minor roads from Llanbedrog), a seventeenth-century National Trust manor house, **Plas yn Rhiw***, overlooks the dangerous waters of Porth Neigwl (Hell's Mouth) and has a pretty cottage garden and woodlands. **Butlin's Starcoast World***, at Pen-y-chain, between Criccieth and Pwllheli, can provide a day out in itself, and is another handy wet-weather fallback.

LUNCHBOX

In **Harlech** it is worth taking refreshments at the Plas tearooms, set in a house once owned by the family of Denys Finch Hatton, whose affair with Karen Blixen was portrayed in the film *Out of Africa*. The Plas offers splendid views of the bay, with the mountains of the Llyn's southern coast ranged along its far side.

The menu at Caffi Llechen Lâs (Blue Slate Café) on Bank Place, off **Porthmadog**'s main street, includes Welsh specialities such as *bara brith* (currant bread) and honey. Owen's Café, on Stryd Fawr (High Street), is a self-service restaurant offering snacks and simple cooked meals.

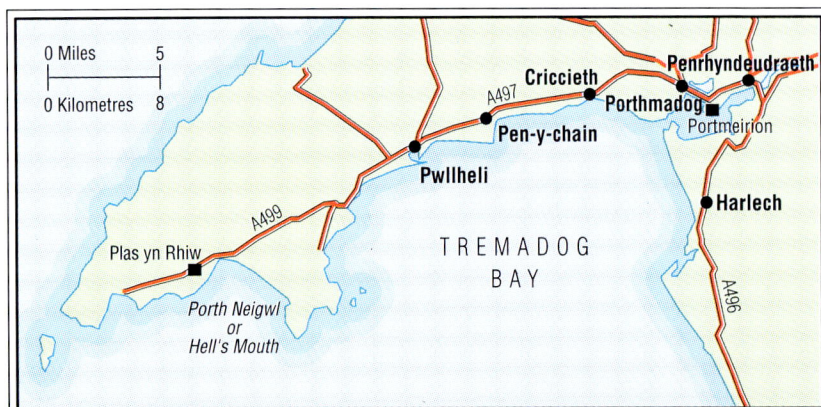

Sports and industrial heritage in Snowdonia

Snowdonia's rugged grandeur and industrial past have given rise to a diversity of activities and tourist facilities.

From leisurely strolls to testing rock-climbs, shooting the rapids in a high-tech canoe or chugging through some of Britain's most spectacular scenery on board an ancient locomotive, this area promises memorable experiences for the whole family. As one of Britain's original industrial heartlands, Snowdonia also offers a fascinating trip through the ages, from the gravity-defying railways of ancient slate mines to the throbbing hub of Europe's biggest hydro-electric power station.

The natural place to begin a trip through Snowdonia is **Betws-y-coed**, a charming clutter of slate-roofed cottages flanking the tumbling waters of the River Llugwy.

Following the river west along the A5, you pass the picturesque Swallow Falls, a pleasant picnic spot, before reaching the turning to Snowdon at Capel Curig. This is the site of the **National Mountain Centre***, a man-made mountaineers' paradise complete with state-of-the-art

♦ **GOOD FOR** Energetic families and those who enjoy leisurely outdoor activities
♦ **TRANSPORT** Car essential
♦ **ACCESS FOR DISABLED PEOPLE** Possible at most attractions
♦ **BEST TIME TO VISIT** All year round, weather permitting

climbing wall and artificial ski slope. The centre offers courses in all levels of skiing, canoeing and mountaineering, and also provides weather forecasts. For keen climbers with families, it is an ideal place to unload the children, who can take part in an all-day adventure programme that includes expert tuition in canoeing, skiing and abseiling.

Heading south along the A4086, you descend into the dramatic heart of Snowdonia, a bleak and craggy wilderness. At the turning to Llanberis, the Pen-y-Gwryd Hotel has established itself as something of a mountaineers' mini-museum. Old boots and ropes are slung from its

Four of the 11 locomotives on the Snowdon Mountain Railway date from the ninteeth century

beams, and its ceilings are signed by the likes of Chris Bonnington and Edmund Hillary, who practised here for their famous Himalayan assaults.

You drive through the daunting Llanberis Pass, its steep, boulder-scattered slopes rising on the left to the lofty heights of Snowdon. A short way along this road you will find the terminus of the famous **Snowdon Mountain Railway***, from where, since 1896, steam locomotives have been heaving a steady stream of sightseers up to the highest point in England and Wales. Trains run at regular intervals from 15 March to 1 November, and more frequently leaving the station between mid-July and early September at half-hourly intervals. On fine summer days the service can become very crowded; get to the ticket office early to secure reservation tokens for a later train. The 3,000-foot climb, traversing a spectacular knife-edge ridge to Snowdon's summit, takes an hour each way, with half an hour at the top. On a clear day you can see all the way to Ireland.

The best way to see Mount Snowdon is of course on foot. From Llanberis, there are several well-trodden paths to the 3,560-foot summit. The most popular and least arduous is the five-mile **Llanberis Path**, which begins above Snowdon Railway Station and follows the track, affording dramatic views over the foreboding depths of Llanberis Pass. Other recommended routes are the more challenging **Pyg Track**, which starts from the car park on the crest of Llanberis Pass, and the **Watkin Path**, arguably the most scenic, from the road through Nant Gwynant. Each walk takes about five to six hours, and detailed instructions can be obtained from the **tourist information office*** in Llanberis.

If the Snowdon Railway is particularly packed, a good

Llechwedd Slate Caverns employed thousands of men, who blasted and drilled in the dark, dank mines

alternative can be found on the other side of the main road at the **Llanberis Lake Railway***, where equally old steam engines ply the attractive north shore of Lake Padarn. The lake forms the centrepiece of the Padarn Country Park, a great day out in itself with its lush nature trails and historic buildings. Beside the railway terminus at Gilfach Ddu, the **Welsh Slate Museum*** offers hands-on experience of the industry that once dominated this region, from demonstrations of tool-making and slate-cutting to encounters with the working locos and compressors and the 56-foot waterwheel, reputedly Britain's largest, that once powered all the machinery.

The scars of the slate industry are most evident on the road back to Capel Curig, on which you pass the ravaged mountainside of **Elidir Fawr**. For the past 15 years, this has been the setting for a more modern industry that has been far kinder to the environment. Half a mile beneath the scarred face of Elidir Fawr is the largest hydro-electric pumped storage power station in Europe.

Dinorwig Power Station is a feat of modern engineering. Beneath the slate-littered hillside, its giant turbines are constantly turning, fed by water draining from its upper reservoir. When the reservoir is dry, the water, up to 1,500 million gallons of it, is pumped back up to begin the process again. The £450-million facility's rapid response capability, the fastest of any pumped storage scheme in the world, is a vital part of the National Grid, providing an immediate reserve of power in the event of plant failure or sudden surges in demand. The **Snowdonia Museum***, on the east bank of Lake Padarn, runs regular tours of Dinorwig complete with a flashy special effects show.

No visit to Snowdonia is complete without a trip to the famous slate mines at **Blaenau Ffestiniog**. Following the A470 south from Betws-y-coed, you descend the scenic slopes of Crimea Pass before suddenly hitting the grim grey outskirts of North Wales' 'slateopolis'. The best underground tours are at the **Llechwedd Slate Caverns***, offering two tours through the gloomy depths of its 160-year-old mine: 'The Miners' Tramway' follows the miners' original route, descending through a succession of eerily lit caverns. Here, recorded narratives and illuminated models give a vivid insight into the lives of the men. 'Deep Mine' plunges you down Britain's steepest passenger railway for a tour guided by the ghost of a young miner. After the rigours of your subterranean excursion, it's worth stopping at Llechwedd's Victorian Village, where the bank sells Victorian coins for buying a 'pennorth' of sweets or a threepenny pint at the Miners' Arms.

There is still some open-cast mining in Blaenau, and a small slice of the action is on show at the **Gloddfa Ganol Slate Mine***, across the road from Llechwedd. In the mine's mill, experienced quarrymen saw and split slate for roofing tiles, and from the safety of its Mining Museum you can watch the open-cast blasting operations that bring the slate to the surface.

The **Blaenau Ffestiniog Railway**, which travels through the Vale of Ffestiniog, is another must for railway addicts.

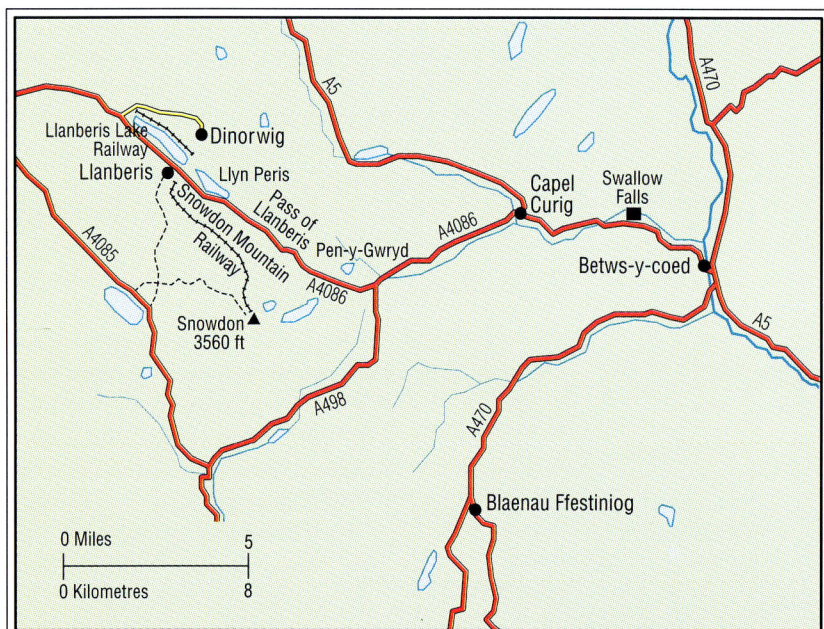

Castles of the Menai Strait

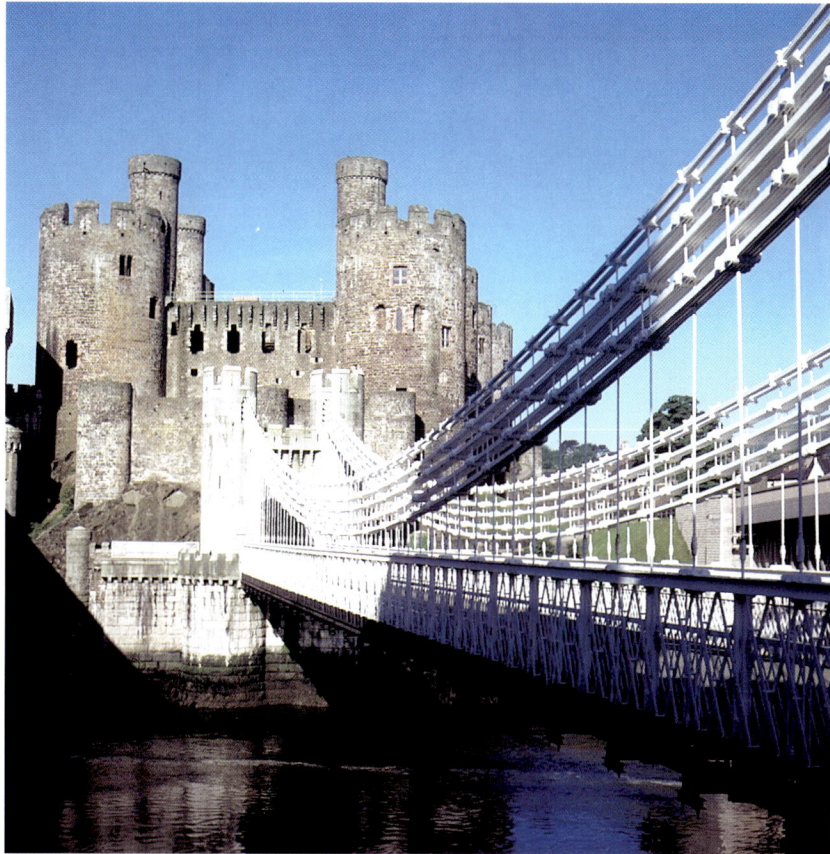

The Conwy Suspension Bridge, built some five and a half centuries after the imposing castle

Wales is dotted with castles – the relics of wealth, war, and conquest. The fortresses of Caernarfon and Beaumaris are survivors of Edward I's thirteenth-century invasion, and Penrhyn Castle is the creation of slate-industry profits in the nineteenth century.

As Edward I carried out his subjugation of the Welsh, he consolidated and protected his gains by building formidable castles. For this purpose he hired renowned craftsmen and hundreds of labourers, and much of their work has withstood the test of time. These symbols of oppression have now become focal points of tourism all around Wales. The fortresses of Caernarfon and Beaumaris are two of the finest examples of Edwardian defensive architecture – along with Conwy, a few miles to the east, where the Menai Strait flows into the sea. Penrhyn Castle, east of the university town of Bangor, pretends to be a Norman fortress but is actually the whim of a slate baron – a

♦ **GOOD FOR** Historical sights and museums with much that is of interest for adults and children alike

♦ **TRANSPORT** There is a British Rail station at Bangor, and buses run regularly from there to Caernarfon, Beaumaris and Penrhyn. Conwy has its own railway station. A car is useful to explore the area more thoroughly

♦ **ACCESS FOR DISABLED PEOPLE** Good access at some sites

♦ **BEST TIME TO VISIT** All year round for Caernarfon and Beaumaris, but Penrhyn is closed in winter

fascinating insight into the decadence of the industrial aristocracy.

In 1282, during the struggle against English forces, the Welsh lost their last native prince, Llywelyn ap Gruffudd. Legend has it that the victorious Edward, having promised his unwilling new subjects a prince who could speak no word of English, fulfilled the vow to the letter by presenting his new-born son, the future Edward II, from the tower of mighty **Caernarfon Castle*** (built between 1285 and 1322). Everything about this castle suggests power and status: the polygonal towers and bands of coloured stone are said to be imitations of the walls of imperial Constantinople, and the virtually complete outer walls still dominate the market town. Exhibitions held in the castle towers include an audio-visual presentation of its history, 'The Eagle and the Dragon', and a museum of the Royal Welch Fusiliers.

Caernarfon itself is a bustling town, well worth a stroll. Details of town walks can be picked up at the **tourist information office*** on Castle Street. Caernarfon's medieval walls can still be seen among the shopping streets: castle and township were built together, and though this is now a distinctly Welsh centre, there was a time when no Welshmen were allowed within its boundaries. On the edge of town, off Beddgelert Road, are the little museum and the excavation site of **Segontium***, the Roman fort built in AD78 where, some say, the Emperor Constantine the Great was born.

The A487 coast road takes you from Caernarfon to the Britannia Bridge (or further to the Menai Suspension Bridge) for the crossing to Anglesey. Turn on to the A545 to reach Beaumaris, a compact and colourful little town overlooking the yachts on the Menai Strait. Tucked in behind its narrow streets and whitewashed houses is **Beaumaris Castle***, the last of Edward's Welsh fortresses, and architecturally the most accomplished. Its perfect

▲ *Built by Thomas Hopper, Penrhyn Castle has a vast collection of paintings and dolls*

symmetry and cunning system of concentric defences are easier to appreciate from the air than from street level, but a tour round its substantial ruins gives some idea of its strength. Surrounded by a moat (and once linked to the sea by a dock), Beaumaris Castle is also guarded by 16 towers and two gates, with 300 crossbow firing-points. The gates and gatehouses of the outer walls were built askew, so that the enemy would have no straight course or view as they attacked. In fact the castle saw very little action, and its sophisticated defensive features were hardly ever used.

If you have more time to spend in Beaumaris, visit the award-winning **Museum of Childhood***, arranged in the rooms of two houses on Castle Street. This is a nostalgic display of clockwork toys, old teddy bears, early cycles and dolls' houses, and the gift shop attached to the museum sells new versions of old toys and games. A rather more grim aspect of life is recalled in the **Beaumaris Courthouse and Gaol***, along Steeple Lane. The renovated 1614 courthouse is still

Caernarfon has a distinguished seafaring past, traced in the **Seiont II Maritime Museum*** on the quayside. Nearby, Porth yr Aur (the Golden Gate) houses the Royal Welsh Yacht Club, where a Caernarfon member, Group Captain Lionel Brabazon Rees, set sail in 1933 in his 34-foot ketch, *May*. He ended up in Miami, Florida, the first man to have sailed the Atlantic alone.

used as a magistrates' court. In the early nineteenth-century gaol the instruments of rough justice are preserved, including punishment cells and a tread-wheel.

Marine life of the Menai Strait can be seen close-up at **Beaumaris Marine World***, where visitors can stroke and feed fish in the 'touch pool'. The centre's Seaview Café offers a clear view across the Strait to the rugged Snowdonia mountain range, a view that can also be enjoyed by strolling along Victoria Terrace beside the sea.

Double back to the Menai suspension bridge for the 4-mile journey to Bangor and take minor roads a further mile and a half to the east of the town for **Penrhyn**

Castle*, a huge and pretentious stately home now owned by the National Trust. Though built to look like an early Norman fortress, this towered and turreted mansion was put together on an existing site in the nineteenth century and furnished in lavish style for the Pennant family, a dynasty of slate magnates. A tour of the rooms reveals just how substantial their fortunes were: look out for the richly carved staircase, the solid slate bed and the room papered with hand-decorated Chinese wallpaper. The castle stands in extensive grounds, where you can wander through the shrubbery enjoying the views. (An insight into the lives of the slate miners themselves at Blaenau Ffestiniog – see *Great Day Out 73* – makes a sobering contrast to Penrhyn's ostentation.)

Although Conwy sits just beyond the point where the Menai Strait flows into the Irish Sea, its remarkable castle and walls make it an interesting addition to the itinerary. **Conwy Castle*** was built in 1287 and is still an impressive sight, its semi-circular towers rising over the harbour. The town's medieval structure is quite clear: Conwy's well-preserved town walls still embrace most of its winding streets, and you can walk along a considerable part of their length. Collect a map of Conwy from the **tourist information office*** at the castle entrance and you can plot a relatively short stroll to take in the main points of interest. These include **Aberconwy House***, a fourteenth-century merchant's house refurbished by the National Trust to reflect various periods of its history; the **Teapot Museum***, which houses pots of all shapes and sizes from the eighteenth century onwards; the **Smallest House** on the quayside, measuring only 9 feet x 5 feet; and, sweeping across the estuary, Thomas Telford's 1826 **Conwy Suspension Bridge**.

LUNCHBOX

Apart from the castle, Beaumaris has several good sights, cafés – including the one at Marine World, mentioned above – and shops and is an excellent place to stop for lunch.

Anglesey through the ages: a circular tour

The Menai Suspension Bridge, which cost £120,000 to build, opened in 1826

Môn Mam Cymru – Anglesey, Mother of Wales – is an island of sheltered bays and mountain views, of low-lying marshland and open seascapes. This round trip takes in its varied scenery and sites ranging from prehistoric to nuclear age.

Separated from the Welsh mainland by the narrow Menai Strait, Anglesey has always enjoyed a distinct character of its own. This was the last stronghold of the druids, religious and cultural leaders of the Celts, and the final Welsh frontier during the Roman occupation, from where painted women screamed across the water at terrified imperial troops. Its long history of settlement is evident in the remains of Neolithic, Iron and Bronze Age structures scattered around the island; and its wealth of sea life draws nature-lovers from all over the world to Puffin Island and South Stack. These and Anglesey's modern tourist-geared attractions provide plenty of scope for a day's visit and more.

♦ **GOOD FOR** Walking in fair weather – there is much varied scenery to take in. Also good for animal-lovers: much wildlife can be seen, including seals, puffins and birds of prey
♦ **TRANSPORT** A car is necessary for the tour (92-mile round trip) unless you plan to go to just one of the sights. There is a train to Llanfair PG
♦ **ACCESS FOR DISABLED PEOPLE** Good access to some sights
♦ **BEST TIME TO VISIT** Spring and summer, as much of the tour is outdoors

Two bridges connect the mainland to Anglesey: the Britannia, a tubular bridge that carries the A5 and the railway; and Thomas Telford's Menai Suspension Bridge, which takes traffic to the town of Menai Bridge

(Porthaethwy). To the east of both is the little yachting town of Beaumaris, a pleasant base for a stay on the island (see *Great Day Out 74*) and the starting point of this tour.

The B5109 leads out of Beaumaris to the easternmost tip of Anglesey, five miles away. At **Penmon** the thirteenth-century remains of an Augustinian priory, built on the site of a Celtic monastery, include a church where services are still held. On the edge of the site is a large stone dovecote; here, drivers must pay a toll to proceed up the narrow road to the shore for a clear view of Puffin Island and the Penmon lighthouse. Cruises around the island are offered by **Starida Sea Services*** and **Cerismar Two***, for closer looks at the puffins, guillemots and cormorants that nest there, and with luck for glimpses of the seal colony.

By backtracking along the B5109 you can join the A5025, following Anglesey's eastern coastline past popular beaches such as Red Wharf Bay (Traeth Coch), near Benllech. Just before Moelfre, signs at a roundabout direct you to **Din Lligwy Ancient Village**, a small scattering of stones surrounding the ruined walls of a chapel, which is set in a field overlooking the sea. These have survived since the early twelfth century, with fourteenth- and sixteenth-century additions. Cross the meadow, keeping the bay below to your right, and follow a track through two kissing gates and into a small wood. The path emerges into a clearing where neat circles and rows of limestone slabs map out the walls of a fourth-century estate, possibly built for a native chief; the massive stone door-posts and steps can still be seen.

Minor roads lead back to the A5025, which swings round to follow the north-western coast, passing a wind farm at close range *en route* to a

The longest place name in Britain was actually invented by a nineteenth-century wag

very different source of energy, Wylfa Power Station. Waymarked nature trails lead from there through woodland to a viewpoint looking out to the Irish Sea.

Return to the coast road, now running across windswept moors. Between Cemaes Bay and Church Bay, signs lead to Llanrhyddlad and the **Anglesey Birds of Prey and Conservation Centre***, where eagles, owls, hawks and falcons are bred and flown. If the flying displays take your fancy, you can buy falconry equipment at the gift shop.

Rejoin the A5025 and carry on to Valley to pick up the A5 north to Holyhead (Caergybi), on Holy Island (Ynys Enlli), where ferries set sail for Dun Laoghaire. Take South Stack Road to the lighthouse and lookout point of **South Stack**. In fine weather this RSPB reserve is a good place for a walk and for spotting the sea birds, puffins, guillemots and razorbills among them, that congregate along the cliffs.

The B4545 takes you across Four Mile Bridge back to the main island to link up with the A5 heading south (signposted Bangor) to the A4080. This route loops around the shoreline and gives access to more ancient sites, including **Barclodiad y Gawres** (the Giantess's Apron), a fascinating Neolithic passage grave near Aberffraw. The tomb is kept locked; you can obtain a key on payment of a deposit at the Coastal Heritage Centre in Aberffraw. Park at the beach and take the path through a kissing gate to reach the partly intact stone chamber. You will need a torch to see the circles, spirals, waves and zigzags – in the style of the Newgrange tombs in Ireland – that decorate five of the slabs.

After the darkness and mystery of prehistoric graves the coastal tour offers something quite different, taking you along the south shore to **Anglesey Sea Zoo***, near Brynsiencyn. This popular tourist spot can take up the best part of a day in itself: as well as the weird and wonderful sea creatures kept and bred here – including dogfish, gurnards and conger eels – children can enjoy activities such as a 'wave cascade' and an adventure playground.

Other sights on this final stretch back are the eighteenth-century National Trust house, **Plas Newydd***, seat of the first Marquess of Anglesey (see below) and home to a Rex Whistler exhibition; and **Pili Palas***, a butterfly palace that also has tropical gardens, snakes, ants and various other creepy-crawlies.

To return to Beaumaris or either of the two bridges to the mainland, carry on to the famous tongue-twister, known to locals as **Llanfair PG**. Towering over the town is the **Marquess of Anglesey's Column**, topped by a statue of Henry Paget, who was made the first Marquess after a brave campaign as second-in-command at Waterloo. The rock on which the column stands was used in ancient times as a hillfort. You can climb the 115 steps for a final bird's-eye view of Anglesey and across the water to the Snowdonia mountains.

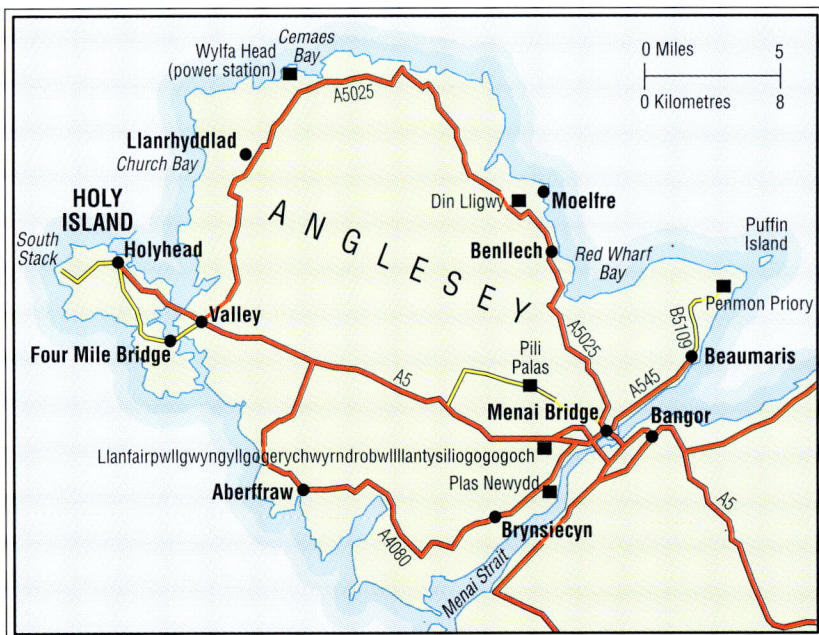

LUNCHBOX

There are various possibilities in Holyhead; also the café at the Anglesey Birds of Prey and Conservation Centre, and the restaurant at Sea Zoo.

'Welsh wonders' in the North Wales Borderlands

Llangollen Railway Station in its unusual position right by the River Dee

Explore some of Wales's most spectacular scenery by rail and canal, admire a few of the local 'wonders', and discover what it was like to live and work in these parts in days gone by.

The North Wales Borderlands around the Dee Valley and Wrexham are full of contrasts and reminders of the past. The River Dee has its own special appeal and our day out provides the opportunity of viewing some high spots by steam train or narrowboat. Wrexham is the industrial heart of the area and the Clywedog Valley is dotted with restored sites that were once its lifeblood. Five of the self-styled 'Seven Wonders of Wales' are in Clwyd: you will see two of them, as well as another stupendous but more recent construction, Telford's mighty aqueduct at Pontcysyllte.

STEAM TRAINS AND SLOW BOATS

Start the day with a jaunt round Llangollen itself: the **tourist**

♦ **GOOD FOR** A great variety of activities
♦ **TRANSPORT** Car necessary; the Clywedog Trail is ideal for cyclists and walkers
♦ **ACCESS FOR DISABLED PEOPLE** Access to some sites; phone to check
♦ **BEST TIME TO VISIT** April to October

information office* in Castle Street will·be able to provide you with advice. If you want to stock up for a picnic Bailey's Delicatessen next door is full of goodies including Welsh fudge.

Just south of the town, off Butler Hill, is **Plas Newydd*** (NT), a splendid black and white 'stately cottage', once occupied by the famous Ladies of Llangollen, romantic runaways whose liberal attitude caused something of a stir among Regency society.

The town centre is dominated by the fourteenth-century stone bridge over the Dee, one of 'The Seven Wonders of Wales'. At this point, the river is wide and unruly, cascading over rocks, foaming around bushy copses and plunging over weirs. There is a pleasant riverside walk here: turn into Parade Street, past the **Victorian School of the 3Rs*** (pick up your slate and take part in a Victorian child's lesson) along the Victoria Promenade and on towards Riverside Park.

As you cross the bridge going out of the town, you can't miss the looming presence of the Hill of Bran, some 900 feet high and crowned by the ruins of **Castell Dinas Bran**, a stronghold of Welsh princes before the English conquest.

Over the bridge, in Abbey Road, is the **Llangollen Railway***. The station itself, deliberately unimproved, is a marvellous evocation of the steam era. Trains meander through the Dee Valley, climbing towards Berwyn and on through the Dee Valley to the present terminus at Glyndyfrdwy – a five-mile journey that takes about 1 hour 15 minutes there and back. (Disabled travellers can be accommodated, but two weeks' advance notice is advisable.)

Not far from the railway, up the steep incline of Wharf Hill, is the **Llangollen Canal Wharf***. A look at the audio-visual displays in the Canal Exhibition Centre will get you in the mood before you take to the water. For the most leisurely and romantic trip possible, book a seat on one of the horse-drawn boats that cruise from the wharf, past the site of the July Llangollen International Musical Eisteddfod and towards Horseshoe Falls. Sturdy Welsh ponies pull the open craft, which look rather like long waterborne bus shelters painted blue and red. The return journey takes 45 minutes.

▲ *Thoroughly recommended: a horse-drawn canal trip on the Llangollen Canal*

Alternatively, go for a longer excursion on the aptly named narrowboat *Thomas Telford* and marvel at 'Telford's triumph', the astonishing **aqueduct** at **Pontcysyllte**. Towering 126 feet above the River Dee, it is a wondrous masterpiece by any standards, more than 1,000 feet long and with 19 gracefully executed arches. Crossing it proves to be an extraordinary sensation – not quite like floating on air, but strangely out-of-this-world in its way. The journey (with live commentary) takes about two hours in each direction.

LIVING IN THE PAST

After lunch, head northwards towards Wrexham to take in some of the prime attractions strung out along the Clywedog Valley. (Follow the A539 out of Llangollen, then pick up the A483 Wrexham by-pass.) The eight-mile **Clywedog Trail**, which runs from Minera to King's Mill, is tailor-made for walking, but you could instead travel by car and choose from any of the attractions you fancied. Obtain full details of opening times and so on, including a map catering for cyclists, walkers and motorists, from the **tourist information office*** in Wrexham.

LUNCHBOX

Gales Food & Wine Bar in Bridge Street, Llangollen is the best spot for lunch; children are welcome. Otherwise, the town has numerous coffee shops, tea rooms and cafés. You can also get refreshments at the station buffets on the Llangollen Railway, at the all-day tea room at Canal Wharf and on board the *Thomas Telford*. There is a restaurant at Erddig. In Wrexham, Bumble Coffee Shop*, Charles Street and the Nag's Head* in Mount Street are recommended.

Signposted 2 miles south of Wrexham off the A483/A5152, **Erddig*** (National Trust) is the finest and most complete 'upstairs-downstairs' property in Britain, and the only one you enter via the servants' quarters. Over the generations the detailed lives of the servants were documented in a uniquely comprehensive manner, so you emerge with a much fuller picture of life downstairs than at most other stately homes. Erddig's formal gardens are home to the National Ivy Collection and all kinds of rare fruit trees and plants; beyond are the wooded expanses of the 200-acre Country Park.

Follow the Clywedog Trail through the park or look for the signs off the

A525 on the south-east outskirts of Wrexham to find the **King's Mill Visitor Centre***. This is a real bonanza for the senses, where you can listen to 'The Miller's Tale' as the old hand tells his apprentice what it was like to work at the mill during the 1770s. Watch the waterwheel turning, feel the grain, make some flour. Youngsters love it.

About 2 miles south-west of Wrexham, just off the A483 after Rhostyllen, look for the signs to **Bersham Ironworks & Heritage Centre***. Bersham tells the story of John 'Iron Mad' Wilkinson and his legendary eighteenth-century ironworks. Here you can soak up the sights and sounds of the foundries that produced cannon for the American War of Independence and cylinders for James Watt's steam engines. Throughout the year, the centre stages all kinds of exhibitions and events, from archaeological excavations to kite-flying workshops.

Continue westwards along the Clywedog Trail (or, from Wrexham, follow the A525 through Coedpoeth, then turn off along the B5426) and look for signs to **Minera Lead Mines & Country Park***, the most ancient lead mines in North Wales. The site gives a vivid glimpse of what it was like during the 1870s: you can take a look at the original shaft, winding engine and boiler house, or climb to the top of the Beam Engine House and admire the views.

Also recommended are the nature trails around **Nant Mill Visitor Centre***, Coedpoeth, on the Clywedog Trail. At Nant Mill itself, children can make rubbings of animal footprints, learn how to count tree rings to age a tree, and – best of all – go down a human-size molehill, complete with dangling roots, wriggling worms, and even a carelessly discarded ring-pull from a can of drink.

Wrexham is worth a visit, especially for its markets, five in all. Go on Monday, if possible, when the vast outdoor open market is in full swing on Eagles Meadow (behind Asda supermarket). And don't miss the tower of St Giles' church, a feature of the skyline since 1520 and another of the 'Seven Wonders of Wales'.

Pottering around the Potteries

The evocatively shaped coal-fired kilns at the Gladstone Pottery Museum

♦ **GOOD FOR** An enjoyable day out during bad weather as all the sights are inside. Good for children, as many museums and factories welcome participation

♦ **TRANSPORT** The China Link bus system takes you round all the sites – see box overleaf

♦ **ACCESS FOR DISABLED PEOPLE** Access to all visitor centres (Wedgwood, Spode, Royal Doulton) and many factory shops

♦ **BEST TIME TO VISIT** If you want to watch pottery being made, you can either go on a factory tour (Monday to Friday, but not during factory holidays) or at one of three visitor centres (Wedgwood, Spode, Royal Doulton); these are open every day all year round, as are the bigger shops. There may be restrictions on the number and age of participants on some factory tours

You do not have to be a china expert to enjoy a visit to the Staffordshire Potteries. The history of the industry and its products is told in a series of excellent museums and factory tours.

An abundance of water, clay and easily mined coal turned the Six Towns of the Potteries (not five, as Arnold Bennett held in his novels that were set in the area) into the ceramic centre of the world in the eighteenth and nineteenth centuries. The industry has since diminished in importance, but many world-famous china companies still have their manufacturing base here, drawing on the skills of local people, honed over many generations, in shaping, firing and decorating clay.

THE GLADSTONE POTTERY MUSEUM*
(Uttoxeter Road, Longton)
The best place to start a Potteries tour is at this award-winning museum, with its distinctive bottle-shaped kilns. Kilns like this were put out of business in the 1950s, when a succession of Clean Air Acts made the use of coal-fired kilns illegal. Today's factories use gas or electricity for firing their ovens, resulting in a cleaner environment and a far higher degree of control

over the firing process. To discover just how much skill was involved in getting the firing temperatures right in the old days of coal, watch the museum's enthralling video, which documents the last-ever firing of museum's own kiln. It also explains that the livelihood of a whole community depended on the outcome: if the firing went wrong, and the vessels in the kiln cracked or warped, nobody got paid, and the work of many weeks, and of many people, was lost.

The skills involved in ceramic production are all demonstrated at the museum by potters and artists who are happy to explain their work, answer questions and let you have a go: they are also very good at getting children involved. Another part of the museum has copious displays of material produced in the Potteries over the centuries, from highly decorated toilet bowls and art nouveau tiles to teapots and Toby jugs. The museum café serves local specialities, such as oatcakes (like pancakes) with various fillings.

You may think twice about shaping a pot yourself at the Gladstone Pottery Museum

THE CHINA LINK BUS
Though once separate settlements, the Six Towns (Tunstall, Burslem, Hanley, Stoke-upon-Trent, Fenton and Longton) have since merged to form one large conurbation called the city of Stoke-on-Trent. One way to ensure that you do not spend a lot of time getting lost is to use the China Link bus system, which does a circular tour departing on the hour from Stoke-on-Trent railway station, calling at all the main museums and factories. If you do decide to travel by car you will find that the main sites are indicated by brown and white signposts. Trail maps and bus details are available from all the sites along the route as well as from the **tourist information office*** at Stoke-on-Trent; the China Experience leaflet lists more than forty factories and outlets (selling seconds and perfect products) in the Stoke-on-Trent area.

THE MINTON MUSEUM*
(Minton House, London Road, Stoke-on-Trent) and the
SPODE VISITOR CENTRE AND MUSEUM*
(Church Street, Stoke-on-Trent)
Two of the best-known names in fine china both have displays of their products dating from the eighteenth century, when the secret art of making porcelain, until then known only to the Chinese, was perfected in Europe. Star of the show at the Minton Museum is the huge pottery peacock. Spode, the oldest factory in the Potteries on its original site (founded 1770), offers a fascinating tour of the works and also has a visitor centre and museum. Both have factory shops where, if you do not mind minor flaws, you can buy seconds at bargain prices, or you can pay full price for the 'best wares'.

LUNCHBOX
Refreshments and light lunches are available at all these sites except for the Etruria Industrial Museum.

THE WEDGWOOD VISITOR CENTRE
(Barlaston)
Josiah Wedgwood was responsible for many of the innovations that gave England the edge in the very competitive ceramics market of the eighteenth century (in perfecting mass-produced tableware, he drove many traditional producers in Delft and elsewhere out of business). You can follow the history of this energetic entrepreneur through displays and videos, see fine examples of Wedgwood designs over the ages and watch potters producing today's masterpieces.

ROYAL DOULTON*
(Nile Street, Burslem)
The Royal Doulton factory has a visitor centre and offers another worthwhile tour. In the Sir Henry Doulton Gallery there are displays covering the output of the works over the last 175 years, including the 'Pretty Lady' and character figurines typical of Royal Doulton, as well as a collection of Toby jugs.

CITY MUSEUM AND ART GALLERY*
(Bethesda Street, Hanley)
If you have now had enough of pottery, come here for the displays on wildlife and archaeology plus the Spitfire aircraft, designed by a local man. You will not escape pots altogether, however, since the social history displays give a fascinating insight into the daily lives of pottery workers. There is also a huge display of over 5,000 pieces of ceramic, providing comprehensive coverage of the industry, including some of its quirkier elements, such as the monstrous and comical birds made by the Martin brothers. This is the largest collection of Staffordshire ceramics in the world.

ETRURIA INDUSTRIAL MUSEUM*
(Lower Bedford Street, Etruria)
By contrast with modern factories, this museum shows how the raw materials for making pottery were produced in the nineteenth century. On the first weekend of every month in season, a working steam engine, *Princess*, drives the crushing mills for the bone and flint that was used to give translucency and strength to bone china. There is also a working forge, a potter's mill and a canal boat typical of those used to transport products from the Potteries to customers all over Britain.

Castles, kings and a forest walk

Stokesay Castle has been used as a grain store and smithy in its time

- ♦ **GOOD FOR** Those interested in kings, their establishments and their battles
- ♦ **TRANSPORT** 40-mile round trip from Ludlow so a car is a must
- ♦ **ACCESS FOR DISABLED PEOPLE** Good for Ludlow Museum and Carding Mill Café and nature information centre
- ♦ **BEST TIME TO VISIT** Spring, summer and autumn; Ludlow festival end June/beginning July; Clun Carnival first Saturday in August. Ludlow flea market (alternate Sundays); 90-minute guided tour of the town at 2.30pm on Saturdays and Sundays (Easter to Sept), starting at the cannon outside the castle; market days Monday, Wednesday, Friday and Saturday in summer, Monday, Friday and Saturday in winter

Tour round the most prominent town, historically speaking, in Shropshire, travel on to one of the earliest fortified manor houses in Britain, and finish with afternoon tea and a paddle in the shadow of a ruined castle.

LUDLOW

We have the French to thank for Ludlow. The town grew up around the castle that they built between 1086 and 1094; it was to become one of the most important fortresses in this border country. They certainly picked a good spot: the castle has formidable defences, falling away to sheer cliffs on two sides, and with steep ground on the others. The surrounding landscape is still predominantly rural, much of it managed by the Forestry Commission. Nearby are remains of hill-top settlements and castles, from the Iron Age to medieval times.

Start with the recently established (1995) **Ludlow Museum*** on Castle Street and you will get the best idea of the foundations on which this town was built. From its early, bloody days through to its height as a wool-trading centre, and on to the fashionable Ludlow of the eighteenth century, the exhibition traces the town's history in some detail.

Next move on to **Ludlow Castle** where, after paying your toll, you will arrive in the outer bailey or 'killing ground'; you can then begin to piece together the stories of marauding invaders and savage skirmishes. If the fine examples of Norman, medieval and Tudor architecture are not to your taste, you cannot fail to be excited by the stories that seem to emanate from every stone in the castle. It was from here that the two young princes Edward and Richard were taken to the Tower of London, where they were eventually killed. Later, Henry VII's sickly eldest son, Arthur, lived here with his wife Catherine of Aragon. After his death she married his brother Henry, who was to become Henry VIII, and so began another gory saga.

A steep climb to the top of the keep gives you great views over the whole town and the Teme Valley. Even if you are not planning to explore Ludlow further, do glance at Castle Lodge, a medieval house rebuilt at the end of the sixteenth century which once housed the prison and later the local parliament. The twelfth-century **parish church** (the largest in Shropshire), with its comical misericords, also deserves a moment or two of your time.

Before you leave you may want a short walk to take in the best view of the castle. Called the Bread Walk, the route heads down Broad Street, over Ludford Bridge and turns right on to Whitcliffe Common. Continue along the riverbank and re-enter the town via Dinham Bridge and Castle Square. The **tourist information office*** can provide details of many more walks in and near the town.

The four-mile geology trail at **Mortimer Forest** (3 miles south-west of Ludlow) is one such walk. With its numbered points of interest it is well worth the exercise. There is also a choice of routes through wooded valleys, across streams and over open commons.

STOKESAY CASTLE*

Not so much a castle as a fortified manor house, English Heritage's Stokesay Castle (8 miles north of Ludlow off the A49) has stood virtually unchanged since the great wool trader Laurence of Ludlow had it built in 1280. The grand yellow-stone house, constructed as a symbol of status, remains highly impressive and from a distance presents an idyllic picture. The great vaulted hall (complete with peepholes so that Lord Laurence could keep an eye on his staff and guests), shuttered windows and Jacobean panelling are all good examples of their kind, and are well explained via a personal-stereo guided tour.

Afterwards, walk around the park; if you find the key a local giant once dropped into the moat you could be

One of the misericords at Ludlow parish church; this was first erected in the twelfth century, but was largely rebuilt some 300 years later

the first to let yourself into the vaults underneath the house and claim the treasure stored there.

THE CLUN VALLEY

The leafy drive along the Clun Valley is pleasant, but A.E. Housman's famous jingle 'Clunton and Clunbury, Clungunford and Clun, Are the quietest places under the sun' is now only half-true, as most of these villages lie on the main B-road through the valley. Unlike the rhyme, the route also includes **Aston on Clun** with its distinctive round houses and the famous Arbor Tree (a new tree now replaces the original).

The eleventh-century **castle at Clun** which has stood in ruins since the 1270s makes a dramatic picnic spot. The village has pubs, tea rooms, historically important buildings, and a thriving craft shop in the main square. However, most people congregate around the fifteenth-century saddleback bridge, with its

stone arches, breakwaters and safe paddling. On your way back take a detour to the Iron Age hilltop settlement at **Bury Ditches** (three miles north-east), which has walks and colour-coded trails.

CHURCH STRETTON AND AROUND

Antiques enthusiasts might want to continue the journey along the A49, which is dotted with antique shops, to the nineteenth-century 'resort' of Church Stretton (15 miles north of Ludlow). Here the Victorians once spilled out of newfangled charabancs to take in the clean air and walk the hills. A mile west of town the National Trust has taken over the turn-of-the-century **Carding Mill*** pavilion, in a cleft in the landscape at the bottom of the Long Mynd, and turned it into a café and nature information centre (closed end October to April).

Also just off the A49, three miles south of Church Stretton, is the **Acton Scott Farm Museum***. Depending on the time of year, the displays at this nineteenth-century working farm vary from butter-making and milking, to sheep-shearing and wool-dyeing.

LUNCHBOX

Ludlow has more than its share of coffee shops and tea rooms. At lunch-time you could join local business people in the Feathers Hotel, which has been serving merchants and traders since 1603. Lunch in the converted schoolhouse at Acton Scott Farm Museum is substantial and inexpensive.

Ludlow Castle, formerly a great fortress, is now used as a theatre during the July festival

The Ironbridge legacy – industry and artefacts

Candle-making is just one of the many crafts re-created at Blists Hill Museum

OTHER SIGHTS TO CONSIDER

Tar Tunnel, Bedlam Furnaces (free), and Rosehill and Dale House, all of them within the gorge, are worth a visit if you have time. Telford Town Park is five miles from Ironbridge and is an excellent destination if the children still have energy to burn off. Free to get in, it has several adventure playgrounds catering for different ages, as well as cafés, an enclosed toddlers' area, and plenty of space to run around.

Scattered along a river gorge internationally famous as the 'birthplace of industry', a variety of museums makes for a day out to suit all ages.

A handful of inventive minds and all the right raw materials (coal, clays and ironstone) combined to make a beautiful Shropshire gorge cut through by the River Severn a world leader in iron-smelting, and therefore manufacturing. The boom period was short-lived, however, and by the mid-nineteenth century the area was deserted. Because no one could even be bothered to knock the buildings down, Ironbridge has been caught in something of a time warp. Looking at the wooded hillsides today, it is hard to imagine a location less representative of the urban sprawl that we associate with industry in the late twentieth century.

Most local traffic bypasses the town itself. The main street, the Wharfage, is leafy and quiet, so you can take a tranquil walk along the riverside picking your way from one

♦ **GOOD FOR** Anyone with an interest in industrial history
♦ **TRANSPORT** All sights are within one and a half miles of the Iron Bridge, spread over six square miles. Each museum has a car park
♦ **ACCESS FOR DISABLED PEOPLE** Most sights have good access. Access guide available on request
♦ **BEST TIME TO VISIT** All year, although some sights close from November to April: check with the tourist information office*

well-designed museum to the next. Here we outline two options.

MUSEUMS FOR CHILDREN

Start with the **Museum of the River**, which gives you a good introduction to the sights to come. First head straight through the exhibition room to the ten-minute slideshow, which traces the history of the gorge from its formation in the Ice Age to the present. After this, everything else falls into place. The exhibition includes a 3-D model of the gorge as it was when royalty visited in 1796. Barges cruise up and down the river, pigs root in cottage gardens, and the chain-making forges are working at full blast. Other displays chart the decline of the area – public notices warning of cholera, and stories of floods.

Just across the car park is the **Merrythought Teddy Bear Shop and Museum**. Goodness knows why teddies thrive in this part of the world, but thrive they do, and have done since the 1930s. Although not strictly part of the nineteenth-century industry programme (although the museum is housed in a former foundry), the shop and museum are a big hit with all softies. The stuffed toys come in all shapes and sizes. A six-foot bear greets you at the door, and inside there are rag dolls, miniature teddies, mice and monkeys.

If the weather is fine you might like to try a river cruise. From the riverbank by the Museum of the River car park, tourist barges leave on the hour for a 45-minute round trip in all but the severest weather. You pass under the elegantly curved Iron Bridge (look up and wonder at the ingenious ribbing), with a running commentary from a guide.

PASSPORT TO THE MUSEUMS

A Museum Trust Passport is worth buying even if you are combining Blists Hill Open Air Museum with only one other sight. It allows you one visit to each museum over whatever timescale you like. The Passport can be purchased from any of the nine museums or from the **tourist information office*** (just up-river from the Iron Bridge), which can also provide you with details on all the sights.

Around 370 tonnes of iron were used in the construction of the Iron Bridge

Before making the two-mile trip from here to Blists Hill Open Air Museum you could take a short stroll past the antique, fudge and tea shops into the centre of town to have a closer look at the eponymous Iron Bridge. If you are really keen on souvenirs, you can buy a certificate declaring that you crossed it.

Blists Hill Open Air Museum is the jewel in the Museum Trust's crown and will easily keep you occupied for the whole afternoon. Covering a site a mile long and half a mile wide, it is a re-creation of a working Victorian town. The 'residents' go about their business in period costume, allowing you to enter their houses and workshops, and to buy goods. Your first stop is Lloyds Bank where you change your tourist pounds for old currency, so that you can buy a penn'orth of gobstoppers from the sweet shop, or quicksilver from the chemist. The project has worked remarkably well with older visitors who stand and reminisce with the 'townsfolk' as much as with the schoolchildren who dash round with clipboards during term-time.

IRON, TILES AND CHINA

The second tour option begins with the Museum of the River (see above) and takes in the **Museum of Iron** further up the valley. Here the exhibits concentrate in some detail on the iron-smelting process and the achievements of the ironmakers, including the Iron Bridge itself, the world's first, which cost £6,000 to build in 1779. The Elton Gallery has temporary art exhibitions, and an inexpensive café-cum-well-stocked arty bookshop.

It is a two-mile drive along the gorge to **Jackfield Tile Museum**. Built to satisfy the Victorian demand for houses, hospitals and civic buildings with decoratively tiled floors and walls, Jackfield is still a producing factory but on a much smaller, more specialist scale. You may be lucky enough to join a free guided tour which takes about 45 minutes and shows you around a tumbledown collection of ovens and storerooms, with rusting pulleys and grass growing where window-frames used to be. The upstairs showroom gives you an idea of the variety of commissions the factory at one time took on, while downstairs you might fancy a rummage through the cut-price reject tiles on your way out.

The **Coalport China Museum** is a mile away, across the new Jackfield Bridge. China hasn't been made here since 1926 when, after more than a century of production, the Coalport works moved to Staffordshire. Today, the large site with its restored kilns and workshops is a museum. The beauty of the product belied the misery of the working conditions.

The explanation of the techniques involved in china manufacturing and the display of the Coalport range of fine china and porcelain is worth an hour of your time before you head over to Blists Hill Open Air Museum for the afternoon.

LUNCHBOX

Blists Hill, the Museum of Iron and Rosehill House have their own cafés. Otherwise, there is a good choice of places to eat at in Ironbridge – the main street along the river is lined with teashops and pubs. The Meadow Inn, a few hundred yards up-river from the Teddy Bear Museum, has a beer garden in a dramatic setting in sight of three huge cooling towers, and an excellent reputation for its bar food.

Teddy bears galore and other furry friends too at the Merrythought Teddy Bear Shop

Heavyweight art and science in Birmingham

Birmingham's superb collection of pre-Raphaelite and European art, its dazzling jewellery heritage and its outstanding industrial history present absorbing and varied possibilities for a day out browsing in fine museums and art galleries.

G rand Victorian buildings now stand cheek by jowl with modern glass structures in Birmingham's regenerated city centre. A large pedestrianised area of linked squares has been created, made stylish and attractive by statues, trees and fountains, and newly opened canalside walks offer another perspective on the city's past. Between visits to the museums and galleries, try to leave time for a stroll around Britain's second largest city. You can obtain more advice from the **tourist information office***.

♦ **GOOD FOR** Pre-Raphaelite art, decorative arts, industrial heritage and Victoriana
♦ **TRANSPORT** Edgbaston is about three miles from central Birmingham, but public transport is reliable
♦ **ACCESS FOR DISABLED PEOPLE** Yes
♦ **BEST TIME TO VISIT** Any time

The Birmingham Museum and Art Gallery* is a splendid Victorian edifice, recently restored. A grand staircase takes you to the Round Room whose picture-covered walls include oils by David Cox, a

The Forward *statue shows the workers of Birmingham moving from the old industrial order to the new*

local artist of the early nineteenth century. The art collection ranges from the seventeenth to the twentieth centuries and includes works by Canaletto, Lely, Stanley Spencer and Lowry. The gallery owns the world's largest collection of pre-Raphaelite paintings and drawings executed by Burne-Jones, Holman Hunt and Ford Madox Brown. However, these highly popular works are often on tour, so you should check before making a special trip to see these or the famous Holy Grail tapestries, which are on limited display for conservation reasons. (Stained-glass windows by Burne-Jones also adorn nearby St Philip's Cathedral.)

In the second-floor Industrial Galleries are splendid displays of pottery, glass and William Morris designs. The vaulted terracotta and turquoise Edwardian Tea-Room is surrounded by wrought-iron galleries and lit by huge lamps in the form of suspended columns. On show is a wide range of items made by local designers – jewellery, pewter, porcelain and architectural ironwork.

The museum's top floor contains a strange mix of objects bequeathed by local benefactors. The darkened geology section is dominated by a life-size grey replica of *Tyrannosaurus rex*, created from newspaper and expanded polystyrene, together with a large collection of stuffed birds and animals, and one memorable giant crab.

The **Birmingham Museum of Science and Industry*** has an extremely broad collection of inventions and locally made machinery from the time of the Industrial Revolution. Its most coveted pieces are the Smethwick Steam Beam Engine, an eighteenth-century device for pumping canal water back into the locks – the oldest working steam engine in the world; and the green and gold City of Birmingham steam locomotive, which pulled express trains from London to Glasgow for 25 years.

Also on view are hydraulic pumps and old pieces of factory equipment which are set in motion on the first and third Wednesdays of each month (depending on staff). Various forms of transport are displayed – Spitfire and Hawker Hurricane planes, old motor cars, the city's only surviving tram and early bicycles (boneshakers to tandems). You can also see optical and astronomical equipment, artisans' workshops and sporting guns. One area children find fun is the hands-on gallery 'Light on Science'.

Before leaving the city centre, check whether there are any temporary exhibitions at the **Royal Birmingham Society of Artists*** or in the huge, refurbished Victorian Gas Hall, adjacent to the Museum and Art Gallery. The **Ikon Gallery*** is a modern building which displays works by contemporary artists.

The **Jewellery Quarter** is a 20-minute walk north-west of the city centre. The **Discovery Centre*** comprises a small exhibition and an old jewellery factory in a converted terrace house. Using audio-visual means and old photos, as well as precious stones, this little display explains how raw minerals are

A youngster measures his own strength at the 'Within Our Power' section of the Museum of Science and Industry

transformed into jewels, and the rise and fall of Birmingham's jewellery industry. Visitors can even have a go at making their own jewellery. The tour takes you round the old factory, which remained in the same family, Smith and Pepper, for 80 years. From a Dickensian office, with old wooden furniture and handwritten order books, visitors go into the cramped workrooms, with bench surfaces covered with burners, dies and punches. In its heyday, overhead belts from 35 motors whirred away, heat and sparks flew from the metals, and cyanide fumes were inhaled daily. Now retired jewellers demonstrate some of the processes, such as polishing.

Close by is Birmingham's latest museum, **Soho House***, an elegant

Georgian building which was the home of Matthew Boulton from 1766 until his death in 1809. Boulton was a button and buckle manufacturer who became a pioneer of the Industrial Revolution and one of Birmingham's greatest entrepreneurs. In Boulton's lifetime the estate covered 300 acres and included a metal factory, employing 800 people and producing silverware, jewellery, swords and coins. The rooms of the house are furnished as Boulton might have chosen, with some of his original purchases and a few outstanding examples produced by his factory, in ormolu, Sheffield plate and silver. Boulton was particularly proud of his magnificent sidereal (star) clock, which stands on a pedestal in a high gilded case.

The Barber Institute of Fine Arts* in Edgbaston, south-west of the city centre, houses a small collection of European works of art (thirteenth to twentieth centuries), as well as sculpture, prints, drawings and coins. Italian works include paintings by Bellini (his earliest signed work – *St Jerome in the Wilderness*), Veronese, Canaletto and Tintoretto. Examples from the Dutch seventeenth-century school include landscapes by van Goyen, Molijn and a rare one by Rubens.

Murillo's *Marriage Feast at Cana* is one of the Institute's prized works, as indeed is its fine clutch of French impressionists – Monet, Degas and Pissarro. English artists are also represented, with portraits by Gainsborough and Reynolds and landscapes by Turner and Wilson. The sculpture collection ranges from an ancient Egyptian head (1500BC) to a bronze by Rodin.

The Travelling Companions *by A.L. Egg at Birmingham Museum and Art Gallery*

LUNCHBOX

Apart from numerous city-centre pubs and restaurants, you could try the Edwardian Tea-Room at the Museum and Art Gallery, or the canalside café of the Science Museum. However, school parties tend to lunch here and also at the small café at the Discovery Centre. Picnic possibilities abound in the new City Centre Park.

A walk around Stratford-upon-Avon

Anne Hathaway's Cottage is a farmhouse with a thatched roof and cottage garden

Spend a full day exploring the historic houses associated with Shakespeare and his family in this delightful but touristy town, perhaps ending the day with a visit to one of Stratford's three theatres.

Stratford is one of Britain's most-visited towns, but you can avoid the queues and crowds by arriving early in the day, before the car parks fill up and the tour buses arrive. The five main sights in Stratford are all managed by the **Shakespeare Birthplace Trust***: all-inclusive tickets are available for the three town-centre properties (Shakespeare's Birthplace, Nash's House and Hall's Croft), or to all five sights (the three above plus Anne Hathaway's Cottage and Mary Arden's House). Ticket-holders are also entitled to a discount on the 'hop-on-hop-off' open-top tour buses which travel around all five properties (every 15 minutes in peak season). Visitors can spend as much time as they like at each property before catching the next convenient bus – worth considering if it is wet or as a means of getting to the out-of-town sights without your car.

♦ **GOOD FOR** There is much of interest for all ages. If you have time aim to see a play
♦ **TRANSPORT** There are open-top tour buses to take you from sight to sight
♦ **ACCESS FOR DISABLED PEOPLE** Ground floors and gardens of historic houses only
♦ **BEST TIME TO VISIT** Spring and autumn, avoiding summer's crowds

SHAKESPEARE'S BIRTHPLACE

Stratford's car parks are well signposted and are all on the eastern side of the town. Conveniently, this is also where the excellent new **tourist information centre*** is situated. Shakespeare's Birthplace is signposted from the car parks, or you can just follow the crowds up shop-lined Bridge Street, across the busy High Street junction and into Henley Street. The entrance to the house is via the modern **Shakespeare Centre**, which hosts occasional exhibitions (for example, of Shakespearean theatre costume).

The timber-framed house, now largely rebuilt, was previously the Swan and Maidenhead pub, which came on the market in 1847 and was purchased by the Shakespeare Birthplace Trust after a public appeal for funds. The house lacks atmosphere, largely due to the crowds, and the upstairs exhibits, explaining what little is known about Shakespeare's life, are rather dull. Look out, though, for the window panes in the bedroom where Shakespeare is supposed to have been born (23 April 1564), scratched with the signatures of such famous nineteenth-century visitors as Sir Walter Scott and Thomas Carlyle.

STRATFORD HIGH STREET

Leaving Shakespeare's Birthplace, turn left into Henley Street and cross into the High Street. On the right is **Harvard House**, former home of Katherine Rogers, mother of John Harvard, founder of Harvard University, Massachusetts. The house is now run as a museum displaying material on the Harvard family. It dates from 1594 and has a flamboyantly carved timber façade. Just beyond, on the left, is the **Town Hall**, a fine classical building.

NASH'S HOUSE AND NEW PLACE

Chapel Street leads to **Nash's House**, which was once owned by Shakespeare's granddaughter, Elizabeth, and her lawyer husband, Thomas Nash. The upstairs rooms display archaeological finds from the Stratford area, including fine jewellery from the Anglo-Saxon cemetery at Bidford-on-Avon.

The house next door used to be the grandest in Stratford and was bought by Shakespeare in 1597. He later retired here and died in the house in 1616. The house, known as **New Place**, was demolished by a subsequent owner, the irascible Reverend Francis Gastrell, who got fed up with the constant stream of visitors, so the site is now a garden.

Turning left out of the house, cross Chapel Lane for a quick look at the **Chapel of the Guild of the Holy Cross**, with its Doom (Last Judgement) painting, then continue down Church Street past a fine row of fifteenth-century timber-framed almshouses, built by the same guild. The first building on the left served as the Guildhall and contained a schoolroom where Shakespeare may have received his early education.

HALL'S CROFT AND HOLY TRINITY CHURCH

Turn left into Old Town and look for **Hall's Croft**, once the home of Shakespeare's daughter, Susanna, and her husband, Dr John Hall. This is the best-furnished and the most likeable of the town's historic houses, and the guides who give a short talk are extremely well informed about its history. There is a large garden to the rear where you can sit and enjoy the relative tranquillity.

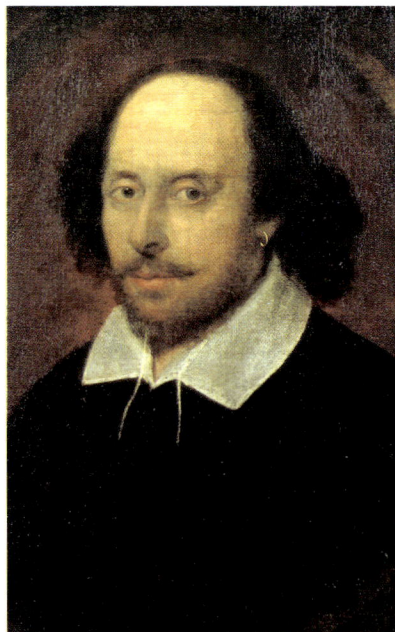

A portrait of the Bard by John Taylor

Turn left from Hall's Croft to reach the stately church of the **Holy Trinity**, surrounded by fine trees. Shakespeare is buried in the chancel, beneath a tomb slab whose famous words – 'Curst be He [that] Moves My Bones' – have invited speculation on what secrets the grave might enclose. To one side is a painted alabaster bust of Shakespeare carved by the Dutch mason Gerard Johnson.

GOING TO THE THEATRE
As well as the famous Royal Shakespeare Theatre, the Royal Shakespeare Company* owns two others: the Elizabethan-style Swan Theatre, used for classic drama, and The Other Place, where modern works are staged. There are tours that take you behind the scenes; advance booking is essential.

RIVERSIDE WALK
Leaving the church by the north door, walk up the lime avenue to the church gate and out into Old Town, then look for a gate on the right which leads into the public gardens lining the west bank of the River Avon. Footpaths will take you past a brass-rubbing centre and the Chain Ferry (boats for hire and ferry crossings to the Butterfly Farm on the opposite bank) to the **Swan Theatre**. The Swan, with its distinctive lead-covered helm roof, is all that remains of the original 1879 theatre, damaged by fire in 1926. It stands next door to the gaunt brick **Royal Shakespeare Theatre** of 1932 (designed by Elizabeth Scott). Turn right at the theatre to enter **Bancroft Gardens**, a festive place in summer, full of visitors and buskers who cluster around the canal basin and its lock, marking the point where the Stratford Canal joins the River Avon.

OUT-OF-TOWN SIGHTS
Anne Hathaway's Cottage stands about a mile west of Stratford, in the suburb of Shottery (well signposted off the A422 Alcester Road). This was the home of Shakespeare's wife before her marriage. Further out at Wilmcote, and well signposted from every direction, is **Mary Arden's House**, the Tudor home of the playwright's mother. It is now the centrepiece of a countryside museum featuring live animals, falconry displays and a working smithy. You will find that children enjoy this museum best of all.

LUNCHBOX
The Garrick Inn on the High Street serves pub lunches; other good choices are Lambs and The Opposition, two bistro-style cafés in nearby Sheep Street. There is a tea room and restaurant alongside Hall's Croft.

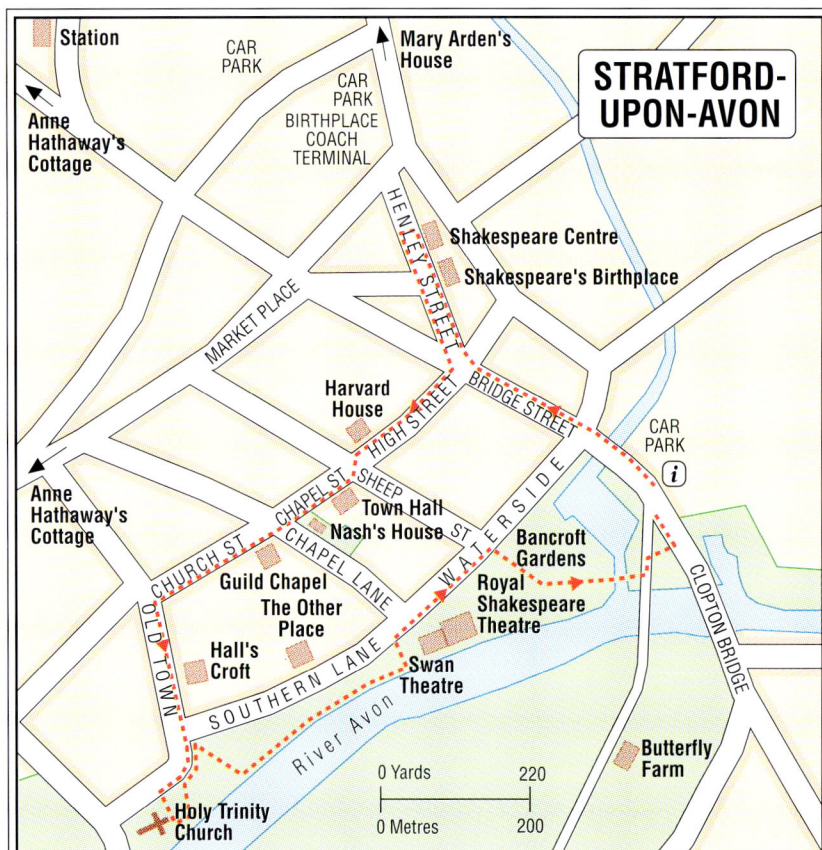

STRATFORD-UPON-AVON

Station
CAR PARK
Mary Arden's House
CAR PARK
BIRTHPLACE COACH TERMINAL
Anne Hathaway's Cottage
HENLEY STREET
Shakespeare Centre
Shakespeare's Birthplace
MARKET PLACE
Harvard House
HIGH STREET
BRIDGE STREET
CAR PARK
Anne Hathaway's Cottage
SHEEP ST
CHAPEL ST
Town Hall
Nash's House
CHURCH ST
CHAPEL LANE
WATERSIDE
Bancroft Gardens
Guild Chapel
The Other Place
Royal Shakespeare Theatre
OLD TOWN
Hall's Croft
Swan Theatre
CLOPTON BRIDGE
SOUTHERN LANE
River Avon
Butterfly Farm
Holy Trinity Church
0 Yards   220
0 Metres   200

The medieval fortresses of Warwick and Kenilworth

Most exhibits in the Doll Museum are British, but some are from France, Japan and Germany

The Warwick District Council Art Gallery and Museum*, in Leamington Spa, has an exhibition of paintings and examples of eighteenth-century glass, as well as local history displays, that paint a vivid picture of this part of England.

Medieval power struggles have left two major memorials in this part of England. Warwick lies within easy reach of Kenilworth, home to another famous castle, while just minutes away is the Regency elegance of Royal Leamington Spa.

WARWICK

Set beside the River Avon, Warwick is a small and compact, partially walled town dominated by its imposing castle, one of the finest medieval strongholds in Europe. The narrow streets that jostle the castle walls are lined with a mix of buildings illustrating architectural styles from every period of the past seven hundred years. It is best to explore on foot with the aid of the informative *Welcome to Warwick* leaflet, available from the **tourist information office***.

Many medieval timbered houses that existed when the castle was built were destroyed in the Great Fire of 1694, which in five hours razed to the ground 460 properties in the town centre; as a result, Warwick has

♦ **GOOD FOR** Perfect for imagining yourself through the ages; take your pick of eras from medieval or Regency or Victorian
♦ **TRANSPORT** Eight miles' travel including Leamington Spa. Railway stations at Warwick and Leamington Spa, bus service runs to Kenilworth
♦ **ACCESS FOR DISABLED PEOPLE** Limited at Warwick Castle; ground-floor access only at Kenilworth Castle and Lord Leycester Hospital
♦ **BEST TIME TO VISIT** All year, although grounds and gardens are at their best in spring and summer

a pleasing medley of Georgian and Tudor houses. A few gabled and timber-framed dwellings survived the blaze, and you should not leave without having a look at a couple of

them. **Lord Leycester Hospital***, in the High Street, is a splendid collection of half-timbered buildings founded as a Guildhall in 1383, then turned into almshouses in 1571. On view to visitors are the courtyard, Banqueting Hall, St James Chapel, the old Guildhall and the Museum of the Queen's Own Hussars.

Along Castle Street is Oken's House, once owned by Thomas Oken, a wealthy benefactor of the town. Today it houses the **Doll Museum*** with displays of eighteenth- and nineteenth-century dolls, toys and games. If time allows, your itinerary could include a visit to **St Mary's Church**, whose fourteenth-century chancel and fifteenth-century Beauchamp Chapel were spared from the fire, and a browse round the County Museum, housed in the old **Market Hall*** dating from 1670.

WARWICK CASTLE*

Wherever you wander, you will never be far away from one of the entrances to the castle, one of the most dramatic and complete in Britain and until recently home to the mighty earls of Warwick. Originally a wooden fortress, supposed to have been built by Ethelfleda, Alfred the Great's daughter, in AD915, it was fortified by William the Conqueror. The castle in its present form was constructed in the fourteenth century: note Caesar's Tower and Guy's Tower.

Time seems to flow backwards as you walk round the castellated ramparts and look out across the surrounding countryside. Various

Exploring Warwick could well take up a whole day. If you intend visiting the castle as well as strolling around town, make use of the free castle car park, as tickets allow you to re-enter the castle at any time during the day.

exhibitions trace the castle's transformation from a military fortress to a sumptuously furnished family home. Start off at the armoury, dungeon and torture chamber, which will send shivers down your spine, before moving on to 'Kingmaker – A preparation for battle', which re-creates the atmosphere of a medieval household making ready for war.

For a complete contrast, return to the Undercroft to enjoy 'an evening of fifteenth-century festivity with stories, songs and a five-course dinner' at the Kingmaker's Feast exhibit. Ornately decorated State Rooms contain collections of furniture, paintings, tapestries and armour and reflect the grandeur of the seventeenth and eighteenth centuries. Victorian times are represented by the award-winning exhibition 'A Royal Weekend Party 1898', a clever reconstruction of an actual event using waxwork figures, including a young Winston Churchill and the future King Edward VII.

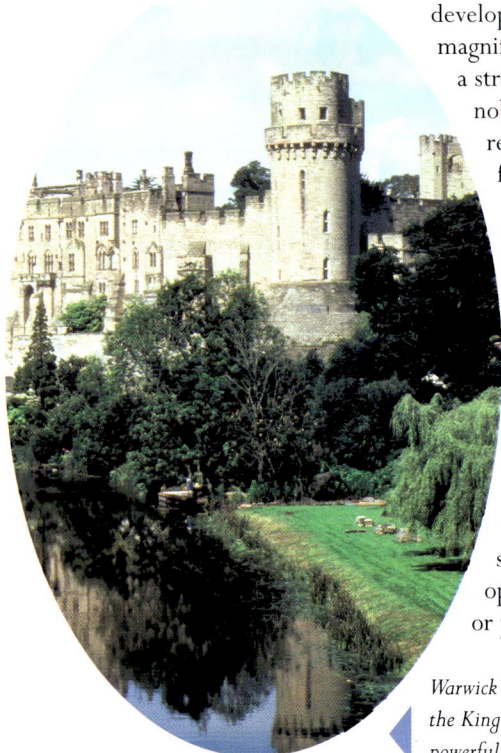

Kenilworth was upgraded to a royal palace in the fourteenth century by John of Gaunt

Make sure you leave yourself enough time to roam the beautiful landscaped riverside grounds, of which there are 60 acres, complete with rose garden, nature trail, picnic areas, café and restaurant.

KENILWORTH CASTLE*

A short drive away, and dominating the old town of Kenilworth, is the shell of Kenilworth Castle (EH), one of the finest and most extensive castle ruins in Britain. Originally a twelfth-century wooden fortress, it developed rapidly, becoming a magnificent red-sandstone castle and a stronghold for the kings and nobles of England. It was remodelled as a palace in the fourteenth century and soon became a place of lavish display and entertainment, Elizabeth I being a regular visitor. Cromwell ordered it to be demolished after the Civil War.

It is an impressive place to stroll round, especially the twelfth-century keep with its immense soaring walls. The scenic grounds are the perfect setting for numerous summer open-air events, or for a picnic; or you could spread your rugs out

in Abbey Fields, next to the attractive old High Street lined with elegant eighteenth- and nineteenth-century town houses.

ROYAL LEAMINGTON SPA*

Rather than seeing two castles in one day you could combine a castle visit with Royal Leamington Spa, only a few minutes by car from Warwick. Its many grand old buildings recall days of prosperity when the rich and famous came here to 'take the waters' during the nineteenth century. Queen Victoria designated it a royal spa on a visit in 1838. The Pump Room of 1814, terraces of Regency, Georgian and Victorian houses, and riverside walks and wide parks, like the beautifully maintained Jephson Gardens are all worth seeing, and the town has an excellent shopping centre.

LUNCHBOX

For imaginative bar food in Warwick head for the Ricochet Inn on Castle Street, and for decent all-day snacks and home-made cakes try Charlotte's Tea Rooms on Jury Street. Excellent, yet simple, meals are served in the original Brethren's Kitchen at Lord Leycester Hospital.

In Kenilworth, Harrington's (near the castle) serves good-value lunches, while in Leamington Spa, Sacher's, a 1930s-style brasserie on the Parade, serves reliable meals all day.

Warwick Castle became the stronghold of Warwick the Kingmaker, Earl of Warwick and most powerful baron during the fourteenth century

The undiscovered villages of Rockingham Forest

Rockingham Castle has views over the Welland Valley and several counties

Northamptonshire's Rockingham Forest, once a favourite hunting ground of Plantagenet kings, lost its trees long ago, but it remains a lovely — and little-known — region reminiscent of the Cotswolds.

This day out takes the form of a circular tour around Corby, the town that nearly died with the collapse of its steel industry in the late 1970s, but which has been transformed, not least by the removal of the grim spoil tips that once dominated the landscape for miles around. Today Corby sits at the hub of some of the Midlands' most attractive countryside, characterised by hamlets of stone cottages with thatched roofs clustering around churches with ornate spires.

Lyddington, three or four miles north of Corby, is just such a village, a delightful place with a main street lined with seventeenth-century houses built from the local iron-rich (and hence rust-coloured) limestone. The Bishops of Lincoln were as fond of the pleasures of the chase as any

♦ **GOOD FOR** Lovers of architecture and history
♦ **TRANSPORT** A round trip of about 26 miles by car or cycle
♦ **ACCESS FOR DISABLED PEOPLE** Difficult
♦ **BEST TIME TO VISIT** Rockingham Castle and Lyddington Bede House are open from Easter to the end of September, and the other sights are open all year

secular prince or monarch, and in the fourteenth century they built a splendid episcopal palace alongside the church. The palace was acquired by the Cecil family of Burghley House (see *Great Day Out 84*) in 1600, and Sir Thomas Cecil, a noted philanthropist, had the building converted into the **Lyddington Bede House*** (EH), an almshouse

for impoverished pensioners. The ancient building, with its massive chimneys, medieval timber roof and handsome chambers, fits perfectly the descriptions of a similar institution whose fortunes are the subject of Anthony Trollope's Barsetshire novel *The Warden*.

From Lyddington, it is a four-mile drive south-east, via Gretton, to **Kirby Hall*** (EH), the magnificent house of Sir Christopher Hatton, constructed between 1570 and 1583 and a fitting place for the entertainment of kings and queens. The fact that the house is now a roofless ruin does not detract one bit from its extraordinary atmosphere. Great master masons, including Nicholas Stone, lavished their skill on the building, copying what were then the most fashionable Renaissance motifs from patterns published in Serlio's work, *De Architettura*. Such is the quality of the local stone that the swags and foliage, the grotesque faces and the acanthus leaves covering the gatehouse and the courtyard walls remain virtually as fresh today as when they were carved.

The southern part of the hall retained its roof when the rest fell into ruin, and artists' impressions are displayed here to give a clearer sense of what the hall would have looked like in the early seventeenth century. You can also look down from the upper windows on to the elaborate garden parterre, which has recently been excavated and the outline of the beds restored.

Lyveden New Bield* (NT) is reached by driving seven miles south-east, via the attractive villages of Upper and Lower Benefield. Less attractive is the bleak landscape around Lyveden New Bield itself, shorn of trees and hedges by agribusiness enterprise. To reach the eccentric and roofless house involves an uphill walk of about half a mile, past the moated remains of an extensive Elizabethan garden and orchard. The Catholic owner of the garden, Sir Thomas Tresham, started building the house as a symbol of his faith in about 1595. When he died ten years later, the masons simply downed tools, leaving the building unfinished. Designed in the shape of the cross, the house has an exterior carved with biblical texts and a frieze made up of the symbols of Christ's Passion. The views from its hilltop site are expansive.

Brigstock, two miles west, glories in its **Saxon church**, one of England's most superb examples, built in the late tenth century. Characteristic of the Saxon architectural style are the triangular windows, and the use of monolithic stones, alternately set vertically and horizontally (and hence called long-and-short-work) at the corners of the tower and nave.

Geddington, another two or three miles west, features England's best-preserved **Eleanor Cross*** (EH), actually triangular in plan and standing some 40 feet tall, with niches containing three lifesize effigies of Eleanor of Castille, the much-loved wife of Edward I. Eleanor died at Harby in Nottinghamshire in 1290, and her grieving husband ordered crosses to be erected at every place

Kirby Hall – a chance to admire the sixteenth- and seventeenth-century stonemasonry

where her funeral cortege rested for the night on its journey to Westminster Abbey, where the queen was to be buried. Of the twelve crosses erected, only three survive (the other two are at Hardingstone in Northamptonshire and Waltham in Essex; the one at Charing Cross in London is a nineteenth-century re-creation). Geddington also has a lovely church, with Saxon triangular windows like those at Brigstock, and a graceful five-arched bridge, built in 1250, which spans the River Ise a short walk away in Bridge Street.

Some four miles west is another of Sir Thomas Tresham's symbolic buildings, **Rushton Triangular Lodge*** (EH); this was built in 1593, with three windows in each of its three walls, three gables, three chimneys and three storeys, all echoing the theme of the Holy Trinity. The English Heritage guidebook explains the meaning of all the symbols carved on the highly ornate exterior of this eccentric little building.

Six miles north of Rushton, **Rockingham Castle*** enjoys a spectacular high vantage point, with views that stretch for miles across the plains and gently rolling hills of Leicestershire and Northamptonshire. The originally Norman castle became a comfortable Tudor house in 1544 and was further improved by the great medievalist, Anthony Salvin, who also restored Windsor Castle and the Tower of London. Everything about the castle has the golden patina of age, from the 300-year-old kitchen table to the romantic medieval Great Hall, though there is also a good collection of modern art, featuring works by Stanley Spencer, Walter Sickert and Augustus John. The panoramic views from the windows of the Long Gallery compete for attention with the original 1838 décor of green and gold wallpaper and rose-red curtains. From the gift shop, an easily missed turret staircase leads to the armoury and rooftop for more fine views. The gardens are justly famous for their roses and yew hedging, but there is much more to see, including a wild garden in a steeply sloping ravine, a fine herbaceous border and some statuesque specimen trees.

Lyveden New Bield: the cruciform, unfinished monument to one man's Catholicism

LUNCHBOX

Refreshments are available at Rockingham Castle. The Green Dragon pub in Brigstock has Chinese and Indonesian bar meals. In Geddington the choice includes the excellent Tea Shop (it also serves lunches) and the Star Inn. The **tourist information office*** in Corby can offer more suggestions.

An architectural feast at Stamford and Burghley

The mellow stone buildings of Stamford, seen from the water meadows

Queen Anne houses, Georgian mansions and fine old churches make this English market town a rare architectural gem. Stamford's rich heritage of fine stone buildings is complemented by the ebullience of Burghley House, one of the largest Elizabethan mansions in Britain.

Stamford started out with several natural advantages, including an abundance of excellent building stone (the name Stamford actually means Stone Ford). From a distance it looks like a miniature Oxford, with its extraordinary number of churches, and 'dreaming spires' thrusting into the East Anglian sky. There is a closer link still with Oxford since a group of rebel undergraduates from Brasenose College attempted to found a rival university here in 1333. The attempt was suppressed, partly at the wish of the townspeople themselves, who did not want their prosperous wool trade threatened by the presence of gangs of noisy and notoriously lawless students.

♦ **GOOD FOR** Those who like old buildings
♦ **TRANSPORT** The nearest railway stations are Stamford and Peterborough. A connection runs between the two. Burghley is 2 miles from Stamford and 9 miles from Peterborough
♦ **ACCESS FOR DISABLED PEOPLE** Access to Burghley House is limited, although parts of it can be seen with help; chair-lift into café
♦ **BEST TIME TO VISIT** Stamford is a day out in its own right at any time of year, but Burghley House is open only from Easter to October

Stamford's medieval streets and warren of cobbled alleys are lined by the quirky and individualistic houses of merchants who made their fortunes in the worsted cloth trade, in the export of wool to Flanders, or in pottery or brewing. **Barn Hill** (familiar as the location for the television serialisation of *Middlemarch*) is a good place to start exploring the town's architecture. The house fronts here are decorated with classical motifs, such as swags, foliage and rams' heads, carved round doorcases and windows, or gracious ironwork, fashioned into intricate fanlights and railings. These houses date mostly from the 1730s, but the older No. 9 Barn Hill was where Charles I spent his last night as a free man in May 1646, before surrendering to Oliver Cromwell's army at Newark.

Broad Street comes next, living up to its name by being wide enough to host the weekly market (Friday). Browne's Hospital, on the north side, is an almshouse dating from 1485. Opposite, the **Stamford Museum*** covers the history of the town and includes wax models of Daniel Lambert, then England's fattest man, who died in 1809 weighing 53 stone, alongside the tiny figure of Charles Stratton, who was only 3 foot 4 inches tall when he died in 1883. Here, too, you can buy several informative town-walk guides.

To one side of the museum, a long alley links Broad Street to the **High Street**, with its many shops. Turn left down the High Street and then right down St George's Street, lined with antiquarian bookshops, to reach the heart of the Georgian town, St George's Square. Here, the prestigious merchants' houses are almost palaces in their scale and grandeur. The people of Stamford's social lives still revolve around the Assembly Room (built 1727) and the Old Theatre (1768), now combined to form the **Arts Theatre**, with its lively programme, plus coffee shop and cellar bar (the **tourist information office*** is also here).

Heading back towards the town centre along St Mary's Street, you will encounter **St Mary's Church** on the left. The south porch is a good place from which to take in views over the Welland and the medieval Town Bridge, still carrying traffic over the river as it has done for centuries. The road on the opposite side of the bridge is lined with coaching inns, of which the most prominent is the George Hotel (a good choice for lunch). Its unmissable 'gallows sign' straddling the street was erected, according to local legend, as a warning to highwaymen.

Beyond the George, on the left, lies Stamford's finest church, **St Martin's**, with its sumptuous marble tomb commemorating Lord Burghley, Elizabeth I's Treasurer and builder of Burghley House. (The road to Burghley House is just beyond the church on the left, and it is also a pleasant walk from here through the park to the house.)

Station Road opposite, alongside the George, will take you to the George Footbridge, giving access to the Welland watermeadows. From this island of greenery and wild flowers there are good views of the spires and rooftops of the town. Across the other side of the island, Castle Dyke will take you back to the

The distinctively bustling skyline of Burghley House, home of the Cecil family

town centre and to the **All Saints Brewing Museum***, where you can view the gleaming coppers and mash tuns of a now disused nineteenth-century brewery, along with a tape-recorded guide.

BURGHLEY HOUSE*

William Cecil, Lord Burghley (1520–98), was friend, *confidant* and financial secretary to Elizabeth I for more than forty years. A man of wide-ranging talents, he designed this extraordinary house himself. It took nearly 30 years to complete and its bizarre skyline bristles with pepper-pot corner towers, chimneys disguised as classical columns, and clock-towers surmounted by stone pyramids. Inside, the fan-vaulted Old Kitchen is hung with gleaming copper pans and has scarcely changed since the house was built. The state rooms are notable for the wonderfully overblown ceiling and wall-paintings of Antonio Verrio (1639–1707), a master of illusionistic painting. In the Heaven

Part of the magnificent west front of Peterborough Cathedral

Room, satyrs, nymphs, gods and goddesses cavort across the ceilings and fly weightlessly across the walls. By contrast, the tormented souls of the damned can be seen being fed into the wide-open mouth of a giant cat on the Hell Staircase.

In the grounds, landscaped by Capability Brown, are an orangery, stables, lake and rose garden.

PETERBOROUGH CATHEDRAL

Another architectural rarity is to be found in Peterborough, designated a New Town in 1967, which has grown rapidly from a small Fenland market town into a city of 150,000 people. The magnificent monastic church at its heart was built between 1116 and 1199 and was not designated as a cathedral until the Reformation. It thereby escaped the constant rebuilding that was the fate of many other Norman cathedrals and is one of the finest examples of Romanesque style in England. The plain and robust Norman nave is topped by an even more unusual survival, a painted wooden ceiling dating from about 1220. This carries the eye eastwards to the semi-circular apse, around which there are several tombs of former monks and abbots. A flourish of fifteenth-century fan-vaulting completes the cathedral, with the so-called New Building at the eastern end.

A meander through historic Cambridge

One of Cambridge's many classic views: Clare College with King's College Chapel behind

Brick-built medieval courtyards, half-timbered halls, spectacular stone chapels, classical façades, mock-Gothic extravaganzas — Cambridge has perhaps the finest concentration of beautiful buildings in Britain. Our suggested walk takes in the best of them.

The ideal way to see Cambridge is from the river, drifting gently downstream in a punt. That way you get the best possible view of the most important college buildings and of the lawns and gardens which run down to the river bank – known locally as 'the Backs'. The punt excursion is designed to be taken in the middle of the day, after a morning's exploration on foot, so that you can combine it with a picnic lunch, but you could equally well start or end the day on the water.

The walk starts at **Queens' College** (near Silver Street bridge). The medieval brickwork of First Court dates from 1449, and Cloister Court next door has a half-timbered Long Gallery above the low red-brick arches. One of the portraits above high table in the college dining hall is

---

♦ **GOOD FOR** Walking between sites means Cambridge is best when the weather is fine
♦ **TRANSPORT** Bus from railway station; most car parks out of centre; Cambridge is the capital city of bicycles
♦ **ACCESS FOR DISABLED PEOPLE** Good access to most sites
♦ **BEST TIME TO VISIT** March: daffodils on the Backs; June: college balls and rowing races; October: start of term and autumn colour on the Backs. Avoid May, when many colleges close for exams. (Note that increasingly colleges are charging an entrance fee.) Punting is usually possible only between Easter and October.

---

of Erasmus – he lived in college for three years, but left after complaining about the beer.

After Queens', head towards King's Parade, the widest street in Cambridge. To get into King's College as a tourist, you have to cut through Senate House Passage at the end of the Parade, just before **Gonville and Caius College**. (Look out for the Gate of Honour, one of three built by John Caius in the sixteenth century to symbolise the progress of the undergraduates. They were supposed to enter through the Gate of Humility, pass through the Gate of Virtue and leave by the Gate of Honour.)

You enter **King's College** by the side gate which leads into the Chapel. It took the imagination, determination and finance of three kings, Henrys VI, VII and VIII, to conceive of and create this astonishing building. The soaring stone pinnacles are impressive enough from the outside, but nothing prepares you for the interior, especially for the grace of the delicate stone tracery which fans out from above the massive stained-glass windows to span the entire ceiling. (In term-time, you can appreciate the Chapel in its full glory at evensong, which is at 5·30 p.m.)

After visiting the Chapel you can walk past the main college lawn down to the river, but you must leave by the same gate – to find the entrance to **Clare College** immediately on your left. The even, seventeenth-century proportions and restrained yellow stonework of Clare's Old Court benefit from the best setting of any college: to one side is the grand prospect of King's, to the other, gardens stretching down to the Cam. Crossing the stone bridge you walk by the Fellows' Garden – the prettiest in Cambridge, with curvaceous lawns overhung by shrubs and trees, a walled herbaceous border, and a sunken garden enclosed by a clipped yew hedge. It is not usually open at weekends, but you can view it from the river and the walk alongside. If you turn right at the back gate of Clare, you can re-cross the river via Garret Hostel Lane and continue past **Trinity Hall** and into Trinity Street. Turning left, you pass the main branch of Heffer's bookshop, with its huge stock of literature and academic books, before coming to the main entrance to **Trinity College**. Through the gate you walk straight into the Great Court, the largest courtyard in Oxford or Cambridge. It was laid out in the late sixteenth century on a magnificent although irregular scale: the six separate lawns which fill the two-acre space are all different sizes and shapes. In the next court, the serene façade of the Wren library overlooks the river. The library is open to the public, so if you have time admire the lavishly carved limewood book shelves and display cases.

Next to Trinity, **St John's College** is more notable for its stunning riverside gardens than the rather dour courts. The **Round Church**, diagonally opposite the main St John's gate house, is also

Church and cycles in St Edward's Passage typify the charm of Cambridge

worth a quick visit. From here you can walk along Sidney Street to **Christ's College**. Christ's has one of Cambridge's most ornate gate towers. The great attraction of the college is the Fellows' Garden (may be closed at weekends), with its extensive lawns, horse-chestnuts, and a three-hundred-year-old mulberry tree.

From Christ's, return to King's Parade by cutting through the stalls of Market Hill (no stalls on Sundays), and through St Edward's Passage, passing G. David, one of Cambridge's best secondhand bookshops. Continue past **Corpus Christi College**, whose Old Court dates from 1352, perhaps fitting in a visit to the nearby church of St Bene't's, the oldest in the city, with its Saxon tower extant. Turning down Silver Street, you come to the bridge – the best place to hire a punt.

The **River Cam** flows soporifically, so heading downstream you can drift gently along the Backs while you eat your picnic lunch and get the hang of pushing and steering with the pole. After the grand prospects of King's College, the most beautiful section is opposite Trinity Library, where the river curves past the levelled lawns and weeping willows towards the so-called Bridge of Sighs, which spans the water at St John's. The open arches of the bridge were fitted with iron bars to prevent undergraduates late back to college from climbing in.

After returning your punt, continue up Mill Lane to **Pembroke College**, notable for its red-brick courtyards and informal gardens, and its tiny stone-faced chapel. This was the second neo-classical church to be built in England (after Inigo Jones' St Paul's in Covent Garden) and the first building to be designed by Sir Christopher Wren.

A visit to the **Fitzwilliam Museum*** on Trumpington Street is a good way to round off the day. If its vast façade – fourteen Corinthian columns support the sculpted pediment – is impressive in itself, the collection is extraordinary in its quality and breadth, from Egyptian sculpture to modern British painting.

CAMBRIDGE

St John's College
Round Church
Bridge of Sighs
Trinity College
River Cam
THE
Gonville & Caius College
Christ's College
GARRET HOSTEL BRIDGE
QUEEN'S ROAD
Trinity Hall
SENATE HOUSE PASSAGE
Clare College
Market Hill
King's College Chapel
PETTY CURY
Guildhall
BACKS
King's Parade
King's College
St Edward's Passage
BENE'T ST
St Bene't's Church
Queens' College
Corpus Christi College
SILVER STREET
MILL LANE STREET
TRUMPINGTON STREET
Pembroke College
Fitzwilliam Museum

0 Yards 220
0 Metres 200

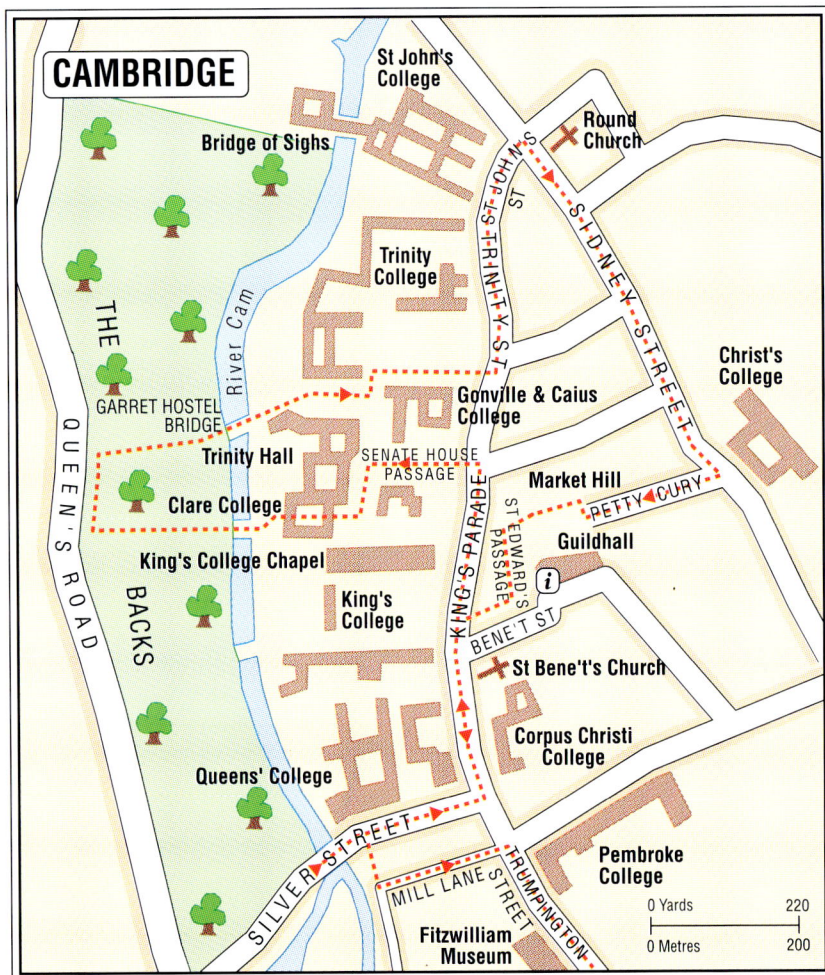

Colchester and the Essex marshes

The Essex Wildlife Trust has 83 nature reserves in its care

ADOPT A PLANT

If you want a living souvenir don't be tempted to plunder wild plants from the reserves. The **Beth Chatto Gardens***, six miles out of town at Elmstead Market, is a must. It is not a tourist attraction as such, but if you are looking for something really unusual, this is the place to go. Alternatively, you could purchase a specimen of Colchester's own rose, 'Colchester Beauty', from the specialist growers **Cant's of Colchester***, Nayland Road.

From Roman history and local culture to parks and marshland nature reserves, this day out encompasses the best of town and country.

Colchester is Britain's oldest recorded town, with 2,000 years of history behind it. The Romans, the Saxons and the Normans have all left their mark here. To understand and appreciate more about the place it is worth visiting the castle and the local museums. Drive a few miles out of the town and you will find yourself in the rich expanses of the Essex marshes, with their wide, shallow estuaries and mudflats. This is prime territory for natural history buffs and anyone who enjoys bracing walks.

COLCHESTER

There are various ways of exploring Colchester. First, you can opt for a walking tour of the town in the company of a guide: allow around two hours for the whole trip. These tours only operate from June to September; obtain details from the local **tourist information office*** in Queen Street (opposite the castle).

♦ **GOOD FOR** History, bird-watching, walking and oysters
♦ **TRANSPORT** Walk around Colchester; car or bicycle necessary for getting from Colchester to Mersea Island (about 10 miles)
♦ **ACCESS FOR DISABLED PEOPLE** Castle Museum is fully accessible; Fingringhoe Reserve has a special path for wheelchair users, and there is a sensory garden for the visually impaired
♦ **BEST TIME TO VISIT** Colchester: all year; Essex marshes: all year, although attractions and points of interest vary from season to season (see details on specific locations)

Staff will also be able to tell you about open-top bus tours.

Alternatively, go your own way, stroll round the ancient market in Vineyard Street (open Friday and Saturday), take a look at Balkerne Gate (the largest surviving Roman gateway in Britain) and follow the

course of the town wall: watch out for the lichens and opportunist wild plants that have rooted themselves among the stonework.

Colchester Castle Museum* holds pride of place in the town and ranks as its main attraction. It was built for William the Conqueror and stands on the site of the Temple of Claudius, once the largest Roman temple in Britain. You can glimpse the remains deep in the underground vaults. The museum also has spectacular collections that map out Colchester's history from prehistoric times to the Civil War Siege of 1648. Visitors can dress up in togas, try on helmets, learn about medieval fashion and take brass rubbings.

For those with an eye for historical treasures, there is the mysterious 'Dagenham Idol' (dating from around 2000BC), the Middleborough Mosaic and a magnificent bronze Roman statue of Mercury, not to mention relics, jewellery and even some remarkably intact Roman military tombstones. The 'Gaoler's Tale' graphically reveals the grisly secrets of the castle prisons.

Over 250,000 bulbs bloom each year in the formal splendour of the Victorian Grade II-listed **Castle Park and Gardens***. Parts of the dried-up moat around the castle have been planted with a jigsaw of geometrically shaped flower-beds, and swathes of green grass slope down towards the lake in Riverside Meadow. The park is also used for cricket matches, fêtes, concerts and other events.

The red-brick Georgian town house in the High Street that contains **Hollytrees Museum***, a stone's throw from the castle, makes an appropriately domestic setting for displays of toys, costumes, curios and knick-knacks from the last two centuries. At the back is a tranquil 'Sensory Garden', which was designed with special thought for people with disabilities; many of the plants are aromatic, and the flower-beds are raised. A level surface has been created for those in wheelchairs or who find walking difficult. At the end of the garden is a shelter from which a pleasant view of the valley and High Woods can be enjoyed. The **Natural History Museum** in All Saints Church, also in the High Street, houses various displays devoted to local natural history, geology and ecology. It makes a good appetiser if you are planning to venture out into the Essex countryside after lunch.

Tymperleys Clock Museum* in Trinity Street, set in a splendid fifteenth-century timber-framed house, is an horologist's delight. The museum focuses on timepieces made in Colchester during the eighteenth and nineteenth centuries.

Oysters have been growing in the waters off Colchester for over 2,000 years

Also on Trinity Street is another museum housed in Trinity Church. The modest **Social History Museum*** gives a lively insight into the way the citizens of Colchester and their rural neighbours have lived and worked over the past 300 years.

THE ESSEX MARSHES

There are more than 1,000 acres of green open space and semi-wild places within the bounds of Colchester itself (details can be obtained from the tourist information office). Even better, however, are the nature reserves in the marshland and open countryside south towards Mersea Island.

Fingringhoe Wick Nature Reserve* (south of Colchester off the B1025 Mersea road) is the headquarters of the **Essex Wildlife Trust***, which should be able to supply information on all nature reserves and notable sites in the county. This reserve is a mixture of saltmarshes and mudflats, heathland and a network of freshwater pools derived from old gravel workings. From the observation tower and hides, you can look out over Geedon

Saltings and the tidal river. The two nature trails take you through clearings, around ponds and along gullies.

Abberton Reservoir is thought to be the most important reservoir in Britain for wintering duck, and bird-watchers flock here to see thousands of mallard, pochard, goldeneyes, widgeon and many other species. There is less activity during the summer months, although mute swans use it as a site for moulting. Visitors have access to the public bird-watching site on the western side of the reservoir.

To get to Mersea Island, you need to follow the B1025 and cross the Strood (the long causeway which takes the road over the path once used by the Saxons). Apart from the caravan sites and the urban development around West Mersea, most of the island is one big, impressive nature reserve. Spectacular bird migrations take place in spring and autumn, acres of beautiful marsh plants are to be seen in summer, while thousands of geese, swans and ducks live here in winter. If you want to explore on foot, the walk from East Mersea along the sea dyke by the Colne Estuary is worth doing.

The picturesque appeal of Constable country

Willy Lott's cottage in Flatford. He was a local villager and friend of Constable

♦ **GOOD FOR** Admirers of painters, paintings – and inspiring countryside
♦ **TRANSPORT** By road, Flatford Mill is 5 miles from Dedham. Sudbury, by way of Stratford St Mary, Stoke-by-Nayland and Nayland, is about 15 miles from Dedham, so a car is necessary
♦ **ACCESS FOR DISABLED PEOPLE** Limited access to Gainsborough's House and the Munnings Collection
♦ **BEST TIME TO VISIT** Avoid Flatford and Dedham at summer weekends. Far fewer tourists are found away from these honeypots. Bridge Cottage at Flatford Mill is open March to November, daily June to September (also guided tours); otherwise closed Monday and Tuesday. Gainsborough's House is open all year except Monday. The Munnings Collection has very limited opening hours between May and September; it is advisable to ring beforehand to check

The focus of the day is painting and painters. Flatford provides the real-life scenes from some of John Constable's best-known works, while the former homes of Thomas Gainsborough and Sir Alfred Munnings have become galleries for their works.

Constable country is synonymous with Dedham Vale, a mellow area to the east of the Stour Valley with water meadows around the banks of the River Stour, gently undulating cornfields and attractive villages made rich in medieval times by the wool trade (see also *Great Day Out 88*). John Constable, probably England's most widely admired landscape artist, was born in 1776, grew up here, and the countryside on the banks of the Stour was his abiding inspiration. Although he showed an early talent for painting and drawing, his originality matured slowly. His fame rests primarily on his realistic depictions of the local scenery, which were unfashionable at a time when idealistic Arcadian scenes were all the

rage. He brought attention to the Suffolk countryside even in his own lifetime. The story goes that once when he was passing through on a stagecoach he overheard a stranger refer to the landscape as 'Constable country'.

Flatford is a magically pretty hamlet on the River Stour. It was the basis for half-a-dozen of Constable's most famous paintings, such as *The Hay Wain* and *The White Horse*. The mill and Willy Lott's cottage, built in about 1600, look much as they did in the paintings. As both the mill and the cottage are used for painting and nature study courses you cannot go inside, but the National Trust does have a visitor centre in **Bridge Cottage***. The shop sells leaflets

which guide you round the lock and mill pool to enjoy the same viewpoints as those which Constable chose for his paintings, or you can take a guided tour to do the same. In the 170 years since Constable painted here little has changed, though you will note how he moved the topographical furniture around a bit to help his compositions.

The mile-and-a-half stroll across the water meadows to Dedham is very popular; alternatively, you can hire a rowing boat. While still at Flatford, you might pop into the Granary Collection, a big thatched barn full of antique bicycles and artisans' tools.

The merit of **East Bergholt** lies less in its picturesque appeal and more in the fact that it is Constable's birthplace. The house where he was born has disappeared, and an early studio has become part of a garage (by the post office). The village church of St Mary has no tower, so the bells are kept in the churchyard in a large sixteenth-century hut called a bell cage. The bells are hung upside-down and are rung by hand.

Dedham, whose broad high street is lined with timbered and brick Georgian buildings, tea shops and gift shops, is more attractive and far more touristy. The **Church of St Mary the Virgin**, the spire of which appears in a number of Constable's paintings, is typical of fine fifteenth-century churches financed by the wool trade. Inside are many commemorations of links with the United States: more Pilgrim Fathers came from Dedham than from any other community in England. The Dedham **arts and crafts centre*** covers three floors of a former church. Inside an endearing small toy museum includes childhood mementoes, china dolls, model trains and teddy bears. Children might also enjoy the **rare breeds farm***.

Just outside Dedham stands Castle House, home of the late Sir Alfred Munnings (1878–1959) and now the **Munnings Collection***. Sir Alfred, a president of the Royal Academy, was an outspoken critic of unrepresentative modern art, so in

Flatford Mill was the original Constable family home and an inspiration to the painter

the rooms of this gentle Tudor and Georgian house and the lovely garden studio you will find plenty of traditional portraits and landscapes, as well as many of the equine studies for which he is best known.

Just west of Dedham lies a collection of ancient, sleepy villages. **Stratford St Mary**'s church was painted by Constable (there is a print inside); flint flushwork spells out the whole of the alphabet on its exterior. **Stoke-by-Nayland**, on the crest of a hill, has another fine 'wool church', and a timbered guildhall and maltings. In **Nayland**, the soft-hued high street is very fetching, as is Fen Street, whose houses are connected to the lane by private footbridges across a stream. John Constable's aunt asked him to paint a picture for the church, which he duly did in 1809, and it is still there.

Thomas Gainsborough (1727-88) became a favourite portrait painter of the Royal Family

Sudbury is the capital of the Stour Valley and the birthplace of Thomas Gainsborough. **Gainsborough's House*** is just off Market Hill, where a statue also evokes the painter, poised with palette and brush. He was born in the Georgian-fronted house in 1727. It now contains what is claimed to be the largest collection of his works in the world. These include his earliest known portrait and his only known sculpture, as well as fine local landscapes; although appreciated first and foremost as a society portrait painter, his love was landscape painting.

Every Thursday and Saturday Sudbury hosts a bustling market selling everything from home-made cakes to letterboxes. The **tourist information office*** in the Town Hall (take the Gaol Lane side entrance) can advise you on other sights in the area.

LUNCHBOX

Refreshments are available at Bridge Cottage, Flatford and the Dedham Arts and Crafts Centre. Picnicking on the water meadows between Dedham and Flatford is popular. In Dedham, try the Marlborough Head Hotel, partly dating from the fifteenth century; the Angel Inn at Stoke-by-Nayland does outstanding food and the Swan Inn at Stratford St Mary is recommended

The wool trade legacy: Suffolk towns and villages

Tudor houses, still lived in today, on Water Street in Lavenham

This little-changed corner of Tudor England possesses arguably England's finest medieval town in Lavenham and, in Kersey, one of its prettiest villages, as well as two particularly fine Elizabethan country houses at Long Melford.

By the end of the fifteenth century Suffolk was producing more wool cloth than anywhere else in England. Wealthy clothiers built churches of a size and quality of stone that showed off their prosperity. Virtually every town and village in the Stour Valley has such a church, often standing next to a superb, timbered guildhall, the cornerstone of the wool trade. But a hundred years later the trade had gone into decline, with the result that some of the region's settlements still look much as they did in late-medieval times.

This tour includes too much to do in a day. Devote half a day to Lavenham, the area's highlight. Spend the other half either in Long Melford's Elizabethan houses or, for less intensive sightseeing, in Hadleigh and Kersey.

♦ **GOOD FOR** Anyone interested in English architecture. Kentwell Hall in particular will appeal to families
♦ **TRANSPORT** No reliable public transport
♦ **ACCESS FOR DISABLED PEOPLE** Only to Melford Hall
♦ **BEST TIME TO VISIT** All the main attractions are closed from November to March, and some open only on certain days, even in summer – phone to check. Kentwell Hall's main 're-creations' take place at weekends from mid-June to mid-July, and on a smaller scale at some spring and other summer weekends

LAVENHAM

At the beginning of the sixteenth century, Lavenham was one of England's richest towns, as is borne out by its 300-plus jettied and timber-framed listed buildings. The town is tiny and virtually every street

is worth seeing. Leave the High Street with its gift shops to take in the unbroken succession of timbered houses along **Water Street** and the marvellous **Shilling Street**, where cottages come in every shade of traditional Suffolk pink. The **tourist information office*** sells leaflets describing the houses' many distinguishing features, such as moulded shafts, oriel windows and mansarded roofs.

In the fine Market Place are two medieval halls. The grey and cream **guildhall***, constructed of English oak, is the town's most impressive secular building. Exhibitions illustrate the manufacture of broadcloth and provide an engaging account of local farming one hundred years ago.

The more modest yellow-plastered **Little Hall*** is very different, having undergone many changes since it originally served as a wool hall. Furniture of the last owners decorates the house, part of which they converted into an artists' dormitory, with decorative washbasins hidden in cupboards.

On Water Street, the **Priory***, completed in 1600, has a pargeted façade (ornamental plasterwork in bas relief) and is still very much lived in. Centuries ago it was the home of Benedictine monks and later of a wealthy wool merchant; today's owners have heavily restored its beamed and vaulted rooms, in the process exposing Elizabethan wall paintings.

The **church** on Lavenham's western edge, in Perpendicular style with flushwork (patterns from knapped flint) and ethereal clerestory windows, is a classic expression of the town's medieval wealth. It was rebuilt between 1485 and 1525 with the money of the local lord John de Vere and clothier Thomas Spring the Third. Their coats of arms and initials appear on the exterior, while inside

Almost unbelievably idyllic – the view from the ford in the village of Kersey

HADLEIGH

This sleepy, untouristy little town benefited greatly in the fourteenth and fifteenth centuries from the wool trade. Its medieval core is a stunning trio of buildings just off the High Street: the triple-storeyed, ochre **guildhall***, the utterly surprising red-brick **Deanery Tower***, built as the gatehouse to the Archdeacon of Suffolk's rectory, and the outsize, flint-faced **church**. (The guildhall is open for guided tours on some days between June and September, and the Deanery Tower only by appointment.) The High Street has the best examples of pargeting and fine pink façades.

KERSEY

Many visitors come to see this one-street village for the thatched and timbered weavers' cottages which descend both sides of the little valley to the ford at the bottom with its ever-present ducks. Aloof on one hill, the **church** has many attractive features, such as fine flushwork on its south porch, and a hammerbeam roof and painted rood screen within.

the detailed carvings on the parclose (wooden enclosure) intended for Spring's tomb is worth seeking out.

LONG MELFORD

This village lives up to its name in its two-mile high street, which suffers from the town not having a bypass. It is said to accommodate no fewer than 20 antique shops. At one end is a giant green and a stunningly light **church**, even finer than Lavenham's and displaying similar features. Here the benefactors are remembered in Gothic script around the exterior, and in both portraits and heraldic devices in the medieval stained-glass windows.

Off the green stand two great Elizabethan manors. The exterior of **Melford Hall*** juxtaposes turrets with later Georgian sash windows. The house, still occupied by a naval family, the Hyde Parkers, who arrived in 1786, is full of family portraits and furniture, but under National Trust administration it has a rather antiseptic air. Its visitors have included Elizabeth I and Beatrix Potter: a selection of the latter's watercolours is on display.

Kentwell Hall*, surrounded by a moat, a controversial modern Tudor-style rose-patterned

courtyard, formal gardens and a rare breeds farm, is altogether less stuffy. The occupants make a point of explaining that this is not a 'stately' home and has few fine contents. They have had a field-day playing about with the interior: for example, creating a Chinese Room and a Roman bathroom. At its large-scale 're-creations' (see Best time to visit) actors dress in costume, talk in a sixteenth-century manner, and perform tasks appropriate to life at that time.

Melford Hall, built for Sir William Cordell in the mid-sixteenth century

Bury St Edmunds and Ickworth House

Ickworth's strange rotunda, set among Italianate gardens

Bury St Edmunds is a compact market town retaining much Georgian architecture. Its ruined Norman abbey, once one of the largest in England, is shown to great advantage in lovely gardens. Close by is Ickworth House, a unique circular building in acres of parkland.

The town is best explored on foot. Head first for the Abbey Gate, rebuilt in 1347, which provides a picturesque entrance to the well-tended **Abbey Gardens**, frequent winner of floral competitions. An aviary, the River Lark, an old-English rose garden and a children's play area add to the attractions. You can also see the old stone Abbot's Bridge (no entry) that once led to a vineyard.

After King Edmund was killed by marauding Danes in the ninth century, Benedictine monks built a wooden shrine to house his bones. Under Abbot Baldwin (1065–97) they began a new stone **abbey**, a project which took the best part of two hundred years to complete. In 1214 the abbey provided the setting

- **GOOD FOR** Churches, paintings, archaeology – all accessible on foot
- **TRANSPORT** Those with cars can park in Ram Meadow in Bury. Ickworth is in Horringer village, about ten minutes away by bus (141, 143 or 144 from St Andrew's Street North in Bury – ask for Sharpe's Corner). Then there is a mile walk each way along the drive
- **ACCESS FOR DISABLED PEOPLE** Not particularly suitable
- **BEST TIME TO VISIT** Gardens and Ickworth are at their best in summer; market days are Wednesdays and Saturdays

for the historic Meeting of the Barons to force King John to accept the Magna Carta. The abbey flourished until the Dissolution of the

Monasteries in 1539 but today little remains apart from the square Norman tower (no entry to the public) which now houses the cathedral bells, and numerous weathered stone stumps. These poke through the tonsured grass like jagged teeth, together with remnants of tall pillars and arches, giving some idea of the abbey's huge proportions. Plaques at strategic spots around the site point out key features, such as the site of the shrine of St Edmund. **The Abbey Visitor Centre***, set in a tower on the west front (the walls are of rubble core as local people used the facing stones to build their own homes), hires out audio cassettes to enable visitors to follow the plaques in sequence.

Two perpendicular-style churches lie within the abbey precinct, both with hammerbeam roofs and carved angels. The Cathedral Church of St James, formerly an early sixteenth-century parish church, became **St Edmundsbury Cathedral** in 1914. **St Mary's Church** has a considerably darker interior: the chancel dates from around 1300 and the tower a century later. Behind the altar is the tomb of Mary Tudor, sister of Henry VIII, and a stained-glass window dedicated to her, which was presented by Queen Victoria.

Angel Hill, running into Crown Street, neatly divides the town between the abbey precinct and the shops and market. Opposite the abbey is the ivy-clad Angel Hotel, mentioned in *The Pickwick Papers*, and the **tourist information office***. The Athenaeum occupies a dominating position: formerly an Assembly House, where Charles Dickens gave readings from his works, nowadays it is used as a function room. Other old buildings in town include the imposing Victorian Corn Exchange and the medieval guildhall.

Bury's medieval abbey ruins look almost like modern sculptures in their weathered state

The new **Manor House Museum*** is a beautifully refurbished Georgian house, with particularly fine plasterwork. Concentrating on horology and art, its exhibits come from several private collections. On the ground floor are many exquisite European and American timepieces, from portable sundials to ornate German Renaissance clocks, as well as English watches; a hands-on gallery allows visitors to activate time-keeping mechanisms. The museum's collection includes Paris fashions from the 1920s, furniture, portraits (by Reynolds and Angelica Kauffmann), objets d'art and early views of Bury. Each exhibit is numbered and a computerised information centre in each room explains everything about it – ideal if there aren't too many other visitors.

In contrast is **Moyses Hall Museum***, a late eleventh-century stone dwelling, which in its time has also served as a jail, workhouse and police station. The vaulted stone undercroft with cobbled floor contains a motley collection of local items – musical instruments, a skeleton and a dolls' house. Upstairs is a more focused exhibition of archaeological finds, including Iron Age coins and Roman pots. Much was retrieved from graves and the best collection is the Isleham hoard – weapons, tools and ornaments from the Bronze Age. Children will be intrigued by the mummified cats and other items of witchcraft. The museum is too small to display everything it owns, so exhibits are changed regularly.

It is worth strolling to the south of the town past handsome Georgian houses to the restored Regency **Theatre Royal***, a delightfully intimate playhouse. The air outside hangs heavy with the smell of malted barley from the **Greene King Brewery***, easily identified by the copper mash tun standing on the pavement. Three-hour brewery tours are conducted each afternoon (except Fridays – book in advance).

ICKWORTH HOUSE PARK AND GARDENS*

Three miles south-west of Bury is an oval rotunda with two low, curved wings. The building was begun in 1795 for the eccentric fourth Earl of Bristol, who planned to live in the rotunda and to display his fine-art and silver collection in the wings. However, he died in Italy before the venture was finished: because of the general unwillingness on the part of sailors to transport corpses his body was brought back to Ickworth packed as a statue. His son later decided to use the rotunda for exhibitions and entertainment.

After the imposing entrance hall, visitors pass through a series of grand rooms, with French furniture, Chinese and French porcelain and serried ranks of domestic family silver. One surprise is that the tall 'marble' columns in some of the rooms are in fact scagliola, sham marble made by applying coloured, pulverised plaster direct to the wooden columns to create a superbly realistic finish. The walls are covered with family portraits by British artists such as Romney, Gainsborough and Reynolds, as well as works by Titian and Hogarth and a charming self-portrait of Madame Vigée Le Brun. A particular favourite with children is a portrait by Velasquez (1635) of Don Balthasar Carlos, the 6-year-old son of King Philip IV of Spain, accompanied by three large dogs almost as large as the *infante* himself. The unusual glass-domed Pompeian room, in red and ochre, has decorations based on a Roman wall-painting, and the more recently added bathroom, with the taps in the corridor, tickles the imagination. The Italianate garden to the south includes a rose garden and orangery, and the surrounding parkland provides several waymarked walks leading to the lake, adventure playgrounds, woods, and, a deer enclosure with a hide.

LUNCHBOX

Bury has numerous eating places, including the Cathedral coffee shop, Alwyne House Tearoom in the Abbey Gardens and Manor House Museum. At Ickworth House, coffees, light lunches and teas are available.

Suffolk's coastal curiosities

A fairy-tale cottage on stilts, the House in the Clouds is visible from miles around

This is very much a day out for pottering about in old-fashioned streets, enjoying some eccentric bits and pieces along this eroded coast, and savouring the salt on your lips and the wind in your hair.

The long shingle beaches and low crumbling cliff-line between Aldeburgh and Southwold are losing their battle against the ravages of the North Sea. Aldeburgh has already lost a whole street to the swirling grey water; Southwold, with its higher cliffs, has suffered less, while at Dunwich just a short row of cottages remains of what was once one of Britain's most prosperous ports.

SOUTHWOLD

Larger, smarter and busier than Aldeburgh down the coast, Southwold is worth a good two or three hours to explore and enjoy the

- ♦ **GOOD FOR** Exploring a stunning coast
- ♦ **TRANSPORT** Car or bicycle
- ♦ **ACCESS FOR DISABLED PEOPLE** Not ideal
- ♦ **BEST TIME TO VISIT** Any time

shopping and the seafront. It's also the best place to eat, so planning for an early lunch here would be a good idea. The attraction of the town, which is largely unsullied by modern development, is its faintly stately air. With its sizeable fifteenth-century church flanked by green open spaces, it almost feels like a small cathedral town. The **parish church of St Edmund** is notable for the screen of

painted angels, apostles and prophets which dates back to the early sixteenth century, and a strange mechanical grotesque called 'Jack of the clock' or 'Southwold Jack', who strikes a bell to mark the beginning of services.

The focus of the town is split between the long seafront promenade, which runs along low cliffs above the shingle beach with its brightly coloured beach huts, and the market square and High Street. Here is an attractive and largely unspoilt mix of Georgian and nineteenth-century houses and shop fronts.

DUNWICH

Once the capital of Suffolk and a thriving port with 18 churches, Dunwich succumbed to a severe storm in 1286; much of the city was swept away. By 1602 it was about a quarter of its original size, and now nothing remains but a few cottages and a pub. But it's still worth a visit to see the tiny museum with its model of the once great city, and to stand on the beach looking out over the devouring sea, and on the cliffs, which still crumble away at the rate of about a metre a year.

The remains of **Greyfriars**, a fourteenth-century friary, are a short walk inland. The impressive walls, the western gate and parts of the refectory still stand.

MINSMERE–DUNWICH HEATH

South of Southwold a pocket of woodland opens into the heathery expanse of Dunwich Heath, spattered with bracken and gorse and a haven for rare birds, including nightjars, stonechats and marsh harriers. Much of it is owned by the National Trust, and the RSPB runs the adjoining **Minsmere nature reserve***. The heath stretches down to the cliff, where there's a National Trust

Fishing boats on the beach at Aldeburgh

car park and visitor centre in a lonely row of whitewashed former coastguard cottages (looming in the distance is the white dome of Sizewell Nuclear Power Station). There are some lovely walks, especially in late summer when the heather is in bloom.

On the way south from here, don't miss **Leiston Abbey** (EH), just off the B1122. The ruins date from 1380 and parts of the presbytery and transepts remain.

THORPENESS

This extraordinary seaside village was conceived of as a sort of upmarket Edwardian Butlin's. In 1911 landowner G. Stuart Ogilvie began building a model holiday village 'for people who wanted to experience life as it was in merrie England'. Most of the houses and shops are half-timbered with mock-Tudor façades or black boarding around the upper storey, but Ogilvie also commissioned a series of architectural fantasies including the bizarre top-heavy House in the Clouds which is actually a water tower.

In the (working) windmill there's a heritage centre explaining the historical and environmental importance of the coastline. The Mere, an artificial lake where you can hire sailing and rowing boats, and the golf course are part of Ogilvie's original scheme for a village devoted to pleasure, but his dream was never fulfilled and most houses were eventually sold to private owners. It is an amazing place nevertheless: to see it to its best advantage, park in the car park and follow the village walk which is marked on the information board.

ALDEBURGH

In many ways, the charm of Aldeburgh lies in its ordinariness. It may have become famous as home to the eponymous music festival inspired by Benjamin Britten and Peter Pears, who lived here from the 1940s and both of whom are buried in the churchyard, but it remains a combination of a slightly melancholy seaside resort and a picturesque fishing village. Lying cheek by jowl are the battered open fishing boats hauled up on the shingle beach, the ramshackle wooden huts from where the fishermen sell their catch – including delicious Dover Sole – and the faded nineteenth-century villas which line the short seafront promenade.

And that's it: two streets wide; you can walk the length of it in ten minutes. The **tourist information office***, in the foyer of the cinema, can provide you with details of many lovely walks in the area. On a bright day, however, Aldeburgh is the perfect place to have tea, watch the life on the beach and round off your day out. Apart from the main venue for the festival concerts, Snape Maltings, a few miles inland, Aldeburgh itself has several attractions. The sixteenth-century **Moot Hall** on the seafront is still the meeting place of the town council and can be visited in the afternoons. The church of St Peter and St Paul on the hill is worth a visit. The porch, nave and chancel are sixteenth-century and there is a beautiful stained-glass window by John Piper in memory of Benjamin Britten.

Merrie England Edwardian-style: the curious architecture at Thorpeness

LUNCHBOX

Ye Olde Cross Keys and the Mill Inn in Aldeburgh both serve fresh fish at lunchtime. The National Trust teashop at Dunwich Heath offers refreshments, but the best places to eat at are the Crown and the Harbour Inn in Southwold.

Norwich – mustard, mammoths and markets

From the soaring grandeur of the cathedral to the microcosm of world art at the Sainsbury Centre, there is much to satisfy visitors in the fine city of Norwich.

O ther English cities may have better individual sights and a fuller historic core, yet the capital of East Anglia appeals for its amalgam of small-scale pleasures. Parts of the city have a faintly bohemian air, thanks to a large student population; elsewhere (apart from the cathedral precincts), it is definitely workaday. Wandering round the lanes of the largely pedestrianised centre, amid modern development and department stores, you will stumble across quaint art galleries, little museums in centuries-old buildings and a host of flint-faced churches. Norwich boasts no fewer than 32 medieval churches (the city once had one church for every Sunday of the year), reflecting its wealth in the Middle Ages when it was second only to London in importance, thanks

- ♦ **GOOD FOR** Churches, wandering and shopping in a medieval setting
- ♦ **TRANSPORT** The BR station is a 15-minute walk from the town centre. The Sainsbury Centre is a 15-minute bus ride from the castle
- ♦ **ACCESS FOR DISABLED PEOPLE** The cathedral, Sainsbury Centre and Castle Museum are all accessible. An access guide to Norwich is available
- ♦ **BEST TIME TO VISIT** All year. The Lord Mayor's Street Procession takes place in July, and the arts festival in October. Several museums are open on Sunday

to a thriving textile industry. Our suggested walk for this day out links these back lanes with the city's three focal points: the Market Place, the castle and the cathedral.

Elm Hill makes a perfect setting for some specialist shopping

CITY WALK
The **Market Place** is home to one of Britain's largest open-air markets. Tapes, underwear, fish, tools, fruit, cheese, rugs, health food – everything imaginable – is sold under this sea of multicoloured, striped awnings. Round the fringes of the market are the flint-chequered **Guildhall**, now housing the **tourist information office*** and the civic regalia (robes and silver plate), and **St Peter Mancroft**, a church of near-cathedral proportions with a fine roof of carved fan tracery and angels, and stained-glass windows.

Leave the Market Place by the art nouveau **Royal Arcade** to reach **Castle Museum***. Building work on the impressive keep with its 'blind arcading' began around 1100, but what you now see is the result of 1830s refacing. Tours take you to the dungeons to see death masks (for many centuries the castle served as a prison) and to the battlements. The castle is also Norwich's main museum, with archaeological, geological and natural history sections, including the bones of a 600,000-year-old *Mammuthus trogontherii*, a very primitive type of mammoth, discovered in the North Norfolk cliffs. If you have limited time, head for the specialist collection of teapots and to the galleries displaying the works of the Norwich School of Artists. These early nineteenth-century landscape painters worked chiefly in oil and water colour and produced typical rural Norfolk scenes.

Leave the castle via the underground tunnel once used by prisoners bound for the courts. The new **Castle Mall** underground shopping complex is worth a browse. Go north to Tombland, from which two superb medieval gates lead into the cathedral's upper close. Take the **Erpingham Gate** and enter the **cathedral***. Building began in 1096,

From bacon rolls to spanners – you can buy almost anything in Norwich's market

but its gracefulness comes from later additions in Perpendicular style. The best of the structure is overhead; along the vaulted nave are hundreds of carved and coloured roof bosses illustrating scenes from the Bible (mirrors on trolleys help prevent neck strain). Other bosses can be seen much closer up in the two-storeyed cloisters, where you can peruse 400 more complex, miniature scenes, mainly depicting the book of the Revelation. Other examples of medieval art, in the form of wall paintings on the reliquary arch, a prized reredos in St Luke's Chapel and fifteenth-century misericords in the choir, are also well worth seeking out.

The **cathedral close** has a collegiate air, as dog-collared clerics and blazered pupils potter between its flint and red-brick buildings, and feels entirely distinct from the rest of the city. Wander from **Upper Close** across to **Lower Close**, with its gardens and Georgian residences,

LUNCHBOX
Norwich excels in cafés in historic surroundings, including in the crypt of **St Andrew's and Blackfriars' Halls**, in **St Michael at Plea**, and a sixteenth-century banqueting hall attached to **Cinema City** on St Andrew's Street. The city's oldest and most appealing pub, the **Adam and Eve** on Bishopgate, does good lunches.

then continue down to **Pull's Ferry**, a fifteenth-century watergate and the city's most scenic spot on the River Wensum.

Retrace your steps to Tombland. At its northern end turn left into **Elm Hill**, the city's prettiest street. The merchants who built the Tudor gabled and half-timbered houses left their homes for more salubrious ones in Georgian times, and by the 1920s the street had become a slum threatened with demolition. Now overlooking its cobbles there are craft shops devoted to everything from pottery to taxidermy.

At the far end of Elm Hill stands a trio of defunct medieval places of worship. The impressive interconnected **St Andrew's and Blackfriars' Halls** were once a Dominican church. **St Peter Hungate*** is a little museum of church art; like **St Michael at Plea**, now an antiques centre, it has a roof adorned with golden angels.

It is a short walk to **Bridewell Alley**; first pop

into the **Mustard Shop**: this quasi-Victorian store pays homage to the 170 years that the local firm Colman's has been in business and sells those distinctive yellow tins of powdered mustard. Then spend an hour in the **Bridewell Museum***. This medieval house, once used as a prison, now serves as a repository for an amazing collection of historical items related to the past trades and industries of Norwich. The sheer number of artefacts – from textile bobbins and yarn winders to printing presses, chocolate moulds and a room full of grandfather clocks – can be somewhat overwhelming.

Just down the road on Charing Cross, **Strangers' Hall*** is a jigsaw puzzle of a building assembled over five centuries. It takes its name from skilled weavers from the Low Countries who lodged here. Furniture from Tudor to Victorian times complements appropriate parts of the building.

Continue into **St Benedict's Street** or **Pottergate**, where there are five more old churches, two of which have become arts centres. St Benedict's Street is also commercial Norwich at its most hip, with shops specialising in second-hand books, prints and musical instruments.

The gracefully apsed chancel of Norwich Cathedral enlightens the spirit

The fishing villages of Blakeney Harbour

Three individual, though equally unspoilt, fishing villages clustered around Blakeney Harbour hold some historic surprises; long walks and sea trips for seal-spotting are other reasons to visit.

In the Middle Ages, Blakeney Harbour was of international importance. The great five-mile arm of sand and shingle which marks the mouth of the River Glaven and encloses the creeks, salt marshes and mud flats provided the last sheltered harbour before Great Yarmouth, well over fifty miles around the coast to the south-east.

Over the years, however, a massive accumulation of sand and mud has silted up the channels, leaving the once-prosperous ports which line the harbour – Blakeney, Cley-next-the-Sea and, to some extent, Morston – bereft of their main source of wealth.

- ♦ **GOOD FOR** Active families – and sailors!
- ♦ **TRANSPORT** You need a car to travel from village to village
- ♦ **ACCESS FOR DISABLED PEOPLE** No
- ♦ **BEST TIME TO VISIT** All year

They have lost little of their charm, however. As the north Norfolk coast faded into economic obscurity, all three villages remained largely unspoilt, retaining their ancient quays, terraces of old flint cottages, some very fine churches, and even one virtually intact windmill. Each village is interesting to visit in its own right, but the large expanses of National Trust beaches

and marshland nearby offer fine walks and excellent wildlife- and bird-watching opportunities.

If you are a strong walker, all three villages can be visited as part of a ten-mile round trip. Park in Morston car park, take the ferry to Blakeney Point; walk along the beach as far as Cley (about five miles), continue to Blakeney along the sea wall (about two and a half miles), then complete the circuit along the sea wall to Morston (another two miles or so). Otherwise, you can simply make the tour by car.

MORSTON

Ironically, it is now Morston, which is of relatively little importance historically, that has the best access to Blakeney Harbour and the sea. The 'quay', as it is rather optimistically called, is signposted down a bumpy track from the main coast road and leads on to a large, rough-and-ready car park. Here is a small National Trust centre, and the point of departure for open ferries which depart every high tide from rickety stagings staked out on the muddy quay for the sand dunes and seals of Blakeney Point. It is best to pre-book your trip in high season: booking details are posted outside the pub and cottages on the main road.

A more romantic way to see the seals is by sailing boat; trips are run by the local sailing school which is based at the pontoon a short walk down the main creek. When the tides are right, the school also offers early-morning trips to Cley at the head of the harbour. The channel is now so narrow that it is rarely used by boats, so this is an almost unique opportunity to follow the old trading route to the quay by Cley windmill. Morston also has a public slipway for launching boats, and if you follow one of the paths leading out on to the marshes it is easy to escape the

Cley windmill in its commanding position amid reed beds

crowds and enjoy listening to the sky larks hovering high above.

Morston village is rather spoilt by the main road that cuts through it, but do not miss the tiny church just by the bend. **All Saints** is a relatively rare example of a Norfolk flint church which escaped improvement by the Georgians or the Victorians. The beautifully simple whitewashed interior remains an outstanding example of Early English thirteenth-century architecture.

BLAKENEY

Old photographs show quite sizeable vessels moored to Blakeney quay at high tide a hundred or so years ago, but the creek has now silted up heavily and there is no more trade or large-scale fishing. Plenty of small sailing boats are still kept here – Blakeney is a rare 'free port' so there are no mooring fees. Other favourite summer activities for visiting families are fishing for crabs in the creeks, and making mud slides from the high banks of the marsh opposite the quay.

Of the three villages, Blakeney is probably the most picturesque. The tiny flint cottages in the steep back streets and the bigger houses which look out over the marsh are undoubtedly very pretty, but Blakeney does get besieged by visitors on warm weekends so try to visit on a weekday or out of high season. By the quay, the remains of the flint guildhall are of some note, while at the top of the town, the sheer size of **St Nicholas Church** is testimony to the former prosperity of the village. The chancel is Early English, but the nave dates from 1435. It is not clear why the church has a tower at each end, but it seems likely that the slender eastern tower was used as a lighthouse and landmark for fishermen and (most probably) smugglers.

Most people in search of some fresh air in Blakeney head off along the sea wall which separates the harbour from the marshes. A more interesting and little-known alternative is to walk to the east end

of the village, beyond the Manor Hotel, and go through the kissing-gate into a stretch of National Trust land below the high flint walls of the old friary. You can follow a short looped walk which has wonderful views to Blakeney Point.

CLEY-NEXT-THE-SEA

Ironically, although Cley (pronounced to rhyme with high) is now virtually cut off from the sea, it is so low that it remains very prone to flooding during high spring tides. One disastrous flood in 1953 completely swamped the village and caused extensive damage.

Like Morston, Cley suffers from the main road which cuts it in half, but while the shops are all on the road, there is plenty to see in quiet corners of the village and some tiny back alleys to explore. Shops include a top-notch delicatessen which sells smoked fish, an excellent tea room, an extremely good pottery shop, a second-hand bookshop – and, most prominent of all, the windmill. It is no longer in working order, but the sails are still in place and you can visit during the afternoons, or bed-and-breakfast in it.

Walking south away from the harbour you will come to the church of **St Margaret of Antioch**, which stands on a low bluff above the village green. If it seems a little removed from the rest of the village, it is because 117 nearby houses destroyed by a fire in 1612 were never fully replaced. With its broad and airy nave, St Margaret's has more of the atmosphere of a small cathedral than a parish church. The superb free-flowing stone decoration would have been even more intricate and impressive, but the money began to run out as Cley lost trade when the channel began to accumulate silt and when the Black Death engulfed the village in 1348.

LUNCHBOX

Both the King's Arms and the White Horse in Blakeney serve decent lunches. Otherwise, try the Whalebone Café in Cley, or the Three Horseshoes pub in Warham about five miles west of Morston. For details of other eating places contact the tourist information office* in Cromer.

Stately houses and gardens in Norfolk

Part of the Jacobean south front of Blickling Hall showing the typical Dutch gables

Norfolk is a county particularly rich in stately homes. Take your pick of Jacobean / Georgian (Blickling), medieval / Tudor (Oxburgh), Palladian (Holkham) or a glorious mix (Felbrigg); all four halls rejoice in some superb treasures as well as fine gardens.

BLICKLING HALL*

Blickling Hall near Aylsham (one of three National Trust properties covered in this Day Out), is approached down an impressive driveway flanked with seventeenth-century yew hedges. The warm red-brick house, built between 1619 and 1627, displays a dominant clock tower and a Dutch-gabled roofline with unusual corner turrets. The hall stands inside the ancient dry moat of the previous house, which was once the residence of the Boleyn family and the birthplace of Anne Boleyn.

♦ **GOOD FOR** Walking, as well as enjoying beautiful buildings, interiors and gardens
♦ **TRANSPORT** No public transport between the sites
♦ **ACCESS FOR DISABLED PEOPLE** There are WCs for disabled people at all the sites, and Braille guides
♦ **BEST TIME TO VISIT** National Trust properties are open between late March and early November; Holkham Hall is open end of May to end of September, plus bank holiday Sundays and Mondays. The gardens may be at their best in spring and early summer

The Jacobean exterior hides a Georgian interior, its centrepiece being the carved oak staircase which winds up in double flights from the hall. Although substantially remodelled in the eighteenth century, the spectacular ornate plaster-moulded ceiling in the 123-foot gallery dates from the 1620s. Further attractions include collections of fine furniture, impressive tapestries (notably a set of eight seventeenth-century Mortlake works), and a library of some 12,000 leather-bound books, many printed before 1500.

The colourful and impressively maintained garden, renowned for its superb herbaceous borders and containing an orangery, gives you a good impression of how it might have looked in Jacobean times. Beyond lies extensive parkland, criss-crossed by a network of footpaths through ancient woodland, as well as a delightful lake (fishing permits available), where you could easily be tempted to spend the rest of the day.

FELBRIGG HALL*

Around 1,700 acres of woods and parkland (accessible from dawn to dusk) surround Felbrigg Hall, near Cromer. The earliest part of this outstanding National Trust mansion is the Jacobean south front, dating from 1620. The red-brick Carolean west wing was added in 1684, with the Georgian east service wing and the castellated neo-Tudor stable block constructed during the eighteenth and nineteenth centuries.

The hall contains a superb collection of original eighteenth-century furniture, much of it introduced by William Windham II after the completion of his Grand Tour of Europe, and a treasure-house of pictures in the handsomely decorated rooms, including an outstanding library. The restored two-and-a-half-acre walled garden is

The north-west corner of Oxburgh Hall with its oriel window

a tranquil area to stroll in, with its fruit trees and herbaceous and cut-flower borders; cooing comes from within the rare octagonal dovecote with nine hundred nesting niches.

Parkland paths lead you to the charming isolated Church of St Margaret, built in 1400 by Sir Simon Felbrigg and probably separated, like the hall, from the village as a result of the plague. Waymarked walks, including a family woodland trail, take you through the Old Deer Park, along the impressive lakeside and the Great Wood.

HOLKHAM HALL*

Holkham Hall, near Wells-next-the-Sea, lies in a vast 3,000-acre deer park on the beautiful North Norfolk coast. This eighteenth-century Palladian mansion is a cache of artistic and architectural history, put together by the Earls of Leicester over seven generations. The tour of the hall starts in the Marble Hall and takes you through the richly decorated State Rooms, adorned with magnificent tapestries, gilded ceilings, fine furniture by William Kent and, among the many works of art, paintings by Rubens, Van Dyck, Poussin and Gainsborough.

After leaving the hall via the old kitchen, complete with original pots and pans, visit the **Bygones Museum**, housed in a stable block. This holds a fascinating collection of over five thousand items, ranging from vintage cars and steam engines to gramophones and toys. An audio-visual guide, dioramas and display models in the **History of Farming Exhibition**, in the Old Porter's Lodge, help explain how the estate evolved, while nearby are a gift shop, an art gallery and Holkham Pottery.

There are invigorating walks across the deer park; or you could take a bracing ramble along **Holkham beach**, one of the best along this coast. The huge expanse of sand is backed by miles of dunes and pine forest and is a haven for birdlife. To reach it follow the straight road opposite the main estate entrance and the Victoria Hotel.

OXBURGH HALL*

Oxburgh (National Trust), near Swaffham, is an impressive moated red-brick manor house built in 1482 by the Bedingfeld family, who still live here. Its outstanding feature is the Tudor gatehouse, which rises 80 feet above the moat (the house was once surrounded by undrained marshland), from the top of which fine views can be had across the Norfolk countryside.

Principal interior rooms demonstrate the transition from medieval austerity to Victorian opulence. One highlight of your tour may be the King's Room (plus priest's hole), where Henry VII slept in 1497, now furnished with a seventeenth-century bed and embroidered wall-hangings worked by Mary Queen of Scots during her captivity in England.

Fine-weather options for afternoon walks abound: amble across the lawns dotted with trees, passing the colourful herbaceous borders and a beautiful parterre garden, explore the Victorian wilderness garden, or enjoy a two-mile woodland walk through Home Covert. The early Victorian chapel in the grounds has a fine altarpiece.

LUNCHBOX

Good bar meals and real ale are served at the Buckinghamshire Arms, which stands at the gates to Blickling Hall; there is also a restaurant at the hall itself. Holkham Hall visitors may like to venture into nearby Burnham Market for lunch at the excellent Hoste Arms. Felbrigg Hall has a licensed restaurant and self-service Turret Tea Room within the converted courtyard stabling area, while Oxburgh Hall offers light lunches and teas in the Old Kitchen.

King's Lynn, medieval fishing and trading port

Custom House: testimony to the importance of King's Lynn as a trading port

CASTLE RISING

A short drive up the A149 north of King's Lynn, the Norman keep of Castle Rising (EH) – still surrounded by the massive earthworks which formed its protective walls and ditch – is worth a detour. The castle was built in around 1140 and, although ruined, the great square bulk of the keep is still intact. It is great fun to explore the surviving skeleton with its stone stairways, first-floor 'wall passages' (which are like elevated cloisters), the tiny chapel and the 'free drop' latrines. The delicate detail of the stonework, such as the interlocked round-arched tracery which survives on the outside walls, is outstanding.

Some excellent small museums and a fascinating array of medieval buildings make King's Lynn a good destination for architecture buffs or simply for a family day out browsing around the town.

This tour starts just outside the centre of the town, which is the ideal place to get a feel for the hard life suffered by the people who worked in Lynn's traditional industry – fishing. **True's Yard Museum*** is on the corner of North Street and St Ann's Street. Here, two tiny one-up, one-down fishermen's cottages, which survived the slum clearances of the 1930s, have been preserved as they would have been in the mid-

♦ **GOOD FOR** Those who enjoy medieval buildings and imaginative museums
♦ **TRANSPORT** King's Lynn has both rail and bus services
♦ **ACCESS FOR DISABLED PEOPLE** No
♦ **BEST TIME TO VISIT** Year round; King's Lynn Festival of Music and the Arts is held in July/August

nineteenth century. As the guides are eager to point out, each cottage

could have housed as many as eleven people, with perhaps nine children sleeping in one bed. The 'Northenders' who lived here were an extremely tough, tight-knit community. They seldom married outside the North End, adultery was rare, and families who lost husbands and fathers to the perils of fishing up to a hundred miles out in the North Sea were looked after by everyone else. The museum next to the cottages contains models of the old fishing smacks and other artefacts associated with the industry. Behind the museum, the houses of Pilot Street date back several centuries and are part of the last surviving remnants of the little community.

Continuing into St Ann's Street, you pass **St Nicholas Chapel** on your left (St Nicholas is the patron saint of fishermen). This extraordinary building has been added to and adapted many times. Two features of particular note are the south porch and the west window. Age and subsidence have distorted the floors and walls alarmingly. (If the chapel is locked ask for the key at True's Yard.) By turning west you pass the **Tudor Rose Hotel**, a half-timbered building still with its original fifteenth-century door. Now you are approaching the large expanse of **Tuesday Market Place**, one of two market places in the town and the setting for the annual St Valentine's Day Fair. The most impressive of the buildings lining the square are the grandiose, pillared **Corn Hall** of 1854, and the seventeenth-century **Duke's Head Hotel**.

Conditions were cramped and the hardships many in the True's Yard fishermen's cottages

From here walk parallel with the town's quays which border the mouth of the Great Ouse, the Fenland river which empties into the North Sea. Many of the buildings along King Street and Queen Street are medieval with Georgian fronts added later. Just beyond Tuesday Market Place is **St George's Guildhall** (NT) of 1410, the largest fifteenth-century guildhall in Britain (Shakespeare is said to have performed here), and now the King's Lynn Centre for the Arts. Further down on the left, the buildings of 28–32 King Street form an interesting combination of architectural styles, including arcaded gable walls from a twelfth-century stone house, and part of a slightly later hall house. The timber shop fronts are late-medieval.

The next important building is the **Custom House** on Purfleet Quay. Built in 1683 from the Dutch-influenced designs of a local architect, Henry Bell, it is expected to open to

the public when the tourist information office moves there in 1997. Towards the end of Queen Street is **Thoresby College** built between 1500 and 1510 by Thomas Thoresby, a former mayor of King's Lynn. It is now used mostly as a home for elderly people. A plaque in the courtyard marks the location of the quay in the thirteenth century; since then, deposits of mud and silt have pushed the river north by many yards.

You are now at the bottom of Saturday Market Place and next to two of the best museums in King's Lynn. The **Town House Museum of Lynn Life*** traces its history from the Norman conquest through to the 1950s with an excellent series of exhibits. Children are well catered for, with hands-on brass-rubbing and a Victorian school slate to try out. Nearby, the **Old Gaol House** is even more fun. You can tour the old cells, learn about witchcraft, ducking stools and being burnt at the stake,

A lesson in crime and punishment – the Old Gaol House

and generally have a gruesome time. (One famous Lynn witch was burnt at the stake in the Tuesday Market Place in 1590 – her heart burst from her body and flew into the crowd.)

Between the two museums is one of Lynn's most important buildings, the **Guildhall of the Holy Trinity** with its remarkable flint and stone chequered façade. The only part open to the public is the undercroft which houses the town regalia (including King John's Cup and Sword) and is visited as part of the tour of the Old Gaol House. Dating from the 1420s, the Guildhall is now used as the Town Hall: the **tourist information office*** is next door.

On the other side of Saturday Market Place is the whitestone **St Margaret's Church**, which was founded in 1104 but now dates mainly from the fourteenth century. The two west towers are Norman. Lynn was a Royalist town, and during the Civil War one of Cromwell's cannon balls shattered the west window. Behind the church is one last clutch of **medieval buildings**: the half-timbered Hampton Court (pre-1350) – you can go into the courtyard only; the Hanseatic Warehouse (1475); the former Valiant Sailor pub, which has a ship's stem-post as its corner timber (pre-Tudor); and Priory Cottages, the remains of a Benedictine Priory of around 1100.

Lincoln's cathedral and a tour of its environs

☂ ❄ 🚐

> *'The most precious piece of architecture in the British Isles', according to John Ruskin*

This under-visited city is home to one of Britain's finest cathedrals, an ancient castle and a most photogenic medieval street. The day out described here is restricted to uphill Lincoln and takes in some of the main sights around the cathedral.

Many of the sights, interesting shops and alluring places to eat and drink in are concentrated in a compact area of Lincoln, so if you are short of time you could ignore modern and commercial downhill Lincoln altogether. Devote a couple of hours to the cathedral, and try to time your visit to tie in with one of the fascinating general tours or a roof tour (on Saturdays only).

CATHEDRAL
Lincoln Cathedral* is a masterpiece of medieval Gothic craftsmanship. Start outside facing its awesome west front. Scaffolding will cover its famous Romanesque frieze for some years to come, but the wonderful, repetitious Gothic arcading is fully revealed. Look up at the statues topping the front's two pinnacles. One pays tribute to Bishop Hugh,

♦ **GOOD FOR** Even if the weather is bad there is enough to keep you amused
♦ **TRANSPORT** Driving is not necessary as the railway station is a 10-minute walk from uphill Lincoln. Once there, all the main places of interest can be visited on foot
♦ **ACCESS FOR DISABLED PEOPLE** Cathedral and castle only
♦ **BEST TIME TO VISIT** Cathedral tours are most frequent in the summer, when the castle also hosts historical enactments. The Victorian-style Lincoln Christmas Market, which takes place over a weekend before Christmas, is worth visiting

who masterminded the rebuilding of the original Norman cathedral after a destructive earthquake in 1185. The other honours the Swineherd of Stow, who donated his life's savings to the reconstruction.

Inside, walk through the vast nave

SOMETHING FOR THE CHILDREN
At the **Incredibly Fantastic Old Toy Show*** you can buy ten old pennies for £1 to operate the many antique mechanical toys. Parents can also introduce their offspring to the icons of their youth, such as a Dalek from *Doctor Who*, the Pink Panther and Andy Pandy.

to the sculpted choir screen. Up close you can see traces of the bright colours in which it was once painted. The rose windows at either end of the transept contain medieval stained-glass and rich tracery; the Dean's Eye faces north, watchful against the devil, while the Bishop's Eye looks south towards the Holy Land to receive the Holy Spirit. Behind the choir screen lies a cornucopia of intricate medieval carving on the oak choir stalls and misericords. Beyond, at the church's far eastern end, the lovely Angel Choir was built to house the shrine of the sanctified Hugh. Only the plinth remains. The choir takes its name from the 28 serene angels above the pillars. However, the face to look for is that of the famous Lincoln Imp, whom the angels turned into stone for intruding into the church (Imp prints can be bought in the cathedral shop).

Don't miss the **chapter house**, whose vaulted ceiling sprouts from its central pillar like a fountain. Edward I is believed to have presided over one of the first English parliaments here, seated in the chair on display. One side of the medieval cloisters has disappeared (a dean needed the stone for his stables) and was replaced by the Wren Library. You can peer into (but not enter) this elegant gallery from the adjacent medieval library. Finally, in summer you can climb the 270-foot-high central tower; an earlier tower, which blew down in 1547, was, amazingly, nearly twice as tall.

▲ *A fine example of Norman architecture, the castle is on a hilltop*

A WALK ROUND UPHILL LINCOLN

Leave the cathedral precincts via Exchequergate and walk across Castle Hill to the **castle***. Begun by William the Conqueror in 1068, the castle has walkable ramparts and climbable towers, which are eclipsed by a display of one of the four surviving 'exemplars' of the Magna Carta. The unornamented sheet of vellum, covered in shorthand Latin, is atmospherically presented, accompanied by a soundtrack of the chanting of some of the text. Equally fascinating is the Victorian chapel of the one-time prison, where the pews were designed to ensure that the prisoners could not see each other.

In the first century AD, Lincoln, as Lindum Colonia, was one of the country's most important Roman settlements. Return from the castle back into Castle Hill and head into **Bailgate** for Lincoln's few Roman sights. In the road are setts that indicate where the columns of a forum once stood. Further on, past a Roman well is **Newport Arch**, still standing after 20 centuries despite the battering inflicted by a lorry carrying fishfingers in the 1960s. Turn right down East Bight, from where you can see bits of Roman wall in back gardens. At the remains of the Roman gate turn right down Eastgate. Look out for the goblinesque figure peering out of the southern wall some 75 yards along.

Turn into the Minster Yard and make your way round past the Georgian and late-medieval houses to the **Bishop's Old Palace***. From its extant jumble of walls, arches and columns you need to apply your imagination to conjure up the splendour in which the bishops lived in the Middle Ages.

Return to Castle Hill again and descend cobbled **Steep Hill**, by far Lincoln's most picturesque street. At the top, window displays of specialist teas, lace and home-made chocolates vie for attention with the ancient buildings themselves. Look out for the twelfth-century **Norman House** and the black-and-white sixteenth-century **Harlequin building**. Further down is **Harding House**, once a merchant's house, now an arts centre, and **Readers' Rest**, an unbeatable second-hand bookshop. Steep Hill soon becomes The Strait. Here stand the **Jew's House** (now a smart restaurant) and the **Jew's Court**, reckoned to have been a synagogue originally, but now selling local history books.

Turn left opposite these medieval buildings to reach the **Usher Gallery***, the city's art gallery, which has a collection of Lincoln cityscapes by Peter de Wint. The **tourist information office*** on Castle Hill is a good source of advice on other attractions in Lincoln.

LUNCHBOX

The city's outstanding old inn is the Wig & Mitre on Steep Hill. It serves upmarket pub fare and first-rate full meals. Browns Pie Shop, also on Steep Hill, is a sweet little restaurant offering interesting fruit, meat and fish pies.

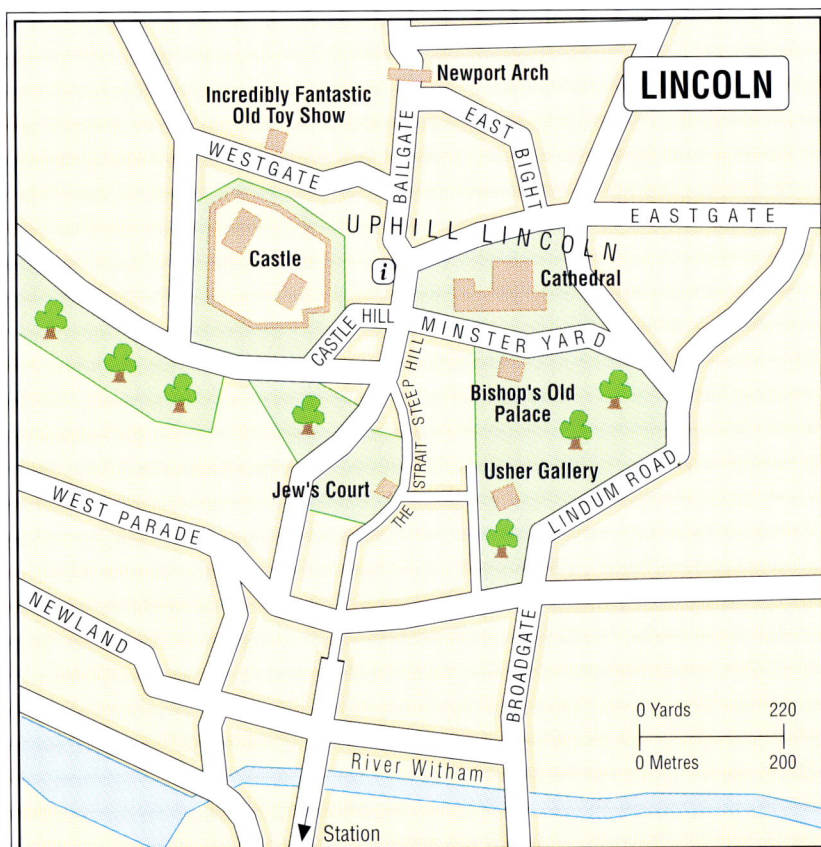

LINCOLN

Newport Arch

Incredibly Fantastic Old Toy Show

WESTGATE

BAILGATE

EAST BIGHT

EASTGATE

UPHILL LINCOLN

Castle

ⓘ

Cathedral

CASTLE HILL

MINSTER YARD

THE STRAIT

STEEP HILL

Bishop's Old Palace

Usher Gallery

LINDUM ROAD

Jew's Court

WEST PARADE

NEWLAND

BROADGATE

0 Yards 220

0 Metres 200

River Witham

▼ Station

Shugborough, Sudbury Hall and Calke Abbey

The cluttered boyhood bedroom of Sir Vauncey Harpur Crewe of Calke Abbey

Each of these three stately homes has some special feature that will appeal to families: the servants' quarters and farm on Shugborough Estate; the Museum of Childhood at Sudbury; and the hotchpotch of possessions of a Victorian aristocrat at the un-refurbished Calke Abbey.

Y ou could easily spend three hours at each of these absorbing National Trust properties, so choose the two that appeal most and take a picnic or have lunch in one of the restaurants (see Lunchbox).

SHUGBOROUGH ESTATE*

Shugborough Estate, five miles east of Stafford, on the edge of Cannock Chase, is an entertaining place, with a good choice of attractions (NT members are admitted to the house and garden for free, but separate admission charges apply for the Servants' Quarters and the Park Farm). The eighteenth-century house is

♦ **GOOD FOR** Hands-on attractions for children; interiors and a slice of social history for everyone who enjoys visiting stately homes
♦ **TRANSPORT** Public transport possible (contact tourist information office* at Derby or Stafford), but car desirable
♦ **ACCESS FOR DISABLED PEOPLE** At Shugborough the Servants' Quarters and Farm are accessible; at Sudbury the Museum of Childhood is accessible; at Calke Abbey only the ground floor is easily accessible
♦ **BEST TIME TO VISIT** Easter to end October: the houses are shut for the rest of the year, though the grounds are open during daylight hours

perhaps best known as the home of the Earl of Lichfield, whose photographs are occasionally on display.

The fine rooms make the most of the garden views and are decorated in classical style. Three of the ceilings have wonderful rococo plasterwork by Vassalli. Sound tours are available, together with children's quiz sheets based on riddles. The gardens reveal eight neo-classical monuments, including the Chinese House, the Tower of the Winds and the Cat's Monument. The Edwardian-style rose garden and the herbaceous border are stunning in summer.

The **Servants' Quarters** in the stable block alongside contain a delightful miscellany of displays, featuring aspects of country life such as the brewhouse, the stables and riding costumes, the gun rooms and the book in which house guests recorded their gambling debts — money was placed on the outcome of such trivial pursuits as racing maggots across the dining table. A section devoted to the children of the estate, and the health and hygiene gallery, with ancient baths and toilets and accounts of food storage in the pre-refrigerator age, have much to fascinate the visitor. There is an Edwardian nursery, and a roomful of puppets of all kinds with which children (and their parents) can play. Best of all, however, are the laundry and the kitchen where you can watch costumed guides washing clothes with a washboard and dolly and often sample delicious home-made toffee and caraway cake.

Park Farm was established as a model farm in the early nineteenth century and continues to be run along traditional lines. The farm-hands take pleasure in explaining their work, and the farm raises rare (and attractive) breeds of cow, horse, pig and fowl, including Staffordshire Longhorn cattle, Gloucester Old

Spot, Tamworth and Iron Age pigs. The best time to visit is feeding time at around 3.30, followed by milking time at 4pm.

You can also explore the cosy rooms of the manager's house and try Staffordshire specialities such as griddle cake in the farm kitchen. Visitors can watch butter and cheese being made in the dairy. A small adventure playground and rides round the farm in a horse-drawn cart will occupy the children.

SUDBURY HALL*

Sudbury Hall, four miles east of Uttoxeter, is a house for connoisseurs of seventeenth-century interior decoration, with its Grinling Gibbons limewood carvings of fruit, flowers, fish and pheasants, its huge royal portraits and a spectacular staircase. However, most families will be drawn to the **Museum of Childhood** in the stable block. Here, children can get a real sense of what it might have been like to be young in the nineteenth century, with reconstructions of a Victorian day nursery and night nursery, and the Cadbury collection of dolls and automata. Childhood in the Victorian and Edwardian periods was not fun and comfort for all young people, however: many were sent up the

Children can join in the lessons in the School Room at the Museum of Childhood

chimneys or down the mines for a living, or put to work in a mill. Children under seven can try the chimney climbs.

In later sections of the museum children are encouraged to play with old-fashioned toys such as whipping tops, skittles, five stones and hoops. Among the numerous surprises are magic mirrors, a Shrinking Corridor and mouseholes in the skirting boards that you can peep into. The last room in the museum is full of books and toys where children can sit and read or play.

CALKE ABBEY*

Calke Abbey, three miles north of Ashby-de-la-Zouch, represents an interesting new approach on the part of the National Trust. Anyone used to the Trust's décor, carefully replicating the original furnishings, is in for a shock. The eighteenth-century house had remained almost untouched since the death of the last baronet in 1924. For 60 years, until the Trust took it over in 1985, little had been replaced or renovated and the result is ripped curtains, peeling wallpaper and shabby carpets. The Abbey's owners threw nothing away. There are rooms of

Cheese-making at Shugborough Estate Farm, using traditional methods

stuffed birds, and others piled high with miscellaneous junk, such as broken toys and abandoned riding boots. By contrast, the star display is the pristine state bed, probably made in the early eighteenth century and left in packing cases until the 1980s when the NT rediscovered this hidden treasure among all the relics. Now in a darkened room to protect the glorious embroidery, it glows with the rich and vibrant colours of Chinese silk.

The Abbey probably gives a truer impression of English aristocratic life than would be the case had the NT carried out its usual programme of meticulous refurbishment to present the house at its best.

The gardens, however, are being carefully restored to their Victorian appearance, with an auricula theatre (planted with auriculas in the spring and pelargoniums in summer), an orangery, an aviary of golden pheasants, walled gardens, a grotto and a kitchen garden.

LUNCHBOX

The Lady Walk restaurant at Shugborough House serves filling meals, including children's helpings. The Coach House tea room at Sudbury Hall serves light lunches and children's portions, and the restaurant in the converted barn at Calke Abbey serves lunches and teas. The Nags Head Inn at Hill Top, Castle Donnington is recommended.

Tram trips in Crich and a bus bonanza in Manchester

You can ride on all manner of trams and enjoy the rural views at Crich

Take a nostalgic trip on a vintage tram at the National Tramway Museum, or hop aboard a bus at the Manchester Museum of Transport and play at being driver or conductor.

◆ **GOOD FOR** Tram and bus enthusiasts
◆ **TRANSPORT** Whatstandwell is the closest rail station to Crich, but it is a steep 1-mile uphill climb to the Tramway Museum; Cromford, Matlock Bath and Matlock rail stations are a bus-ride away. By car take junction 28 off M1 and follow the A38 to Alfreton, then signposted. The Manchester Museum of Transport is 1 mile from city; buses (134, 135 or 136) from Piccadilly
◆ **ACCESS FOR DISABLED PEOPLE** It is possible to explore static exhibits, but not to access trams and buses
◆ **BEST TIME TO VISIT** National Tramway Museum: Easter to end October; Manchester Museum of Transport: Wednesdays and weekends all year

Instead of tackling both these museums on the same day, we suggest you combine a trip to the National Tramway Museum at Crich with a visit to Cromford and Matlock Bath (see below); the Manchester Museum of Transport could be fitted in with a visit to the Museum of Science and Industry in Manchester (see *Great Day Out 105*).

THE NATIONAL TRAMWAY MUSEUM*

Where do old trams go when they retire? A very large number of them, from as far away as Prague and New York, have ended up in this enjoyable museum at Crich, near Matlock, where they gain a new lease of life and run up and down a mile-long stretch of track in the Derbyshire countryside. The National Tramway Museum was founded in the 1950s when tramlines throughout Britain were being torn up and the tram-cars scrapped. Today, the tram has been rediscovered as a rapid and cheap form of mass transport, and trams are back on the streets of Manchester and Sheffield.

The rise and fall of Britain's tramways is the major theme of this museum, and one senses a certain evangelical zeal in the way that the story is told, through audio-visual material, reconstructions of street scenes built around lovingly restored trams, and sheds full of vintage examples – open and closed top, single- and double-decker, horse-drawn, steam-driven and electric. The Turn-of-the-Century Trade Exhibition reconstructs an actual trade fair at which scores of manufacturers demonstrated their wares, from ticket-issuing machines and conductors' uniforms to varnishes, paint and upholstery – an imaginative way of drawing together the museum's vast collection of tram-related memorabilia.

The working trams form the central attraction of this museum, and you can take as many rides as you like, trying out any of the half-dozen or so restored tramcars that ply the rails in an abandoned limestone quarry. For the first part of the journey, they trundle alongside a reconstructed street that features the rebuilt façade of the Derby Assembly Rooms, shops, pubs and cafés. Soon, however, the track rises over the crest of a hill into open countryside, with sweeping views over the

Derwent Valley – a strange experience for those who think of trams as being essentially an urban form of transport.

MATLOCK BATH AND CROMFORD

To enjoy some more stunning views of this typical Derbyshire scenery, not to mention some diverting 'seaside' culture, venture three miles north-west of Crich to **Matlock Bath**. Complete with fish and chip shops and busy amusement arcades, the village is like an inland seaside resort. From August bank holiday until the last weekend in October you can enjoy night-time illuminations and 'Venetian Nights' (trips up the River Derwent in illuminated boats). The village, which sits in a deep limestone gorge, developed as a spa in 1853 and has become a victim of its own success. Even with two large car parks it can be difficult to park at the height of the season. If you can bear the crowds and traffic jams, seek out the **Peak District Mining Museum***. It includes pumping

Learn about life on the buses as a clippie or a driver

engines and rare minerals and really brings home the dirty, wet and arduous conditions under which local miners used to work. Follow this with a visit to the **Heights of Abraham Country Park*** and the caverns, reached by means of cable cars or a steep walk, and featuring an informative and lively audio-visual account of the region's geology.

Between Crich and Matlock, **Cromford** offers slightly quieter pleasures. Here you can park and

stroll by the **Cromford Canal**, or go on a guided tour of **Arkwright's Mill***, a landmark building for the Industrial Revolution, since it was here that Richard Arkwright established the world's first water-powered cotton-spinning mill in 1771. It is now slowly being restored.

MANCHESTER MUSEUM OF TRANSPORT*

If you specialise in collecting double-decker buses, you need a jolly big shed in which to store them. Appropriately enough, this museum is in a huge former bus depot in Cheetham, now home to some 70 vintage buses, crammed in so tightly that there is scarcely room for visitors to explore. The museum also boasts a large number of non-transport items: a collection of ancient wheelchairs and invalid carriages, for example, plus a shiny Salford fire-engine, several telephone boxes, numerous street signs and a handful of postmen's regulation-issue bicycles, not to mention the pillar boxes dotted around, including a splendidly ornate Victorian one painted green and gold.

The curators clearly have a sense of humour: there is a reconstruction of some roadworks halfway round the museum, and the café is a real trip down memory lane to the days of draughty old bus-station canteens with hideous and uncomfortable furniture (to complete the sense of nostalgia, this one serves cups of hot Bovril). One exhibit is not an antique – a gleaming up-to-date Manchester tram. If you have ever wanted to sit in the cab and play with the controls, now's your chance.

The views from the Heights of Abraham are worth the cable-car ride

LUNCHBOX

Refreshments are available at the Tramway Museum. The remote Druid Inn at Birchover, Ye Olde Gate Inn (said to be haunted) at Brassington and the White Horse Inn at Woolley Moor, near Matlock, all serve interesting pub food. Matlock Bath and Cromford offer a selection of eating places.

Three outstanding Derbyshire houses

Kedleston Hall's Saloon, featuring coffered dome and gilded rosettes

- ♦ **GOOD FOR** Devotees of the English stately home
- ♦ **TRANSPORT** Car necessary
- ♦ **ACCESS FOR DISABLED PEOPLE** To the ground floor of Kedleston and Hardwick; not to Haddon Hall
- ♦ **BEST TIME TO VISIT** Easter to September/October

Derbyshire is particularly rich in stately homes: these three — Kedleston, Haddon and Hardwick — are prime examples of the builder's art, and have remained little touched by later generations.

KEDLESTON HALL (NT)*

The design of Kedleston Hall (5 miles north-west of Derby) is a first-rate example of eighteenth-century Palladian architecture. The architect who devised the basic form of the house, a central block with two wings attached by corridors, was Matthew Brettingham. Later, James Paine and then Robert Adam were brought in. The house has barely altered from when it was finished in the 1760s — for the newly elevated first Lord Curzon, whose family, the Scarsdales, had already lived on this site for the best part of 600 years. Dr Johnson dismissed Kedleston as ostentatious, but most people enjoy its grandeur and Adam's work here is thought to be amongst his best.

You enter through Adam's Marble Hall with its pink alabaster colonnades, which is still considered one of the finest rooms in Europe. From here you pass through to the Music Room with its musically themed paintings and its chamber organ case (designed by Adam), and through the Drawing Room with its sixteenth- and seventeenth-century Italian paintings. You carry on through the Library (note the Rembrandt) and the Saloon, based on Rome's Pantheon and meant as a showcase for Lord Scarsdale's neo-classical sculpture collection. Next you will see the State Apartment, which consists of an Ante-Room, Dressing Room and State Bedroom — the latter contains two paintings by Sir Peter Lely. The brown, white and beige Dining Room follows, then the Indian Museum on the ground floor (one of the Curzons was Viceroy of India in the late nineteenth century).

Behind the right-hand wing (as you face the building), which houses the enormous kitchens, stands a thirteenth-century church — all that remains of the village of Kedleston when it was moved to make way for the new house.

The 400-acre park contains a fishing pavilion and an elegant bridge, both by Adam, over the lake. This area has superb rhododendrons and azaleas — at their peak in May and June — but a guided evening tour of the gardens (free of charge) or an independent walk following one of the marked routes would be a pleasant diversion at any time.

HADDON HALL*

Like Kedleston, Haddon Hall, 2 miles south-east of Bakewell, is also a fine example of its kind, an archetypal medieval English manor house. Standing on a hill overlooking the

Haddon Hall, a former home of the Dukes of Rutland

River Wye, it was built by several generations of the Vernons, a Norman family who came over with William the Conqueror, but the construction of the present house was carried out largely in the fourteenth and fifteenth centuries. More work was done in the late sixteenth century, when the house passed by marriage to the Earls of Rutland, but from the early eighteenth century it fell into disuse. It was made habitable again only in the early twentieth century, by the ninth Duke of Rutland.

Haddon, with its battlements, mullioned windows, high ceilings and preponderance of aged wood, remains true to its origins: no attempt has been made to turn it into a Tourist Attraction. Its main reception rooms are authentically short on furniture, the dearth of seating reflecting the habit of the day to stand, rather than sit, more than we do nowadays.

Upstairs the Great Chamber (Haddon's main room of state), the seventeenth-century Long Gallery (built for exercise and as a display room) and the Orpheus Room (once the State Bedroom) all boast beautiful wood panelling and carving, plaster friezes and sixteenth- and seventeenth-century tapestries. Downstairs the Parlour has a splendid painted ceiling. Other notable features include frescoes in the chapel, a fifteenth-century porch tower and a medieval kitchen still with much of its original equipment and utensils. A fine oak roof was put on the banqueting hall and minstrels' gallery in the renovations of 1923–5.

The walled terraced gardens, one of the highlights of Haddon, are Jacobean. It is unusual in England to find gardens left in true seventeenth-century style: the tidal wave of landscaping in the following century swept most of them away. Rosebeds and clipped yews grace the terraces, which jut out above a packhorse bridge.

The statue of Mary, Queen of Scots, at Hardwick Hall, where she was a long-term resident

HARDWICK HALL (NT)*

Built in 1591–7 by the ambitious septuagenarian Bess of Hardwick after she had buried her fourth husband, 'Hardwick Hall, more window than wall' is a testament to her wealth, power and energy. (She also built the first Chatsworth House – see *Great Day Out 100*.) You can clearly see Bess's initials, 'ES' (Elizabeth of Shrewsbury), on all six towers as you face the symmetrical three-storey house. This is simply one of the best Elizabethan houses in the whole of England.

Everywhere there are wonderful examples of furniture, glass, textiles, tapestry and needlework, including cushion covers embroidered by Bess herself in the Drawing Room, unusual painted cloths in the Chapel and a series of sixteenth-century Brussels tapestries in the High Great Chamber depicting the story of Ulysses. The Paved Room, Bess's private dining-room, contains some needlework by Mary, Queen of Scots, who was her contemporary and the erstwhile prisoner of her husband, kept in his charge at Hardwick for 15 years. (The National Trust advises a visit on a bright day if seeing the tapestries and textiles is a particular priority.)

Other reasons for visiting Hardwick are its phenomenal plasterwork and its feeling of space, more that of a palace than a home, albeit a stately one. The remains of Hardwick Old Hall, Bess's previous home, can be seen in the grounds, which contain pleasant walled gardens, simply designed.

Eyam plague village: a tale of self-sacrifice

A tragedy told in stone — the Plague Cottages and headstones

The extraordinary history of the village of Eyam during the plague years of the 1660s, with its tales of courage and tragedy, makes for a fascinating and unusual day out.

The terrace of grey stone cottages next to Eyam (pronounced 'eem') church at first seems no different from many others dotted throughout the villages of the Peak District. Look a little closer, however, and you notice that each cottage is marked by a small plaque. In fact, all around the village are tell-tale signs bearing witness to a remarkable episode of local history, when the villagers of Eyam, hit by an isolated outbreak of the Great Plague, made a decision of immense courage and self-sacrifice.

Inspired by the enlightened leadership of their parish priest, William Mompesson, they went into voluntary isolation to prevent the disease spreading to other villages. Once the decision had been made, nearly all the villagers abided by it, and virtually no one left until the threat had passed. In the end, 90 of the 350 inhabitants survived. But

♦ **GOOD FOR** All ages will be gripped by the moving stories from this village
♦ **TRANSPORT** There is no regular public transport
♦ **ACCESS FOR DISABLED PEOPLE** No wheelchair access to cottages; Museum is accessible, Hall at ground level only
♦ **BEST TIME TO VISIT** The Hall and Museum are open from April to October

their sacrifice was not in vain — the surrounding villages were spared.

Remarkably, many of the events of those years can still be traced. You can identify the houses where many of the victims died, the gravestones where they were buried and the 'boundary stone' where food and provisions were left. The natural amphitheatre where the villagers worshipped, fearing that the disease would spread if they gathered in church, is now private land owned by Eyam Hall (see overleaf).

The best place to start is at the **Plague Cottages** next to the church. Although there is some controversy as to how the disease reached Eyam, it is well documented that the first victim died here. The source of infection is thought to have been a box of damp cloth sent from London, where the Great Plague was in full spate. George Viccars, a tailor who was lodging in one of the cottages, received the box in September 1665. It is assumed that infected rat fleas carrying the disease were released when Viccars hung the cloth out to dry. He was bitten, and was dead within a week. You can see how the plague started to spread by walking down the row of cottages. The plaques list five more victims who died within that first month.

At this point it is a good idea to pay a visit to the **church***, which was kept closed during the plague years. It now has an excellent collection of booklets, maps and memorabilia, as well as an exhibition summing up the key events and explaining the myriad superstitions of the time. One of the contemporary treatments for plague was to 'take a pigeon and pluck the feathers off her tail very bare and set her tail to the sore and then she will draw out the venom till she die'.

Outside in the graveyard, near the weather-beaten Celtic Cross, is one of the most poignant sights: the **tomb of Mompesson's wife**. Tireless in ministering to the victims, Catherine Mompesson for a long time seemed immune to the disease, and as the plague began to wane in the summer of 1666 it appeared that she might be a lucky survivor. Then in August she began to show the signs of infection — glandular swellings, running sores, sneezing — and by the 25th she too had died. The letter Mompesson wrote to his children (who had left to live with relatives in the early days of the plague) begins: 'This brings you the doleful news of your dearest mother's death; the greatest loss that could befall you. I am deprived of a kind and loving consort, and you are bereaved of the most indulgent mother that ever poor little children had. Dear children, your dearest mother lived a holy life and made a comfortable end, though by means of sore pestilence, and she is now invested with a crown of righteousness.'

Head back past the Plague Cottages, beyond **Eyam Hall*** (built in 1672) towards the old stocks on the green. Down the hill is **Cucklet Delf**, which served as the open-air church (access is by permission only). It was also the scene for illicit meetings between two lovers: Emmott Sydall from Eyam, and Rowland Torre who lived nearby in Stoney Middleton. They met secretly each day, until in April 1666 Emmott failed to appear. Rowland could know nothing of her fate until Eyam was finally re-opened to the outside world at the end of the year. He was the first to enter the village; he was so heart-broken at the news of her death that he never married.

At Mompesson's Well coins were left in the water to pay for provisions

Walking back up to the village and continuing roughly north, you pass **Margaret Blackwell's cottage** in Rock Square. She is reputed to have recovered from her symptoms after drinking hot bacon fat which she mistook for milk. Turn right up Hawkhill Road to the **Eyam Museum*** in the Methodist Chapel. Here a small but impressive exhibition recounts many of the stories associated with the village's battle with the plague.

From the museum you can continue for a few hundred yards to Town Head to see **Marshall Howe's cottage** – he acted as a self-appointed gravedigger and buried many of the victims. Returning past the church towards the Square, look out for the **Miners Arms** in Water Lane, the croft of which was used for plague burials. To the south, Lydgate – once the main road into the village but now a track which peters out into a footpath – leads past the graves of Thomas and Mary Darby, known as the **Lydgate Graves**. If you continue down the lane you will come to open countryside with beautiful views over the ridges and valleys of the Peak

The sundial over the priest's door in Eyam Church was erected in 1775

District. About half a mile along the path, on its own in a field, is a boulder. Known as the **boundary stone**, it used to mark the entrance to the village and was where medicines and provisions were left for the beleaguered villagers. Six holes were drilled in the top for coins to be placed in payment – they were dipped in vinegar in the belief that it would prevent infection.

Two other excursions around the outskirts of the village are worth doing on foot. The **Riley Graves**, standing rather bizarrely surrounded by a low stone wall in the middle of a field, are about ten minutes' walk out of Eyam; take a left-hand track leading off New Road (signposted). The seven headstones mark the graves of the Hancock family; within eight days in August 1666 Elizabeth Hancock lost her husband and six of her seven children. She is said to have become so distraught that she fled to Sheffield with her surviving son.

If you return to the village and turn up Water Lane, you can continue up the steep hillside to **Mompesson's Well** – about half an hour's walk in all. This is in fact a spring and, like the boundary stone, was also used as a provisions point. Again, the splendour of the Peak District countryside enhances these two rambles.

LUNCHBOX

The Miners Arms serves good pub fare and there is a tea shop in the square. There is a Buttery at Eyam Hall and a Craft Centre.

Chatsworth House and neo-classical Buxton

☂

The honey-coloured stone of Chatsworth, seen from its park

Chatsworth, one of Britain's most spectacular stately homes, is set in over 1,000 acres of impressive parkland overlooking the River Derwent.

The first Chatsworth House was built by the formidable Bess of Hardwick (see *Great Day Out 98*) and her second husband, Sir William Cavendish, in the 1550s. Their descendant, the first Duke of Devonshire, rebuilt the house on a massive scale in the late 1700s, and in the early 1800s the sixth ('Bachelor') duke made further numerous alterations and improvements.

CHATSWORTH HOUSE*

Chatsworth, still a family home, has no organised tours, so visitors may wander at their own pace through the succession of grand rooms. Make your way from the main entrance into the Painted Hall, noting the wrought-iron work, then upstairs into the first duke's lavishly

♦ **GOOD FOR** Art lovers and garden enthusiasts
♦ **TRANSPORT** The nearest BR station is Chesterfield (12 miles from Chatsworth). A bus service runs from there to Chatsworth, and from Chatsworth to Bakewell, where you must change to get to Buxton
♦ **ACCESS FOR DISABLED PEOPLE** Access to grounds only
♦ **BEST TIME TO VISIT** The house is open from March to October. The gardens are open all year except the first weekend in September but they are at their best from May to September

decorated State Rooms, designed to display *objets d'art* of every description. The house is liberally endowed with wood carvings, leather hangings, ceiling and wall paintings by Verrio and Laguerre,

silver and tapestries, and the porcelain includes some attractive Delft tulip-vases. Look out for the famous *Violin Door*, a mid-seventeenth-century *trompe l'oeil* by Jan van der Vaart.

You now pass through the Sketch Gallery, which originally housed a collection of Old Masters but which is now hung with paintings of the family, and down the West Staircase; this takes you to the Chapel. Unlike the rest of the house, which has grown and changed with the centuries, the baroque Chapel, one of the finest in England, has been altered very little. The painting of *Doubting Thomas*, over the splendid alabaster altar, is by Verrio; the other works are by Laguerre; the seventeenth-century woodwork by Samuel Watson is outstanding.

Walk through the Oak Room and once again through the Painted Hall, continue up the eighteenth-century Oak Staircase (this boasts the only Grinling Gibbons carving in the house), and into the Library with its medieval illuminated manuscripts. From here you can view the three Van Dyck portraits in the Great Dining Room. Carry on into the Sculpture Gallery, which is full of Old Masters and the 'Bachelor' duke's favourite sculptures. Access to the gardens is through the Orangery, which is now a gift shop.

Chatsworth's magnificent gardens, not to be missed, have undergone many changes since the first duke established them in the seventeenth century. They were remodelled by Capability Brown and the fourth duke in the 1760s, and then again by Chatsworth's head gardener Joseph Paxton and the sixth duke starting in the 1820s. In the course of these operations a bend in the Derwent was made straight and a whole village relocated out of sight of the house.

If you are using the Flora's Temple entrance, the rose-fringed Broad Walk takes you southwards to the famous **Cascade** (1696), with panoramic views. The wooded backdrop to the cascade features Asian and North American trees and is particularly fine in the autumn.

The West Front Garden and the South Lawn are private, but if you bear to the right you can walk past the Ring Pond to the famous lime tree-fringed Canal Pond, built for the first duke in 1703. The water from the canal was used for making ice. Today, however, it is the spectacular **Emperor Fountain** that people come to see. Spurting up to 290 feet, this was a great feat of engineering by Paxton, who was helped in its design by the 'Bachelor' duke. At the southern end of the Canal Pond stands the *War Horse* by Elisabeth Frink (1991). Here is one of the best views in Chatsworth: the house seems to float on the water.

The main walk then leads to the Azalea Dell and thence up to the Ravine, a steep wooded wilderness, only for the fit, and the pine-filled Pinetum. This can be avoided by those who wish by taking a broader path around the dell and past the Grotto Pond where it joins up with the Ravine path.

The yew-hedge maze at Chatsworth, established in 1962

As you wander back towards the house you will pass the site of Paxton's Great Conservatory, the glass, wood and iron forerunner to the Crystal Palace of the 1851 Great Exhibition. The area is filled with flowers and trees, and the middle part is now occupied by a yew-hedge maze. To the north is Paxton's Strid Waterfall, which is named after the natural gorge in Bolton Abbey.

BUXTON

Buxton, a graceful neo-classical town, 15 miles from Chatsworth, is the capital of the Peak District. The fifth Duke of Devonshire decreed that it should be a spa resort, but the harsh Derbyshire winters overruled him.

Dominating the entrance to the town is the elaborate **Devonshire Royal Hospital**, which was originally built to provide stables. From here the visitor can walk to Buxton's centre, the **Crescent**, built by John Carr of York to rival the Royal Crescent at Bath.

The source of Buxton water can still be seen through a glass door at the **tourist information office***; the water pours out of the ground at 32,000

The Wellington Bedroom at Chatsworth showing the helmet-like corona above the bed

litres (1,540 gallons) per hour. Opposite is **St Ann's Well**, where visitors can queue to drink the water free. Beside the well is the former Pump Room.

Behind the Crescent is the sumptuously restored **Opera House**, known as the 'Theatre in the Hills' because of its beautiful setting, and the iron and glass **Pavilion**, both nineteenth-century creations. The latter hosts Buxton's Music and Arts Festival in July and August. Opposite the Crescent lie the Slopes, steep gardens leading to Buxton's museum.

WELL-DRESSING IN TISSINGTON

In days gone by every village economy depended on fresh water supplies from wells and local springs. The wells in Tissington (to the south of Chatsworth on the way to Ashbourne) are decorated every Ascension Day, following an originally pagan tradition of thanksgiving to the water gods. Clay-covered boards are decorated with flowers, cones, berries and beans to form a large picture or design; nowadays the images are usually Christian. It is thought that an old custom was revived after the Black Death epidemics, when the medicinal properties of the pure Peak District water were believed to ward off the plague.

Well-dressing also takes place in Buxton, Wirksworth and Youlgreave, but why this tradition survives only in Derbyshire is not known.

Macclesfield silk and other treats

Young and old alike can uncover the secrets of silk at the Silk Museum

The silk museum and mill in Macclesfield, the black and white splendour of the timbered Tudor Little Moreton Hall and the unexpected eccentricities of Biddulph Grange Garden provide the ingredients for a diverse and absorbing day out.

Macclesfield has been associated with silk since the seventeenth century, when wives and daughters supplemented the family income by making the intricate buttons of embroidered silk that were all the rage among fashionable Londoners. This tradition of cottage-industry skilled work was the foundation for the town's later industrial development. In 1743, Charles Roe, one of Macclesfield's leading button merchants set up the town's first silk-spinning mill, and within 50 years the town's silk industry was booming, given impetus by the almost total disappearance of silk production in France during the turbulent decades of the Revolution and the Napoleonic Wars.

Just as quickly, however, the British silk industry declined because of competition from cheap imports and the invention of less costly synthetic fabrics. One or two mills still continue production in the town, concentrating on the upmarket end of the fashion industry.

An exploration of the town's silk heritage should begin at the **Silk Museum** at the **Heritage Centre*** in Roe Street, where an audio-visual programme tells the story of the industry as a prelude to displays on everything from the life cycle of the silk worm to costume design through the ages. The shop attached to the museum sells modern Macclesfield silk, as well as leaflets suggesting various routes around the town that take in the most interesting buildings.

A short walk from the Heritage Centre is **Paradise Mill***; although it closed as a working mill in 1981, it is kept in working order by former employees who give guided tours. The tours are fascinating and detailed – young children might find the level of detail too much – and cover every stage in the process of turning raw silk into beautifully light and colourful woven fabric.

LITTLE MORETON HALL*

In many ways, the wonderfully flamboyant timber framing of Little Moreton Hall (NT) is as pleasing to the senses, and as intricately patterned, as Macclesfield silk. The moated manor house lies some 12 miles south of Macclesfield, between Congleton and Kidsgrove, and was built in the fifteenth century as an expression of the optimism and prosperity of the age. In this part of the Midlands, timber was the principal building material, and landowners flaunted their wealth by using far more than was strictly necessary for structural stability, filling the timber box frame with highly decorative herring-bone patterns and curved windbraces.

♦ **GOOD FOR** Families with older children and gardening aficionados in particular
♦ **TRANSPORT** A drive of about 15 miles; no easy public transport
♦ **ACCESS FOR DISABLED PEOPLE** Wheelchair access possible at Silk Museum and Paradise Mill. Biddulph Grange difficult
♦ **BEST TIME TO VISIT** Easter to end September, Wednesday to Sunday. Paradise Mill is closed Monday. Little Moreton Hall and Biddulph Grange are closed Monday and Tuesday

▲ *Little Moreton Hall – possibly the best-preserved half-timbered building in Britain*

The marvellous oriel windows and overhanging upper storeys, called jetties, add to the architectural character of the house. The effect of the jetties is to increase the floor area, so that, in contrast to many modern houses, there is far more space on the upper storeys than on the ground floor. This is exploited to great effect in the huge open area of the light-filled Long Gallery, with its allegorical wall paintings of Destiny, Knowledge and Fortune. Some late sixteenth-century wall paintings of biblical scenes within an elaborate frieze were discovered behind Georgian panelling. Other features of note in the unfurnished house include the plasterwork coat of arms of Elizabeth I in the Withdrawing Room and the massive brick chimneys added in 1600 (before then, the smoke simply dispersed through the roof).

BIDDULPH GRANGE GARDEN (NT)*

This 15-acre garden, situated just north of Biddulph village and seven miles north of Stoke-on-Trent, has

been described as one of the most innovative gardens of the nineteenth century. James Bateman, the son of a wealthy industrialist, designed the garden on what was then bleak and swampy moorland. Paths thread through twisting canyons of rock in which various novelties are hidden, leaving every visitor charmed and (quite probably) utterly disoriented. Much is packed into quite a small space by using the sloping hillside site to best effect, with tunnels and paths that double back on each other to visit a series of gardens within gardens, each planted in a different style. The gardens are themed and walking around them is like making a miniature tour of the world: China contains a pagoda, a joss house and an ornamental bridge; Egypt offers a pyramid of

clipped yews, a sphinx and a stone demon. Other attractions include the Scottish glen, the American garden (given over to rhododendrons), the pinetum with unusual conifers, and the Stumpery. The latter is a Victorian confection, like a rockery only using roots instead of rocks.

Restoring the garden has been an astonishing feat, given how overgrown it was when acquired by the National Trust in 1988. An exhibition in the cellars beneath the garden entrance details the history of the garden and the scale of the restoration work.

The novelty value of the maze of narrow footpaths, and the occasional surprises such as the fat ceramic frogs and tinkling temple bells in the Chinese garden, are sufficient to amuse many visitors, but the garden is also very satisfying from a horticultural point of view, with planting schemes planned for colour and interest from spring to autumn. Perhaps the garden is at its most spectacular when the azaleas and rhododendrons flower in May and June, but high summer has its delights, too, from the bright colours of the massed blooms in the Dahlia Walk.

◄ *In a corner of the Chinese garden stands a golden water buffalo*

Quarry Bank Mill and Styal Country Park

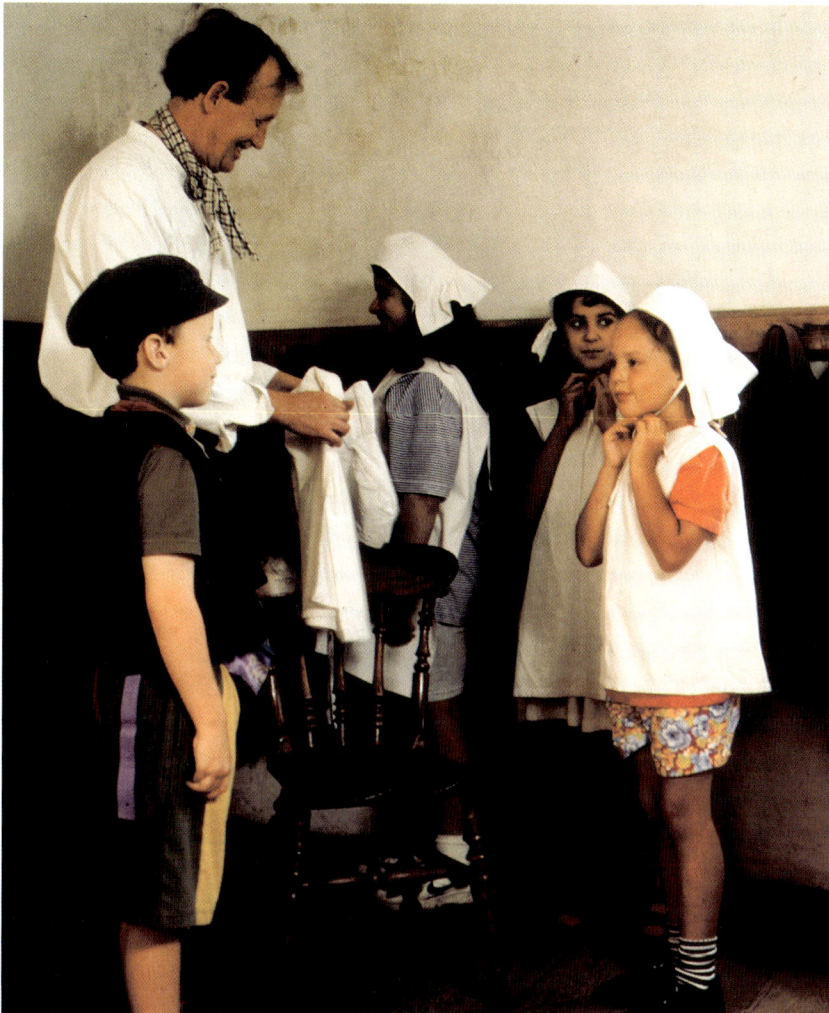

Children trying on clothes at the Apprentice House

Quarry Bank Mill, founded in 1784, is still a working mill, producing cotton cloth on a commercial basis, so you can see and hear the machinery at work, experience what it was like to work in a mill and enjoy walks in the beautiful valley of the River Bollin.

One of the great attractions of Quarry Bank Mill, for children especially, is the Apprentice House, where generations of orphans and children from poor families lived when they were not hard at work in the mill. Guides explain the harsh and highly disciplined life led by the apprentices, and children can try dressing in apprentice clothing, sleeping in their beds and tasting the unpleasant medicines that were meted out. Admission to the house is by timed ticket, and tours (afternoons only, except at weekends and in school holidays) soon get booked up, so it is best to obtain your ticket as soon as possible after arrival. A plan for the day might be to visit the mill first, then have lunch and a walk to Styal village or around the country park, followed by the Apprentice House tour in the afternoon.

- ♦ **GOOD FOR** Families especially
- ♦ **TRANSPORT** No car is needed on site, although it would be useful for getting there. Public transport is not particularly good. There is a railway station at Styal (limited service); or a bus service from Manchester airport
- ♦ **ACCESS FOR DISABLED PEOPLE** To parts of mill and Apprentice House by ramp and lifts; there is a wheelchair route through the country park
- ♦ **BEST TIME TO VISIT** All year, but the Apprentice House has restricted hours so ring in advance

QUARRY BANK MILL*

A tour of this fascinating place begins on the top floor of the mill, where there is a scale model of the building in its setting. This serves as the basis for a miniature *son et lumière* show, with taped commentary, relating how Samuel Greg first exploited the fast-flowing waters of the River Bollin in 1784, using them to drive the newly invented spinning jenny, a machine for spinning raw cotton fibres into thread. The Greg family business grew into one of the biggest in Britain by the 1840s, expanding to cover the whole process of turning cotton into printed cloth, and the mill became the centre of a small community, with houses, shops and churches built by the mill owners in order to attract and maintain a loyal workforce.

Alongside the model are displays that explain the characteristics of cotton, with a number of hands-on exhibits to show you, for example, how fibres are given strength by being twisted into yarn. These are followed by working models of the key inventions that gave birth to the Industrial Revolution; guides in costume demonstrate the spinning, carding and weaving machines that were used when textile production was still a cottage industry.

Downstairs, visitors are shown some of the marvellously intricate and complex machines that were used for spinning, carding, winding and warping, once this became a fully automated factory process. At one end cotton thread as fine as cobweb is fed into the machines; by the time it reaches the other end it has been transformed into an exceedingly strong thread, ready for weaving.

The story of weaving is continued on the floor below. To get there you pass through a section on dyeing and pattern-making, where children can use woodblocks to print their own designs. The rest of the middle floor is taken up by exhibits on the social history of the mill, looking in intimate detail at the home and working lives of the mill owners and their employees. The abiding impression left by the clattering looms in the weaving sheds, on the floor below, is of just how noisy the factory would have been in its heyday. The looms that remain are now used to weave textiles for the 'Styal Collection' of fabrics.

The basement may prove to be the most exciting part, filled as it is with Heath-Robinson-style machines, demonstrating how water can be used to power machinery. These exhibits serve as a prelude to the waterwheel itself that drives the factory nowadays, a huge and enormously impressive piece of engineering.

Mill workers' houses in the village of Styal

COUNTRY PARK AND VILLAGE

Touring the mill may take up to two hours, and several more can be spent exploring the idyllic woodland, threaded by the River Bollin that stretches for some four miles south and west of the mill complex. As it is close to Manchester airport, the peace is disturbed by aircraft from time to time, but the woods still host rich wildlife. Herons and kingfishers can be seen by the water. A leaflet with suggested walks is available from the shop, and the footpaths are easy to follow. **Styal village**, comprising farm buildings which the mill owner converted for his workers and new buildings built in the years 1806–22, is just a short stroll away across well-marked field paths. Here you can see the church, chapel, school and

A loom in one of the weaving sheds at Quarry Bank Mill

shops, linked by cobbled paths that pass between neat rows of cottages with their colourful front gardens.

Apart from the church and chapel, you can view the buildings of the village only from the outside, since they are still inhabited or in use, but you can join a tour of the **Apprentice House**. You are also encouraged to ask questions, touch objects and even sample the medicines doled out to sick children, deliberately made to taste horrible on the principle that they could not be doing you any good unless they made you suffer. Exhausted from a long day's work in the factory, barely nourished by a monotonous diet of gruel and boiled potatoes, the apprentices must have dropped exhausted every night into their hard beds – no wonder so many tried to run away, only to be punished severely on being recaptured.

LUNCHBOX

The country park is full of picnic spots with tables and chairs, accessible from the car park. The food at the mill restaurant is adequate but not special, and the choice includes a range of cooked meals, sandwiches and salads; children's helpings are available.

Sightseeing and shopping in historic Chester

The Eastgate clock, which celebrates Queen Victoria's Diamond Jubilee

Chester's unique attractions are the Rows, two-tiered medieval shopping arcades, and the only complete city walls in Britain.

Chester began as a Roman fortress called Dewa (or Deva), established in AD79. Excavations show that through Saxon, Norman, Tudor, Georgian and Victorian times buildings were erected on top of the foundations of previous ones. Architecture and remains from almost all these periods can be found all over the city. Some of the most intriguing sights are hidden away in The Rows' shops, so sightseeing and shopping for quality goods can become happily confused.

Chester's centre is pleasantly compact – everything is within walking distance – but there is too much to see in one day. We have picked out a day's worth of sightseeing suggestions, with a couple of extra ideas for families with young children. The **tourist information office*** is situated in the Town Hall, opposite the cathedral.

♦ **GOOD FOR** Shopping and historical sights; adults and children alike will find plenty to keep them busy
♦ **TRANSPORT** Chester is small enough to walk round, and the railway station is a 15-minute walk from the city centre
♦ **ACCESS FOR DISABLED PEOPLE** Access to cathedral, Chester Zoo and Dewa Roman Experience only
♦ **BEST TIME TO VISIT** Chester's main attractions are open all year round. As the shopping is so good, try the January sales as well as before Christmas. The city gets very crowded in summer

THE ROWS AND SHOPPING

The Rows run along parts of the city's four main streets: Watergate, Eastgate, Northgate and Bridge streets. No one is exactly sure of the origins of their strange configuration, although the most likely explanation is that in the thirteenth century they were built around Roman débris, the shops on the ground level against the rubble, those on the first floor and the covered arcades on top of it. The most eye-catching buildings rise for many storeys, have exposed timber frames and sharp gables, and are painted black and white. Many of the façades are inscribed with dates, indicating which are Tudor and which are Victorian fake. The streets meet at the fifteenth-century **Cross**, haunt of street entertainers and the Town Crier (noon and 2pm Tuesday to Saturday, May to October).

Watergate Street has a cornucopia of antique shops and traditional galleries. Some old buildings are immediately striking, such as the Bishop Lloyd's House (No. 41) with carved and painted panels of biblical scenes, and the house with the inscription 'God's Providence is mine inheritance', which indicates that the house was the only one in the city not to lose a life during an outbreak of bubonic plague in 1647. Other buildings need to be entered to be appreciated. Watergates Wine Bar (No. 11) has the city's finest medieval crypt. The Sofa Workshop (No. 21), also known as Old Leche House, has a two-storey gallery and painted plasterwork.

Eastgate Street's 'magpie' houses are mainly Victorian. Here you will find chain stores and fashionable clothes shops, as well as the long-established department store, Brown's.

On **Bridge Street**, Bookland (No. 12) has another medieval crypt, and Owen Owen (Nos. 48–50) is Chester's top delicatessen. Across the street, Lowe & Sons (No. 11) is a fine jeweller's established in 1770 in a beautiful, galleried shop. Do not miss the basement of Spud-u-like (No. 39); in this unlikely venue, you can see a section of a Roman underfloor heating system (or hypocaust).

THE MAIN SIGHTS

In Georgian times, the whole of the two-mile-long city walls was converted into a promenade. The northern and eastern sections are generally considered to be the most interesting, so start your tour of the walls here. The section of wall east of Northgate is partly Roman and it runs dramatically above the Shropshire Union Canal. King Charles Tower in the north-east corner is so called because Charles I is supposed to have seen his troops defeated at the battle of Rowton Moor from here in 1645. Continue down the eastern section of wall to Kaleyards Gate, created by Edward I for monks to reach their vegetable plot outside the walls.

Leave the walls and go down handsome Georgian Abbey Street to reach the **cathedral***. Much of the red sandstone building was heavily restored by the Victorians, but the choir retains superb examples of medieval craftsmanship in its carved bench ends, corbels beneath the stalls' dizzyingly intricate canopies, and misericords. The medieval monastic buildings – a magnificent

The Rows on Bridge Street, typical of Chester's 'magpie' buildings

refectory (see Lunchbox), lovely vestibule and chapter house, and undercroft with a good exhibition on the buildings' history – are equally enjoyable.

St Werburgh and Eastgate streets bring you to back to the walls at Eastgate. Walk south to Newgate, leaving the walls again to visit the remains of the largest **Roman amphitheatre** to be found in Britain (unfortunately, a wall cuts the circle in half), a collection of Roman masonry in a pretty garden and the predominantly Norman **St John's Church**, with massive, leaning pillars.

Return to the city centre via Pepper and Grosvenor streets to the large, free **Grosvenor Museum***. It incorporates a seventeenth-century house with set-piece rooms, and has good fine-art and silverware galleries, but the highlight is its two Roman exhibitions. One is devoted to tombstones, arranged like a cemetery, many of which are engraved with fascinating inscriptions and scenes. The other displays a plethora of finds to illustrate common-or-garden life in Dewa, such as lead waterpipes, boot soles, brooches and glass perfume bottles.

CHESTER FOR CHILDREN

The **Dewa Roman Experience***
should appeal to all the family. A reconstructed Roman galley and a street representing Dewa, with gossipers in the baths, stallholders at the market and a snoring centurion, are excellently executed. You can also take a serious look at current archaeological work in large excavation pits, and see and handle some of the finds.

Chester Zoo* is the largest and one of the best in Britain. Three miles north of the city (buses leave from outside the Town Hall), it contains all the favourite zoo animals, as well as unusual ones, such as rheas and guanacos. It has conservation and breeding programmes, and the animals are kept in large, usually uncaged enclosures. You need half a day to do it justice.

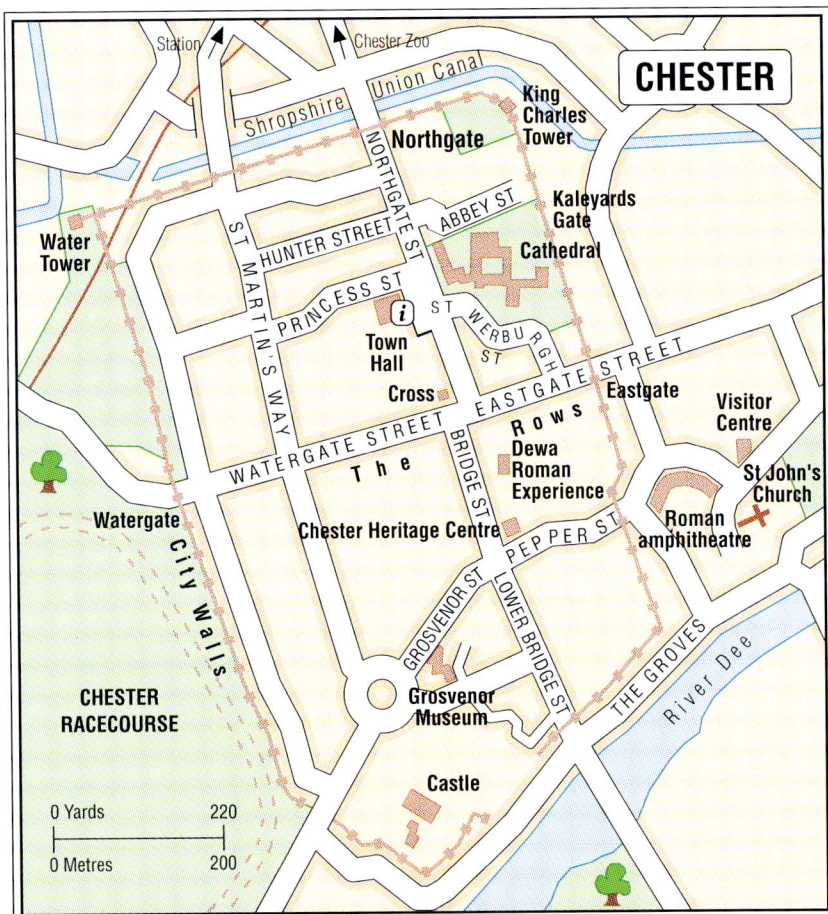

CHESTER

- Station
- Chester Zoo
- Shropshire Union Canal
- King Charles Tower
- Northgate
- Water Tower
- Kaleyards Gate
- Cathedral
- HUNTER STREET
- ST MARTIN'S WAY
- PRINCESS ST
- NORTHGATE ST
- ABBEY ST
- ST WERBURGH ST
- Town Hall
- Cross
- EASTGATE STREET
- Eastgate
- Visitor Centre
- WATERGATE STREET
- The Rows
- BRIDGE ST
- Dewa Roman Experience
- St John's Church
- Watergate
- Chester Heritage Centre
- PEPPER ST
- Roman amphitheatre
- City Walls
- GROSVENOR ST
- LOWER BRIDGE ST
- THE GROVES
- River Dee
- CHESTER RACECOURSE
- Grosvenor Museum
- Castle
- 0 Yards 220
- 0 Metres 200

Liverpool, the Beatles and the Albert Dock

View across the dock to the Pier Head, including the Royal Liver, Cunard and Port of Liverpool buildings

LIVER BIRDS

Liverpool's emblem is the 'liver bird'. Two of these mythical creatures, resembling cormorants, crown the twin towers of the Royal Liver Building by the Pier Head. They measure 18 feet in height and can be seen from many parts of the city.

Beatles and boats, sculptures and 'scouse' are just some of the memorable features of Liverpool life. No one can fail to be struck by the city's pride, vigour and sheer variety of attractions.

Liverpool is all things to all people – a port of distinction, a centre of art and culture, hotbed of rock music, football, horse-racing and much more. If you enjoy buildings for their own sake, Liverpool has more than its share of architectural treasures, from the Cunard Building by the Pier Head to the great Anglican Cathedral (the largest in Britain, with the highest Gothic arches, the mightiest organ and the heaviest ring of bells). And then there is its Roman Catholic counterpart, the Metropolitan Cathedral of Christ the King, nicknamed 'Paddy's Wigwam' because of its astonishing design.

This day out concentrates on two of the city's most cosseted assets: the Beatles and the Albert Dock development. The most significant sights can be seen on foot or by bus,

- ♦ **GOOD FOR** Beatles fans
- ♦ **TRANSPORT** Excellent both to and within the city
- ♦ **ACCESS FOR DISABLED PEOPLE** Albert Dock sights accessible; Beatles Story has lift
- ♦ **BEST TIME TO VISIT** Attractions and events throughout the year

refreshments are everywhere, the attractions are geared to young and old, able and disabled alike.

'PLACES I REMEMBER'

Kick off your day at the **Merseyside Tourism Welcome Centre*** in Clayton Square Shopping Centre: here you can pick up street maps, details of ferries and so on. Kick off with the **Beatles Trail**.

Turn left out of the centre, walk down Church Street, cross over on to Lord Street, then right into North

John Street. A little way down on your right is Mathew Street and the Cavern Quarter. In front of you, on the right, is 'where it all began'. The red door marks the entrance to the Cavern Club where, one February lunchtime in 1961, four local boys set about changing the course of pop music history. On the other side of the street is Arthur Dooley's controversial statue of Mother Liverpool cradling the 'four lads who shook the world'. Further down is the Grapes, one of the group's favourite drinking haunts and nearby, inset into a wall, is the sculpted head of a man: Liverpool is 'the pool of life', reads the inscription (attributed to Carl Jung).

If you want to purchase some memorabilia, head for the **Beatles Shop*** (31 Mathew Street), which sells every imaginable bit of gear for the devoted fan. Walk down to Stanley Street and you will see the statue of 'Eleanor Rigby', sculpted by Tommy Steele and sold to the city for half a sixpence.

The mood of this area is soulful, hard-edged, brimming with activity and music. There is also a touch of poignancy: Cynthia Lennon designed the motifs and exterior decorations for the nearby shopping centre – roses (John's favourite flowers) and doves (symbolising love and peace) are its most striking details.

'There are places I remember all my life' runs the opening line of a famous Lennon and McCartney song. If you want to discover where the members of the group lived, went to school, played gigs and got inspiration, you can **See Beatles Liverpool by Taxi*** or take a ticket to ride by contacting **Cavern City Tours*** or the Merseyside Tourism Welcome Centre.

DOCKLANDS

Spend the rest of the day at Albert Dock. (If you are footsore, SMART bus services, routes 1 and 2, run every 15 minutes from the city centre; contact **Merseytravel Line*** for details.) Otherwise, make your way on to Whitechapel (off Stanley Street) and walk down Paradise Street, following the signs. As you stroll over the rising ground by Canning Place, the skyline and its complexion change dramatically. Suddenly, the dark Victorian cityscape is replaced by light, airy redevelopment. Cross Strand Street and you will see Canning Dock to your right, Salthouse Dock to your left. Albert Dock lies behind the latter.

Turn left to find the **tourist information office*** in the Atlantic Pavilion. **Albert Dock** was originally designed and built by Jesse Hartley and opened by Prince Albert in 1846. The redevelopment of the dock was begun in the early 1980s and the process continues. The dock's rectangular design has been cleverly exploited and, as a result, it is possible to walk from one attraction to another with ease. Most of the sights are also under cover, making the whole complex a great draw whatever the weather. Here you will find shops selling high fashion and designer chic, ethnic artefacts, books, football souvenirs and much more.

There are three major attractions around the dock. Walking clockwise from the tourist information office, the first big feature is the **Beatles Story***, housed in Britannia Vaults. This multi-media show charts vividly the

The Cavern: where the Fab Four began

group's rise to fame, from their early days in Hamburg in the latter half of 1960 as a five-man rock 'n' roll band (including Stuart Sutcliffe), playing at the Kaiserkeller and Indra clubs, through the steamy heat of the Cavern Club to the headiness of flower power. You can even board the Yellow Submarine.

The next place worth visiting is the **Tate Gallery*** in the Colonnades. This is the major centre for twentieth-century art in the north of England. (Its sister gallery in London – see *Great Day Out 45* – was a gift to the nation from the Liverpool sugar magnate Henry Tate.) Displays from the National Collection are bolstered by major international exhibitions, which are stunningly laid out on three floors (there are great views of the River Mersey from two of them).

Your final port of call should be the huge **Merseyside Maritime Museum***, which has enough exhibits to keep anyone occupied for several hours. An anchor marks the entrance

A 'liver bird' on the Royal Liver Building at the Pier Head

and inside there are five floors of displays, galleries, floating exhibits, craft demonstrations and hundreds of curios illustrating Merseyside's maritime past. Recent additions include a special feature on Transatlantic Slavery and 'Anything to Declare?' (**HM Customs & Excise National Museum**) – weird and wonderful exhibits of confiscated goods, a look at the tricks of the smuggling trade and even sniffer dogs in action. The Maritime Museum also incorporates the **Museum of Liverpool Life** (formerly the Labour Museum), an intriguing look at the life and work of the people of Liverpool over the last century. The museum covers social, industrial and leisure history and includes exhibitions on such diverse topics as *Brookside*, ethnic minorities in Liverpool, the suffragette movement, dockers, and the printing industry. In the summer there are Punch and Judy shows and an old-time music hall.

As a final excursion you might want to take a '**ferry across the Mersey**': the 50-minute cruise from the Pier Head (a few minutes' walk from Albert Dock) across to the Wirral is a great way of seeing Liverpool's historic waterfront. Those of you old enough to remember Gerry and the Pacemakers can sing along to the tape as the boat docks. For details, contact **Mersey Ferries Ltd***.

YOU ARE WHAT YOU EAT

Sailors working out of Liverpool often lived on a diet of 'lobscouse', a dish of meat, vegetable and ship's biscuits. The name was shortened to 'scouse', and people who ate the dish became 'scousers'. If you want to sample a modern version of this local delicacy, go to the Scouse House Kitchen, Edward Pavilion, Albert Dock.

LUNCHBOX

Albert Dock is packed with eating places of all kinds, and major attractions such as the Tate Gallery also provide refreshments. Two family-friendly pubs offering sustenance are the Pump House and Hartley's.

Manchester's urban heritage park

All manner of flying machines can be seen at the Air and Space Gallery

Manchester's former dockland is being transformed into an urban heritage park, including three major venues: the immensely popular Granada Studios Tour and the more challenging museums of Science and Industry and of People's History.

These three fascinating and sharply contrasting attractions stand virtually side by side and are well signposted on all approach roads into Manchester (follow signs for Castlefield). The Museum of Science and Industry and the Granada Studios both have their own car parks. Attempting to do justice to all three sites in one day would prove quite exhausting: the Granada Studios Tour certainly warrants a day in its own right but the two museums could perfectly well be combined.

♦ **GOOD FOR** Plenty to absorb visitors of all ages
♦ **TRANSPORT** 15-minute walk from city centre; nearest BR station Deansgate; nearest Metrolink tram stop is G-Mex; also on several bus routes
♦ **ACCESS FOR DISABLED PEOPLE** Excellent
♦ **BEST TIME TO VISIT** All year, but ring to check Granada Studio opening times in advance, since they open to a complex schedule and are closed most Mondays; the People's History Museum is also closed on Mondays

GRANADA STUDIOS TOUR*

In return for a (substantial) entrance fee, you are given a timed and numbered ticket. This admits you to the studio tour itself, a fascinating but all-too-short trip behind the scenes to see how TV programmes are made. One or two very lucky members of the tour get to operate cameras, read the news or present a highly fictitious weather forecast, but the pace of the tour is too fast to allow everyone to have a go.

To enjoy the tour it helps if you are a fan of *Coronation Street*, since 'the Street' and its characters form the focus of the costume department and the studio sets, but there is much else to enjoy, including a convincing mock-up of No. 10 Downing Street (built because filming is no longer allowed in the real Downing Street, for security reasons).

Do not be daunted if you are told on arrival that you will have to wait several hours: there are some dozen or so shows to keep you entertained while you wait. Queues do build up for some of these, but you rarely have to stand in line for more than 30 minutes to get in.

Most popular is the Robocop ride, a cinematic experience in which your seats move with the screen action to simulate crashes, explosions, and motorcycle jumps, tricks and skids. So violent is the motion that you have to be strapped to your seat and children under a certain height are not allowed in, effectively barring the show to those under six or seven years of age. Several of the other attractions also carry 'health warnings' to deter those who are easily frightened or suffering from a heart condition.

For children up to five or six, the Sooty Show is perfect, and the 3D Rock Laser Show, though billed as noisy and potentially disturbing, is full of captivating visual effects that

One of the nation's favourite TV pubs on the Granada Studios Tour

Hands-on at Xperiment! at the
Museum of Science and Industry

young children will love. For older children, the UFO Zone puts you in the position of a TV reporter investigating the crashed wreckage of an alien spacecraft, and there are two excellent shows in which special-effects experts show how the blood, gore and sound effects are put into horror movies.

THE MUSEUM OF SCIENCE AND INDUSTRY IN MANCHESTER*

Although right next door to Granada Studios, this museum is a world away in spirit, for, while there are many entertaining exhibits, the underlying purpose is educational. The museum is huge and occupies a number of redundant warehouses grouped around the terminus of the Liverpool and Manchester Railway. At weekends you can take a ride on one of the trains in the museum's large collection of early steam railway engines, and the vast Power Hall is full of working, hissing, clanking engines, covering the evolution of power from waterwheels to the internal combustion engine.

Three highlights will grab the attention of all visitors. The first is the **Xperiment!** gallery, which is full of robust hands-on scientific experiments that are designed to be fun at the same time as imparting information about sound, light or electricity (don't miss the mirror that turns you into a ghost, or the entrancing musical sonar that allows you to play music by moving your hands in the air, just like the rock musician Jean-Michel Jarre).

The second highlight is the **Underground Manchester** display, dedicated to the engrossing topics of toilets, sewage and the supply of fresh water through the ages, complete with a replica sewer, pongs, rats and excrement.

The last, in an old Victorian market, is the **Air and Space Gallery**, packed with exhibits covering flight and the history of space exploration. As well as the many examples of RAF service planes, early passenger

The Anamorphic Ball and Cone: reflected in the cone are pictures of the great inventors, such as Faraday

aircraft, fighter planes and helicopters on display, there are numerous private planes by Manchester makers. Upstairs are some amusing comparisons between science fiction and reality.

THE PUMP HOUSE: PEOPLE'S HISTORY MUSEUM

Housed in an Edwardian pumping station by the banks of the River Irwell, this museum is a branch of the National Museum of Labour History and is most likely to appeal to those who subscribe to left-of-centre politics. The museum tells the story of the rise of the trades unions and the Labour Party. There are some fascinating exhibits, including a collection of trades-union banners and another of Labour party campaign posters of the immediate post-war era. The temporary exhibits shown on the upper floors can also be worth a look.

LUNCHBOX

There is no shortage of eating places on site at the Granada Studios Tour, and the choice ranges from hot dogs and beefburgers to pub food and full restaurant meals, though prices are on the high side. Catering at the Museum of Science and Industry in Manchester is pitched at families, with a good range of hot and cold drinks, snacks and hot meals. The café at the People's History Museum serves a good range of vegetarian food, exotic breads and interesting salads.

Manchester's magnificent palaces of culture

☂ ❄ 🚌 ♿

Cheetah and Stag with Two Indians by
George Stubbs (Manchester City Art Galleries)

England's third-largest city boasts an outstanding array of civic buildings, including a fine Victorian town hall and three major museums and galleries, all of them packed with delights and treasures.

Manchester's Town Hall and City Art Galleries are in the centre of the city, while the Manchester Museum and Whitworth Art Gallery are about a mile out, on the Oxford Road, with numerous bus and tram connections between the two.

THE MANCHESTER MUSEUM*

The Manchester Museum belongs to the glorious tradition of encyclopaedic Victorian museums that combine geology, natural history, archaeology and ethnology in one vast, cathedral-like building – in this case a very elegant construction of stone, iron and glass designed by Alfred Waterhouse, who also built Manchester's Town Hall, not to mention the Natural History Museum in London (see *Great Day Out 44*). The exhibits are outstanding and have been reworked to appeal to modern tastes without having to discard the original Victorian cabinets. Tigers leap from their jungle hiding place and skeletons rear out of ornate Egyptian tomb chests. In the warmth of the top-floor vivarium

♦ **GOOD FOR** Uplifting the spirit on a wet day in Manchester
♦ **TRANSPORT** All museums and galleries are accessible by bus and Metrolink tram
♦ **ACCESS FOR DISABLED PEOPLE** City Art Galleries not easily accessible to wheelchair users, all others are
♦ **BEST TIME TO VISIT** Year round, Monday to Saturday (on Sundays the museums and galleries are either closed, or open in the afternoon only)

there is even a small live collection of basking crocodiles, snakes and exotic frogs.

The ground floor is taken up by the large geology section, which contains displays on the landscapes and resources of the Peak District, with explanations of how various commercially valuable minerals are used. Upstairs, as part of the splendid Egyptian collection, there is an account of the unwrapping of Mummy No. 1770, with a reconstruction of what the skeleton might have looked like in her lifetime, and grim photographs of the parasites that inhabited her body.

From this it is a short step to displays on human biology and evolution, and to the ethnography collection, full of colourful exhibits of masks, costumes, jewellery and musical instruments that humankind has made through the ages to use in rituals – be it war, marriage or death.

THE TOWN HALL*

Manchester's neo-Gothic Town Hall, built in 1868–75, is one of an imposing group of civic buildings at the heart of the city. Alongside is the 1930s art deco Town Hall extension (where you will find the **tourist information centre***) and the temple-like Central Library. The style of the Town Hall was inspired by similar buildings in Antwerp, Bruges and other cities in the Low Countries from which Flemish weavers emigrated to establish the Manchester cotton industry. Visit the rib-vaulted sculpture hall on the ground floor, with its busts and memorials to famous citizens, then climb the superb stone spiral staircases to the suite of public rooms on the first floor.

The finest room is the Great Hall, which is used for concerts and receptions; it is decorated with murals by Ford Madox Brown commemorating key moments in the history of the city, from the founding of the Roman fort in AD80 to John Dalton's experiments with marsh gas that led him to develop the atomic theory in the late eighteenth century. The murals have a lively theatrical quality that even manages to perk up such mundane events as 'the proclamation regarding weights and measures in 1556'. As you leave the Great Hall, note the mosaic floors of the corridors, decorated with stylised cotton flowers and bees, symbolising industry. The other rooms are more functional in appearance, but many contain fine examples of woodwork, stone carving or needlework, plus

▲ Hylas and the Nymphs *(1896) by J.W. Waterhouse in the Pre-Raphaelite room at Manchester City Art Galleries*

portraits of public figures and notable city benefactors.

MANCHESTER CITY ART GALLERIES*

Manchester has two City Art Galleries, side by side: the main Mosley Street gallery for the permanent collections, and the Princess Street gallery for changing exhibitions. The former may have only nine rooms devoted to paintings but nearly every picture is a masterpiece. (A suite of rooms on the ground floor covers the decorative arts from all periods.) The works are hung chronologically, starting with the Renaissance and ending with works by such twentieth-century artists as L.S. Lowry and Lucien Freud.

In Room 1 the show is stolen not by a painting but by the striking gilded frame to Giovanni Battista Gaulli's (Il Baciccio) *John the Baptist*; the frame was designed by

William Kent the architect for Devonshire House, the Piccadilly (London) home of William Cavendish. Room 2 tellingly places Claude Lorraine's *Adoration of the Golden Calf* (1660) alongside Turner's canvas called *Thomson's Aeolian Harp* (painted in 1809 and referring to a poem by James Thomson), so that Turner's debt to the French artist can be observed. Here, too, are works by Canaletto and a Gainsborough *Peasant Girl* (1782) looking more like an aristocratic beauty.

Room 3 contains Stubbs' gorgeous and exotic *Cheetah and Stag with Two Indians* (1765), and there is another Turner, this time a seascape, in Room 4. Room 5 is the most popular on account of its pre-Raphaelite paintings, including Holman Hunt's *The Hireling Shepherd* (1851), and Ford Madox Brown's epic painting *Work* (1852–65). Room 6 has historical genre

◄ *Part of the lively display at Manchester Museum's Egyptology Gallery*

paintings and the many semi-draped classical figures in Room 7 include a brooding *Sappho*, and George Frederick Watts' powerful *The Good Samaritan*, which is based on a Michelangelo *Deposition*. Room 8 is for the Impressionists and Room 9 brings the account up to date with changing displays of twentieth-century works by artists such as Sickert, Nicholson, Ernst and Giacometti.

The gallery has a small shop selling examples of contemporary art and craft, and a good café serving vegetarian dishes, roasts, filled baked potatoes, salads and home-made cakes.

THE WHITWORTH ART GALLERY*

The Whitworth, on Oxford Road, is home to a vast collection of historic British watercolours, textiles (including some by William Morris) and wallpapers, as well as an impressive range of modern and historic prints, drawings, paintings and sculpture. Displays from these collections are changed regularly, and a programme of temporary exhibitions runs throughout the year. The gallery is also known for its lectures, concerts and workshops, and is fortunate in its excellent bistro, and a well-stocked bookshop covering the visual arts.

Forging links with Sheffield past and present

☂ ❄ 🚐 ♿

The imposing Town Hall in Sheffield celebrates the city's legacy of steel

Here is a chance for enthusiasts to look at Sheffield's great steel-making tradition. If, after visiting the numerous museums devoted to industry, you still have time, pop into some of its excellent art galleries.

Unlike the other great commercial cities of the north, Sheffield rose to prominence through steel and iron production rather than textiles. The industry developed as the power of the city's fast-flowing rivers was harnessed, and by the end of the eighteenth century 150 water-powered cutlery and tool-grinding workshops were in operation. More recent innovations include stainless steel, first produced here in 1913 and the brainchild of one Harry Brearley.

Heavy bombing in the Second World War saw many of the city's splendid Victorian civic buildings destroyed, and these were controversially replaced by some of the worst bland, concrete architecture imaginable. Although little remains of the city's glory days, the museums described below provide an insight into those times and some nineteenth-century

♦ **GOOD FOR** Those interested in industrial history
♦ **TRANSPORT** Sheffield is well served by public transport
♦ **ACCESS FOR DISABLED PEOPLE** Good except at Traditional Heritage Museum and South Yorkshire Railway
♦ **BEST TIME TO VISIT** Any time

buildings still stand proud: the exterior walls of the Town Hall are covered in friezes depicting industrial scenes, and the 210-foot roof is topped by a statue of Vulcan, Roman god of fire and smithies. More art galleries and museums are opening, and Sheffield has an abundance of leafy green public parks (the legacy of all that Victorian philanthropy). In the city centre the canal basin around Victoria Quays in Park Square has been rejuvenated with a mix of shops, restaurants and cafés.

INDUSTRIAL MUSEUMS

Kick off your tour with a visit to the **City Museum*** in Weston Park, which has an entire section devoted to locally produced cutlery, the largest collection of Sheffield plate in the world and a display of Bronze Age and prehistoric antiquities.

The **Kelham Island Industrial Museum*** in Alma Street, to the north of the city centre, is to be found in a dour old power-generating station. It contains a huge variety of items created at the height of the city's engineering output; a 10-ton bomb and a silver-plated penny-farthing made for the Tsar of Russia are among the most unusual exhibits, while the largest is the grand old River Don Engine, weighing in at 400 tons and still operational, belching out steam with all its 12,000-horsepower might. You can see craftsmen at work in the fully functional period **Little Mesters** workshops, demonstrating long-forgotten precision skills involved in cutlery-making.

Further out of the city centre to the south, on the A621, is one of Sheffield's largest water-powered sites, at **Abbeydale Industrial Hamlet***. This little village – purpose-built for the local foundry-workers, who produced agricultural implements and scythes – grew over a hundred years between the early eighteenth and nineteenth centuries. The foundry was still operating at full capacity as recently as 1933. As you wander round the village, you will see the four vast waterwheels powering the world's oldest surviving crucible forge, water-driven hammers belting up and down on molten metal in the tilt forge, a grinding hull for sharpening cutlery, blast furnaces and fully functioning workshops. A couple of the workers' tiny terraced cottages and the manager's house (which of course is slightly grander) have been refurbished and are open for visitors to explore.

Just to the north-west of Abbeydale is the **Shepherd Wheel*** in Whitely Woods. Here a grinding works was driven by the waters of the River Porter, producing a mixture of sharp, steel-edged knives, ranging in size from meat carvers to penknives. The peaceful setting of the old factory building, in acres of tranquil woodland, belies the atrocious conditions found within – cramped, dark and filthy. No consideration had been given to the safety of the workforce who kept this site going profitably until the 1920s.

On Ecclesall Road, just south of the city centre, is the **Traditional Heritage Museum***, which pays homage to Sheffield's highly skilled steel workers. It has on display exquisite examples of local silverwork and cutlery, as well as samples of basket-making and shoe-making – not to mention some wooden clogs. The opening hours of this intriguing little museum are somewhat haphazard, but it is possible to make appointments for private visits.

For over a hundred years Sheffield thrived from supplying the steel that went to make railway lines across the

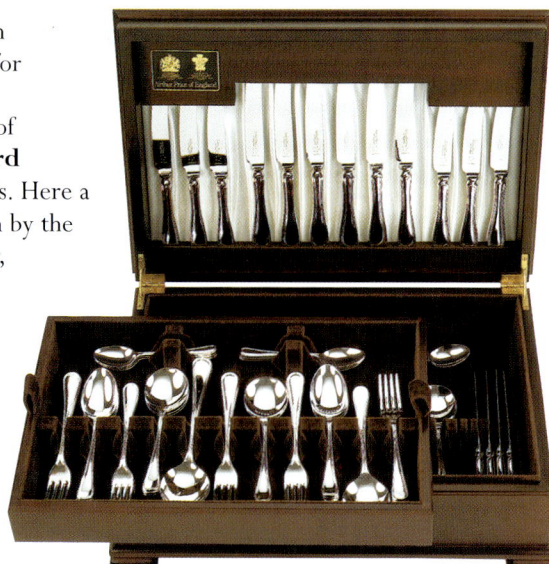

Cutlery – Sheffield's best-known export

world, and the local steam service was halted only 25 years ago. As a tribute both to the vast profits reaped from the railways and to the elegance of rail travel under steam power, some 30 steam engines, carriages, wagons and signal boxes have been preserved with the aim of eventually re-opening a 3½-mile stretch of the old railway line between Chapeltown and Meadowhall. In the meantime, to the delight of train buffs, the relics are exhibited at **South Yorkshire Railway***, Meadowbank.

Not surprisingly, the Cutlers' Company was the richest and most important guild in Sheffield and the **Cutlers' Hall***, built in 1832 in Church Street to house its members,

is appropriately lavish. It is now home to a priceless collection of silverware (open by private appointment) and a rather bacchanalian annual dinner known as the Cutlers' Feast.

ART IN SHEFFIELD
The City Museum shares its nineteenth-century neo-classical home with the **Mappin Art Gallery***, which has a permanent collection of eighteenth- and nineteenth-century British paintings and frequently changing exhibitions of contemporary work.

At the **Ruskin Gallery*** on Norfolk Street, you will find a fabulous, if eclectic, collection of paintings, illuminated manuscripts, plastercasts and minerals, all put together by watercolourist John Ruskin and donated to the Guild of Saint George in 1875 to 'educate' the people of Sheffield, although he never actually lived in the city. The exhibition is accompanied by notes on Ruskin's life and a well-stocked library. Adjoining this is the **Ruskin Craft Gallery**, which features temporary exhibitions of local crafts and occasional workshops. Close enough to warrant a call is the **Graves Gallery*** on the third floor of the City Library, which has a strong collection of British art from the sixteenth century onwards and some good watercolours and prints. The focal point of the small decorative arts section is the Grice Collection of carved Chinese ivories.

Old workshops in Abbeydale Industrial Hamlet

Humberside's seafaring heritage

The Old Harbour in Hull, evidence of the city's status as a fishing port

SING FOR YOUR SUPPER!

The International Sea Shanty Festival – a riotous bonanza of music and fun – is staged in early September on Hull Marina, Kingston Street. In Grimsby, there are often summertime performances by local hero John Connolly and Immingham tugboatman Shanty Jack. Sessions take place, weather permitting, outside the Heritage Centre. Details of these and other events can be obtained from the appropriate tourist information offices or from the Yorkshire & Humberside Tourist Board*.

From the thrills and dangers of life on a trawler to the relics of the whaling industry, this day out in two east-coast ports provides a vivid glimpse into Britain's rich maritime heritage. (Plenty of fish and chips are on offer too...)

For centuries, the Humber Estuary was the heartbeat of the British fishing industry, and both Hull and Grimsby (or, to give them their correct titles, Kingston upon Hull and Great Grimsby) were ports without rival. But have you ever wondered what life was really like on board ship, and how the fish for your tea was actually snatched from the waters and brought home? This day out, which children will enjoy as much as adults, explores 'cod's kingdom', and much more besides.

Our suggested day out starts in Grimsby and ends in Hull, but you could just as easily re-jig your plans and travel in the opposite direction. Either way, you will get the chance to see – and, if you wish, travel over – the Humber Bridge.

The National Fishing Heritage Centre* on Alexandra

- ♦ **GOOD FOR** As near a real-life nautical adventure as you will get without actually running off to sea
- ♦ **TRANSPORT** Grimsby to Hull is about 25 miles; there are good bus connections between the two
- ♦ **ACCESS FOR DISABLED PEOPLE** Good except for *The Ross Tiger*
- ♦ **BEST TIME TO VISIT** All year, but most lively during summer and early autumn when carnivals, festivals and other events are staged

Dock in Grimsby is a wonderfully compact set-up. The **tourist information office*** is on-site, refreshment spots are near at hand and you can either park by the main building or follow the walkway from town over West Haven (note the effigies of fish etched in cement beneath your feet).

The (piped) sound of seagulls and the creaking of ships' timbers set the tone. When you enter, you sign on, and you can choose to be anything from cook or engineer to the ship's cat. You then embark upon a journey from the streets of Grimsby to the Arctic fishing grounds and back again on a trawler in the mid-1950s. Feel the chill of the icy deck; get your sea legs as the vessel pitches and rolls; mop your brow in the heat of the engine room; wonder how it was possible to sleep in such cramped conditions; join in the celebrations as the catch is hauled in.

The centre also offers an evocative slice of social history conjuring up home life in the 1950s, the heyday of the fishing industry on Britain's east coast. This is the world of early rock 'n' roll 78s and Brylcreem, the BBC Light Programme on the wireless, black saloon cars with leather upholstery, and the taste and smell of that childhood panacea, cod-liver oil. There is a lot to see and do, and you should allow about three hours for the complete works.

Stroll along the waterside towards Corporation Bridge to see some of the old ships and other maritime exhibits on display. In the far distance (don't forget your binoculars) you should be able to spy the Dock Tower, a 312-foot hydraulic tower once used

Scrimshaw, appropriately on a sperm whale tooth, showing a whale hunt

to operate the lock gates and now the town's most famous landmark. If you like smoked fish, head for the **Alfred Enderby*** works in Fish Dock Road where you can see traditional methods of curing, smell the smoke and buy at wholesale prices.

After lunch you could hop aboard **The Ross Tiger**, a restored 1950s 'side-winder' trawler berthed just beyond the Lincoln Castle pub. Once it worked the fishing grounds off North Scotland and the Faroe Islands; nowadays it is a tourist showpiece, and visitors can go on a 45-minute guided tour above and below decks. Tickets for this can be obtained in the Heritage Centre.

Alternatively, if travelling by car, buy a toll ticket for the **Humber Bridge** from the tourist information office and set off for Hull. The quickest route is inland via the A180, then right on to the A15. The bridge itself is possibly Humberside's most

stunning photographic opportunity, and a rare feat of civil engineering. It is the longest single-span suspension bridge in the world – almost a mile from tower to tower – and is an awesome sight by any standards. (There is also a footway across, if you are brave enough.)

Drive a further five miles, following the signs to the centre of Hull. The **Town Docks Museum*** in Queen Victoria Square is housed in an eye-catching Victorian building. This three-domed stone edifice is flanked by **Queen's Gardens**, seven acres of fantastic flowers and fountains that make a good informal picnic spot. The building was once occupied by the offices of the Hull Dock Company; therefore it is appropriate that a maritime museum devoted to the port's history is now to be found here.

Much of the ground floor is concerned with fishing vessels, from shrimpers and Yorkshire cobles to stream trawlers. To the right of the main entrance are the whaling

galleries, testament to a trade that was once part of the city's lifeblood. In particular look out for the mighty baleen skeletons on show (these were mentioned in *Moby Dick*), the displays of Eskimo art and scrimshaw (carvings on whalebone, walrus tusks and shells fashioned by seamen to while away the time when the seas were empty or they were icebound). These designs and scenes conjure up a curiously potent, hand-crafted vision of the Arctic landscape.

Upstairs, you can get to grips with the story of Hull, the men and the ships who made this Britain's most important fishing port for centuries. The Romans and Vikings had made their way up the estuary for conquest and profit, but it was not until the reign of Edward I that Kingston upon Hull was founded as a port for coastal and European shipping. Today it depends for its livelihood on deep-sea ships, ferries, container vessels and floating factories.

The **Ferens Art Gallery*** nearby has a permanent display called 'Hull through the eyes of the artist', with paintings and prints exploring the city's relationship with the sea. Also worth visiting is the **Spurn Lightship***, a floating lighthouse which was in use for over 50 years at Spurn Point.

LUNCHBOX

At Grimsby, the Paddle Steamer Lincoln Castle – the last ferry to sail across the Humber, and now transformed into a pub/restaurant – is moored directly outside the Heritage Centre. However, if you are looking for the best fish and chips in town, head for Leon's Family Fish Restaurant. For a pint of real ale try the Tap & Spile, Haven Mill, or the Hope & Anchor, Victoria Street South. In Hull, try the Queen's Dock Coffee Saloon.

The smokehouses at Alfred Enderby have been used for 80 years

Industrious Leeds, past and present

☂ ❄ 🚐

The Victorian magnificence of Leeds' Corn Exchange, now housing over 50 retail outlets

England's third-largest city offers its visitors not only art galleries and museums but impressive shops, great and small, and many insights into its industrial past. Nearby are fine country estates.

Manufacturing, of many kinds, and especially the ready-to-wear clothing business, made Leeds important, but only relatively recently has its potential as a tourist venue been recognised, its assets spruced up and re-presented in their full glory. The museums and galleries evoke Leeds' industrial past, the once-abandoned canals are bordered by shops and restaurants, the majestic Victorian civic buildings stand proud and clean, and the ornate arcades are brimming with shops and cafés. Close by in picturesque countryside are opulent stately homes such as Harewood House.

Leave your car in one of the multi-storey car parks on the outskirts of the centre, and explore on foot. The shopping is superb – worth a day in itself. Quite apart from major department stores such as Schofield's, and the avant-garde Bond Street Centre, Leeds has a unique series of covered markets and arcades,

♦ **GOOD FOR** Families with older children
♦ **TRANSPORT** Car necessary for visiting out-of-town sites; walk around the city
♦ **ACCESS FOR DISABLED PEOPLE** At some sites
♦ **BEST TIME TO VISIT** Any time

Victorian and Edwardian wonderlands that have been fully refurbished, with decorative balconies, arched roofs covered with stained-glass and wrought-iron, and brightly tiled floors. All are full of unusual shops. Look out for the vast dome of the Corn Exchange, and explore County, Thornton's and Queen's arcades, the Victorian Quarter and Edwardian Kirkgate Market, the largest covered market in England (where the Marks & Spencer empire kicked off with a penny stall in 1884).

A conspicuous success story is **Granary Wharf*** in the arches between the River Aire and the Leeds–Liverpool Canal, south of City

Square, where hundreds of buzzing little shops sell crafts, paintings, clothes and exotica. Every weekend, a big outdoor market is held here, and the atmosphere changes from busy to frenetic. Entertainers play, sing and juggle; the canal-side paths heave with people and canal boats putter by. (The entrance to Granary Wharf is difficult to find: look for a small sign under the railway bridge indicating the 'Dark Arches'.) For information on canal trips, contact the **Gateway Yorkshire Regional Travel and Tourist Information Centre***.

Close by along the waterfront is the circular brick, glass and steel building of **Tetley's Brewery Wharf***, where the story of the English pub is told. An eccentric 'pubs through the ages' tour takes visitors to a fourteenth-century monastic brewery, introduces Elizabethan brewery workers in their cramped lodgings and looks to the future in the Star and Crater, *circa* 2053. For many people, though, the main attractions of their visit will be the patient shire horses which still pull the drays. (There are also playgrounds and a restaurant.) A little further east the **Royal Armouries*** bring to the public gaze the collection formerly housed at the Tower of London.

For modern art head off to the imposing Victorian **City Art Gallery*** on the Headrow, which has a Henry Moore sculpture photogenically draped over the entrance. Inside is a light and airy gallery with a strong collection of Victorian and Post-Impressionist paintings. Permanent exhibits include works by Lowry, Sickert and Stanley Spencer. Adjoining, but with the entrance at 11 Cookridge Street, is the **Henry Moore Institute**, which holds many of Moore's best pieces. The complex houses a gift shop and small café.

To glimpse the industrial history of Leeds, head for **Armley Mills***along the A65 two miles west of the city. Once the world's largest woollen mill, this gaunt building by the river is now an award-winning museum. Vast eighteenth-century machines spin yarn and there are demonstrations of static steam engines and waterwheels. The displays of tools, machinery and cloth evoke working Leeds exceptionally well, from the first days of the Industrial Revolution to the sweat shops of the 1940s. Do not miss the thought-provoking, first-ever, flickering black-and-white moving pictures, shot in Leeds in 1888 and shown in the museum's 1920s cinema. Bringing the city's story up to date is an account of the development of the ready-to-wear clothing industry.

The social implications of the rapid industrialisation of Leeds are examined a little further out of town on the same road. The **Abbey House Museum*** is in the Gothic gatehouse to **Kirkstall Abbey**, itself an austere Cistercian relic from the twelfth century, worth wandering round for half an hour. Within the museum, rows of shops and back-to-back houses have been re-created to represent little Victorian working-class streets. Each domestic interior has been assembled in full, accurate detail and the shops, such as an ironmongery and a pipemaker's, contain authentic stock and fittings. Children will enjoy the Victorian slot machines in the Toy Gallery.

An interesting detour to the south of Leeds along the A61 is **Thwaite Mills***, a fully operational water-powered grinding mill straddling the land between the River Aire and the Calder Navigation Canal. Tours by costumed guides lead past the two great waterwheels and grinding stones, and the little workers' cottages.

As a diversion, or an alternative to the industrial museums, you could opt to drive out of

The ruins of Kirkstall Abbey, just west of Leeds

Leeds on the A61, turning off to Roundhay Park and **Tropical World***. Here exotic plants, insects and animals abound in tropical habitats; the Butterfly House is alive with fluttering moths and butterflies, and in the gloom of the Nocturnal House fruit bats, bushbabies and monkeys scurry around. (Avoid school holidays.)

Seven miles down the unlovely A61 towards Harrogate is **Harewood House***, set in stunning landscaped parkland and entered through a pair of vast wrought-iron gates. This yellow stone Palladian mansion, home to the Lascelles family, was designed in 1759 by the York architect John Carr. Much of the exquisite interior is by the Scottish designer Robert Adam and the majority of the furniture is by Thomas Chippendale, Yorkshire's master cabinet-maker. The thousand-acre estate was laid out by Capability Brown and

Old buildings by the canal, now converted to housing

the formal knot gardens at the rear of the house were created by Sir Charles Barry. Allow at least half a day for this stately colonnaded masterpiece and its grounds.

The attractions include the brand new Watercolour Rooms, dedicated to the works of English painters, an unsurpassable collection of Crown Derby china, and masterly Renaissance works by Bellini, El Greco, Titian and their peers. Be sure to leave time for the four-acre Bird Garden, where flamingoes, owls, hummingbirds and chatty parrots compete raucously for attention. Boat trips are available on the lake, and woodland walks can be taken all over the estate.

LUNCHBOX

The streets and arcades of Leeds are full of wine bars, cafés and restaurants; the most famous, and the oldest, pub in Leeds is Whitelocks in Turk's Head Yard, off Briggate, with a long, narrow bar and good pub food. Other city institutions include Bibi's, Greek Street, close to the station, one of Yorkshire's first Italian restaurants, Bryan's Fish and Chip Shop, Weetwood Lane, and the Flying Pizza on Street Lane (look for the Ferraris parked outside – and the vast plates of pizza and pasta served inside). At Harewood, try the Courtyard Café or the Harewood Arms.

Bradford's high-tech regeneration

The elaborate façade of the City Hall in Bradford

From exploring the quirky, fascinating high-tech museums and a Victorian village to sampling Bradford's famous Indian restaurants, there is much to see and do in this gruff northern city.

At one time there were 120 textile mills in Bradford, making it the world centre in cloth production and bringing huge wealth to the area. But after the Industrial Revolution the city went into decline and for the last hundred years it has suffered the reputation of a sooty, pigeon-spattered slum. Now things are changing, however, and the city fathers have embarked on a major clean-up campaign to entice visitors to the many historic mills, houses and museums.

The town centre is a monument to Victorian architecture: follow the

- ◆ **GOOD FOR** Industrial heritage, technology, colour and curries
- ◆ **TRANSPORT** Rail and bus
- ◆ **ACCESS FOR DISABLED PEOPLE** All sights are accessible; ground floor only at Bolling Hall
- ◆ **BEST TIME TO VISIT** Some venues have reduced opening hours in the winter; telephone first

City Trail (details from the **tourist information office***) to see highlights of Bradford's heritage, which include the massive, mock-Gothic **City Hall** on Norfolk

Gardens, with its complex façade featuring statues of all the British monarchs; the Italianate **Wool Exchange**, built in 1867 and one-time hub of the world textile trade, being redeveloped as a shopping complex; and the area to the east of the centre known as **Little Germany**, where wealthy immigrant textile barons built their vast warehouses in the late nineteenth century. The glamorous **Alhambra Theatre** on Morley Street dates from Edwardian times and has recently been restored to its former gilded glory.

Bringing you abruptly into the late twentieth century is the **National Museum of Photography, Film and Television*** opposite the Alhambra Theatre (be warned – it is often overrun with schoolchildren). On the lower ground floor of this bland glass and concrete building, the **Kodak Museum** takes you through the history of the camera, from ancient box Brownies to modern digital miracles. The **Television Galleries** allow visitors behind the screens to operate TV cameras, read the news and take a magical 3D carpet ride; other sections include lots of technical hands-on exhibits and gimmickry. Undoubtedly the focal point of the museum is the massive **IMAX** screen, which stands five storeys high, provides surround-sound and features horrifyingly realistic footage of sharks, bears and the Rolling Stones, as well as state-of-the-art big-screen journeys through the workings of computers, across the sky and deep into space. Another great draw is the curved **Cinerama screen** at the Pictureville Cinema to the left of the museum's main entrance; this shows an entrancing mixture of films old and new.

Bradford's award-winning **Colour Museum*** is a few minutes' walk away off Westgate. It opened in 1978

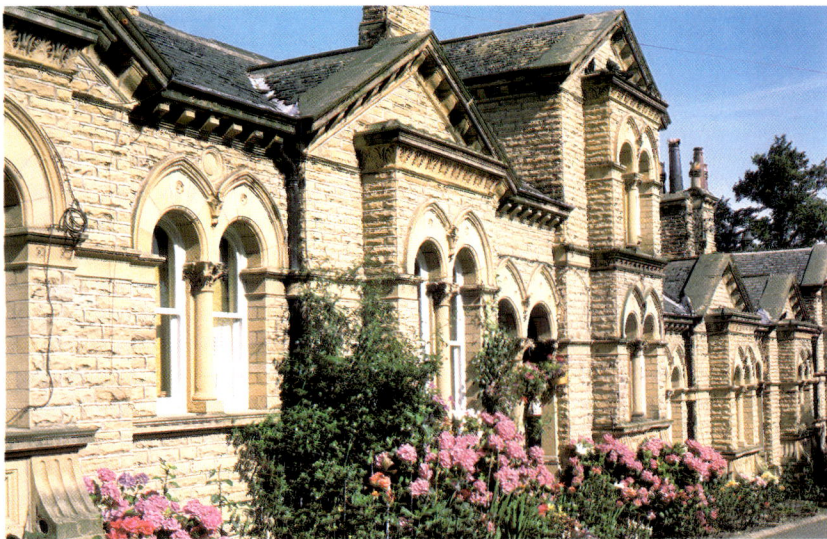

Almshouses at Saltaire, perhaps the finest factory village in Britain

in a hall which originally belonged to the Society of Dyers and Colourists. This fascinating little museum is separated into two galleries: one examines the nature of colour and our understanding of it; with the use of multi-media it shows the world through the eyes of a dog or a bee, and produces extraordinary computer-generated colour illusions. The second gallery concentrates on the history of dyeing and printing textiles and gives you the chance to mix and match your own dyes or to analyse all manner of substances using the latest technology. Audio-visual presentations, push-button displays and colourful temporary exhibitions all add to the fun; a shop sells unusual jewellery and toys.

Youngsters with an interest in the history of transport should demand a detour to **Transperience***, just south of Bradford on the M606. At this new fun park children can 'drive' buses and trains in computerised simulators, explore five separate themed exhibition halls, hitch a ride on carefully restored trams and solve a trivia quiz which leads them all round the park.

Very young children will enjoy the adventure playground with its miniature train; there are also two restaurants, a picnic area and two souvenir shops.

For those more interested in history, art and architecture, several sights are worth a glance. The **Industrial Museum***, in an old spinning mill two miles from the centre, relates the story of the textile industry using working displays of steam-driven machinery. Other attractions include a terrace of Victorian workers' cottages furnished in the style of different periods, a mill manager's house in late Victorian style (see how the other half lived), Victorian stables with resident shire horses, a display of urban workhorses and an exhibition of the local car, the Jowett. The mock-Baroque **Cartwright Hall Art Gallery*** – arched, colonnaded and turreted – is set in beautiful Lister Park and houses permanent exhibitions of nineteenth- and twentieth-century British art as well as a new gallery of decorative arts from India and Pakistan.

Bradford's recently restored Alhambra Theatre

The beautiful Jacobean mansion and pele tower of **Bolling Hall*** is noted for its fine collection of North Country furniture and a huge stained-glass window showing 24 coats of arms.

SALTAIRE

This model factory village north of the city was built by Victorian philanthropist Sir Titus Salt between 1852 and 1872. Having made his fortune in alpaca, Salt became mayor of Bradford in 1848 and was so incensed by working conditions in the mills that he relocated his factory and 2,500 workers to a rural spot in the Aire Valley on the banks of the Leeds–Liverpool Canal. He took as his architectural influence the buildings of the Italian Renaissance, probably because he considered himself the leader of a new, northern, renaissance, and named most of the wide, cottage-lined streets after members of his family. The llamas and angora goats to which he owed his wealth are commemorated in statues and design motifs throughout the village. The church was the first building to be completed, positioned right opposite the gates of the four-storey Salt's Mill, which was itself styled as a neo-Gothic *palazzo* and was the largest factory in the world when it first opened. The factory was surrounded by schools, houses, a hospital, library and elaborate almshouses, all of mellow sandstone and all virtually unaltered. Pubs were banned.

Knick-knack and antique shops, tea rooms, cafés and restaurants have now infiltrated every corner of Saltaire. The **1853 Gallery** on the ground floor of Salt's Mill contains the national collection of works by local artist David Hockney, including studies of his dachshund Boodge.

LUNCHBOX

There are hundreds of curry houses around Bradford's centre. The city's first Asian restaurant was the Kashmir. Near the National Film Museum, it is cheap, café-style and seves a full menu including vegetarian dishes. Refreshments are also available in Saltaire, the Industrial Museum and Cartwright Hall.

Brontë country: a literary tour of Haworth

Anne, Emily and Charlotte Brontë painted by their brother Branwell

Even if you haven't read Wuthering Heights *or* Jane Eyre *since you were at school, a visit to Haworth will bring the memories flooding back and inspire you to read them again.*

A day out exploring Haworth and Brontë country falls into two distinct halves – a tour of the village and the family parsonage and a walk on the nearby moors up to Top Withins, the ruined farmhouse that inspired Wuthering Heights. Which you visit first could depend on the weather – if it is a fine morning, take your chance and head up to Top Withins; if it is raining, visit the Parsonage and hope it clears for the afternoon!

HAWORTH VILLAGE

Haworth's cobbled **Main Street** runs directly uphill towards the church near the top and the moors beyond. Many of the buildings lining the street date from before 1820 when the Brontës first arrived in the

♦ **GOOD FOR** Excellent for combining history and literature with a bracing walk in the rugged countryside
♦ **TRANSPORT** British Rail or National Express bus to Keighley. Buses run every 20 minutes from there to Haworth. Medium-sized car park by Parsonage
♦ **ACCESS FOR DISABLED PEOPLE** Not really
♦ **BEST TIME TO VISIT** The summer is the best time to visit if you are keen to walk up on to the moors; the heather is wonderful in August/September. The Parsonage is open all year round

village. Indeed, the **Black Bull** pub, which you pass about three-quarters of the way up, is where Branwell, profligate brother of Anne, Charlotte and Emily, drank himself into an early

grave. Before you get to the church you pass the excellent **tourist information office***, worth visiting for the background it provides on the Brontë family and Brontë country in general.

The church itself, to which Patrick Brontë was appointed as parson in 1820, has changed radically since the family worshipped there – it was rebuilt in 1879 on the same site. It is still interesting to visit, however, and the Brontë tomb, now buried beneath a pillar, is marked by a plaque.

The **Parsonage*** has also changed since it served as an incubator for some of the most evocative writing of the nineteenth century. The original façade and many of the rooms are intact, but a new wing was built on shortly after the Brontës left.

However, you are unlikely to be disappointed by your visit. The impression inside is of the family home much as it was when the Brontës lived there. Most of their furniture has been restored to the original rooms, including Emily's piano, the sofa where she died in 1848, little more than a year after her only novel was published, and Anne's writing desk and rocking chair. The kitchen where the children's imaginations were fired by the fairy stories of their maid, Tabitha, was lost when the house was extended but it has now been reconstructed, as far as possible, with much of the original furniture back in place.

Upstairs are the sisters' bedrooms, Patrick Brontë's room, and Branwell's studio, hung with some of his rather clumsy portraits (he trained as an artist). The tiny study at the front of the house is particularly associated with Emily and includes a self-portrait sketch from her diary together with her dog, Keeper, and her cat.

Once you have explored the original parts of the house you can

Two lone trees mark the ruins of Top Withins farm, high on the bleak moors above Haworth

walk directly through Branwell's studio into the new visitor centre. Two exhibition rooms display exhibits and memorabilia including watercolours and sketches by the sisters, letters, manuscripts and fascinating examples of the tiny books in which they and Branwell composed stories of imaginary kingdoms during a childhood in which all entertainment was self-created.

THE WALK TO TOP WITHINS
(about 7 miles)
While a visit to the Parsonage gives an insight into the ordered family life of the Brontës, it is only once you head out on to the moors that you get a feel for the raw energy that saturates Emily's writing, and the brooding, wind-blown landscape that inspired the demonic passion and cruelty of her character Heathcliff. As Charlotte Brontë put it, here is 'the wild workshop' that produced *Wuthering Heights*, a novel 'moorish and wild, and knotty as the root of heath'. Make sure you are well prepared before walking up on to the moors (see box).

From the back of the Parsonage follow the sign to **Haworth Moor**. After about a mile, mostly along country roads, you reach the

> **WALKING**
> Before you set out for the moors bear in mind that, although you should never be more than a couple of miles from civilisation, this is wild country, so be prepared for bad weather – the Ordnance Survey Outdoor Leisure Map 21 is useful to keep track of where you are in case the mists descend.

beginnings of the open moorland. (Alternatively, follow the path from the church graveyard and skirt round Penistone Hill.) There are a few signposts pointing to Top Withins, and the path is very clear.

Once out of Haworth, the atmosphere that infuses *Wuthering Heights* becomes quickly apparent. In autumn and winter the skies lower above the rolling moors, rain flurries whip in over the peaty hummocks, the brown heather and the weather-blasted rocks. From the pockets of snow left frozen on the northern slopes, you get a sense of the treacherous weather and landscape that set the tone for the beginning of the novel when the narrator, Mr Lockwood, is trapped at Wuthering Heights and dreams of the return of Cathy's ghost. Visit in spring or summer, and the happier days of Cathy and Heathcliff rambling over

the moors come to mind.

After about two miles of easy but gentle uphill walking, you reach the so-called **Brontë Falls**. Here, recently married and newly pregnant, Charlotte Brontë was caught in a rainstorm and contracted a fatal chill.

Signposts then point you over the steepish hillside opposite, and you soon glimpse the gaunt, squat, roofless ruins of **Top Withins** farm, about a mile away, just below the top of the moor. It's much smaller than the impression given in the novel, but its wild location on a moor called Withins Heights suggests that Emily had this farmhouse in mind as the model for Wuthering Heights itself.

From the house you can re-trace your steps back to Haworth, head off on a longer circular route across the moors (make sure you have a map and a compass) or follow the easiest route back to Haworth – the two-mile walk along the 'B' road via Stanbury.

> **LUNCHBOX**
> For lunch either take a picnic up on to the moors or if the weather isn't good try the Quarry House Inn, off the A629 1½ miles east of Haworth, or the Bay Horse Inn on the A6033 Hebden Bridge to Keighley road.

Old Lancaster and the Lancashire coastline

The 600-year-old gatehouse of Lancaster Castle

From the distinctive silhouettes of the Lancaster skyline to sunsets over Morecambe Bay, this is an away-from-it-all glimpse of old Lancashire.

Since the eighteenth century, Lancashire's coastline has served the recreational needs of crowds from the urban centres of the north and beyond. The prosperity of this area depends on the holiday trade and huge amounts of money have been ploughed into entertainment and leisure facilities.

The ancient villages of Morecambe (formerly Poulton-le-Sands) and Heysham have merged over the years and now constitute a five-mile-long resort with every attraction imaginable. The celebrated illuminations are switched on in Happy Mount Park at the beginning of August (until late October).

This day out is a reminder that there is more to this part of

♦ **GOOD FOR** Walkers, cyclists, nature lovers and those interested in historic buildings
♦ **TRANSPORT** Bus or train to Lancaster
♦ **ACCESS FOR DISABLED PEOPLE** A few sights in Lancaster offer wheelchair access
♦ **BEST TIME TO VISIT** April to October

Lancashire than theme parks and amusement arcades. One of the best ways to see the sights is by walking or cycling. The county town of Lancaster has many fine old buildings and historic associations. After a tour, you could follow the cycle path down to Glasson Dock. For walkers, there is the alternative prospect of crossing Morecambe Bay – that huge tidal basin spanning 50 square miles between Lancashire and Cumbria.

LANCASTER
The heart of old Lancaster lies to the west of the city and most of its historic sights are grouped around the **tourist information office*** at the bottom of Castle Hill. From there you can climb up to the medieval **castle***, a grand edifice owned by Her Majesty the Queen in her capacity as Duke of Lancaster. After the steep trek, you come upon the magnificent gatehouse, built by John of Gaunt's son in about 1400. Parts of the castle – including the dungeons and Hadrian's Tower – are open to the public; a stroll around the perimeter affords breathtaking views of the town as well as of Morecambe Bay and the Lakeland hills.

Close by is the **Priory and Parish Church of St Mary***, founded in 1094 on the site of an early Benedictine monastery. Also take a look at the **Judges' Lodgings*** (reputedly the town's oldest dwelling) that now houses the Museum of Childhood and a fine collection of furniture from Gillow, a local cabinet-maker. Nearby are the remains of the **Roman Bath House** and the fragments of a fourth-century fort wall just off Vicarage Lane.

If the west of Lancaster is dominated by the castle, the east looks to the **Ashton Memorial**, a grandiose folly that looms dramatically above the skyline. No wonder Lancaster is sometimes known as 'the city of silhouettes'. The memorial itself was commissioned by Lord Ashton, who was a Lancaster linoleum magnate at the turn of the century. It stands in 38 acres of grounds now occupied by **Williamson Park*** – a high-flying local attraction with a tropical butterfly house, mini-beast centre, exotic birds and all kinds of exhibitions.

Lord Ashton also gave the city its Town Hall, a Classical building

The Ashton Memorial dominates the city of Lancaster

incorporating a large concert hall.

Lancaster was once a premier-league port, handling more tonnage than Liverpool, and the town takes its maritime history seriously. From the castle, walk along St George's Quay, with its tall stone warehouses, workshops and storage yards. Two hundred years ago the air would have been filled with the heady aromas of turpentine, rum and molasses. To find out more, pay a visit to the **Maritime Museum***, set in the converted eighteenth-century Customs House by St George's Quay. This conjures up the sights, sounds and smells of the Roman harbour, the slave trade, legendary coach journeys across the tidal sands and the modern-day Morecambe gas field.

THE COASTAL PATH TO GLASSON DOCK
A trip down the coastal path from Lancaster to Glasson Dock is a pleasant way of occupying an afternoon: we suggest cycling. Sturdy mountain bikes are the order of the day: hire one in the town (details from the **tourist information office***). The tracks are also suitable for walking or you could go by bus (contact **Ribble Motor Services Bus Enquiries***).

Pick up the signs for the cycle path alongside St George's Quay, past the Maritime Museum. From Marsh Point, the path cuts due south through fields and footpaths until it reaches Aldcliffe (look for the remains of the old level crossing). From here, the route follows the tracks of the disused Lancaster–Glasson Railway, opened in 1887 to provide a connection between the dock and Preston. The limestone ballast and rugged embankments have been colonised by scores of wild plants that thrive in these conditions.

The route then passes Ashton Park Golf Course and Ashton Hall, where a private wooded platform was built specially for one of its previous incumbents. Further on is Conder Green – once a station but now a popular picnic site. This area, a designated Sight of Special Scientific Interest, offers many opportunities

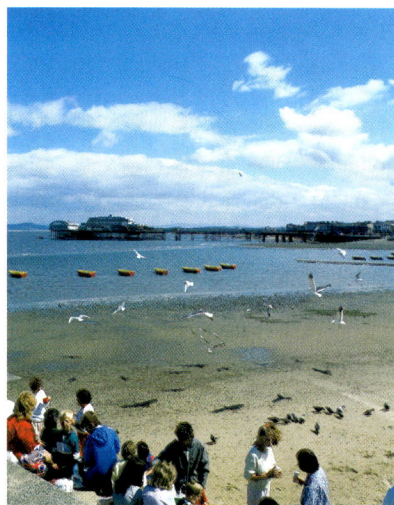

The beach at Morecambe, popular with bathers and birdlovers alike

for spotting birds, animals and plants of the Lune estuary all year round. Wildfowl swoop in during the autumn, while flocks of waders poke around for worms and shrimps on the mudflats in the winter.

The last part of the cycle path takes you to Glasson itself. Built as a wet dock in 1787 as an alternative to Lancaster, it failed to attract enough business to be viable. Now the canal basin has been transformed into a marina and there is always plenty of loading and unloading to watch.

LANCASTER SANDS
As an alternative to cycling, you can head for the coast and embark on one of the regular **Cross Bay walks*** over the sands of Morecambe Bay (telephone for details). Some walks begin at Hest Bank, but the most popular is from Arnside, north of Morecambe on the Lancashire/Cumbria border.

When J.M.W. Turner (1775–1851) painted *Crossing Lancaster Sands*, horse-drawn coaches carried travellers all the way between Lancaster and Ulverston across the vast tracts of sand. Nowadays you can undertake a shortened version of the journey on foot, although you should never try to do it without a guide. The tides can ebb and flow unexpectedly, there are tidal rivers to negotiate and you need to beware of quicksand. Even so, it is quite an experience: the air is exhilarating, the expansiveness and light are astonishing. The area is a mecca for ornithologists, attracting migrant winter flocks and breeding birds.

Touring the Yorkshire Dales National Park

The low, flat Aysgarth Falls are the most visited waterfalls in the Dales

YORKSHIRE DALES NATIONAL PARK
The route described here lies within the Yorkshire Dales National Park, an area of outstanding natural beauty. Dotted around are six national park centres, three of which are at Hawes*, Aysgarth Falls* and Malham*. In addition, Horton in Ribblesdale, Muker, Kettlewell and Reeth have information points. The centres and points provide a complete information service for those exploring the park.

Indoor sights are few in the Dales; this is a place to be outside — on foot, in a car, on a bicycle or on horseback. Although feasible as a day trip, our route has enough in it for a week of leisurely exploration.

The treasures of the Dales come free: unspoilt grey-stone villages nestling beneath green hillsides grazed by Swaledale sheep; spectacular limestone features such as Malham Cove; and the nuances of colour and character that distinguish one dale from another.

The tour starts at **Settle**, following the wonderfully scenic **Settle-Carlisle railway** (see *Great Day Out 121*) as far as Ribblehead, passing **Horton in Ribblesdale**. This is the usual starting point for the tough Three Peaks Walk, a challenging 22-mile route attempted by dozens of hardy hill-yompers virtually every weekend. Those managing the route within 12 hours can become members of the Three Peaks of Yorkshire Club, based at the café at Horton. The three peaks are

♦ **GOOD FOR** This is a day out *par excellence* for revelling in wonderful countryside
♦ **TRANSPORT** Car essential if you want to do the whole route in one day; it is a round trip of some 85 miles
♦ **ACCESS FOR DISABLED PEOPLE** Please contact the national park centres for advice
♦ **BEST TIME TO VISIT** All year, although major centres such as Malham get very busy at weekends and other peak times, and roads can be treacherous in mid-winter

Ingleborough, Pen-y-ghent and Whernside. **Ingleborough** is riddled with caves and potholes, the most famous being **Gaping Gill**, into which you can enter on certain bank holidays by winched chair. **Whernside**, Yorkshire's highest mountain (which it shares with

Cumbria) rises to 2,414 feet and can be climbed from near the spectacular Ribblehead Viaduct. The market town of **Hawes** stands in the centre of Wensleydale, a wide, mellow dale threaded by the River Ure. The **Dales Countryside Museum*** has all manner of objects including items relating to local hand-knitting, lead-mining and cheese-making. The last activity can be seen in action at the creamery on the edge of the village; the recipe for Wensleydale cheese was concocted by medieval monks from nearby Jervaulx Abbey (see *Great Day Out 114*).

The nearby hamlet of Hardraw gives its name to **Hardraw Force**, entered through the Green Dragon Inn (fee payable), where a column of water plummets 96 feet. Follow the moorland road high over the **Buttertubs Pass**, so-called because the natural limestone 'sinks' beside the top of the road were formerly used for cooling butter while it was being brought to market. You now reach **Swaledale**, the remote beauty of which makes it a favourite of many visitors; yet in the nineteenth century the area was busy with lead-mining. Hardy Swaledale sheep and stone barns dot the stone-walled pastures. At **Keld**, a superb short section of the Pennine Way leads beneath the slopes of Kisdon Hill above Kisdon Force towards Muker and runs parallel to the swift-flowing Swale.

A breathtakingly remote road leads up to the **Tan Hill Inn**, at 1,732 feet above sea level England's highest pub, placed amid lonely moors once frequented by drovers and coal miners. The route continues into **Arkengarthdale**, the most northerly of the dales, its slopes scarred with relics of lead-mining. Its settlements are no more than tiny hamlets memorable for their names – Whaw, Arkle Town, Eskeleth and Booze. **Langthwaite** is entered via a bridge that is familiar to many from the opening sequence of the TV series *All Creatures Great and Small*, based on the James Herriot vet stories. **Reeth**, with its spacious, sloping green, is beautifully sited just north of where Arkle Beck merges into the Swale. Across the Swale, **Grinton** boasts the church

Swaledale, with its characteristic dry-stone walls

grandiosely dubbed 'the cathedral of the dales', founded in Norman times but rebuilt in the fifteenth century; until Muker church was built in the sixteenth century, this was Swaledale's only consecrated burial ground, and coffins had to be carried for miles along a route known as the Corpse Way.

Head south to enter Wensleydale near **Bolton Castle** (the village it quite dwarfs is Castle Bolton), a huge, partly ruined stronghold built in 1379. Mary, Queen of Scots, was imprisoned here on her journey southwards to eventual execution. This dale's most famous beauty spot is **Aysgarth Falls**, where the Ure tumbles over limestone terraces for half a mile. A trail leads from the national park centre here through woodland to the falls. Visit the **Yorkshire Museum of Carriages and Horse-drawn Vehicles***, which occupies the former Yore Mill by the road bridge.

South of Aysgarth, **West Burton** spreads around a long village green, presenting a classic scene of rural England. The road south-west from here heads up Bishopdale and drops into the heart of **Wensleydale**. Drive on to **Hubberholme**, where the church has a splendid sixteenth-century rood-loft and modern pews by Robert Thompson, who left his signature in the form of his carved 'Kilburn mice'.

Kettlewell is another village that grew with lead-mining, and is a centre for walks – along the Wharfe, along green lanes over the hillside or high up to Great Whernside to the east. South of the village, enter Littondale, branching left at **Arncliffe** to reach **Malham Tarn**. Sedges, brown mosses and purple moor-grasses grow on its swampy shore. Just to the south lies one of Britain's most striking limestone landscapes, with the huge cliff of **Malham Cove** topped by a natural limestone pavement, and the dramatic gorge of **Gordale Scar**, where a stream somersaults between forbidding crags. A trail which starts at the national park centre at Malham takes in both Malham Cove and Gordale Scar. On the final stretch into Settle, pause at **Kirkby Malham**, which has another unspoilt country church with box pews.

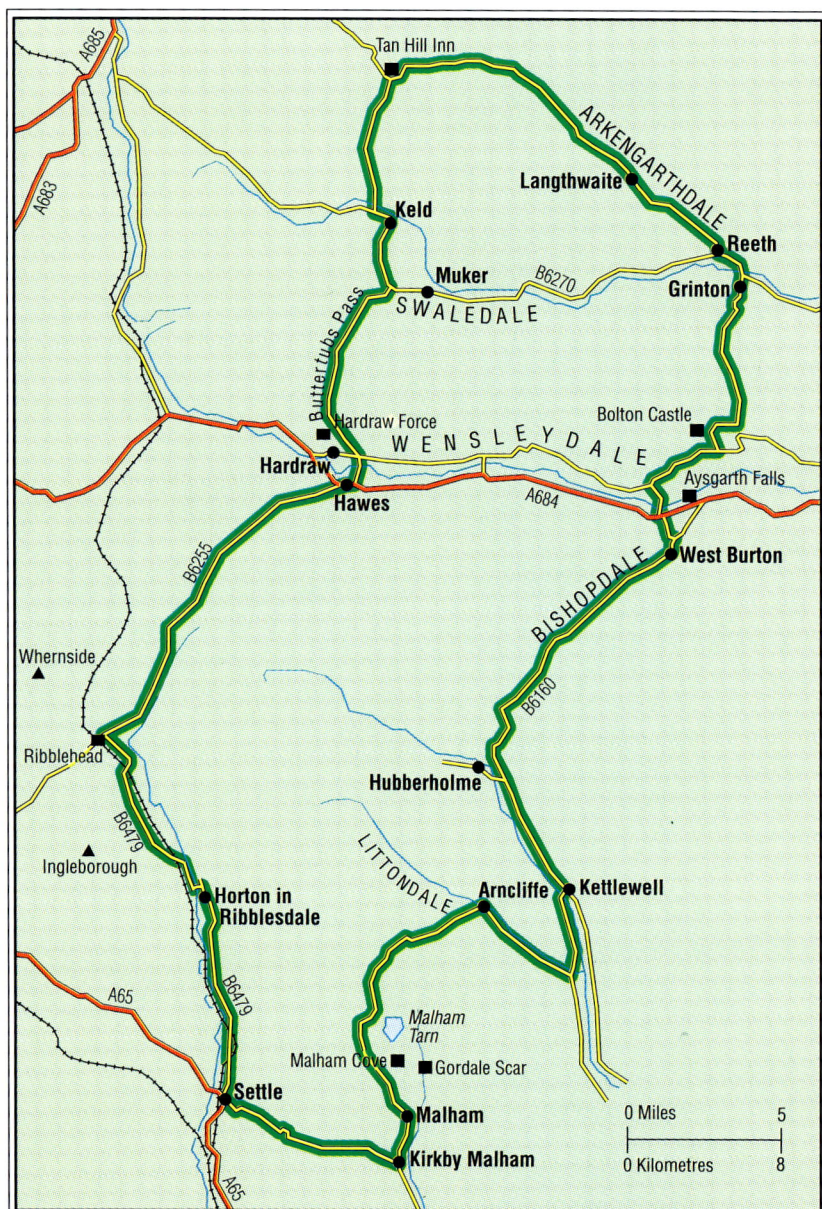

LUNCHBOX

This is prime picnic territory; supplement your sandwiches from pubs along the route.

The abbeys of the Yorkshire Dales

The graceful and vast ruins of Bolton Abbey overlook the River Wharfe

On this tour you will see the oldest and most complete abbey ruins in Britain. The short drives in between are through the spectacular countryside of the Yorkshire Dales National Park.

The Norman Conquest (1066) gave rise, gradually, to a resurgence of religious activity after the Vikings' wholesale destruction of monasteries in the eighth and ninth centuries. At one time there were over 80 abbeys in the north of England, and several have survived in Yorkshire. As an order, the Cistercians in particular were stricter than their increasingly lax brethren from other orders (such as the Benedictines), and the rigours of living in this wild and relatively isolated county suited them: of the three abbeys covered by this tour, two – Jervaulx Abbey and Fountains Abbey – were Cistercian.

BOLTON ABBEY (PRIORY)*

Somewhat confusingly, the actual ruins on the Bolton Abbey estate are those of a priory, not an abbey.

♦ **GOOD FOR** Families with older children
♦ **TRANSPORT** A car is necessary if you wish to do all three abbeys in one day, but Bolton Abbey can be reached by taxi from Skipton railway station about 2 miles away; for Jervaulx, take a taxi from Ripon; for Fountains, take the bus from Harrogate or a coach to Ripon and a bus to the abbey
♦ **ACCESS FOR DISABLED PEOPLE** Generally good. Wheelchairs are available at Bolton Abbey and Fountains Abbey
♦ **BEST TIME TO VISIT** Any time of year but ideally not in wet weather. Fountains is not open on Fridays in the winter

The estate is the Yorkshire home of the Dukes of Devonshire and, situated as it is in the valley of the River Wharfe, offers superb opportunities for long or short walking tours, through open moorland and forest or by the river.

Bolton Priory was originally built for an Augustinian order in 1154 on the site of a Saxon manor, and was destroyed during the Dissolution of the Monasteries (1536–40) by Henry VIII, who resented their growing influence and wealth. During the Dissolution, the nave of Bolton Priory was walled off by a quick-thinking priest, thus changing its status from a monastery to a parish church and enabling it to survive. The ruined choir and transepts can be seen, as can the Old Rectory, built from the ruins of the priory and used as a school. The remains testify to the enormous riches accumulated by the monks, through wool trading.

There are 30 miles of footpaths in the grounds of Bolton Abbey. Walking highlights include a visit to the **Strid**, so-called because at this point the River Wharfe is narrow enough for a person to stride across. Take care if you are crossing as the river is extremely fast-flowing and dangerous. An area has been set aside for fly fishers.

Twelve miles from Bolton Abbey is the excellent and popular **Malham walk**, with its stunning limestone scenery. The entire route is 7 miles long and takes about 4 hours with stops but it can be shortened to suit the walker, or indeed combined with one or more of the abbeys (see also *Great Day Out 113*).

JERVAULX ABBEY*

It takes about 40 minutes to drive from Bolton Abbey (30 minutes from Ripon) to Jervaulx Abbey. Now in the heart of the Yorkshire Dales National Park, this is the only privately owned abbey in England and is regarded as one of the most picturesque. Jervaulx was founded in 1156 by Cistercians and suffered greatly during the Dissolution. The ruins are extensive and require explanation, so the present owners, the Burdon family, have put together an illustrated booklet that provides visitors with a route to follow and detailed explanations as to what each building was used for.

The largest fragment from the twelfth century is the Monks' Dorter (dormitory), with its two-tier wall and arched windows; a Tudor fireplace can still be seen. The Infirmary acted not only as a hospital but also as a kind of old people's home when it was built in the thirteenth century, and in those austere times it was one of the few buildings in the abbey to have a fireplace. The existence of the fourteenth-century Abbot's Lodging indicates increasing laxity among the brothers; the abbot was supposed to live as an ordinary monk, but by the time the building was constructed he had elevated himself to a point where he needed to house many servants. The enormous fifteenth-century Meat Kitchen next door – complete with serving hatches – bears witness to the monks' abandonment of their rule of vegetarianism.

The Cellarium in Fountains Abbey is remarkably intact

FOUNTAINS ABBEY*

From Jervaulx it takes about 40 minutes to drive to Fountains Abbey (quite a bit longer if you are coming from Bolton Abbey). The sandstone abbey's ruins are the most complete in Britain, and are extraordinarily atmospheric. The spectacular water garden of Studley Royal Park (see below) is nearby.

Set in a wooded valley and built in 1132–3 by the Cistercians, Fountains Abbey got its name from the springs that abound in the area. The abbey ruins include those of the chapter house, cloisters, abbot's house, kitchen, infirmary, refectory and storehouse. Highlights include the well-preserved Undercroft and the Chapel of Nine Altars, an ornate building with 59-foot-high windows at either end dating from the first half of the thirteenth century. The vaulted Undercroft was used for storing wool, which the monks sold to Italian wool merchants. Its 295-foot length is a good indication of the monks' increasing prosperity. Nearby is the manor

house of **Fountains Hall**, built in the early seventeenth century with stones from the ruined abbey and now under renovation. The design of its Great Hall is attributed to the sixteenth-century architect Robert Smythson, and the room incorporates a minstrels' gallery.

The adjoining **Studley Royal Park** was acquired by John Aislabie, then Chancellor of the Exchequer, in 1720 after he bought the whole estate including the abbey ruins. He immediately started work on the water garden, landscaping it in typical eighteenth-century Classical style and this work was carried on by his son, William. The park contains over 700 deer. Sights worth taking in include two follies, the Temple of Piety and the Temple of Fame, and Anne Boleyn's Seat, from which there is a superb view of the abbey.

Studley Royal Park contains lakes, cascades and canals and will take about two hours to explore. For those with the time and the energy, the beautiful **Seven Bridges walk** is less than 1½ miles away. It takes up to an hour.

LUNCHBOX

Bolton Abbey offers the licensed Cavendish Pavilion near the river, and also the Tea Cottages, for snacks, in the village. There is a tea room by the car park at Jervaulx (closed from approximately Christmas to Easter). Fountains has two restaurants on the estate, one in the abbey's visitor centre and the other near the Studley Royal Park admission point.

Wild flowers blossom delightfully in the ruins at Jervaulx

York: Vikings, 'fat rascals' and snickleways

Life with the Vikings, 1,000 years ago, at Jorvik Viking Centre

This historic city retains many of its Roman, Anglo-Saxon, Viking, medieval and later associations, and a single day's visit can only scratch the surface. From museums to archaeological theme parks, the Minster and lively shopping streets, the possibilities are endless.

The sign by Micklegate Bar – York's south-western gate – tells visitors that the severed heads of traitors were spiked and left on public display here. Part of the fun of discovering York is picking up on historical asides of this sort – like the story of highwayman Dick Turpin, who was tried at York, or the grim fate of Margaret Clitherow, the butcher's wife who was crushed to death in 1586 as a penalty for harbouring Jesuits.

Although there are several **bus tours** of the city (and **river cruises** from Lendal Bridge), most of York's historic centre is pedestrianised, and you will see much more of the city if you move about on foot. If you are feeling energetic you could get your bearings by walking around the **city**

♦ **GOOD FOR** Families (especially the Jorvik Viking Centre). York city centre is particularly good for shopping and has many interesting old buildings
♦ **TRANSPORT** Motorists should use the park-and-ride facilities. In the city, walk or take the bus – or a river cruise
♦ **ACCESS FOR DISABLED PEOPLE** Access available for some sights
♦ **BEST TIME TO VISIT** Visit in February for the Jorvik Festival, May to October for the York races, and early December for the St Nicholas Fair. Otherwise, visit at any time of year: York has plenty to see indoors in the event of bad weather

walls (allow at least two hours). Despite a threat by the Victorians to demolish a section around Bootham Bar owing to 'traffic problems', these impressive medieval fortifications still form a virtually complete circle round the centre.

Otherwise, walking between the sights that interest you most and taking the occasional detour down some of the narrow alleys (or snickleways) for which York is well known is the easiest way to enjoy a day out. One street you should not miss is the **Shambles**, which used to be the city's butchers' row. Although it suffers from streams of tourists, this narrow lane retains much of its historic appeal, lined as it is with crooked timber-framed buildings whose upper storeys and steep-pitched roofs precariously overhang the cobbles below. Shoppers, meanwhile, whether looking for York ham, home-made fudge, books, glass and china or simply keen to window-shop, will find a huge variety of retail outlets in the streets and lanes between **Coppergate** and **Deangate**, as well as a daily open-air market nearby.

More formal guided walks are available free of charge most days – contact the **tourist information centre*** for details.

YORK MINSTER
It took 252 years to complete this, the largest medieval building in Britain and one of the most impressive cathedrals in Europe (the last stone was put in place in 1472). The result is an extraordinary combination of architectural styles, which were developed and adapted during its building. The crypt, for instance, is Norman and the oldest part of the present structure, the transepts retain the plain features of the thirteenth-century early English style, the soaring arches of the nave are more characteristic of the decorative fourteenth century, while the slightly later choir is in the Perpendicular style. The stained-glass

Micklegate Bar, previously part of the main route from London to Scotland

– from the great Rose Window to the Pilgrimage window in the nave, which includes a monkey's funeral – dates from virtually every period in the Minster's 800-year history. Try the walk along the city walls between Bootham Bar and Monk Bar for the best views of the exterior.

JORVIK VIKING CENTRE*
Inspired by the archaeological excavations in Coppergate, this is a highly effective way of getting a feel for everyday life in York 1,000 years ago. Electric 'time-cars' take you back through history and into an exact reconstruction of Coppergate as it was in Viking times. Sound and smell effects (the latter particularly strong near the fishing boat and the latrines) increase the realism. Actual finds from the dig are also displayed, with good descriptions.

OTHER SIGHTS
The **ARC*** (Archaelogical Resource Centre), housed in the carefully restored medieval church of St Saviour, has plenty of hands-on displays to give children (and adults) a chance to 'hold history in their hands', try ancient crafts, write their names in runes and use interactive video and databases.

The **Barley Hall***, a splendid house dating from 1480, has only just been re-discovered. The rooms are slowly being restored to their full fifteenth-century glory.

Fairfax House* is a superb Georgian town house containing a fine collection of eighteenth-century furniture.

Merchant Adventurers' Hall*, one of the three surviving guildhalls – there were once nine – bears witness to the power and importance of these institutions. Its 1350s open-timbered roof is one of the finest in Europe.

The **Museum of Automata*** in Tower Street contains a small but extraordinary collection of toys, sculpture, musical boxes, clocks and other mechanical

The Roman method of making shoes, at the ARC

contraptions which range from the historic to the modern.

Originally built in medieval times for the Minster's treasures (the treasure was confiscated in 1547), the **Treasurer's House*** is now a rather gloomy National Trust property at the north-east corner of the Minster. It was heavily restored 100 years ago when Frank Green, its obsessively precise owner, added his own eccentric touches.

The **York Castle Museum*** is a huge folk museum celebrating everyday household objects. It incorporates a full-size re-creation of a Victorian shopping street and the condemned cell in which Dick Turpin spent his last night before being hanged. Allow two hours for the full tour. From the walls of **Clifford's Tower**, next door, you can enjoy good views of the city. The tower was the keep of York Castle, of which little survives.

The **Yorkshire Museum*** is an extensive collection of finds and exhibits associated with York's turbulent past, from the arrival of the Romans.

The **National Railway Museum*** explores the progress of British railways to the present day – see *Great Day Out 120*.

York's medieval buildings and spooky snickleways are the ideal setting for tales of poltergeists and haunted houses. As a result, **ghost walks** are immensely popular and definitely worth trying if you still have the energy and can stay until about 7.30 or 8pm. The arrangements for different walks vary throughout the year, so phone the tourist information centre for details.

LUNCHBOX
York is famous for its teas – almost every street has a tea room of some description, many of a very high standard. The most famous (especially noted for its 'fat rascal' fruit buns) is Betty's on St Helen's Square. For real Yorkshire ale, try the Tap and Spile on Monkgate. Other good choices would be the King's Arms on Kings Staithe by the river (prone to flooding – a mark on the wall shows that the 1982 floods reached head height); Lendal Cellars (26 Lendal), and Ye Olde Starre Inne on Stonegate, the oldest pub in York.

Castle Howard and Rievaulx Abbey

Castle Howard, home of the Howard family, set in a 1,000-acre estate

WALKING

A mile from Rievaulx is the beginning of the North York Moors, and the famous long-distance walk known as the Cleveland Way. For those who would like something a little gentler there is a 2–3 mile circular walk starting and finishing in Helmsley. The National Trust's Rievaulx Terrace, less than half a mile from the abbey, will delight those who appreciate neo-classical follies and landscaped gardens.

This day out is about architectural splendour, from the most opulent of Yorkshire's stately homes to the ruins of one of its greatest medieval abbeys, taking in some superb scenery between the two.

CASTLE HOWARD*

If you approach Castle Howard from the north (rather than taking the A64 up from York), travelling south from the B1257 via Coneysthorpe, your first, breathtaking sight of the house across the lake will be the one that became familiar to millions from the 1980s television adaptation of Waugh's *Brideshead Revisited*. The palatial mansion was always intended by the ambitious Charles Howard, third Earl of Carlisle, as a showcase of beauty and a status symbol. His ancestors had been close advisers to royalty since Tudor times, and he wanted a fittingly sumptuous setting for his aristocratic family.

To this end, he commissioned a

♦ **GOOD FOR** Families with older children and anyone who appreciates beautiful buildings
♦ **TRANSPORT** Car essential for the 15-minute drive between sites, via Helmsley
♦ **ACCESS FOR DISABLED PEOPLE** At Castle Howard, but not at Rievaulx
♦ **BEST TIME TO VISIT** Rievaulx Abbey is open all year except Christmas; Castle Howard is open March to October, although its grounds are open all year

designer of no previous architectural experience but no shortage of grandiose ideas – Sir John Vanbrugh. After the initial plans were accepted in 1699, work proceeded relatively quickly. The main body of Castle

Howard was completed by 1712, mainly under the supervision of Nicholas Hawksmoor, who had been Wren's clerk of works. (Vanbrugh's second country house was Blenheim Palace – see *Great Day Out 55*.)

It can take as long as a day to do justice to Castle Howard. There is much to see within the house and in the extensive parklands surrounding it – the latter can be toured by tractor-drawn carriages.

Visitors usually enter through the West Wing (1753–9), which houses the Chapel with its stained-glass windows by the nineteenth-century artists William Morris and Edward Burne-Jones. Here too is the Long Gallery, where many great paintings by artists such as Holbein and Van Dyck are on display; among them are many portraits of the family.

The Antique Passage, which is lined with a great variety of eighteenth- and nineteenth-century collectables, leads to the centre of the house and the domed Great Hall. This amazing 66-foot-high room has grand neo-classical columns, typical of the architecture of the time, and a circular gallery. The wall paintings are by Pellegrini.

Also on view are the Grand Entrance, the Museum Room, the Dressing Room (including the bed in which Queen Victoria slept in 1850), the Music Room – for the beautifully decorated fireplace, carved by a

Huguenot refugee – and the bedroom which contains Chippendale furniture. The East Wing is the residential part of Castle Howard where the descendants of the Howard family still live.

Castle Howard was gutted by fire in the 1940s and rebuilt only recently; an exhibition document all the renovations that have taken place here.

The splendid grounds are landscaped in typical eighteenth-century style with lakes and hillsides and small stands of trees. Within these green acres are a walled garden, a massive mausoleum by Hawksmoor, a stable block by John Carr and a marvellous eighteenth-century folly known as the Temple of the Four Winds, which was designed by Vanbrugh shortly before his death in 1726.

Castle Howard is one of the most child-friendly stately homes in the

The soaring tiers of arcades that form part of the remains of Rievaulx Abbey

north: younger visitors will love the adventure playground in the grounds near the walled garden.

RIEVAULX ABBEY*

The medieval ruins of Rievaulx Abbey (pronounced Reevo) are a vivid contrast to Castle Howard. Rievaulx (EH) enjoys a spectacular position in the wooded Rye valley.

Built by innovative architects as a monument to the glory of God, the abbey was founded in 1132 by a group of 12 Cistercians from Clairvaux in France. At one point under abbot Aelred (1147–67), it accommodated 140 monks together with over 500 lay brothers.

Its three-tier arcades of pointed arches are unforgettable, and give a clear indication of how prosperous the abbey was in its heyday, but by the time of the Dissolution in 1539 parts had been demolished and only 22 monks were in residence.

The abbey ruins are almost totally surrounded by steep banks, which forced the monks to build on a north-south axis rather than a west-east axis as was usual for ecclesiastical buildings.

Vanbrugh's Temple of the Four Winds, in the grounds of Castle Howard

The remains of the Norman nave, built 1135–40, predate any remaining in France: the stumps of the pillars and the outer walls give a good impression of what it was like. The transepts and the beautiful early thirteenth-century choir are the highlights of Rievaulx. Part of the main cloister arcade has been reconstructed, and from the extensive remains you can also clearly visualise the living quarters: refectory, infirmary, warming room (the only room in which a fire was permitted) and kitchens. Rievaulx's visitor centre incorporates an interesting exhibition on the austere life led by twelfth-century monks.

The North York Moors by road and rail

Farndale, ablaze with daffodils in April, is beautiful any time of year

THE NORTH YORKSHIRE MOORS RAILWAY*

One of Britain's most ambitious privately owned nostalgia trips, the railway runs steam and diesel-hauled trains from Grosmont (in Eskdale, west of Whitby) to Pickering, an 18-mile journey slicing through the North York Moors. The hour-long ride stops at Goathland, Newton Dale Halt and Levisham (note that Levisham village is a mile from the station). Grosmont's Loco Shed is crammed full of engines and old carriages. Walkers can follow the course of the original line, which opened in 1836 as a horse-drawn tramway and took in a 1 in 15 incline at Beck Hole; this proved to be too much for horses or traction so a new 'deviation' line was constructed in 1865. This trail is one-way; walkers can return on the train itself.

Brookside strolls, visits to a castle and two folk museums, and a ride on a steam train punctuate this car tour through the highly distinctive dales-and-moorland scenery of the North York Moors National Park.

The tour begins at **Danby**, where the **Moors Centre***, run by the North York Moors National Park, has displays about the area. The village is one of a string in Eskdale, through which the Esk threads eastwards to Whitby. Carry on west to Castleton and follow the road going south, which leads up to the high moor. This very distinctive heathery landscape makes up 40 per cent of the park and constitutes England's largest continuous expanse of heather moor. Right on top the road passes close to the two windswept Ralph Crosses – 'Young Ralph' is the national park emblem – that like all the crosses in the area were erected in medieval times, probably as waymarkers. The road then leads along Blakey Ridge, with typically panoramic views opening up over green dales. A diversion into **Farndale** will enable you to go on a short, very attractive

♦ **GOOD FOR** Children will enjoy the North Yorkshire Moors Railway, the folk museums and the walk to Mallyan Spout

♦ **TRANSPORT** Car essential; beware of sheep straying on to unfenced roads

♦ **ACCESS FOR DISABLED PEOPLE** Some 80 per cent of Ryedale Folk Museum is accessible, also lower floor of Beck Isle Museum and parts of Pickering Castle; travel on the North Yorkshire Moors Railway possible: phone in advance

♦ **BEST TIME TO VISIT** Hutton-le-Hole and Thornton Dale can get packed at weekends and in the summer. Pickering Castle open April to October; Ryedale Folk Museum open mid-February to October; Beck Isle Museum open March to October. Farndale has wild daffodils in early spring, and the heather on the North York Moors is spectacularly in bloom in July, August and early September. North Yorkshire Moors Railway: note that steam services run only in summer; in winter, diesel locos are used

walk along the river from a car park at the hamlet of Low Mill for a mile or so to the pub at Church Houses.

Hutton-le-Hole is an idyllic village with a broad, hummocky green dissected by the clear Hutton Beck and grazed by sheep. Park at the top of the village. Limestone-walled, pantile-roofed cottages line the streets, and Hutton-le-Hole's open-air **Ryedale Folk Museum*** features an absorbing assemblage of rural buildings and local bygones, ranged around a grassy expanse. Begun in 1964, the collection now extends to a fully fledged village within a village, presided over by a thatched manor house of about 1600 and incorporating some more modest cottages (one complete with a musty-smelling parlour), England's oldest photographic studio, a smithy, cobbler, tinsmith and a village shop.

Make sure you do not miss **Lastingham**, a village nestling in a dip between Rosedale and Farndale which contains a remarkable sight. **St Mary's Church** looks pleasantly conventional from the outside, but its

Norman crypt, complete and virtually unchanged in 900 years, was built as a shrine for St Cedd (a monk from Lindisfarne who founded a monastery here in AD654) and is unique in Britain for having a nave and side aisles. The altar is just a simple slab, carvings of rams' heads adorn the capitals of the columns, and the whole church-within-a-church is lit only by a tiny window.

The bustling market town of **Pickering** (Monday is market day) has plenty to justify a possibly prolonged wait for a trip on the North Yorkshire Moors Railway (see box), which starts here. William I founded the **castle*** (EH), which survives as an excellent example of the motte and bailey pattern favoured by the Normans and was frequently used as a royal hunting lodge. Although the structure was damaged in the Civil War, the motte is still crowned by a substantial keep, and the curtain wall is impressive.

At the top of the town is the sizeable parish church of **St Peter**

Thornton Beck swirls through lovely little Thornton Dale

and St Paul, whose fifteenth-century wall paintings were discovered in 1851 but then whitewashed over by a disapproving vicar, only to be uncovered once more 27 years later. An intriguing

motley collection awaits at the **Beck Isle Museum of Rural Life***, where an astonishing number of mementoes of nineteenth- and twentieth-century life is crammed into a series of rooms that are refreshingly bereft of glass cases.

Thornton Dale is something of a coach-tour stopover, dominated by tea shops and souvenir stalls; the most enticing parts of it are up at the Scarborough end of the village, where there are cottage gardens, seventeenth-century almshouses and a very pretty brook. The route joins the A169, which bends round at the roadside viewpoint into the **Hole of Horcum**, a huge hollow gouged out by glacial meltwater and popular with hang-gliding enthusiasts. High-security MOD fencing on Fylingdales Moor surrounds the prominent **Raytheon ballistic missile early-warning system**, a truncated pyramid that in 1991 replaced the giant 'golf balls', or radomes.

Goathland, the setting for the TV series *Heartbeat*, has almost a mile of sheep-nibbled verges. A path beside the Mallyan Spout Hotel leads down into the leafy gorge of the West Beck to the **Mallyan Spout** itself, a drizzling waterfall of a subsidiary stream; the stroll can be agreeably extended along the gorge to a point now crossed by this car tour. A road detour or an extended walk (an Ordnance Survey map is essential) leads to **Wade's Causeway**, Britain's best-preserved stretch of Roman road, discovered in 1914, and now for walkers only; for 1¼ miles you tread on the original surface of flat stones on gravel – the path is raised in the middle to facilitate drainage. It originally ran from Malton to Goldsborough, a hamlet between Staithes and Whitby, where there was a Roman signal station.

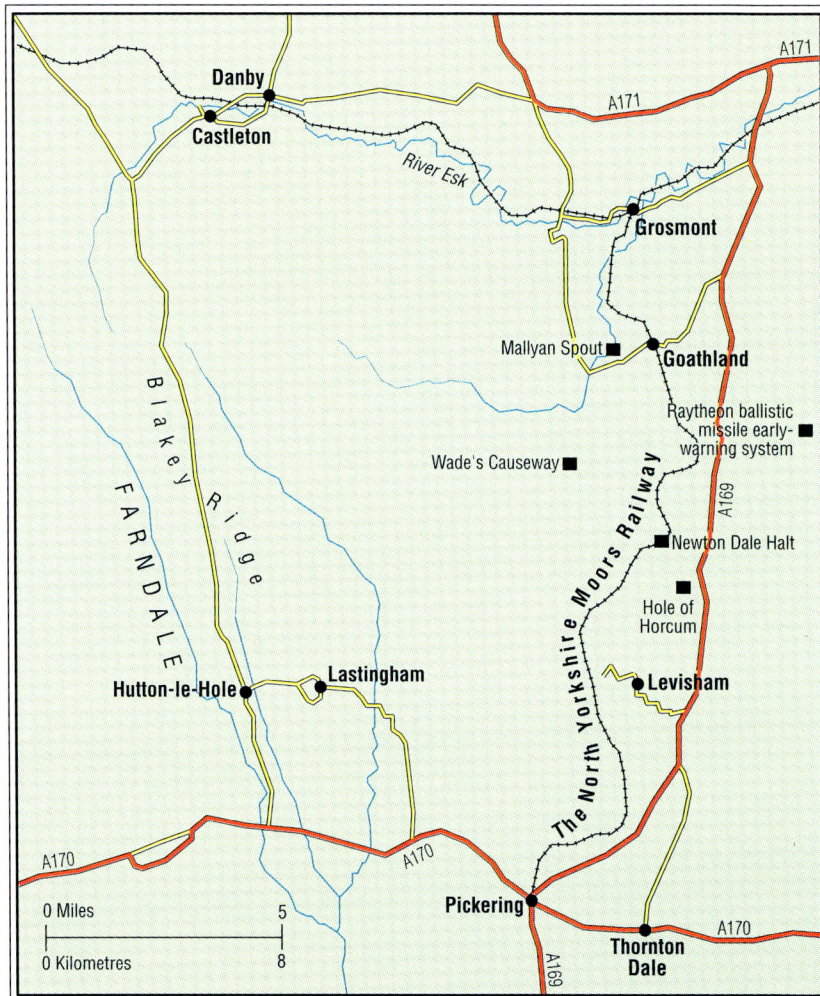

LUNCHBOX

Birch Hall Inn at Beck Hole (near the Grosmont end of the North Yorkshire Moors Railway), the Mallyan Spout Hotel at Goathland and the White Swan at Pickering are good watering-holes; there are also tea rooms and cafés in Thornton Dale, Hutton-le-Hole and Pickering. Phone the **tourist information office*** at Pickering for details and more suggestions.

[Map with labels:]

Danby, Castleton, River Esk, A171, A171, Grosmont, Mallyan Spout, Goathland, Raytheon ballistic missile early-warning system, Wade's Causeway, Blakey Ridge, FARNDALE, The North Yorkshire Moors Railway, A169, Newton Dale Halt, Hole of Horcum, Hutton-le-Hole, Lastingham, Levisham, A170, A170, A170, Pickering, Thornton Dale, A169

0 Miles 5
0 Kilometres 8

Scarborough on a rainy day

Let Gypsy Rose Lee tell your fortune at Scarborough Fair, Millennium

Marine and leisure centres, sports facilities and theatres make historic Scarborough the ideal place to be in when the weather is poor.

On top of the many delights Scarborough has to offer on fine, hot sunny days (ask at the **tourist information office***) the town is well accustomed to catering for more than just the occasional rainy day.

Although now a blend of tat and faded gentility, Scarborough has had its great moments – in Victorian times the spa was justly known as the 'queen of watering places' – and its history goes back two thousand years to Roman times and beyond. Iron Age, Roman and Norman relics have been found around the castle that stands on the rocky headland to the east of the town, and there is evidence of a Viking settlement, which may have been known as *Skarthaborg*. This rich culture is presented at award-winning

- ♦ **GOOD FOR** Traditional and not so traditional seaside diversions
- ♦ **TRANSPORT** Rail or bus, as well as car
- ♦ **ACCESS FOR DISABLED PEOPLE** Varies from sight to sight – telephone to check details
- ♦ **BEST TIME TO VISIT** Any time, but more activities in summer

Millennium*, a journey through a thousand years of local history combining sounds, smells, convincing models and a script by the local playwright Alan Ayckbourn. Enjoy a trip back to Viking times in a 1930s steam train, admire the castle in Norman times, witness a siege in the 1645 Civil War, see the development of Georgian Scarborough and experience the scandal caused by Victorian sea-bathers.

Another must for children is the **Sea Life Centre***, an easy stroll along North Bay from Millennium, but get there early on a rainy day – it can get unbearably packed. Housed in a series of ultra-modern white pyramids, the centre has a perspex underwater tunnel from which stingrays, sharks and other horrors of the deep can be observed, a Sea Lab full of piscine information and around 30 displays depicting aspects of marine life round the British coastline. Sammy the Seal plays host to young children, and the centre caters for large parties and birthdays in the restaurant.

Older children will be intrigued by the circular Georgian **Rotunda*** in the Valley Gardens. This was one of Britain's earliest purpose-built museums, designed by William Smith, an avid geologist and collector. The unusual shape of the building is reflected inside, with curved mahogany cabinets displaying their curious contents, including a brain in a test tube, a self-pouring teapot, a pair of false teeth made from hippopotamus bone and a variety of local archaeological relics, as well as cross-sections showing the geology of the coastline.

Other museums worth a glance include **Wood End Museum***, once the home of the Sitwell family and now an odd combination of a two-storeyed Victorian conservatory stuffed with tropical plants, a vast aquarium, museum of geology and natural history, and a literary shrine to the erstwhile owners – the West Wing of the house contains most of the Sitwells' major works and many of their family portraits.

In the same sweeping Regency crescent as Wood End is the **Art Gallery***, an elegant nineteenth-century villa housing eminent English paintings from the seventeenth century to the present day, a

Scarborough's huge South Bay and Foreshore with Castle Hill and the harbours beyond

collection of nineteenth-century oils, including works by Lord Leighton and Atkinson Grimshaw, and watercolours by local artists.

Boating enthusiasts should head for the **Hatherleigh**, a deep-sea trawler permanently moored off Lighthouse Pier as a reminder of the days when the east coast of Yorkshire had a massive fishing fleet. Anyone exploring the cramped, rusty interior will be amazed at the conditions the fishermen endured (opening times are eccentric, so check with the tourist information office). Another odd little place which may appeal is **Seeing is Believing***, a fascinating display of holograms and mind-boggling hands-on scientific exhibits, hidden away in an arcade on the Foreshore and open only during summer months.

If the children are clamouring to let off steam, there are several options in a downpour. **Scarborough Sports Centre*** organises special courses for children and Kids' Krazy Kapers runs holiday activity programmes during the school holidays. The centre has a packed timetable, including squash and badminton and the Shapeshop fitness room. It also boasts a solarium. **Scarborough Indoor Pool*** at Northstead also has a fitness centre, a solarium suite, sunbeds (so you can pretend you saw the sun) and great splashy, fun sessions for children on huge, brightly coloured inflatables. The **Olympia Leisure*** complex on Foreshore Road provides ten-pin bowling in high-tech surroundings and the **Alexandra Bowls Centre*** on Peaseholm Road has eight indoor rinks.

No one should visit Scarborough, whatever the weather, without making a visit to the tea rooms in the **Vitadome***, a vast, elaborate, Victorian frippery which dominates the seafront. From May to September you can treat yourself to a traditional afternoon tea and panoramic views over the surrounding cliffs, beaches and coastline, accompanied by the soft sounds of a chamber orchestra.

Scarborough, in common with so many seaside resorts, has a strong musical and theatrical heritage; Alan Ayckbourn was born here and his plays are all premiered at the **Stephen Joseph Theatre in the Round***. He is often to be found directing other works here, so it is worth checking to see what's on. The town also has numerous music halls and children's theatres, some of which offer a summer-long programme of entertainment. Try **The Corner*** for nightly comedy shows and special parties for all the family, or the **Spa Ocean Room***, which features coffee dances, talent competitions, all-star wrestling and fun shows for children. The **Spa Suncourt** holds Palm Court and other concerts every morning during summer, and the **Futurist Theatre*** provides a repertoire of big names in comedy, music and dance.

To add a literary touch to the day you could visit the grave of Anne Brontë (1820–49), the author of *The Tenant of Wildfell Hall* and *Agnes Grey*. She died in Scarborough of tuberculosis and is buried in St Mary's Church near the castle.

Opened in 1829, the Rotunda was declared 'a temple of curiosities'

In the footsteps of Captain Cook

The ruins of Whitby Abbey are a glorious example of Early English architecture

From the suburbs of Middlesbrough to weather-beaten fishing villages via legend, bloodshed and vampires, this day out takes you to some of the places associated with the early life of Captain James Cook (1728–79), one of the most famous of British explorers.

Captain Cook's three great voyages between 1768 and 1779 included the exploration of New Zealand and the discovery of Christmas Island, Hawaii and other Pacific isles. He was also the first to survey the eastern seaboard of Australia (the existence of which had been recognised from 1606).

At Cleveland Shopping Centre in Middlesbrough is a scale replica of HM Bark *Endeavour*, a modified collier vessel known as a Whitby cat, on which Cook made the first of his voyages. A Captain Cook Heritage Trail, taking in some of the places described below, starts from there.

Cook's birthplace at **Marton** has now been absorbed into the southern suburbs of Middlesbrough, but it is

- ♦ **GOOD FOR** Seascapes, clifftop walks, seafaring memorabilia
- ♦ **TRANSPORT** Car necessary
- ♦ **ACCESS FOR DISABLED PEOPLE** Cook Birthplace Museum at Marton is fully accessible; the Schoolroom at Great Ayton and the Heritage Centre at Staithes have steps up to entrance; Whitby Museum should present no problems
- ♦ **BEST TIME TO VISIT** Whitby hosts a regatta and folk week in August, and the Captain Cook festival in October

commemorated by the **Captain Cook Birthplace Museum***. Re-creations of the shop in Staithes where he worked (see below) and the quayside at Whitby – complete with sound effects – set the scene; most of

the rest of the museum focuses on his voyages and includes Aboriginal artefacts picked up by Cook along the way and extracts from his log.

Ironically – given the name of the museum – you can also see the clubs allegedly used by natives to kill Cook in Hawaii. Cook's last voyage in 1776 was undertaken to discover a north passage from the Pacific to the Atlantic; *en route* he discovered Hawaii. The Hawaiians initially showered Cook with gifts, but relations soured as food supplies ran short. When a mast of his ship was damaged by a storm, Cook returned to the island to a hostile reception; a ship's boat was stolen and he tried to take their king hostage, whereupon a crowd clubbed and stabbed him to death.

Outside the museum, in Stewart Park, an urn marks the site of Cook's birthplace. Nearby, St Cuthbert's church holds the original entry for Cook's baptism and has two stained-glass windows in his memory. On Marton's green are stones from Point Hicks in Australia, the first point on the continent that Cook's party spotted on the first voyage.

The Cook family moved when James was eight to **Great Ayton**, a village typical of the area, with houses ranged along a long green. Nothing remains of the house Cook's father built: the entire structure was shipped in packing cases to be resurrected in Melbourne, Australia. An obelisk marks the spot where it stood. The **Schoolroom Museum***, rebuilt in 1785, which James attended from the ages of eight to twelve, is now a tiny museum of memorabilia of his life and voyages. During that time his father worked at nearby Airey Holme Farm, and James had his first job there. The farm is not open to the public but can be seen from Gribdale Gate car park, 2 miles east of Great Ayton and a mile east of the railway station; from the car park

This arch celebrates the time when Whitby was the foremost whaling port in Britain

you have a choice of viewpoints (both involve uphill walks) – southwards for a short mile leads to **Captain Cook's Monument**, erected in 1827 by a Whitby banker, Robert Campion; northwards for an exhilarating couple of miles leads to **Roseberry Topping**, a hill which, as its name suggests, resembles a pudding (albeit one scooped out by collapsed ironstone mines), for a superior view encompassing Teesside, the Vale of York and the Pennines.

At the age of 16 Cook was put to work with William Sanderson, a grocer and haberdasher in **Staithes**. He soon discovered his ambitions lay elsewhere. The **Captain Cook Heritage Centre*** tells the story of his life in this period. Staithes has survived as one of the most memorably authentic, weather-beaten fishing villages on the east coast, huddled in a valley leading out to the headland of Cowbar Nab, and ranged along narrow streets and crooked alleys. A lifeboat station chronicles Staithes' precarious co-existence with the sea; 13 houses have been lost to coastal erosion, and the Cod and Lobster Inn has been washed away and rebuilt three times. In 1953, amid scenes reminiscent of *Whisky Galore*, the entire cellar stock of the inn floated out. The most

memorable approach to the village is from **Runswick Bay** (3 miles each way; 1½ miles each way if you start from Port Mulgrave), a charming jumble of red-roofed cottages lying snug against the cliff. Walk up the road to the top of the village, where the acorn-waymarked Cleveland Way to the right takes a route along the clifftops, passing **Port Mulgrave**, high above the old jetty which once served the local ironstone industry; Staithes soon appears in dramatic fashion.

Whitby straddles the mouth of the Esk, spanned by a swing bridge. Steep lanes rise on either side of the busy fishing harbour. To the west, Captain Cook's statue stands by a whalebone arch; between 1753 and 1833 more than 2,700 whales were brought into Whitby, together with seals and the occasional polar bear. The arch frames a view of **Whitby Abbey**, an

eleventh-century Benedictine foundation which was built over a pre-Norman abbey, where in 667 the Synod of Whitby fixed the dates of Easter. It was shelled by German battle-cruisers in the First World War. A flight of 199 steps, known as Church Stairs, makes a testing ascent to the abbey and nearby **St Mary's Church**, whose churchyard was the setting for the opening of Bram Stoker's novel *Dracula*. The church has Norman and medieval work but is particularly memorable for its array of Georgian furnishings, including a hotch-potch of box pews and a triple-decker pulpit. A handful of shops in town sell ornaments made from Whitby jet, a form of fossilised wood; there are further choice examples, along with some wonderful local fossils, in the eclectic **Whitby Museum***.

From 1746 to 1749 Cook was apprenticed to John Walker, a Quaker ship-owner from Whitby. Walker and Cook got along well and Cook excelled. His seafaring knowledge expanded, and in 1755 he enlisted with the Royal Navy, where he gained swift promotion. Walker's house, where Cook lived, is now the **Captain Cook Memorial Museum***. Two rooms downstairs are furnished in Quaker style. Upstairs exhibits evoke Cook's time in Whitby and his voyages, complete with original letters and pictures by artists who travelled with him and models of the ships he sailed in.

Captain James Cook learnt sailing skills on ships in Whitby Harbour

The railway museums of Darlington and York

A replica of Stephenson's Rocket *(1829) at York, the blueprint for the age of steam*

For a nostalgic day out, visit one of these two great railway museums and examine the steam engines of a bygone age.

It was in 1825 that George Stephenson, engineer, and Edward Pease, entrepreneur from a wealthy Quaker family, first brought together the steam engine and the public railway: previously, steam engines had been used only on private railways and horses had pulled public rolling stock. As early as the 1830s other entrepreneurs were taking their chances and buying up large sections of railway line. Men such as George Hudson from York realised vast profits as heavy industry came increasingly to rely on rail transport to move goods across the country, and as passengers took to rail travel with alacrity. With such rich beginnings, it is small wonder that the railway museums in Darlington and York are both exceptional.

♦ **GOOD FOR** If you aren't a rail buff beforehand you may well be afterwards
♦ **TRANSPORT** Darlington and York are both served by British Rail and bus services
♦ **ACCESS FOR DISABLED PEOPLE** Yes
♦ **BEST TIME TO VISIT** All year

DARLINGTON

George Stephenson's *Locomotion* puffed off from Shildon via Darlington on its historic journey to Stockton-on-Tees in 1825, hauling the very first passenger steam train. A horseman armed with a red flag rode before the engine to warn of its approach, and Stephenson himself was at the controls – after all, they were travelling at 15 miles per hour. The Stockton and Darlington line became the world's first steam-driven public railway; the novelty of this form of transport soon caught on, with railway lines all over the country being used to carry people as well as industrial commodities. Darlington rapidly became a major rail engineering centre, fed by the vast steel mills of the north-east, and the town remained a wealthy industrial centre until Parliament began to block off all but the main arteries of the rail network, which eventually led to the engineering works closing down in 1966.

Trains still stop at Darlington's North Road Station (built in 1842) but the major part of the station building has been renovated, and its primary function is now of **Railway Centre and Museum***. While Stephenson's *Locomotion* is the main attraction, pristine and shining, other locally made engines to look out for include the *Derwent*, built in 1845 and the oldest surviving locomotive to be constructed in Darlington. Many other engines and rolling stock are on display, together with items such as posters, tickets, station signs and signals. A former goods shed used by the Darlington Railway Preservation Society as a restoration workshop is also open to the public on occasion, and a group of enthusiasts plan to assemble a new steam locomotive, to be called *Tornado*, in the old carriage works.

The **Ken Hoole Study Centre*** was opened in 1992; this esoteric reference collection contains huge numbers of photographs, newspaper cuttings, official reports on railway accidents between 1872 and 1987, route maps and timetables – everything for the rail history fanatic. There are occasional steam weekends, when the locomotives pull visitors a few hundred yards along the private track by the museum. Check with the **tourist information office*** for details.

A 'composite' carriage at Darlington: first- and second-class compartments in one coach

YORK

The **National Railway Museum*** in York is the largest in the world, and somewhat glitzier than that at Darlington. One of its halls deals with the history of rail travel and the development of engines, while the other is concerned with the social aspects of the growth and decline of the railways.

The **Great Hall** contains about 50 engines of all types dating from the 1830s onwards, with a star attraction taking a turn on the revolving 70-foot turntable in the middle of the hall. As well as a 1934 replica of George Stephenson's *Rocket* – the *Concorde* of its day, outstripping all rival locomotives in terms of speed and efficiency – you will find the *Lode Star* locomotive built for Great Western Railways in 1907, the 1938 *Mallard*, the world's fastest steam engine at 126 miles per hour, and masses of others, including a 1972 prototype of today's High Speed Train. In one corner of the vast space a cross-section of the Channel Tunnel shows all the working components; the narrow-gauge 'muck truck' close by is on loan from Eurotunnel (see *Great Day Out 37*).

The **South Hall** is reached by subway underneath Leeman Road and creates the feel of a period railway station, with the exhibits pulled up alongside a series of old platforms. For many people the most appealing section deals with the complexities of royal train travel: on display are the highly elaborate day compartment from Queen Victoria'a Royal saloon, dated 1869, the fashionably sparse day room from Edward VII's train of 1902 and the utilitarian sitting-room of the 1941 royal train, which was used by Queen Elizabeth II until 1977. Paraphernalia including gold-plated footwarmers and special headlamps resplendent with the royal crest are further evidence of the great royal railroad show.

Also here are sleeping cars, lavatory carriages and diners, posters advertising the facilities available on various privately owned lines, and several pieces of art, in particular a pair of oil paintings by George Earl from the 1890s depicting an aristocratic shooting party heading to Perth and their subsequent return to King's Cross.

Locomotives and carriages are operated regularly in the South Yard during school holidays, giving children the chance to see engines in action. Check with the museum in advance to see whether the miniature railway will be operating to give rides. Among the other special events geared to youngsters are re-enactments of railway history by Platform 4, the resident drama group, which can be quite disconcerting as they take place among the displays with little warning. The interactive exhibition at **Magician's Road** is open to everyone and explains the simpler principles of rail technology. Children can try their hand at wheel-tapping, driving a simulated InterCity 125 and even building a bridge.

The only engine to take part in all three anniversary celebrations (1875, 1925 and 1975) of the Stockton and Darlington Railway

LUNCHBOX

A café is open at the Darlington museum during the summer. York Railway Museum's licensed Brief Encounter restaurant is in the South Hall (as is a gift shop), and a little barbecue is often on the go during the summer months.

The Settle to Carlisle railway

The spectacular Ribblehead viaduct has 24 arches, 100 feet high

TICKETS, TIMETABLES AND WALKS
The trip from Leeds to Carlisle is 112 miles and takes about 2 hours 45 minutes. From Settle to Carlisle is some 72 miles, a journey of 1 hour 45 minutes. Contact **British Rail, Carlisle*** for fares and timetables. There is also an invaluable connecting bus service between different stations and destinations in the area (telephone **Travel Link*** for details).

Throughout the year, on Saturdays and Sundays, there are also guided walks from various stations: if you are interested, send an s.a.e. to the Walks Co-ordinator, 16 Pickard Court, Leeds LS15 9AY.

A trip on one of Britain's most remarkable railways provides a unique glimpse of dramatic north-country scenery, from awesome Pennine fells to lush Lakeland valleys, via charming villages and country towns.

Enthusiasts revere it as one of the wonders of the North and historians wonder why it was ever built at all, but the Settle to Carlisle railway is an outstanding railroad. It took over six years to build and was hewn out of the wild landscape by thousands of navvies, who lived in shanty towns along the route. In recent times the line has teetered on the brink of extinction but, thanks to vigorous local support, it is now very much alive.

You are most likely to be transported on a modest two-coach 'Sprinter', which does not quite have the same romantic charge as a steam-powered locomotive. However, steam excursions are organised periodically by **Waterman Railways***, in Derby. You could combine the train journey with walks in and around the towns along the way.

Leaving **Leeds**, the line follows the meanderings of the River Aire,

♦ **GOOD FOR** Travelling through beautiful countryside by train – and on foot
♦ **TRANSPORT** Trains, buses (see Tickets, timetables and walks box)
♦ **ACCESS FOR DISABLED PEOPLE** Possible on the train, but you have to book in advance
♦ **BEST TIME TO VISIT** All year, but very bad weather can make the line impassable

past the waterside developments that have rejuvenated the city. Beyond Bingley and Keighley it ventures into North Yorkshire, passing Ilkley Moor and Skipton. At Gargrave, the line says goodbye to the Aire Valley and moves on through Hellifield, where it picks up the River Ribble and follows its course through Long Preston and Mear Beck.

Settle junction marks the start of the 'Long Drag', 22 miles of continuous uphill gradient that must

have stretched the power of old steam engines to the limit. Settle itself is a prosperous little town, dominated by the venerable edifice of Giggleswick School. The Tuesday market held around the Shambles is fruitful territory for shoppers. You can find out more about Settle from the **tourist information office***.

The line climbs again, through **Horton in Ribblesdale**, up a thousand feet towards perhaps the most stunning sight on the entire journey, **Ribblehead viaduct**. At one time a train-spotter's greatest triumph was to catch on camera the steam trains crossing the expanses of the viaduct, billowing smoke into the incandescent skies. A few minutes later the train plunges into the 1½-mile-long corridor of Blea Moor tunnel: you enter in North Yorkshire and emerge in Cumbria. After that you cross Dent Head and Arten Gill viaducts (the latter fashioned from a fossil-filled local sandstone known as Black Marble).

Be warned: **Dent** station is the highest on the English main line (1,150 feet above sea level); it is also more than four miles from the village. The trek downhill is exhilarating, the climb back a real slog. The dazzling scenery makes up

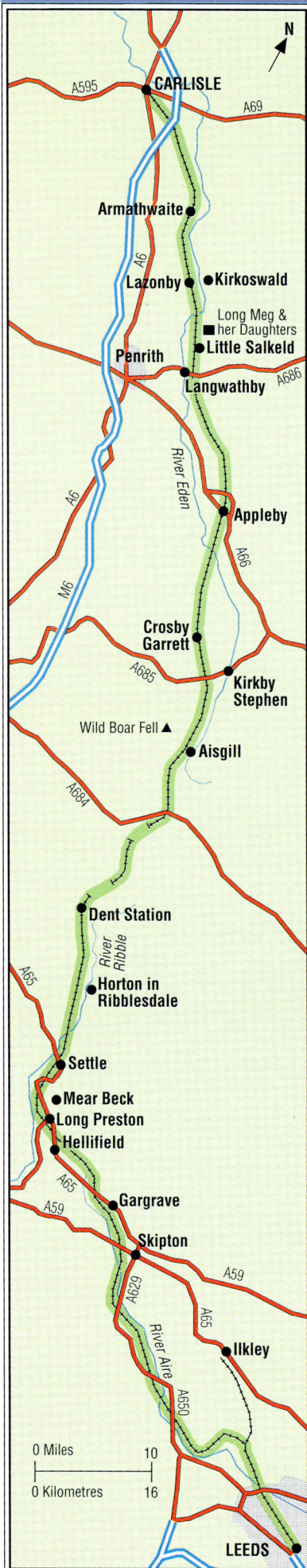

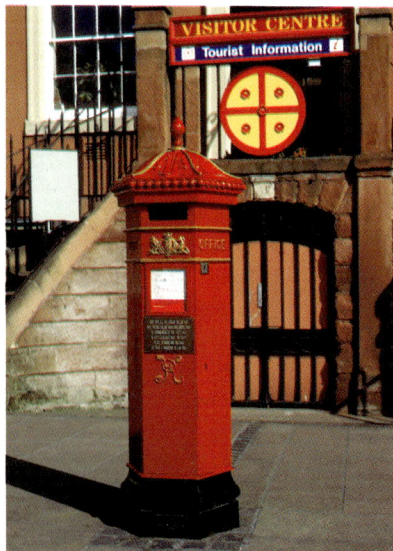

A replica of England's first red postbox stands in Carlisle

for it and Dent's cobbled streets are worth exploring.

From Dent, the line dips briefly back into Yorkshire before setting its sights on the pastoral landscapes of the **Eden valley**. On the way it passes Aisgill, the highest mainline summit in England and also the source of the River Eden. If you are thrilled by scenery, this is a moment to savour. To your left is the looming shadow of Wild Boar Fell; to your right, in the valley bottom, is the bleak, stony ruin of Pendragon Castle, reputedly the home of Prince Uther (father of King Arthur).

Kirkby Stephen station is more than a mile from the village, but it is a pleasant and refreshing stroll. A historic butter market ringed by cobblestones, a handsome red sandstone church and a stately home or two can be seen here. For details contact the **tourist information office***, Market Square.

From here the line descends through Crosby Garrett and across the broad plain of the lower Eden Valley. As this is the halfway point between Settle and Carlisle, the next stop – Appleby – is the ideal place at which to break your journey.

Once the county town of old Westmorland, **Appleby** exudes history. Its tree-lined main street, proud Norman castle and medieval churches give the place an air of civilised dignity. Attached to the castle, and right by the river, is the **Conservation Centre*** with many rare breeds of farm animals, birds of prey and nursery gardens. In June, Appleby takes on a different

complexion when it is overrun by hundreds of gypsies and traders who gather for the rumbustious annual horse fair (call the **tourist information office*** for details).

Travelling out of Appleby, the line passes through **Langwathby**, then on towards **Lazonby and Kirkoswald**; on the way it cuts through a lovely wooded gorge and skirts Little Salkeld (known for its organic flour mill) and the Neolithic stone circle nicknamed **Long Meg and her Daughters**. The next stop is **Armathwaite**, a pleasing village clustered round a bridge over the Eden. It is worth paying a visit to the **Eden Valley Woollen Mill***, where you can watch craftsmen working at restored Victorian looms.

The final stretch of the line snakes along beside the river, then heads westward to its destination, **Carlisle** Citadel station. The ancient and frequently fought-over capital of north-west England warrants a couple of hours' exploration. Lawless feuding families from both sides of the England-Scotland border squabbled over this land for centuries and much 'reiving' (wanton criminal activity) took place. To find out whether you are descended from these outlaws, consult the audio-visual display in the marvellous **Tullie House Museum & Art Gallery***, opposite the city's equally imposing **castle*** (EH). Also take a look at the modest **cathedral*** (founded in 1122) and the restored medieval **guildhall***; the **tourist information office*** is a good source of material on Carlisle.

LUNCHBOX

In Settle, try the Royal Oak or Liverpool House. Stone Close in Dent is a beamed teashop; the Sun Inn serves bar snacks and beers from the Dent Brewery. In Kirkby Stephen, picnic in Jubilee Park, or have a bar lunch in the Kings Arms. Options in Appleby include the Royal Oak and the café in the Conservation Centre. In Carlisle, the Garden Restaurant in Tullie House Museum, the Prior's Kitchen in the cathedral and Mamma's Ristorante, Pizzeria and Coffee Shop in the guildhall are all handy.

Children's stories in the Lake District

Kep talks to the hound puppies in front of the Tower Bank Arms (Jemima Puddle-Duck)

From Beatrix Potter's watercolour gallery to adventure sailing in the wake of Arthur Ransome, this is an exciting family day out with a nostalgic literary theme.

Whether you want to sail into the Hidden Harbour of Wild Cat Island, or explore the world of Peter Rabbit and Benjamin Bunny, the landscape around Lake Windermere and Coniston Water is rich in associations with classic children's literature. Both Arthur Ransome and Beatrix Potter drew heavily on their own childhood memories of holidays on the lakes, and much of the world they immortalised is still easily recognisable. Here we outline the most important elements that are within easy reach of each other, so that you can focus your day out on just one author, or combine a mixture of sights.

♦ **GOOD FOR** Families will find plenty to do, both in and out of doors
♦ **TRANSPORT** This day out is best done by car if you want to cover everything: the round trip is about 25 miles from Windermere
♦ **ACCESS FOR DISABLED PEOPLE** No
♦ **BEST TIME TO VISIT** Spring, summer, autumn – National Trust houses and sights are normally closed in winter

THE TRAIL OF BEATRIX POTTER

A good way to bring the stories to life for youngsters is to begin the day with a visit to the **World of Beatrix Potter Exhibition*** in Bowness-on-Windermere, with its video screens, 3D tableaux and special effects. The permanent heart of the walk-through exhibition is now Mr McGregor's garden – you can visit his potting shed – but changes are made each year. Other highlights include a moving model of Jemima Puddle-Duck and 'scent' effects in Mrs Tiggy-Winkle's laundry.

A short drive across Lake Windermere (use the chain ferry), among the idyllic white-washed and slate-roofed cottages of Near Sawrey, is **Hill Top*** – the little seventeenth-century farmhouse bought by Beatrix Potter in 1905 and bequeathed (along with several Lake District farms) to the National Trust in 1943. It has been kept exactly as she left it, and since she used the rooms and furniture as a setting for many of her illustrations, walking into the flagstoned kitchen with its iron range is just like stepping into one of the pages from *Samuel Whiskers* or *Tom Kitten*. Copies of the books are kept at the house and it's great fun for children (and adults) to compare the originals with reality. The only problem with the house is its size – visitors may have to queue. It's best to avoid the first hour after opening, which is often the most popular time.

If there is a long queue, or you want to explore Near Sawrey after visiting Hill Top, don't miss the Tower Bank Arms – the local pub used in *Jemima Puddle-Duck* – and Buckle Yeat house, which was the Duchess's house in *The Pie and the Patty Pan*. There's also a good walk out on to the fells and up to Moss Eccles Tarn: follow the lane running roughly north opposite the pub. It's about half a mile each way. (*The Tale of Samuel Whiskers* has a wonderful plate depicting a view of the lane and some Near Sawrey rooftops which you can still see from the upstairs windows at the back of Hill Top.)

POSTMAN PAT
(and his black and white cat)

There is another 'literary' connection for children in the Lake District: the creator of Postman Pat and Jess, his black and white cat, John Cunliffe, based 'Greendale' on Longsleddale, which is a few miles north of Kendal. The lake is modelled on Grasmere and 'Pencaster' is Kendal (although the canal in the story is fictional). For aficionados there's a room dedicated to the world of Postman Pat at the Abbot Hall Museum of Lakeland Life and Industry* in Kendal. The museum also has some of Arthur Ransome's personal possessions in a mock-up of his study.

The final stop is the nearby village of Hawkshead, where the **Beatrix Potter Gallery*** has a permanent exhibition of original watercolour illustrations for her books. The gallery, which is owned by the National Trust, was her solicitor husband's office, and the creaking floors, small rooms and low lighting (to protect the watercolours) help create an old-fashioned atmosphere, in keeping with the works on display.

SWALLOWS AND AMAZONS FOR A DAY!

Although Arthur Ransome based most of his children's adventures on real places, the map which forms the frontispiece to the books is a fictional lake, similar to Lake Windermere but with details taken from Coniston Water. So you need a bit of imagination to piece together the Lake District of *Swallows and Amazons* – but that of course is half the fun of the day out.

The best starting point is the **Windermere Steamboat Museum***, which has the old steam yacht *Esperance* on display. It's generally agreed to be Captain Flint's house boat and has been immaculately restored. The little sailing boat that inspired *Amazon* (originally named *Mavis*) is also on show, but sadly *Swallow*, Ransome's own boat, no longer survives.

The ideal way to enjoy tracking down the other sights is to hire a sailing dinghy (details of hire-centres are available from the **Cumbria Tourist Board***). However, it's perfectly possible to see many of the

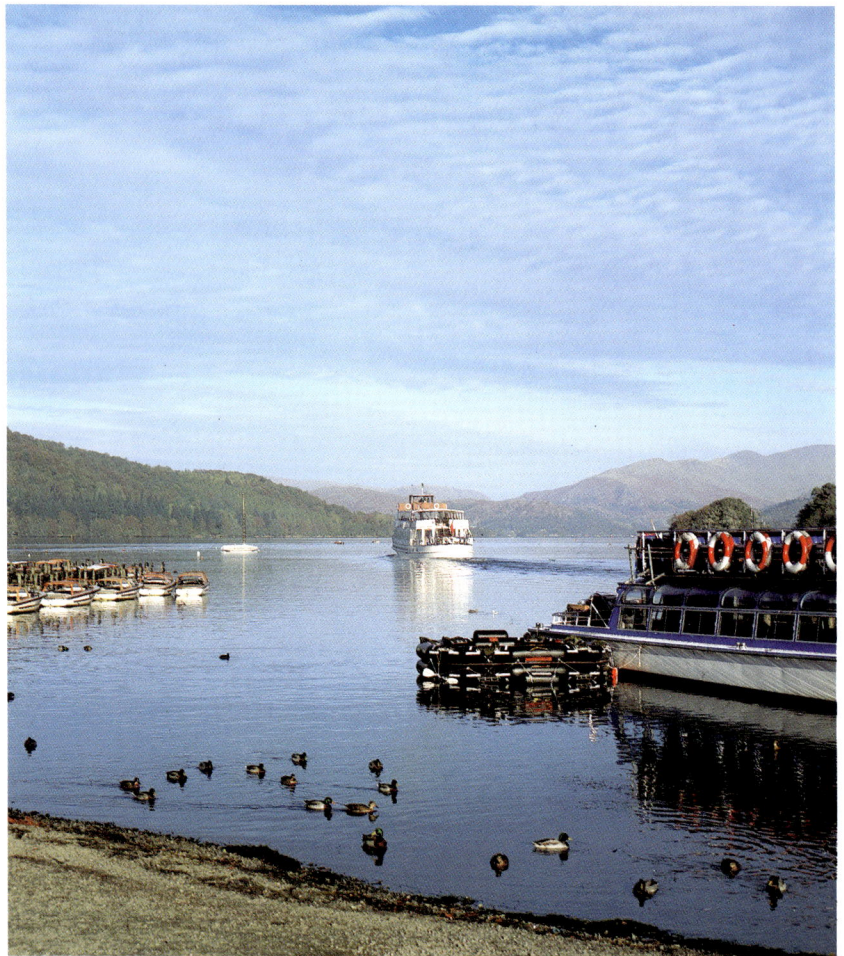

Rio (alias Bowness-on-Windermere) with one of the lake's steamers

islands and bays from one of the lake steamers, or from the road. Another possibility is to mount an expedition following one of the adventures as described in the books – the ascent of Kanchenjunga, for instance (the mountain was based on the Old Man of Coniston), or the trip to the North Pole (which is marked by a plaque on open ground near Waterhead).

Key sights on Windermere are Long Island (Belle Island in real life), Shark Bay (White Cross Bay), Cormorant Island (the tiny Silver Holme) and Rio (Bowness). House Boat Bay, where Captain Flint (a self-portrait of Ransome) moored his boat, is thought to be just south of Bowness.

To see the other main features of the Swallows and Amazons' map you'll have to make the short trip to Coniston Water, perhaps combining Beatrix Potter's Hill Top, or the Gallery in Hawkshead on the way. The houses which served as models for Holly Howe, where the Swallows stayed, and Beckfoot, home of the Amazons, are clustered around High

Bank and How Head at the north-eastern tip of the Water. Octopus Lagoon and the River Amazon were based on Allan Tarn and the River Crake, which flows from the southern end. Wild Cat Island itself resembles Coniston's Peel Island. To find the Hidden Harbour where *Swallow* took refuge after careful navigation between the rocks, you'll need to take to the water since it's difficult to see from the shore.

A good source for identifying other landmarks in the books is the simple but excellent map *Arthur Ransome in Lakeland*, published by the Lake District Art Gallery and Museum Trust and available locally.

LUNCHBOX

The Tower Bank Arms in Near Sawrey has a small restaurant, and allows children inside at lunchtimes. It also has a beer garden at the back. The Queen's Head Hotel in Hawkshead has a family room and a children's menu. Good picnic spots include Moss Eccles Tarn, and the quieter, eastern shore of Coniston Water.

Wordsworth: a Lake Poet from birth to death

Dove Cottage — once a pub, now a shrine for Wordsworth fans

- ♦ **GOOD FOR** Walking and those interested in Wordsworth's life and work
- ♦ **TRANSPORT** Car essential to visit all three sites
- ♦ **ACCESS FOR DISABLED PEOPLE** At Rydal Mount, ground floor only; at Dove Cottage, good access; at Wordsworth House, garden only
- ♦ **BEST TIME TO VISIT** Avoid Bank Holidays and summer weekends. Rydal Mount has limited opening in the winter, Dove Cottage is closed mid-January to mid-February and Wordsworth House is open only from April to October

William Wordsworth (1770–1850), the great Romantic poet, spent most of his life in the Lake District, the beauty of which inspired many of his poems. This day-trip takes in three of his homes — Dove Cottage, Rydal Mount and his birthplace — and the area around them.

The area north of Windermere teems with Wordsworth associations: there is scarcely a hillside or dale which is not mentioned somewhere in his or his sister Dorothy's writings. To appreciate fully the sources of Wordsworth's inspiration, try to build in a walk into this day out. Even from the car — you will need one if you want to see all three of the houses in one day — you can revel in the ever-changing views of rolling hills and sparkling water. The route described here starts at the southernmost house and goes north (and backwards chronologically); it would be just as easy to do it in the opposite direction.

The first of Wordsworth's homes on this tour is **Rydal Mount*** (in the tiny hamlet of Rydal off the A591 and near Rydal Water). Rydal Mount was the most permanent (and grandest) of Wordsworth's homes — he lived here from 1813 until his death — although it was not where he spent his most productive years. As Poet Laureate he never wrote a line of official verse; he concentrated most of his efforts instead on landscaping the 4½-acre garden.

Among the many visitors he entertained in the summerhouse in his much-loved garden were the foremost literary figures of the day, including Southey, De Quincey and Coleridge. The interior of the house remains much as it was in the poet's lifetime, with his possessions, his study, a set of first editions and much other memorabilia.

When Wordsworth moved to Rydal Mount he bought a plot of land below the house, known today as **Dora's Field** (NT). In spring Dora's Field is spectacularly carpeted with daffodils (although this was not the scene that inspired Wordsworth's best-known poem — the 'host of golden daffodils' that he saw was some miles to the north-east, on the shores of Ullswater).

If you continue westwards, either by car or on foot – the walk, known as the 'coffin trail', is highly recommended and takes around 45 minutes – you will reach **Grasmere**. This touristy village adjoins the lake of the same name and its backdrop is a picturesque view of fells. It has a rectangular green at its centre, surrounded by shops. At the southern end of the village stands **Dove Cottage***, the first home of

Wordsworth's that he could call his own, and where he spent his happiest years. He moved with Dorothy to this small, dark, damp cottage in 1799. It had been built in the early seventeenth century as a pub, the Dove and Olive Bough, serving traffic on the old Ambleside to Keswick road, and is a humble building with stone walls, lattice windows and a slate roof. Interestingly, Wordsworth never knew it as Dove Cottage.

In 1802 he married Mary Hutchinson, and the two of them and Dorothy resided here in a state of 'plain living and high thinking'. This spartan lifestyle was obviously conducive to Wordsworth's creative abilities – it was at this time that he produced some of the greatest poetry in the English language, including the 'Intimations of Immortality' ode, 'I Wandered Lonely as a Cloud' (popularly known as 'Daffodils') and 'Ode to Duty'.

The cottage itself retains the atmosphere it must have had when Wordsworth lived here. Only a little of the original furniture is in it; a lot of what you can see there now belonged to him, but in other residences. One of the poet's favourite objects, a cuckoo-clock which used to hang at Rydal Mount, is now installed here; it was the one that was chiming midnight when Wordsworth died. De Quincey

Rydal Mount, where fans would gather to catch a glimpse of the poet

moved into Dove Cottage after Wordsworth moved out, and some of his belongings – including his opium scales – are on display too.

Next door is the excellent **Wordsworth Museum**, containing numerous original manuscripts and pictures associated with Wordsworth and the other poets who lived and wrote in the area. Among the more light-hearted items is a glass case full of Wordsworth's effects, including his buckles, 'ww' monogrammed socks, silk umbrella and purse.

Grasmere **church**, dedicated to St Oswald, has several Wordsworth connections. Above the nave is a memorial to the poet; his prayer book is preserved in a glass case near the organ. In the churchyard are the graves of William, Mary, Dorothy and three of the poet's children.

Another option for a walk is in **Easedale**, a short valley north-west of Grasmere, explorable only on foot: to the magnificently sited tarn and back is 3½ miles.

Leave Grasmere and head for Keswick, from where you have choice of the A591 or the A66 – the former is slower but the scenery is better – to Cockermouth, best known as Wordsworth's

A bust of Wordsworth at Cockermouth, where the poet was born

birthplace. **Cockermouth** is a small, bustling market town founded in the twelfth century and surprisingly untouristy. The main attraction here is **Wordsworth House*** (NT), where the poet lived until he was eight.

Situated at the west end of Main Street and overlooking the River Derwent, the seventeenth-century house is the most impressive building in sight, though it narrowly escaped being demolished to make way for a bus station in the 1930s. As well as some of Wordsworth's furniture and effects, it also boasts artefacts belonging to other Lakeland poets, such as Southey, and an early painting by Turner. At the back of the house are a walled garden and terrace which have a pleasant view over the river.

Cockermouth also has a thirteenth-century **castle**, privately owned and open to the public during the Cockermouth Festival (August).

LUNCHBOX

In Grasmere, try the Rowan Tree and Baldry's for snacks, White Moss House and Michael's Nook for full meals. At Cockermouth, in addition to the refreshment rooms at Wordsworth House there are bars and bistros near Main Street, such as the Courtyard Coffeehouse for the mornings and a bar called Cheers for the evenings. The **tourist information offices*** in both towns can provide more suggestions.

The historic city of Durham

Built on a rocky peninsula, Durham has just one unmissable sight, its awesome Norman cathedral. A tiny city, with scenic riverside walks, it is easily explored in a day.

Durham's colossal cathedral rising majestically above the arboreal banks of the River Wear is one of England's most memorable images and reason alone to visit Durham. Having exhausted its dramatically austere interior and its fascinating treasures, wander along the virtually traffic-free streets of the surrounding peninsula and the paths around the severe loop of the river. During the summer months, you can take to the water on a **short cruise** or in a **rowing boat** (these are hired from Brown's Boathouse*; departures from under Elvet Bridge), thereby seeing the city from a different perspective.

♦ **GOOυ FOR** Those who like exploring handsome, medieval towns
♦ **TRANSPORT** The railway station is a ten-minute walk from the city centre, and all the main sights are best visited on foot
♦ **ACCESS FOR DISABLED PEOPLE** To cathedral and treasury
♦ **BEST TIME TO VISIT** Autumn is the prettiest time, when the leaves on the wooded riverbank are turning; in summer, there are tours of the cathedral and precincts, the castle is open daily and there are river cruises and rowing boats for hire; the Durham Regatta takes place in June, and the Miners' Gala in July; the city is far less crowded out of university term-time

CATHEDRAL*

Devote about a couple of hours to exploring this fortress of a cathedral – in Walter Scott's words 'half church of God, half castle 'gainst the Scot'. Built largely between 1093 and 1133, it is a triumph of early Norman architecture, unsurpassed in the British Isles. Along the nave, Herculean pillars carved with zigzag and chevron patterns rise up towards a roof in an innovative rib-vaulted style. Pilgrims once flocked to the shrine of St Cuthbert, a seventh-century bishop from Lindisfarne, at the church's east end in the Gothic Chapel of the Nine Altars. At the west end, the Venerable Bede (eight century), author of *The Ecclesiastical History of the English People* and called the 'father of English history', is entombed in the moorish Galilee Chapel. Originally, in AD735, he was buried in Jarrow, but a monk stole his remains and brought them here.

The fit should take the 325 spiral steps up to the **roof** of the main tower for the views. Everyone should visit the **treasury**. Here you'll find remnants of St Cuthbert's coffin, the religious carvings on which are still clearly visible, and beautiful relics of the saint such as his pectoral cross and comb. Look, too, for the original, grotesque-faced twelfth-century sanctuary knocker: once at the north-west door of the church (where there's now a replica), fugitives could, under medieval law, claim sanctuary by clinging to it. Lastly, glance into the glorious **monks' dormitory**, completed in 1404 and retaining its impressive roof timbers. It now doubles both as a library and a museum of Anglo-Saxon carved stonework.

A WALK AROUND DURHAM

Directly north of the cathedral lies handsome **Palace Green**, on whose

The sanctuary knocker is now housed in the treasury in the cathedral

spacious sward students sometimes play croquet in summer. The surrounding buildings, now university lecture rooms and a library, were in previous centuries the administrative heart of the Palatinate of Durham. This was a semi-autonomous state set up by the

Normans which stretched from the Tees to the Tyne: the oldest building on the green (nearest the castle and dating from the fifteenth century) was the palatinate's exchequer. Head of the state was the prince bishop, appointed by the English monarch. The **castle*** was the bishops' palace until the 1830s, when it became the foundation college for Durham University. The most ancient part, dating from around 1080, is the atmospherically gloomy Norman Chapel, while the Black Staircase and the aptly named Great Hall, where students dine, are both impressive. You can visit the castle only on a guided tour, led by a student whose lively patter will give you something of a feel for collegiate life.

Return to Palace Green and head down to Saddler Street, where you'll find Durham's few gift shops. Pass through the Market Place, where the **tourist information office*** is to be found, and down Silver Street to medieval Framwellgate Bridge. Paths lead from here alongside the River Wear beneath steep banks coated in beeches, oaks and horse-chestnuts. Take the nearside path south down to the weir, which links a pair of picturesque old mills. The **Old Fulling Mill*** has been converted

DURHAM UNIVERSITY ORIENTAL MUSEUM*

If the weather is foul, consider dropping in to see this extraordinarily rich collection, about a mile south of the city centre near Van Mildert and Trevelyan colleges. The vast array of largely antique displays covers pots, masks and figurines from Egypt, India, Tibet, China and Japan. Those without specialist knowledge may find the highly educational sections on the history of writing (including examples of Mesopotamian cuneiform) and ancient Egypt (obelisks, mummies, hieroglyphics, exquisite statuettes) the most rewarding.

into a small archaeological museum containing some inscribed Roman stones and Samian pottery (tableware made in Roman Gaul). Further along the bend in the river, pedestrian **Prebends' Bridge** is the city's most scenic spot. From here in 1834 Turner painted the cathedral's towers erupting out of the tree tops.

Take a detour across the bridge and up to Georgian **South Street** for a fabulous, unbroken view of the west end of the cathedral. Return across Prebends' Bridge and follow the peninsula's prettiest street, **South Bailey** (cobbled and lined with Georgian brick façades), up to an impressive gateway a few hundred yards up on the left. On its other side lies the serene **College** or cathedral close, with venerable old buildings such as the Deanery and the fourteenth-century Priors' Kitchen. You can wander through on your own or in summer take one of the infrequent guided tours, which include a fascinating visit to the stonemasons' yard. A passage takes you back to the cloisters and the cathedral itself, the starting point of the walk.

LUNCHBOX

The best pitstop is the seventeenth-century Almshouses on Palace Green, which serves sophisticated cafeteria fare. The Undercroft Restaurant, off the cathedral cloisters, provides interesting food as well but can get crowded (the bookshop next door does a roaring trade in prints of the cathedral). The most appealing city-centre pub is the diminutive Shakespeare on Saddler Street.

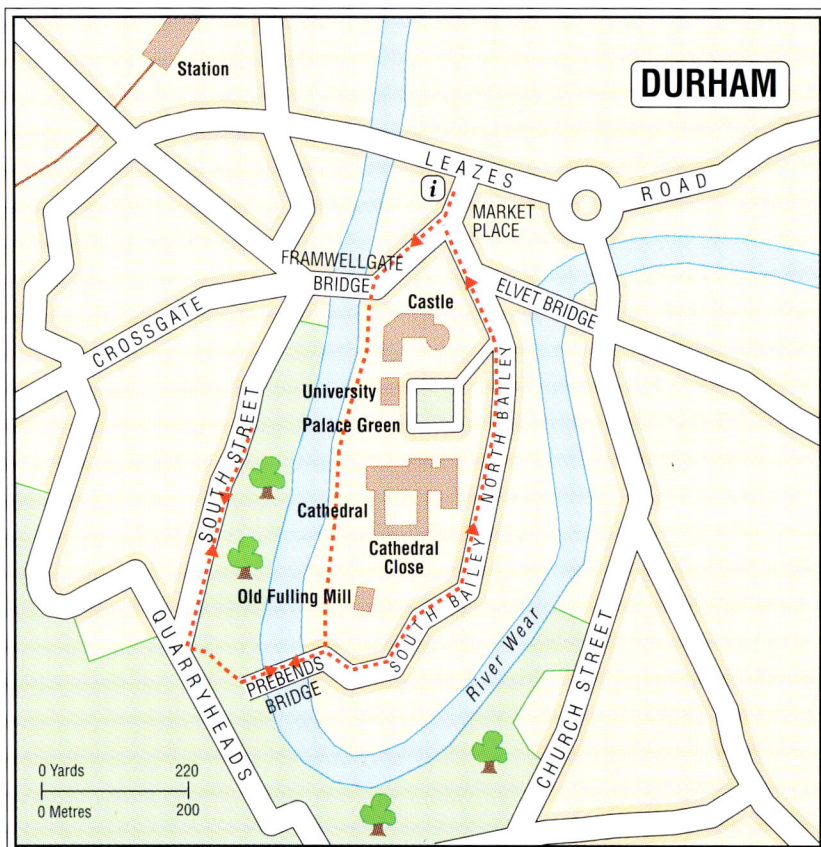

DURHAM

Station

LEAZES ROAD

MARKET PLACE

FRAMWELLGATE BRIDGE

ELVET BRIDGE

CROSSGATE

Castle

University

Palace Green

NORTH BAILEY

Cathedral

Cathedral Close

SOUTH STREET

Old Fulling Mill

SOUTH BAILEY

QUARRYHEADS

PREBENDS BRIDGE

River Wear

CHURCH STREET

0 Yards 220
0 Metres 200

Beamish's museum in the open air

Ride on a tram, go down a coal mine, see a printer at work. Then discover what school was like in 1913, experience the terrors of the dentist's surgery and learn the pianoforte – all in the space of one day. This is your chance to experience life in the early 1900s.

Beamish, the North of England Open Air Museum* is one of the few museums where it really is possible to be diverted, entertained and educated for an entire day. It is a museum like no other in Britain. Set up in 1970 on 300 acres of wooded land crossed by the Beamish Burn, it re-creates a vanished way of life. Entire buildings have been moved from their original sites, re-erected and refurbished; others have been built from scratch. The Drift Mine, Home Farm and Pockerley Manor were all here already.

Don't expect exhibits in glass cases, labels or the other trappings of traditional museums. What you will find here are real people (in costume) – young and old – acting out everyday life as it was in a north country town in the year before the outbreak of the First World War. Dramatised history,

♦ **GOOD FOR** An exhilarating dip into life just before the First World War
♦ **TRANSPORT** Car: take the A1(M) to the turn off for Chester-le-Street and follow the 'Beamish Museum' signs along the A693 towards Stanley (4 miles). From the north-west take the A68 south to Castleside, near Consett, and follow the signs along the A692 and A693 via Stanley
♦ **PUBLIC TRANSPORT** Durham City and Newcastle Central BR stations are equally convenient: bus services run regularly between the station and the museum. Ring **Travel-Line*** for details
♦ **ACCESS FOR DISABLED PEOPLE** Possible though not easy
♦ **BEST TIME TO VISIT** April to October; the 'Town' and tramway are open all year

you might call it. The players in this drama are also 'guides': part of their job is to answer questions. Curiosity invariably pays dividends.

Take a tram-ride back in time to a way of life before the Great War

Beamish recently acquired a new dimension in the shape of **Pockerley Manor & Horse Yard**, which depicts the life of a yeoman farming family in the 1820s, just before the dawn of the Industrial Revolution. We recommend a day out during the summer season, when the whole site is open: during the winter you can still visit the 'Town' and use the tramway, but other areas of the museum are closed.

It is worth allowing a couple of hours both before and after lunch to take in the main areas of interest. There is no set route, although most people tend to head straight for the Town. On busy days, queues for the Drift Mine are longest in the afternoon and only limited numbers can be ferried underground on each trip. Also, if you are running late you may have to skip Pockerley Manor. It is best to visit both the Mine and the Manor earlier rather than later.

You can explore Beamish on foot or ride on the fleet of trams and buses. A **tram circuit**, the longest tramway of its kind in Britain (1½ miles), connects most parts of the museum and it is certainly the most enjoyable way of seeing the sights. The oldest tram is the *Blackpool 31*, built in 1901. If you want to travel by **bus**, sit on the open top of the replica 1913 omnibus that once ran between Chester-le-Street and Gateshead. You can also ride in the Armstrong Whitworth limousine.

Catch a tram at the entrance and get off at the **Colliery Village**. A descent into the dark depths of the **Drift Mine** is one of Beamish's prime attractions. The mine itself dates from the 1850s and was here long before the museum. You can find out what life was like underground, as well as looking at the steam winder and other heavy equipment used to keep this industry working.

The grocery department of the Co-op: the bacon was cut to order, the coffee hand ground

If you visit Beamish during the winter, the best plan is to tour the museum in the morning, then explore the sights of Durham after lunch (see *Great Day Out 124*). Alternatively, phone the **Northumbria tourist information office*** to see if there are any special events in the area.

The nearby row of pit cottages started life at Hetton-le-Hole before being brought to Beamish; along the back street you can see sheds or 'crees' that were put up by the pitmen as workshops and greenhouses. **Pit Hill Chapel** was erected in 1854 to provide spiritual nourishment for the mining community: here, you can watch a magic lantern show depicting festive celebrations and warning townsfolk about 'the Demon Drink'.

Going to school in 1913 was all about discipline and learning by rote. **Beamish Board School** originally belonged to the village of East Stanley before being transplanted to the museum. Take a look at the biological exhibits, the posters and charts illustrating everything from acts of heroism in the British Empire to basic hygiene.

Then stroll across to **Home Farm**. Notice the traditional breeds of livestock – Teeswater sheep, saddleback pigs and shorthorn cattle. Watch the blacksmith at work, and the farmer's wife at her chores in the kitchen. Buy a sample of Beamish cheese from the dairy.

Next stop is **Pockerley Manor & Horse Yard**, where you are straight away caught up in the life of a yeoman farmer. The series of formal gardens, vegetable plots and orchards here is particularly interesting. The latter are planted with old-fashioned varieties such as 'Damask Blush' and 'Pompom de Bourgogne' roses and Hessle and Jargonelle pear trees.

After Pockerley, set a course for the **Town**. If you have worked up a thirst, have a drink at the **Sun Inn**. All the trappings of an old north country pub are here, but don't expect pre-war prices. Draught beers are served using a traditional beer engine. Then call in at **Jubilee Confectioners** to watch sugar being boiled in huge copper pans and the cutters fashioning sweets into myriad shapes – buy some humbugs to suck as you walk around.

Nearby is the **Co-op Store**, amply stocked with beechwood casks of butter, whole cheeses and bags of coffee, as well as working clothes, pots and pit lamps. **The Motor & Cycle Works** re-creates a typical Edwardian town garage; look at the Model T Ford undergoing repairs. The town also has its own **Newspaper Office**, **Dentist's Surgery** and **Solicitor's Office**. And if you fancy a music lesson, visit No. 2 Ravensworth Terrace, the home of Miss Florence Smith, spinster and pianoforte teacher.

To round off your day, make a detour to the **Railway Station**, with its wagons, locomotives, wrought-iron footbridge, weighbridge and signal box. The passenger station building once stood at Rowley, near Consett, and was lit by oil lamps. Finally, have some fun among the carousels and coconut shies on the **Fairground**.

The interior of one of the Pit Cottages at Beamish

LUNCHBOX

Ideally, bring a picnic; several sites are laid out around the Museum. There is a coffee shop by the entrance and a self-service tea room above the Co-op – not to mention the Sun Inn.

A journey into the past along Hadrian's Wall

This is an area steeped in Roman history, vividly brought to life by fragments of Hadrian's Wall, abandoned garrison sites and a trio of well-endowed museums. Walkers will find the countryside challenging and scenic, while the less energetic can explore medieval Hexham.

The best way of seeing the wall is to walk beside it, though bear in mind that the terrain is uneven and undulating and that the ridge can be windy. Three museums and open-air sites vie for your attention – Chesters, Housesteads and Vindolanda – as well as the small market town of Hexham.

Roman armies invaded Britain in AD43 and remained here for the next 350 years, building roads and bridges, towns and temples. It had proved impossible to control the northern tribes, so Emperor Hadrian came up with the idea of defining the northernmost limits of his empire by erecting a wall from coast to coast. He came to Britain in AD122 to oversee the start of the construction, a task which was to take about ten

◆ **GOOD FOR** Family adventures in Roman forts
◆ **TRANSPORT** Haltwhistle and Herham have railway stations and are pick-up points for the Wall Bus (see box)
◆ **ACCESS FOR DISABLED PEOPLE** Access is good for Hexham Abbey, Vindolanda Museum, Chesters
◆ **BEST TIME TO VISIT** All year as long as the weather is fine

years, with constant modifications. The western part of the wall from Bowness to the River Irthing was first made from turf and timber, and the eastern part from locally quarried stone. The wall was a complicated structure, about 18 feet high, with a military way running alongside and a ditch on either side. Every (Roman)

Hadrian's Wall runs for 80 Roman miles (73½ modern miles) from the Tyne to the Solway

The Hadrian's Wall bus operates two services which overlap along the middle section of the wall. The East Bus runs from Hexham to Birdoswald (May to September, weekends and bank holidays), and the West Bus from Carlisle to Vindolanda (May to October, weekdays). From the last week in July until the first weekend in September the East Bus operates every day. Ask for the leaflet *Hadrian's Wall Bus.*

mile there was a fort guarding a gateway (milecastle), with observation posts (turrets) between them. It has been calculated that, with all the posts manned, operating a 24-hour shift system, 10,000 men must have been needed.

Vindolanda (Chesterholm) served as the garrison of several Roman cohorts, and this site has yielded the best finds. The **museum*** is a 15-minute walk from the entrance and contains an outstanding collection of artefacts backed up by taped commentaries. Most exciting are the letters written on thin sheets of wood (shown by enlarged photos), which have been deciphered to reveal party invitations and requests for more beer. On display are hundreds of domestic and personal items, as well as tools, weapons and a reconstructed Roman kitchen. The site (three times larger than the other two) contains many replicas: an attractive Roman temple with painted walls set in a garden with pseudo-Roman tombstones, and two reconstructed turrets, which give you an idea of the original height of the wall. Real remains include the headquarters building with its courtyard and storerooms.

Housesteads (Vercovicium), a fort for 1,000 infantry and a large civilian population, stands on a steep ridge adjoining the south side of the wall and covers five acres. It can be reached only on foot, either by

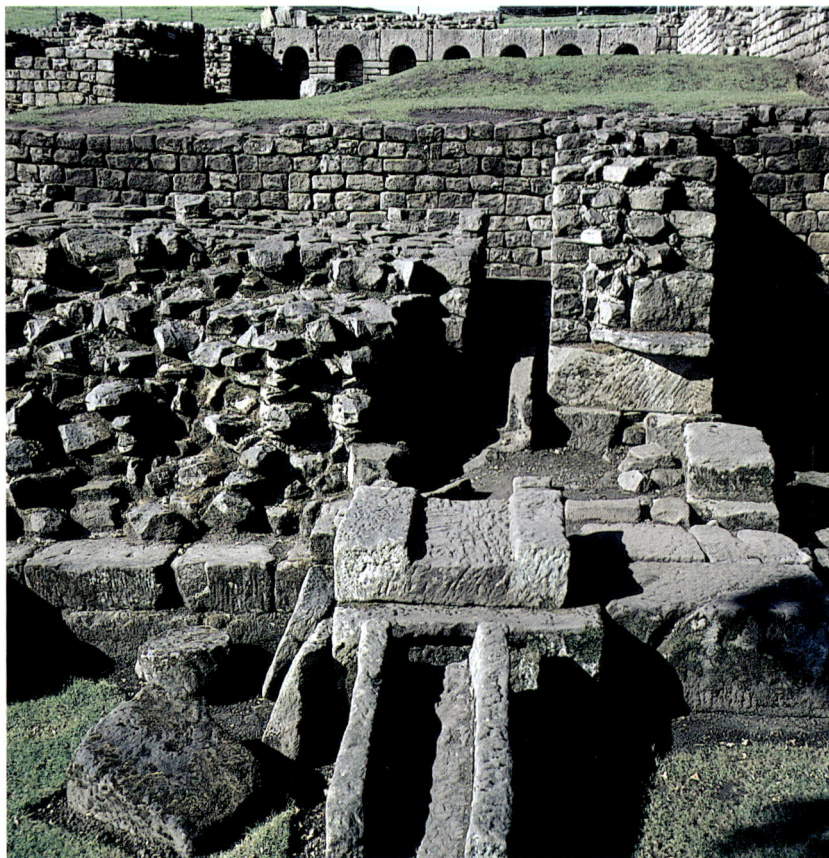

A Roman military bath house, just part of one of the many civilian settlements that grew up around the forts

One popular 2½-mile walk (allow two hours) is eastwards from Steel Rigg, north of Once Brewed National Park Visitors' Centre* to Housesteads. The route is a footpath alongside the wall (walking on the wall itself is discouraged), which starts steeply and then follows a ridge, giving spectacular views of the wall dramatically snaking over the craggy moorland. Highlights are three ruined milecastles, blue Crag Lough below, and a section of shady woods. From Housesteads you can return to Steel Rigg by a lower route.

walking along the wall, or from the car park at the National Trust Visitors' Centre, about half a mile's walk uphill. The **museum*** is by the site and comprises one large room with good descriptions, and a few excavated finds, including jewellery, cooking utensils and stone altars, as well as a lifesize model of a Roman soldier. At the site, visitors see low stone walls, representing outlines of buildings and rooms; aim to see the unique latrine (apparently flushed by water from nearby tanks), the hospital and the granaries.

The Roman cavalry occupied the fort of **Chesters** (Cilurnum) on an attractive site on the bank of the River Tyne. The highlight here is the well-preserved bath-house, with its underfloor heating system, rooms of different temperatures and a changing room with niches for statues. Other

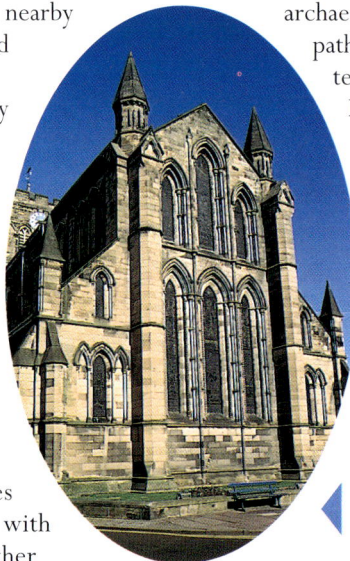

buildings, separated from each other by wire fencing to keep out sheep, include the commandant's house and the barrack blocks as well as some gateways. In the **museum*** is a cluttered array of objects, mostly stone sculptures and reliefs, discovered at many points along the Wall.

If you drive past **Brocolitia** *en route* to Chesters, it's worth visiting this unexcavated fort to get an idea of the daunting tasks faced by archaeologists. Follow the path downhill for about ten minutes to the Roman temple of Mithras; the altars are reproductions, but do create an evocative atmosphere.

Hexham (market day is Tuesday) is set on a hilltop and is dominated by its

The nave of Hexham Abbey was pillaged by the Scots in 1297 and restored only at the beginning of the twentieth century

ancient **abbey***. Formerly a Benedictine monastery founded by St Wilfred in AD674 it was severely damaged by the Danes in the ninth century. The ruins were rescued in 1113 by Augustinian Canons who created a magnificent priory in Early English style; the choir and transepts survive. A worn stone staircase, down which the monks used to enter the church, is a rare relic of the Dissolution of the Monasteries. Try to find a member of the abbey staff to accompany you down the steep stairs of the dank and low-ceilinged Saxon crypt constructed from stones from Corstopitum (Corbridge), some of which bear Latin inscriptions. The abbey is richly furnished and its treasures include the Frith Stool, a sanctuary stone stool thought to have been used by St Wilfred, the tombstone of a first-century Roman standard bearer and a 'Breeches' bible.

Hexham has two other medieval buildings, both rather severe in style: the Town Gaol, now housing the **tourist information office*** and the **Border History Museum***, and the Moot Hall, used for exhibitions. The small museum concentrates on the border warfare of the fifteenth-century reivers by use of tableaux, videos and commentaries, with displays of weapons and armour. The town has narrow streets, some pedestrianised.

LUNCHBOX
Light refreshments are available at small restaurants at Chesters and Vindolanda, and at Housesteads National Trust Visitors' Centre by the car park. There are plenty of eating places at Hexham and Haltwhistle.

Northumberland's secluded National Park

Cragside's 900-acre park becomes aglow with rhododendrons in early summer

KEEP OUT

The 4,000 acre-section of the National Park between the north side of the A68 and the Cheviot Hills is owned by the Ministry of Defence, and most of it is inaccessible to the general public at all times. There are a number of walks and rides around the perimeter of the firing range, but the sign-posted safety regulations should be strictly followed. If you wish to walk in this area and have any doubts about which paths to follow, check with the **Range Control Officer***.

There are two sorts of day to be had in the Northumberland National Park: combine a short walk along Hadrian's Wall (see Great Day Out 126) *with time at Kielder Water; or take a longer walk in nearly 400 square miles of forest, valley and hillside around the Pennine Way.*

The National Park covers a large chunk of Northumberland, stretching from Hexham in the south to the Scottish border in the west, and bounded by Wooler and the B6351 in the north. The area is rich in history: as well as Hadrian's Wall in the south of the area, you can see the Iron Age settlements high above on Otterburn and the fourteenth- and fifteenth-century bastles (fortified farmhouses) and pele towers used by the little farming communities to defend themselves against the marauding reivers of the border country. To the north are acres of bracken-strewn hillsides, bubbling rivers and burns, woodland, valleys and bleak heather moorland – a haven for wildlife; skylarks, curlews and finches circle and chatter overhead in spring and

- ♦ **GOOD FOR** Walkers and lovers of scenery
- ♦ **TRANSPORT** Car necessary
- ♦ **ACCESS FOR DISABLED PEOPLE** Most of the sites are inaccessible to disabled people
- ♦ **BEST TIME TO VISIT** Spring and summer and with care in autumn

summer, while foxes, deer and elusive otters roam freely. To the north-west **Kielder Water** (a man-made reservoir some 30 miles round) has been developed into a magnificent water-sports centre, and facilities for rock-climbing, horse-riding and off-road cycling are available (in the Border Forest Park), as well as many miles of marked woodland trails and some serious hill-walking in the Cheviots.

Drivers wishing to explore the park by road should aim to start off

from **Bellingham** and reach **Wooler** at the end of the day. Bellingham itself is a plain little village which boasts a tiny **Heritage Centre*** with descriptions of local farming practices; it is the starting point for many marked walks leading west into the spruce-planted **Border Forest Park** and north along the **Pennine Way** (see box). From here, the B6320 wiggles along by the side of the North Tyne river; you might like to detour to the right, seven miles along tiny lanes, to look round the roofless, heavily-fortified, sixteenth-century Black Middens Bastle House.

Back on the B6320, the road passes through heavily wooded countryside to Kielder Water. Children will love the reindeer herd and the local Cheviot goats at **High Yarrow Farm***, and will enjoy the sailing, canoeing and windsurfing facilities and tuition available at **Leaplish Waterside Park***. A more leisurely approach would be to take a boat on the reservoir – contact **Kielder Water Cruises***. Fishing permits are available from the **Tower Knowe Visitor Centre***, which also houses an exhibition on the area's history, a restaurant and picnic area, and the walks up into Kielder Forest begin at the **Kielder Castle Visitor Centre***.

From the little settlement of Kielder past the end of the reservoir,

▲ *Sheep-grazing plays an important role in the Cheviot Hills' arable system*

a rough 16-mile toll track owned by the Forestry Commission winds among the trees to the main A68 road just south of **Byrness**, a tiny village and campsite in the Redesdale valley. Turn right at this junction and head ten miles along the side of the River Rede into **Otterburn**, site of a decisive battle in which the Scots routed the English in 1388.

Winding B roads lead north-east from Otterburn to the popular walking centre of **Rothbury**. Here the staff at the **Visitor Centre*** give out expert information about walking routes and weather conditions in the surrounding Coquet valley, Simonside Hills and the Breamish, College and Harthope valleys which run down from the Cheviot Hills. The eastern end of the village is overlooked by **Cragside** (NT)*, the grandiose mock-Tudor home of the eccentric industrialist Lord Armstrong, which in 1880 became the first house in the world to be heated and lit by hydro-electric power. The gloomy, ponderous interior is saved by William Morris's wonderful stained-glass and a marvellously over-the-top pastiche of a Renaissance fireplace in the main drawing-room.

From Rothbury either follow the A697 north to Wooler or drive alongside the River Coquet to **Chew Green Roman Camp**, where the foundations of the massive fort are still clearly etched into the ground. Further north, the Cheviot Hills provide more hearty walking country, including the arduous trek up **Cheviot** itself, at 2,700 feet the highest hill in the range (this climb can also be done as part of the walk along the Pennine Way, but is not recommended for a family day out).

Wooler, a small market town, lies seven miles north-east of the Cheviot; another main walking centre, it has a **tourist information office***, a few youth hostels, a campsite, a couple of decent cafés and the **Earle Hill Museum***, with a strange collection of farm machinery. James IV of Scotland was killed in fierce fighting at nearby Flodden in 1513; the Iron Age hill fort at Yeavering Bell north-west of Wooler affords extensive views across the battlefield.

THE PENNINE WAY

Perhaps the most popular way to view the National Park is along the Pennine Way, which enters the National Park at Greenhead by Hadrian's Wall before wandering off to the north through the spruce-planted Wark Forest to Bellingham and Byrness, skirting around the Otterburn firing range and up through the foothills of the Cheviots, thence to Kirk Yetholm at the northern extremity of the park. This part of the Pennine Way covers 64 miles, but it can be divided into quite manageable sections for a family ramble. Remember that the weather in the park can be extremely changeable, so always take sound footwear and warm clothing with you.

For gentle walks, try the sections of the Pennine Way between Bellingham and Stonehaugh to the south, Bellingham and Hareshaw Burn to the north or a shorter stroll along the River Rede into Byrness. More strenuous is the section between Hadrian's Wall and Bellingham (15 miles' hard slog across wild moorland); from Byrness the Pennine Way heads 27 miles north across hill country to Kirk Yetholm and across the border into Scotland.

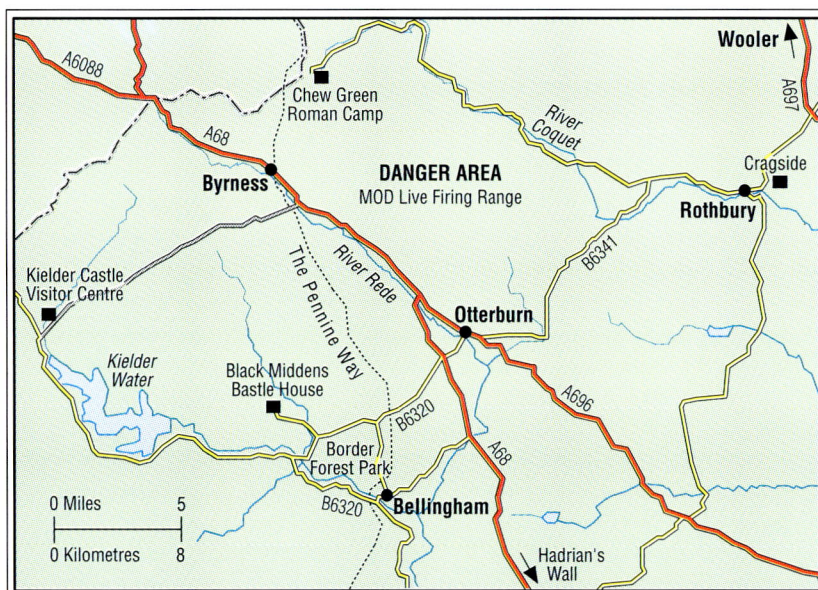

The rugged, windswept Northumberland coast

Boats in Lindisfarne Harbour, with Bamburgh Castle in the distance

This extensive itinerary takes in exploring the islands, castles and towns of the rugged coastline between Bamburgh and Berwick, an area steeped in early Christian history and rich in wildlife.

There is far too much to do in this unspoilt corner of Northumberland in one day, so choose from the suggested possibilities to suit your party. You can visit an island wildlife sanctuary, explore the religious centre of Holy Island, tour Bamburgh Castle or promenade around the Elizabethan walls of Berwick-upon-Tweed. If you have young children and the weather looks promising, take a picnic and combine a boat ride to the Farne Islands with a trip to one of the many quiet beaches like Spittal, or Druridge Bay further south.

From Seahouses (south-east of Bamburgh) take a boat out to the **Farne Islands**, a string of rocky islets scattered a couple of miles off the coast; full details of cruises are available from the **tourist information office***. The islands are run as a nature reserve by the

- ♦ **GOOD FOR** Sea birds, and early Christian and Border history
- ♦ **TRANSPORT** Car necessary
- ♦ **ACCESS FOR DISABLED PEOPLE** Museums only
- ♦ **BEST TIME TO VISIT** Spring, summer

National Trust, providing a summer refuge for thousands of migratory sea birds and for one of Britain's biggest colonies of grey seals. Only **Staple** and **Inner Farne** are open to tourists; on the latter a small exhibition features the teeming wildlife of the islands, and you can peer into a tiny fourteenth-century chapel built in honour of St Cuthbert, an early Christian hermit who spend many years here.

Bamburgh is the next port of call, three miles north of Seahouses, a pretty little village clustered round an open green and dominated by a

formidable **castle*** glaring sternly out to sea. The site has been a fort since Roman times, and later the Angle kings ruled Northumbria from here, but the present stone edifice, with its extended keep (12 feet thick in places), dates from Norman times.

Over the years, the castle was extended, abandoned and rebuilt several times, eventually falling into disrepair before it was bought by the industrial magnate Lord Armstrong in 1893. He oversaw extensive refurbishment, including the enormous wooden-ceilinged Grand King's Hall, which boasts delicately worked animal carvings by Fabergé. Like nearby Cragside (see *Great Day Out 127*), Armstrong's previous residence, the castle is crammed with gloomy late-Victorian prints and paintings, heavy furniture and elaborate porcelain; a collection of armour can be seen in the basement of the Norman keep. The **Armstrong Museum**, which celebrates the life of the founder of the family fortune, is housed in the former laundry, and odd bits of flying memorabilia are displayed in the **Aviation Artefacts Museum**.

The village of Bamburgh itself is notable chiefly for the **Grace Darling Museum***, which pays homage to the local girl who became a national heroine in 1838 when she and her lighthouse-keeper father rescued the crew of a sinking steamship called the SS *Forfarshire*, preventing them from being dashed against rocks off the Farne Islands. The museum contains a motley assortment of Grace's clothes and belongings. Her ostentatious mock-Gothic grave lies in the churchyard opposite the museum.

Ten miles north of Bamburgh, cut across the tidal flats on a three-mile causeway, eerily bordered by sodden marker poles, to **Holy Island**. Remember to check tidal

Lindisfarne Castle: gaunt fortress outside, comfortable home inside

information with the **tourist information office*** in Berwick – otherwise you may be delayed while the tide ebbs (there are also notices at both ends of the causeway). Also known as **Lindisfarne**, the island is long-famous as the birthplace of English Christianity; the first priory was founded here in 635 by St Aidan of Iona at the invitation of Oswald, king of pagan Northumbria. St Cuthbert was bishop for a short while, but scuttled back to his hermetic existence on Inner Farne, having found life on Holy Island too hectic. The monks of Holy Island became great scholars and were responsible for crafting the beautifully illuminated **Lindisfarne Gospels**, preserved in the British Museum (see *Great Day Out 44*).

After the Norman invasions in the eleventh century, Lindisfarne was taken over by French Benedictine monks. It is the ruins of their **priory** that you see today, all sweeping Romanesque arches and decorative brickwork, with the thirteenth-century ruins of the Church of St Mary the Virgin abutting. The **Visitor Centre*** explains how the medieval monks and scholars lived, and charts the decline of the monastery. Close by in the little stone village is a statue of St Aidan staring out to sea, his hand raised in supplication.

A ten-minute trek away is **Lindisfarne Castle***, built on top of a steep crag in 1550 to protect the harbour from attack by the Scots. This threat had receded by the seventeenth century and the castle fell into disuse; it was not until 1901 that it was rescued from ruin, when the publishing entrepreneur Edward Hudson fell in love with it, bought it and persuaded the architect Edwin Lutyens to turn in into a cosy family home. It still retains its austerity, however, with vast stone fireplaces, arches and columns adorning enormous panelled rooms. Even in this storm-battered place, Lutyens' collaborator Gertrude Jekyll managed to design a thriving walled garden.

Children will enjoy seeing rare breeds of farm animals at **Saint Coombes Open Farm***. For those wishing to stay overnight, there are a couple of bed and breakfast places on the island.

The best time to see puffins on the Farne Islands is between April and July

Otherwise, return across the water to **Berwick**, a smart town 12 miles north on the border and scene of countless skirmishes between the Scots and English. Berwick's changing fortunes reflected this cross-border warfare; the prosperous thirteenth-century Scots port declined into an impoverished garrison town when the English isolated it from its trading routes, and by the 1550s it was a tatty backwater. Queen Elizabeth I then decided to repair Berwick's crumbling fortifications, and spent a fortune on the construction of ramparts around the town. Peace between England and Scotland meant that these defences never saw military action. Today they stand pristine, 1½ miles long, 20 feet high and monstrously thick – and quite the best place to walk round and admire the old town, the architecture of Georgian mansions such as **Quay Walls** on the riverside, the extensive views along the Northumbria coast and the three great bridges spanning the River Tweed.

Unsurprisingly, Berwick has several museums; the **Barracks*** complex houses three such, although the one likely to be of most interest is the **Borough Museum***, featuring aspects of local history and a marvellous art collection given by the Glasgow millionaire Sir William Burrell (see also *Great Day Out 135*). The **Town Hall and Cell Block Museum*** provides yet more historical artefacts and the chance to ring the town bells, and in the **Wine and Spirit Museum*** you will find pottery and brewing equipment as well as a reconstructed Victorian chemist's. There is also an arts centre at the **Maltings***, with theatre, exhibitions, café, bar and restaurant.

LUNCHBOX

At Bamburgh castle meals and snacks are available in the Clock Tower Tea Rooms, while on Holy Island oysters are the speciality at the Crown and Anchor pub. In Berwick, for a fabulous seafood extravaganza try the Rob Roy restaurant on Dock Road, or Humble Pie on Marygate for good vegetarian cooking. The King's Arms on Hide Hill has three decent restaurants, including an Italian-style café.

Marauding in the Borders: four ruined abbeys

The ruined medieval abbeys and majestic castles of the Border country, with its troubled past, provide wonderful settings for a day out that combines the rugged outdoors with extravagant interiors.

King David I, who reigned from 1124 to 1153, founded the four great medieval abbeys of Jedburgh, Kelso, Dryburgh and Melrose; he had his reasons. The Borders had suffered constant raids by the English and had also taken a battering from continual local feuding. The abbeys were offered to various powerful monastic orders as a sweetener by which the monarch hoped to gain the support and allegiance of the monks, who had enough economic and political sway to influence the local folk. To a certain extent this ploy was successful, and the region enjoyed a period of relative stability until the sixteenth century, when the English started raiding the Borders again in the run-up to the Reformation.

The Gothic ruins of **Jedburgh Abbey** (founded in 1138) stand on a hill overlooking Jed Water. The abbey flourished until the late thirteenth century, when civil war reduced the

- ◆ **GOOD FOR** Ruins, views, river walks and fabulous interiors
- ◆ **TRANSPORT** Car necessary
- ◆ **ACCESS FOR DISABLED PEOPLE** Access is good at Dryburgh and Jedburgh
- ◆ **BEST TIME TO VISIT** Spring and summer; some sights are closed in winter

power of the Scots monarchy; it was repeatedly damaged and rebuilt before the Reformation in 1560, when even the most determined monks gave up and left. A beautiful rose window is still intact, as is the three-storey nave of breathtaking architectural complexity.

The abbey's history is recounted in its **Visitor Centre***; evocative Gregorian chant punctuates the story at intervals. Close by is the **Mary, Queen of Scots House and Visitor Centre*** in a many-storeyed fortified stone tower-house where, it is said, Mary spent a night in 1556.

The exhibition tells the tragic story of Mary Stuart's life from her birth in 1542 to her execution at Fotheringay Castle in 1587. Castlegate is dominated by castellated **Jedburgh Castle Jail***, built in 1820 to a design by the popular architect Archibald Elliot. Reconstructed rooms and period costume depict prison life in the early nineteenth century.

The A698 runs north from Jedburgh to **Kelso**, a small town on the banks of the River Tweed. Here King David commissioned a Romanesque abbey for the Tironensian order in 1128. This took 80 years to build and survived relatively unscathed for four centuries until 1545 when the worst of three razings by the English, led by Henry VIII's envoy, the Earl of Hertford, left it devastated. Only a vast arched buttress at the west end, adjoining a central tower remains. The **Kelso Museum Turret House***, found in Abbey Court, is an unusual white-washed tower owned by the National Trust for Scotland; it contains a skinner's workshop, a reconstructed market, a Victorian classroom and the requisite history of the abbey.

The most splendid of the Borders castles, **Floors**, is just north of Kelso on the A6089 – a lovely walk along the meandering River Tweed will take you there from the town centre. Set in rolling parkland, this huge pile, with its turrets, towers and wings, is the largest inhabited castle in Scotland and home to the Duke of Roxburghe. Only ten rooms of William Adam's spectacular creation are open to the public, but they are decorated with priceless works of art and opulent furnishings, and the estate is a delight to wander around.

Mellerstain House, six miles north of Kelso, was also partly built by William Adam; the wings were completed in 1725, and Adam's son

Mellerstain's interior is perhaps the finest monument to Georgian caprice in Scotland

STAYING AT TRAQUAIR
Bed and breakfast accommodation is available at Traquair House, in huge bedrooms with romantic canopied beds. The fly-fishing for trout and salmon on this stretch of the River Tweed is superb, and other attractions in the grounds include a traditional brewery producing beer to a secret recipe, craft workshops, tea rooms and a gift shop.

Robert added the main bulk of the house 40 years later – a novel way of building a house but, here at least, eminently successful. The interior has twisted colonnades and ornate moulded ceilings which offset the classic proportions of the elegant, richly furnished rooms. The gardens are terraced and formal, with views across the park down to the lake.

Back on the abbey trail, follow the winding A6105 down to **Dryburgh Abbey**, passing Smailholm Tower (see *Great Day Out 130*) to the left. David's third monastery, beside the Tweed, did not flourish as the others did; it was presented to a renegade monastic order known as the White Canons, who squabbled among themselves. The abbey was partly destroyed during the Wars of Independence in the fourteenth century, before finally being razed in 1545 at the same time as Kelso Abbey. These ruins are perhaps the most beautiful and best-preserved of the four and are surrounded by massive cedar trees and carefully kept lawns. The abbey contains the tomb of Sir Walter Scott (see *Great Day Out 130*), and Field Marshal Earl Haig is also buried here.

Melrose Abbey boasts the tomb of Robert the Bruce, or at least that of his heart. The abbey was founded for the Cistercians in 1136; they were a worldly order who made money from selling wool, but their success was short-lived as the abbey suffered throughout the Wars of Independence before being destroyed in 1545 by the Earl of Hertford. The remains are an intricate lattice-work of arches and windows, mainly dating from the fifteenth century when the monks stoically rebuilt the abbey several times. A museum in the **Commendator's House** next to the abbey illustrates its history and displays finds from a Roman dig at nearby Trimontium.

Nearly 30 Scots and English monarchs have visited historic **Traquair House*** (80 miles from Melrose, just south of Innerleithen, via Galashiels and the A72). The oldest part of the building dates from the tenth century and it has been continually inhabited by the Maxwell-Stuart family ever since. Half-house, half-fortress, the whitewashed building grew piecemeal to look like a cosy, miniature baronial castle, topped with turrets and towers. It is less grand than Floors, but has more hidden priest's holes and priceless bric-a-brac collected down the ages from various aristocratic guests. Historically, the family was staunchly Catholic, as a result of which the fifth earl spent two years in the Tower of London for his part in the Jacobite Rebellion of 1745. Legend has it that the Bear Gates at the back of the house were swung shut after Bonnie Prince Charlie's defeat, never to be opened until a Stuart king sits on the British throne. For more information about these sights, phone Hawick **tourist information office***.

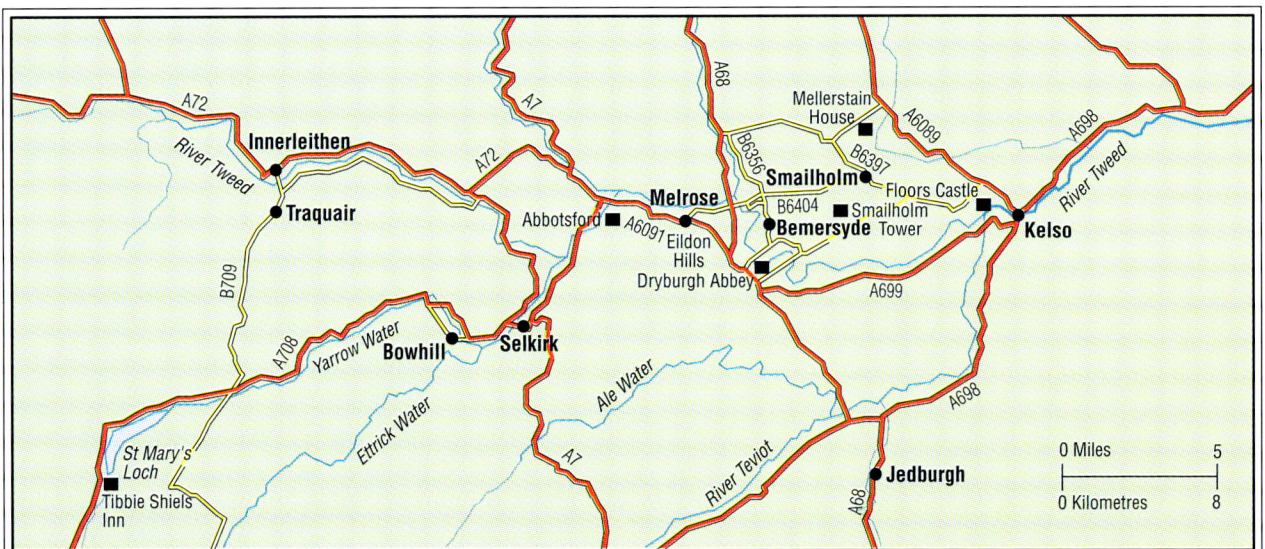

Walter Scott's beloved country

Abbotsford House, where Scott relished the role of Tweedside laird

A historic literary tour through the Border country following in the patriotic footsteps of Sir Walter Scott.

Ruined medieval abbeys, brave little towns that withstood years of siege from the English raiders, old family castles and mansions and the rich loveliness of the River Tweed – these are just a few of the pleasures to be discovered in this little-visited region.

The poet and novelist Sir Walter Scott (1771–1832), with his sentimental tales of noble Scots and their fiery passions, probably did more than anyone to extol the beauty and charm of his country. He grew up in Edinburgh, the son of a wealthy professional family, and was a brilliant, though sickly, scholar. After qualifying as a Writer to the Signet (lawyer) he left Edinburgh to live in the Borders, an area he had grown to love during the summers he spent

- ♦ **GOOD FOR** Landscape and literature
- ♦ **TRANSPORT** A car is essential
- ♦ **ACCESS FOR DISABLED PEOPLE** Easy at Teddy Bear Museum and Bowhill House; ring other venues for details
- ♦ **BEST TIME TO VISIT** April to October

convalescing at his grandfather's farm at Sandyknowe near the tiny hamlet of **Smailholm**. By his early teens he had become adept at romanticising the bloodthirsty feuding and constant attack by the reivers (thieves) that formed the backdrop of Borders history.

Sir Walter Scott bought Cartley Hall farm, on the banks of the River Tweed, in 1812 with the proceeds of his poems and novels, and lived there for the last 20 years of his life. He

demolished most of the original building, re-named it and gradually added a stepped gable here, a turret there, another wing, a beautiful baronial entrance hall, buttresses and towers until he had customised **Abbotsford House*** into an architectural fantasia, his mellow-stoned 'conundrum castle'. The interior is just as grandiose and eclectic; Scott borrowed ideas from local abbeys and castles and incorporated them into his dream.

Sir Walter was a passionate collector of historic relics and a tour of the house includes such curiosities as Rob Roy's gun, Napoleon's writing case, a lock of Bonnie Prince Charlie's hair, breastplates and helmets from the Battle of Waterloo and a pearl-inlaid crucifix belonging to Mary, Queen of Scots. Don't miss the panelled study, the library lined with over 9,000 rare volumes, an armoury and the dining-room in which Scott died in his bed on 21 September 1832. He had suffered a stroke earlier that year and had travelled to the Mediterranean to recover. However, he was taken ill and on his return he requested that his bed be brought down to the dining-room so he could look out at his 'beloved Tweed'. Outside in the gardens, a line of classical arches and fortified walls set off the manicured lawns and topiary trees. Beyond all the artifice, the tree-laden hills slope gently down to the Tweed.

Nearby **Melrose** was Scott's local town and today it is home of the **Teddy Bear Museum***, where Winnie the Pooh and Paddington are waiting to greet you. The abbey ruins (see *Great Day Out 129*) dominate the little town. From here, you can walk in the sweeping **Eildon Hills** and along the **Tweed Valley**, both sources of inspiration for Scott. The **Melrose Motor Museum*** (full of automotive curiosities) and

St Mary's Loch is popular with sailors and anglers and can be crowded at weekends

Priorwood Garden* (NTS) (specialising in plants for drying) make interesting diversions for those wishing a less literary diet.

Follow the A6091 from Melrose and turn on to the B6356 north to steep Bemersyde Hill and **Scott's View**, the writer's favourite spot for quiet reflection, with far-reaching vistas taking in the Tweed, the undulating Cheviot Hills, the forests and fields. Continue to **Dryburgh Abbey** (see *Great Day Out 129*), where Scott is buried.

Beyond the silent ruins of Dryburgh on the B6404 stands **Smailholm Tower** (Historic Scotland), open between April and September. The tower was built in the sixteenth century as a fortified house and safe haven from raids by English mercenaries. It reaches to an impenetrable 57 feet, with walls six feet thick, made of great, heavy boulders. The tower was further protected by its position atop a grass-covered mound by the side of a tiny, reedy lochan. According to local legend, the tower owes its preservation to Walter Scott, who persuaded the local laird to save it in return for one of his ballads. Its gaunt and threatening appearance is somewhat belied nowadays by the exhibition of costumed dolls depicting characters from Scott's *Minstrelsy of the Scottish Borders*.

Twelve miles west in **Selkirk** the **Scott Monument** dominates the Market Place and celebrates Scott's role as sheriff of the county for 33 years. Two other monuments stand close by: one to explorer and doctor Mungo Park (1771–1806), the other honouring the Scottish victory at the Battle of Flodden Field in 1513. The **tourist information**

Dryburgh Abbey is the resting place of Sir Walter Scott and Field Marshal Earl Haig

office* is in the Market Place in **Halliwell's House***, now an excellent museum of local history. At a glass-making factory on the outskirts of town you can watch paperweights being made.

Continue west down the A708 to the magnificent early nineteenth-century **Bowhill House***, seat of the dukes of Buccleuch (house open only in July). A stunning collection of Old Master paintings, including a Leonardo da Vinci, is on display. The expansive wooded estate is open daily in the summer and offers nature trails, walking, bike hire and a riding centre – another day out in itself.

St Mary's Loch is a few miles on from Bowhill through the Yarrow valley. A crooked, reedy stretch of water overlooked by the Wiss (1,993 feet), it is at the heart of the walking country of the Southern Uplands. **Tibbie Shiel's Inn***, at the southern end of the loch, is famous for the nineteenth-century *literati* that drank there – Robert Louis Stevenson and Thomas Carlyle were frequent recipients of Scott's hospitality here. Now the inn welcomes walkers and Scott pilgrims alike for a pint of local heavy and a solid meal.

To the north of St Mary's Loch is **Innerleithen**. Scott based his novel *St Ronan's Well* on the **natural springs** in the hills behind the town and, predictably, when his readers identified this fact, they rushed in their thousands to take the waters, bringing their money, which all seemed to fall into the hands of the local landowners, the earls of Traquair. The National Trust for Scotland also runs **Robert Smail's Printing Works*** – a museum which provides a fascinating insight into the life of a jobbing printer from the early nineteenth century onwards. Pride of place goes to a water-driven printing press.

LUNCHBOX

Abbotsford House offers refreshments. In Melrose, Burts Hotel has long been popular with tourists and locals alike. Tibbie Shiel's Inn and the Crook Inn, near Broughton, produce excellent food and have the added bonus of being haunts of literary figures such as Walter Scott, Robert Burns and John Buchan.

The banks and braes of Burns country

❄ ♿

The Auld Kirk in Alloway where Tam o' Shanter saw 'warlocks and witches in a dance'

Follow in the footsteps of Scotland's best-loved poet, Robert Burns, around the lush and peaceful countryside of south-west Scotland.

Robert Burns loved, lost and fell in love again so often that it is a wonder he had the time or energy to write any poetry at all. But write he did, while travelling all over this tranquil area of rolling hills, soft glens and forest wedged between the Irish Sea and the Solway Firth. The main tourist routes rush northwards from the border, leaving Dumfries and Galloway unspoilt and uncrowded and – Burns is not the only attraction here – dotted with stately homes, gardens, castles and wildlife parks. In fact, the **Burns Heritage Trail**, which starts in Ayr, is so comprehensive that all but the most ardent of his fans will probably prefer to concentrate on Dumfries and Alloway.

The story of 'Caledonia's Bard' begins in **Alloway**, a small village

♦ **GOOD FOR** Appreciating the quiet corner of Scotland that is most closely associated with Robert Burns
♦ **TRANSPORT** A car is necessary
♦ **ACCESS FOR DISABLED PEOPLE** Possible at most sights but no wheelchair access to National Burns Memorial in Mauchline
♦ **BEST TIME TO VISIT** Any time of year

just south of Ayr. Burns was born here on 25 January 1759, the son of a poor farm labourer. He grew up to be a charismatic, handsome man with a fearsome reputation for womanising. The little thatched, whitewashed cottage where he was born is part of the **Burns Cottage and Museum*** complex. The story of the poet's life is told alongside a display of ephemera such as the

family's bible and some of his original manuscripts.

Just down the road to the left is the **Tam o' Shanter Experience***. This is housed in a modern museum, updated in early 1995, and incorporates the Land o' Burns Centre. It is an excellent introduction to Burns' life and work, transporting visitors back to eighteenth-century Alloway by means of multimedia presentations to bring alive his most famous character, the rogue Tam o' Shanter. On sale in the bookshop are editions of his poetry, several biographies and histories of the region.

Almost opposite is the roofless shell of the **Auld Kirk**, built in 1510 and the scene of drunken Tam's encounter with the dancing witches. Beyond is the **Auld Brig o'Doon**, the hump-backed, thirteenth-century bridge across which he fled in terror from the 'hellish legion' on his gray mare Meg.

Overlooking the River Doon is the elaborate **Burns Monument***, a folly built in 1823 as a neo-classical temple, with exotically carved colonnades supporting a dome topped by dolphins and a Grecian urn. The interior is somewhat plainer; a small room where bibles, locks of hair and other treasures belonging to some of Burns' lovers, and even a translation of his work into Esperanto, are on display. The verdant gardens surrounding the monument are planted with rare flowers and shrubs, and a little pavilion shelters stone statues of Tam o' Shanter and his drinking companion the cobbler Souter Johnny.

More Rabbie Burns nostalgia is on offer in nearby **Mauchline**, where several of his children are buried in the church in the centre of the village. The **tourist information office*** is in the base of the **National Burns Memorial***, a tower with a local history museum on the second floor, and splendid views across hills and rich farmland from the viewing platform at the top. At **Mossgiel** (on the outskirts of Mauchline) Burns farmed for several years, and at **Tarbolton** he socialised long and rowdily with a debating group which met at the **Bachelor's Club*** in a property now owned by the National Trust for Scotland.

You can also encounter the spirit of Burns in other parts of Ayrshire: in Irvine, Kilmarnock and Kirkoswald, before you head towards Dumfries on the A76.

Some seven miles north of Dumfries is the small farm of **Ellisland***, which was home to Burns, his wife Jean Armour and infant son Robert from 1788 to 1791; a second son, Francis, was born here in 1789. Burns built the cosy, whitewashed farmhouse where he produced some of his best-known works, including 'Tam o' Shanter' and 'Auld Lang Syne'. The farm buildings and cottage have recently been restored and you will find an audio-visual presentation as well as general Burns memorabilia. There are also some peaceful walks along the River Nith. Sadly, the farm could not yield sufficient to support Burns and his family and he was forced to move on to Dumfries to work full-time as an exciseman.

Dumfries itself is an old sandstone town through which the River Nith wanders on its way to the Solway Firth. The largest town in south-west Scotland, with a

Some Burns memorabilia in his cottage in Alloway

population of about 32,000, it is the hub of an agricultural community stretching to the west to the hills and moors of Galloway.

In 1791, Burns and his family moved into three small rooms on the second floor of a red-brick worker's cottage at **11 Bank Street**. His regular haunts included the **Globe Inn** just off the High Street. (The barmaid gave birth to Elizabeth, his first daughter.) The panelled snug bar is crammed with Burnsian memorabilia, including his chair. After a year at Bank Street, the birth of another (legitimate) daughter made the lodgings too cramped and the family moved again to 24 Mill Street (now **Burns Street**). Burns wrote a great deal here, including 'My love is like a red

red rose', and died in 1796, probably of rheumatic heart disease. The cottage now forms the **Burns House Museum*** and contains a fascinating collection of personal belongings and original furniture, such as his writing desk and chair.

Burns was buried in **St Michael's** churchyard. When his neo-classical **Mausoleum**, complete with a statue of him communing with a Muse, was completed in 1815, his remains were removed here; many of his family and dearest friends lie in the same churchyard (there is an explanatory plaque at the entrance to the graveyard). Following his death, a huge, sparkling white **statue of Burns** was erected outside Greyfriars Church in Dumfries High Street. He clutches a tiny bunch of flowers and his dog Luath is curled at his feet. The dog was said to be the inspiration for the poem 'The Twa Dogs'.

The **Robert Burns Centre*** in Mill Street was opened in 1986 in the town's old water-mill. This award-winning centre now contains an audio-visual theatre, temporary exhibitions concentrating on Burns' life in Dumfries and a bookshop.

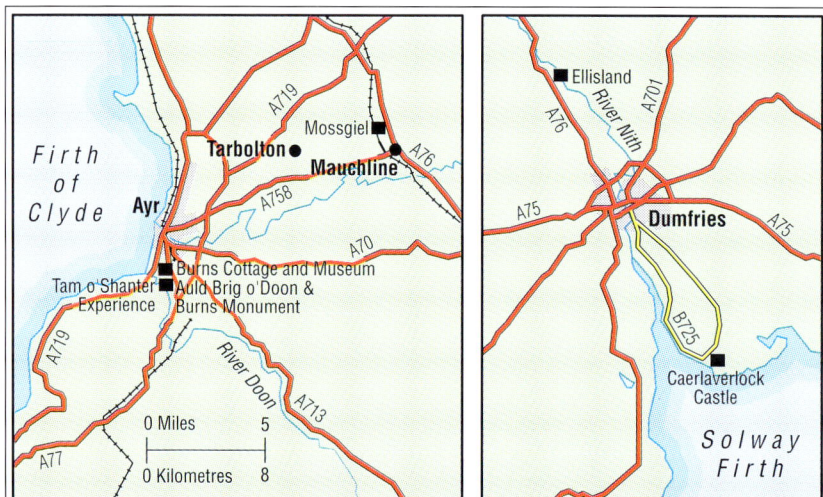

The glories of the Galloway Forest Park

Glen Trool and the Southern Upland Way: prime walking country

Two interesting attractions on the southern edge of the Park are the **Mill on the Fleet Heritage Centre***, a fascinating conversion of a former bobbin mill at Gatehouse-of-Fleet which portrays the industrial history of this handsome little place (good for scones too). Further east, the **Creetown Gem Rock Museum*** is a treasure trove of minerals and spectacular rocks.

The Galloway Forest Park, like a photo on a shortbread tin but without all the tartan trimmings, is the largest park of its kind in Britain. It covers over 300 square miles of hills, lochs and, naturally, forest and is a walker's paradise.

Mile upon mile of conifer, but also plenty of mixed woodland and natural features: the Galloway Forest Park has grand scenery in abundance. The plantings across this rugged area were first planned more than seventy years ago to produce timber for industrial purposes – paper, chipboard and sawn wood. This is Forestry Commission territory so there are no problems getting around, except where local conditions or felling operations temporarily close off tracks or trails (of which there are more than 200 waymarked miles).

From Newton Stewart at the southern approaches to the Forest Park, drive north along the A714, enjoying fine views north-east over the woods by the River Cree to the big, bare hills of the interior. Follow signs into Glen Trool beyond Bargrennan, turning into the deep

♦ **GOOD FOR** Woodland walks and stupendous scenery
♦ **TRANSPORT** A car is essential (80 miles round trip)
♦ **ACCESS FOR DISABLED PEOPLE** Possible at Glen Trool Visitor Centre and Clatteringshaws Forest Wildlife Centre
♦ **BEST TIME TO VISIT** Any time – but check local weather forecast. Early summer for Wood of Cree; the visitor centres are closed out of season

woods. Stop at the **Glen Trool Visitor Centre*** by Stroan Bridge, where you can stock up on leaflets galore on the various walks and trails (and some good home-bakes, too).

Then drive to the road end overlooking **Loch Trool**. Here is quintessential Galloway scenery, which you can view from the top of a knoll. With loch, wooded slopes and high hills it is quite a surprise if you

expect such scenery only in the 'real' Highlands of Scotland.

The English army of occupation which passed this way in 1307 had no time for enjoying the views. During the campaign of the Scots Wars of Independence, Robert the Bruce, Scotland's King Robert I, and his men ambushed them just across the loch, rolling boulders down from the heights above. An inscribed stone recalls the event. This is also the starting point for climbing the **Merrick**, the highest hill in the Southern Uplands, best given a full day. Below you, a walk also goes round Loch Trool – but if you want to take in the overall shape of the Forest Park, then that also should wait for another day.

Make your way back along the glen, this time going left beyond Stroan Bridge to follow a slightly claustrophobic back road through the conifers; then go left to emerge between the woods and the River Cree, parallel to the A714 but on the other bank and with a more pleasant and open outlook. Watch for signs for the RSPB reserve at the **Wood of Cree**. Follow the nature trail here, at least as far as the viewpoint over the marshy river, to compare the impoverished, almost monotonous, plantings in places of the mass coniferous with the richness of the flora and fauna to be found in this ancient fragment of semi-natural oakwood. One bird you are bound to see is the handsome little black and white pied flycatcher, but there are plenty of other species singing madly in late spring, such as warblers and pipits by the hundred (look out for the nesting boxes).

Join the A712 north-east of Newton Stewart. This main road is known as the Queen's Way. Note in passing on your right the parking space at **Glen of the Bar**, where Forest Enterprise has erected a particularly imaginative viewing platform and display board. The text describes a hunt by Bronze Age warriors long before the area was swathed in conifers. Further on, **Murray's Monument**, high on the left, recalls Alexander Murray, who was born in 1775, the son of a poor shepherd living nearby. In spite of his humble origins he rose to become Professor of Oriental Languages at Edinburgh University. His monument is also close to a **wild goat park**. These shaggy creatures in various shades of brown, white and grey used to roam the hills before the forests were planted. Now they are conserved as a useful gene pool should they ever be required to introduce a hard-wearing strain of cashmere. Of the many forest walks nearby, one goes off to the **Grey Mare's Tail Waterfall**.

Again, only a few minutes further on – distances seem short hereabouts – you will come upon the

Bruce's Stone in Loch Trool recalls the Scottish ambush of the English troops in 1307

Clatteringshaws Forest Wildlife Centre*. Whereas the Glen Trool Visitor Centre takes a historic theme, this place tells you about the wildlife. Then backtrack along the A712 until you see the Raider's Road Forest Drive sign.

The **Raider's Road** follows the line of an old drove road and joins the A762 to the east. Along the way, make sure you stop at the **Otter Pool**, a delectable spot where the River Dee flows between flat rocks and islets in a sheltered grove, scented with bog myrtle. Another good stop, especially if you find old railway structures

romantic, is the peaceful **Stroan Loch**, where the former main line to Stranraer (the 'Port Road') crossed the River Dee on a handsome viaduct. The line closed in 1965, but the viaduct stands poignantly as a monument to Victorian engineering and a vanished way of life. A pleasant walk goes south, under the arches. Continue to the A762, where you could turn south to return to Newton Stewart via an unclassified road that runs from Laurieston to Gatehouse of Fleet, then take the very scenic B796 to Creetown, leaving only a short stretch on the busy A75.

SOUTHERN UPLAND WAY

This is Scotland's only east-west 'official' long-distance footpath, taking a switchback route 212 miles across the grain of the Southern Uplands between Portpatrick and Cockburnspath. It passes through the Galloway Forest Park along the opposite bank of Loch Trool to the road – useful if you are planning to 'circumnavigate' the loch on foot.

THE QUEEN'S WAY

The route of the A712 lies on or close to the old pilgrim road which led down to the Machars (below the Park) and on to Whithorn, the earliest Christian community in Scotland. It is associated with the Stewart monarchs, notably Mary, Queen of Scots, although it received its official title of the Queen's Way only in 1977 with the jubilee of Queen Elizabeth I (of Scotland).

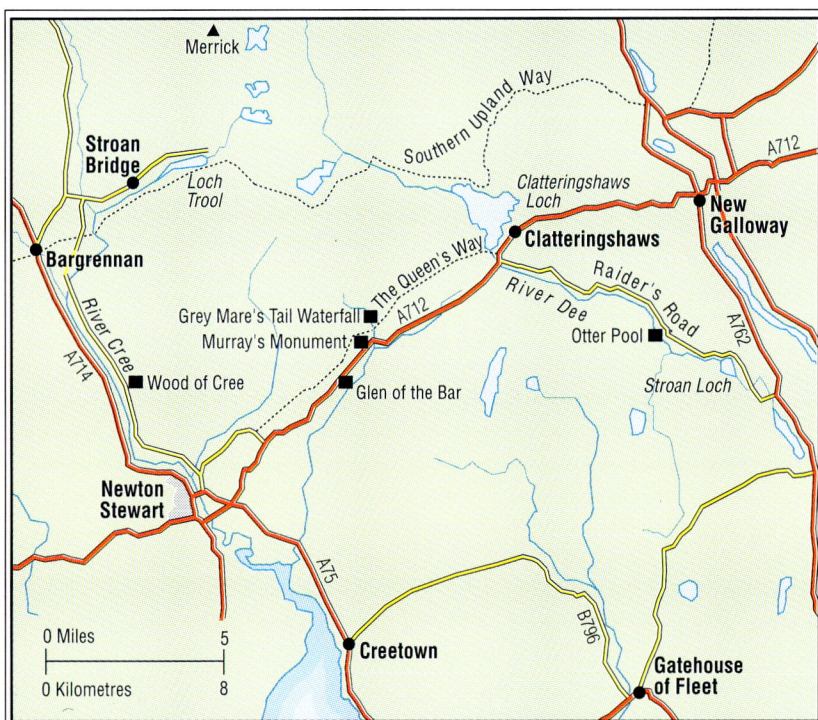

The best of Edinburgh's Old and New Towns

☂ ❄ 🚐

Pipers beating the retreat on the Esplanade of Edinburgh Castle

Here we suggest a whistle-stop tour of Edinburgh's major sights, from the medieval castle to the Georgian New Town, also taking in the Palace of Holyroodhouse and attractions all along the Royal Mile.

Edinburgh is divided into two parts, the Old and New Towns, by the gorge of Princes Street gardens. It is a rugged and beautiful city, imbued with history and culture, from the dour granite castle that dominates the west end of Princes Street to the neo-classical elegance of the spacious squares of the New Town. In between are palaces, museums, galleries, monuments, statues and Arthur's Seat, the famous volcanic landmark on the eastern edge of the city.

Inevitably, the **castle*** is the starting point for exploring the Old Town. It stands high over the city on a great crag of stone and from the steep, battlemented **Esplanade** there are unparalleled views across

- ♦ **GOOD FOR** Anyone with a love for art and history
- ♦ **TRANSPORT** Waverley BR station is right in the centre. Parking is difficult and expensive in the city
- ♦ **ACCESS FOR DISABLED PEOPLE** In general not good, although a lift, ramps and a courtesy vehicle enable disabled visitors to gain access to parts of the castle
- ♦ **BEST TIME TO VISIT** Late August for the festival, otherwise all year round

to the Firth of Forth and Fife beyond. First fortified in the Iron Age, the castle grew haphazardly into a stern citadel hidden behind massive walls. The Esplanade is surrounded by buildings, churches and halls, and from here the main features of the castle are signposted.

Head for the Honours of Scotland walk-through display of the royal crown, sword and sceptre, which were last used in the coronation of Scots King Charles II. **St Margaret's Chapel**, a tiny Norman church on the King's Bastion, is thought to be the oldest surviving building in Edinburgh.

A vast fifteenth-century cannon known as **Mons Meg** lurks in the cellars, and, on the right of Crown Square the **Scottish National War Memorial**, designed by the Fife architect Sir Robert Lorimer and opened in 1927, has a Gallery of Honour paying tribute to the victims of the First World War. On the south side of the same square is the **Great Hall**, a late medieval banqueting hall, extensively rebuilt by James IV in the fifteenth century and the setting for some gruesome political shenanigans. **Queen Mary's Apartments** are in the **Old Palace**, and although she gave birth to James VI here in 1566 she preferred the gentler environment of Holyroodhouse.

The **Royal Mile** sweeps down through the Old Town to that palace, with sights aplenty along its length, as well as many cafés, bars, restaurants and shops. A maze of narrow alleys and wynds, twisting stairs and tenement blocks surrounds the street to form the heart of the Old Town. On the way down you could call by at several quirky museums: claim your free tot in the **Scottish Whisky Heritage Centre*** and see Edinburgh upside down through the camera obscura at the **Outlook Tower**, both on Castle Hill. Further down is **Gladstone's Land**, on the left of Lawnmarket, a six-storey tenement built in 1617 for a wealthy merchant and preserved intact with painted ceilings and period furniture. Stroll down past **Brodie's Close**, home

The Scott Monument shelters statues of the author and his dog

to Deacon Brodie, who inspired Robert Louis Stevenson to write *Dr Jekyll and Mr Hyde*. **St Giles' Cathedral** stands halfway down the street in Parliament Square, squat witness to rioting between religious factions in the sixteenth century. The interior has been restored but it retains its bare Calvinist gloom, with the exception of Sir Robert Lorimer's Chapel of the Thistle (1911). The *Heart of Midlothian* insignia can be seen in the paving in front of the church.

The oldest house on the Royal Mile belonged to **John Knox**, the fiery-tempered preacher who clashed with Mary, Queen of Scots. On the first floor of this tenement, on the left of the Royal Mile beyond the bridges, is a small exhibition about the man and his work.

In the shadow of Athur's Seat at the end of the Royal Mile lies the **Palace of Holyroodhouse***. It is still the monarch's official residence in Scotland and scene of much pageantry during June and early July, when the Queen is in residence (the palace is closed to the public during Her Majesty's visits). The palace was built around 1500 and is largely a dreary place, somewhat enlivened by tales of the antics of Queen Mary, who married her dissolute lover, Darnley, here, helped murder the courtier Rizzio and subsequently married the Earl of Bothwell. Bonnie Prince Charlie held court here for five brief weeks in 1745 before his fateful march south to defeat.

From the palace, either wander round the foot of **Arthur's Seat** or retrace your steps up the Royal Mile, turning right down the **Mound**, the majestic sweep connecting the Old and New Towns that started life as a medieval rubbish dump. On the right is the neo-Palladian splendour of the **National Gallery of Scotland***, begun in 1850 by William Playfair. This has one of the best collections in the UK, small but well-chosen, with Canova's sculpture *The Three Graces* in among some good Scots works and paintings by Poussin, Gainsborough, El Greco, David, Holbein, Raphael and Titian, to name but a few. A collection of 38 Turners can be viewed with advance permission.

Just along Princes Street on the right is the Gothic **Scott Monument**, erected in 1840 to honour the Romantic author who did so much to boost Scotland's image (or, as some say, sold her down the line) – see also *Great Days Out 129* and *130*.

Walk back along Princes Street, then turn up into **Charlotte Square**, a New Town square built in the late-eighteenth century when the old town on the hill had become squalid and overcrowded. In an ambitious scheme Charlotte Square is one of a pair of counter-balancing squares, interconnected by sweeping crescents, wide streets and parks that back on to the northern side of Princes Street. The NTS has restored the lower floors of the **Georgian House*** on the north side of this square; it is a beautifully decorated monument to the rich merchant classes of the time, with sumptuous furnishings and many original utensils in the kitchen.

LUNCHBOX

Finding any type of refreshment is never a problem in Edinburgh, a cosmopolitan city with an abundance of choice. The **tourist information office*** on Princes Street can make specific suggestions.

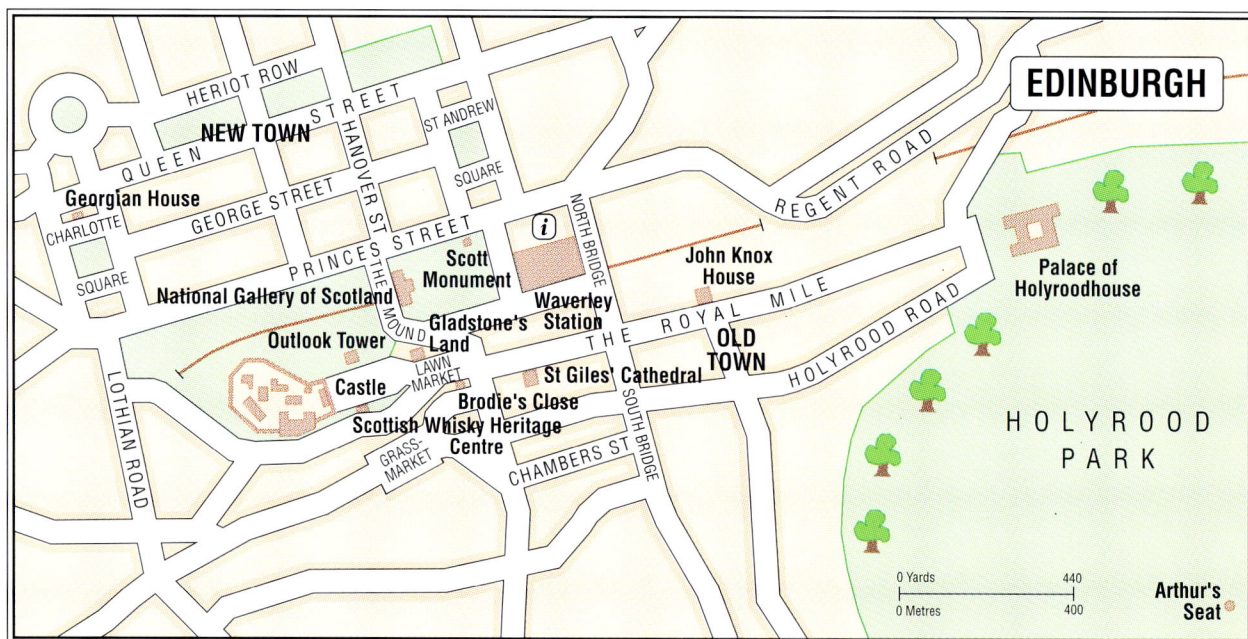

EDINBURGH

Mainly for children – in and around Edinburgh

Best foot forward at Edinburgh Zoo's summer afternoon penguin parade

THE FORTH BRIDGES

The Rail Bridge took seven years to build and was finally completed in 1890, to a design by the eminent Victorian engineers Benjamin Baker and John Fowler. Its four arches span a mile and a half across the Firth of Forth between South and North Queensferry, connecting Edinburgh to Fife. The railway line is 157 feet high and its round steel girders are hollow, allowing the construction workers to move up and down inside them. In all, it takes seven years to paint the bridge from one side to the other.

The Road Bridge, on the other hand, belongs to the modern age; a single-span suspension bridge of hardy reinforced concrete, it opened in 1964. Nowadays the bridge takes such a weight of traffic that morning and evening rush hours are to be avoided.

A day out for the kids, featuring animals, insects, fish, a swimming-pool complete with waves and flumes, and even a ghost or two.

When the children (or you) have had enough of history and culture in Edinburgh, here are some alternative options for indulging them. The attractions we have picked are mostly to the north and west of the city; they include a large, modern zoo, an underwater fantasy world, countryside trails and wildlife, as well as the two huge man-made wonders spanning the Firth of Forth. Children may like to choose their own itinerary from the following ideas.

Edinburgh Zoo* has long been committed to the preservation of endangered species and has earned one of the best reputations for this approach in Europe. Situated about

♦ **GOOD FOR** Families with children of all ages
♦ **TRANSPORT** Car essential
♦ **ACCESS FOR DISABLED PEOPLE** Most sights fully accessible; Hopetoun House grounds only (steps into house itself)
♦ **BEST TIME TO VISIT** Spring, summer

four miles to the west of central Edinburgh on the A8 at Corstorphine, it boasts the largest – and noisiest – penguin pool in Europe. At two o'clock every afternoon in the summer months, the penguins parade for their public, a sight not to be missed as they waddle around full of self-importance. Other

animals to be seen include tigers, brown bears, giraffes and rare red pandas, as well as all manner of creepy-crawly creatures.

From the zoo, it is an easy drive west to the airport and **South Queensferry**. This pretty little town was the departure point for the ferry that used to ply the waters of the Firth of Forth before the Road Bridge was opened in 1964. Nowadays it is virtually squashed under the rusty red expanse of the Forth Rail Bridge, which seems to leap out of a cliff across the water. The **Queensferry Museum*** in Burgh Chambers details the history of the bridge's construction (see the box). Next to the old ferry ramp is the **Hawes Inn**, which features in the novels of Robert Louis Stevenson.

On the way out of South Queensferry towards Edinburgh, the early nineteenth-century **Dalmeny House*** with its fine mock-Gothic façade sits in rolling grounds overlooking the Firth. It has long been the home of the Earls of Rosebery and the Rothschild

BUTTERFLY AND INSECT WORLD
At Lasswade, south of Edinburgh, is the little-known Butterfly and Insect World*, a small covered garden given over to the preservation of scores of pretty species of butterflies and insects. Most young children are fascinated by them.

Collection of paintings, silver, tapestries and antique furniture. (Opening periods are limited.)

Two miles to the west along the A904 coast road is **Hopetoun House***, probably Scotland's most distinguished Adam mansion. You approach it through beautifully manicured grounds culminating in a semi-circular courtyard, round which the splendid neo-classical mansion is arranged. The entrance stairs are imposing, the interior grand. The State Apartments are crammed full of works by Titian and other Old Masters, and the walls hung with luscious silks and damasks spun with gold and silver thread. Of more interest to children, however, will be the grounds, which have been converted into a wildlife park where deer and rare St Kilda sheep graze; nature trails and woodland walks wend their way across the estate and along the river.

The Forth Rail Bridge, like nose-to-tail dinosaurs, and the simpler Road Bridge

A drive up the A90/M90 across the single-span Forth Road Bridge (a toll bridge) takes you off at the first exit to North Queensferry and Deep Sea World, one of the most high-tech aquariums in the world (see *Great Day Out 141*).

Another option would be to visit the **Royal Botanic Gardens*** in Inverleith, with its wildly colourful herbaceous borders and glasshouses full of steaming tropical vegetation. Or take the coast road to **Leith Waterworld*** in Easter Road for a headlong dash down the flumes and water runs into the wave pool. For exhausted parents there is also a spa.

If you plan to head back into the city centre, be sure to visit the **Museum of Childhood***, sometimes a bit of a squash in its steep and narrow building, but fascinating to parents and

In the Old Town, on the corner of Candlemaker Row and George IV Bridge, is the statue to Greyfriars Bobby, a Syke terrier who stood watch over his master's grave for 14 years

children alike. It was founded in 1955 by a man who opined that 'children are tolerable only after their baths and on their way to bed'. Joseph Murray's tongue-in-cheek humour is still to be found on many of the caption cards. Exhibits include some wonderful dolls' houses and unusual automata and slot machines (including a gruesome execution), as well as railways, board games, theatres, teddy bears and toy soldiers.

Legend has it that the Old Town of Edinburgh (*see Great Day Out 133*) is full of spooks and spectres that flit around the alleys and wynds at night. For those with a strong constitution, several companies give fascinating guided walking tours in the evening. The trips are led by experts whose commentaries are based on sound historical fact (and you may even spot a ghost…). For more information on the times of individual tours, phone the **Edinburgh Tourist Board***.

LUNCHBOX
The Hawes Inn at South Queensferry serves food, and there is also a little tea room at Dalmeny House and a restaurant at Hopetoun House.

The galleries of Glasgow: ancient and modern art

Seaside cottages with dovecote *by Edward Walton, one of the Glasgow Boys*

Besides its magnificent nineteenth-century architecture, Glasgow boasts an impressive range of galleries, bringing together paintings by foreign and Scottish artists (both famous and lesser-known), sculpture, furniture, ceramics and, of course, the all-embracing Burrell Collection.

Glasgow has long competed with Edinburgh for supremacy in the art world and, for the moment, it would seem the two cities are running neck and neck; both play host to annual international arts festivals and both have a superb range of galleries. However, it was not always so. Until the early nineteenth century Edinburgh dominated Scotland culturally and financially, and it was only when the wealthy industrialists and commodities importers of the west coast became connoisseurs and patrons of the arts that Glasgow became a cultural force to be reckoned with.

The mid-eighteenth-century physician William Hunter laid the foundations of two great collections which he bequeathed to the University of Glasgow. These were originally housed together in the Hunterian Museum (see *Great Day Out 136*) but his art collections were moved in 1980 to a purpose-built gallery, the **Hunterian Art Gallery*** on Hillhead Street. There are three main attractions here. The first is a major series of work by

- ♦ **GOOD FOR** Anyone who enjoys art, architecture and the decorative arts
- ♦ **TRANSPORT** All the galleries are near public transport
- ♦ **ACCESS FOR DISABLED PEOPLE** No wheelchair access to Art Gallery and Museum Kelvingrove (although motorised chair available); ground floor only at Haggs Castle
- ♦ **BEST TIME TO VISIT** All year

nineteenth- and twentieth-century Scottish artists, including the powerful, orientally influenced work of James Guthrie and Edward Hornel of the Glasgow Boys – a realist movement sparked off in the mid-nineteenth century in reaction to the work of the Scottish Romantic painters, and one that was much decried by contemporary collectors. Secondly, a vast number of James Whistler's works hang here, a mixture of pastels, landscapes and exquisite full-length portraits given and bequeathed in 1935 and 1958 to the University of Glasgow.

The gallery has the largest collection of prints in Scotland and

OTHER GALLERIES IN GLASGOW

Glasgow's newest attraction is the **Gallery of Modern Art***, situated in the distinctive neo-classical former Royal Exchange Building in Queen Street in the heart of the city. The content of the galleries in this new venture is as innovative as the theme of the four floors which have been specially designed to reflect the elements of Fire, Earth, Water and Air. From the spectacular creative centre of the basement Fire Gallery, with its interactives and computer-generated images, to the splendid rooftop café designed by young Scottish artist Adrian Wiszniewski, the gallery offers a unique and dynamic vision of contemporary art. Works by some of the biggest names in the field, including David Hockney, Niki de Saint Phalle and Sebastião Salgado, feature together with examples of the talent of young Scottish artists such as Alison Watt, Peter Howson and Stephen Campbell. In addition, there are diverse and dramatic works from as far afield as Papua New Guinea, Mexico, Russia... and even England.

Also worth a visit if you have time: the **McLellan Galleries*** in Sauchiehall Street have ever-changing temporary exhibitions, usually of modern, controversial work; and the **Centre for Contemporary Art*** (also in Sauchiehall Street).

many important paintings by the likes of Stubbs, Pissarro and Sisley, but the third major reason to come here is found in a three-storey side gallery, the **Mackintosh House**, in which replicas of the hall, dining-room, drawing-room and bedroom of Charles Rennie Mackintosh's marital home have been recreated. Many original pieces of his furniture were brought here when his house was demolished, and others came from a building he designed in Northampton.

By Kelvingrove Park, closer to the city centre, stands the **Art Gallery and Museum Kelvingrove***, a red sandstone, fussy, mock-Gothic edifice with pinnacled towers, buttresses and great arched windows that was purpose-built in 1902. There is almost too much to see here in one visit, so you could skip the ground floor, with its displays of weapons, and head straight up the grand staircase to the galleries upstairs. The enormous collection of paintings is hung in a series of galleries in roughly chronological order from the Renaissance, including works by Botticelli and Filippo Lippi, through to the Dutch School, featuring Rembrandt's *Man in Armour*, to the Victorian Romantics such as Henry Raeburn, Alexander Nasmyth and Edward Burne-Jones, the Modern tradition and the Impressionists. Among the works on display are examples of the Scottish Colourists including Francis Cadell and Modern masters such as Picasso and Dufy.

However, Glasgow's most impressive gallery is the **Burrell Collection***, situated 20 minutes from the city centre in the rolling countryside of Pollok Park. (It is accessible by car, bus and train.) Set aside at least half a day to do it justice, although it really requires more. The collection is the personal treasure trove of the wealthy shipbuilder William Burrell, who had squirrelled away over 8,000 finds by the time of his death in 1958. He bestowed this priceless collection on

Characteristic chairs designed by Charles Rennie Mackintosh

the city of Glasgow, along with strict instructions as to how and where his precious pieces should be displayed.

It was not until 1983 that the gallery fulfilling all Burrell's conditions was completed: an airy, prize-winning confection of light stone, glass corridors, vast picture windows and archways. Incorporated into the design are medieval stone doorways bought from William Randolph Hearst, the reclusive American newspaper magnate who had installed them in his fantastic San Simeon retreat in California; and delicate sixteenth-century stained-glass heraldic panels, lined up along the windows to catch natural light.

There is so much to see in this beautiful and eclectic gallery that it is possible to mention only some of the major exhibits: in the entrance hall is a cast of the famous bronze, *The Thinker*, by Rodin; in the courtyard, the Warwick Vase from the Emperor Hadrian's summer villa

in Tivoli outside Rome, and artefacts from Mesopotamia, Iraq and Iran as well as Greece, Rome and Egypt. About a quarter of the entire exhibition consists of Oriental Art, ranging from carved jade dating from the Stone Age and exquisitely decorated porcelain of the fifteenth-century Ming dynasty to a placid, bemused-looking stone Lohan, sitting cross-legged against the window. William Burrell's own favourites are found in the Medieval and Post-medieval European Art section – ecclesiastical and secular tapestries, still vivid in colour, stitched in phenomenal detail and worth a fortune. On the first floor is a series of nineteenth-century French paintings, including *Jockeys in the Rain* by Degas, and some early Flemish work, particularly a beautiful *Annunciation* by Hans Memling.

The weakest part of the gallery (in design, not content) is the mezzanine floor, which is dingy enough to spoil a series of wonderful paintings by the Impressionists.

If you have chosen to spend the whole day at the Burrell, follow a little track across the field to **Pollok House***, a stern, grey stone mansion completed by William Adam and his son Robert in 1752. Here is a magical collection of big, gloomy Spanish paintings, including Goyas, El Grecos and Murillos.

Just north of Pollok Park on St Andrew's Drive is **Haggs Castle***, a sixteenth-century baronial mansion that today houses a hands-on, interactive Scottish history museum for children – a great antidote to all those paintings.

The vast centre hall of the Art Gallery and Museum Kelvingrove

LUNCHBOX

Try Joe's Garage (pizza and pasta, close to the university) or the Willow Tea Room (see *Great Day Out 136*) at the reasonable end of the scale, or the Ubiquitous Chip, with its creeper-covered patio, for super Scottish food at the top end of the market, in the West End. There are also open-air bars and cafés in the streets round the Italian Centre in the city centre.

Glasgow museums: tenements, trams and tea

The Museum of Transport will delight adults and children alike

Glasgow's museums are as good as they come, with exhibits ranging from the sacred to the profane, from dinosaurs to prams, plus a helping of Charles Rennie Mackintosh for good measure.

Glasgow's West End and city centre are splendid Victorian enclaves, with sweeping vistas, gracious townhouses, up-market shops, restaurants, cafés, imposing public buildings and a more than efficient underground system, known as the 'Clockwork Orange'. The city, richly deserving of its designation as UK City of Architecture and Design 1999 offers a fine array of galleries and museums, all of which have free admission. (See *Great Day Out 135* for Glasgow's magnificent art galleries.)

Kelvingrove Park stands to the west of the city and is near the University of Glasgow and two museum and gallery complexes: the Hunterian and Kelvingrove. The **Hunterian Museum*** on University Avenue is Scotland's oldest public museum (opened in 1807) and contains the collections bequeathed to the University of Glasgow by an eminent doctor, William Hunter. It boasts most of Scotland's rare dinosaur remains, along with numismatic, geological and archaeological collections.

♦ **GOOD FOR** Curiosities, trams, social history and tea
♦ **TRANSPORT** All sights are on or near public transport
♦ **ACCESS FOR DISABLED PEOPLE** Full access to People's Palace, Transport Museum and St Mungo Museum; Art School access to Mackintosh Room and Library but not to Furniture Gallery
♦ **BEST TIME TO VISIT** All year, but particularly exciting and busy during Mayfest, which rivals the Edinburgh Festival

Close by in Burnhouse Road is the enormous, fascinating **Museum of Transport***, devoted to the history of transport over land and sea. Exhibits include horse-drawn circus caravans, old steam engines (some over a hundred years old), trams, buses, fire engines and even prams. Models of fishing boats, and liners built in the thriving shipyards on the river in the city's Victorian heyday, are displayed in the Clyde Room; these combine with old film footage to serve as a poignant reminder of Glasgow's industrial heritage. Children will enjoy the reconstructed 1938 street, complete with an Italian deli, a bank and an underground station.

In the city centre, the **Glasgow School of Art*** on Renfrew Street is Glasgow's shrine to Charles Rennie Mackintosh (1868–1928), a visionary architect and designer much underrated during his lifetime. The school was built in two parts and finally completed in 1909. Each façade is different, and enthusiasts will be able to trace Mackintosh's influences from Elizabethan mansion to Scottish baronial. The angular exterior hides an interior flooded with light and full of Mackintosh's characteristic high-backed chairs, stark wrought-ironwork and sombre, severe furniture. The irreverent presence of the art students who double as guides lightens the atmosphere, but restricts the times when the school can be visited. Ring to check when tours are available.

Round the corner, along the precinct of Sauchiehall Street, is the **Willow Tea Room***, an exact reconstruction of one of four tea rooms designed by Mackintosh for his patron Kate Cranston. Perch on a reproduction Mackintosh chair and drink your tea within the luscious silver and purple interior of the 'Room de Luxe'.

Over 800 years of Glasgow's turbulent history are explored at the People's Palace, of which the Winter Gardens shown here form part

Another place worth seeking out can be found in Buccleuch Street, four blocks north of Sauchiehall Street. Now owned by the National Trust for Scotland, the **Tenement House*** was home to eccentric Agnes Toward from 1911 to 1965, during which time she threw away almost nothing. Her private letters, photographs, clothes and other memorabilia are exhibited on the ground floor of the museum and form a tribute to her ordinary life; upstairs the hall, parlour, bedroom, bathroom and kitchen remain almost as they were in Edwardian times. Glasgow's Victorian population was housed in many variations of the tenement, ranging from 10-roomed apartments with live-in staff to 'single-end' slums. Where possible, tenements are now being restored (as in Merchant City to the east of Princes Square) or re-invented by progressive architects.

In the ancient heart of the city is a square, softstone house, built as the manse to St Nicholas' Hospital in 1471. **Provand's Lordship*** houses a museum with period displays; the reconstruction of the rooms of a rather puzzled fifteenth-century ecclesiastical clerk contrasts nicely with the more secular exhibits and the stories collected from sleazy low-lifes in the last century. In the grounds of the house is a newly created medieval-style garden.

The glorious landmark **Cathedral** and **Necropolis** are opposite Provand's Lordship, as is the **St Mungo Museum of Religious Life and Art***. Opened in 1993, the latter has the distinction of being the only museum in the world to look at all the major faiths. It has three galleries with white-painted walls, focusing separately on religious art, world religions and the turbulent history of religion in Scotland. The highlights are a specially commissioned statue of Ganesh, the many-armed Hindu elephant god, the stunning but intensely gloomy *Christ of St John on the Cross* by Salvador Dali, poorly hung and so losing some of the impact of its weird perspective, and a Japanese Zen garden, truly a calm, reflective spot.

Indulge in some tea and style at the Willow Tea Room

LUNCHBOX
Refreshments are available at the Transport Museum, St Mungo Museum, the Winter Gardens and, of course, the Willow Tea Room. See also *Great Day Out 135*.

If it is the weekend, wend your way through the huge market of the **Barras** on Gallowgate to the **People's Palace*** on the northern tip of Glasgow Green. This imposing Victorian museum, completed in 1898 and now with the massive Winter Gardens conservatory moulded on to its back, relives Glasgow's history from 1175 to the present day. The ground floor offers rather standard fare, with recreated rooms showing Glasgow families and houses through the ages; upstairs are presented the different visions which have shaped the city – those of the Capitalist, the Civic and the People. Other displays examine how things work and tell the stories of celebrated and less well-known Glaswegians, while Billy Connolly, that most Glaswegian of comedians, is featured in a portrait wearing patchwork denim flares and a star-embroidered jacket. The opulent water gardens, towering plants and café make the **Winter Gardens** an ideal place to put your feet up at the end of a long day's sightseeing.

The island of Bute and a Gothic extravaganza

Mount Stuart: a high Victorian Gothic fantasy in red sandstone, marble and stained glass

The island of Bute, in the Clyde estuary, is a peaceful place once you get away from the traditional resort of Rothesay. The second largest island in the Firth of Clyde, it offers the extraordinary stately home of Mount Stuart, sweeping bays and stunning scenery.

No visitor could do justice to Bute in one day, so here we concentrate on Rothesay and the south-western corner of the island. Spend some time in town, taking in a castle and a museum, and then head south. Nothing can prepare you for what you will see only a few minutes out of Rothesay – a fabulous Gothic stately home, quite unexpected on a quiet island like this. If you have the time, and a car, wander around the coast to the south and west. Here you can see, in addition to panoramic views of the sea, a church rebuilt in the twelfth century.

There is a fine view of **Rothesay** from the sea. The town had its heyday when the Clyde estuary was criss-crossed by steamer services, and the annual holiday exodus 'doon the watter' (down the water, i.e. the Clyde) was the big event in the lives of industrial Glasgow's working

♦ **GOOD FOR** Diversity: bays, beaches, a resort town and an amazing Gothic palace
♦ **TRANSPORT** You could take your car with you (useful for exploring the island) or leave it at Wemyss Bay on the mainland and catch the ferry. The journey to Rothesay takes half an hour, and a bus service runs between Rothesay and Mount Stuart and other parts of the island
♦ **ACCESS FOR DISABLED PEOPLE** There is limited access to Rothesay Castle and Mount Stuart
♦ **BEST TIME TO VISIT** Summer for better weather but there is plenty to see inside if it is bad

population. Some of the handsome Victorian hotels and residences have seen better days, but the seafront still has a certain charm. Male visitors can even sample a restored Victorian gents' loo. (Women use a modern facility next door.) A useful

tourist information office* is located near the pier.

Moments from the harbour-front is **Rothesay Castle***. The curious design of the castle, which was originally circular and without towers, is possibly linked to that of certain castles in Cornwall. What is seen today includes a circular curtain wall and four massive round towers; the walls were breached by raiding Vikings in 1230. The massive square frontal tower dates from the sixteenth century, when the castle assumed strategic importance with the Stuart kings as a base from which they could quell the unruly Highlanders of the west.

Bute Museum*, opposite the castle, also deserves a few minutes just to set the island's ancient story in context. This is a no-nonsense traditional museum, though perhaps with too many stuffed animals for some tastes. It displays carved crosses and religious artefacts, and material dating from neolithic times. You will find, too, in pictures and documents, a hint of the resort's 'golden age'. For instance, a little enamelled sign says to the novice sea voyagers on their day out, 'Persons are warned not to row towards steamers and to take care changing seats'.

Mount Stuart* is only a few minutes' drive to the south of Rothesay. This is definitely the stately home for people who do not usually like stately homes. It was the vision, or indulgence, of one man, John Patrick Crichton-Stuart, third Marquess of Bute, who, at his coming of age in 1868, was believed to be the richest man in Britain. Later, after a fire destroyed the central block of his previous property on his Bute estates, he commissioned the Mount Stuart seen today.

Its centrepiece is the awesome **Marble Hall**, more cathedral than family home, with its columns and arches of rare Italian marble soaring up to a roof painted with stars and surrounded by stained glass. But this is no religious edifice: the theme is astrology, with the twelve signs of the zodiac. Note the marble staircase and the magnificent wood panelling in the dining-room and library. Idiosyncratic, perhaps even eccentric, the whole concept of Mount Stuart seems to overwhelm the rare and exquisite furniture and almost overshadow the priceless portraits – Reynolds, Ramsay and Batonia among others – and vast tapestries. Not a great number of rooms are open, but each is quite extraordinary.

If you emerge reeling from the sumptuousness of it all, there's a cup of tea to be had in the little tearoom housed in one of the Georgian wings. There are also vast grounds to explore, with green avenues rolling out to a vanishing point far off beneath the tall trees, a shoreline to discover, and a mild and sheltered spot called 'The Wee Garden' (only five acres) to lose yourself in.

OFF THE BEATEN TRACK
Rothesay and Mount Stuart could take up most of the day, but it is well worth exploring further into the island so do leave some time for this.

St Blane's Chapel is worth seeing for its carved columned Romanesque arch in the chancel

Rejoin the main road by Mount Stuart and follow it south. Past Kingarth, where a road goes off for Kilchattan Bay, go left at a cemetery on a minor road, still going south.

The road goes up and over a ridge and, if you have armed yourself with the endearingly earnest nature-trail books written by the Buteshire Natural History Society, you can learn all about the ancient volcanic activity around here, as well as the fort on the headland on your right. Otherwise, just enjoy the breathtaking skyline of Arran, filling the south-western

horizon, and park at the road end, where a sign points to **St Blane's Chapel**. A short walk brings you to a roofless chapel and a circular kirkyard. Here, in AD788, the Vikings attacked the small religious settlement founded by St Blane in the sixth century. The descendants of these raiders-turned-settlers built another church in the twelfth century. Worship ceased in the eighteenth century, and nowadays the spot, in a mossy bowl below the trees, is peaceful and half-forgotten.

You can take various walks, down to the shore or over by Suidhe Hill and Kilchattan Bay. Make your way back to the main road, going left on the A844 to head north along the west side of the island, passing various tempting sandy bays, including an attractive panorama from a lay-by overlooking the sandy reaches of Scalpsie Bay. Further on is the even more extensive Ettrick Bay, only minutes away from Rothesay, while the north end of the island (beyond the Highland Boundary Fault crossed at Scalpsie Bay) is much more rugged and wild.

FERRIES ACROSS THE CLYDE
Full details of Clyde ferry services to Rothesay are available from Caledonian MacBrayne. In addition to the Wemyss Bay–Rothesay (non-bookable) connection, there is a five-minute crossing from Colintraive to Rhubodach, which links the island to the attractive area of Cowal on the mainland and is useful if you are planning a longer tour.

Ettrick Bay is typical of the scenery in the southern half of Bute

Loch Lomond, Glasgow's summer playground

Ben Lomond is the most southerly of Scotland's 30 munroes (hills that reach over 3,000 feet)

A day of walking, boating and fresh air round Scotland's most famous loch – with a spot of shopping thrown in for good measure.

Loch Lomond – 23 miles long and up to five miles wide in the south – is Britain's largest stretch of inland water. As it is close to Glasgow and on one of the main routes into the Highlands, it becomes Glasgow's playground in the summer. The villages along the lochside heave with people and the usually serene loch is crowded with little craft of all kinds. However, before you dismiss the idea of a visit out of hand, be advised – Loch Lomond is incredibly beautiful. In the early morning it has a mirror's stillness, with the heavily wooded hills rising up to Ben Lomond on the eastern side, and a little scattering of islets at its southern end.

Balloch, at the southern tip of the loch, straddles the River Leven as it pours towards the River Clyde. This is a holiday resort, with hotels, camp sites, fishing, water-skiing, tennis courts, bowling and a marina.

♦ **GOOD FOR** Beautiful scenery, waterscapes, mountain climbing, walking and sailing
♦ **TRANSPORT** Car essential; boat trips
♦ **ACCESS FOR DISABLED PEOPLE** No
♦ **BEST TIME TO VISIT** Summer

You can hire a boat or take a leisurely cruise round the little wooded islands (**Mullen's Cruises*** or **Sweeney's Cruises***), or you can hire dry and wet fishing tackle to have a go at catching some of the loch's teeming trout (but not its powan – freshwater herring – as these are an endangered species). The **Balloch Castle Country Park*** stretches over acres of garden and woodland scenery to the east of the town.

THE EASTERN SIDE
Crouching in the hills at the foot of the loch to the east is the little town of **Drymen**, crossroads for people travelling from the Trossachs (see *Great Day Out 140*) and buzzing with walkers and climbers in summer. From here you can drive to **Balmaha**, a sheltered hamlet ranged round a busy harbour, from where **MacFarlane's*** run cruises on the loch. **Rowardennan** is an even smaller settlement at the end of the East Loch Lomondside road, a starting point for gentle walks up into the gloriously wooded Queen Elizabeth Forest Park (again, see *Great Day Out 140*), and also for the strenuous three-hour climb up Ben Lomond (3,192 feet). The **West Highland Way** meanders round the east side of the loch from Milngavie and continues northwards, up and down glen towards Fort William. The **ranger services*** will advise on individual itineraries, weather conditions and suitability of routes. Watch out for timid roe deer and, in spring, the swathes of blossom all down the hillside right to the water.

THE WESTERN SIDE
The western side of Loch Lomond is more accessible and much busier; the A82 follows the shoreline to the north, joining a series of small tourist villages all bristling with hotels, restaurants and marinas.

Inchmurrin is the biggest island in the loch, reached by boat from the tiny hamlet of Arden, which has Scotland's grandest and most haunted youth hostel. The grim ruins of Lennox Castle on the island are a reminder of the area's turbulent history, dominated by clan feuding and grisly murders. Some of the biggest troublemakers were the Macgregors, whose traditional burial place is on **Inchcaillach**, an island at the eastern side of the loch and now owned by Scottish National Heritage. It is criss-crossed with nature trails.

Luss is an exceptionally pretty conservation village halfway along the loch, famous as the location of the Scots soap opera *Take the High Road* and thus very crowded in summer. In addition to the **Loch Lomond Visitor Centre*** and a popular kilt shop, the village has a quiet sandy beach hidden in a little sheltered bay. Just to the south on the A82 is the **Thistle Bagpipe Works***, something of an institution and worth a visit for curiosity's sake to see how these extraordinary musical instruments are made.

From **Inverbeg** you can take the single-track road north-west up across Glen Douglas to Loch Long, a sea loch bordering the heavily wooded Roseneath Peninsula. To the east of Inverbeg, a ferry hops across Loch Lomond to Rowardennan and the hills beyond. You can hire self-drive motor cruisers from the **Inverbeg Inn***. Further north is grey-stone **Tarbet**, framed by craggy hills. There are a couple of hotels and restaurants here but the

See how bagpipes — one of Scotland's most vivid emblems — are made in Luss

busy road now dominates the village. North of Tarbet, on the left-hand side of the road, visit the **handloom weaver's** workshop, where fine-quality tartans for kilts and warm woolly blankets are produced. These are for sale in the adjoining shop.

Peaceful **Ardlui** stands at the extreme upper tip of Loch Lomond, overshadowed by towering peaks. There is a tiny, friendly hotel here, overlooking the quiet marina, a great base from which to explore the serene reaches of this northern end of the loch.

ALSO WORTH VISITING

At the southern end of the loch in **Alexandria**, a couple of miles south of Balloch on the A82, you can visit the **Antartex Village Visitor Centre***. A guided tour of the factory, where garments are made from sheepskin and leather, is followed by a visit to the British Antarctic Survey Exhibition, where a mock-up of the base at the South Pole displays equipment and clothing used there. Hunt down some bargains in the mill and factory shops, which offer knitwear, tartans and pure woollen clothes, and browse around the craft workshops.

Nearby **Helensburgh** was built in the eighteenth century to an elegant grid-plan design, and its wide streets, bordered with fine town houses, lead down to the sea at the entrance of Gare Loch. Sports facilities are excellent, with sailing craft for hire, a swimming-pool and eighteen-hole golf course. The town is more famous, however, as the birthplace of John Logie Baird, inventor of television, and for **Hill House*** in Upper Colquhoun Street, designed by Charles Rennie Mackintosh, Scotland's favourite architect (see *Great Days Out 135 and 136*). Mackintosh undertook it as a private commission for the publisher William Blackie in 1902 and it is now owned by the National Trust for Scotland.

LUNCHBOX
The Buchanan Highland Hotel near Drymen offers delicious fresh fish and seasonal local game. The Weaver's Restaurant and Coffee Shop near Tarbet serves refreshments, while excellent views across the loch are a bonus to the good food at the Inverbeg Inn. There is a café at Hill House in Helensburgh.

Inveraray and around Loch Fyne

The name Rest and Be Thankful recalls the days when cars could be seen cooling off at the top of the hill

A wildlife park, sub-tropical gardens, a jail and a majestic castle are all to be found around the shores of Loch Fyne and the beautiful but austere town of Inveraray.

T he long, narrow arm of Loch Fyne snakes 40 miles inland from the sea, separating the Cowal Peninsula to the south from Knapdale and Kintyre in the north. Inveraray, the main town, is perched on a little offshoot of the loch called Shira, and has an imposing castle and a jail. Just south of Inveraray is a fascinating open-air museum chronicling the history of the Highlands. If the weather is fine, head for the area around Loch Fyne: you can choose from walking in a superb forest park, watching animals in a wildlife park or strolling through lovely gardens, or do all three. The area is also famous for its oysters, mussels, trout and salmon, all farmed from the loch.

Approach **Loch Fyne** from the A83 through Glen Kinglas, known locally as Rest and Be Thankful. It is a dour road overshadowed by dark

- ◆ **GOOD FOR** Nature lovers and walkers – the area abounds in forests, gardens and wildlife; children will find Inveraray Jail especially fascinating
- ◆ **TRANSPORT** Car essential
- ◆ **ACCESS FOR DISABLED PEOPLE** There is access to the Argyll Wildlife Park and the Auchindrain Museum, and limited access to the Castle
- ◆ **BEST TIME TO VISIT** Spring and summer as most sights close during the winter months

peaks, but the landscape softens as it descends towards the head of gentle Loch Fyne and winds round to Inveraray. **Inveraray Castle** looms up first, on the right-hand side of the road, an impressive, square, grey-stone building with fortified round towers at each corner and a square, crenellated tower appearing to rise

LUNCHBOX

At the head of Loch Fyne, near **Cairndow**, is the Loch Fyne Oyster Bar, where you can treat all the family to spanking fresh seafood and oysters without breaking the bank. There is also a shop in the complex which sells local specialities, such as venison pâté and home-baked bread, for picnics. At **Portsonachan**, on the eastern side of Loch Awe, there is a cosy family hotel that has a fish and seafood restaurant with vast windows overlooking the loch. Food here is not cheap, but a bar menu is also available. **Auchindrain Museum** has an excellent tea room and bookshop.

through the roof. It was begun in 1770 for the third Duke of Argyll, leader of Clan Campbell. Robert and William Morris contributed to the design, and the interior shows off the fine decoration by Robert Mylne. The tour of the castle (April to October) includes the State Dining Room, with delicately painted walls and ceilings, and the Tapestry Room, featuring a unique set of 200-year-old Beauvais tapestries. Also on view is an extensive collection of weapons, ornate silver displays and portraits of the Argyll family by Gainsborough, Raeburn and others, among them one of Queen Victoria's daughter Louise, who married the ninth duke. The Combined Operations Room in the Stable Block tells of Inveraray's curious role in the Second World War: Loch Fyne was used in practice runs for the D-Day landings, and over half a million troops were secretly billeted in town.

Inveraray itself is a new town – built in the eighteenth century. It was the oldest settlement in Argyllshire, but no trace remains of this ancient past as it was demolished in 1744 by the third duke and moved half a mile down the road: he wanted his castle to be where the town had been. The

Prisoners were first locked up in Inveraray Jail, where conditions were extremely cramped, in 1849

work took 40 years to complete, and now Inveraray is an attractive little Georgian town, although the elegant, white-washed, colonnaded buildings can look harsh in the grey rain of a West Highland winter day.

The **parish church** is in the middle of the main street, and the **Episcopalian church**, a few yards away in the Avenue, has a 126-foot granite tower, from which the view of the castle and surrounds is quite stunning. This church, built after the First World War at the behest of the tenth Duke of Argyll, has a ten-bell peal which is rung in tribute to the Campbells who lost their lives during the war. Many of the shops sell knitwear, walking gear and crafts, and, despite the influx of tourists in summer, there are some bargains to be had. The **tourist information office*** is on Front Street.

Probably the most popular attraction is the award-winning **Inveraray Jail***, a series of stern buildings held in by rounded stone walls abutting the loch. These have been turned into an ingenious museum, using life-like models, actors, recordings and hands-on exhibits to show conditions in the crowded old prison blocks. It also has a mock-up of a trial in the semi-circular Georgian courthouse.

OUT OF INVERARAY

About two miles south of Inveraray is the **Argyll Wildlife Park***, a 60-acre site open all year and worth popping into for the owls, wallabies, badgers, deer and foxes, with wildfowl scuttling around.

Further down the A83 as it winds its way round the shoreline of the loch is the open-air **Auchindrain Museum*** (open from Easter to September). For anyone with more than a passing interest in the turbulent history of the West Highlands, this is an absolute must. The museum has been established in a deserted township of about 20 eighteenth- and nineteenth-century cottages, each carefully restored to its original state and refilled with artefacts pre-dating the Highland Clearances. Wandering round the primitive 'but and bens' (two-roomed white-washed cottages), barns and smithies, you will appreciate just how hard the lives of the crofters were. In those days, the crofters had joint tenancy over agricultural land and they established a rota system, called strip farming or 'runrig', enabling each family to farm the most fertile land in turn. Whoever farmed the best land paid the lion's share of the rent that year – a simple system that worked for many years and can now only be seen demonstrated here.

Three beautiful gardens are to be found around Loch Fyne: **Ardkinglas Woodland Garden*** is at the head of the loch, off the A83 at Cairndow; **Kilmory Woodland Park*** in the grounds of Kilmory Castle, south of Lochgilphead, overlooks the loch; and **Crarae Glen Garden***, ten miles south of Inveraray, is thought by many people to be quite the loveliest in Scotland. The last of these is enclosed in a tiny, rocky glen, with pathways running to and fro across a tumbling burn. Azaleas and rhododendrons poke out among the rock faces, and maples burn bright in the autumn months.

Much of Argyll is inaccessible by road, so it remains a paradise for walkers and a safe haven for wildlife. One such area is **Argyll Forest Park*** between Lochs Long and Fyne. Here the forests of Ardgarten, Benmore and Glenbranter together form 60,000 acres of wild and dramatic scenery, encompassing scores of forest walks through old estate woodlands. There are a number of marked short forest walks, and many longer trails that lead up into the hills. The route through Puck's Glen goes past cascading waterfalls, while the Lauder Walk is best followed in late spring, when all the rhododendrons are in bloom. One of the Lochgoilhead Forest Walks leads up to **Rob Roy's Cave** in Glen Shira, behind Inveraray. In summer there are guided walks through the glens and woodlands.

The township at Auchindrain Museum is an original West Highland village

The Trossachs without the crowds

Callander, at the heart of the Trossachs, is the ideal touring base

Breadalbane is the unruly, rugged walking and climbing country to the north of the Trossachs, steeped in legend. Its ancient territory was traditionally populated by giants, fairies, spirits, saints and warriors who fought endlessly. These local tales have now been brought together in the **Breadalbane Folklore Centre*** in **Killin**, a pretty village that straggles along by the impressive Falls of Dochart (turn right off the A85 on to the A827 seven miles north of Lochearnhead). The museum is a monument to clan history, and brings local legend to life through clever use of audio-visual, interactive video and electronic trickery. Across the road there is a jolly good pub, the Salmon Lie.

Walk through beautiful forested glens alongside rushing rivers and burns, pay homage to the folk hero Rob Roy, see sheepdogs being trained, and maybe even water-ski on Loch Earn.

This tiny region is singularly beautiful, squashed between the Lowlands and the foothills of the Highlands, scattered with peaceful little towns and lochs of breathtaking serenity. Fishing, walking, climbing and water-sports facilities – these are what attract tourists by the thousand every spring and summer.

The trick with the Trossachs is to visit when everybody else has gone home. The area is so accessible and popular that in summer it almost grinds to a standstill. However, by mid-September the little towns have reverted to their sleepy pace.

Callander is a late eighteenth-century town with a wide main street dotted with art galleries, craft shops and cafés. The town is better known as the fictional Tannochbrae, the setting of A.J. Cronin's *Dr Finlay's Casebook*, but a somewhat wilder character dominates its streets.

Rob Roy is big news here. Whether you accept Sir Walter Scott's sentimental view of him as folk hero,

- ◆ **GOOD FOR** Scenery, walking, folklore, water sports
- ◆ **TRANSPORT** Car necessary
- ◆ **ACCESS FOR DISABLED PEOPLE** Rob Roy Centre and Scottish Wool Centre are fully accessible; the Breadalbane Folklore Museum is accessible at ground-floor level
- ◆ **BEST TIME TO VISIT** Autumn – not only will the crowds have gone, but the hills will be carpeted with gold and russet (but note that the boat service on Loch Katrine runs only from April to end September)

immortalised in the novel of 1817, or believe he was simply the rogue leader of the notorious Macgregor clan, you can discover more about him at the **Rob Roy and Trossachs Visitor Centre***. The multivision theatre and the exhibition provide an insight into the life of a clan chieftain.

The Trossachs are walking country; follow the trails up from Callander to the spectacular **Falls of Bracklinn**, to the **Callander Crags** or along the nine-mile cycle path to the north

through the **Pass of Leny** and past **Loch Lubnaig** to **Strathyre**. The Rob Roy Centre has details.

From Callander, the A81 creeps south-west along the feet of the Menteith Hills to the **Loch of Menteith**, which holds a double delight: it is a fantastic spot for fly-fishing, and Mary, Queen of Scots, was hidden away on a little island here in her childhood. Her refuge, **Inchmaholme Priory**, was an Augustinian priory built in 1238, and is now in gaunt ruins. A ferry runs to the island in summer months, stopping at the end of September.

It was in the manse at **Aberfoyle** that Sir Walter Scott conceived the idea for his novel *Rob Roy*. Indeed, a more inspirational location is hard to imagine, with heavily wooded mountains stretching away from the town in all directions. At the **Scottish Wool Centre*** there you can follow the story of wool from the sheep's back to yours. In the **amphitheatre**, visitors are treated to the history of

LUNCHBOX

The **tourist information offices*** in Aberfoyle and at the Rob Roy Centre* can supply plenty of ideas.

The SS Sir Walter Scott, *named after the man who brought mass tourism to the area, plies the calm waters of Loch Katrine*

upland sheep farming, as told by the sheep, and in the **Sheepdog Training School** dogs and shepherds go through their paces. You will find real woolly lambs at the centre's **Children's Farm** and at the nearby **Farmlife Centre***, and toy ones in the shops and craft studios, which also sell good-quality woollen goods.

Aberfoyle is a springboard for forays into the surrounding hills and forests – options include walks into Loch Ard forest and over to Loch Lomond (see *Great Day Out 138*), and long hikes past **Loch Ard** to remote **Loch Chon** – all in all, 180 miles of forestry track are open for walkers. The **Queen Elizabeth Forest Park*** covers a 50,000-acre area of wild, unspoilt glens; the Visitor Centre is on the A821. If you don't want to walk, stay in the car and drive through the stunning **Duke's Pass**, a road built especially for tourists in Victorian times, which leads from Aberfoyle through the Queen Elizabeth Forest Park back towards Callander. The **Achray Forest Drive** dives into the trees four miles to the right down this road; it is beautifully landscaped, with picnic facilities that are hard to beat. A small toll is payable.

Depending on the time of year, detour off to the left under the shadow of Ben Venue, down to Loch Katrine. Here you could take a trip on the famous cruiser SS *Sir Walter Scott* – this is the only way for motorists to explore this majestic loch, the isolated hamlet of Stronachlachar and wild Glen Gyle beyond, as the track that runs down the northern side of Katrine is privately owned (cyclists and walkers are welcome).

Back on the A821, head back towards Callander, through Brig-o'-Turk along the shores of **Loch Venachar**, turn left on to the A84 and drive through heavy woodland past Loch Lubnaig. Turn left at Kingshouse up a single-track road to desolate Loch Voil and **Balquhidder**, Rob Roy's home village. He was buried in the little churchyard in 1734; his grave is surprisingly unspoilt, considering his immense following. In **Stronvar House*** you will find a museum of bygones associated with him.

Seven miles away up Glen Ogle on the A84 is **Lochearnhead**, a tiny settlement standing at the western end of Loch Earn and completely given over to water sports; speed boats, yachts, water-skis and wind surfers are for hire everywhere, and there are more hotels than houses.

The Forth Estuary: old town, new world under water

Here you can explore the home environments of a rich merchant in an old Scottish burgh and, nearby, sea creatures of all kinds.

T he small burgh of **Culross** (pronounced koo-riss) sits on the north bank of the estuary of the River Forth (in an area that was effectively cut off from the rest of Scotland by the estuary in the Dark Ages). 'Burgh' was the name given to a community with rights to hold fairs and markets, to elect its town council and to dispense local justice. Bypassed by the Industrial Revolution, Culross's seventeenth- and eighteenth-century domestic architecture escaped redevelopment. The old town having decayed significantly by the 1930s, the National Trust for Scotland stepped in and initiated a 50-year programme of restoration that has made Culross one of the most handsome small towns in Scotland. The Trust aimed to improve living standards for the people living in Culross, without taking away the old burgh's character.

♦ **GOOD FOR** Families with children over 7
♦ **TRANSPORT** 53-mile round trip from Edinburgh city centre. The car park in Culross is at the far west of town. Although there is a car park right next to Deep Sea World in North Queensferry, you can avoid the congestion in the narrow streets by using the overspill car park. This is linked to the visitor centre at peak times by a shuttle bus service running every few minutes
♦ **ACCESS FOR DISABLED PEOPLE** Possible only at Deep Sea World
♦ **BEST TIME TO VISIT** Main season for Culross, but Deep Sea World gets very busy during school and public holidays

Take junction 1 from the Forth Bridge, going west on the A985. Culross is signposted from this road. The old houses that you see running up from the foreshore may be sanitised and quaint but are as close as

Little now remains to suggest that Culross was once one of Scotland's major trading ports

you are likely to get to a sense of bygone times in Scotland, before the loss of independence, when the Scots nation looked to Europe, trading with the Low Countries and the Baltic. The red pantiles were originally brought back as ballast in the vessels in which coal, salt and other Scottish materials were exported.

On the left is a building associated with the man who shaped this early town. The **Palace*** of Sir George Bruce is no ornate confection, but a complex of stout, small-windowed buildings, with the characteristic, Dutch-influenced, crow-stepped gables – in short, a rich merchant-industrialist's house. Its first phase was completed in 1597, according to the the date on the pediment above the dormer window.

Buy your ticket on the ground floor, then climb the worn steps to the interiors furnished in period style. You will take some time to adjust from the brightness outdoors to the brown panelled walls and heavy, dark furniture lit only by those small windows. NTS guides will point out the main features, notably the preservation of painted wall and ceiling decorations dating from the late sixteenth to the early eighteenth centuries. The north (detached) wing has 1611 carved on a window pediment. As well as the obvious surviving wall and ceiling decorations, look for the faint traces of a seventeenth-century wall painting which was lost to view only in recent years. A small copy of it hangs nearby. It was drawn by a government inspector, just before time and the poor condition of the building immediately post-war erased the extraordinary image of King James VI dressed as Solomon.

Walk to the **Town House*** built in 1626, the very heart of the burgh. An audio-visual exhibition here tells the story of the town. A further stroll

Midway between Culross and Deep Sea World is the substantial town of **Dunfermline**, birthplace of the millionaire philanthropist Andrew Carnegie. The cottage where he was born is now the site of a museum, which tells his life-story. Dunfermline's role as a former leading manufacturing centre for damask linen is portrayed in Dunfermline Museum.

brings you to a house called the **Study*** of 1612, with its Outlook Tower corbelled out from the face of the wall. Its main room is furnished in period, and you can squeeze up the claustrophobically narrow spiral staircase for a view over the Forth.

These are the only buildings open to view in Culross, but there are many other handsome little houses, all around the Mercat (market) Cross. You can climb the brae (slope) to the ruins of the abbey, founded in 1217, and a reminder of the antiquity of Culross. Nearby, in the churchyard, try working out the trades of those buried by the marks and the tools on the tombstones. The **tourist information office*** in Dunfermline will provide you with more details about the area.

The Palace in Culross: see how prosperous seventeenth-century merchants lived in Scotland

DEEP SEA WORLD

Drive east and cross under the main M90. Follow tourist signs (white lettering on brown) for Deep Sea World within the shadow of the Forth Rail Bridge at North Queensferry. Deep Sea World has the largest single fish tank in the world (1 million gallons of water), with over half a million visitors a year, and is seen from the longest underwater tunnel (112 meters) in the northern hemisphere.

The main exhibition hall has plenty to divert children, including a waist-high rock pool which allows cautious exploration.

Divers/presenters are on duty here, wading around to bring up specimens for closer examination. They answer questions and explain to children such facts as how the fish move and eat and where they sleep.

Nearby are other special exhibits with octopus, lobsters and several other well-presented specimens, as well as plenty of displays on a variety of ecological marine topics. The new fresh-water display features 200 piranhas (ranging from 1 to 9 inches) in a setting that resembles the Amazon river,

Deep Sea World cost the consortium that developed it £5.5 million in 1993

with jungle plants, sounds and smells. The centre aims to educate its visitors about the jungle and environmental issues as well as the fish. It has a classroom and two full-time teachers who give talks to visitors.

Next you pass the pirate displays, faintly incongruous yet gory and realistic (older children love it, but younger ones are likely to be terrified by the smoke, smells and yelling). Down a sloping cavern-like walkway — also possibly a bit scary — you reach what appears to be the seabed, then enter an acrylic tunnel which winds below what could be a crystal-clear sea. Slow-flapping skate and shoals of unblinking cod steer silently around you, menacing sharks power past (some of the sand-tiger sharks that live in the tank are as much as 9 feet long), and conger eels gape from holes in the rock. Be careful: half the floor is a moving walkway and, before you realise, children could be silently propelled 20 meters further on.

You move around this circular tunnel at your own pace — most visitors go right round several times and there is no pressure to move on. You can alternate your time between the displays upstairs and the excursions down to seabed level.

LUNCHBOX

At Deep Sea World an eating area called the Shark Bite Café offers straightforward family fare.

Comely villages in the East Neuk of Fife

Many would say that Crail's little harbour is the prettiest in Fife

An adventurous family day out that combines time spent exploring curious museums and grand houses with walks around picturesque fishing villages and along sandy beaches. There is even a National Nature Reserve island to explore.

'Neuk' is the old Scots word for corner and here applies to the scenic eastern peninsula of the old Kingdom of Fife; a string of colour-washed, red-roofed little villages clings to the coastline, while inland, the rich farming country undulates towards the sea. Fishing has been part of local life since the ninth century, when Crail exported salt fish to Europe. This seafaring tradition lives on around the bustling harbours but East Neuk offers many other attractions.

Travel south-east out of St Andrews (see *Great Day Out 143*) on the A917, passing through fertile countryside – and round some very nasty bends. Eight miles on the left is **Cambo***, just past a village called

♦ **GOOD FOR** Fishing villages, a Cold War bunker, birds, beaches and a castle
♦ **TRANSPORT** Car essential
♦ **ACCESS FOR DISABLED PEOPLE** No
♦ **BEST TIME TO VISIT** Spring or summer

Kingsbarns. Built at the tail end of the nineteenth century, after the previous mansion had mysteriously burnt down, this massive old pile was constructed expressly to be the largest house in Fife. It still is, and thought by some to be the ugliest too, but it does have beautiful, rolling parkland, carpeted with snowdrops and daffodils in spring, a landscaped two-and-a-half-acre walled garden built around a little stream, complete with waterfall and

oriental bridges. Old-fashioned roses bloom all summer, dahlias in autumn.

Just before Crail you might like to turn right on the B940 to the **Secret Bunker*** at Troywood. This labyrinthine underground hideout, built during the Cold War, was to be the command centre for government and military leaders in the event of nuclear war. The operations rooms, computer rooms, broadcast studios and living quarters are all on view, enhanced by an audio-visual theatre. There is also a café and gift shop.

On to **Crail**, with its pastel-washed little houses, cobbled streets and photogenic harbour. It is worth enduring the throngs of artists and tourists in summer to wander round this beautifully preserved village. The **tourist information office*** and **Crail Museum and Heritage Centre*** are in an eighteenth-century fisherman's house at 62 Marketgate. The museum provides an insight into the past life of this ancient royal burgh, its seafaring tradition and 200-year-old golf club. It is said that the devil hurled the large blue stone that now rests at the gate of the twelfth-century **church of St Mary** from his hideout on the **Isle of May** (visible some five miles out to sea). The island, now a National Nature Reserve, teems with raucous birdlife, with eider duck, razorbills, puffins and gulls all competing for territory and food. Seals also have breeding grounds here.

Trips to the Isle of May and sea-angling tours can be arranged through **Anstruther Pleasure Trips*** in the attractive little town of that name to the south-west. Here, in a series of old, higgledy-piggledy buildings, is the **Scottish Fisheries Museum***, which charts the development of whaling and

Pittenweem is the thriving home port for the Fife fishing fleet

fishing in the area with lots of reconstructed interiors and old boats.

A possible detour here is **Kellie Castle***, just inland (see map). The original house dates from the fourteenth century, but today's building is mostly sixteenth- and seventeenth-century, an excellent example of Scottish domestic architecture and elegantly manicured gardens. The famous Scots architect Sir Robert Lorimer designed the walled garden and garden house.

Back on the coast road (the A917), **Pittenweem** has a frenetic, early-morning market where local restaurateurs come to buy fish from the morning's catch. The National Trust for Scotland has been hard at work here, renovating the square, gabled tower of **Kellie's Lodgings** in the High Street and a cluster of old houses called the **Gyles** by the harbour. A mile further down in **St Monance** steep wynds lead down to the cottage-lined harbour.

Besides the golf links and popular Ship Inn down on the harbourside,

the award-winning beach at **Elie** is probably this small town's main attraction. It is long, clean, clear and sandy – and occasionally seals can be seen basking on the little rocks in the bay. At the south-west end of the beach is **Kincraig Point**, round which an ancient **Chain Walk** winds. Great fun on a calm sunny day, the chains (firmly embedded in the rock) lead you round the headland, and you scramble up and down well-worn rockfaces to a cave. Stories vary as to whether this served as a storage place for pirates' booty or where Macduff hid from a vengeful Macbeth in the eleventh century.

From Earlsferry **Largo Bay** opens up to the west. This is mainly residential, with holiday homes scattered round the bay. The beach and golf links are closer to Edinburgh than those to the north and consequently more crowded. **Lower Largo** was the birthplace of local hero Alexander Selkirk, born here in 1676 – he was marooned on a tiny island in the Pacific Ocean for five years and provided the inspiration for Daniel Defoe's *Robinson Crusoe*. A statue in the square commemorates Selkirk. On a fine day, venture off up the main A915 towards St Andrews and climb **Largo Law**, an odd volcanic plug that rises out of the surrounding countryside to a height of 948 feet. It's not a difficult climb and the views across the rolling hills of inland Fife, and out over the sea, are superb.

The royal and ancient town of St Andrews

Whether you come to enjoy the unspoilt stretches of Fife's longest beach, explore the old castle, visit the new high-tech Sea Life Centre or play a game of golf on one of the famous courses, you need never be at a loose end in this part of Scotland.

Tucked away in a corner of the picturesque East Neuk of Fife, St Andrews is first and foremost a historic university town and second a mecca for golfers. The castle and the cathedral are medieval, steeped in violent legend from the days that saw Protestant martyrs regularly burnt at the stake. Many buildings date from the early fifteenth century, when Scotland's oldest university was founded here. In recent years this beautiful little seaside town has pulled itself into the twentieth century. Its facilities, for both tourists and golfers, are now second to none.

The best way to see St Andrews is to park on one of the three main streets – the town centre basically consists of Market Street (where a

♦ **GOOD FOR** Adults and children will find plenty to do and see here, both in and out of doors; a must for golfers

♦ **TRANSPORT** It is best to park the car in town and walk around

♦ **ACCESS FOR DISABLED PEOPLE** Access is limited at the cathedral and the castle (rough terrain), the university grounds (some gravel paths) and the Sea Life Centre; the British Golf Museum and the Craigtoun Country Park are fully accessible

♦ **BEST TIME TO VISIT** Spring and summer. If you want a quiet time, don't go when a golf international is on

helpful **tourist information office*** can be found), North and South Streets – and explore on foot. Car parks are also provided in Murray Place and City Road. All

Thousands of pilgrims visited the cathedral in medieval times to pray at the shrine of St Andrew

roads lead to the **cathedral**, which is where you should head first. This was built in 1160 and was once the biggest in Scotland, with 31 altars. It has stood in ruins since 1559, when Calvinist zealots stripped it of its riches, but the vast twin towers still dominate the skyline.

The little Cathedral Museum is full of odd bits and pieces, and if it is not too blustery, you might like to climb the 158 stone steps that lead to the top of **St Rule's Tower**, which stands bluff and gaunt behind the cathedral. From the tower, you will be rewarded with a stunning view over the neat town, fishing harbour and miles of soft, sandy beaches. It is a short walk from here through the Pends, a huge, vaulted fourteenth-century gatehouse, once the entrance to the priory, by the side of the castle walls to the **harbour**. Here, after church on Sunday during term-time, red-gowned students still make their traditional pier-walk. Little boats buzz in and out of the harbour, nets lie in heaps, and seagulls circle overhead; it is very much a working harbour. The beach just to the south is the East Sands, popular in summer but bitterly cold in winter, when winds blow in from Siberia. The **leisure centre*** here, with pool, water slides, squash courts, snooker, bar and restaurant, is ideal for children on days when the weather is not too good.

To the north of the beach, the Scores runs along the coast, lined with baronial buildings that house some of the university's departments, to the ruins of **St Andrews Castle**. The peaceful aspect of the ruins belies the castle's turbulent past: power struggles within the Church were played out here until the sixteenth century, and many martyrdoms and revenge killings took place. Prisoners and dead bodies alike were summarily

Golf was first played on the Old Course, the renowned home of golf, in 1400

Golf was invented by the Scots in the early fifteenth century, so it is natural that its spiritual home is in Scotland. It was a game for members of the aristocracy, because only they had the time to indulge in such a hobby, and was played on sandy spaces close to the shoreline, called 'links'. In 1754, a party of gentlemen golfers got together and formed the Society of St Andrews Golfers, which acquired its present title of The Royal and Ancient Golf Club when William IV became the club's patron in 1834. Called the R&A by those in the know, the club sets the rules for golf throughout the world.

flung into the infamous bottle dungeon, a 24-foot-deep pit hewn out of solid rock and still visible in the Sea Tower; few escaped. A secret passage here was burrowed into the cliff sides in 1546 (a new Visitor Centre offers more information).

Turn right up the Scores from the castle and left up Butt's Wynd, a comically named little alleyway that leads into North Street, and peer through a great stone archway into the university's elegant main quadrangle, part of **St Salvator's College**, founded in 1450. Legend has it that the face of heretic martyr Patrick Hamilton is burnt into the stone – look to the left of the arch. To the right of the arch is St Salvator's Chapel, traditionally the university's main church, which contains the pulpit from which John Knox preached. Guided tours of the university start from the porter's lodge (mid-July to September only).

On South Street is pretty, tree-lined St Mary's Quad, home of the theological college. The **St Andrews Museum***, in Hepburn Gardens, tells the story of the relationship between town and gown.

A ten-minute walk up North Street to the opposite end of the town transports you into golfing heaven. Here, the squat stone shape of the Royal and Ancient Golf Club presides over the hallowed greens of the Old Course, where the British Open is held. It is the ruling body of golf, and although the clubhouse is not open to the public, the **British Golf Museum*** is just across the road. Pictures of golfing heroes and a mishmash of clubs, memorabilia and video footage trace the history of the game. The rules for admission to the Old Course are very strict; it is also possible to book in advance and play on other courses in the area, including the Balgove, the Jubilee, the Strathtyrum and the Eden – ring **St Andrews Links*** for details.

Children who want a bit of light entertainment will revel in the **Sea Life Centre***, just off the Scores. It contains hundreds of specimens of British marine life, great walk-through tanks and some huge, rather scary fish. The vast stretch of the West Sands falls away to the left, a wonderful stretch of beach which is a safe haven for swimmers. In the summer Fife can be surprisingly warm and sunny, making this lovely beach unbeatable. It is sandy, long enough not to get horribly crowded and the sea can be quite warm.

A couple of miles south-west of St Andrews on the B939, the beautifully landscaped 50-acre **Craigtoun Country Park*** stands in the grounds of grand old Mount Melville House. Here you will find a model Dutch village in the middle of an ornamental lake, a miniature railway, boating, crazy golf, a formal Italian garden, picnic areas and many woodland trails.

LUNCHBOX

There are lots of good pubs, wine bars, cafés and restaurants in and around St Andrews. If you want peace and quiet, visit the tranquil Rufflets Hotel on the road to Craigtoun Park, but if you prefer to see the students at play, you should try the Victoria Café on St Mary's Place at the west end of Market Street.

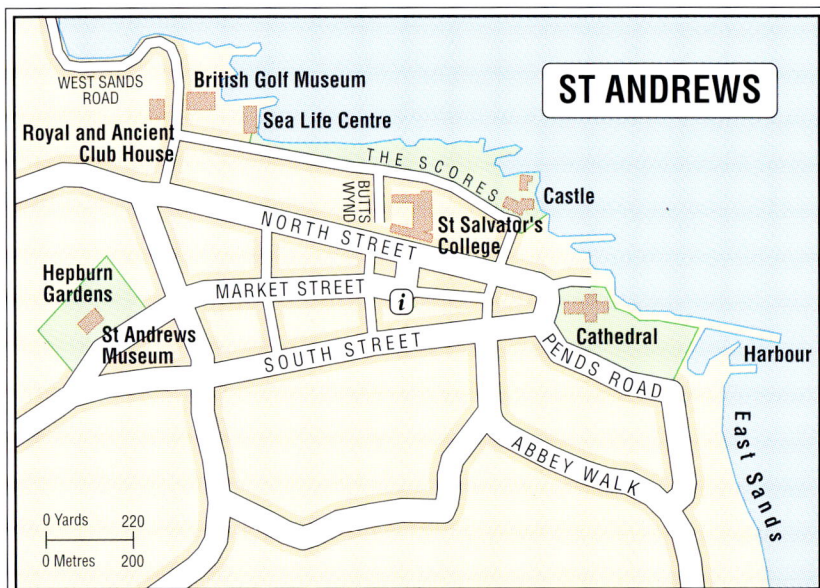

ST ANDREWS

WEST SANDS ROAD
British Golf Museum
Sea Life Centre
Royal and Ancient Club House
THE SCORES
BUTTS WYND
NORTH STREET
Castle
St Salvator's College
Hepburn Gardens
MARKET STREET
St Andrews Museum
SOUTH STREET
Cathedral
PENDS ROAD
Harbour
ABBEY WALK
East Sands

0 Yards   220
0 Metres   200

The wild beauty of the Angus glens

Glen Esk, the northernmost glen, is a long haul through rolling scenery

GET TO KNOW THE GLENS ON FOOT

The Glen Doll car park is the starting point for walks of all grades from full-scale mountain expeditions (for the experienced and well-shod only) to shorter strolls. You could, for example, take the route signposted north from the car park (that is, away from Glen Doll itself) – a pleasant walk by the burn which leads towards woodland, about a mile from your starting point. This is the Capel Mounth track, an ancient way that crosses high ground to drop eventually into Glen Muick and Deeside. You need go only as far as the end of the woodland for a superb view of the craggy glen and a hint of the empty stretches of the plateau lands above.

Unsung and unspoilt, the Angus glens offer plenty to delight the birdwatcher, botanist and walker. This day out covers a large area of the glens, from Edzell in the east to Glen Clova in the west, and takes in castles, a museum and hilltop forts, all set in spectacular scenery.

The Angus glens lie between the central belt of Scotland and the northlands, and between the rich farmlands of Strathmore and the high Grampian peaks. These extremely long, lonely, silent glens running deep into the hills are comparatively unknown, although the main glens all have public roads for much of their length. Allow enough time for exploration, bearing in mind, for example, that it is 18 miles from Kirriemuir to the car park at the head of Glen Clova.

HILL TOWNS AND LONELY ROADS

Glen Esk is the northernmost of the Angus glens, with the sleepy little village of **Edzell** as its gateway. Two miles north-east, an inconspicuous road sign by a red phone box leads to a secret world penetrating far into the uplands. In the lower reaches the open

- ♦ **GOOD FOR** Those who enjoy walking
- ♦ **TRANSPORT** A car is a must to get to this remote area. The trip described here is nearly 80 miles long
- ♦ **ACCESS FOR DISABLED PEOPLE** Parts of Edzell Castle and the Glenesk Folk Museum are accessible; there is a lift at Barrie's house but passageways are narrow
- ♦ **BEST TIME TO VISIT** Spring for snowy hills, autumn for colour. The properties are closed for the winter

fields are lush and green below the brown hills. At the cluster of houses, which is **Tarfside,** long-distance walkers stock up with home bakes. Nearby, at a former shooting lodge called the Retreat, you will find the **Glenesk Folk Museum*** (opens at noon), which reveals much of the everyday life of the glens. Further up the glen, birchwoods and pine, a guardian castle and the tumbling

River North Esk set the scene.

All these glens are ancient through-routes to the north; over the centuries pedlars, packmen, priests and predatory armies have gone before today's visitors, up and over the Grampian plateau. The right-of-way signposts bearing names in Royal Deeside to the north are very tempting, and if you have never visited the glens before you may experience itchy feet at the road-end car park (beware, it may strike again in Glens Clova and Isla). Instead, turn the car round, perhaps after a stroll to Invermark Castle, a tall and grim four-square fort guarding the pass, and make your way back to Edzell. Close by is the red tower of sixteenth-century **Edzell Castle***, with its unique 'pleasance', a walled garden laid out in heraldic patterns.

On the minor road running south-west from Edzell you will find the **White and Brown Caterthuns** signposted by Historic Scotland. The views are spectacular from the Iron Age hilltop forts, now tumbled ramparts of stone – an atmospheric spot where you can wonder at the sheer effort of those builders of 2,000 years ago.

Edzell Castle, the seat of the Crawford Lindsays, was built in the sixteenth century

Make your way by minor roads to the junction at **Memus**. Then go right for Dykehead and Glen Clova; this route shows the characteristic U-profile of a Scottish glen, gouged out by glaciers, with pastures along the river-flats and steep slopes rolling down. At the car park beyond Braedownie at the mouth of **Glen Doll** (which joins the head of Glen Clova) the atmosphere is positively alpine. High above are the grey crags of the **Winter Corrie**, a hanging valley sculpted by long-melted glaciers. At your feet, even quite close to the car park, you will find examples of the flora that make the Clova area one of the most exciting in all of Scotland for botanists. As at Glen Esk, many walkers' routes meet at the car park, with rights of way leading off in all directions (see box).

Retrace your route towards Memus, noting that a section of the glen has a road on either side. By now if you have dallied in Esk or

You may not be able to cover more than Glens Esk and Clova in a day, unless you intend to spend most of the time in the car. If you do extend your stay, explore Glens Prosen and Isla, which are nearby. **Glen Prosen** is very scenic and is associated with Captain Robert Falcon Scott (Scott of the Antarctic), who planned his ill-fated South Pole expedition from a house in the lower reaches (now an art gallery). A memorial cairn can be seen nearby. **Glen Isla** is bare and wild in its upper reaches but offers a choice of walking routes, including a through way into Deeside, the Monega Pass, sometimes described as Britain's highest right of way.

Clova the day will be well advanced. There are many more sights to see in the area, if you have the time – you could, for example, make your way by minor roads south-west to **Kirkton of Kingoldrum** for displays of exclusive knitwear designs. Continue west to **Bridgend of Lintrathen** and go round to the south of the Loch of Lintrathen – Dundee's water supply – to reach Peel Farm, with its farm trail and gift shop. Moments away from Peel Farm is the **Reekie Linn**, where the River Isla tumbles out of the Highlands – actually over the Highland Boundary Fault – in a spectacular waterfall which sends up spray to create a misty rainbow. Take care, as the shady path to the fall is unfenced.

Finally, return east via Kirriemuir, the southern gateway to the Angus glens, noting on the way back the **Loch of Kinnordy**, a nature reserve in the care of the RSPB. **Kirriemuir** is a handsome red-sandstone town with cobbled, winding streets. It is best known for its association with the creator of *Peter Pan*, J.M. Barrie. The National Trust for Scotland looks after his **birthplace***, home to a *Peter Pan* display.

Take a picnic with you or else have lunch or afternoon tea at the Glenesk Folk Museum, which serves good, plain home cooking. The Drovers Inn at Memus is a favourite lunch spot for those in the know. Excellent home bakes can be bought at Peel Farm near the Loch of Lintrathen.

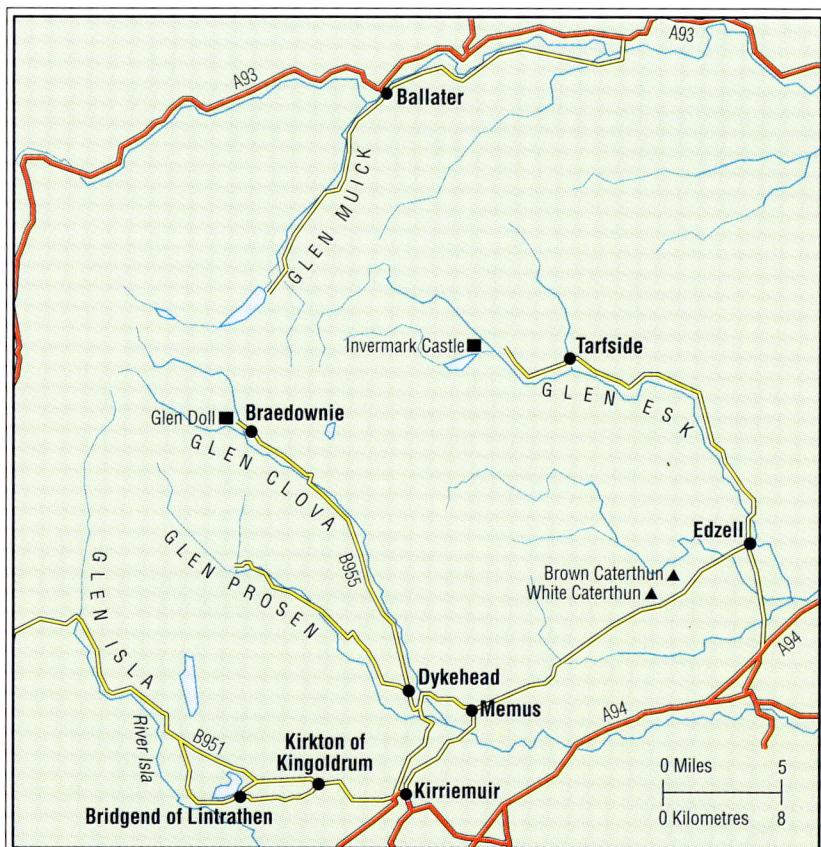

Royal Deeside: highland walks and Balmoral Castle

The granite turrets of Balmoral Castle amid gorgeous autumn forest colours

A favourite royal venue since the mid-nineteenth century, when Prince Albert checked the weather statistics and chose it as the ideal holiday destination for Queen Victoria, the wooded valley of the River Dee attracts visitors from far and wide.

The royal family acquired the estate in 1852 and work on Balmoral Castle, formerly a country house, began immediately. The area is very picturesque, from the well-ordered fields and woodlands down-river towards Aberdeen to the harmonious pinewood and hill scenery of the upper reaches, where the Dee emerges from the high Cairngorms. As there is more than enough to see in one day, the riverside excursion described here can only be selective.

Between Aberdeen and Banchory lie the National Trust for Scotland properties of **Drum Castle*** and **Crathes Castle***, part of the area's rich architectural heritage. Crathes has the bonus of a fine garden. (Another option for a day out would be to take

♦ **GOOD FOR** Superb Highland scenery – but you would be lucky to spot royalty
♦ **TRANSPORT** Hourly bus service (201) from Aberdeen to Braemar serves all Deeside villages
♦ **ACCESS FOR DISABLED PEOPLE** No
♦ **BEST TIME TO VISIT** Autumn for landscape colour

the Castle Trail and see the region's finest buildings in succession.)

If you press on along the main A93 beyond Banchory to the upper reaches of the Dee, you will notice the hills beginning to close in. After Aboyne, look for a granite boulder with the legend 'You are now entering Highlands' cut into it. The road continues through extensive

birchwoods. Turn right up the A97, going north for a few minutes until you see a car park on the left and a small visitor centre. This is the starting point for the short **Burn o'Vat walk**, a stroll (on duckboards) through the trees to reach a half-hidden rocky hollow on the Vat Burn. Here the local outlaw, Gilderoy (a kind of downmarket Rob Roy Macgregor), hid his rustled cattle. Follow the path's wooden steps for a fine view, through the birch and pine, over Loch Kinnord. This walk is part of the Muir of Dinnet National Nature Reserve.

Return to the main road to reach **Ballater**, where you can count the 'By Royal Appointment' signs displayed above several shops, suppliers to the royal household at Balmoral Castle. Goods on sale range from basic foodstuffs to antiques and outdoor wear. From Ballater, you can make a worthwhile excursion to the south-west, across the Dee, to take in **Glen Muick**. Red deer are all but guaranteed near the car park at the road's end and you will even find a pair of binoculars thoughtfully provided at the little visitor centre to help you spot them.

Take the Glen Muick option only if you reach Ballater early in the day, but in any case cross the Dee to take the South Deeside Road (B976), where the **Royal Lochnagar Distillery*** offers displays, tour, whisky-tasting, shop and so on – the complete distillery experience. The scones in the café are usually good, too. **Balmoral Castle*** is nearby, though its opening hours are limited (see box).

The South Deeside Road rejoins the main A93 at Balmoral. Continue west through an increasingly impressive pinewood setting to cross the Dee once more. Downstream from this bridge is the **Old Bridge of Dee** with a shoulder of high Lochnagar in the background – one of the most photographed views for

▲ *The heather-clad hills beyond the Brig o' Dee near Braemar*

BALMORAL CASTLE
Typically, when he had Balmoral Castle rebuilt in 1852–5, Prince Albert made sure that many of his own ideas were incorporated. The castle's pleasant grounds and the ballroom, with paintings from the Queen's private collection, are open for three months of the year only – May, June and July. Before visiting, check the times at any tourist information office in the valley, such as the one at Braemar*. (Park on the Crathie side of the bridge.) For the rest of the year Balmoral is a private home under high security. However, unless you are a dedicated royal-watcher, you will find more interesting places to see on Deeside.

miles around, replicated on a multitude of shortbread tins.

Look for **Braemar Castle*** on the approaches to Braemar itself. This Highland village was the unlikely birthplace for Robert Louis Stevenson's adventure novel *Treasure Island* (1881), part of which he wrote when he and his family spent a holiday here in wet weather. The **Braemar Highland Heritage Centre*** tells the story of the village and its famous association with the Braemar Gathering, the best-known of the Highland games, held annually in September. There are some fine walks up **Morrone Hill** behind the village, with views towards the Cairngorm massif.

Rather than heading on into the Cairngorm heartlands immediately to the west, the main road sheers off south. However, a minor road continues up-river and is well worth

taking for three different natural attractions, all involving rocks and water. The first of these entails a walk up Glen Ey, which runs south from the Dee by the little settlement of Inverey. The Ey Water pushes through the steep, rocky cleft known as the **Colonel's Bed**. It was used as a hiding-place by Colonel John Farquharson after the Battle of Killiecrankie in 1689, the climax of the Jacobite uprising.

A little further on, the road loops back over the **Linn of Dee**. Before it broadens into the brown pools where the salmon lie, the young Dee is constricted at the Linn by narrow rocky shelves through which the waters roar and foam. You may be tempted to leap the river here, but would be wiser not to risk it – and beware of slippery tree roots.

Finally, if you keep going to the end of the public road, a walk up

through the trees, northwards, brings you to yet another scenic watery place, the **Earl of Mar's punchbowl**. This spot, where the rolling stones of the little River Quoich have hollowed out several circular bowls in the rocky banks, polished and silvery grey, is ideal for a picnic. The vicinity offers many other possibilities for walks.

By way of a change, when you return to Braemar you can take the South Deeside Road from Ballater towards Aberdeen. On the way, near Aboyne, you pass the entrance to **Glen Tanar**, one of the finest of the Deeside glens. As well as the pinewoods, which offer a good variety of walks on to the open hills for another day, the **hardy tree nursery** is worth visiting: if the trees prosper here, high on a northern hill, they should flourish in your garden.

LUNCHBOX
Picnicking is recommended. Otherwise, Ballater has the widest choice of eating places in the valley.

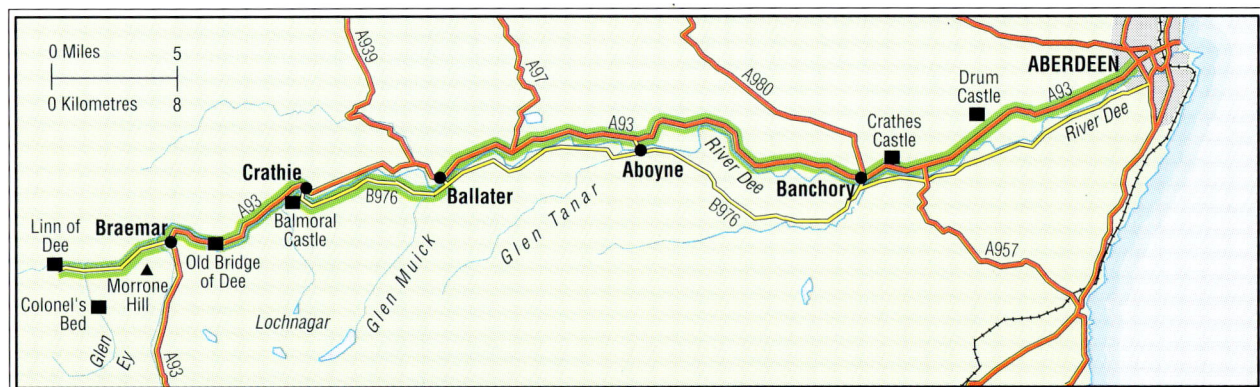

The delights of Britain's northernmost city

Aberdeen's splendid architecture spanning several centuries, superb art gallery and remarkable horticultural displays will appeal to adults and older children; youngsters can have fun (and learn) in an interactive science museum and burn up the calories in an adventure playground.

Although you may perceive Aberdeen as being a long way from anywhere, it is only a couple of hours by road from Edinburgh and has good air and rail connections. Its most attractive feature is its silvery granite townscape, and it glories in its floral decorations, spending large sums of money on stunningly colourful displays from early crocuses to high summer roses in parks, public places and even the central reservation of the ring road.

There is enough to do and see in Central Aberdeen for a day, so the suggestions below are restricted to this area. If you have more time, go and admire the venerable buildings of Old Aberdeen and laze on the 2-mile-long sandy beach to the north.

♦ **GOOD FOR** The whole family – art and architecture for the adults, activities both mental and physical for the children
♦ **TRANSPORT** Aberdeen is well connected by train and air; bus services within the city are good
♦ **ACCESS FOR DISABLED PEOPLE** Art Gallery and Satrosphere are fully accessible; Provost Skene's House accessible only at ground-floor level; no access at Marischal Museum
♦ **BEST TIME TO VISIT** Any time; summer is best for rose displays

Scotland's third city is compact and easy to get around. You could follow the route described here using public transport or take advantage of Aberdeen's park-and-ride schemes.

The Granite City is a regular winner of the Britain in Bloom trophy

Alternatively, use the multi-storey car park above or beside the Bon Accord Shopping Centre.

Start at the excellent **Art Gallery*** in Schoolhill. It boasts a cross-section of most painting styles, although it favours the eighteenth to twentieth centuries. You may notice the preponderance of British – especially Scottish – artists, but the French are well represented, notably the Barbizon School, the precursors of the Impressionists. It also has a good watercolour section, where you can see works by Blake and Turner. Note, in passing, the pillars just inside the gallery entrance hall, each made from a different kind of granite, from silver grey to rich red.

Make your way west along Schoolhill and up Kirkgate towards Marischal College, which is part of Aberdeen University. The college is the second-largest granite building in the world, and has an unmistakable rippling façade topped with gilded flags. As well as university departments, the college is home to the **Marischal Museum*** (at the far end of the quadrangle), which contains a diverting mix of local and rather eclectic ethnographic material from around the world.

Opposite the museum, dwarfed by the ugly modern block of St Nicholas House, is **Provost Skene's House***, a steeply gabled, rubble-built townhouse. It is the oldest domestic house in Aberdeen and dates in part from 1545. In it are several furnished period rooms.

Next make your way up to the top or west end of Union Street, the main thoroughfare of the city, to **Satrosphere***. It has been described as an 'interactive science and technology exhibition centre', but in reality is much more fun. It pitches itself at a wide age range (including, surprisingly, the very

ACCOMMODATION
Because of Aberdeen's involvement in the oil industry, it is extremely well provided with hotels for the business sector in particular. However, given that business folk tend to go home at weekends, you should be able to secure a short break at a budget price, as some hotels discount room rates at weekends.

A taste of the tropics in the Winter Gardens at Duthie Park

young), offering a variety of 'hands-on' equipment with a scientific theme. Children can spin a giant wheel to demonstrate centrifugal force, fiddle with microscopes and experiment with sound waves, soap bubbles, inertia wheels, photosensitive walls, periscopes and chain bridges. There is a host of things to jump on, twiddle, look or speak into, or, in the case of the huge panpipes, hit with sticks to make music. All in all, an absorbing couple of hours can be spent here.

If Satrosphere represents an intellectual challenge, **Ramboland*** has no such pretensions. It is a large and imaginatively designed adventure playground, part of **Aberdeen Amusement Park*** (which claims to be Scotland's largest permanent funfair) and is noisy and

garish. You can buy any number of fixed-price tickets to the park, depending on which rides you want. This applies also to entry to Ramboland, for which you will need nine tickets. Admission to the park's slides, walkways and other adventurous paraphernalia works not on the basis of age but of size. Only children less than 4 foot 6 inches (137cm) tall – and you can measure them on the spot to check – can go in. It is open daily all-year round, well into the evening (around 10pm) in summer.

Ramboland is tucked inside the covered part of the entertainment complex and appears as a separated-off area of rope walkways, nets, chutes, tunnels and stairs stretching up and out of sight. A junior, softer, safer version is adjacent for under-3s. Attentive staff help you to keep an eye on exuberant youngsters climbing, bouncing, swinging and shrieking.

If you can tear the children away, slow them down a little by taking them, via the harbour area and the banks of the River Dee, to **Duthie Park***. Here

Painted ceilings and local history displays can be seen in Provost Skene's House

you will find what is described as the largest covered glasshouse in Europe, the Winter Gardens. This is a good place for very young children – they will enjoy seeing fat goldfish and carp, a giant frog that mysteriously rises and sinks, a talking cactus (sometimes) and the exotic vegetation with winding walkways and little bridges.

An open-air alternative would be **Hazlehead Park**, which has a children's zoo (mainly of the tame goats and rabbits variety) and – quite a novelty for Scotland – an old-established maze. Its dense, high privet hedging ensures no cheating.

Other options for your itinerary include Aberdeen's **Maritime Museum***, within walking distance of the Marischal Museum and telling the story of the city's sea-going connections. A new oil-related exhibition is scheduled to open here in 1997. Moments away is the **Tolbooth Museum***, where you can do a tour of the old cells in what was once the administrative centre of Aberdeen. At the mouth of the harbour the quaint fishing village of **Footdee** (Fittie) is well worth a visit.

LUNCHBOX
Refreshments are available at the Art Gallery, Provost Skene's House, Ramboland and the Amusement Park. The **tourist information office*** is a good source for more details.

The whisky trail through glorious Speyside

☂ ❄ ♿

The massive copper stills at Glen Grant Distillery, dwarfing the stillsman

MAKING MALT WHISKY

Producers outside Scotland have never been able to match the quality and variety of Scottish malts, which are made from pure, soft spring water, home-grown barley, and yeast. Production is a complex process: initially the barley is soaked, allowed to germinate and gently dried in a kiln, under which peat may be burned to influence the flavour. The 'malt', as the barley is now known, is crushed and mashed with the spring water at 64°C. Mashing converts the barley starches to sugars. The resulting sweet liquid ('worts') is cooled and yeast added to ferment the sugars to alcohol. After fermentation the liquor ('wash') is distilled twice in copper pot stills. It is the stillsman's responsibility to select and keep the best of the second distillation, which is matured in oak casks for a number of years. The wood serves to mellow and round the spirit, imparting the colour and flavour that give the whisky its unique character. When the time is right, the spirit is reduced to bottling strength. After bottling, the whisky is packed and despatched worldwide.

This route takes you through the beautiful Spey valley, bordered to the east by the Cairngorm mountains. On the way you have the chance to sample some of the most exclusive malt whiskies in the world.

A long the course of the River Spey, climate and geology conspire to produce the optimum conditions for the soft water used in making the very finest whisky – its Gaelic name, *uisge beatha*, means 'water of life'. The result of this happy collusion of nature is the highest concentration of malt whisky distilleries in the world. Unless you are an aficionado of the merits of individual malts you will probably want to select just a couple of distilleries to visit and otherwise just enjoy the drive, the colours of the landscape and the sight of the burns rushing down the bleak foothills of the Cairngorms.

Note that if you have young children with you they may not be allowed into the distilleries' production areas.

The modern chimney stacks of **Glenlivet Distillery*** are ten miles north of Tomintoul, alongside the

♦ **GOOD FOR** Seeing superb countryside while educating the palate
♦ **TRANSPORT** 70-mile trip; volunteer the non-drinking driver in your party. As an alternative, the little Speyside Rambler bus can be taken to some of the sights from Tomintoul
♦ **ACCESS FOR DISABLED PEOPLE** Possible at the distilleries
♦ **BEST TIME TO VISIT** All year

River Avon on the B9136. In 1824 this became the first distillery to go into legal production, following concessions by the Parliament of the day, which realised that by decriminalising and taxing liquor it could create a source of revenue. Exhibits here include an assortment of ancient, mysterious tools used in the distilling process.

Ten miles from Glenlivet Distillery along the B9009 is Dufftown, centre of distilling country

and home of one of the most famous distilleries in the world, **Glenfiddich***. It does not occupy the most attractive of sites, having a backdrop of forest-denuded hills and the untidy ruins of Balvenie Castle close by. Glenfiddich is still a family concern, owned by the Grants, and the only distillery that still bottles on the premises. It offers a small exhibition, audio-visual display, picnic area and gift shop, where you can buy presentation bottles and very old malts at very serious prices.

At Craigellachie to the north-west is **Speyside Cooperage***, where over 100,000 oak casks are repaired and refurbished annually for individual distilleries. Here you can see skilled coopers and their apprentices at work and savour the sights, sounds and smells of the largest independent cooperage in

Strathisla Distillery is the oldest operating distillery in the Highlands

Britain. This traditional industry is thriving again thanks to the upsurge in whisky export and tourism.

Turn left on the A95 to Ballindalloch to find the **Glenfarclas Visitor Centre***, completed in 1973, with its distinctive pagoda-

style entrance. The premium malt whisky produced here by five generations of the Grant family is much praised, and visitors are well catered for, with a gift shop, audio-visual facilities and picnic area.

(Nearby stands **Ballindalloch Castle**, filled with the memorabilia of eight generations of Macpherson-Grants, including an excellent collection of Spanish paintings. The grounds are home to an exceptionally fine herd of Aberdeen Angus cattle.)

Taking the B9102 from Grantown-on-Spey or joining it between Rothes and Craigellachie you arrive in Knockando, where, in Victorian times, a woman named Helen Cumming struck an early blow for feminism by establishing **Cardhu Distillery*** (illegally) in 1811. It was legitimised in 1824 and moved

to its present site in 1884. Cardhu is now owned by the Johnnie Walker Company. The old soft stone buildings, sited round a picturesque pond, have been joined by a modern production plant, coffee shop, exhibition and picnic area.

Dallas Dhu Historic Distillery*, one mile south of Forres, slightly off the tourist track, is probably the most interesting of all the distilleries, perfectly preserved in its Victorian glory. The process of whisky production is brought to life through exhibitions incorporating life-size models and evocative photographs, displayed in sparkling white buildings clustered round a courtyard bordered with flowers. Wander around as you please, watch the video and sample the whisky.

Glen Grant Distillery*, five miles north of Craigellachie, was established in 1840 and is now run from a turreted baronial manse at Rothes. Glen Grant was once Scotland's largest producer of malt whisky. Today, the highlight is perhaps the carefully laid-out Victorian garden.

Chivas Regal owes a great deal of its character to the single malt produced since 1786 at **Strathisla***, Keith, to the east of Rothes along the B9015. Serene and rather snug-looking, the distillery squats by an offshoot of the River Isla, fronted by a huge waterwheel and two malting towers. Here you are left to look around in your own time, with complimentary handbook, before being offered a tutored whisky 'nosing', coffee, shortbread and souvenir brochure.

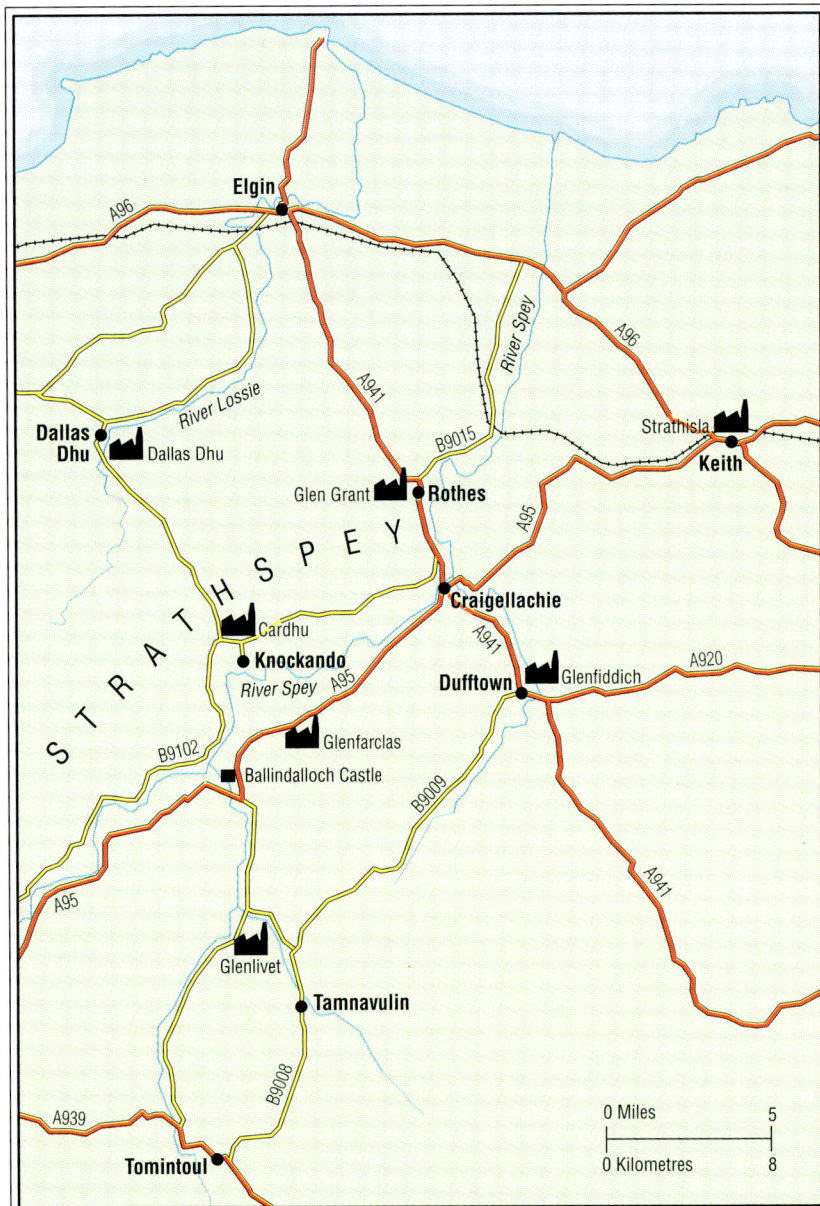

LUNCHBOX
Those in search of local food specialities might try the Delnashaugh Inn at Ballindalloch or the Rothes Glen Hotel (both closed in winter).

The undiscovered Moray Firth coastline

Sunnyside is a blissfully uncommercialised beach with plenty of golden sand

This excursion takes in tiny cottages clinging to the wild shoreline below sheer cliffs, old fishing ports a fishy museum — and an elegant country-house gallery. You could combine a bracing walk and even a spell on a beach with visiting the man-made attractions.

Along the Moray Firth coast in north-east Scotland, the immediate hinterland of much of Moray and Aberdeenshire comprises productive farmland or woods, rather than the acid peaty moorland, the 'wet desert' of the west, which so appeals to visitors. This overlooked narrow strip of wild cliff and sandy beach has plenty of wildlife interest, from rare plants to seabird colonies, as well as picturesque fishing villages built gable-end to the sea.

Wherever your base, perhaps in Banff or somewhere inland, start this route at **Pennan**, where a little sign from the switchbacking coastal road points steeply downhill. After nosing your car tentatively round the last

- ♦ **GOOD FOR** Pottering along a splendid coast; even in the rain you will be rewarded by dramatic seascapes
- ♦ **TRANSPORT** Car essential: Pennan to Buckie is a 33-mile drive
- ♦ **ACCESS FOR DISABLED PEOPLE** To main indoor attractions
- ♦ **BEST TIME TO VISIT** Any time

bend you descend from the rooftop level of the village's single strip of houses to a street where the sea is at your elbow. The car park is at the far end of the street. A great red cliff rears to the east. Below it is a harbour, while halfway along is the red phone box that found fame as a location for the film *Local Hero*,

starring Burt Lancaster. The houses huddle between a roaring pebbly shore and a tumbled rocky green slope. Once you have absorbed the atmosphere of this extraordinary sea-girt place, and maybe looked in at the pub, there is nowhere else to go but out again by the same road.

Further west another sign points to Cullykhan and Fort Fiddes, where there is another parking place if you want to explore some wild cliffs. (The area is not suitable for children, though some amazing seabird colonies are to be found here.) A gash in the rocks nearby is named Hell's Lum (Scots for chimney), because during storms the seaspray emerging from it appears to smoke.

The road to Crovie is a few minutes' drive further west. If Pennan is an unlikely setting for habitation, **Crovie** seems impossible – a crescent of cottages, prettified and tidy, but alarmingly close to the high-tide mark. There is no road access for visitors' cars. You can look down on the village from a spectacular viewpoint, exposed to the searing wind. Next, westward, clinging to the cliff-face, is the village of **Gardenstown** (Gamrie to the locals). Rather than clog up another cul-de-sac road which leads down to the village harbour, continue past the main access road and look instead for the bumpy track signed **Kirk of St John**. Try to do the superb walk, which offers a breathtaking view over both Gamrie and Crovie from the car park down to this ancient ruined church.

If, after this, you head for Macduff and Banff, you will be leaving behind the wildest stretch of this coast. **Macduff** is a workaday fishing port. Its neighbour on the other side of the River Deveron is **Banff**, which has a **tourist information office***. This handsome little town's Georgian

The precariously sited Crovie is best appreciated from the cliff-top

architecture can be admired in the surviving townhouses on its old High Street but reaches its epitome in **Duff House***, in the nearby parkland. Banff is hardly on a main route yet in Duff House it boasts the premier outstation of the National Galleries of Scotland. This Palladian mansion has many art treasures on view, including an El Greco, and it is worth allowing a reasonable amount of time to see the place properly.

Continuing west by the main road, you will reach **Portsoy** in just a few minutes. In addition to three antique shops and a marble workshop, it has a seventeenth-century harbour and charming dwellings and warehouses clustered along the waterfront, which has been used more than once as a period film set. (You will find a good café down the side street by the chemist.)

One of the finest of the beaches can be enjoyed at **Sandend**, five minutes further west, where you can

also buy excellent locally cured smoked fish. Between Sandend and Cullen, signposted off the main road, is the curious ruin of **Findlater Castle**, on a rocky headland, reached on foot from a car park in the middle of a farmstead. **Sunnyside Beach** can also be accessed only on foot. It is perhaps the most perfect little strand for miles in either direction – no ice-cream vans, no cars, no facilities of any kind: it offers just rock, cliff and golden sand.

At **Cullen**, the character of the coast changes again. Cullen is very appealing: a nineteenth-century planned settlement on a hill above the old sea-town. Separating the two are the viaducts of the old Great North of Scotland Railway, closed since 1968 and a visible indictment of the power of the local laird, who forced the railway to build them in order to keep the tracks off his land. Further west lies a string of small fishing hamlets showing the typical

north-east coastal taste for painted stonework with the mortar picked out in a contrasting colour. Portknockie has this attractive feature, as does Findochty, its neighbour. Between them is a good coastal path, where the linnets sing in the clifftop gorse and black guillemots nest in the tumbled rock below. Findochty's harbour, long deserted by the larger commercial fishing boats, takes on a positively Mediterranean air in the sunshine, with its yachts and little pleasure craft snugly moored below the colourful houses on terraces above.

The coastal road runs into Buckie, a grey and busy fishing town not aspiring to the picturesque. However, it does offer the **Buckie Drifter***, down by the quayside, which tells the story of the town's important role in the development of the herring fishery. Open-decked boats, then steam drifters and finally diesel-engined craft went out for decades after the shoals of the 'silver darlings', which were usually salted and packed in barrels, often for export, making fortunes – sometimes – for the curers. This was the basis for the prosperity of the coast, but at some human cost to those who sought a living from the sea. The Buckie Drifter, known as the 'fishiest museum in Moray' has an exciting fish gallery with interactive and hi-tech displays. You can also try your hand at various sea-related activities including packing fish in a barrel.

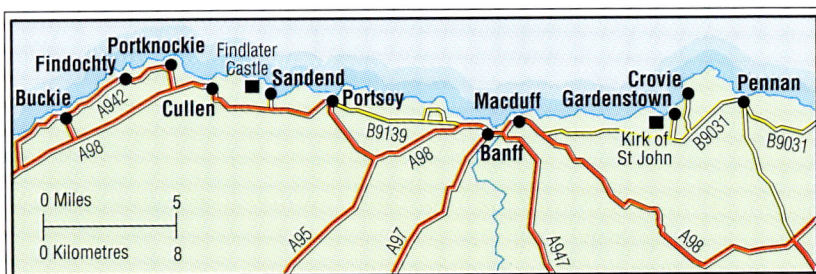

Glen Coe, where history's ghosts linger still

The dramatic skyline of Glen Coe, scene of dark deeds in days gone by

THE GLEN COE MASSACRE
The overwhelming beauty of this glen is matched by the tragic tale of the massacre during a blizzard one night in the winter of 1692. The rebel clan chief (and common sheep rustler) Alastair Macdonald of Glen Coe had been slow to swear a statutory oath of allegiance to King William III (it arrived six days after the deadline). While he was holed up high on the side of the lower part of the glen, to the south of the road, the King used this as an excuse to punish his troublesome subject, sending troops into the glen to billet with Macdonald. Clan tradition dictated that hospitality must be offered to all, so Campbell of Glenlyon and his 128 soldiers were welcomed into the little community, where they stayed for ten days enjoying generous Highland hospitality. In the early hours of 13 February Campbell and his troops arose and murdered 38 of their hosts, forcing the women, children and old men to flee into the icy hills, where many died of exposure. Henceforth, the Macdonalds and Campbells were locked in hatred.

Scotland's most infamous glen offers superb opportunities, in fine weather, for walking and marvelling at the spectacular, brooding scenery and, with luck, wild animals and birds of prey. Mountains, skiing, several small museums and craft shops are among other local attractions.

Most people have heard of Glen Coe – the Glen of Weeping – and, perhaps, of the horrific massacre that took place here in 1692, but few will be prepared for the glen's intense, unforgiving beauty. The glen is highly accessible, a two-and-a-half hour drive north from Glasgow along the newly modernised A82; Fort William is only 16 miles north on the same road.

Glen Coe is best approached from the south across the rain-sodden desolation of Rannoch Moor. On an icy but sunny winter day the moor looks stunning, pock-marked with frozen little lochans, everything still apart from a few birds. Sadly, it is

♦ **GOOD FOR** Those who enjoy walking and beautiful scenery
♦ **TRANSPORT** A car is a necessity
♦ **ACCESS FOR DISABLED PEOPLE** The day is mainly about walking
♦ **BEST TIME TO VISIT** Summer, when the weather is at its most gentle, late winter for the skiing and winter mountaineering

much more likely that you will see the moor with glowering rain clouds hanging low over the peaty ground, with the peaks disappearing behind straggles of mist and dew. The road wends its way across the moor before descending into Glen Coe itself, which used to be marked by

a lone piper in full regalia; even though he is no longer there the atmosphere can still be one of doom and menace.

The drive down to the **National Trust Visitor Centre***, just short of the little white-washed village of Glencoe, takes you past ragged raw crags, often topped with snow. In spring, melt-water cascades down these mountainsides to form spumey white waterfalls and tumbling rivers, strewn with boulders that have been dragged along by the sheer power of the water. Away from the main road the glen is even more breathtaking, and offers some of the best climbing in the Highlands.

Walking enthusiasts might like to try a popular hike that leads up from **Black Corries Lodge** (take the first turning on the right as you come into the glen from Rannnoch Moor) to the youth hostel at Corrour on

Red deer, a common sight throughout the glens

WALKING AND CLIMBING

This is not a glen for amateurs; if you are going to climb or walk in the hills, be sensible. Discuss the routes and your ability with the rangers at the Visitor Centre or at the **climbing hostel***, both at Clachaig, two miles east of Glencoe village, tell them which route you will take and equip yourself properly. The weather in this valley changes so quickly and becomes so severe that anyone can be caught out.

Loch Ossian, ten miles away over the hills and round the eastern end of Blackwater Reservoir. This is inaccessible by road; you are guaranteed total tranquillity and the chance to spot some wildlife: red deer, wild cats, pine martens, falcons and golden eagles – about 300 pairs of these huge birds of prey now nest in the Highlands – quite apart from the woodlands and alpine flora.

Many easier, and shorter, walks in the glen are detailed at the **Visitor Centre***, which offers an exhibition on the history of mountaineering in Glen Coe, an audio-visual presentation on the massacre (complete with blood-curdling sound effects), a snack bar and picnic area, all of which can get rather over-populated in the height of the summer.

At the head of the glen is a **skiing centre***, open between January and September. The chair-lifts go up to 2,400 feet and are an ideal way of seeing Glen Coe on a clear summer's day. Also located here are a small **Museum of Scottish Skiing and Mountaineering** and a licensed restaurant. In winter the skiing is good and quiet, comparatively sheltered and enjoys more hours of sunshine than other ski areas in Scotland. The glen also boasts the country's longest vertical ski descent – 2,600 feet.

If the weather is bad go to the **Glen Coe and North Lorne Folk Museum*** in Glencoe village. Situated in a group of thatched houses, it is full of relics from Jacobite times including weapons, costumes, tools, domestic utensils and old photographs. A couple of gift shops sell local craft items. Newly opened in Ballachulish is **Highland Mysteryworld***, a virtual reality experience of five different aspects of local history. Ballachulish also has a well-equipped **tourist information office*** (open Easter to October), and just across the distinctively arched Ballachulish Bridge is the **Confectionery Factory Visitor Centre***, specialising in Scottish foods and sweet, brittle fudge known as tablet.

LUNCHBOX

The seafood at Pier House, fifteen miles down the coast at Port Appin, is superb and not expensive. Otherwise, there are plenty of traditional Scots hotels dotted along the roadside, including baronial houses like the Ballachulish Hotel.

Black Rock Cottage, Glen Coe, frequented by many a mountaineer

Inverewe Gardens and a tour of Wester Ross

Loch Maree is a well-known fishing loch and a favourite in the area

A driving tour through stunning countryside between Loch Carron and Ullapool, taking in the tropical gardens at Inverewe.

Wester Ross is perhaps the most beautiful area of the sparsely populated North Highlands, flanking the coastline from Loch Carron in the south to Loch Inver in the north. It is crammed with stark mountains edged by peaceful lochs, unspoilt beaches warmed by the Gulf Stream, bays dotted with small islands, and pretty little towns. The gardens at Inverewe, an impressive monument to the Victorian obsession with the collecting and ordering of nature, are well worth a visit.

Start your tour at **Lochcarron**, the small town which stands at the head of Glen Carron. Here there is an excellent tweed factory, where you should be able to pick up some bargains. The little village of **Applecross** is off the A896, on a spectacular road winding down a bleak glen and known here as *Bealach na Ba*, Gaelic for the Pass of the Cattle. It is quite stupefyingly steep and has a series of tortuous hairpin bends, but persevere and you will be rewarded by the sight of the Cuillin

- ◆ **GOOD FOR** People who like remote, yet magnificent, scenery
- ◆ **TRANSPORT** Car essential: this is a one-way journey of 133 miles
- ◆ **ACCESS FOR DISABLED PEOPLE** There is disabled access to Inverewe Gardens
- ◆ **BEST TIME TO VISIT** Spring and early summer: late summer sees the advent of the midge!

Hills of Skye on the horizon, and the beauty of Applecross, full of flowers in spring and summer. Snug on the west side of a little peninsula, the village has the Flowertunnel Restaurant and a sandy beach in a sheltered bay.

From here, follow the coast road round the southern shore of Loch Torridon into **Torridon** village, much of which is now owned by the NTS, which has set up a visitor centre at the junction with the road signposted to Upper Loch Torridon. This provides information for walkers and has a small museum that highlights the importance of the magnificent red

deer to the profits of the vast sporting estates that made up much of the area. Drive onwards through the **Beinn Eighe National Nature Reserve***, past the menacing peaks of Liathach, often swathed in grey cloud. Here, the pine forest is home to foxes, pine martens, mountain goats, wildcats, deer, buzzards and the occasional golden eagle.

Eight miles north across this wild, lochan-splattered glen from Torridon, at the junction with the main A832 from Inverness, is the hamlet of Kinlochewe. Turn left here and head north-west along **Loch Maree**, arguably the loveliest loch in Scotland; it is peppered with islets and bordered with slopes carpeted with rhododendron bushes – an exquisite sight when in flower in late spring. Savour the view as you head away from the loch towards Kerrysdale, past the dramatic Victoria Falls tumbling down on the left. Queen Victoria stayed close by at the Loch Maree Hotel, and her enthusiasm for the area was a direct cause of the increase of Highland tourism.

Follow the A832 through the village towards **Gairloch**, which is a surprisingly tame, cultivated holiday resort with big Victorian hotels, a splendid long beach and the fascinating **Gairloch Heritage Museum***. This tiny place is a tribute to the history of Gaelic culture, featuring the reconstructed interior of a crofter's house and a school-room, a portable pulpit, an illicit still and thousands of Gaelic recordings of the reminiscences of local characters. The town also offers masses of water-sports facilities, sea-angling, diving and sailing. The **tourist information office*** here is open all year round.

Poolewe is an eight-mile drive away across the hills, with Loch Tollaidh nestling in the hills to your right. As the road descends into

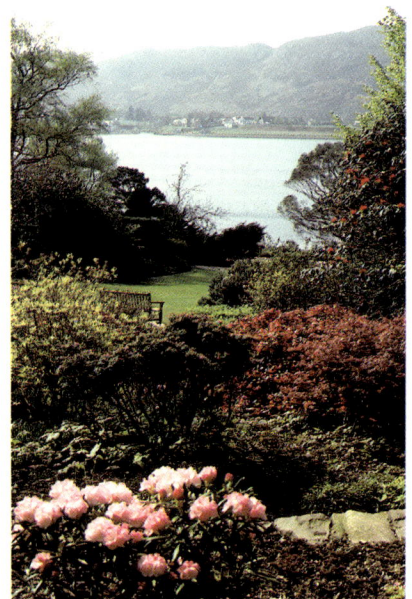

The site of Inverewe gardens, once barren, now a famous botanical display

Poolewe, stop and look at the torrent of water raging down from Loch Maree into the more sheltered sea water of Loch Ewe. **Inverewe Gardens*** are just north of the

INVEREWE GARDENS

These extraordinary gardens were created by the eccentric botanist and local laird Osgood Mackenzie in 1862. It was not an easy task as there were no roads and every scrap of soil had to be transported here, but thanks to the freak warming effect of the Gulf Stream and a lot of human help the exotic collections thrive at a Siberian latitude. Belts of pines were first planted along the shoreline as windbreaks, and now eucalyptus, magnolias, rhododendrons, Himalayan lilies, azaleas and giant forget-me-nots from South America produce a staggering display of colour – May and June are particularly good months to visit. There are about 2,500 different species of plant in this 50-acre sub-tropical fantasy land so it is worth engaging a guide to walk you round the narrow little paths. The gardens are run by the NTS, which has created a massive car park, a display in the visitor centre explaining the origins of the gardens, a small restaurant and a shop.

village, perched on the hillside looking out over Loch Ewe.

From Inverewe, the road wiggles round the shores of Loch Ewe to **Aultbea**, a NATO naval base, then crosses the hills again towards **Laide** and **Gruinard Bay**, with its sinister history. The island that lies in the middle of the inlet was contaminated by anthrax spores during biological-warfare testing in the Second World War. It was decontaminated in 1990 but still stands deserted. If you have time, take the tiny road from Laide to the quaintly named hamlet of **Mellon Udrigle**, where there is a peaceful sandy beach to relax or picnic on. Skirt round **Little Loch Broom**, passing a number of crofting communities and another enormous waterfall at **Ardessie**, and start climbing again at Dundonnell for a particularly scenic drive through forest to the Braemore Junction with the A835 at the head of Loch Broom. Sections of this road were built by locals during the potato famines of the nineteenth century: it is known as Destitution Road, because without such employment that is what the crofters would have faced. Just before

the Braemore Junction is **Corrieshalloch Gorge**, a deep, narrow ravine with the waters streaming from lochans on the hillsides into Loch Broom.

The A835 tears off round the northern shores of Loch Broom into **Ullapool**, a strangely cosmopolitan little town developed by the British Fishery Society in 1788. It is very popular with tourists and provides the main ferry-link to the Outer Hebrides, as well as being a commercial fishing centre, as the waters of the sea loch provide deep-water anchorage. Russian factory ships often stop here, but there is nothing exotic about the harbour; it is gritty, salty and dirty, but full of life. Ullapool was a departure point for displaced crofters during the Highland Clearances; two little museums capture this troubled time: the **Loch Broom Museum*** with its odd jumble of flotsam, including Lord Nelson's razor, and the **Ullapool Museum***, better organised and featuring a fine collection of old local photographs.

Ullapool's wide streets were laid out in grid fashion. It is a pretty place to stop at overnight and wander around for the craft and souvenir shops. The Ceilidh Place in West Argyle Street is probably the hotel to go for, a comfortable combination of bookshop, restaurant, hotel and events centre, with classical music playing in the background.